PRONOUNCING SHAKESPEARE'S WORDS

A Guide from A to Zounds

DALE F. COYE

GREENWOOD PRESS
Westport, Connecticut

Library of Congress Cataloging-in-Publication Data

Coye, Dale F.
   Pronouncing Shakespeare's words : a guide from A to Zounds / Dale
F. Coye.
      p.   cm.
   Includes bibliographical references and index
   ISBN 0-313-30655-9 (alk. paper)
      1. Shakespeare, William, 1564–1616—Language—Pronunciation.
   2. Shakespeare, William, 1564–1616—Language—Glossaries, etc.
   3. English language—Early modern, 1500–1700—Pronunciation—
Dictionaries.   I. Title.
   PR3081.C87   1998
   822.3′3—dc21   97–44868

British Library Cataloguing in Publication Data is available.

Library of Congress Catalog Card Number: 97–44868
ISBN: 0–313–30655–9

First published in 1998

Greenwood Press, 88 Post Road West, Westport, CT 06881
An imprint of Greenwood Publishing Group, Inc.

Printed in the United States of America

The paper used in this book complies with the
Permanent Paper Standard issued by the National
Information Standards Organization (Z39.48–1984).

10 9 8 7 6 5 4 3 2

Contents

Preface

First, what this book is not: It is not about how Shakespeare might have pronounced his words four hundred years ago. It is a guide to how they are pronounced today. It is a book for students, actors, readers, and teachers of Shakespeare who find themselves wishing there were pronunciation notes for all of the unfamiliar words they otherwise must guess at or take the time to look up in a dictionary.

Readers of Shakespeare, especially those confronting him for the first time, often feel overwhelmed by his language. Much of this has to do with unfamiliar meanings, but part of the difficulty also arises from questions of pronunciation. This is something which actors obviously must struggle with, and this book is certainly intended for them, both at the amateur and professional levels, but by far the largest number of people reading Shakespeare do so in classrooms, usually with very little understanding of how to speak the lines or pronounce the unfamiliar words. One professor who read this manuscript commented that Shakespeare classes at the college level, and English courses in general, seldom include any effort on the part of the teacher to have students read out loud. Surely this is unfortunate, for when students are encouraged to speak the verse themselves, their experience inevitably becomes richer, more personal and immediate than would otherwise be the case if hearing the language only through lectures, films, or tapes. This *Guide* then, was written with students in mind, to help them confidently negotiate metrical and pronunciation difficulties on their own. But it was also written for teachers, both at the high school and college levels, who are themselves often uncertain about many of these archaic or literary words. Here they will find an authoritative, up-to-date, comprehensive guide to pronunciation. The hope is that this volume will encourage teachers to read with their students, helping them to discover the rhythms of the verse as they learn to savor the sound of the spoken word.

Anyone who has ever opened a volume of Shakespeare knows how quickly the barrage of unfamiliar words begins. Although obscure meanings are noted in any good edition, no Shakespeare glossary or edition of his work offers any consistent guidance to the pronunciation of obsolete or literary words, leaving the reader to struggle with the dictionaries. But dictionaries are not always very helpful. Some of these "Shakespearean" words are not listed in the average college dictionary or even in the thickest unabridged volumes. The *Oxford English Dictionary (OED)* lists nearly all of them with the British pronunciation, but for some archaic words gives only meanings without pronunciation guidance. Furthermore, proper names are not included in the *OED*, and if they are given in other dictionaries, it would be hopeless to expect that the many obscure people and places mentioned in Shakespeare would be listed.

Dictionaries can also be misleading. Consider Shylock's cry of triumph:

This is the fool who lent out money *gratis*. (MV 3.3.2)

Gratis is a literary word rarely used in our everyday, spoken language. Students seeking advice on its pronunciation would find different answers depending on where they looked (symbols have been translated to the system used in this volume).

From British sources:

Collins Cobuild English Language Dictionary, 1987	/GRAYT iss, GRAT iss, GRAHT iss/
English Pronouncing Dictionary, 14th ed., 1988	/GRAYT iss/, less commonly /GRAHT iss, GRAT iss/
Oxford English Dictionary, 2nd ed., 1989	/GRAYT iss, GRAT iss, GRAHT iss/
Longman Pronunciation Dictionary, 1990	UK /GRAT iss/, less commonly /GRAYT iss, GRAHT iss, -us/; US /GRAT iss/.
BBC English Dictionary, 1992	/GRAT iss, GRAHT iss/

From American sources:

A Pronouncing Dictionary of American English, 1953	/GRAYT iss/
Webster's Third New International Dictionary, 1961	/GRAT iss, GRAYT iss/
Random House, 2nd ed., 1987	/GRAT iss, GRAYT iss/
American Heritage, 3rd ed., 1992	/GRAT iss, GRAHT iss, GRAYT iss/
Merriam-Webster's Collegiate Dictionary, 10th ed., 1993	/GRAT iss, GRAYT iss/

In this case, the dictionaries generate more questions than they answer: Are all three pronunciations really used today, and if so, by whom? Are some of them old-fashioned? Is one pronunciation more often heard in England and another in the United States? What method did each of these dictionaries use to determine which pronunciations are actually in use?

To give another example, a reader seeking the pronunciation of *quietus* in Hamlet's "To be or not to be" soliloquy will find only one pronunciation given in nearly every dictionary: /kwī EE tus/, although two other variants are commonly used by scholars and actors, /kwī AY tus/ and /kwee AY tus/. What are the implications of this discrepancy? Is there a right and wrong way to pronounce it?

Then there is the question of *bade*. Whenever a group of students or even a company of professional actors rehearses a Shakespeare play there is always an argument over the pronunciation of this word, as well as of *wont, adieu, wassail, zounds* and many others commonly found in Shakespeare's works. In all of these cases an appeal to the authority of the dictionaries will only yield a list of variants without further comment.

Recordings are also of limited value as sources. First, because most of them were produced in Great Britain, reinforcing the unfortunate tendency of North American students to shift into their notion of a British accent whenever they speak Shakespeare's lines. Second, because actors on recordings sometimes use obsolete or even incorrect pronunciations. *Peize* in one recording of *King John* was pronounced to rhyme with *size*, rather than as /peez/ or /payz/. *Counterfeit* ends in /-feet/ in some of the recordings, an unusual pronunciation in the United Kingdom today and unheard of in the United States.

This volume is unique in its use of a survey of American, Canadian, and British Shakespearean scholars who were asked for their recommendations on how to pronounce over 300 of Shakespeare's words. The results from the Survey show, for example, in the case of *gratis,* that the form common to most dictionaries, /GRAY tiss/, is virtually non-existent today, while the pronunciation least cited, /GRAH tiss/, is now used more often than /GRAT iss/ in the United States and the United Kingdom. The Survey also shows that even among the experts great uncertainty exists in some instances. Over half of the Shakespearean scholars in the United States said they were not sure how to pronounce *oeillades, artere,* and *gimmal. Puissance* was given eleven different pronunciations; *importune* had eight. This multiplicity of forms usually boils down to a question of traditional pronunciations vs. innovations based on spelling, a distinction that is often poorly understood by students, actors, and scholars alike.

There are other sources of pronunciation difficulty in Shakespeare, some arising from the verse form of the plays. Many readers are unaware that the iambic verse sometimes demands a shift in stress for some common words (*access, exploit, princess*) while others are expanded or compressed. Then there are the proper names and foreign phrases liberally scattered throughout the plays. Again, many of these names are not listed in any ordinary dictionary, while the glossaries that do exist like Helge Kökeritz's *Shakespeare's Names*

(1959), though valuable, are sometimes out of date or incorrect in their American vs. British distinctions.

Together these factors make reading Shakespeare a frustrating experience for many beginning students, while even seasoned Shakespearean actors and teachers find themselves baffled at times over choices of pronunciation. Other works in this field, like Kökeritz's *Shakespeare's Pronunciation* (1953), Viëtor's *Shakespeare's Pronunciation* (1906), and Cercignani's *Shakespeare's Works and Elizabethan Pronunciation* (1981) all focus on the development of the Elizabethan sound system and are decipherable only by the philologist. Some recent studies are helpful in understanding how the demands of verse affect pronunciation and line readings, notably Wright's *Shakespeare's Metrical Art* (1988), Spain's *Shakespeare Sounded Soundly* (1988), and Linklater's *Freeing Shakespeare's Voice* (1992), but none of these discuss pronunciation comprehensively or serve the reader in the line-by-line difficulties that arise from the text.

In this volume the reader and actor will find a straightforward guide to the pronunciation of the "hard" words in Shakespeare's plays and poems. The hope is that it will add to the enjoyment of the casual reader, professional actor, or Shakespeare scholar as it removes some of the obstacles inherent in working with a form of speech that is four centuries old.

This book would not have been possible without the assistance of the many scholars who took time to answer the postal questionnaire and the email surveys. I'm grateful to all who contributed. In addition I owe special thanks to R. Whitney Tucker, best known for his work with ancient Greek, but whose knowledge of Latin is also formidable. His assistance in determining the pronunciation of the Latin entries, particularly the Anglo-Latin variants, was invaluable.

I would also like to mention two Shakespeare scholars at my alma mater, St. Lawrence University. The first, Stanley Holberg, unwittingly inspired this study many years ago when he made the startling announcement to our class that *zounds* was derived from *God's wounds* and should be pronounced accordingly, not, as was commonly believed, to rhyme with *hounds* (but see the entry under *zounds*). The second, Thomas Berger, was kind enough to recommend this volume to Jane Garry at Greenwood Press. I'm grateful to both Tom and Jane for their support.

Further inspiration came from my friends and family. I'm grateful to Nan and Ian Twiss for reading through long lists of words, and to Jamie Horton and Isabel Tourneau for encouraging me to just do it. Thanks finally to Leah for your Prospero, to Adria for your Titania, to Julie for the many nights of reading the comedies together, and to Ben and Bev for letting me disappear so often in order to immerse myself in the world of vowels and consonants.

Pronunciation Key

a, ă- bat	ī- high	oy- boy
ah- mama	ih- divide	p- pay
ah^n- French sans	ĭr- mirror	r- road
air- pair	j- jump	s- so
ăir- marry	k- kill	sh- shell
a^n - French fin	l- lose	t- tea
ạr, ar- car	ł- little	ṭh- that
âr- war	m- moon	ᵺ - thin
aw- law	n- no	U, Ŭ- but
ay- bay	ṇ- listen	u, ŭ- about
ḅ- bad	ng- sing	ụ- bull
c, ck- duck	o- old	ü- French vu,
ch- chill	ŏ- hot	German müde
d- dead	ö- French peu, Germ.	uh- about
e- bet	Goethe	UR- fur
EE- bee	oh- boat	ur- under
ee- very	oh^n- French bon	v- vow
eer- peer	oo- mutual	w- will
ĕr- merry	o͞o- wood	wh- why
f- fill	o͞o- moon	y- yell
g, ĝ- give	oor- tour	z- zoo
h- how	or, ōr- or	zh- measure
i- bit	ow- how	

Word Stress (accent) is shown with upper case letters: /SHAYK speer/

Abbreviations

THE WORKS OF SHAKESPEARE

AC	Antony and Cleopatra	MM	Measure for Measure
AW	All's Well That Ends Well	MND	A Midsummer Night's
AYL	As You Like It		Dream
Cor	Coriolanus	MV	The Merchant of Venice
CE	The Comedy of Errors	MWW	The Merry Wives of
Cym	Cymbeline		Windsor
E3	Edward III	O	Othello
Ham	Hamlet	P	Pericles
1H4	Henry IV part one	R2	Richard II
2H4	Henry IV part two	R3	Richard III
H5	Henry V	RJ	Romeo and Juliet
1H6	Henry VI part one	T	The Tempest
2H6	Henry VI part two	TA	Titus Andronicus
3H6	Henry VI part three	TC	Troilus and Cressida
H8	Henry VIII	TGV	The Two Gentlemen of
J	King John		Verona
JC	Julius Caesar	TmA	Timon of Athens
L	King Lear	TN	Twelfth Night
LLL	Love's Labor's Lost	TNK	The Two Noble Kinsmen
M	Macbeth	TS	The Taming of the Shrew
MA	Much Ado About Nothing	WT	The Winter's Tale

REFERENCE WORKS

EPD	*English Pronouncing Dictionary*	*LPD*	*Longman Pronunciation Dictionary*

| OED2 | Oxford English Dictionary, 2nd ed. | W3 | Webster's Third New International Dictionary of the English Language |
| RH2 | Random House Dictionary, 2nd ed. | | |

OTHER ABBREVIATIONS

adj.	adjective	Ital.	Italian
Am.	American	mod.	modern
angl.	anglicized	n.	noun
Ang.Lat.	Anglo-Latin	prep.	preposition
App.	Appendix	Q	quarto
cf.	compare	RP	Received Pronunciation (Standard British)
Class.Lat.	Classical Latin		
CN	Canada	Shk	Shakespeare
ed.	editor	Sp.	Spanish
F	folio	s.v.	sub verbo (under that word)
Fr.	French	UK	United Kingdom
Germ.	German	US	United States
Gk.	Greek	v.	verb

Introduction

USING THE *GUIDE*

The *Guide* lists all the words in Shakespeare's plays and poems which the average college student or actor might find difficult to pronounce. The words are listed by act, scene, and line in the order they appear in each play or poem.

> **Before turning to the individual plays and poems readers should first become familiar with the two lists on pp. 33–40:**
>
> **"The Most Common 'Hard' Words in Shakespeare"**
> **"The Most Common Reduced Forms"**

Knowing the pronunciation of these words is an absolute prerequisite for anyone attempting to speak Shakespeare's lines. They will not be found in the scene-by-scene listings because they appear so often that including them would have meant repeating the same words many times throughout the *Guide*.

The Basic Text: *The Riverside Shakespeare*

The Riverside Shakespeare (1974) edited by G. Blakemore Evans provides the basic text, and line numbers refer to this edition.[1] However the *Guide* is intended as a companion volume for any modern text edition of Shakespeare a reader may be using. *Riverside's* line numbers will not correspond exactly to

---

1. The second edition of Riverside (1997) edited by Evans and J.J.M. Tobin serves as the base text for *Edward III*. Line numbers throughout the second edition are the same as in the first.

those in other editions, but they will help place a word generally and will be especially useful when a scene or play is read from beginning to end. In general, the longer a scene and the more prose passages, the greater will be the discrepancy between line numbers of different editions. In some cases the way scenes are divided will differ from edition to edition. This poses a more serious difficulty to finding the word, but it is relatively rare, and if the reader is reading the scenes in order, the words will still occur in their proper sequence. The scene divisions of one other edition, Wells and Taylor's *The Complete Oxford Shakespeare* (1987), have been included in parentheses where they differ from *Riverside*.

Of the many editions of Shakespeare's works, *Riverside* was chosen as the basic text for several reasons. First, because it is usually considered the standard text for use in critical works on Shakespeare (Thompson, et al. 1992, 16). It also serves as the basis for Marvin Spevack's *Harvard Concordance to Shakespeare* (1973), an invaluable tool in any study of Shakespeare's language. Perhaps even more important is the conservative editing. Though *Riverside* is a modern spelling text, it does not modernize as many words as most other editions. Instead, it retains what it considers legitimate older forms which may indicate distinctive Elizabethan pronunciations (*Riverside* 1974, 39). In other words, the editor is trying to make it possible for the reader to experience more of the flavor of sixteenth- and seventeenth-century English by using older forms like *murther* for *murder*, *vild* for *vile*, and *bankrout* for *bankrupt*.

Readers should be aware that an edition other than *Riverside* may not contain every example listed in the *Guide* because the editor may have preferred another choice at that point. However, most of these alternatives have also been included.

Riverside has been criticized for retaining too many archaic forms which may interfere with the reader's or listener's comprehension. It has also been criticized for including many inferior line readings (S. Wells 1979, 5; S. Wells 1984, 19-20; Thompson, et al. 1992, 16). Alternative readings are listed in *Riverside's* textual notes and the *Guide* includes some of these and others proposed by various editors. Specifically, the editorial choices of *The Complete Oxford Shakespeare* (1987) have been included for nearly all entries in the *Guide*.

But again a reminder: the *Guide* lists only those archaic words or alternative readings which would puzzle the average reader. *Shrowdly* vs. *shrewdly* appears because it is not clear whether the archaic form is pronounced with /ow/ or /oh/. However, *corse* vs. *corpse* is not listed because the pronunciation in either case is clear from the spelling.

Which Words Are Included?

Shakespeare's works are full of difficult words and, naturally, the more inexperienced the reader, the greater the number of unfamiliar words he or she will confront. The words in this *Guide* were chosen based on what an average college student might find difficult. Where to draw the line inevitably requires some arbitrary decisions. Some readers will wonder why *hie* or *deign* are included, but *adage* is not. It will be impossible to satisfy everyone on this score.

In general, words were included if they fell into one of the following categories:

1. Uncommon words whose pronunciation is not evident from the spelling: *gimmal, cerements, accompt, chough*
2. More common literary words whose pronunciation varies, or which are often mispronounced: *boor, bulwark, wassail, waft, heinous, jocund*
3. Words stressed differently in current English than in the line in question: *obscure, complete, frontier, antique*
4. Proper names whose pronunciation is not evident from the spelling, or whose pronunciation varies: *Holofernes, Thetis, Dunsinane, Bianca*
5. Foreign phrases

Common words which vary in today's English, either within one country's borders or between North America and the United Kingdom, are not included (*calm, either, often, hover, accomplish*), but some are listed in Appendix A. This is an important category of words to note because the influence of Standard British is so great that sometimes Americans make the mistake of assuming that the UK forms are the only correct ones for a Shakespeare play or poem.

Notation

The aim of the *Guide* is to allow readers to produce the correct pronunciation with minimal reference to a chart containing unusual symbols and diacritic marks. For that reason the International Phonetic Alphabet is not used, since it is unfamiliar to many potential users of the *Guide*. Instead, a system similar to that used by American dictionaries has been adopted in which letter symbols are keyed to simple, unambiguous vowels and consonants (see p. xiii). The major difference from dictionary notation is, that diacritic marks over vowels have been avoided as much as possible, and word stress (accent), is indicated by upper case letters rather than by a stress mark. For example, *bruited* is given as /BROOT id/ where the /OO/ indicates the vowel of *too* and carries the stress.[2]

---

2. Since the goal is for the reader to be able to deduce a word's pronunciation correctly, the same sound may be symbolized in two different ways if it will increase the reader's likelihood of producing the correct pronunciation. /s/ in *gratis* is symbolized with a double *s*, /GRAT iss/, because if the final syllable were written /is/ readers might

Variants are listed according to syllable. For example,

methinks /mee-, mih ~~TH~~INKS/

indicates that the first syllable may be either /mih-/ or /mee-/. Variants that are used less frequently are given in square brackets [ ], and those specific to the United States, Canada, or the United Kingdom are indicated where appropriate.

One of the difficulties in writing a pronunciation guide for the English language is that there is no universally accepted standard on which to base it. Even within Standard British, which has been defined sound-by-sound and given the name Received Pronunciation (RP), there are accepted variations that reflect distinctive accents (J.C. Wells 1982, 2: 279). This makes it difficult for a pronunciation guide to be accurate, comprehensive, and efficient at the same time. If the International Phonetic Alphabet were used, each national or regional variant would have to be listed for each word (cf. *LPD*), but using the key-word notation usually makes a more efficient entry possible without sacrificing accuracy. Speakers will simply substitute the sounds of the key words as they normally pronounce them in whatever dialect they speak. This approach makes the *Guide* accessible to speakers anywhere in the English-speaking world, as long as care is taken in the choice of key words. Some minor confusions that may arise are discussed in Appendix C.

Pronunciation Variants within the United States

In a word like *apricot,* different vowels are used in different regions of the United States (/AYP rih kŏt/ vs. /AP rih kŏt/). Both sounds exist in the repertories of each group, but historical and social considerations have caused one to be favored over the other, giving rise to regional variation. Other examples of this sort are *bath* with the vowel of *bat* in most parts of America, and /ah/ in Standard British and parts of New England; *greasy* has /s/ in the northern and western United States and /z/ in the South. Americans living along the East Coast and in parts of the South pronounce words like *Morris, historical, Horace* with the vowel of *car*, while most other Americans use /or/. More and more Americans are pronouncing the /l/ in *calm, palm*, etc., but many speakers retain the

---

say /iz/. In other cases, primarily at the beginning of words, the single /s/ can be used unambiguously.

A diacritic mark is sometimes placed over or under a vowel to avoid ambiguity. For example, in a word like *bulwark*, there are two possibilities for the first syllable. The transcription /BUL wurk/ is ambiguous so diacritics are added: /BŬL wurk/ indicates the vowel of *dull*, and /BU̱LL-/ is used for the variant with the vowel of *bull*.

Syllable division may seem inconsistent, but again the chief goal is to elicit the desired pronunciation. The various pronunciations of *adieu* are written with syllable breaks in different places (/uh DYOO, ad YOO/), with primary consideration given to avoiding potentially confusing notations like /a DYOO/ where a reader would be left wondering which value to give /a/ by itself.

older /l/-less pronunciation. These differences occur in a variety of common words and are important to note, especially for actors and directors who may not realize that theirs is a regional pronunciation, and consequently either less or more acceptable depending on their intended audience. The *Guide* points out some of these differences in common words in Appendix A, but variant forms are only included in the scene-by-scene lists for literary or unusual words like *lazar, satyr,* or *orison,* and it is usually difficult to ascertain whether a speaker's regional origin plays a role in these variations.

In some cases where a regional phonological feature is common to a category of words, geographical notations are made in the lists. The southern United States tends to preserve the glide /y/ in words like *duke, new, tune (*/dyo͞ok/, etc.) and this is carried over into some listed words like *importune.* Some speakers from eastern New England use the vowel /ah/ in *mask, bath, half,* and this applies to *masque, blasphemy,* etc. in the lists. On the eastern coast of the United States there are a number of vowel sounds before /r/ followed by another vowel which differ from the rest of the country and must be taken into account (*Harry: hairy* have different vowels on the East Coast, but are the same for most Americans, see App. C). It should be noted, however, that regional factors are constantly changing, and when a variant in the *Guide* is given a label like "Eastern New England," the implication is not that all speakers from that area would use the given pronunciation, only that many do.

How the Pronunciations Were Determined

The pronunciations listed in this *Guide* were researched in two ways. First the words were checked in the following dictionaries:

American
A Pronouncing Dictionary of American English (1953)
Webster's Third New International Dictionary of the English Language (1961)
The Random House Dictionary of the English Language, 2nd edition (1987)
The American Heritage Dictionary of the English Language, 3rd edition (19 92)

British
English Pronouncing Dictionary, 12th, and 14th editions (1964, 1988)
Collins Cobuild English Language Dictionary (1987)
The Oxford English Dictionary, 2nd edition (1989)
Longman Pronunciation Dictionary (1990), which contains both American and British
     pronunciations.
BBC English Dictionary (1992)

Those words which were not listed in any of these sources were checked in *Webster's New International Dictionary* (1934) and in Worcester's *A Universal Critical and Pronouncing Dictionary of the English Language* (1856), both of which contain many obscure Shakespearean entries.

A significant number of words are listed in these sources as having variant pronunciations. Sometimes they indicate that the differences are American vs. British. Especially valuable in this regard is the *Longman Pronunciation Dictionary* (1990), though at times the American entries are inaccurate.[3] In most dictionaries, however, variants are simply listed without comment.

In order to ascertain whether these variant pronunciations still have any currency, a survey was conducted of college professors of Shakespeare in the United States, Canada, and the United Kingdom, asking them in a questionnaire how they would recommend pronouncing these words and some others that were listed without variation in the dictionaries.[4] This was supplemented by a smaller survey of dramaturges and literary consultants at theatres and drama schools in North America specializing in Shakespeare performances. In addition, surveys were conducted via email discussion groups which included classicists, historians, and professors of literature.[5] Words that were included in any

---

3. For example, *anybody* is listed only with /-bŏd ee/, omitting the common pronunciation /-bud ee/; /ketch/ for *catch* is listed as non-standard, and words beginning with *wh-* are said to be pronounced /hw/ in General American (770), a statement based on data that is now out of date (Dale Coye, "A Linguistic Survey of College Freshmen: Keeping up with Standard American English," *American Speech* 69 (Fall 1994): 260–284).

4. Ideally surveys would have also been conducted in other English-speaking countries, particularly Australia and New Zealand, but it was logistically difficult. Then too, once you begin to report by nation, it is hard to know which countries to leave out. South Africa, India, and Ireland, all deserve to be counted as well.

5. The Carnegie Foundation for the Advancement of Teaching's *Classification of Institutions of Higher Learning* (Princeton, 1994) was used as a base document to select American colleges and universities for the main postal survey. After excluding specialty colleges (agriculture, technology, the arts), every seventh college was selected from the lists in the following categories: Research Universities I and II, Doctoral Universities I and II, Master's Colleges and Universities I, Baccalaureate Colleges I. Telephone calls to those institutions determined the name of a professor teaching Shakespeare. 107 questionnaires were sent in the United States, and 38 returned. Using a similar method 12 questionnaires were returned from Canadian universities, and 19 from the UK (the source for the Canadian lists was the *Directory of Canadian Universities* 29th ed., Association of Universities and Colleges of Canada, and for the UK *Commonwealth Universities Yearbook 1993*, Association of Commonwealth Universities). These numbers include only professors who are still teaching in the country where they learned English. Respondents' years of birth ranged from 1925 to 1966, with over one-third of the informants in each country falling in the years 1939–43. Over 300 words were asked in the US and UK surveys and slightly less for Canada. Because the word list was so long, it was divided seven ways (with some overlap) and distributed, with an additional 25 words of special interest sent to all informants. See App. D. *puissance, surety* for examples of the responses. It was more difficult to engage the theatres, with only 7 responses from places such as the Stratford Festival in Ontario, New York's Public Theatre, and Julliard.

The email respondents came from various lists which serve as forums for professors, grad students, and others with an interest in the specific subject areas. For example, 38 names like *Atropos, Bacchus, Charon* were submitted to the classics list (asking for the

of these surveys are indicated by an asterisk. The results show that some variations in pronunciation are still in force, but others listed in the dictionaries appear to be extinct. In other cases pronunciations not listed in any source books are being used with great frequency.

When Is a Variant Pronunciation "Wrong"?

This raises the question of mispronunciation. Should every pronunciation found in the surveys or in a dictionary be listed and accorded the status of a correct, acceptable pronunciation? In other words, does the fact that somewhere a professor of English pronounces a word in a given way, define it as Standard English, or can they sometimes be "wrong"?

There are different schools of thought on mispronunciation. Some would have us believe that there are strict standards of pronunciation, defined by language experts and listed in source books that should serve as bibles to the uninformed. Others believe that the whole notion of what constitutes a mispronunciation is relative. *Webster's Third* defined standard speech in a way that has been largely accepted by American dictionary-makers. It rejected the idea of a single standard of pronunciation for the United States as a whole and defined the standard speech in any area as that used by a "sufficient number of cultivated speakers" (1961, 38a). In other words, when large numbers of well-educated people from Syracuse say *orange pajamas* as /ornj puh JAM uz/, while those in New York City say /AHR inj puh JAH muz/, neither group is incorrect. There are a number of words that vary in this way from region to region in the United States, and even more that differ between North American and British English (see Appendix A).

Orange is a word used regularly in daily life and the variations in its pronunciation arose through normal linguistic change, the same sorts of changes that created the differences between Old, Middle, and Modern English as the entire sound system shifted in various ways over the centuries, forming dialect regions that are sometimes radically different from each other. Book words—words that are found most often in writing but are rarely spoken—change as well but in a somewhat different way. When the communal memory of a word's pronunciation has been lost, or when speakers who have never heard a book word pronounced attempt it, then spelling will play a key role in determining the new pronunciation.

Bade is a case in point. This was once a much more commonly used word than it is today and was pronounced /bad/. In most dictionaries in the early part of the twentieth century this was the only pronunciation given, but at that time, as people became increasingly literate and the standard pronunciation faded

---

pronunciation they would recommend if the name appeared in a work of English literature). 26 responded from the US, 3 from Canada, and 7 from the UK. The 18th century list was asked 50 literary words like *augury, environ, prerogative*. 45 responded from the US, 8 from Canada, and 13 from the UK.

from the collective memory, /bayd/, based on spelling and in existence for at least a century, rapidly gained ground. The Survey shows that in the United States /bayd/ is rarely used by those professors born before 1940 but is preferred by half of those born after that date. In keeping with this change among educated speakers, about twenty years ago dictionaries began to include /bayd/ alongside /bad/, it being now deemed an acceptable standard pronunciation, though some traditionalists would disagree.

Another word of this sort is *gyves* /jīvz/ 'fetters,' which was originally pronounced with /g/, not /j/. As the word fell out of use after the Elizabethan era, a new pronunciation based on the spelling arose and completely conquered the field by the end of the nineteenth century (*OED2*, s.v.). Similarly *avoirdupois* is listed as /AV ur duh poiz/ in many current dictionaries, but recently a bevy of spelling pronunciations based on French has made the older pronunciation obsolete.

Sometimes spelling pronunciations are applied to whole categories of words, for example, those ending in *-or*. *Mentor, orator* and other words of this class that are not commonly used in day-to-day life (including "Shakespearean" words like *servitor, proditor, paritor*) are often pronounced on- and off-stage with /-or/, but the traditional pronunciation is /-ur/, as found in most of our common words ending in *-or* (*actor, instructor, doctor*). Another example is found in a group of words containing *th*. *Apothecary, Arthur, author* were loaned into English from French with /t/, but sometime after the Elizabethan era were changed to /th/ because of their spelling (Kökeritz 1953, 320).

Conservatives often have little patience with spelling pronunciations. Spain calls the pronunciation of *bade* as /bayd/ a "gross mispronunciation" and deplores the practice in modern dictionaries of simply listing without comment the pronunciations which exist, even those "not worthy" of use (1988, 201, 210). Kökeritz scorned the spelling pronunciation of *Jaques* as /JAY kweez/ or as /JAY kwiz/, stating unequivocally that the pronunciation Shakespeare intended was /JAY kis/ (1959, 3). Despite his pronouncements /JAY kweez/ still dominates today.

The point for readers of Shakespeare is that there will always be an argument brewing over how certain words are pronounced. Conservatives and purists, looking to the history of the word, condemn spelling pronunciations outright and would have the reader adhere to traditional forms. On the other hand, many listeners will be unfamiliar with traditional pronunciations like /bad/, and may even believe that the performer is saying the word wrong.

The *Guide* reports which pronunciations are currently most in favor based on the Survey, pointing out which are traditional and which innovations based on spelling or analogy. Tension will always exist because the language changes and in some cases the choice between variants must be left to the reader. However, some basic guidelines can be set down. *Heinous*, for example, has traditionally been pronounced /HAY nus/ and is exclusively cited this way in nearly every dictionary,[6] but a small number of highly educated individuals, including professors from both sides of the Atlantic, use a newer pronunciation /HEE nus/. Generally a new pronunciation of a word based on spelling, like /HEE nus/, is subject to a collective displeasure in its infancy from those who pronounce it in the traditional way. In other words, if only a small segment of the educated population says /HEE nus/ it is easier to label it a mispronunciation. Those speakers who use the new pronunciation might agree that they were guessing from the spelling, and try to conform to the traditional form. Certainly high school students go through this process with some regularity in words like *epitome* which many meet first in print and pronounce /EP ih tohm/.

However, as more and more speakers use a new pronunciation, or as it acquires a base within a specific group (speakers within a geographic area, or younger speakers, for example), it becomes more difficult to call it incorrect. There comes a time when the linguist, if not the purist, must admit that a significant percentage of educated speakers does indeed say /bayd/ for *bade* and acknowledge it as an acceptable variant.

On the other hand, it is difficult to label fading traditional pronunciations incorrect until they are completely extinct. It is now possible to say that using a "hard" /g/ for *gyves* is wrong, but even if only one percent of the country were to say /bad/ for *bade*, would we be justified in calling it incorrect when it is the older, standard pronunciation? The *Guide's* goal in these cases is to make the speaker aware that the conflict exists, and that until /bad/ disappears completely, it must still be considered acceptable. Using the *Guide*, readers can chose variants themselves.

However, the *Guide* offers some recommendations, generally urging readers to avoid newer, relatively rare, spelling pronunciations. /HAY nus/ is recommended, /HEE nus/ is not, which is another way of saying that the vast majority of educated speakers consider it non-standard.[7] Among other pronunciations not recommended are *doth* and *dost* with /ō/, and *choler* as /KOH lur/, all used by some of the professors in the Survey. Further, when an archaic word like *phthisic* has a wide variety of pronunciations, most of them based on guesswork from the spelling, tradition should be the deciding factor, making /TIZ ik/ the choice. Similarly when the educated community is divided over words like *bade, quietus,* and *liege* the weight of history should tip the scales in favor of /bad/, /kwī EE tus/, and /leej/ for the student or actor trying to decide which pronunciation to use.

A final note is needed on RP (Received Pronunciation), the British standard pronunciation. Half a century ago RP had an undisputed prestige in England and was used in all formal situations, including Shakespeare recitations and performances. Daniel Jones' *English Pronouncing Dictionary* was the final arbiter on what was RP and what was not, today supplemented by the *Longman Pro-*

---

6. The exceptions are *W3* which lists "sometimes" /HEE nus/ or /HĪ nus/ and *LPD* which lists as non-standard /HEE nus/ and as incorrect /HAY nee us/.

7. Though apparently in the UK the majority is not so vast. The Survey showed that in that country 4 out of 11 professors were using /HEE-/; in the US only 1 out of 17.

nunciation Dictionary and others. Recently the situation has changed for Standard British as many regional features have crept into the sound system, creating variants that previously did not exist. Judging from the results of the Survey, many of the most highly educated members of society—the professors, lecturers and instructors at universities—use what *EPD* and *LPD* consider non-RP forms of English. To give two examples, the RP form of *satyr* is /SAT ur/ according to *LPD* and *EPD14*, but 30 percent of the professors surveyed from the UK say /SAY tur/. These dictionaries also report that the final syllable of *plantain* is RP /-tin/, but five out of six professors say /-tayn/. Perhaps the question, "what is the RP form" is of diminishing interest to the educated Briton. As in North America, the question should be: "what pronunciations are now being used by educated speakers, and are they different from older standard forms?" The *Guide* will indicate these discrepancies where they occur, again leaving the choice to the British reader.

Mannered Pronunciations and the Influence of British English in North America

Speaking Shakespeare's verse demands clear articulation, however there is a danger of going too far. For example, there is a tendency, sometimes encouraged by vocal coaches, to replace normal weak, unstressed vowels with full vowels in inappropriate places. In the United States *offend, opinion, official* are normally /uh FEND/, /uh PIN yun/, etc, yet in the theatre it is not uncommon to hear /oh FEND/, /oh PIN yun/. Other examples occur in words like *condemn, contempt*, pronounced with /kŏn-/ rather than normal /kun-/, *provide, pronounce* with /proh-/ rather than /pruh-/,[8] or *capitol* with /-tŏl/ instead of /-tł/. These are "mannered" or "stage" pronunciations. The speaker is altering the usual pronunciation of these words toward his or her perception of a correct standard of speech—a standard which in fact is used by virtually no one in real life. Mannered speech also affects some "Shakespearean" words. The final syllable of *recreant* and *miscreant* should be /-unt/, but actors sometimes use /-ant/ (cf. *important, significant, defiant*). *Vizard* should rhyme with *wizard*, yet it is sometimes given the vowel of *hard*. If no one but an actor says /oh POHZ/, then that pronunciation is an affectation and should be avoided (unless of course the actor is trying to make the character sound affected—Malvolio, for instance).[9]

There is a related problem specific to North America where Standard British (RP) has enormous influence when it comes to Shakespeare. Because recordings and films of Shakespeare's works are almost invariably produced with British actors using RP, American actors, from superstars to neophytes, con-

---

8. *LPD* lists /kŏn-/ in these words as a non-RP form. It also labels *offend, provide* with /oh-/ as non-RP pronunciations.

9. Note however that some unstressed vowels do vary normally. In American English *enough, eleven* may begin with either /ee-/ or /ih-/. Certain prefixes like *ex- (extend, explore)* vary between /eks-/ and a reduced form /iks-/.

sciously or unconsciously, alter their pronunciation toward the British. It is very common to hear college students shifting to British accents, sometimes without realizing it, when reading Shakespeare. Some of these shifts are encouraged by speech teachers or directors in the name of "good" pronunciation, despite the fact that American pronunciations have as rightful a claim to historical legitimacy as their British counterparts. In acting schools in both North America and the United Kingdom actors are sometimes taught what is called a "Mid-Atlantic Accent." This refers to a sort of pronunciation that is neither British nor North American, that is to say, an attempt is made to neutralize regional features to the point where an audience is unable to tell where the actor is from. It is certainly possible to cover up native speech patterns to a degree, but if an American actor starts moving his pronunciation in the direction of RP the audience will very likely be aware of it, and the effect is often a very stagey one. Some of the changes that American actors make in the direction of British are:

1. Changing the vowel in *bath, ask, can't* etc. to /ah/. Often American amateur actors go too far, making the change in the wrong places, for example in *can, and, had.*
2. Adding the glide /y/ in words like *new* /nyōō/, *duke* /dyōōk/, *tune* /tyōōn/, *lute* /lyōōt/,[10] instead of using the usual /nōō, dōōk/ etc.
3. /t/ between voiced sounds: The following pairs are homonyms in normal American English but not in British: *metal : medal, butting : budding,* and *letter* rhymes with *redder.* Yet on the stage or in readings Americans will usually pronounce the /t/ as the British would: unvoiced, with a slight puff of air.
4. Most importantly, the loss of /r/ at the end of a word or before a consonant. *Bark, far, ear, sure* are changed to /bahk/, /fah/, /ih-uh/, /shōō-uh/.[11]

Unless the play is being staged in a British setting (one of the histories for instance) with deliberately British accents, there is no reason American performers should alter any of their ordinary American vowel and consonant sounds, as long as they are following the patterns of the "cultivated" speakers in their region. Even in the case of a history play there is a good argument for using the North American accent. For if we are to lend color to the play by using British accents to portray British subjects, should we then use Scottish accents in *Macbeth* or Italian accents in *Romeo and Juliet*? We are not pronounc-

---

10. In everyday American English /nyōō, dyōōk/, etc. are usually heard only in the South and even there it is becoming less frequent, see Betty S. Phillips, "Southern English Glide Deletion Revisited," *American Speech* 69 (Summer 1994): 115–127. Elocutionists sometimes insist on the glide for the classical theatre, but it makes little sense to say /dyōōk/ on the stage and /dōōk/ in real life. /lyōō-/ was once standard in the UK as well and used for the classics. Today however, many *lu-* words like *Luke, Lucy, Lucifer, lunacy* are no longer normally pronounced with /lyōō-/ in Standard British, but simply as /lōō-/, though some RP speakers may use /lyōō-/ in other *lu-* words, like *lubricate, lucid, lucrative, illuminate, lute,* and, according to *LPD,* especially *lure, lurid* and *alluring* (see the British dictionaries listed in the references, s.vv.).

11. In some American dialects—parts of New York City, eastern New England, and the South—/r/ does not occur in these positions, but the vast majority of Americans naturally use /r/ and should do so on stage.

ing the words as Shakespeare did in any case, nor did Shakespeare write in the language used by King John, or Richard II. The audience is being asked to suspend disbelief and there is no reason why the American, Canadian, Australian, Irish, or South African languages may not serve as the medium as well as Standard British.

Lost Rhymes and Puns

> He is gone, he is gone,
> And we cast away moan (Ham 4.5.197–98)

When an Elizabethan Ophelia sang this song this was a true rhyme, probably with *gone* pronounced with the vowel of *go,* though *moan* may have been shortened (Cercignani 1981, 115). There are many other instances in Shakespeare of word pairs that no longer rhyme in modern English because of a shift in vowel sounds: *love-prove, come-doom,   food-good-flood.* Some of these rhymes may have been only eye rhymes even in Shakespeare's day, poetic fossils from an earlier era (Kökeritz 1953, 31). Besides ignoring them and pronouncing the word in the modern manner, the reader is left with few options. In some cases it may be possible to nudge different vowels toward each other. For example, in the lines:

> He who the sword of heaven will bear
> Should be as holy as severe; (MM 3.2. 261–62)

it is not too difficult to alter the pronunciation of *bear* toward *severe* and vice-versa.

In other cases there is little the performer can do. For example, one of the most common types of rhyme in Shakespeare is illustrated in these lines:

> My ear should catch your voice, my eye your eye,
> My tongue should catch your tongue's sweet melody.
> (MND 1.1.188–89)

Nouns ending in *-y* and adverbs and adjectives in *-ly* were rhymed with either /ī/ or with /ee/ by Shakespeare, exhibiting a variation that goes back to Middle or even Old English. In the example given, presumably the Elizabethan performer would have said /MEL uh dī/, but today on stage words in this class are always given their normal, modern pronunciation, and the rhyme is lost.

A similar problem affects some puns which are hopelessly lost because of pronunciation shifts. The following lines lose their resonance because the noun *ache* has lost its pronunciation as /aytch/, common until the eighteenth century:

> I had a wound here that was like a T,
> But now 'tis made an H. (AC 4.7.7–8)

In the *Guide* only those puns which require explanations will be pointed out, for example, *Person: pierce-one* LLL 4.2.82–84 (see Kökeritz 1953, 86–157 for a thorough description of puns in Shakespeare).

Proper Names

Many of the entries for proper names given in earlier glossaries are now out of date. For example, nearly every sourcebook gives *Laertes* as /lay UR teez/. This is indeed the traditional form, however the Survey found that two-thirds of American college professors today use /lay AIR teez/, a partially "restored" pronunciation (see p. 14). Comparing entries in Kökeritz's *Shakespeare's Names* (1959) to the current survey reveals a number of other differences, for example:

Table 1
Recommendations for the Pronunciation of Proper Names

	Kökeritz, 1959	Majority of UK professors in the current survey	Majority of US professors in the current survey
Adonis	/uh DOHN iss/	/uh DOHN iss/	/uh DŎN iss/
Bianca	/bee ANG kuh/	/bee ANG kuh/	/bee AHNG kuh/
Bolingbrook	/BŎL-, BULL ing brŏŏk/	/BŎL ling brŏŏk/	/BOHL ing brŏŏk, BULL-, BŎL-/
Dr. Caius	/keez/	/KĪ us/	/KAY us/
Dunsinane	/dun sih NAYN/	/DUN sih nayn/	/DUN sih nayn/
Eros	/EER ŏss, ĔR-/	/EER ŏss, ĔR ŏss, ĔR ohss/	/ĔR ŏss, -ohss/
Fleance	/FLEE unss/	/FLEE unss, FLAY-/	/FLEE ahnss, FLAY unss/

Probably as long as Shakespeare has been in print certain names have been given variant pronunciations. The *Guide* sorts through the variants and offers a truer picture of how these names are pronounced today. At the beginning of each play are two lists entitled "People in the Play" and "Places in the Play." Here the reader will find only those names which pose a difficulty for the average native speaker. The lists include names from the cast of characters, frequently mentioned places, and people not in the cast who are mentioned throughout the play.

Foreign Words and Phrases

Latin, Italian, and French words and phrases are common in the plays. Some guidance is given on how to pronounce these words, but the notation is unable to capture the sounds of these languages completely. The reader or actor must also bear in mind how the character speaking these lines would pronounce the phrase. Pistol would probably pronounce French very badly, King Henry V might speak it better, and the Frenchmen and Frenchwomen perfectly. French pronunciations are often given without indication of word stress because in that language stress is variable. So if *Gerard de Narbon* is to be pronounced as in French in its only verse instance (AW 2.1.101), then *Gerard* could be stressed on either the first or second syllable and is given as /zhay rahr/. The meter dictates however that *Narbon* must be stressed on the first syllable, written as /NAHR boh^n/.

The pronunciation of Latin words is especially problematic. Up until the beginning of the twentieth century the normal pronunciation taught in all Latin classes and used by all English-speaking scholars was an anglicized Latin which was quite different from both classical Latin and that spoken on the continent (Allen 1978, 102–8). This Anglo-Latin has a long history dating from Middle English. It took part in the regular sound changes of English and is still used in many of the more commonLatin names today, for example, *Caesar* /SEE zur/, *Cato* /KAY toh/, *Titus* /TĪ tus/. Latin phrases were commonly pronounced as though they were English: the tombstone inscription *hic jacet* (AW 3.6.62–63) 'here lies' in Anglo-Latin was always /hick JAY sit/, while in classical Latin it would have been /heek YAH ket/.

At the end of the nineteenth century scholars began a campaign to rehabilitate these wayward vowels and consonants, claiming that, for example, that part of the brain known as the *pia mater* should no longer be /PĪ uh MAY tur/ as it had been for centuries, but /PEE ah MAH těr/, the pronunciation which was probably used in ancient Rome. The restoration of classical Latin sounds has been a great force in the last hundred years and has resulted in two competing pronunciations for Latin words, each with its own legitimacy. Sometimes there is a notable difference between North America and the UK, especially in the treatment of unstressed syllables. Names like *Lucius, Cassius, Ephesians,* and *Pallas* are most commonly /LŌO shus, CASH us, ih FEE zhunz, PAL us/ in the United States, reflecting the normal development of these sounds in English (cf. *vicious, fictitious, vision, terrace),* while the majority of speakers in the United Kingdom have either tenaciously held on to forms from Middle and Early Modern English (and ultimately classical Latin or Greek) or restored them recently to /LŌO see us, CASS ee us, ih FEE zhee unz, PAL ǎss/. To the American ear many of these restored forms sound overly precise or even bizarre.

Many of these words also show mixed forms with one syllable retaining an Anglo-Latin vowel, while the other has acquired the classical Latin. For example, the goddess *Ate* is traditionally /AY tee/, or in its restored form /AH tay/, but /AH tee/ was sometimes reported in the Survey as well. Similarly *quietus,* whose traditional form is /kwī EE tus/, sometimes has its second syllable restored but not its first: /kwī AY tus/. To add to the confusion, church Latin, based on the Italian version of classical Latin, is widely known in English-speaking countries through its use in singing. Choral groups are often taught to say *excellcis*, for example, as /eks CHEL seess/, and many would guess that *hic jacet* should therefore be /heek YAH chet/.

The main point to be made is that using a restored, classical Latin pronunciation is not the only correct way to pronounce these words. For one thing, the reforms have not really restored the classical Latin sounds precisely. Typically only those sounds which already exist in English are used. Further, it is unthinkable to go back to the past and transform all the Latin words in English into their ancient Roman forms. This would mean altering words like *Caesar* to /KĪ sahr/. The reader must again decide what would be appropriate for the character speaking the lines, keeping in mind the audience's expectations. But again, the Anglo-Latin forms have the weight of an older tradition behind them, so when all else is equal, the recommendation is to choose the pre-restoration pronunciations for all names. Latin phrases are probably best pronounced as in classical Latin, at least in the United States.

French names in English also have a history of anglicization. Some of our common pronunciations of the French names that appear in Shakespeare are fully anglicized (*Paris, Verdun*), others only in part. Today, however, there is a tendency to pronounce some of these words with a full French pronunciation. This also applies to common English words that "feel" French. *Liege,* for example, is now most commonly heard in the United States as /leezh/, as in French, whereas *siege* is usually pronounced /seej/, though both share the same lineage. Other words of this sort are *nonpareil, adieu,* and *denier,* which in traditional English should be /nŏn puh REL, uh DYOO/, and /DEN yur/ or /duh NEER/.

Italian names also appear frequently in Shakespeare's plays. Some are typically pronounced as in Italian, while others have anglicized vowels: *Tranio* always has Italian /AH/, but in the United Kingdom *Bianca* usually is heard in its anglicized form /bee ANK uh/. Some directors prefer to give all names their modern Italian pronunciations. In that case a name like *Vincentio* becomes /veen CHEN tsee oh/, rather than the traditional /vin SEN shee yoh/. Both forms are listed in the *Guide*. Again it should be repeated that it is impossible to reproduce all of the phonetic nuances of a foreign language using the notation of this volume, or any other broad notation for that matter. For that reason the long French scenes in *Henry V* are not included. The best course for a performer who wants to pronounce these lines accurately is to consult a native speaker of that language.

Regional, Foreign, and Lower Class Accents

Making fun of people with foreign accents was as popular in the Elizabethan era as it is today. Perhaps the most famous example in Shakespeare is the argument over the art of war in *Henry V* between the Scot, Jamie, the Irishman,

MacMorris, and the Welshman, Fluellen.   These accents are hinted at in Shake-speare's spelling, but by no means does he provide all the clues an actor would need to reproduce the dialect fully.   Providing a notation for a regional or foreign accent is beyond the scope of this *Guide*.   However some tips are given at the appropriate section in the line-by-line guide in order to help the reader decipher some of the spellings used in the text.

It is common on recordings and films of Shakespeare's plays to hear the kings, queens and courtiers speaking Standard British while the clowns and riff-raff speak with a Cockney or regional British accent.   Again the reader should consider the play and the character.   The gravedigger in *Hamlet* is a Dane, and since we are asking the audience to use its imagination and accept English as the language of communication, it should be able to accept American as well as British.   In the United States there are also lower- and upper-class accents, and the pronunciation can be tailored to the character.   In any case Shakespeare provides only hints of these characters' accents which the actor or reader must then fill out in order to correctly reproduce whatever style of speech has been chosen.

ALTERING MODERN PRONUNCIATION TO FIT THE VERSE

Shakespeare wrote some scenes of his plays in prose, but most of them are written in verse using iambic pentameter as the metrical form.   The iamb is a weakly stressed syllable followed by a strongly stressed one.   Each iamb comprises a foot, with generally five feet per line (*penta*—Greek 'five').   The normal iambic pentameter line can be illustrated using x to represent a weak stress and / a strong stress:

> x / x   / x / x / x /
> The law hath yet another hold on you (MV 4.2.345)

> x / x / x   / x / x /
> O, pardon me, thou bleeding piece of earth (JC 3.1.254)

There are several good studies available on reading iambic verse.[12]   For the purposes of pronunciation, it is important to recognize that the rhythmic requirements of these verse lines sometimes demand a pronunciation change for certain words, either by shifting the main stress to a different syllable, compressing the word, or adding an extra syllable.   In order to understand when these

---

12. Linklater 1992 and Wright 1988 are among the best. The most important precept is beautifully summed up by Linklater: "The iambic pentameter is a pulse; it is the heartbeat of Shakespeare's poetry. Like your pulse it does not keep a steady, dull pace; it races with excitement, dances with joy or terror, slows down in contemplation . . . . There is nothing mechanical about the rhythms of great poetry. If they seem mechanical, *you* have made them so" (140).

alterations should be made it is first necessary to become familiar with some of the common variations to the basic iambic pentameter line.[13]

Variations of the Basic Iambic Pentameter Line

1. **Inversion** of a foot, in which the strong stress precedes the weak one. It may occur anywhere in the line except in the last foot where it is very rare, and it must be followed by a normal iambic foot with a strong final stress. In other words, the inverted foot and the following foot form the pattern strong-weak-weak-strong. Inversion is especially common in the first foot:

> /   x   x   / x /   x   / x   /
> *Conscience* is but a word that cowards use (R3 5.3.309)

> *Dying* with mother's dug between its lips (2H6 3.2.393)

Here the fourth foot is inverted:

> That were our royal faiths *martyrs* in love (2H4 4.1.191)

However, if it occurs in the middle of a line it is most commonly found after a pause, as in this line with two inversions, one in the first foot, and one in the third:

> *Tamer* than sleep, *fonder* than ignorance (TC 1.1.10)

2. Some lines have an extra weak syllable at the end, the **feminine ending** or **double ending**:

> x /   x   / x /   x / x   / x
> How ill white hairs becomes a fool and jester! (2H4 5.5.48)

3. A **caesura**[14] is a break in mid-line, often, but not always, indicated by punctuation. Sometimes the regular iambic rhythm is not affected by the break:

> x /   x/ x / x /   x   /
> O damn'd Iago! O inhuman dog! (O 5.1.62)

In other cases the caesura may be preceded and followed by a weak stress, giving the line two weak stresses in a row and eleven syllables instead of the usual ten. This is called an **epic caesura**. Its effect is to create a feminine ending

---

13. See Sipe 1968, 32–35; Wright 1985, 366–67; Spain 1988, 10–21, 47–61 and especially Wright 1988, 116–206 for more details on these and other variations.

14. US /sih ZOOR uh/; UK /-ZYOOR-/; *also* /-ZHOOR-/ in both countries.

before the break, with the iambic rhythm resuming on a weak stress with the next phrase:

x   /   x / x   x / x / x   /
Observe my uncle.   If his occulted guilt . . . (Ham 3.2.80)

x / x / x / x   x / x /
For by the dreadful Pluto,   if thou dost not . . . (TC 4.4.127)

4. Some lines have twelve syllables, producing six feet, a **hexameter**. This is also called an **alexandrine**:[15]

x   /   x   /   x   /   x   / x   /   x   /
Coy looks with heart-sore sighs; one fading moment's mirth
(TGV 1.1.30)

Sometimes the fifth strong stress is followed by two weak stresses. This is not strictly speaking a hexameter, but a **triple ending**.

x   / x /   x   / x / x   / x x
And for I know thou'rt full of love and *honesty* (O 3.3.118)

 It often occurs in lines ending in a name: *Angelo, Horatio, Octavia, Cassio,* and it may indicate that the two final weak syllables were meant to be reduced to one (/ANJ loh, huh RAY shyoh, ŏk TAYV yuh, KASS yoh/). The same is true of words like *courtier,* which in modern English is usually pronounced with three syllables, but can easily be reduced to two, and must be in many other instances in Shakespeare:

x   / x /   /   x x   / x / (x)x
Oh worthy fool! One that hath been a courtier (AYL 2.7.36)

5. There are also **short lines**, which come in different variations and lengths, including shared lines which together make up a complete line of iambic pentameter:

/   x   x /
Cornwall: Bind him, I say.

x   /   x / x / x
Regan: Hard, hard. O filthy traitor! (L 3.7.32)

---

15. /heck SAM ih tur/; /al ig ZAN drin/ is the oldest pronunciation; /-drīn/, /-dreen/ are newer and more common.

6. Omission of a syllable including:

a. **headless lines**, which do not contain the first, unstressed syllable. These are relatively rare in Shakespeare:

> / x / x / x / x / x
> They were all in lamentable cases (LLL 5.2.273)

Note *lamentable* in its usual UK form.

b. **broken-backed lines**, which lack an unstressed syllable after a caesura:

> ... the hour prefix'd ...
> x / x / / x / x / x
> Comes fast upon. Good my brother Troilus (TC 4.3.1–3)

7. Verse that is not iambic pentameter is also used, for example, in a long section of Act 3 Scene 1 of *The Comedy of Errors* written with four beats to the line:

> x x / x (x) / x /(x) x x /
> I should kick, being kick'd, and being at that pass,

> x x / x x / x x / x x /
> You would keep from my heels, and beware of an ass. (CE 3.1.17–18)

8. Shakespeare sometimes includes an **anapest** /AN uh pest/ (two weak stresses followed by a strong one in a single foot) among the iambic feet. This, however, is rare. Line 55 below could be scanned in two ways: with an anapest in either the third foot (slightly stressing *with* and *craft*) or in the fourth (stressing *you* and *craft*):

> ... she purpos'd,
> By watching, weeping, tendance, kissing, to
> O'ercome you with her show, and in time
> *(When she had fitted you with her craft) to work*
> Her son into th' adoption of the crown (Cym 5.5.52–56)

Once in a great while a line begins with two weak syllables:

> I am a subject,
> x x / x / x / x / x / x
> And I challenge law. Attorneys are denied me (R2 2.3.133–34)

However, usually lines that seem to contain anapests have extra syllables which were meant to be compressed to fit the iambic shape (see p. 21).

Shifting the Stress of a Word to Maintain the Iambic Rhythm

Shakespeare stressed some of his words differently than we do today. If the words occur in prose passages, there is usually no difficulty in maintaining our modern pronunciation. But if they appear in verse, the meter demands an adjustment from our current pronunciation. Sometimes in the process the words are transformed so much that recognition becomes difficult for an audience. Today *revenue* is stressed on the first syllable, and in North America is pronounced /REV uh n$\overline{oo}$/ or in the South /REV uh ny$\overline{oo}$/, but in Shakespeare's verse it is sometimes stressed on the second syllable /ruh VEN y$\overline{oo}$/:

x / x / x /   x /   x   / x
That no revenue hast but thy good spirits (Ham 3.2.58)

A naive audience hearing this pronunciation may not understand the word. To give another example, some on hearing the line

> And as mine eye doth his /ef FIJ eez/ witness
> Most truly limn'd and living in your face (AYL 2.7.193–4)

might not recognize the word *effigies*, especially since it is not a plural, but an archaic singular form. Another fairly common example is *persever* /pur SEV ur/ (modern *persevere*), but there is a long list of others.

The most common words which require a stress shift from their modern pronunciation (28 or more occurrences) are listed among the words on pp. 33–38. They are not included in the scene-by-scene lists, but all others are. The reader must decide whether to preserve Shakespeare's intended accentuation in these words, following the dictates of the meter, or at times to break with the meter, using the modern pronunciation in order to enhance the listener's understanding. A compromise is often possible. For *revénue*, for example, the reader can emphasize the second syllable slightly more than usual, while lessening the stress on the first. The same is true in phrases like *upon my sécure hour* and *a thousand cómplete courses.*

Marking the stress shifts in the *Guide* is complicated somewhat by regional differences. *Defect, princess, translate* are examples of words that may today be stressed on either the first or second syllable, depending on where the speaker is from. If Shakespeare's meter shows that *translate* must be pronounced with stress on the second syllable, that would be unusual for most Americans and normal for the British. Words of this sort are included in the *Guide* to cue those who would otherwise miss them. However, if a word can generally be pronounced with varying stress in all varieties of modern English, it is not included in the lists (for example, *perfume, mankind, adverse*, all of which show varying stress in Shakespeare).

Compressing Words

If the following line:

And hath given countenance to his speech, my lord (Ham 1.3.113)

is spoken in normal, modern English it is difficult to find the rhythm we expect in Shakespeare. There are twelve syllables rather than the ten found in a normal iambic pentameter line, and it almost seems that there are four major beats, one on each of the syllables *giv-, count-, speech,* and *lord*. To fit the verse into the proper iambic shape it is necessary to delete two syllables. In this case *given* must be reduced to /givn/, and *countenance* to /COWNT nunss/. The deletion of an entire syllable is known as **syncope** /SINK uh pee/ or **syncopation**. It is very common in Shakespeare, and sometimes, but not always, indicated by an apostrophe. In polysyllabic words it is especially common when the deleted vowel is followed by /l, r, n/: *exc'llent* /EKS lunt/, *gen'ral* /JEN rl/, *rev'rend* /REV rund/, *card'nal* /CARD nl/.

The word may also be compressed when two vowel sounds are next to each other. This occurs in three different ways:

1. The first of two adjacent vowels, each carrying a syllable, becomes a glide:
    chariot /CHĂIR ee ut/ ⇒ /CHĂIR yut/
    glorious /GLOR ee us/⇒ /GLOR yus/
2. Compression of two adjacent vowels across a word boundary:
    many a ⇒ /MEN yuh/
    be unworthy⇒ /byun WUR thee/
 3. The loss of the second of two adjacent vowels, each of which carries a syllable:
    diadem /DĪ uh dem/ ⇒ /DĪ dem/
In this last category some compressed forms have become standard in much of the United States. Three that occur in Shakespeare are:
    diamond /DĪ mund/, *violet* /VĪ lit/, *diaper* /DĪ pur/.

The reader should always be alert to the possibility of compression. *Borrower* and *borrowing* should be pronounced with two syllables in verse. The following words are often monosyllabic: *being* /beeng/, *knowing* /noing/, *flower,* which can almost be pronounced as /flar/. Nearly all examples of comparatives and superlatives of words ending in -*ly* and -*y* must be compressed so that *holier, heavier, mightier, prettiest, worthiest,* etc. should be /HOHL yur, HEV yur, MĪT yur, PRIT yist, WURTH yist/.[16]

---

16. In Elizabethan English these words were pronounced /HOHL ir, HEV ir, etc./ or /HOHL ur, HEV ur/ (Dobson, 1968, 2: 877; Kökeritz 1953, 288), but the modern reader and audience will probably be more comfortable with the forms given above.

Compression may occur in unexpected places, for example, across a word boundary when the second word begins with /h/:

> *bury him* ⇒ /BĔR yim/
> *pity him* ⇒ /PĬT yim/

It may also occasionally occur in names that otherwise are pronounced fully. It is found at least once for *Priam, Diomed,* and *Hermione,* while *Lewis* almost always calls for a monosyllabic pronunciation in Shakespeare, compressed from /LŌŌ iss/ to /lŌŌss/ (Cercignani 1981, 282).

Contractions of verbs and pronouns are another sort of compression not always indicated in the text. To avoid introducing an extra unstressed syllable, *I am* should sometimes be read as *I'm*; *he will* as *he'll*; *thou hast* as *thou'st*; *thou art* as *th'art* etc. :

> x   / x / x / x / x   / x
> *We are* glad the Dolphin is so pleasant with us (H5 1.2.259)

It should be noted that the same word is not always consistently syncopated or compressed. Some words can be pronounced with one or two syllables, depending on where they fall in the verse line: *giv(e)n, heav(e)n, warr(a)nt*; some can have either two or three: *dang(e)rous, prosp(e)rous, temp(o)ral, beck(o)ning, flatt(e)ry, desp(e)rate.*

None of the examples of compression or syncopation given thus far place any particular strain on the modern reader, actor, or audience. More difficult are those instances in which the meter indicates the need for a greater departure from our current pronunciation.   For instance, in Shakespeare's time /v/ was sometimes lost between vowels, in a process going back to Middle English (Kökeritz 1953, 324–25; Dobson 1968, 2: 965). This is familiar to most readers in the common poetic forms *e'en, o'er, e'er* for *even, over, ever.* But it may give the modern speaker pause when the meter demands a monosyllable for *having, heaven, seven, given, devil,* and also for some words with /ţh/ and /r/ between vowels, as in the following examples:

> x / x / x /   x / x /
> Be absolute for death: *Either* death or life
> Shall thereby be the sweeter.   (MM 3.1.5-6)

> x   / x / x / x / x   /
> *Marry,* thou dost wrong me, thou dissembler, thou— (MA 5.1.53)

Other examples occur in *whether* (sometimes written *whe'er*), *whither, spirit, Sirrah,* and *warrant* (Wright 1988, 152).   It is possible that in Shakespeare's time all of these words were pronounced with a weakened /ţh/ or /r/, but in most cases Elizabethan spellings do not indicate that the consonant in question was actually lost.[17]

But the important question is not how Shakespeare pronounced these words, but how we should pronounce them in order to make the meaning clear to a modern audience. Words like *o'er* and *e'er* pose no problem, but to weaken the /r/ of *spirit* or *warrant* to the point of omission might prevent the listener from understanding the line. However there are other ways to maintain the rhythmic integrity of the verse in these cases. *Spirit* can also be pronounced as one syllable by deleting the final vowel, /spĭrt/; *warrant* can be *warr'nt*. *Heaven* and *seven* can be pronounced more or less monosyllabically as /hevn, sevn/, with the /v/ and /n/ spoken almost simultaneously. *Marry* used explosively as an oath could be reduced to one syllable by deemphasizing the /r/, realizing it almost as /may/, In the case of *either, whither, whether,* the best solution is to retain the modern pronunciation or the lines become unintelligible.

The same common sense must govern choices involving syncopation. In the line

Thou hast so wrong'd mine innocent child and me (MA 5.1.63)

innocent should be pronounced /IN sunt/ if the meter is followed strictly. Other examples of words that sometimes demand a radical syncopation are *maj'sty, vag'bond, el'quence, imped'ment, count'feit, rec'mend, lib'tine, carc'sses* (Wright 1988, 152). To completely delete these syllables may make audiences feel too much has been sacrificed in the interest of meter. One alternative is to reduce these syllables to a hint of a vowel when syncopation is demanded, producing a sort of half-syllable (Wright 1988, 158). If a word listed in the scene-by-scene guide contains a syllable which should be syncopated in this way, that syllable is enclosed in parentheses to remind the reader that some sort of reduction is called for. The reader then may chose how far to proceed in each case.

---

17. Elizabethan commentators on pronunciation almost never recorded monosyllabic *heaven,* which may indicate it was a rare variant, perhaps used by poets artificially (Dobson 1968, 2: 911). The same may be true for most of the words with *th* or *r* in this category, many of which have no written forms that show consonantal deletion, but only the evidence of the meter to indicate something is different. Dobson 1968 and Cercignani 1981 are silent on the subject of an Elizabethan deletion of /th/ and /r/ between vowels. Kökeritz believes /th/ was deleted (1953, 322). Wright speculates that the poets heard /v, th, r/ between vowels as "less than fully formed" (1988, 152). S. Wells states that Shakespeare did not expect these words to be contracted (1979, 23). That full deletion was possible can be demonstrated by looking at some modern dialects. In parts of the southern United States /r/ is lost in this position (*story, Carol*) (Donna Christian and Walt Wolfram, *Dialects and Education: Issues and Answers,* Englewood Cliffs, NJ: Prentice Hall Regents, 1989, 133); and in the dialect of Belfast, N. Ireland /th/ is deleted between vowels (*feather*) (John Harris, *Phonological variation and change: Studies in Hiberno-English,* Cambridge, UK: Cambridge University Press, 1985, 58).

Compression of the word *the* should also be noted. Before a vowel or *h-*, which was more often silent in Shakespeare's time than it is today, *the* can be easily attached to the following word to rid the line of an extra syllable:

> The rugged Pyrrhus, like *th'Hyrcanian* beast (Ham 2.2.450)
> ⇒ /th⁷ur KAYN yun/

Note that these instances are not always marked with an apostrophe:

> A blanket, in *the alarm* of fear caught up (Ham. 2.2.509)
> ⇒ /th⁷uh LARM/

Before a consonant, if *the* creates an extra syllable, it is usually attached to a preceding preposition that ends in a vowel. In the following line there are two such instances:

> /   x x   /   x /   x   /   x   /
> Even to the court, the heart, *to th'* seat *o'th* brain (Cor 1.1.136)
> ⇒ /tooth SEET uth BRAYN/

A reader's tendency would be to substitute full *the* in both the fourth and fifth feet: *to the seat of the brain.* This may in the end be necessary for clarity but to do so changes the rhythm of the line from what Shakespeare intended (see p. 27). Note again that these instances are not always marked by apostrophes:

> Tweaks me *by the* nose, gives me the lie i'th' throat (Ham 2.2.574)

One final example of reduction from our modern pronunciation needs to be mentioned, the possessive form in words ending in /s/. In Shakespeare's verse words like *Pyrrhus', Phoebus'* would nearly always have two syllables, not three. This form appears relatively often in Shakespeare's works:

> She is sad and passionate at your Highness' tent (J 2.1.544)
> ⇒ /HĪ niss tent/, not /HĪ niss iz tent/.

Note also the contraction of *She is* and syncopation of *passionate* to /PASH nut/.

Only those examples of syncopation and compression which otherwise present pronunciation problems are given in the scene-by-scene lists. So, for example, the reader will be expected to find the syncopated form of *enemy* whenever it occurs, but the unfamiliar *hebona* /HEB (uh) nuh/ is listed with syncopation indicated.

Expanding Words

Sometimes a word will not fit the meter unless an extra syllable is added. In some cases this means shifting our modern pronunciation back to what it was a few centuries ago. The most important example is the verb ending *-ed*. In ordinary speech the Elizabethans pronounced this ending much as we do, but in their verse the older, Middle English syllable was sometimes retained (Dobson 1968, 2: 885; Wright 1988, 50-51). A word like *saved* is now, as in 1600, /sayvd/, but in the poetry of the day it could sometimes be /SAY vid/. Today the meter demands that we follow the Elizabethan lead or the verse sounds poorly written, and this is the common stage practice.

In some editions of Shakespeare the *-ed* ending is spelled out if it must be expanded to a separate syllable, while an apostrophe is used if it is reduced. *The sea enraged is not half so deaf* (J 2.1.451) would require the pronunciation /en RAY jid/.[18] Modern /en RAYJD/ would be indicated if it were written *enrag'd*. Other editions use an accent over the *e* for a full syllable (either *-èd* or *-éd*) and unmarked *-ed* to indicate our usual pronunciation. The reader should be cautious if using reproductions of the folios and quartos where the apostrophe is used inconsistently to mark elision of the syllable.

Other examples of expansion are found in suffixes like *-tion*. In Shakespeare's time this ending was sometimes pronounced with one syllable (/-syun/ or modern /-shun/) and sometimes with two (/-sih un/) as in Middle English (Dobson 1968, 2:957-58). For example, the meter tells us that in the line:

> x   /   x / x /   x / x/
> Whose power was in the first proportion (1H4 4.4.15)

the suffix was pronounced as two syllables, while in the next example the meter indicates one syllable:

> x / x /   x / x   / x /
> I will survey th'inscriptions back again (MV 2.7.14)

Other examples of words that sometimes demand expansion are those that end in *-ial, -ient, -ian, -ious, -iage*:

> Too flattering-sweet to be *substantial* (RJ 2.2.141)

> I can no longer hold me *patient* (R3 1.3.156)

> By'r Lady, he is a good *musician* (1H4 3.1.231)
>   (with contraction of *he is*)

---

18. In the *Guide* the *-ed* ending immediately following a stressed syllable will be symbolized /-id/ though it may vary between /-id/ and /-ed/.

Confess yourselves wonderous *malicious* (Cor 1.1.88)
(with inversion in the 3rd foot and syncopation to *wond'rous*)

To woo a maid in way of *marriage* (MV 2.9.13)

Your mind is tossing on the *ocean* (MV 1.1.8)

If the meter demands two syllables for *-tion*, *-tial*, etc., the reader is again faced with the choice of making the verse limp by leaving out the extra syllable, or of sounding odd to an audience by putting it in as /-shee un/. The *-ed* ending may also be somewhat jarring the first time it is heard, but it is such a widely accepted convention that it is soon taken for granted. However, even when the meter demands it, the *-tion* ending is rarely pronounced with two syllables on the stage and to use it may make the reading sound odd or affected. Again a "half-syllable," with a hint of the extra vowel may be a possible solution (Spain 1988, 38).

Monosyllabic words may also occasionally be expanded, especially if /r/ or /l/ are involved:

/   x   x   /x   /   x   /   x   /   x
Therefore in *fierce* tempest is he coming (H5 2.4.99)

x /   x   /x   /   x /x   /
This ignorant present, and I *feel* now (M 1.5.57)

Other words of this sort are *weird, more, bear, fourth, gules*. There are also instances of words which are usually two-syllables in both Elizabethan and modern English, expanding to three. One of the most common is *business:*

x / x   /   x /   x   / x/
I must employ you in some *business* (MND 1.1.124)

Some of these expanded words sound distinctly odd today, and the extra syllable should be ignored or pronounced as lightly as possible:

captain /KAP ih tun/, *angry* /ANG gur ee/,
Henry /HEN ur ee/, *children* /CHILL dur un/

This group of "unusual expansions" is listed as each word appears in the scene-by-scene guide to alert the reader that a change is indicated. However other expansions which are not much different than the modern pronunciation are not included, but are left for the reader to discover:

monstrous /MŎN stur us/, *fiddler* /FID ł ur/,
rememberance /ree MEM bur unss/, *prisoners* /PRIZ uh nurz/

Why Follow the Iambic Meter?

With attention to the demands of the iambic meter, seemingly irregular lines can be made regular by expansion, compression, or shifts in syllable stress. But does it really matter if an extra weak syllable is inserted into a line occasionally, or if the rhythm deviates beyond the common variations listed at the beginning of this section? A much debated topic in Shakespearean scholarship has been how strictly the syllables of the verse line should follow the iambic pattern.[19] Some scholars believe that it should be followed as much as possible. Others maintain, and many actors and directors agree with them, judging by the way they pronounce the words on stage, that Shakespeare never intended the meter to be so strictly followed; that the iambic line is not as important as the rhythm of the natural spoken phrase (Wright 1988, 12). This school of thought would claim that it is not the end of the world to break from the iambic pentameter and its permissible variants to produce four-beat lines, or pronounce two weak stresses together in the form of an anapest. If this argument were taken to its logical extreme there would be no need to compress, expand, or shift the stress of any word like *revenue* or *persever* to fit the meter.

To illustrate the difference, the following passage could be spoken with four strong beats and two or more weak stresses in between:

> This music mads me, let it sound no more,
> x   /   x x   /   /   x x x   /
> For though it have holp mad men to their wits,
> In me it seems it will make wise men mad. (R2 5.5.61-63)

but giving it its iambic reading means lightly stressing *have* and *to*, thereby changing the melody and the emphasis of the line.

If the line already cited from *Coriolanus* were expanded fully to modern English there would be three anapests after an initial inversion:

> / x   x x /   x /   x x / x x /
> Even to the court, the heart, to th' seat o'th brain (Cor 1.1.136)

Obviously there is no loss in meaning in this line when it is expanded in this way, in fact it could be argued that the words are clearer than if an attempt were made to pronounce *to th' seat* as /tōōth SEET/. But the feel of the verse is slightly different.

This difference is even more evident in the following passage. A reading using the accents of modern English would produce:

---

19. See Wright 1988, 10–12, 151, 154; Kökeritz 1953, 26–27; Kökeritz 1969, 208–12 for a description of that debate.

```
  x  /  x  x  /    x  x  /  x  /  x
As many farewells as be stars in heaven,
     x    x /    /    x  x  /    /  x  /   x
With distinct breath and consign'd kisses to them,
He fumbles up into a loose adieu;  (TC 4.4.44-46)
```

An iambic reading, however, places first syllable stress on *distinct, consign'd* and *farewells,* producing a very different sort of rhythmic flow.

Proponents of strict iambic readings contend that by following the rhythm more precisely than many contemporary actors do, we find subtle indications of Shakespeare's intentions while at the same time making the line more verse-like; it retains its identity as poetry, rather than drifting into prose (Spain 1988, 22-36; Linklater 1992, 132; Wright 1988, 193-94). Moreover, by following the iambic rhythm generally, the acceptable variations (the inversions, caesuras, alexandrines, etc.) highlight subtle meanings and point to irregularities in the thoughts of the characters, disturbed emotional states, or heightened feelings.[20] Poets, like composers, set their words to specific rhythms with great deliberation. Changing iambic feet to anapests is like ignoring the dot on a dotted eighth note or playing in three-quarter time instead of six-eight. The words may be the same, but the "meaning" of the piece changes.

However there is a danger of going too far. Once the reader understands the scansion of the line, he or she must choose whether or not to carry out any indicated changes. Should *Lewis* really be pronounced /lōoss/ just because the meter demands a monosyllable? Should *commendable* be pronounced with stress on the first syllable or is the modern pronunciation the best choice? Kristin Linklater calls these choices "negotiable artistic option over the rule of prosodic law"(1992, 139) and warns of the danger of becoming too pedantic in the pursuit of the perfect rhythm.

In the end, pronunciation decisions should be made by weighing the need to preserve the verse's form against the need to deliver the author's meaning. Whenever a compression, expansion, or stress shift is demanded, the reader must keep in mind that there will sometimes be a trade-off between audience understanding and strict adherence to the meter. Any deviation from modern pronunciation must be accompanied by a certain amount of common sense. It is clear that Shakespeare intended his verse to be spoken iambically, so as a general rule, readers should maintain the iambic rhythm as much as possible by altering their pronunciation in the ways outlined in this section. However, in a line like the following:

Like to a vagabond flag upon a stream (AC 1.4.45)

---

20. See for example Wright 1988, 160–73. Wright finds in some syncopations and compressions, ambiguous half-syllables that "crowd the air with meanings only half-spoken" (1988, 158).

where *vagabond* must be pronounced /VAG bŏnd/ to maintain the meter, the speaker should pause and ask whether an audience will be more annoyed at the alteration than pleased because it feels the verse. Again, using a half-syllable /VAG ^{uh} bŏnd/, with a hint of a vowel after the first syllable, may be the best compromise.

A Pronouncing
Guide to the Plays
and Poems

Each play or poem appears in alphabetical order and the words are arranged by scene in the order they appear. The form given in *The Riverside Shakespeare* is listed first, with alternatives from other editions following in bold face type. Some variants from the quartos and folios which were not found in any edition are also listed in italics.

At the beginning of each play or poem are listed the names of people who either appear in or are repeatedly mentioned in that work. This is followed by a list of frequently mentioned places. Only those people and places are listed whose names would pose difficulties for the average native speaker.

Before turning to a play the reader should become familiar with the two lists on pp. 33–40.

1.   **The Most Common "Hard" Words in Shakespeare**
2.   **The Most Common Reduced Forms**

These words will not appear in the scene-by-scene lists because each occurs so frequently that to include them would have involved considerable repetition.

Special symbols used in the lists
* included on one of the surveys (see p. 6)
( ) meter demands that the enclosed syllable either be deleted or suppressed (see p. 23)
[ ] less common pronunciations.
Q and F refer to the quarto and folio versions of Shakespeare's work.

Reminders

1. *Mars' drum, Theseus' love, Proteus' birth.* A possessive after /s/ or /z/ does not create a new syllable: /marz drum/ not /MARZ iz drum/.

2. *Octavius, Antonio, Hortensio.*   Some names ending in *-io, -ius, -ea,* etc. are pronounced with two final unstressed syllables in prose /an TOHN ee oh/, but in verse they often should be compressed:

> Let good Antonio look he keep his day (MV 2.8.25)
> ⇒ /an TOHN yoh/.

However, at the end of a line of verse the two weak syllables may be maintained (a **triple ending**), or compressed to form a **feminine ending**:

> What mercy can you render him, Antonio? (MV 4.1.378)
> ⇒ /an TOHN yoh/ or /-ee oh/.

3. If undecided about a choice of pronunciations, use the older, traditional English forms. The label "older" refers to the form normally used in English until interference from spelling, restored Latin, etc. occurred. It does not refer to ancient Roman or Middle English pronunciations. The "older" form of *huswife* would be /HUZ if/; *liege* would be /leej/; *Actaeon* would be /ak TEE un/.

THE MOST COMMON "HARD" WORDS IN SHAKESPEARE

These words occur over twenty-eight times according to the *Harvard Concordance to Shakespeare* (1973) (the number of occurrences appears in parentheses). Because they occur so often, they will not be listed in the scene-by-scene guide.

Some words are listed because they are stressed differently in Shakespeare's verse than they are in modern English. Words like *offense* /uh FENSS/ present no problems to British speakers, but are included because Americans sometimes use an inappropriate form /AW fenss/, based on sports usage. Note also that some of these words may retain their modern English accentuation if the foot can be inverted (see p. 17). In prose they may also be pronounced as in modern English.

*abhor (-s, -r'd, -r'dst, -red, -ring, all-abhorred) /ab-, ub HOR/ [-OR] to loathe, be horrified by (51).

*adieu (-s) /uh DYŌO, ad YŌO/ goodbye.   Other alternatives not recommended, except in cases where a French character would use the French pronunciation. Some speakers prefer a French pronunciation for this word, but the angl. form has a long history in English and is necessary for some rhymes (107).

afeard /uh FEERD/ afraid. Still used in some dialects of SW England (33).

anon /uh NŎN/ 'soon' or 'at once' (137).

aspect (-s) in verse /ass SPECT/ usually with meaning 'face' (33).

ay /ī/ yes (785). Note that **aye** 'ever' is /ay/, though a newer pronunciation /ī/ is often used, but not recommended. Confusion is rampant because in many non-Shakespearean texts the spellings are reversed: **aye** means 'yes' and **ay** is 'ever.'

*bade /bad, bayd/ past tense of *bid*, 'ordered, greeted, summoned.' /bayd/ is newer. Both are used equally among scholars in CN, but /bad/ is preferred in the UK and US. Among the general population /bayd/ is the overwhelming choice (47).

   forbade /for BAD, for BAYD/ did not permit (4).

besiege see **siege**.

business (-es) may be either /BIZ niss/ or /BIZ ih niss/ depending on meter. The latter is virtually unknown in mod. English (253).

ă-bat, ăir-ma**rry**, air-**pair**, ạr-**far**, ĕr-me**rry**, ĝ- get, ī-high, ĭr-mirror, ł-little, ṇ-listen, ŏ-hot, oh-go, ōō-wood, ōō-moon, oor-**tour**, ōr- or, ow-how, ţh-that, ŧh-thin, Ŭ-but, UR-f**ur**, ur-under.   ( ) - suppress the syllable   see p. xiii for complete list.

*censure (-s, -d, -ing) /SEN shur/; US, CN *also* [-chur] (n) judgement, (v) to find fault with. /-syoor/ is not recommended (see App. D *-ure*) (34).

*choler (-s) /CŎL ur/ anger. /COH lur/ is not recommended (28).
  *choleric depending on meter: /CŎL ur ik, CŎL rik/ 'prone to anger.' Never /cuh LĔR ik/ in Shakespeare (10).

contrary /cŏn-, cun TRĔR ee/ or with 1st syllable stress, which in the US is /CŎN trĕr ee/ [-truh ree]; UK /-truh ree/ (49).

*courtier (-s, -'s, -s') in verse /COR tyur/; US, CN *rarely* [COR chur] man of the court. May be /COR tee ur/ in prose or at the end of a line in a triple ending (45).

coz /CUZ/ cousin (44).

cozen (-'d, -s, -er, -ers, -ing, coz'ning, -age, coz'nage) /CUZ in, -ŋ/ deceive (36). *Cozenage, cozening, cozener* may need to be reduced to two syllables (/CUZ nij/, etc.) depending on meter.

*cuckold (-ed, uncuckolded) /CUCK łd, CUCK old/ (n) husband of an adulterous woman, (v) to deceive a husband by committing adultery (44).

defense (UK **defence**) **(-s)**, /dih-, dee FENSS/. US /DEE fenss/ will not fit the meter (46).

Dian (-'s) /DĪ un, -an/ Diana, Roman goddess of the hunt and of chastity (28).

discharge (-'d, -ed, -est, -ing) in verse (n, v) /dis CHĄRJ/ (53).

*discourse (-ed, -er, es) in verse /dis CORSS/ (n) speech, (v) speak (66).

*dispatch (-'d,) (n, v) in verse /dih SPATCH/ often with meaning 'hurry' (97).

dost /DUST/ 2nd person sing. indicative of *do.* /dŏst/ not recommended (451).
  *doth /DUŦH/ does. /dŏŧħ/ not recommended (1072).

doublet (-s) /DUB lut/ man's garment worn over a shirt (29).

ducat (-s) /DUCK ut/ gold coin (59).

ere /air/ before (397); **ere't** /airt/ before it (5); **erewhile** /air WHĪL/ hitherto (3).

*err (-s, -ing) to make a mistake. US, UK /ur/ [ĕr]; CN /ĕr/ [ur]. /ĕr/ is the newer form and is non-standard in the UK.   Among the general population /ĕr/ is strongly preferred (28).

*exile (-'d) (v, n) 1st or 2nd syllable stress in verse. Today in the US /EGG zīl/ [EK sīl]; CN uses both equally; UK /EK sīl/ [EGG zīl] (33).

farewell (-s) usually with 2nd syllable stress as in modern English, but sometimes stressed on the 1st syllable (380).

feign (-'d, -ed, -ing) /fayn/ 1) to fabricate, 2) to pretend; *feigning* 'pretending, imaginative' (23).
   unfeigned (-ly) /un FAY nid/ honest, true (7).

fie /fī/ expression of disgust or shock (167).

*flourish (-'d, -es, -eth, -ing) US, CN /FLUR ish/, *sometimes newer* [FLŌŌR-, FLŌR-]; UK, E.COAST US /FLUH rish/ (n) embellishment, (v) to thrive (35).

forbade see **bade**.

gallant (-s) (adj) 'brave, full of spirit' is always /GAL unt/. The noun 'man of fashion, ladies' man' is also /GAL unt/ in verse, but in prose may be /guh LĂNT/, a common modern form (71).

hie (-s, -d) /hī/ hurry (61).

import (-s, -ing, -ed, -eth, -less) (n) importance, (v) to mean. Whether noun or verb always /im PORT/ in verse except once at AW 2.3.276 where it is /IM port/ (42).

*Jesu Jesus. US /JAY zōō/ [JEE-, JAY sōō, YAY zōō]; UK /JEE zyōō/ [-zōō], *rarely* [JAY-, YAY-, -sōō]. The recommended forms are the oldest, /JEE zyōō/ in the UK,   /JEE zōō/ in North America.   The others are newer, based on classical and church Latin (28).

levy (-ies, -ied, -ing) /LEV ee/ usually meaning (n) army, (v) raise an army or money. **Levying** may be /LEV ying/ or /LEV ee ing/ depending on meter (30).

*liege (-'s) overlord; **liegeman, -men** vassals, subjects. /leej/ is older and more common in the UK; in North America /leej/ and newer /leezh/ are used equally (145).

ă-bat, ăir-marry, air-**pair**, ạr-far, ĕr-merry, ĝ- get, ī-high, ĭr-mirror, ł-little, ṇ-listen, ŏ-hot, oh-go, ōō-wood, ōō-moon, oor-**tour**, ōr- **or**, ow-how, ṭh-**that**, t̶h̶-thin, ŭ-but, UR-**fur**, ur-under.   ( ) - suppress the syllable   see p. xiii for complete list.

madam (-'s, -s) /MAD um/ form of address to a middle or upper class woman. Note the difference from Fr. **madame** /mah DAHM, MAH dahm/, found only in H5 3.4, a Fr. language scene (530).

medicine, med'cine (-s) despite the spellings, each of these may be pronounced either /MED ih sin/ or /MED sin/ depending on meter. The latter is the most common UK form, but is unknown in the US (31).

*****methinks** /mee-, mih ~~THINKS~~/ it seems to me. The former is favored slightly in the US, UK, and strongly in CN (162).
    methought /mee-, mih ~~THAWT~~/ it seemed to me (53).

monsieur (-s) depending on meter: /muh SYUH, -SYUR/ or with 1st syllable stress /MŏŏS-, MUH-/. French form of address to a middle or upper class man. The Fr. pronunciation /mö syö/ can also be stressed on either syllable (40).

offense (UK **offence**) (-'s, -s, -less, -ful) /uh FENSS/. US /AW fenss/ will not fit the meter (150).

princess (-') /PRIN sess/ or /prin SESS/ depending on meter. The most common Standard British pronunciation is /prin SESS/, which is almost unheard of in the US (63).

*****prithee** /PRIŢH ee/, *sometimes newer* [PRI~~TH~~ ee] I pray thee, please (229).

quoth /kwoh~~th~~/ said (117).

rapier (-s, -'s) /RAY pyur/ type of sword. /RAY pee ur/ will not usually fit the meter in verse, but may be used in prose (29).

recompense /REK um penss/ (v) to pay back, (n) payment (33).

requite (-s, -ed) /rih-, ree KWĪT/ to return love or repay something.   Once stressed on the 1st syllable TmA 4.3.522 (33).
    requital /rih-, ree KWĪT ł/ repayment (7).

seignieur see **signior.**

*****siege** (-s) /seej/; US, CN *also newer* [seezh]. Usually 1) military blockade of a town, but also 2) seat, 3) rank, 4) excrement (34).
    besiege (-'d, -ed) US, CN /bee-, bih SEEJ/ [-SEEZH]; UK /bih SEEJ/ to lay siege to (16).

signior (-s) /SEEN yor/ form of address to a middle or upper class man, based on Italian. Some eds. prefer Ital. **signor** for the Italian names (pronounced the same way), Fr. **seignieur** angl. /SEN YUR/; Fr. /sen yör/ for the French names, and Sp. **señor** /sayn YOR/ for Armado in LLL. In verse they are all stressed on the first syllable (139).

*sinew (-s, -ed, -y) /SIN yo͞o/; US *also* [SIN o͞o] 1) tendon, 2) nerve, 3) strength (30). In addition *Riverside* has the archaic variants **sinow (-s, -y)** /SIN oh/ (7).

sirrah form of address to a servant or inferior (152). /SĬR uh/ is generally used, but if the word had survived into modern English, /SUR uh/ would also have been common in North America (cf. *syrup, stirrup* with both /UR/ and /ĬR/).

strook *Riverside* uses this archaic form, possibly pronounced /stro͞ok/, or perhaps simply a variant spelling of **struck** (cf. *flood, blood*) (55).
  strooken is usually modernized to **strucken** or **stricken** (6).

*subtle, subtile (-ly, -ties, -ty, -er) /SUT ł/ 1) sly, 2) tricky, 3) delicate. /SUB-/ is not recommended (47). *Subtly, subtilly* are always two syllables /SUT lee/ in verse.

*surfeit (-er, -ed, -ing, -s) /SUR fit/ (n) too much of something, (v) to have too much of something (38).

swounds see **zounds.**

thereas, thereat, etc. see **whereas.**

*thither toward a place. In the US, CN the newer form /THITH ur/, with initial *th* as in *thin,* is much more common. In the UK the older form /T͟HIT͟H ur/, with initial *th* as in *then,* is preferred and the newer form is non-standard (98).

toward (-s) (prep.) usually one syllable in verse, but sometimes two are indicated. If two syllables, then /TOH urd/ or /tuh-, to͞o WÂRD/ (as in *war*), depending on meter; if one, /tōrd, twōrd/. In the UK, CN the usual pronunciation is /tuh-, to͞o WÂRD/; in the US /tōrd, twōrd/ (156). Note the difference from adj., adv. **toward (-ly)** 'about to take place, obedient' which is usually /TOH wurd, -urd/ (17).

*troth (-s) /trohth/ truth. Two other common alternatives /trŏth/ and US /trawth/ will not fit the rhymes (112).

unfeigned see **feign.**

unwonted see **wont.**

ă-bat, ăir-marry, air-pair, ạr-far, ĕr-merry, ĝ- get, ī-high, ĭr-mirror, ł-little, ṇ-listen, ŏ-hot, oh-go, o͞o-wood, o͞o-moon, oor-tour, ōr- or, ow-how, t͟h-that, th-thin, ŭ-but, UR-fur, ur-under.   ( ) - suppress the syllable   see p. xiii for complete list.

*usurp (-ed, -'d, -er(s), -er's, -s, -'st, -ing(ly), -ation) take over unlawfully. US /yo͞o SURP/ [-ZURP]; CN both /s, z/ forms used equally; UK /yo͞o ZURP/ [-SURP] (69).

vild (-er, -est, -ly) /vīld/ archaic variant of **vile** (57).

*visage /VIZ ij/ face. /VISS ij/ not recommended and is non-standard in the UK (41).

vouchsafe (-'d, -ed, -s, -ing) /vowch SAYF/ to grant.   Alternatively, both syllables may be evenly stressed (62, including 4 instances of the archaic form **voutsafe** /vowt SAYF/).

*wanton (-ly, -ness, -'s, -s) /WŎN tun/; US *also* [WAWN tun] (adj) morally loose, (n) a morally loose person (91).

wherefore 'why.'   The usual pronunciation is with 1st syllable stress, even at the beginning of a line where it could have 2nd syllable stress: *Whérefore should I curse him?* It occasionally shows stress shift to the 2nd syllable (144).
   Note that **whereas, whereat, whereby, etc.** as well as **thereat, thereby, etc.** also vary, but usually have 2nd syllable stress.   **Therefore**, however, like *wherefore,* is pronounced as it is in mod. Eng. with 1st syllable stress.

whiles /whīlz/; **whilest** /WHĪL ust/; **whil'st** /whīlst/.   All three forms mean 'while' (122).

*withal /wi h AWL/; US, CN *also* /wi h -/ with.   In the UK /wi h -/ is non-standard (151).   So also **therewithal** with main stress on either the first or last syllable (9).

without usually stressed on the 2nd syllable, as it is today, but 29 times with 1st syllable stress.

wot (-s, -st. -ting) /wŏt/ know (33).

*wont US /wohnt, wawnt, wŏnt/; CN, UK /wohnt/ [wŏnt] 'custom,' **wonted** 'accustomed,' **unwonted** 'unusual' (64).   Among the general population /wawnt/ is the most common in the US.

*zounds, swounds /zowndz, zo͞ondz/ by God's wounds.   Both pronunciations were used in Elizabethan English.   By the end of the nineteenth century /zowndz/ alone was recommended, but /zo͞ondz/ was restored during the twentieth century, and now predominates in the UK.   Both are used equally among scholars in North America and both can be justified on historical grounds (29).

THE MOST COMMON REDUCED FORMS

'a he (183). *'a was a merry man.* Best pronounced as *he* is in modern, informal speech: "He was a merry man." Note in weak position, modern *he* also may lose /h/: "Did 'e go?" /did ee GO/. The unstressed sound spelled *a* could vary between /uh/ and /ih/ in older dialects, hence the spelling variations like *Ursula-Ursley, sirrah-sirry.* Today this final unstressed /ih/ has become /ee/ in most American dialects.

a' /uh/ of, on, in (195). *'a God's name.*

'a' /uh/ have (7). *She might 'a' been.*

e'en /een/ even (36). Note that as an adv. **even** spelled fully (*even till they wink*) should usually be pronounced as one syllable, either as /een/ or with the /v/ and /n/ pronounced nearly simultaneously.

e'er /ĕr/ ever (177); so also **howe'er** (9), **howsoe'er** (5), **howsome'er** (2), **soe'er** (6), **some'er** (1), **whatsome'er** (2), **wheresoe'er** (10), **wheresome'er** (1), **whoe'er** (10), **whosoe'er** (3). Ev'r is occasionally used, and also indicates that the meter demands one syllable.

ha' /hă/ have (25). *I'll ha' thee burnt.* Our normal /hav/ may be substituted for better clarity. **ha't** /hat, havt/ have it (11).

h'as /hʸaz/ he has (24). Our normal modern contraction *he's* /heez/ may also be used.

i' /ih/ in (400). Usually in the combinations:
i'faith /ih FAYTH/ in faith (a mild oath).
i'th' in the. *i'th' name of Beelzebub!* Meant to be pronounced /ith/ in verse to preserve the iambic meter, but in practice *in the* is often substituted (see p. 24).

ne'er /nĕr/ never (234). **Nev'r** also is used which should be pronounced as one syllable.

o' /uh/ of (284). *any kind o' thing.* Sometimes with meanings 'on, one.'
o'th' of the. *the frown o' th' great.* Meant to be pronounced /uth/ in verse to preserve the iambic meter, but in practice *of the* is often substituted (see p. 24).

ă-bat, ăir-marry, air-pair, ạr-far, ĕr-merry, ĝ- get, ī-high, ĭr-mirror, ł-little, ṇ-listen, ŏ-hot, oh-go, o͞o-wood, o͞o-moon, oor-tour, ōr- or, ow-how, ţh-that, t͟h-thin, ŭ-but, UR-fur, ur-under.   ( ) - suppress the syllable   see p. xiii for complete list.

o'er /or/ over (219 plus many compounds).

't it. Attached either to the preceding or following word *take't, by't* /taykt , bīt/; *'t may* /tmay/.

t' to. Attached to the following word *t'invite, t'accept;* /tin VĪT, tak SEPT/. It is also possible to use the form /tw-/ to make it clearer that *to* is intended without adding an extra syllable: /twin VĪT, twak SEPT/.
   t'other the other. /TUŢH ur/.

ta'en /tayn/ taken (104). So also **mista'en, underta'en, overta'en, o'erta'en**.

th' usually 'the,' sometimes 'thy, thou, they' (1,424). When used as a shortened form of 'the' before a vowel it is attached to the following word. *Th'end* is a single syllable /ţhʸend/, not two distinct syllables /ţhee END/.   Before a consonant it is usually attached to a preceding preposition.   Shakespeare probably intended this to be spoken as one syllable, but sometimes for clarity it should be spoken as two (see p. 24):
   i'th', o'th' (see above under **i', o'**).
   by th' *hung by th' wall* /hung bīţh WAWL/ or in reduced form /buţh/. This is especially common in oaths like *by th' mass* /buţh MASS/.
   to th' *to th' vulgar eye* /tōōţh-, tuţh VUL gur/.

whe'er, whe'r /whĕr/ whether (16).   For clarity may also be pronounced /WHEŢH ur/ (see p. 22).

Some common non-spoken words

dramatis personae cast of characters. /DRAM uh tiss pur SOH nee/; restored Latin /DRAHM ah tiss pĕr SOH nī/.

exeunt stage direction 'they exit.' /EK see unt/.

manet stage direction 'he or she remains' or **manent** 'they remain.' /MAY nut, -nunt/; restored Latin /MAH net/, /MAH nent/.

The Plays

All's Well That Ends Well

People in the Play

Austringer see **a Stranger.**

Bertram /BUR trum/.

Diana Capilet /dī ANN uh   KAP ih let/.

Dumaine (First and Second French Lords) US /doō MAYN/;
UK, SOUTH. US /dyoō-/; Fr. /dü MEN/.

***Florentine(s)** US /FLŌR in teen/ [-tīn]; E.COAST US /FLŎR-/;
UK /FLŎR in tīn/ [-teen] person from Florence.

Gerard de Narbon angl. /juh RAHRD duh NAHR bun/. In the sole verse
instance the foot may be inverted, /JĚR ard, -urd/. Some eds. prefer Fr. **Gérard**
/zhay rahr duh NAHR boh^n/.

Helena /HELL in uh/.

Lafew, Lafeu /luh FYOO/. *Lafeu* in Fr. would be /lah FÖ/.

Lavatch /luh VATCH/.

Mariana /mair ee ANN uh/, or *newer* /-AHN uh/. Her name is not spoken.

***Parolles, Paroles** US, CN /puh ROHL iz/ [-iss], *rarely* [-RŎL iss, -iz];
UK /puh ROHL iz, puh RŎL iz/ [-ROHL iss, -RŎL iss]. /puh ROHLZ/ is also
used, but its final syllable would have to be treated as two syllables to meet the
metrical requirements of the verse.

Rinaldo /rih NAL doh, -NAWL-, -NAHL-/. Some eds. prefer **Reynaldo** /ray-/.

Rossillion 3 or 4 syllables depending on meter /ruh SILL (ee) yun/. Some eds.
prefer **Roussillon** /roō-, roō-/. The Fr. /roō SEE yoh^n/ will not expand to 4
syllables.

a Stranger (F3) Mentioned in a stage direction in 5.1. Some eds. prefer F1's
astringer /ASS trin jur/, variant of **austringer** /ŎSS-, AWSS-/ 'falconer.'

ă-bat, ăir-m**a**rry, air-p**ai**r, a̱r-f**a**r, ĕr-m**e**rry, ĝ- g**e**t, ī-h**i**gh, ĭr-m**i**rror, ɫ-litt**le**, ṇ-list**e**n,
ŏ-h**o**t, oh-g**o**, oō-w**oo**d, oō-m**oo**n, oor-t**ou**r, ōr- **o**r, ow-h**ow**, ţh-**th**at, t̶h̶-**th**in, ŭ-b**u**t,
UR-f**u**r, ur-**u**nder.   ( ) - suppress the syllable   see p. xiii for complete list.

People in the Play (cont.)

Violenta angl. /vī oh LEN tuh/, /vee oh LEN tuh/ is based on Ital. Some eds. do not include her in 3.5, making her the same character as Diana.

Places in the Play

Rossillion see "People in the Play."

St. *Jaques le Grand. The most common angl. forms are US /saynt JAY kweez luh GRAND/; UK /sn̩t-, sint-/. Other forms are [jayks], or *rarely* US [JAY kiz, -keez, -kis]; UK [JAY kwiz, -kwes]. Some eds. prefer Fr. **St. Jacques le Grand**, which would normally be pronounced /să^n ZHAHK luh GRAH^N/. However in some lines *Jaques / Jacques* should be two syllables, which in Shk's time would have been /JAY kis/.

Act 1 Scene 1

34. **fistula** US /FIS chuh luh/; UK *also* /-tyoo luh/ a long, round ulcer.

76. **comfortable** here should be /CUM fur tuh bł/.

88. **collateral** US /cuh LAT rł/; UK *also* [cŏ-] indirect.

91. **hind** /hīnd/ doe.

98. **his reliques, relics** /REL iks/ reminders of him.

113. **barricado** barricade. /băir ih KAY doh/ is older, /-KAH doh/ is newer.

126. **politic** /PŎL ih tik/ good policy.

158. ***brooch** /brohch/ ornament. US [brōōch] not recommended.

172. **dulcet** /DULL sit/ sweet.

Act 1 Scene 2

1. **The Florentines and *Senoys* are by th' ears** may have been /SEEN oyz/ or /SEEN (oh) eez/, archaic form of **Sienese** which here would have to be /SEE (uh) neez/ or /SYEN eez/. /see uh NEEZ/ is also possible with *the* pronounced fully in a hexameter.

8. **Prejudicates** /prih-, pree JOOD ih kayts/ prejudges.

11. **credence** /CREED n̩ss/ trust.

14. **Tuscan** /TŬSS kun/ of Tuscany, a region in Italy.

17. **exploit** here should be /ek SPLOYT/.

53. ***plausive** /PLAW ziv/ [-siv] praiseworthy.

Act 1 Scene 3

25. **barnes** /ba̩rnz/ dialect word for 'babies.' A more commonly known dialect variant preferred by some eds. is **bairns** /bairnz/, still found in Scotland and North.Eng.

49. ***ergo** /UR go/ is older, /ĔR go/ is newer. The former is more common in the UK, the latter in the US, but both forms appear in all countries.

52. **Charbon** angl. /SHAHR bun/; Fr. /shahr boh^n/. Some eds. prefer Fr. **Chairbonne** /shair bŏn/ 'good-flesh,' i.e., Protestant.

52. **Poysam** /POY sum, -zum/. Some eds. prefer **Poisson** Fr. /pwah soh^n/ 'fish,' i.e., Catholic.

52. **papist** /PAYP ist/ Catholic.

57. **calumnious** /cuh LUM nee us/ slanderous.

73. ***Priam's** King of Troy. US, CN /PRĪ umz/ [-amz]; UK /-amz/, *rarely* [-umz]. Normal development would favor /-um/.

85. **tithe-woman** /TĪṬH-/ tenth woman.

94. **surplice** /SUR pliss/ white priest's garment.

119. **sithence** /SI̶T̶H̶ unss/ since.

144. **enwombed mine** /en WOOM id/ born of my womb.

191. **appeach'd** /uh PEECHT/ informed against.

ă-bat, ăir-marry, air-pair, a̩r-far, ĕr-merry, ĝ- get, ī-high, ĭr-mirror, l-little, n̩-listen, ŏ-hot, oh-go, oͦo-wood, o͞o-moon, oor-tour, ŏr- or, ow-how, t̶h̶-that, t̶h̶-thin, Ŭ-but, UR-fur, ur-under. ( ) - suppress the syllable   see p. xiii for complete list.

202. **intenible** (F2), **intenable** /in TEN ih bł, -uh bł/ leaky. Some eds. prefer F1's **intemible, inteemible** /in TEEM ih bł/ 'letting nothing pour out.'

202. **sieve** /siv/ strainer.

Act 2 Scene 1

16. **questant** /KWEST unt/ seeker.

35. **I am your accessary, and so farewell** /AK sess ree/ makes the line regular. /AK sess ĕr ee/ (which in the UK would be /-uh ree/) is possible before an epic caesura, or, if *I am* is *I'm*, mod. /ak SESS uh ree/ can be used.

42. **Spinii** Ang.Lat. /SPIN ee ī/; Class.Lat. /SPIN ih ee/.

43. **Spurio** /SPUR-, SPOOR ee oh/; Ital. /SP$\overline{\text{OO}}$R-/.

43. **cicatrice** /SIK uh triss/ scar.

57. **dilated** /dih-, dī LAYT id/ expansive.

76. **Pippen, Pippin** /PIP in/ father of Charlemagne. Some eds. prefer **Pepin** /PEP in/, or Fr. **Pépin** /PAY pă^n/.

77.***Charlemain, Charlemagne** US /SHĄR luh mayn/, *rarely* [shąr luh MAYN]; CN /SHĄR luh mayn/; UK /SHĄR luh mayn/ [SHĄR luh mīn, shąr luh MAYN], *rarely* [shąr luh MĪN]. /-mīn/ is a newer pronunciation. Fr. /shąrl mahn^y/.

97. **Cressid's uncle** /CRESS idz/ Pandar, who brought Troilus and Cressida together.

122. **empirics** /EM pur iks/ quack doctors.

122. **dissever** /dih SEV ur/ sever.

155. **imposture** archaic variant of F3's **impostor**, both pronounced /im PŎS tur/ (see App. E).

162. **diurnal** /dī UR nł/ daily.

164. **Hesperus** /HES pur us/ the evening star.

167. ***infirm** /in FURM/ diseased.

170. **venter** /VEN tur/ archaic variant of **venture**.

172. **Traduc'd** slandered. /truh DY$\overline{OO}$ST/; US *also* /-D$\overline{OO}$ST/. /-J$\overline{OO}$ST/ is considered non-standard in the UK.

173. **ne** (F1) /nee/ or when unstressed /nih, nuh/, an old negative. Some eds. prefer F2's **no**.

180. *****estimate** /ES tih mayt/ value. Here rhymes with *rate*. /-mut/ would otherwise be more common in the US.

183. **intimate** /IN tih mayt/ argue.

204. **resolv'd** here should be /REE zŏlvd/ with mind made up.

Act 2 Scene 2

18. **quatch-buttock** /KWŎTCH but uck/ flat buttock.

22. **taffety** /TAF uh tee/ a silk-like cloth worn by whores. Variant of **taffeta** /TAF uh tuh/.

26. **quean** /kween/ ill-behaved woman.

54. **is very sequent** /SEE kwunt/ properly follows.

60. *****huswife** /HUZ if/ is traditional, /HUSS wīf/ is a newer, spelling pronunciation. The former is the most common form in the UK, the latter in the US. In CN both are used equally. In North America /HUSS wif/ is also sometimes used. Some eds. prefer mod. **housewife**.

Act 2 Scene 3

4. **ensconcing** /in SKŎNSS ing/ sheltering.

11. **Galen** /GAY lin/ Gk. doctor.

11. **Paracelsus** /păir uh SEL sus/ famed physician of the 16th century.

29. **facinerious** /fass ih NEER ee us/ wicked. Variant of **facinorous** /fuh SIN ur us/.

ă-bat, äir-**marry**, air-**pair**, ạr-**far**, ĕr-**merry**, ĝ- g**et**, ī-high, ĭr-m**ir**ror, ł-little, ṇ-listen, ŏ-hot, oh-go, $\overline{oo}$-wood, $\overline{oo}$-moon, oor-tour, ōr- or, ow-how, ţh-that, t̶h̶-thin, ŭ-but, UR-f**ur**, ur-under.   ( ) - suppress the syllable   see p. xiii for complete list.

34. ***debile** /DEE bīl, DEB īl/; US *rarely* [DEB ł] weak.

41. **Lustick** /LŬS tik/ merry. Some eds. prefer **Lustig**, pronounced the same way if angl., or as in Germ., /Lo͞oS tik/.

43. ***coranto** courant, a fast dance. US /coh-, cuh RAHN toh/ [-RAN-]; UK /cŏr AHN toh, -AN toh/.

44. **Mort du vinaigre** angl. /mor do͞o vin AY gruh/ pseudo-Fr. for 'death of the vinegar.' Fr. /mor dü veen AYG ^ruh/.

59. **Curtal** /CURT ł/ name of a horse with a short tail.

79. **ames-ace** /AYMZ ayss/ two aces, i.e. ones, lowest throw in dice. Some eds. prefer **ambs-ace** which is sometimes [ĂMZ ayss].

88. **eunuchs** /Yo͞o nuks/ castrated men.

152. **misprision** /mis PRIZH un, -ŋ/ misconduct.

158. ***travails** here should be /TRAV aylz/ labors.

178. **Smile upon this contract.** If /cŏn TRACT/ as elsewhere in Shk, then the first foot is inverted with a slight stress on *this*. Mod. /CŎN tract/ works as either a headless line, or an inverted first foot with *smile* considered two syllables.

204. **bannerets** /ban ur ETS/, or, especially in the UK, /BAN ur ets/ banners.

216. **egregious** /ih GREE jus/ extraordinary.

259. ***pomegranate** US, CN /PŎM uh gran it/; US *also* [PUM-, PŎM gran it, PUM ih gran it]; UK /PŎM uh gran it/ [PŎM gran it].

273. **Tuscan** /TŬSS kun/ of Tuscany, a region in Italy.

282. **curvet** here should be /cur VET/ a leap on horseback.

293. ***capriccio** whim. US /kuh PREE chyoh, -choh/, *rarely* [-PRITCH-]; UK /kuh PREE chyoh, -choh/ [-PRITCH-].

Act 2 Scene 4

41. *__prerogative__ /pur RŎG uh tiv/ [prih-, pree-] right. /pree-/ non-standard in the UK.

Act 2 Scene 5

81. __timorous__ /TIM (uh) rus/ frightened.

92. __coraggio__ /coh RAH joh/ Ital. 'courage.'

Act 3 Scene 2

31. __misprising, misprizing__ /mis PRĪZ ing/ undervaluing.

66. __moi'ty, moiety__ /MOY tee/ portion, half.

114. __caitiff__ /KAYT if/ scoundrel.

117. __ravin, raven, ravine__ (F1) all pronounced /RAV in/ ravenous.

Act 3 Scene 3

2. __credence__ /CREED ṇss/ trust.

6. __th' extreme__ here should be /ṬHᵞEK streem/.

Act 3 Scene 5

24. __lim'd__ /līmd/ coated with lime, i.e., paste.

76. __Antonio__ /an TOHN yoh/; Ital. /ahn-/.

77. __Escalus__ /ES kuh lus/.

85. __jack-an-apes__ /JACK uh nayps/ monkey, impertinent fellow.

94. __enjoin'd__ here should be /EN joynd/ bound by oath.

ă-bat, ăir-__marry__, air-__pair__, ạr-__far__, ĕr-__merry__, ĝ- get, ī-high, ĭr-__mirror__, ł-little, ṇ-listen,
ŏ-hot, oh-go, ōō-__wood__, ōō-__moon__, oor-__tour__, ōr- or, ow-how, ṭh-that, t̶h̶-thin, Ŭ-but,
UR-__fur__, ur-under.   ( ) - suppress the syllable   see p. xiii for complete list.

Act 3 Scene 6

3. **hilding** /HILL ding/ good-for-nothing.

26. **leaguer** /LEEG ur/. Some eds. prefer **laager** /LAH gur/. Both mean 'camp.'

35, 65. **stratagem** /STRAT uh jum/ scheme.

62. *__hic jacet__ here lies, i.e., I would die trying. Ang.Lat. /hick JAY sit/; Class.Lat. /heek YAH ket/. Some eds. prefer **hic iacet**, pronounced as in Class.Lat. Occasionally Church Latin /-chet/ is used.

67. **magnanimious** /mag nuh NIM ee us/ archaic variant of **magnanimous** /mag NAN ih mus/.

68. **exploit** /ek SPLOYT/ in verse, but here may be mod. /EK sployt/.

Act 3 Scene 7

37. **persever** /pur SEV ur/ persevere, carry out the plan.

44. **assay** /uh-, ass SAY/. Some eds. prefer **essay** /es SAY/. Both mean 'attempt, test.'

Act 4 Scene 1

11. **linsey-woolsey** /LIN zee WŌŌL zee/ cloth of linen and wool, i.e., mix of words.

19. **choughs', chuffs'** /chufs/ jackdaws'.

21. **politic** /PŎL ih tik/ cunning.

26. *__plausive__ /PLAW ziv/ [-siv] plausible.

38. **exploit** /ek SPLOYT/ in verse, but here may be mod. /EK sployt/.

42. **Bajazeth's** some eds. prefer **Bajazet's**, both pronounced /BAJ uh zets/ or more rarely /baj uh ZETS/. A variant with /th/ is also used.

50. **stratagem** /STRAT uh jum/ scheme.

58. **fadom** /FAD um/ archaic variant of **fathom** /FĂTH um/.

69. **Muskos', Muscos'** /MŬS kohss/.

76. **poniards** /PŎN yurdz/; UK *also newer* [-yardz] daggers.

Act 4 Scene 2

1. **Fontibell, Fontybell, Fontibel** /FŎNT ih bel/ or / FŎNT ee bel/.

37. **persever** /pur SEV ur/ persevere.

38. **scarre** uncertain meaning, perhaps pronounced /skahr/. Some eds. prefer **snare, surance**.

44, 48. **obloquy** /ŎB luh kwee/ speaking ill of someone.

70. **sate** archaic variant of **sat**. May have been /sayt/ or /sat/.

Act 4 Scene 3

59. **rector** /REK tur/ priest or governor. See App. D *-or*.

86. **abstract** /AB stract/ summary.

87. **congied, congeed** /CŎN jeed/ or /cun-, cŏn JEED/ taken formal leave. Some eds. prefer **congéd** angl. /CŎN-, COHN zhayd/, or with 2nd syllable stress; a Fr. pronunciation is also possible /coh^n zhayd/.

99. **module** /MŎD yo͞ol/; US *also* /MŎJ o͞ol/ image. *Module* was formerly confused with **model**.

100. **prophesier** /PRŎF uh sī ur/ prophet.

101. **sate** archaic variant of **sat**. May have been /sayt/ or /sat/.

123. ***pasty** meat pie. US /PĂSS tee, PAYSS-/; UK /PĂSS tee/ [PAYSS-]. /PAYSS-/ is newer.

141. **militarist** /MIL ih tur ist/ military man.

ă-bat, ăir-marry, air-pair, ạr-far, ĕr-merry, ĝ- get, ī-high, ĭr-mirror, ł-little, ṇ-listen, ŏ-hot, oh-go, o͞o-wood, o͞o-moon, oor-tour, ōr- or, ow-how, ṭh-that, ᵵh-thin, ŭ-but, UR-fur, ur-under.   ( ) - suppress the syllable   see p. xiii for complete list.

142. **theoric** /~~THEE~~ uh rik/ theory.

143. **chape** /chayp/ metal tip on the end of a sheath.

161. **Spurio** /SPUR-, SPOOR ee oh/; Ital. /SPŌOR-/.

162. **Sebastian** US /suh BĂS chun/; UK /suh BĂST yun/.

162. **Corambus** /koh-, kuh RAM bus/.

163. ***Jaques, Jacques**. Since this is a prose passage it may be pronounced with one or two syllables and Fr. /zhahk/ may be the best choice. In other instances in Shk it is commonly pronounced /JAY kweez/ (see "Places in the Play"—*St. Jaques le Grand*.)

163. **Guiltian** /ĜIL shun/ is traditional, /-shee un, -tee un/ are also used. Some eds. prefer **Guillaume** Fr. /ĝee yohm/.

163. **Lodowick** /LŎD oh wik, LOHD-, -uh-/.

164. **Gratii** Ang.Lat. /GRAY shee ī/; Class.Lat. /GRAH tih ee/. A mixed form /GRAH tee ī/ is also used.

165. **Chitopher** /CHIT uh fur, KIT uh fur/. *Christopher* may have been intended.

165. **Vaumond** /VOH.mund, -mŏnd/; Fr. /voh moh^n/.

165. **Bentii** Ang.Lat. /BEN shee ī/; Class.Lat. /BEN tih ee/. A mixed form /BEN tee ī/ is also used.

169. **cassocks** /KĂSS ucks/ soldiers' long coats.

183. **inter'gatories** questions. US /in TUR guh tor eez/; UK /-tur eez, -treez/.

187. **shrieve's** /shreevz/ archaic variant of **sherrif's**.

213. **advertisement** /ad VURT iss munt, -iz-/ warning. In this prose passage it could be pronounced /AD vur tīz munt/ as in mod. Am. Eng., but since the meanings are so different, the former, older pronunciation is recommended.

220, 300. **lascivious** /luh SIV ee us/ lustful.

236. **armipotent** /ạr MIP uh tunt/ powerful in arms.

251. **Nessus** /NESS us/ centaur who tried to rape Hercules' wife.

254. **volubility** /vŏl yuh BIL ih tee/ quick wit.

267. **tragedians** /truh JEE dee unz/ actors of tragedies.

267. **belie** /bih-, bee LĪ/ slander.

278. **cardecue** /CAR dih kyōō/ Fr. coin. Some eds. prefer **quart d'écu**, pronounced the same way if angl., or quasi-Fr. /CAR day kyōō, car day KYŌŌ/.

306. **pestiferous** /pes TIF ur us/ harmful.

Act 4 Scene 4

3. ***surety** guarantee. Here should be two syllables, though in mod. English, three syllables are more common, /SHUR (ih) tee, SHOOR-, SHOR-/ (see App. D).

4. **perfect** here should be /PUR fict/ fully accomplish.

7. **Tartar's** /TAR turz/ people of Central Asia.

9. **Marsellis** /mar SELL iss/ archaic variant of **Marseilles**. The usual mod. pronunciation /mar SAY/ will not fit, but another modern variant from the UK will: [mar SAY łz].

Act 4 Scene 5

1. **snipt-taffata, taffeta** /TAF uh tuh/ type of cloth slashed to show lining beneath.

2. **saffron** /SAFF run/ yellow food-coloring used in pastry and in starch for clothes.

6. **humble-bee** pronounced with the same stress as *bumble bee.*

14, 17. **sallets** /SAL its/ herbs or greens for salads. Some eds. prefer **salads**.

ă-bat, ăir-**marry**, air-**pair**, ạr-**far**, ĕr-**merry**, ĝ- **get**, ī-**high**, ĭr-**mirror**, ł-**little**, ṇ-**listen**, ŏ-**hot**, oh-**go**, ōō-**wood**, ōō-**moon**, oor-**tour**, ōr- **or**, ow-**how**, ţh-**that**, th-**thin**, ŭ-**but**, UR-**fur**, ur-**under**.   ( ) - suppress the syllable   see p. xiii for complete list.

16. **marjorom** type of herb. Archaic variant of **marjoram**, both pronounced /MAR jur rum/.

20. **Nebuchadnezzar** US /neb uh kud NEZ ur/; UK /neb yuh-/ king of Babylon.

39. **name** (*maine* F1). Some eds. prefer **mien** /meen/ appearance, manner.

40. **fisnomy** /FIZ nuh mee/ face. Archaic variant of **physiognomy* /fiz ee ŎG nuh mee/, *rarely older* /fiz ee ŎN uh mee/.   Some eds. prefer **phys'nomy** /FIZ nuh mee/ or **phys'namy** (to make clear a pun with *name* in line 39).

66. **patent** US /PAT n̩t/; UK /PAYT n̩t/ [PAT-] license.

80. **Marsellis** /mar SELL iss/ archaic variant of **Marseilles**. In this prose passage the mod. pronunciations may be used /mar SAY/; UK *also* [mar SAY ɫz].

101. **carbinado'd** slashed. Archaic variant of **carbonado'd*, both pronounced /car buh NAH dohd/; UK *rarely older* [-NAY dohd].

Act 5 Scene 2

16. **Foh** indicates an expression of disgust made with the lips /pff/! or /pfuh/! Sometimes rendered as /foh/ or *faugh* /faw/.

17. **close-stool* US /CLOHSS sto͞ol, CLOHZ-/; UK /CLOHSS-/, *rarely* [CLOHZ-] chamber pot enclosed in a stool.

33. **cardecue** /CAR dih kyo͞o/ Fr. coin. Some eds. prefer **quart d'écu**, pronounced the same way if angl., or quasi-Fr. /CAR day kyo͞o, car day KYO͞O/.

Act 5 Scene 3

16. **survey** here should be /sur VAY/ sight.

25. **relics** (F3), **reliques** (F1) /REL iks/ remains.

48. **perspective** here should be /PUR spek tiv/.

57. **compt** /cownt/ archaic variant of **count**. Both mean 'account.' See App. D. *accompt*.

72. **cesse** /sess/ a variant of **cease** which here rhymes with *bless*.

86. **reave** /reev/ bereave, rob.

101. **Plutus** /PLOOT us/ god of riches.

108, 297. ***surety** pledge, guarantee. The first instance can be two syllables or
a triple ending, the second should be two syllables, though in mod. English three
syllables are more common /SHUR (ih) tee, SHOOR-, SHOR-/ (see
App. D).

---

134. **suppliant** /SUP lyunt/ someone who asks humbly for something.

139. ***protestations** US /proh tess-, prŏt ess TAY shunz/;
CN /prŏt ess-/ [proh tess-]; UK /prŏt ess-/.

197. **sequent issue** /SEE kwunt/ subsequent generation.

250. **equivocal** /ih KWIV uh kł/; US *also* /ee-/ arguing both sides of an issue.

254. ***orator** US, CN /OR uh tur/; UK, E.COAST US /ŎR-/. Sometimes /OR ayt ur/
is used, but it is not recommended. See App. D *-or*.

260. **Sathan** archaic form of **Satan**, both pronounced /SAYT ņ, -un/ the devil.

321. **handkercher** /HANK ur chur/ archaic variant of **handkerchief**.

ă-bat, äir-**marry**, air-**pair**, ạr-**far**, ĕr-**merry**, ĝ- g**e**t, ī-h**i**gh, ĭr-**mirror**, ł-litt**le**, ņ-list**en**,
ŏ-h**o**t, oh-g**o**, o͞o-w**oo**d, o͞o-m**oo**n, oor-t**our**, ōr- **or**, ow-h**ow**, ţh-**th**at, t̶h̶-**th**in, ŭ-b**u**t,
UR-f**ur**, ur-**under**.   ( ) - suppress the syllable   see p. xiii for complete list.

Antony and Cleopatra

People in the Play

Aemilius see **Lepidus**.

Agrippa /uh GRIP uh/.

Alexas /uh LEK sus/.

Antony 2 or 3 syllables depending on meter /ANT (uh) nee/. F1's **Anthony** was pronounced the same, and still is in the UK.
    Antonio /an TOHN yoh/.
    Antonius /an TOHN yus/.

Canidius 3 or 4 syllables depending on meter /kuh NID (ee) yus/. Some eds. prefer **Camidius** /kuh MID (ee) yus/.

*Charmian usually 2 syllables, but may also be 3 /CAR m(ee) yun, CHAR-, SHAR-/. Classical names spelled *ch-* are always /k/ making /CAR-/ the best choice.

Cleopatra US /clee oh PAT ruh/; UK *also* /-PAHT ruh/.

Decretas (F2) /DEK ruh tus, duh CREE tus/. Some eds. prefer F1's **Dercetas** which is normally /DUR sih tus/ but may be /dur SEE tus/ at 5.1.5 in the only appearance of this name, depending on whether *I'm* or *I am* is used.

Demetrius /dih MEE tree yus/ his name is not spoken.

Diomedes /dī uh MEE deez/.
    Diomed(e) 2 or 3 syllables depending on meter /DĪ (uh) med, -meed/.

Dolabella /dŏl uh BEL uh/.

Domitius (Enobarbus) /duh MISH us/.

*Enobarbus /ee nuh-, ee noh BAR bus/, *rarely* [en oh-].

*Eros US /ĔR ohss, -ŏss/ [EER-]; CN /ĔR ŏss/ [EER-]; UK /EER ŏss/, *rarely* [-ohss]. /EER-/ is older, /-ohss/ is newer.

Euphronius /yōō FROH nee yus/ the schoolmaster. This name is not spoken.

People in the Play (cont.)

Fulvia usually 2 syllables /FŬL vyuh/ Antony's wife, mentioned throughout.

Gallus /GAL us/.

Herod /HĔR ud/ king in Judea in Jesus' lifetime, mentioned throughout.

Iras US /Ī rus/ [-răss]; UK, CN /-răss/ [-rus]. Normal development would favor /-rus/.

Lamprius /LAMP ree us/ appears in 1.2. His name is not spoken.

Lepidus, M. Aemilius /LEP ih dus/. *Aemilius* /ih MIL ee us/ is not spoken.

Lucillius /lōō SILL ee yus/ appears in 1.2. His name is not spoken (for /lyōō-/ see App. D *lu-*).

Maecenas, Mecaenus, Mecenas /mee-, mih SEE nus/; **Mae-** has a restored Latin form /mī-/.

Mardian 2 or 3 syllables depending on meter /MAR d(ee) yun/.

Menas US /MEE nus/ [-năss]; UK, CN /-năss/ [-nus]. Normal development would favor /-nus/.

Menecrates /muh NEK ruh teez/.

Octavia 3 or 4 syllables depending on meter /ŏk TAY v(ee) yuh/.

Octavius usually 3 syllables /ŏk TAY v(ee) yus/.

Philo /FĪ loh/.

Pompeius, Sextus /pŏm PEE yus SEK stus/.
  Pompey /PŎM pee/.

Proculeius /proh kyoo LEE yus/.

Rannius /RAN ee us/ appears in 1.2. His name is not spoken.

Scarus /SKAIR us/.

ă-bat, ăir-m**arr**y, air-p**air**, a̧r-f**ar**, ĕr-m**err**y, ĝ- **g**et, ī-h**igh**, ĭr-m**irr**or, ł-litt**le**, n̩-list**en**, ŏ-h**o**t, oh-g**o**, ōō-w**oo**d, ōō-m**oo**n, oor-t**our**, ōr- **or**, ow-h**ow**, t̯h-**th**at, t̶h̶-**th**in, ŭ-b**u**t, UR-f**ur**, ur-und**er**.   ( ) - suppress the syllable   see p. xiii for complete list.

People in the Play (cont.)

Seleucus /suh LOO kus/ (for /lyoo-/ see App. D *lu-*).

Sextus see **Pompeius.**

Silius /SILL yus/.

Thidias /THID ee yus/. Some eds. prefer *Thyreus /THĬR ee yus/ [-yooss], though a newer pronunciation /THĪ ree yus/ is now commonly used. See App. D *-eus.*

Varrius /VĂIR ee yus/.

Ventidius (F2) /ven TID yus, -TIJ us/. Shk probably used the latter.

Places in the Play

Nilus /NĪL us/ the Nile.

Parthia /PAR thyuh/ in NW Iran.
  Parthian /PAR thyun/.

Philippi /fih LIP ī/. Occasionally the Gk. form with 1st syllable stress is used in mod. Eng., but will not fit the meter in Shk.

Act 1 Scene 1

1. **dotage** /DOHT ij/ love-sickness.

8.*reneges** denies. US /ree-, rih NEGZ, -NIGZ/ [-NEEGZ, -NAYGZ]; CN /-NEGZ, -NAYGZ/; UK /rih NAYGZ/ [-NEEGZ, -NEGZ, -NIGZ].

16. *bourn** /born, boorn/ boundary. North American [burn] not recommended. Normal development would favor /born/.

31. **Is Caesar's *homager** /HŎM ij ur/; US *also* /ŎM ij ur/ does homage to Caesar.

33. **Tiber** /TĪ bur/ main river of Rome.

35. **dungy** /DUNG ee/ contemptible, filthy.

Act 1 Scene 2

12. **banket** /BANK it/ light meal of fruit. Archaic variant of **banquet**.

21. **his *prescience** foreknowledge. Here a mock title. US /PRESS ee unss/ [PRESH unss]; CN, UK /PRESS ee unss/, *rarely* [PRESH unss].

29. ***homage** /HŎM ij/; US *also* /ŎM ij/ acknowledgement of allegience.

47, 49. ***presages, -eth** /PRESS ih jiz/ [pree-, prih SAY jiz] foretells.

53. **prognostication** omen. US /prŏg nŏss tih KAY shun/; UK /prug-/ [prŏg-].

64-73. **Isis** /Ī sis/ chief goddess of Egypt.

89. **Lucius** /LOO shus /, /LOO syus/. The former is nearly universal in the US, the latter is most common in the UK. Normal development would favor /LOO shus/ (for /lyoo-/ see App. D *lu-*).

99. **Labienus** /lab ee EE nus, layb-/.

101. **Extended Asia; from Euphrates** /yoo FRAY teez/ is the normal mod. pronunciation, but here /YOO fray teez/ is indicated, with *Asia* having 3 syllables.

103. **Ionia** /ī OH nee yuh/.

113-9. **Sicyon** city in Greece. Normal anglicization would produce /SISH un/. Other angl. forms are /SISH yun, SISS yun/; restored pronunciation /SIK yŏn/.

117. **dotage** /DOHT ij/ love-sickness.

125. **low'ring, louring** threatening. /LOWR ing/, with the vowel of *how*.

144. **celerity** /suh LĔR ih tee/ speed.

193. **courser's** /COR surz/ warhorse's.

Act 1 Scene 3

49. **condemn'd** here should be /CŎN demd/.

ă-bat, ăir-**marry**, air-**pair**, ąr-**far**, ĕr-**merry**, ĝ- **get**, ī-**high**, ĭr-**mirror**, ł-**little**, ṇ-**listen**, ŏ-**hot**, oh-**go**, ōō-**wood**, ōō-**moon**, oor-**tour**, ōr- **or**, ow-**how**, ţh-**that**, th-**thin**, ŭ-**but**, UR-**fur**, ur-**under**.   ( ) - suppress the syllable   see p. xiii for complete list.

61. **garboils** /GAR boylz/ disturbances.

84. *****Herculean** here should be /hur KY$\overline{OO}$L yun/. Today stress is usually on the third syllable /hur kyōō LEE un/.

Act 1 Scene 4

6, 17. **Ptolemy** /TŎL uh mee/ Cleopatra's dead husband/ brother.

9. **th'abstract** here ignore the apostrophe: /ţhee AB stract/ summary, epitome.

11. **enow** /ih NOW/; US *also* /ee-/ archaic variant of **enough**.

20. **stand the buffet** /BUFF it/ exchange blows.

41. **primal** /PRĪ mł/ original.

56. **lascivious** /luh SIV yus/ lustful.

56. *****wassails** carousing. Here stressed on the 1st syllable US /WŎSS łz, -aylz/, *rarely* [WĂSS łz]; CN /WŎSS aylz/ [WŎSS łz]; UK /WĂSS aylz/ [WŎSS-]. Normal development would favor /WŎSS-/.

57. **Modena** here should be /muh-, moh DEE nuh/. Newer /-DAY-/ is also used.

58. **Hirtius** (F2), **Hirsius** (F1), **Hircius** all pronounced /HUR shus/. Sometimes restored /-tyus, -syus/ are used.

58. **Pansa** /PAN suh, -zuh/.

58. **consuls** /CŎN słz/ Roman officials.

63. **deign** /dayn/ accept.

Act 1 Scene 5

4. **mandragora** here should be /man DRAG uh ruh/ a narcotic.

8, 10. **eunuch** /Y$\overline{OO}$ nuk/ castrated man.

23. *****demi-Atlas** /DEM ee-/ i.e., one of the strongest men.

24. ***burgonet** /BURG uh net/; US *also* /burg uh NET/ helmet, i.e., defense.

28. **Phoebus'** /FEE bus/ god of the sun.

70. **Isis** /Ī sis/ chief goddess of Egypt.

71. ***paragon** US /PĂIR uh gŏn/ [-gun]; CN /-gŏn/; UK /-gun/ [-gṇ] compare.

Act 2 Scene 1

10. ***auguring hope** /AWG y(u)r ing/ [AWG (ur) ing] hope which looks into the future.

21. **wan'd** /waynd/ faded.

23. ***libertine** /LIB (ur) teen/, *rarely* [-tīn] person who acts without moral restraint.

24. ***epicurean cooks** here with 3rd syllable stress /ep ih KYOOR yun/; US *also* /-KYUR-/ fancy cooks.

26. **prorogue** /pruh-, proh ROHG/ postpone.

27. **Lethe'd** /LEE̶T̶H̶ eed/ *Lethe* was the river of forgetfulness.

48. **cement** here with 1st syllable stress /SEE ment, SEM ent/.

Act 2 Scene 2

34. **derogately** disparagingly. /DĔR uh gut lee/; UK *also newer* [DEER-].

55. **defects** here should be /dih-, dee FECTS/.

67. **garboils** /GAR boylz/ disturbances.

69. **Shrowdness** /SHROHD niss/ cunning. Archaic variant of **shrewdness**.

74. **gibe** /jīb/ mock.

116. **A' th' world** /uth/ of the. Some eds. prefer **O' th' world**.

ă-bat, ăir-**marry**, air-**pair**, ạr-**far**, ĕr-**merry**, ĝ- **get**, ī-**high**, ĭr-**mirror**, ł-**little**, ṇ-**listen**, ŏ-**hot**, oh-**go**, o͞o-**wood**, o͞o-**moon**, oor-**tour**, ōr- **or**, ow-**how**, t̠h-**that**, t̶h̶-**thin**, ŭ-**but**, UR-**fur**, ur-**under**.　　( ) - suppress the syllable　　see p. xiii for complete list.

160. **Misena** /mih SEE nuh/ some eds. prefer **Misen(i)um**
/mī-, mih SEEN yum, -um/.

187. **Cydnus** /SID nus/.

203. ***divers-color'd** various-colored. Here should be stressed on the first
syllable US, CN /DĪ vurss, -vurz/; UK /DĪ vurss/ [-vurz].

206. **Nereides** sea nymphs. The normal plural form would be **Nereids**
/NEER ee idz/ but Shk may have intended /neer EE ih deez/ after an epic
caesura.

211. ***yarely** /YAIR lee/; US *also* /YAR-/ smartly.

226. **eat** /et/ dialect variant of **ate**, which is also commonly /et/ in the UK.

231. **defect** here with 2nd syllable stress /dih-, dee FECT/.

Act 2 Scene 3

20. ***daemon** guardian spirit. US /DEE mun/ [DAY-]; CN /DAY-/ [DEE-];
UK /DEE-, DAY-/. /DEE-/ is older. /DĪ-/ is a recent pronunciation based on
classical Latin, often written *daimon* today, as in Gk.

Act 2 Scene 5

3. **billards** (F1) /BILL urdz/ archaic variant of F2's **billiards**.

5. **eunuch** /YOO nuk/ castrated man.

22. **tires** /tīrz/ headdress.

23. **Philippan** /fih LIP un/ of Philippi.

50. **allay** /uh LAY/ diminish.

51. **good precedence** here should be /pree-, prih SEED unss, -nss/ preceding
good news.

53. ***malefactor** /MAL ih fak tur/, *rarely* [mal ih FAK tur] evil doer. See
App. D *-or*.

95. **cestern** /SESS turn/ archaic variant of **cistern** /SISS turn/.

116. **Gorgon** /GOR gun/ monster.

Act 2 Scene 6

15. ***Cassius** US /CĂSS yus, CASH us/; UK /CĂSS yus/. Normal development would favor /CASH us/.

22. **scourge** /SKURJ/ harshly punish.

35. **Sardinia** /sạr DIN yuh/.

38. **unhack'd** here should be /UN hackt/.

39. **targes undinted** light shields. Here should be one syllable /TẠRJ (i)z/. The /z/ can be attached to *undinted*.

68. **Apollodorus** /uh pŏl uh DOR us/.

73. **toward** /TOH wurd, -urd/ about to take place.

110. ***Caius Marcellus** US, CN /KĪ us/, *rarely* [KAY us]; UK /KĪ us, KAY us/. Ang.Lat. /KAY us/; Class.Lat. /KĪ ōōs/. Another angl. form /keez/ is also sometimes used but not recommended. **Marcellus** /mar SELL us/.

117. **prophesy** /PRŎF uh sī/ predict the future.

Act 2 Scene 7

5. **alms-drink** drink given in charity. /AHMZ-/ is older; /AHLMZ-, AWLMZ-/ are newer. In the UK the latter are non-standard.

12. **as live** as soon. May have been /liv/ in Shk's time. Variant of **as lief** /leef/. In the US **lieve** /leev/ is still found in some dialects and can also be used here.

20. **foison** /FOY zun, -zṇ/ plenty.

34. **Ptolemies'** /TŎL uh meez/ kings of Egypt.

35. **pyramises** /pih RAM ih siz, -seez/; US *also* /pĭr-/ archaic variant of *pyramids*.

ă-bat, ăir-marry, air-pair, ạr-far, ĕr-merry, ĝ- get, ī-high, ĭr-mirror, ł-little, ṇ-listen, ŏ-hot, oh-go, ōō-wood, ōō-moon, oor-tour, ōr- or, ow-how, ţh-that, ŧh-thin, ŭ-but, UR-fur, ur-under.   ( ) - suppress the syllable   see p. xiii for complete list.

52. **epicure** /EP ih kyoor/; US *also* /-kyur/ glutton.

104. ***bacchanals** wild dances. US /bahk uh NAHLZ/ [back uh NALZ, BACK uh nłz]; UK /BACK uh nalz/ [back uh NALZ, bahk uh NAHLZ]. The /ah/ vowel is newer.

108. **Lethe** /LEE̶T̶H̶ ee/ river of forgetfulness in Hades.

114. ***Bacchus** god of wine. US, CN /BAHK us/ [BACK us]; UK /BACK us/ [BAHK-]. /BAHK-/ is newer.

114. **eyne** /īn/ dialect form of *eyes*.

134. **says 'a** says he. Some eds. substitute **Sessa** /SESS uh/ uncertain meaning, perhaps 'hurry' or 'cease.'

Act 3 Scene 1

4. **Pacorus** /PACK uh rus/.

4. **Orodes** /oh-, uh ROH deez/; UK *also* /ŏ-/.

5. **Crassus** /CRĂSS us/.

7. **Media** /MEED ee yuh/.

17. **Sossius** /SŎSH us, SŎSS ee yus/. Normal development would favor /SŎSH us/.

Act 3 Scene 2

11. ***nonpareil** one without equal. /nŏn puh RELL/ is the oldest form, still common in the US, but now vanished from the UK and CN, where it has been replaced with /nŏn puh RAYL/ [-RAY], based on mod. Fr. /-RAY/ is also common in the US. /-RĪ, -RĪL/ are occasionally heard, but not recommended. Sometimes 1st syllable stress is used.

29. **cement** here with 1st syllable stress /SEE ment, SEM ent/.

57. **rheum** /rōōm/ cold.

62. **wrastle** /RĂSS ł/ archaic variant of **wrestle**.

Act 3 Scene 3

15, 43. **Isis** /Ī sis/ chief goddess of Egypt.

Act 3 Scene 4

3. **semblable** /SEM bluh bł/ similar.

32. *****solder** US /SŎD ur/; UK /SOHL dur/ [SŎL dur] join metal together.

Act 3 Scene 5

8. **rivality** /rī VAL ih tee/ rivalry.

Act 3 Scene 6

3. *****tribunal** /trīb YO͞ON ł/ [trib-] platform.

6. **Caesarion** /see-, sih ZAIR ee un/. Sometimes newer /-ŏn/ is used, but is not recommended.

9. **stablishment** /STAB lish munt/ rule.

15. **Ptolemy** /TŎL (uh) mee/ Cleopatra's dead husband / brother.

16. *****Cilicia** US /sih LISH uh/ [sih LISS yuh]; UK /sih LISS yuh/. Normal development would favor /sih LISH uh/. /sī LISH uh/ not recommended.

16. *****Phoenicia** /fuh NEESH uh/ [-NISH-, -yuh]; UK *also* [fih-]. Normal development would favor /fuh NISH uh/.

17. **In th'abiliments** /thʸuh BIL (ih) munts/ clothes. Variant of **habiliments**. As written it is a headless line, but it also works as an inversion in the first foot if *the* is full.

17. **Isis** /Ī sis/ chief goddess of Egypt.

28. **triumpherate** (F1) /trī UM fur ut/ mistake for or variant of F2's **triumvirate** /trī UM vur ut/ 'ruling body of three persons.'

ă-bat, ăir-**marry**, air-**pair**, ạr-**far**, ĕr-**merry**, ĝ- **get**, ī-high, ĭr-**mirror**, ł-little, ṇ-listen, ŏ-hot, oh-go, o͞o-**wood**, o͞o-**moon**, oor-**tour**, ōr- **or**, ow-**how**, t̟h-**that**, t̶h̶-t̶h̶in, ŭ-**but**, UR-**fur**, ur-und**er**.   ( ) - suppress the syllable   see p. xiii for complete list.

30. **revenue** here should be /ruh VEN yo͞o/.

61. **abstract** /AB stract/ summary. Some eds. prefer **obstruct** /ŎB struct/ obstruction.

69. **Bocchus, Bochus** /BŎCK us/.

69. **Archelaus, Archilaus** /ark ih LAY us/.

70. **Cappadocia** /kap uh DOH syuh, -DOH shuh, -DOH shyuh/. Normal development would favor /-shuh/.

70. **Philadelphos** US /fil uh DEL fus, -fŏs/; UK /-fŏs/ [-fus]. A newer pronunciation /-ohss/ is also used, especially in the US. Normal development would favor /-us/.

71. **Paphlagonia** /paf luh GOHN yuh/.

71. **Thracian** /T̶H̶RAY shun/.

71. **Adallas** /uh DAL us/. Some eds. prefer **Adullas** /uh DULL us/.

72. **Manchus** /MANG kus/. **Maucus** (F1) /MAW kus/. Some eds. prefer **Malchus** /MAL kus/.

72. **Pont** /pŏnt/.

73. **Mithridates** /mit̶h̶ rih DAY teez/.

74. **Comagena** /cŏm uh JEEN uh/. Some eds. prefer **Comagene** /CŎM uh jeen/.

74. **Polemon** /PŎL (ih) mun, -mŏn/. /-ŏn/ is usual in the US and is increasingly common in the UK. /puh LEE mun, -ŏn/ has also been recommended. Both will fit the meter. See App. D -*on*.

74. **Amyntas, Amintas** /uh MIN tus/.

75. **Mede** /meed/.

75. **Lycaonia, Licaonia** /lī kay OH nee yuh/.

Act 3 Scene 7

13. **Traduc'd** slandered. /truh DYO͞OST/; US *also* /-DO͞OST/. /-JO͞OST/ is considered non-standard in the UK.

14. **Photinus** /FOHT in us, FŎT ih nus/.

14. **eunuch** /YO͞O nuk/ castrated man.

21. **Tarentum** /tuh REN tum/.

21. **Brundusium** traditionally it would be /brun DO͞O zhum/, UK *also* /-DYO͞O-/ here expanded to 4 syllables /-ee um/; *sometimes* /-zee um/. Restored Latin /bro͞on DO͞O see o͞om/ variant of **Brundisium** /-DIZ ee um, -DIZH ee um, -DIZH um/.

23, 55. **Toryne** US /TOR in/; E.COAST US, UK /TŎR in/.

---

24. **Celerity** /suh LĔR ih tee/ speed.

31. **Pharsalia** /far SAYL yuh/.

35. **muleters** /MYO͞O l(ih) turz, -teerz/. Some eds. prefer mod. **muleteers** /myo͞o lih TEERZ/, which would mean that the line is a broken-backed hexameter.

36. **impress** here should be /im PRESS/ forcing men to join the service.

38. *****yare** /yair/; US *also* /yạr/ smart, quick.

51. *****Actium** /AK tee um/. Traditional /AK shum/ is now obsolete.

54. **descried** /dih SKRĪD/ found out.

60. *****Thetis** /T̶H̶E̶E̶ tiss/, *sometimes newer* [T̶H̶E̶T iss] a sea nymph.

64. *****Phoenicians** /fuh NEESH unz/ [-NISH-, -yunz]; UK *also* [fih-]. Normal development would favor /fuh NISH unz/.

72. **Justeius, Justeus** /juss TEE yus/.

73. **Publicola** /pub LICK uh luh/.

ă-bat, ăir-marry, air-**pair**, ạr-far, ĕr-merry, ĝ- get, ī-high, ĭr-mirror, ł-little, ṇ-listen, ŏ-hot, oh-go, o͝o-wood, o͞o-moon, oor-tour, ōr- or, ow-how, t̪h-that, t̶h-thin, ŭ-but, UR-fur, ur-under. ( ) - suppress the syllable see p. xiii for complete list.

73. **Caelius, Celius** /SEEL yus/.

78. **Taurus** /TOR us/. Some eds. prefer **Towrus** /TOW rus/ as in _tower_.

Act 3 Scene 8

1. **Taurus** /TOR us/. Some eds. prefer **Towrus** /TOW rus/ as in _tower_.

5. **prescript** /PREE script/ directive.

Act 3 Scene 10

2. **Th'Antoniad** /ţhʸan TOHN ee ad/.

5. *****synod** US, CN /SIN ud/ [-ŏd]; UK /SIN ŏd/ [-ud] council of the gods.

10. **ribaudred** /RIB baw durd/ rotted by sexual license. The only occurrence in the language of this word. Some eds. prefer *****ribald** 'bawdy, vulgar' which fits the meter better: US, UK /RIB łd/ [-awld], _rarely_ [RĪ-]; CN /RĪ bawld/ [RĪ błd, RIB łd, RIB awld]. /RIB łd/ is the traditional pronunciation. Other suggestions are **ribanded, riband-red** 'ribboned, ribbon-red' which here should be /RIB (ŋ) did/, /RIBN red/.

14. **breeze** some eds prefer **breese**. Both mean 'gadfly' and are pronounced /breez/.

17. **loof'd, luff'd** sailed close to the wind. Standard Eng. is /lŭft/ but in the northern dialects of Eng. both spellings would be pronounced /lo͞oft/.

20. **heighth** /hīth/ or /hītth/ archaic variants of **height**. /hītth/ is still used today, though non-standard.

25. *****lamentably** here should be /LAM un tuh blee/ the usual UK pronunciation.

30. **Peloponnesus** /pel uh puh NEE sus/.

Act 3 Scene 11

37. *****Cassius** US /CĂSS yus, CASH us/; UK /CĂSS yus/. Normal development would favor /CASH us/.

63. **palter** /PAWL tur/ use tricky or vague arguments.

73. **viands** /VĪ undz/ food.   /VEE undz/ not recommended.

Act 3 Scene 12

18. **Ptolemies** /TŎL (uh) meez/ kings of Egypt.

32. **edict** /EE dict/ decree.

Act 3 Scene 13

10. **mered question** /MEER id/ sole point at issue. Some eds. prefer **mooted** 'the question of dispute' or **meted** /MEET id/ 'measured.'

79. **combating** here should be /CŎM buh ting/; UK *also* [CUM-].

104. **arrant** /ĂIR unt/ archaic variant of **errand** 'message.'

118. **Cneius** (F2), **Gneius** (F1), **Cneus** (Plutarch), or some eds. prefer **Gnaeus**. The angl. form of all these is /NEE yus/.

127. **Basan** /BAY sun, -sn̩/.

131. *****yare** /yair/; US *also* /yạr/ smartly, quick.

147. **th' abysm** /t̩hʸuh BIZM/ variant of **abyss** /uh BISS/.

149. **Hipparchus** /hih PARK us/.

149. **enfranched** /en FRĂNCH id/ freed.

153. **terrene** /TĔR een/ earthly.

162. **Caesarion** /see-, sih ZAIR yun/. Sometimes newer /-ŏn/ is used, but is not recommended.

197. **diminution** US /dim ih NOO shun/; SOUTH. US, UK /-NYOO-/ decrease.

Act 4 Scene 2

7. **Woo't** /woot/ variant of **wilt** in the sense 'wilt thou.'

ă-bat, ăir-**marry**, air-**pair**, ạr-**far**, ĕr-**merry**, ĝ- **get**, ī-**high**, ĭr-**mirror**, ł-**little**, n̩-**listen**,
ŏ-**hot**, oh-**go**, oo̅-**wood**, o̅o̅-**moon**, oor-**tour**, ōr- **or**, ow-**how**, t̩h-**that**, ~~th~~-**thin**, ŭ-**but**,
UR-**fur**, ur-**under**.   ( ) - suppress the syllable   see p. xiii for complete list.

39. **dolorous** /DOH lur us/ painful. See App. D *-or.*

Act 4 Scene 4

13. **dafft** /dăft/ take it off. Archaic variant of **doff 't** /dŏft/; US *also* /dawft/.

Act 4 Scene 7 (*Complete Oxford* 4.8)

6. **clouts** /clowts/ cloths.

8. **'tis made an H** play on *ache* which as a noun was pronounced /aytch/.

Act 4 Scene 8 (*Complete Oxford* 4.9)

2. **gests** /jests/ stages of a royal journey.   Some eds. prefer F1's **guests**.

5. **doughty-handed** /DOWT ee/ strong-, brave-handed.

7. **Hectors** /HEK turz/ *Hector* was a Trojan hero. See App. D *-or.*

16. **triumphing** here should be /trī UM fing/.

29. **Phoebus'** /FEE bus/ god of the sun.

36. **brazen** /BRAY zun, -zŋ/ brass.

37. **taborines, taborins, -our-** /TAB ur inz/ small drums. See App. D *-or.*

Act 4 Scene 9 (*Complete Oxford* 4.10)

6. **Stand close** /clohss/ keep hidden.

8. **record** here should be /rek-, rik ORD/.

29. **raught** /rawt/ reached.

Act 4 Scene 12 (*Complete Oxford* 4.13)

4. ***auguries** /AWG yur eez/ [AWG ur eez]; UK *also* /-yoor-/. Some eds. prefer **augurs** /AWG yurz, -urz/, **augurers**. In any case the meaning is 'prophets.'

21. **spannell'd** (*pannelled* F1) /SPAN łd/ fawned. Archaic variant of **spaniel'd** /SPAN młd/ (cf. *Dan'el*). Some eds. prefer **pantled** /PAN tłd/ 'panted.'

27. **crownet** /CROWN it/ small crown.

30. **Avaunt** /uh VAWNT/ begone!

34. **plebeians** here /PLEB ee yunz/ common people. /PLEEB-/ is an obsolete pronunciation.

43. **shirt of Nessus** /NESS us/ shirt that tortures its victim.

44. **Alcides** /al SĪ deez/ Hercules.

45. **Lichas** Hercules' servant. US /LĪ kus/ [-kăss]; UK, CN /-kăss/ [-kus]. Normal development would favor /-kus/.

Act 4 Scene 13 (*Complete Oxford* 4.14)

2. **Telamon** /TEL (uh) mŏn, -mun/ Ajax, Gk. hero at Troy. /-ŏn/ is usual in the US and is increasingly common in the UK. See App. D -*on*.

2. **Thessaly** /THESS uh lee/ region in Greece.

Act 4 Scene 14 (*Complete Oxford* 4.15)

10. **dislimns** /dis LIMZ/ blots out. Some eds. prefer **dislimbs**, or **distains** /dih STAYNZ/ dims.

25. **eunuch** /YŌŌ nuk/ castrated man.

53. **Dido** /DĪ doh/ Queen of Carthage.

53. **Aeneas** /ih NEE yus/; UK *also* /EE NEE yus/ Prince of Troy.

63. **exigent** /EGZ-, EKS ih junt/ necessity.

74. **corrigible** US /COR ih jih bł/; E.COAST US, UK /CŎR-/ punishable.

83. **precedent** /prih-, pree SEED unt, -ṇt/ preceding.

ă-bat, äir-**ma**rry, air-**pair**, a̧r-**far**, ĕr-**me**rry, ĝ- get, ī-high, ĭr-mirror, ł-**little**, ṇ-**listen**, ŏ-hot, oh-go, ōō-wood, ōō-moon, oor-**tour**, ŏr- or, ow-how, t̩h-**that**, t̶h̶-**thin**, ŭ-but, UR-**fur**, ur-**under**.   ( ) - suppress the syllable   see p. xiii for complete list.

120. **prophesying** /PRŎF uh sī ing/ predicting the future.

Act 4 Scene 15 (*Complete Oxford* 4.16)

19. ***importune** /im POR chun/ beg (for a delay). See App. D.

23. **th'imperious** /t͡hʸim PEER yus/ imperial.

25. ***brooch'd** /brohcht/ adorned. US [bro͞ocht] not recommended.

44. ***huswife** /HUZ if/ is traditional, /HUSS wīf/ is a newer, spelling
pronunciation. The former is the most common form in the UK, the latter in the
US. In CN both are used equally. In North America /HUSS wif/ is also
sometimes used. Here means **hussy**.

59. **woo't** /wo͞ot/ variant of **wilt** in the sense 'wilt thou.' May be pronounced
/wilt/ for clarity.

75. **chares** /chairz/ archaic variant of **chores**.

Act 5 Scene 1

1. **Dolabella, Dollabella** /dŏl uh BEL uh/.

2. **frustrate** /FRUSS trut, -ayt/ defeated.

19. **moi'ty, moiety** /MOY tee/ portion.

Act 5 Scene 2

2. **paltry** /PAWL tree/ worthless.

54. ***chastis'd** punished. Here should be /CHĂSS tīzd/, the usual US
pronunciation, also used in CN; in the UK 2nd syllable stress is usual.

61. **pyramides** /pih RAM ih deez/; US *also* /pĭr-/ archaic form of *pyramids.*

61. **gibbet** /JIB it/ post from which they hung corpses after hanging.

82. **bestrid** /bih-, bee STRID/ straddled.

91. **crownets** /CROWN its/ small crowns, i.e., princes.

121. **project** here should be /PROH ject/ set forth.

135. **scutcheons** /SKUTCH unz/ escutcheons, coats of arms.

214. **lictors** /LIK turz/ Roman officials. See App. D -*or*.

215. **scald** /skawld/ scabby.

217. **Extemporally** /ek STEM p(ur) ruh lee/ composed on the spur of the moment.

228. **Cydnus** /SID nus/.

231. **chare** /chair/ archaic variant of **chore**.

283. ***Yare** /yair/; US *also* /yạr/ smartly, quick.

293-352. **aspic('s)** /ASS pik/ asp.

304. **intrinsicate** /in TRIN sih kut, -zih-/ intricate.

317. **Phoebus** /FEE bus/ god of the sun.

318. **awry** /uh RĪ/ askew.

334. ***augurer** /AWG yur ur/ [AWG ur ur]; UK *also* /-yoor-/ prophet.

342. ***diadem** /DĪ uh dem/ [-dum] crown.

ă-bat, ăir-**marry**, air-**pair**, ạr-**far**, ĕr-**merry**, ĝ- **get**, ī-**high**, ĭr-**mirror**, ł-**little**, ṇ-**listen**, ŏ-**hot**, oh-**go**, o͞o-**wood**, o͞o-**moon**, oor-**tour**, ōr- **or**, ow-**how**, ţh-**that**, ŧh-**thin**, ŭ-**but**, UR-**fur**, ur-**under**.   ( ) - suppress the syllable   see p. xiii for complete list.

As You Like It

People in the Play

Aliena /ay lee EE nuh/ Celia's pseudonym.

Amiens /AM yenz, -yunz/ are the most common angl. forms. Another angl. variant formerly used was /AYM yenz/. /AM yah^n/ is a more recent semi-angl. form with the wrong Fr. ending; Fr. would be /AHM yă^n/. Used only once.

Celia 2 or 3 syllables depending on meter /SEE l(ee) yuh/.

Corin US /COR in/; E.COAST US, UK /CŎR in/.

Duke Frederick 2 or 3 syllables depending on meter /FRED uh rik, FRED rik/.

Duke Senior /SEEN yur/.

Ganymed /GAN ih med/ or /GAN ee-/ archaic variant of ***Ganymede** /-meed/ Rosalind's pseudonym.

***Jaques** /JAY kweez/ [jayks] in all countries. Other endings are only rarely used: US [JAY keez, -kiz, -kis]; UK [JAY kwiz, -kwis]. In some lines it should be two syllables, but in others it can be one or two. The normal pronunciation in Shk's time was /jayks/ or if two syllables, /JAY kis/.

Le Beau /luh BOH/.

Phebe, Phoebe /FEE bee/.

Rosalind /RŎZ uh lind/ is the traditional form, but for Orlando's rhymes in 3.2 /-līnd/ is indicated.

Rowland de Boys de Bois /ROH lund duh BOYSS, -BOYZ/ Fr: /roh lah^n duh BWAH/.

Silvius 2 or 3 syllables depending on meter /SIL v(ee) yus/.

Places in the Play

Arden, Ardenne /AHR din/; Fr. /ahr den/.

Special Note

Riverside uses the archaic form (still found in some dialects) **wrastle** /RĂSS ł/ 'wrestle' which occurs throughout the play.

Act 1 Scene 1

13. **manage.** Some eds. prefer **manège** US /mah NEZH, -NAYZH/; UK /man AYZH/ [-EZH, MAN ayzh]; Fr. /mah nezh/. Both words mean 'horsemanship.'

19. **hinds** /hīndz/ menial laborers.

39. **penury** /PEN yur ee/; UK *also* /PEN yoor ee/ poverty.

50. **albeit** /awl BEE it/ although.

55, 56, 59. **villain.** Some eds. prefer to make a contrast in this passage between **villain** and in line 56 **villein** 'a type of serf' which on historical principles should also be /VIL un/ but which is sometimes /-ayn/ to differentiate it from *villain.*

73. **allotery** /uh LŎT ur ee/ allotment.

87. **Holla** /huh LAH/ a call to attract attention.

92. *****importunes** /im POR chunz/ asks insistently, begs. See App. D.

102. **revenues** sometimes in verse /ruh VEN yōōz/, but in this prose passage may be mod. Eng. US /REV in ōōz/; UK, SOUTH. US /-yōōz/.

146. **as lief** /leef/ as soon.

156. **anatomize** /uh NAT uh mīz/ analyze in detail.

171. **mispris'd, misprized** /mis PRĪZD/ despised.

Act 1 Scene 2

31. *****huswife** /HUZ if/ is traditional, /HUSS wīf/ is a newer, spelling pronunciation. The former is the most common form in the UK, the latter in the

---

ă-bat, ăir-**marry**, air-**pair**, ar-**far**, ĕr-**merry**, ĝ- **get**, ī-**high**, ĭr-**mirror**, ł-**little**, n-**listen**, ŏ-**hot**, oh-**go**, ōō-**wood**, ōō-**moon**, oor-**tour**, ōr- **or**, ow-**how**, ţh-**that**, th-**thin**, ŭ-**but**, UR-**fur**, ur-**under**.   ( ) - suppress the syllable   see p. xiii for complete list.

US. In CN both are used equally. In North America /HUSS wif/ is also sometimes used. Some eds. prefer F1's **housewife**.

42. **lineaments** /LIN ee yuh munts/ distinctive features.

51. *****Peradventure** perhaps. /PUR ad VEN chur/;
US *rarely* [PĔR-, PUR ad ven chur];
UK, CN *also* [PUR-, PĔR ad ven chur, pĕr ad VEN chur].

97. **Bon jour** Fr. /boh^n ZHOOR/ good day.

181. **mispris'd, misprized** /mis PRĪZD/ despised.

251. **quintain** US /KWINT n̩, -in/ wooden target used in tilting.

251. **liveless** /LĪV liss/ archaic variant of **lifeless**.

262. **Albeit** /awl BEE (i)t/ although.

265. **misconsters** /mis CŎN sturz/ misconstrues.

Act 1 Scene 3

74. **eat** /et/ dialect variant of **eaten**.

83. **irrevocable** here should be /ih REV uh kuh bł/; US *also* /ĭr-/.

120. **martial** /MAR shł/ warlike.

129. **assay'd** /uh-, ass SAYD/. Some eds. prefer **essayed** /es SAYD/. Both mean 'attempted.'

Act 2 Scene 1

19. **translate** transforming. Here should be stressed on the 2nd syllable, the normal UK pronunciation. US /trănss LAYT, trănz-/; UK /trănss LAYT/ [trănz-, trahnz-, trahnss-, trunss-, trunz-].

23. **burghers** /BURG urz/ citizens.

24. **confines** territories. Here should be /cŏn-, cun FĪNZ/.

31. *antique (*anticke* F1) ancient. Here /AN teek/, *rarely older* [AN tik].
Some eds. prefer antic /AN tik/ grotesquely shaped.

Act 2 Scene 2

10. Hisperia Ang.Lat. /hih SPEER ee uh/; Class.Lat. /-SPĔR-/.

14. sinowy /SIN (oh) wee/ muscular. Archaic variant of sinewy
/SIN y(oo) wee/; US *also* [SIN (oo) wee].

Act 2 Scene 3

8. priser, prizer /PRĪZ ur/ prize fighter.

57. *antique ancient. Here /AN teek/, *rarely older* [AN tik].

65. In *lieu of US, CN /lo͞o, lyo͞o/; UK /lyo͞o/ [lo͞o] in return for.

Act 2 Scene 4

51. peascod /PEEZ cŏd/ 'peapod,' but here apparently 'pea plant.'

66. Holla /huh LAH/ a call to attract attention.

75. succor (UK succour) /SUCK ur/ help. See App. D -*or*.

81. little reaks, recks /reks/ takes no care.

Act 2 Scene 5

18, 19. stanzo(s) /STANZ oh/ archaic variant of stanza. /STAN zuh/ could also
be indicated by the -*o* ending because unstressed /oh/ was often reduced to /uh/.

54. *Ducdame US /do͞ok DAYM/ or /duck-, do͞ok DAH mee/;
CN /duck DAM ee, do͞ok DAH mee/; UK /do͞ok DAH may, duck DAYM/. In the
US, UK many other variants were reported, with first syllable /duck-, do͞ok-/, and
final syllables /-DAH may, -DAY mee/. Probably a nonsense word with 3
syllables to match *come hither* in the previous stanza. Shk probably intended
the latter part of the word to be /DAY mee/ or /DAM ee/.

ă-bat, ăir-marry, air-pair, a̧r-far, ĕr-merry, ĝ- get, ī-high, ĭr-mirror, ł-little, n̦-listen,
ŏ-hot, oh-go, o͝o-wood, o͞o-moon, oor-tour, ōr- or, ow-how, t̠h-that, t̶h̶-thin, ŭ-but,
UR-fur, ur-under.   ( ) - suppress the syllable   see p. xiii for complete list.

62. **banket** /BANK it/ light meal, often of fruit. Archaic variant of **banquet**.

Act 2 Scene 7

5. **compact** /cum-, cŏm PACT/ composed of.

13-58. **motley** /MŎT lee/ costume of different colored cloth worn by fools.

30. ***chanticleer** a rooster. US /CHĂNT-, SHĂNT ih cleer/; UK /CHĂNT-/, *rarely* [CHAHNT-, SHAHNT-]; *rarely* with 3rd syllable stress in both countries.

31. **contemplative** here should be /cun TEMP luh tiv/ thoughtful.

32. **sans** /sănz/ without.

56. **anatomiz'd** /uh NAT uh mīzd/ examined in detail.

64. **mischievous** here should be /MIS chiv us/. /mis CHEEV us/ is considered non-standard in all countries.

65. ***libertine** /LIB ur teen/, *rarely* [-tīn] person who acts without moral restraint.

88. **eat**. The second *eat* is /et/, a dialect variant of **eaten**.

114, 121. **knoll'd** /nohld/ archaic variant of *knell'd* rung.

115. **sate** archaic variant of **sat**. May have been /sayt/ or /sat/.

144. **Mewling** /MYO͞OL ing/ whining.

154. ***capon** US /KAY pŏn, -pun/; CN, UK /KAY pŏn/ [-pun] chicken. See App. D -*on*.

158. ***pantaloon** foolish old man. US, UK /PANT uh lo͞on/ [pant uh LO͞ON]; CN /pant uh LOON/ [PANT uh lo͞on].

166. **Sans** /sănz/ without.

180-190. ***Heigh-ho** US /hay ho, hī-/; CN /hī-/, *rarely* [hay-]; UK /hay-/. Shk intended /hay/. In speech the syllables are evenly stressed or spoken as if sighing, with 1st syllable stress.

193. **effigies** /ef FIJ eez/ archaic form of **effigy**, both of which are singular.

194. **limn'd** /limd/ described.

Act 3 Scene 2

44. ***parlous** /PAR lus/ archaic variant of **perilous**.

50, 68. ***uncleanly** /un CLEN lee/, or newer /un CLEEN lee/.

64, 67. **civet** /SIV it/ a type of perfume.

67. **perpend** /pur PEND/ consider.

88. ***Inde** the Indies. Here /ĭnd/ in keeping with the other rhymes in this passage.

90. **wind** here the archaic pronunciation /wīnd/ should be used, in keeping with the other rhymes.

101. **hind** /hīnd/ doe.

117. **graff** US /grăf/; E.NEW ENG., UK /grahf/ archaic variant of **graft**.

118, 120. **medlar** /MED lur/ an apple-like fruit.

139. **quintessence** here should be /KWIN tih senss/ or /kwin tih SENSS/ rather than mod. /kwin TESS n̯ss/.

146. **Cleopatra's** US /clee oh PAT ruz/; UK *also* /-PAHT ruz/.

147. **Atalanta's** /at uh LAN tuz/ the swiftest runner in Gk. myths.

148. **Lucretia's** Roman who commited suicide after being raped. /lōō CREE shuz/ (for /lyōō-/ see App. D *lu-*).

150. ***synod** US, CN /SIN ud/ [-ŏd]; UK /-ŏd/ [-ud] council of the gods.

176. ***Pythagoras'** US /pih ~~THAG~~ uh rus/ [pī-]; UK /pī-/ Gk. philosopher.

179. ***Trow you** US, CN /troh, trow/; UK /trow/ [troh] do you know. Shk's rhymes elsewhere indicate /-oh/.

ă-bat, ăir-marry, air-**pair**, a̱r-**far**, ĕr-**merry**, ĝ- **get**, ī-**high**, ĭr-**mirror**, ɫ-**little**, n̩-**listen**, ŏ-**hot**, oh-**go**, ōō-**wood**, ōō-**moon**, oor-**tour**, ōr- **or**, ow-**how**, t̪h-**that**, ~~th~~-**thin**, ŭ-**but**, UR-**fur**, ur-**under**.   ( ) - suppress the syllable   see p. xiii for complete list.

193. **hooping** /HO͞OP ing, Ho͞oP-/ i.e., power to speak. Variant of *whooping
/WHO͞OP ing/ [Ho͞oP-, HO͞OP-, WHo͞oP-].

195. **caparison'd** /kuh PĂIR ih sṇd/ decked out.

225. **Gargantua's** US /gar GAN choo uz/; UK *also* /-tyoo uz/.

228. **catechism** /KAT uh kiz um, -kizm/ series of questions and answers.

232. **atomies** /AT uh meez/ tiny particles.

244. **holla** /HŎL uh/ or /huh LAH/ whoa.

244. **curvets** /cur VETS/; US *also* /CUR vits/ type of leap on horseback.

254. **as lief** /leef/ as soon.

257. **God buy you** good bye. Some eds. substitute **God b'wi' you**
/gŏd BWEE yo͞o/ or some other variation of that phrase.

268. **stature** /STATCH ur/ size.

277. **Atalanta's** /at uh LAN tuz/ the swiftest runner in Gk. myths.

308, 309. ***divers** various. US, CN /DĪ vurss, -vurz/ [dī-, dih VURSS];
UK /DĪ vurss/ [-vurz, dī VURSS].

315. **se'nnight** /SEN it, -īt/ week.

324. **penury** /PEN yur ee/; UK *also* /PEN yoor ee/ poverty.

339. ***cony** /KOH nee/, *rarely older* [KUN ee] rabbit.

354. **halfpence** /HAYP ṇss, -unss/.

362. **elegies** /EL uh jeez/ sorrowful poems.

364. ***fancy-monger** love peddler. US /FAN see mŏng gur/ or /-mawng-/,
[-mung-]; CN /-mung gur, -mŏng gur/; UK /-mung gur/.

365. **quotidian** /kwoh TID ee un/; UK *also* [kwŏ TID ee un] type of fever.

378. **revenue** sometimes in verse /ruh VEN yo͞o/, but in this prose passage may
be mod. Eng. US /REV in o͞o/; UK, SOUTH. US /-yo͞o/.

382. **point-devise, -device** /POYNT dih VĪSS/ fastidious.

383. **accoustrements** /uh CUSS tur munts/ clothes. Archaic variant of **accoutrements** /uh CO͞OT ruh munts, uh CO͞OT ur munts/.

Act 3 Scene 3

8. **Ovid** /ŎV id/ Roman poet.

9. **Goths** /gŏ~~th~~s/; US *also* /gaw~~th~~s/ Germanic tribe. Shk pronounced it /gohts/ or /gŏts/, hence the pun with *goats.*

74. **God 'ild you** God reward you, thank you. /gŏd ILD yo͞o/; US *also* /gawd-/. Some eds. prefer **God 'ield you** /-EELD-/.

78. **motley** /MŎT lee/ here means 'fool.' See 2.7.13.

79. **bow** /boh/ yoke.

87. ***wainscot** /WAYNZ cŏt, -cut/; US, UK *also newer* [-coht] type of wooden interior siding.

103. **Wind** /wīnd/ wander.

Act 3 Scene 4

24. **concave** /CŎN-, CŎNG kayv/ or /cŏn-, cun KAYV/.

42. ***traverse** /truh VURSS, TRAV urss/; UK *also* /TRAV URSS/ across.

43. **puisne** /PYO͞O nee/ archaic variant of **puny**.

Act 3 Scene 5

13. **atomies** /AT uh meez/ tiny particles, specks of dust.

17. **swound** archaic variant of **swoon**. In Shk's time the vowel could be either /ow/ or /o͞o/.

23. **cicatrice** /SIK uh triss/ mark.

ă-bat, ăir-**marry**, air-**pair**, ạr-**far**, ĕr-**merry**, ĝ- **get**, ī-**high**, ĭr-**mirror**, ł-**little**, n̥-**listen**, ŏ-**hot**, oh-**go**, o͞o-**wood**, o͞o-**moon**, oor-**tour**, ōr- **or**, ow-**how**, ţh-**that**, ~~th~~-**thin**, ŭ-**but**, UR-**fur**, ur-**under**.   ( ) - suppress the syllable   see p. xiii for complete list.

56. **lineaments** /LIN yuh munts/ distinctive features.

95. **erst** /urst/ formerly.

105. **yerwhile** may have been /yair-/ variant of **erewhile** /air WHĪL/ 'before,'

108. **carlot** /CAR lut/ peasant.

123. **damask** /DAM usk/ pink or light red.

Act 4 Scene 1

14. **politic** /PŎL ih tik/ shrewd.

31. **God buy you** good bye. Some eds. substitute **God b'wi' you**
/gŏd BWEE yōō/ or some other variation of that phrase.

38. *****gundello** /GUN duh loh, -luh/ boat of Venice. Archaic variant of **gondola**
/GŎN duh luh/.

52. **as lief** /leef/ as soon.

55. **jointure** /JOYN chur/ marriage settlement. See App. D -*ure*.

75. *****orators** US, CN /OR uh turz/; UK, E.COAST US /ŎR-/. Sometimes
/OR ayt urz/ is used, but it is not recommended. See App. D -*or*.

97. *****videlicet** namely (abbreviated *viz.*). The older, anglicized pronunciations
are US /vih DELL ih sit/ [-DEEL-, vī-]; UK /vih DEEL ih sit/ [vī-, -DELL-].
Newer pronunciations mix in restored Latin syllables, for example, /-ket/ or
/-DAYL-/. These are not recommended.

100. **Leander** /lee AN dur/ he swam the Hellespont to be with Hero.

103. **Hellespont** /HEL iss pŏnt/ the Dardenelles.

106. *****Sestos** US /SESS tus, -tŏs/; UK /-tŏs/ [-tus]. A newer pronunciation /-ohss/
is also used, especially in the US. Normal development would favor /-us/.

150. **Barbary** /BAR buh ree/ region in North Africa.

156. **hyen** /HĪ in/ variant of **hyena**.

Act 4 Scene 3

8, 21. **contents** here should be /cŏn TENTS/.

11. **tenure** archaic variant of **tenor**, both /TEN ur/.

27. *****huswive's** /HUZ ivz/ is traditional, /HUSS wīvz/ is a newer, spelling pronunciation. The former is the most common form in the UK, the latter in the US. In CN both are used equally. In North America /HUSS wivz/ is also sometimes used. Archaic variant of **housewive's**.

35. **Ethiop** /EETH yŏp/ an Ethiopian, i.e., black.

50. **eyne** /īn/ dialect form of *eyes*.

76. **purlieus** US, CN /PUR lōōz, -lyōōz/; UK /PUR lyōōz/ /-lōōz/ tract of land on the edge of a forest.

79. *****osiers** US /OH zhurz/ [OH zyurz]; UK /OH zyurz/ willows.

97. **handkercher** /HANK ur chur/ archaic variant of **handkerchief**.

168. *****Heigh-ho!** US /hay ho, hī-/; CN /hī-/, *rarely* [hay-]; UK /hay-/. Shk intended /hay/. Spoken with evenly stressed syllables or as if sighing, with 1st syllable stress.

Act 5 Scene 1

43, 44. **ipse** /IP see/ himself. Restored Latin is /IP say/.

48. *****boorish** US, CN /BŌŌR ish/, *sometimes* [BOR-]; UK /BŌŌR ish, BOR-/ peasant (language).

54. *****bastinado** beating with a stick. /bas tih NAH doh/;
UK *rarely older* [bas tih NAY doh].

Act 5 Scene 2

4. **persever** /pur SEV ur/ persevere. Since it is prose, mod. /pur suh VEER/ may be substituted.

ă-bat, ăir-**marry**, air-**pair**, ạr-**far**, ĕr-**merry**, ĝ- **get**, ī-**high**, ĭr-**mirror**, ł-**little**, ṇ-**listen**, ŏ-**hot**, oh-**go**, ōō-**wood**, ōō-**moon**, oor-**tour**, ōr- **or**, ow-**how**, ŧh-**that**, th-**thin**, ŭ-**but**, UR-**fur**, ur-**under**.   ( ) - suppress the syllable   see p. xiii for complete list.

11. **revenue** sometimes in verse /ruh VEN yo͞o/, but in this prose passage may be mod. Eng. US /REV in o͞o/; UK, SOUTH. US /-yo͞o/.

26. **sound** archaic variant of **swoon**. In Shk's time the vowel could be either /ow/ or /o͞o/.

26. **handkercher** /HANK ur chur/ archaic variant of **handkerchief**.

31. **thrasonical** /t̶h̶ruh SŎN ih kł/ [t̶h̶ray SŎN ih kł] boastful.

43. ***nuptial** wedding. US, UK /NUP chł/ [-shł]; in CN both are used equally.

Act 5 Scene 3

17. **nonino, nonny-no** /NŎN ee NOH/ a nonsense word.

40. **God buy you** good bye. Some eds. substitute **God b'wi' you** /gŏd BWEE yo͞o/ or some other variation of that phrase.

Act 5 Scene 4

5. **compact** plot. Here should be /cŏm-, cum PACT/.

35. **toward** /TOH wurd, -urd/ about to take place.

41. **motley-minded** /MŎT lee-/ foolish. See 2.7.13.

45. **politic** /PŎL ih tik/ shrewd.

54. **God 'ild you** God reward you, thank you. /gŏd ILD yo͞o/; US *also* /gawd-/. Some eds. prefer **God 'ield you** /-EELD-/.

65. **dulcet** /DULL sit/ sweet.

130. **contents** /cun TENTS/ contentments.

184. **convertites** /CŎN vur tīts/ converts to a religious life.

189. **allies** here with 2nd syllable stress.

192. **victuall'd** /VIT łd/ provided with food.

Epilogue

11. *conjure entreat. US, CN /CŎN jur/, *rarely* [CUN-]; UK /CUN jur/ [CŎN-], *rarely* [cun JOOR]. The older pronunciation for this meaning is /cun JOOR/.

ă-bat, ăir-marry, air-pair, ạr-far, ĕr-merry, ĝ- get, ī-high, ĭr-mirror, ł-little, ṇ-listen, ŏ-hot, oh-go, ŏŏ-wood, ōō-moon, oor-tour, ōr- or, ow-how, ţh-that, th-thin, ŭ-but, UR-fur, ur-under.   ( ) - suppress the syllable   see p. xiii for complete list.

The Comedy of Errors

People in the Play

Abbess /AB iss/, also called **Aemilia**.

*Adriana US /ay dree AHN uh/ [ad ree AHN uh, ay dree ANN uh];
CN /ay dree ANN uh/ [-AHN-]; UK /ad ree AHN uh/ [-ANN-, ay dree AHN uh].
Recommendation: the oldest angl. form /ay dree ANN uh/.

Aegeon see **Egeon**.

Aemilia, Emilia /ee-, ih MEEL ee yuh/. Older /-MILL-/ is now rare. Also
called the **Abbess**.

Angelo /AN juh loh/.

Antipholus /an TIF uh lus/.

*Balthazar, Balthasar /BAL thuh zar/. The scansion is uncertain at 3.1.19 and
22, but the stress could be on the first syllable. A variant form /bal THAZ ur/ is
also possible, though rarely used today. Likewise a form with third syllable
stress is rare.

*Courtezan, Courtesan US /CORT ih zun, -zan/, *rarely* [cort ih ZAN];
CN /CORT ih zan/ [-zun], *rarely* [cort ih ZAN]; UK /CORT ih zan, cort ih ZAN/.
This word is not spoken in the play.

Dromio 2 or 3 syllables depending on meter /DROH m(ee) yoh/.

Egeon, Aegeon /ih-, ee JEE un/ is usual, but /-ŏn/ is sometimes used. See
App. D *-on*.

Emilia see **Aemilia**.

Luce /looss/. Some eds. call this character **Nell** (for /lyoo-/ see App. D *lu-*).

*Luciana US /loo see AH nuh, -chee-, -shee-/ [loo see ANN-, loo chee ANN-];
CN /loo see ANN uh/ [-chee AHN-, -chee ANN-]; UK /loo chee AHN uh/
[-see AHN-, -chee ANN-]. Recommendation: the oldest angl. form
/loo shee ANN uh/. /-chee-/ and /-AHN-/ are Ital. forms (for /lyoo-/ see
App. D *lu-*).

Solinus /soh-, suh LĪ nus/.

Places in the Play

The Centaur /SEN tor/ an inn.

Ephesus /EF ih sus/.

Epidamium (F1) /ep ih DAYM yum/. The usual mod. form of this city is
Epidamnus. Some eds. prefer the form **Epidamnum** /ep ih DAM num/.

The Porpentine /POR pin tīn/ an inn. Archaic variant of **Porcupine**.

*****Syracuse** US /SĬR uh kyo͞oss/; UK /SĪ ruh kyo͞oz/ [SĬR-, -kyo͞oss].
  Syracusa angl. US /sĭr uh KYO͞OZ uh/; UK /sī ruh-/ [sĭr uh-];
  Ital. /see rah KO͞O zah/.
  Syracusian(s) US /sĭr uh KYO͞O zhun(z)/; UK /sī ruh-/ [sĭr uh-].
  Syracusan is prefered by some eds. /-sun, -zun, -sn̩, -zn̩/.

Act 1 Scene 1

8. **guilders** /ĜILL durz/ type of money.

11. **intestine** /in TESS tin/; UK *also* [-teen] internal or deadly.

13.*****synods** US, CN /SIN udz/ [-ŏdz]; UK /-ŏdz/ [-udz] councils.

20. **confiscate** confiscated. Here should be /cŏn FISS kayt, -ut/.

42. **randon** /RAN dun/ archaic form of **random**.

87-111. **Corinth** US, CN /COR inth/; UK, E.COAST US /CŎR-/.

---

92. **amain** /uh MAYN/ with full speed.

93. **Epidaurus** /ep ih DOR us/.

120, 141. **mishap(s)** here /mis HAP(S)/.

122. **dilate** /dih-, dī LAYT/ tell in detail.

126. *****importun'd** /im POR chund/ asked insistently. See App. D.

ă-bat, ăir-**marry**, air-**pair**, a̱r-**far**, ĕr-**merry**, ĝ- **get**, ī-**high**, ĭr-**mirror**, ł-**little**, n̩-**listen**,
ŏ-**hot**, oh-**go**, o͞o-**wood**, ō͞o-**moon**, oor-**tour**, ōr- **or**, ow-**how**, th-**that**, th̶-**thin**, ŭ-**but**,
UR-**fur**, ur-**under**.   ( ) - suppress the syllable   see p. xiii for complete list.

144. **disannul** /dis uh NŬL/ annul.

145. **advocate** /AD vuh kut/ someone who supports a person or cause.

158. **liveless** /LĪV liss/ archaic variant of **lifeless.**

Act 1 Scene 2

2. **confiscate** /CŎN fiss kayt, -ut/ confiscated.

28. **consort** /cun SORT/ keep company with.

44. ***capon** US /KAY pŏn, -pun/; CN, UK /KAY pŏn/ [-pun] chicken. See App. D -*on.*

55. **sixpence** /SIKS punss, -pṇss/; US *also* /SIKS penss/.

79. **sconce** /skŏnss/ head.

96. **o'erraught** /or RAWT/ cheated.

101. **mountebanks** /MOWNT uh banks/ quack doctors.

Act 2 Scene 1

16. ***situate** US /SITCH (oo) wut/ [-wayt]; UK /-wayt/ situated.

22. ***Indu'd** /in DYŌOD/; US *also* [-DŌOD] supplied.

38. **unkind** here should be /UN kīnd/.

72. **arrant** /ĂIR unt/ archaic variant of **errand.**

86. **low'reth, loureth** threatens. /LOWR ith/ with the vowel of *how.*

92. **voluble** /VŎL yuh bł/ easily flowing.

104.***homage** /HŎM ij/; US *also* /ŎM ij/ acknowledgement of allegience.

Act 2 Scene 2

34-7. **sconce** /skŏnss/ double meaning: head, fort.

38. **insconce** /in SKŎNSS/ fortify.   Most eds. prefer **ensconce** /en-/.

58-62. **Basting** /BAYST ing/ beating.

75. **periwig** /PĚR ee wig/ *also* /PĚR ih-/ wig.

77. **niggard** /NIG urd/ miser.

109.***wafts** beckons.   US, CN /wŏfts/; SOUTH. US /wăfts/;
UK /wŏfts/ [wăfts, wahfts].   /wăfts/ is newer and considered non-standard by
many.

122. **undividable** /un dih VĪ duh bł/.

122. **incorporate** /in COR pur rut, -rayt/ united in body.   /-ut / is more usual for
an adj.

131. **licentious** here should be /lī SEN chee us/ lustful.

132.***consecrate** /CŎN suh crut, -crayt/ consecrated.

133.***contaminate** /cun TAM ih nut, -ayt/ contaminated.

136. **harlot** /HAR lut/ whore.

140. **adulterate** /uh DULL trayt, -trut/ defiled with adultery.   /-ut/ is more usual
for an adj.

158. **buffet** /BUFF it/ strike.

161. **compact** here should be /cŏm-, cum PACT/ plot.

177. **dross** /drŏss/; US *also* /drawss/ impure matter, rubbish.

193. **prat'st** /praytst/ chatter.

215. **persever** /pur SEV ur/ persevere.

ă-bat,   ăir-m**arry**, air-p**air**, ạr-f**ar**,   ĕr-m**erry**,   ĝ- g**et**, ī-h**igh**, ĭr-m**irror**, ł-l**ittle**, ṇ-l**isten**,
ŏ-h**ot**,   oh-g**o**,   ōō-w**ood**, ōō-m**oon**, oor-t**our**,   ōr- **or**, ow-h**ow**, t̬h-t**hat**, th-t**hin**, ŭ-b**ut**,
UR-f**ur**, ur-u**nder**.   ( ) - suppress the syllable   see p. xiii for complete list.

Act 3 Scene 1

4. **carcanet** /CAR kuh net/ necklace.

27. **niggardly** /NIG (ur)d lee/ miserly.

28. **cates** /kayts/ food.

31. **Cic'ly, Cicely** /SISS lee/.

31. **Gillian** /JILL yun/.

31. **Ginn** /jin/.

32. *__capon__ US /KAY pŏn, -pun/; CN, UK /KAY pŏn/ [-pun] chicken. See App. D *-on.*

34. *__conjure__ here should be /cun JOOR/ summon by magic.

77. **hind** /hīnd/ menial laborer.

101. **rout** /rowt/ crowd.

121. **elsewhere** here with 2nd syllable stress, a form still used in the UK, but unknown in the US.

Act 3 Scene 2

4. **ruinous** /ROO ih nus/. F1 has an archaic variant **ruinate** /ROO ih nut/.

7. **elsewhere** here with 2nd syllable stress, a form still used in the UK, but unknown in the US.

10. *__orator__ US, CN /OR uh tur/; UK, E.COAST US /ŎR-/. Sometimes /OR ayt ur/ is used, but it is not recommended.   See App. D *-or.*

12. **harbinger** /HAR bin jer/ a messenger sent in advance.

22. **compact** /cum-, cŏm PACT/ composed of.

43. *__homage__ /HŎM ij/; US *also* /ŎM ij/ acknowledgement of allegience.

102. **Swart** /swōrt/ black.

114. ***spherical** US, CN /SFEER ih kł/ [SFĔR-]; UK /SFĔR ih kł/.

128. **rheum** /rōōm/ mucus.

137. **armadoes** /arm AY dohz/ archaic form of **armadas** /arm AH duz/ fleets.

137. **carrects** /KĂIR ucts/ large ships. Archaic variant of **carracks** /KĂIR uks/.

137. **ballast** /BĂL ust/ ballasted, loaded with ballast, weight.

138. **Belgia** /BEL juh/ Belgium.

146. **curtal dog** /CURT ł/ dog with tail cut short.

Act 4 Scene 1

1. **Pentecost** /PEN tih cŏst/; US *also* /-cawst/ seventh Sunday after Easter.

2. ***importun'd** /im POR chund/ asked insistently. See App. D.

4. **guilders** /ĜILL durz/ type of money.

22. **holp** /hohlp/ helped.

28. **charect** /KĂIR uct/ archaic variant of **carat** /KĂIR ut/ a unit of weight.

48, 59. **dalliance** play, frivolity. The first instance is /DAL yunss/, the second /DAL ee yunss/.

53. ***importunes** /im POR chunz/ asks insistently. See App. D.

87. **fraughtage** /FRAWT ij/ cargo.

89. **balsamum** /BAWL suh mum/ balsum or balm, a healing oinment.

89. ***aqua-vitae** distilled liquor, e.g., brandy. US /AHK-, AK wuh VEE tī/, *rarely* [-VĪ tee]; CN /AK wuh VEE tī/ [AHK-]; UK /AK wuh VEE tī/ [-VEE tuh]. /AK wuh VĪ tee/ is the oldest surviving form. /-VEE tay/ not recommended.

95. ***waftage** passage. US, CN /WŎFT ij/; SOUTH. US /WĂFT-/; UK /WŎFT-/ [WĂFT-, WAHFT-]. /WĂFT-/ is newer and considered non-standard by many.

ă-bat, ăir-marry, air-**pair**, ạr-**far**, ĕr-**merry**, ĝ- get, ī-high, ĭr-mirror, ł-little, ṇ-listen, ŏ-hot, oh-go, ōō-wood, ōō-moon, oor-**tour**, ōr- or, ow-how, ţh-**that**, ŧħ-**thin**, ŭ-but, UR-**fur**, ur-under.   ( ) - suppress the syllable   see p. xiii for complete list.

98. **rope's, ropës** here 2 syllables are indicated /ROH piz/.

110. **Dowsabel** /DOW suh bel, -zuh-/ i.e., Luce.

Act 4 Scene 2

19. **sere** /seer/ withered.

32. **Tartar** /TAR tur/ hellish.

37. ***countermands** forbids. /COWNT ur măndz/; E.NEW ENG., UK /-mahndz/.
More rarely the stress falls on the last syllable. Here should rhyme with *lands*.

58.***bankrout** /BANK rowt/ [-rut] archaic variant of **bankrupt**.

Act 4 Scene 3

27. **suits of *durance** /DYOOR unss/; US *also* /DOoR-/ [DUR-]. Double
meaning: 'durable cloth' and 'imprisonment.'

28. **exploits** /ek SPLOYTS/ in verse, but here may be mod. /EK sployts/.

28. **morris-pike.** Some eds. prefer **Moorish pike** /MOOR ish/ [MOR-] a pike
of moorish origin.

48, 49. **Sathan** archaic form of **Satan**, both pronounced /SAYT n̩, -un/ the
devil.

56. ***ergo** /UR go/ is older, /ĔR go/ is newer. The former is more common in
the UK, the latter in the US, but both forms appear in all countries.

69. **diamond** here should be /DĪ uh mund/, the standard UK form.

79. **Avaunt** /uh VAWNT/ begone!

Act 4 Scene 4

41. **respice finem** Ang.Lat. /RESS pih see FĪ nem/;
Class.Lat. /RESS pik ay FEE nem/ look to your end.

54. **Sathan** archaic form of **Satan**, both pronounced /SAYT n̩, -un/ the devil.

61. **saffron** /SAFF run/ yellow.

71. **Perdie, Perdy** /PUR DEE/ indeed (originally 'by God'). Some eds. prefer the variant **Pardie** /par DEE/.

73. **Sans** /sănz/ without.

75. **Certes** /SUR teez/ certainly.

79. **contraries** /CŎN truh reez/ behavior opposite to what is expected.

82. **suborn'd** /sub ORND/ persuaded someone to do wrong.

101. **harlot** /HAR lut/ whore.

103. **abject** /AB ject/ contemptible.

108. **wan** /wŏn/ pale.

Act 5 Scene 1

20. **controversy** here should be /CŎN truh vur see/, the normal US pronunciation.

37. **priory** /PRĪ (uh) ree/ convent.

97. **assaying** /uh-, ass SAY ing/. Some eds. prefer **essaying** /es SAY ing/. Both mean 'attempting.'

114. ***prostrate** /PRŎS trayt/, US *rarely* [-trut] lying face down.

170. **a-row** /uh ROH/ one after the other.

185.***halberds** US, CN /HAL burdz, HAWL-/; UK /HAL-/ [HAWL-] spears with blades on the end.

192. **bestrid** /bih-, bee STRID/ stood over protectively.

205. **harlots** /HAR luts/ lewd men.

217. **Albeit** /awl BEE (i)t/ although.

ă-bat, ăir-**marry**, air-**pair**, ạr-**far**, ĕr-**merry**, ĝ- **get**, ī-**high**, ĭr-**mirror**, ł-**little**, ṇ-**listen**, ŏ-**hot**, oh-**go**, o͞o-**wood**, o͞o-**moon**, oor-**tour**, ŏr- **or**, ow-**how**, th-**that**, th-**thin**, ŭ-**but**, UR-**fur**, ur-**under**.   ( ) - suppress the syllable   see p. xiii for complete list.

239. **mountebank** /MOWNT uh bank/ quack doctor.

271. **Circe's** /SUR seez/ a sorceress.

311. **untun'd** here stressed on the first syllable.

314. ***conduits** blood vessels. Here must be 2 syllables /CŎN dwits/;
UK *also* [CUN dwits, CŎN dywits, CŎN dits, CUN dits].

352-366. **Corinth** US, CN /COR inth/; UK, E.COAST US /CŎR-/.

361. **children** here /CHIL dur in/ is indicated.

369. **Menaphon** /MEN uh fun, -fŏn/. /-ŏn/ is usual in the US and is increasingly
common in the UK. See App. D *-on*.

392. **diamond** here should be /DĪ uh mund/, the standard UK form.

401.***travail** here should be /TRAV ayl/ suffering (of childbirth).

Coriolanus

People in the Play

Aedile (**Edile** F1) /EE dīl/ Roman official.

Agrippa see **Menenius Agrippa**.

Aufidius 3 or 4 syllables depending on meter /aw FID (ee) yus/.

Brutus see **Junius Brutus**.

***Caius (Martius)** US, CN /KĪ us/, *rarely* [KAY us]; UK /KĪ us, KAY us/.
Ang.Lat. /KAY us/; Class.Lat. /KĪ ōōs/. Another angl. form /keez/ is sometimes
used, but doesn't fit the meter.

Cominius 3 or 4 syllables depending on meter /kuh MIN (ee) yus/.

Coriolanus 4 or 5 syllables depending on meter /cor (ee) yuh LAY nus/;
restored Latin [-LAHN-].

Junius Brutus /JŌŌN yus BRŌŌT us/.

Lartius /LAR shus/.

Lictors /LIK turz/ Roman officials. Not spoken in this play. See App. D -*or*.

Martius 2 or 3 syllables depending on meter /MAR shus, MAR shee yus/.

Menenius Agrippa /muh NEEN yus   uh GRIP uh/.

Nicanor /nī KAY nur/. See App. D -*or*.

Sicinius Velutus 3 or 4 syllables in *Sicinius* depending on meter
/sih SIN (ee) yus   vuh LŌŌT us/ (for /lyōō-/ see App. D *lu*-).

Tullus (Aufidius) /TŬLL us/.

Valeria /vuh LEER (ee) yuh/. At 1.3.26 it appears to be /VLEER ee uh/ but it
may have been intended as a prose passage.

ă-bat, ăir-**marry**, air-**pair**, ar-**far**, ĕr-**merry**, ĝ- **get**, ī-**high**, ĭr-**mirror**, ł-**little**, n̩-**listen**,
ŏ-**hot**, oh-**go**, ōō-**wood**, ōō-**moon**, oor-**tour**, ōr- **or**, ow-**how**, t̠h-**that**, t̶h̶-**thin**, ŭ-**but**,
UR-**fur**, ur-**under**.   ( ) - suppress the syllable   see p. xiii for complete list.

People in the Play (cont.)

Velutus see **Sicinius Velutus**.

Virgilia /VUR JIL ee uh/.

The Volscians Ang.Lat. /VŎL shunz/. Sometimes a restored pronunciation /-skyunz/ is used.

Volsce /vŏlss/, plural **Volsces** /VŎL siz/ the Volscians. Sometimes a restored pronunciation /VŎL skee/ is used, but this will not always fit the meter when the singular demands one syllable.

Volumnia /vuh LUM n(ee) yuh/.

Places in the Play

Corioles 3 or 4 syllables depending on meter /kuh RĪ (uh) lus/. Some eds. prefer *****Corioli** /koh-, kuh RĪ (uh) lee/. Ang.Lat. would be /kuh RĪ (uh) lī/. Sometimes restored Latin /-REE-/ is used. 3rd syllable stress will not fit the meter.

The Tarpeian Rock /tar PEE un/.

Special Words

consul /CŎN sł/ Roman official.

plebeians the common people. /plih BEE unz/ is the mod. pronunciation and can be used in prose passages. In verse it should be /PLEB ee yunz/ or /PLEB yunz/ depending on meter. There was also a pronunciation /PLEEB-/, now obsolete. Note that at 3.1.101 the stress may fall on the first or second syllable, depending on whether the line is scanned with an epic caesura.

*****tribune** here always with stress on the 1st syllable /TRIB yoͦn/.

Act 1 Scene 1

29. **commonalty** /CŎM un ł tee/ commoners.

58. **fortnight** /FORT nīt/; US *also* [FORT nit] two weeks. Virtually obsolete in the US.

68. **staves** /stayvz/ staffs.

81. **edicts** /EE dicts/ decrees.

82. **usury** /YOO zhur ee/; UK *also* [-zhyoor ee, -zhoor ee] lending money for interest.

82. **usurers** /YOO zhur urz/; UK *also* [-zhyoor urz, -zhoor urz] those who lend money for interest.

100. **viand** /VĪ und/ food.   /VEE und/ not recommended.

118. **muniments** /MYOON ih munts/ defenses.

121. *****cormorant** /COR m(uh) runt/; US *rarely* [-ant] a fishing bird, i.e., devouring.

130. **incorporate** /in CORP rut, -rayt/ united in one body. /-ut/ is more usual for an adj.

151. **weal** /weel/ welfare.

164. **dissentious** /dih SEN shus/ quarrelsome.

250. **mutiners** it is not certain whether Shk pronounced this /MYOOT n̩ urz/ or as in mod. **mutineers** /myoot n̩ EERZ/.

Act 1 Scene 2

20. **pretenses** (UK **pretences**) designs. Here should be /prih TENSS iz/, the normal UK pronunciation, or /pree TENSS iz/ based on the most common US pronunciation /PREE tenss iz/.

Act 1 Scene 3

40. **Hecuba** /HEK yoo buh/ Queen of Troy.

41, 42. **Hector ('s)** /HEK tur/. See App. D *-or*.

65. **mammock'd** /MAM ukt/ tore to pieces.

70. *****huswife** /HUZ if/ is traditional, /HUSS wīf/ is a newer, spelling pronunciation. The former is the most common form in the UK, the latter in the

---

ă-bat, ăir-**m**arry, air-**p**air, ạr-**f**ar, ĕr-**m**erry, ĝ- **g**et, ī-**h**igh, ĭr-**m**irror, ł-**l**ittle, n̩-**l**isten, ŏ-**h**ot, oh-**g**o, ŏŏ-**w**ood, ōō-**m**oon, oor-**t**our, ōr- **or**, ow-**h**ow, t͟h-**th**at, t͟h-**th**in, ŭ-**b**ut, UR-**f**ur, ur-**u**nder.   ( ) - suppress the syllable   see p. xiii for complete list.

US. In CN both are used equally. In North America /HUSS wif/ is also sometimes used. Some eds. prefer mod. **housewife**.

83. **Ulysses'** in verse always /yōō LISS eez/; US *also* /yōō-/, but in this prose passage the less common UK pronunciation /YŌŌ lih seez/ may also be used.

84. **Ithaca** /ITH uh kuh/ Ulysses' home.

84. *****cambric** fine linen cloth.   /KAM brik/, or older [KAYM brik].

Act 1 Scene 4 (*Complete Oxford* 1.5).

9. *****'larum** US, CN /LAHR um/ [-LĂIR-]; UK /LĂIR um, LAHR um/ call to arms.

38. **agued** /AY gyōōd/ fevered.

57. **Cato's** /KAYT ohz/ Roman moralist.

Act 1 Scene 5 (*Complete Oxford* 1.6)

3. **murrain** US, CN /MUR in/; E.COAST US, UK /MUH rin/ plague.

5. **drachme** (F1) /DRAK mee/ Gk. coin. Variant of **drachma** /DRAK muh/.

Act 1 Scene 6 (*Complete Oxford* 1.7)

22. **flea'd** /fleed/ archaic and dialect variant of **flayed** /flayd/ skinned.

25. **tabor** /TAY bur/ small drum. See App. D *-or*.

31. *****nuptial** wedding. US, UK /NUP chł/ [-shł]; in CN both are used equally.

32. **tapers** /TAY purz/ slender candles.

32. **bedward** /BED wurd/.

53. *****vaward** US /VAW wurd, VAY-/ [VOW-]; UK /VAW wurd/ [VAY-, VOW-, VAW WURD]. The vowel of *war* not recommended in the second syllable. Archaic variant of **vanguard**. See App. D *-aun-*.

53, 59. Antiates /AN shee ayts/ citizens of *Antium* which is usually /AN tee um/ today, formerly /AN sh(ee) um/.

58. endure 'always remain.' Here with 1st syllable stress.

Act 1 Scene 8 (*Complete Oxford* 1.9)

7. Hollow me /HŎL uh, -oh/ hunt me. Variant of **Holla** /HŎL uh/ 'hunting cry.' Stress could also fall on the 2nd syllable.

11. Hector /HEK tur/. See App. D *-or*.

12. progeny race, family. /PRŎJ ih nee/; UK *also* [PROH-], a newer form.

Act 1 Scene 9 (*Complete Oxford* 1.10)

12. caparison /kuh PĂIR ih sn̩/ an ornamental cloth worn by a horse.

14. *extol praise. /ek STOHL/; UK *sometimes* and US *rarely* [-STŎL].

22. traducement slander. /truh DYŌŌS munt/; US *also* /-DŌŌS-/. /-JŌŌS-/ is considered non-standard in the UK.

48. *debile /DEE bīl, DEB īl/; US *rarely* [DEB ł] weak.

51. hyperbolical /hī pur BŎL ih kł/ exaggerated.

70. howbeit here should be /how BEE (i)t/ nevertheless.

Act 1 Scene 10 (*Complete Oxford* 1.11)

22. Embarquements /em BARK munts/ restraints. Some eds. prefer **Embargements**.

26. hospitable here should be /HŎS pih tuh bł/.

Act 2 Scene 1

1. *augurer /AWG yur ur/ [AWG ur ur]; UK *also* /-yoor-/ prophet.

ă-bat, ăir-marry, air-pair, ạr-far, ĕr-merry, ĝ- get, ī-high, ĭr-mirror, ł-little, n̩-listen, ŏ-hot, oh-go, ōō-wood, ōō-moon, oor-tour, ōr- or, ow-how, ţh-that, ŧħ-thin, Ŭ-but, UR-fur, ur-under.   ( ) - suppress the syllable   see p. xiii for complete list.

44. ***magistrates** /MAJ ih strayts/; US *also* [-struts].

49. **allaying** /uh LAY ing/ diminishing the effects of.

49. **Tiber** /TĪ bur/ main river in Rome.

54. **wealsmen** /WEELZ min/ statesmen.

55. **Lycurguses** /lī CUR guh siz/ Lycurgus was a Spartan lawgiver.

64. **beesom** /BEE zum, -sum/ blind. Variant of **bisson** /BISS ṇ/.

64. **conspectuities** US /cŏn spek TOO ih teez/; UK, SOUTH. US /-TYOO-/ eye-sight.

71. **forset-seller** probably /FŎSS it/ in Shk's day, pronounced without the *r*. Archaic variant of **faucet**.

71. **rejourn** /ree-, rih JURN/ postpone.

72. **threepence** /T̶H̶R̶E̶P̶ unss, -ṇss/ [T̶H̶R̶U̶P̶-, T̶H̶R̶I̶P̶-, T̶H̶R̶o͞o̶P̶-].

74. **colic** /CŎL ik/ stomach ache.

82. **giber** /JĪ bur/ witty fellow.

91. ***predecessors** US /PRED ih sess urz/; UK /PREE dih sess urz/; in CN both /PREE-/ and /PRED-/ are used equally. Rarely with stress on the 3rd syllable. See App. D *-or*.

92. **Deucalion** father of the human race. /dyoo KAY lee un/; US *also* /doo-/. Sometimes newer /-ŏn/ is used, but is not recommended.

92. ***peradventure** perhaps. /PUR ad VEN chur/;
US *rarely* [PĚR-, PUR ad ven chur];
UK, CN *also* [PUR-, PĚR ad ven chur, pĕr ad VEN chur].

93. **God-den** /gud-, good EN/ good evening. Some eds. prefer **Good e'en**.

117. **Galen** /GAY lin/ Gk. doctor.

117. **empiricutic** /em pĭr ih KYOOT ik/ quackish.

131. **fidius'd, fidiussed** /FID ee yust/ Aufidius'd, i.e., thrashed.

148. **cicatrices** /SIK uh triss iz/ scars.

150. **Tarquin** /TAR kwin/ former king of Rome.

208. ***malkin*** US /MAWL kin/; UK /MAW kin/ [MAWL-, MŎL-] wench.

209. **lockram** /LŎCK rum/ cheap linen cloth.

209. **reechy** /REECH ee/ grimy.

211. **leads** /ledz/ lead roofs.

213. **flamens** /FLAY munz/ priests.

216. **damask** /DAM usk/ pink or light red.

218. **Phoebus'** /FEE bus/ god of the sun.

218. **poother** /PŌ͝OTH ur/ or /PUTH ur/ commotion. Archaic variant of **pother** /PŎTH ur/.

234. **vesture** /VES chur/ clothing, covering. See App. D *-ure*.

251. **provand** /PRŎV ṇd/ food for animals.

264. **handkerchers** /HANK ur churz/ archaic variant of **handkerchiefs**.

Act 2 Scene 2

54. **convented** /cun VENT tid/ summoned.

76. ***alarum*** here 2 syllables are called for, /uh LARM/ call to arms.

85. **haver** /HAV ur/ one who has.

88, 94. **Tarquin ('s)** /TAR kwin(z)/ former king of Rome.

91. **Amazonian** /am uh ZOHN yun/ here, 'beardless.'

92. **bestrid** /bih-, bee STRID/ stood over, with legs apart.

93. **oe'rpress'd Roman** here should be /OR prest/.

ă-bat, ăir-**marry**, air-**pair**, ạr-**far**, ĕr-**merry**, ĝ- **get**, ī-**high**, ĭr-**mirror**, ł-**little**, ṇ-**listen**, ŏ-**hot**, oh-**go**, ō͝o-**wood**, ōō-**moon**, oor-**tour**, ōr- **or**, ow-**how**, ṭh-**that**, th-**thin**, ŭ-**but**, UR-**fur**, ur-**under**.   ( ) - suppress the syllable   see p. xiii for complete list.

117. **fatigate** weary. /FAT ih gut, -ayt/, but /-ut/ is more usual for an adj.

143. *****predecessors** US /PRED ih sess urz/; UK /PREE dih sess urz/; in CN both /PREE-/ and /PRED-/ are used equally. Rarely with stress on the 3rd syllable. See App. D *-or*.

Act 2 Scene 3

19. **abram** /AY brum/ variant of *abran* /AY brun/ 'light yellow.' Later confused with **auburn** (F4) /AW burn/ 'reddish brown.'

28. **wadg'd** /wăjd/ archaic variant of **wedged**.

81. **alms** charity for the poor. /ahmz/ is older; /ahlmz, awlmz/ are newer. In the UK the latter are non-standard.

91. **scourge** /SKURJ/ instrument of punishment.

115. **toge** /tohg/ toga.

119. *****antique** ancient. Here /AN teek/, *rarely older* [AN tik].

139. **Endue** /en DY$\overline{OO}$/; US *also* [-D$\overline{OO}$] endow.

181. **weal** /weel/ commonwealth

184. **plebeii** /PLEB ee ī/ the common people.

189. **Translate** here may be stressed on either syllable. 1st syllable stress is usual in the US, final syllable stress in the UK. US /trănss-, trănz-/; UK /trănss-/ [trănz-, trahnz-, trahnss-, trunss-, trunz-].

205. **rectorship** /REK tur ship/ government.

225. **gibingly** /JĪ bing lee/ sarcastically.

238. **Martians** /MAR shunz/.

239. **Ancus Martius** /ANK us MAR shus/.

239. **Numa's** US /N$\overline{OO}$ muz/; UK /NY$\overline{OO}$ muz/.

240. **Hostilius** /hŏs TIL yus/.

241. **Publius** /PUB lyus/.

241. **Quintus** /KWIN tus/.

242. ***conduits** water pipes or channels. Here must be 2 syllables /CŎN dwits/;
UK *also* [CUN dwits, CŎN dywits, CŎN dits, CUN dits].

243. **Censorinus** /sen suh RĪ nus/.

243. **surnam'd** here should be /sur NAYMD/.

244. **censor** /SEN sur/ Roman official. See App. D -*or*.

Act 3 Scene 1

11-18. ***Antium** Ang.Lat. /AN shyum/; Class.Lat. /AHN tih ōōm/. /AN tyum/
is the most common form today.

43-125. ***gratis** at no cost. US, UK /GRAHT iss/ [GRAT-],
UK *rarely* [GRAYT-]; CN /GRAT-/ [GRAHT-].

---

44. **suppliants** /SUP lyunts/ those who ask humbly for something.

47. **sithence** /SITH unss/ since.

58. **palt'ring** /PAWL tring/ trickery.

66. **meiny, meinie** /MAYN ee/ common people.

89. ***Triton** a god of the sea. /TRĪT n̩/, but /-ŏn/ is also increasingly heard. See
App. D -*on*.

92. **reakless, reckless** /REK liss/ heedless.

94. **peremptory** here should be /PĔR um tur ee/; US *also* /-tor ee/ overbearing.

99. **lenity** /LEN ih tee/ leniency.

104, 201. ***magistrate(s)** /MAJ ih strayt/; US *also* [-strut].

ă-bat, ăir-ma**rry**, air-**pair**, a̩r-**far**, ĕr-me**rry**, ĝ- g**et**, ī-h**igh**, ĭr-mi**rror**, l̩-li**ttle**, n̩-li**sten**,
ŏ-h**ot**, oh-g**o**, ōō-w**ood**, ōō-m**oon**, oor-**tour**, ōr- **or**, ow-h**ow**, t̩h-**that**, th-**thin**, ŭ-b**ut**,
UR-**fur**, ur-un**der**.   ( ) - suppress the syllable   see p. xiii for complete list.

---

156. **multitudinous tongue** US /mŭl tih T͞OOD (ih) nus/;
UK, SOUTH. US /-TY͞OOD-/ tongue of the multitudes, i.e, the tribune.

175. **weal** /weel/ welfare.

177. *****surety** support, bail. Here should be two syllables, though in mod.
English, three syllables is more common, /SHUR (ih) tee, SHOOR-, SHOR-/
(see App. D).

261. **Tiber** /TĪ bur/ main river in Rome.

268. **severity** /suh VĔR (ih) tee/.

275. **holp** /hohlp/ helped.

284. **peremptory** here should be /PĔR um tur ee/; US *also* /-tor ee/ determined.

302. **kam, cam** /kam/ twisted.

303. **awry** /uh RĪ/ askew.

305. **gangren'd** here should be /gang GREEND/; US *also* /gan-, gayn-/.

311. **unscann'd** here should be /UN skand/ thoughtless.

325. **humane** here should be /HY͞OO mayn/; US *sometimes* [Y͞OO mayn].

Act 3 Scene 2

45. **Tush** /tŭsh/ expression of disdain.

66. **louts** /lowts/ oafs.

70. *****salve** heal. US /salv/ [sav]; NEW ENG. *also* [sahv];
CN /salv/ [sahlv, sav, sahv]; UK /salv/. Normal development would favor
the *l*-less form (cf. *halve, calve*).

75. **bussing** /BŬS ing/ kissing.

99. **sconce** /skŏnss/ head.

112. **harlot's** /HAR luts/ whore's.

113. **quier'd** archaic variant of **choired**, both pronounced /kwīrd/.

114. **eunuch** /Y$\overline{OO}$ nuk/ castrated man.

120. **alms** charity for the poor. /ahmz/ is older; /ahlmz, awlmz/ are newer. In the UK the latter are non-standard.

121. **surcease** /sur SEESS/ cease.

132. **mountebank** /MOWNT uh bank/ here, 'persuade them using deceit.'

135. **return** here should be /REE turn/.

Act 3 Scene 3

4. **Antiates** /AN shee ayts/ citizens of *Antium* which is usually /AN tee um/ today, formerly /AN sh(ee) um/.

17. *__prerogative__ /pur RŎG uh tiv/ [prih-, pree-] right. /pree-/ non-standard in the UK.

27. **chaf'd** /chayft/ angered.

32. *__hostler__ US, CN /HŎSS lur, ŎSS lur/; UK /ŎSS lur/ [HŎSS lur] innkeeper.

70. **sate** archaic variant of **sat**. May have been /sayt/ or /sat/.

89. **fleaing** /FLEE ing/ variant of **flaying** /FLAY ing/ skinning.

114. *__estimate__ US /ES tih mut/ [-mayt]; UK /-mayt/ [-mut] reputation.

114. **increase** here should be /in CREESS/ offspring.

135. **elsewhere** here with 2nd syllable stress, a form still used in the UK, but unknown in the US.

Act 4 Scene 1

4. **trier** /trīr/ something that tries, tests.

28. **solace** /SŎL us/ comfort.

33. **cautelous** /KAWT (uh) lus/ deceitful.

ă-bat, ăir-**marry**, air-**pair**, ạr-**far**, ĕr-**merry**, ĝ- get, ī-high, ĭr-**mirror**, ł-little, ṇ-listen, ŏ-hot, oh-go, $\overline{oo}$-**wood**, $\overline{oo}$-**moon**, oor-**tour**, ōr- **or**, ow-**how**, ţh-**that**, ṭh-**thin**, ŭ-but, UR-**fur**, ur-und**er**.   ( ) - suppress the syllable   see p. xiii for complete list.

36. **exposture** /ik SPŎS chur/; UK *also* /-tyoor/ exposure. See App. D *-ure.*

Act 4 Scene 2

52. **puling** /PYO̅O̅L ing/ whining.

Act 4 Scene 3

43. *****centurions** US, CN /sen TOOR ee unz, -TYOOR-, -CHOOR-/ [-CHUR-, -TUR-]; UK /-TYOOR-/ [-CHOOR-] Roman soldiers.

44. **billeted** /BILL it id/ enrolled.

Act 4 Scene 4

1-8. *****Antium** Ang.Lat. /AN shyum/; Class.Lat. /AHN tih o̅o̅m/. /AN tyum/ is the most common form today.

Act 4 Scene 5

3-4. **Cotus** /COH tus/.

48. **prat'st** /praytst/ chatter.

69. **extreme** here should be /EK streem/.

78. **Hoop'd** /ho̅o̅pt, ho̅o̅pt/, *****Whoop'd** /who̅o̅pt/ [who̅o̅pt, ho̅o̅pt, ho̅o̅pt].

85. **wreak** /reek/ vengence.

104. **divine** here should be /DIV īn/.

150. **strooken** /STRo̅o̅K in/ or perhaps simply a variant spelling of **strucken.**

176. **as live** as soon. May have been /liv/ in Shk's time. Variant of **as lief** /leef/. In the US **lieve** /leev/ is still found in some dialects and can also be used here.

187. **carbinado** slashed piece of meat. Archaic variant of *****carbonado**, both pronounced /car buh NAH doh/; UK *rarely older* [-NAY doh].

200. **sowl** /sowl/ drag, yank.

202. **poll'd** /pohld/ shorn.

212. **conies** /KOH neez/, *rarely older* [KUN eez] rabbits.

223. **apoplexy** /AP uh plek see/ paralysis.

Act 4 Scene 6

7. **Dissentious** /dih SEN shus/ arguing.

20-1. **Good-en** /gŏŏd-, gud EN/. Some eds. prefer **Good e'en**.

50. **record** here should be /rek-, rik ORD/.

73. **contrariety** /cŏn truh RĪ uh tee/ contradiction. May be a double or triple ending. Some eds. prefer **contrarieties**.

81. **holp** /hohlp/ helped.

82. **leads** /ledz/ lead roofs.

85. **cement** here with 1st syllable stress /SEE ment, SEM ent/.

Act 4 Scene 7

34. **aspray** presumably /ASS pray/, archaic variant of **osprey** /ŎS pray, -pree/ a fish-eating hawk.

39. **defect** here should be /dih-, dee FECT/.

43. **casque** /kăsk/; UK *also* [kahsk] helmet.

51. **commendable** here should be /CŎM en duh bł/.

53. **T'*extol** praise. /tek-, twek STOHL/; UK *sometimes* and US *rarely* [-STŎL].

Act 5 Scene 1

26. **noisome** /NOY sum/ disgusting.

ă-bat, ăir-ma**rry**, air-**pair**, ạr-**far**, ĕr-me**rry**, ĝ- **get**, ī-**high**, ĭr-**mirror**, ł-**little**, ṇ-**listen**, ŏ-**hot**, oh-**go**, ōō-**wood**, ōō-**moon**, oor-**tour**, ŏr- **or**, ow-**how**, ṭh-**that**, ~~th~~-**thin**, ŭ-**but**, UR-**fur**, ur-**under**.   ( ) - suppress the syllable   see p. xiii for complete list.

Act 5 Scene 2

22. **leasing** /LEE zing/ lying.

44. **palsied** /PAWL zeed/; UK *also* [PŎL-] trembling.

44. **dotant** /DOHT ṇt, -unt/ someone who is senile.

60. **arrant** /ĂIR unt/ archaic variant of **errand** 'message.'

62. **guardant** /GARD ṇt/ guard.

> 67, 101. **swound** archaic variant of **swoon**. In Shk's time the vowel could be either /ow/ or /ōō/.

69.*__synod__ US, CN /SIN ud/ [-ŏd]; UK /SIN ŏd/ [-ud] council.

75.*__conjure__ entreat. US, CN /CŎN jur/, *rarely* [CUN-]; UK /CUN jur/ [CŎN-], *rarely* [cun JOOR]. The older pronunciation for this meaning is /cun JOOR/.

84. **revenge** here should be /REE venj/.

86. **Ingrate** here could be either a noun 'ungrateful person' or adj. 'ungrateful.' Because an inverted foot is possible, stress could fall on either the 1st or 2nd syllable. In the US 1st syllable stress /IN grayt/ would be usual for a noun.

Act 5 Scene 3

35. **instinct** here should be /in STINCT/.

59. **Fillop** /FILL up/ variant of **fillip** /FILL ip/ 'strike smartly.'

63. **holp** /hohlp/ helped.

64. **Publicola** /pub LICK uh luh/.

68. **epitome** /uh PIT uh mee/; US *also* /ee-/ summary.

71. **supreme** here should be US /SŌŌ preem/; UK, SOUTH. US *also* [SYŌŌ-].

85. **T'allay** /tuh LAY/ or /twuh-/ calm.

95. **bewray** /bih-, bee RAY/ reveal.

114. **recreant** /REK ree yunt/ coward.

115. **With manacles *through* our streets, or else.** Another syllable is needed in this line, and some eds. substitute **thorough**, archaic variant of *through,* used when the meter demands two syllables. It is often pronounced as mod. *thorough* on stage, with 1st syllable stress. Using /-o͞o/ in the final syllable will bring it closer to the pronunciation of mod. *through.*

131. **sate** archaic variant of **sat.** May have been /sayt/ or /sat/.

170. **To his surname** here should be /SUR naym/; *To his* is one syllable /twiz/.

Act 5 Scene 4

1. **coign** /coyn/ variant of *quoin* 'corner stone.'

20. **corslet** /CORSS lit/ body armor.

43. **the Tarquins** /TAR kwinz/ former royal family of Rome.

49. **psalteries** a stringed intstrument. Here should be 3 syllables /SAWL tur eez/; UK *also* [SŎL-]. In mod. Eng. sometimes 2 syllables /-treez/.

50. **Tabors** /TAY burz/ small drums. See App. D -*or.*

Act 5 Scene 6

10. **alms** charity for the poor. /ahmz/ is older; /ahlmz, awlmz/ are newer. In the UK the latter are non-standard.

19. **pretext** here should be /pree-, prih TEKST/ motive.

35. **holp** /hohlp/ helped.

45. **rheum** /ro͞om/ tears.

79. **Antiates** /AN shee ayts/ citizens of *Antium* which is usually /AN tee um/ today, formerly /AN sh(ee) um/.

ă-bat, ăir-**marry**, air-**pair**, ạr-**far**, ĕr-**merry**, ĝ- **get**, ī-**high**, ĭr-**mirror**, ł-**little**, ṇ-**listen**, ŏ-**hot**, oh-**go**, o͝o-**wood**, o͞o-**moon**, oor-**tour**, ōr- **or**, ow-**how**, t̪h-**that**, t̶h̶-**thin**, ŭ-**but**, UR-**fur**, ur-**under**.　　　( ) - suppress the syllable　　　see p. xiii for complete list.

Cymbeline

People in the Play

Arviragus /ạr vih RAY gus/.

Belarius /buh LAIR yus/; E.COAST US *also* /-LĂIR-/.

Britain /BRIT ṇ/ resident of the British Isles. Some eds. prefer **Briton,** pronounced the same way.

Cadwal /KAD wawl/ Arviragus' pseudonym.

*****Caius Lucius** US, CN /KĪ us/, *rarely* [KAY us]; UK /KĪ us, KAY us/. Ang.Lat. /KAY us/; Class.Lat. /KĪ o͞os/. Another angl. form /keez/ is sometimes used, but doesn't fit the meter.   **Lucius** /LO͞O shus/, /LO͞O syus/. The former is nearly universal in the US, the latter is most common in the UK. Normal development would favor /LO͞O shus/ (for /lyo͞o-/ see App. D *lu-*).

*****Cloten** /CLOHT ṇ, CLŎT ṇ/. The former predominates, but the latter is attractive because it sounds like *clod* and *clotpole* 4.2.184.

Cornelius /cor NEEL yus/.

Cymbeline /SIM buh leen/.

Euriphile /yoor RIF ih lee/; US *also* /yur-/, former nurse of Arviragus and Guiderius, mentioned throughout.

Fidele Imogen's pseudonym. /fih DEE lee/ is the traditional angl. form, but /fih DEL ee/ or restored Latin /fee DAY lay/ are also used, as is the mixed form /fih DAY lee/.

Filario see *Philario.*

Gaolers UK spelling of **Jailers**, pronounced the same way.

Guiderius 3 or 4 syllables depending on meter /gwih DEER (ee) yus/.

*****Jachimo** /YAH kih moh/; US, CN *also* [-kee moh]. Only rarely is the form Shk probably intended used in any of the countries surveyed, [JACK ih moh], from Ital. **Giacomo** /JAH koh moh/. 2 syllables at 2.5.14 /YAH k(ih) moh/. Some eds. prefer **Iachimo**, which leads to the erroneous pronunciation /ĭ AK ih moh/.

People in the Play (cont.)

Imogen 2 or 3 syllables depending on meter /IM (uh) jin/, Some eds. prefer **Innogen** /IN (uh) jin/.

*Leonatus /lee oh NAY tus/, /lee uh-/; restored Lat. /lay oh NAH tōōs/. /-NAH tus/ is the most common form in all countries, with some use of /-NAY tus/ in North America.
   Leonati /-NAY tī/; restored Lat. /lay oh NAH tee/.

Lucius see **Caius Lucius**.

Philario, Filario /fih LAHR yoh/.

Philarmonus /fil ahr MOH nus/.

Pisanio 3 or 4 syllables depending on meter /pih ZAHN (ee) yoh/.

Polydore /PŎL ih dor/ Guiderius' pseudonym.

Posthumus /pŏst HYŌŌ mus/ or /PŎS tyoo mus/ [-choo-. chuh-] depending on meter. US *also* [pŏst YŌŌ mus]. May be /PŎS chmus/ at 1.1.41.

Places in the Play

Britain /BRIT n̩/ the British Isles.

Gallia, -n /GAL yuh/ France.

Act 1 Scene 1

29, **Sicilius** /sih SILL yus/.

30. **Cassibelan** /kass-, kuh SIB uh lun/ uncle of Cymbeline.

31. **Tenantius** /tuh NAN shus/.

50. **dotards** /DOHT urdz/ old men.

59. **swathing** /SWAYŢH ing/; US *also* /SWŎŢH ing/ archaic variant of **swaddling** /SWŎD ling/.

ă-bat, ăir-**marry**, air-**pair**, ạr-**far**, ĕr-**merry**, ĝ- **get**, ī-**high**, ĭr-**mirror**, ł-**little**, n̩-**listen**, ŏ-**hot**, oh-**go**, ōō-**wood**, ōō-**moon**, oor-**tour**, ōr- **or**, ow-**how**, ţh-**that**, ~~th~~-**thin**, ŭ-**but**, UR-**fur**, ur-**under**.   ( ) - suppress the syllable   see p. xiii for complete list.

76. **advocate** /AD vuh kut/ someone who supports a person or cause.

112. **diamond** here should be /DĪ mund/, the most common form in the US.

116. **cere** /seer/ seal.

140. **puttock** /PUTT uk/ a bird, the red kite.

Act 1 Scene 3

18. **diminution** US /dim ih NŌŌ shun/; SOUTH. US, UK /-NYŌŌ-/ decrease.

32. ***orisons** prayers. US, CN /OR ih zunz, -zṇz/ [-sunz, -sṇz]; E.COAST US /ŎR-/;
UK /ŎR ih zunz, -zṇz/.

Act 1 Scene 4

20. ***lamentable** US /luh MEN tuh bł/ [LAM en tuh bł];
CN, UK /LAM un tuh bł/ [luh MEN-].

24. ***sojourn** reside temporarily. US, CN /SOH jurn/; UK /SŎJ urn/
[SOH-, SUJ-, -URN]. Stress also sometimes falls on the 2nd syllable.

35. **Orleance** /OR lee yunss, OR leenss, or LEENSS/. Archaic variant of
Orleans /OR lee yunz, OR leenz, or LEENZ/. Other eds. prefer
Fr. **Orléans** /or lȧy ahⁿ/.

49. **arbiterment** /ạr BIT ur munt/ settlement. Archaic variant of **arbitrement**,
arbitrament /ạr BIT ruh munt/.

73-151. **diamond** in these prose passages may be either /DĪ uh mund/ or US *also*
/DĪ mund/.

---

80. ***unparagon'd** US /un PĂIR uh gŏnd/ [-gund]; CN /-gŏnd/; UK /-gund/ [-gṇd]
unequaled.

108. **moi'ty, moiety** /MOY tee, MOY uh tee/ portion.

Act 1 Scene 5

22. **Allayments** /uh LAY munts/ antidotes.

26. **noisome** /NOY sum/ noxious.

64. **cordial** US /COR jł/; UK /COR dył/ restorative.

80. **liegers**, **leidgers** (F1) resident ambassadors. Also written **ledgers, legers, legiers** or **leaguers** and pronounced /LEJ urz, LEE jurz, LEE gurz/.

83. **cowslips** /COW slips/ a yellow flower.

83. **primeroses** may have been pronounced /PRĪM roh ziz/ or as its mod. variant **primroses** /PRIM roh ziz/.

Act 1 Scene 6

4. **supreme** here should be US /SOO preem/; UK, SOUTH. US *also* [SYOO-].

20. **Parthian** /PAR ~~th~~yun/ inhabitant of NW Iran.

41. ***mows** /mohz/ [mowz] grimaces. Both were used in Shk's time but his rhymes elsewhere indicate /mohz/.

47. ***trow** US, CN /troh, trow/; UK /trow/ [troh] I wonder. Shk's rhymes elsewhere indicate /-oh/.

48. **satiate** /SAYSH yayt, -yut/ satisfied, filled. /-ut/ is more usual for an adj.

49. **ravening** /RAV (i)n ing/ devouring.

85. ***Lamentable** here should be /LAM un tuh bł/ the usual UK pronunciation.

86. **solace** /SŎL us/ comfort.

105. ***Slaver** US, UK /SLAV ur/ [SLAHV-, SLAYV-]; CN /SLAYV-, SLAV-/ drool. /SLAV ur/ is older, the others are newer spelling pronunciations.

120. **empery** /EM pur ee/ empire.

123. **diseas'd** here should be /DIZ eezd/.

137. **runagate** /RUN uh gayt/ fugitive, renegade.

139. **close** /clohss/ secret.

ă-bat, ăir-**marry**, air-**pair**, ạr-**far**, ĕr-**merry**, ĝ- **get**, ī-**high**, ĭr-**mirror**, ł-**little**, ṇ-**listen**, ŏ-**hot**, oh-**go**, o͞o-**wood**, o͞o-**moon**, oor-**tour**, ōr- **or**, ow-**how**, ţh-**that**, ~~th~~-**thin**, ŭ-**but**, UR-**fur**, ur-**under**.   ( ) - suppress the syllable   see p. xiii for complete list.

159. **assur'd** here with 1st syllable stress.

163. **affiance** /uh FĪ unss/ trust.

Act 2 Scene 1

3. **jack-an-apes** /JACK uh nayps/ monkey, impertinent fellow.

11. **curtal** /CUR tł/ cut short. Archaic variant of **curtail** /cur TAYL/.

23. ***capon** US /KAY pŏn, -pun/; CN, UK /KAY pŏn/ [-pun] chicken. See App. D *-on.*

43. **derogation** /dĕr uh GAY shun/; UK *also newer* [dee ruh-] lessening of honor.

44, 47. **derogate** lessen one's honor. /DĔR uh gayt/; UK *also newer* [DEER-].

57. **divine** here should be /DIV īn/.

Act 2 Scene 2

5, 19. **taper** /TAY pur/ slender candle.

12. **Tarquin** /TAR kwin/ king of Rome who raped Lucretia.

14. **Cytherea** /sith uh REE uh/ Venus.

17. ***unparagon'd** unequaled. US /un PĂIR uh gŏnd/ [-gund]; CN /-gŏnd/; UK /-gund/ [-gn̩d].

22. ***azure** blue. US /AZH oor/ [AZ yoor, AZH ur]; UK /AZH oor, AZ yoor/ [AY zyoor, -zhyoor]. Normal development would favor /AZH ur, AY zhur/. See App. D *-ure.*

27. **contents** here /cŏn TENTS/.

38. **cinque-spotted** /SINK SPŎT id/ with 5 spots.

39. **cowslip** /COW slip/ a yellow flower.

45. **Tereus** he raped Philomel. /TEER yus/ [-yōōss]. See App. D. *-eus.*

46. **Philomele** /FILL uh meel, -oh-/ the nightingale. Variant of **Philomel** /-mel/.

Act 2 Scene 3

21. **Phoebus** /FEE bus/ god of the sun.

21. **gins** /ĝinz/ begins.

23. **chalic'd** /CHAL ist/ having cup-like blossoms.

30. **eunuch** /Y$\overline{OO}$ nuk/ castrated man.

56. **Albeit** /awl BEE (i)t/ although.

114. **alms** charity for the poor. /ahmz/ is older; /ahlmz, awlmz/ are newer. In the UK the latter are non-standard.

123. **hilding** /HILL ding/ good-for-nothing.

124. **Profane** here should be /PROH fayn/.

143. **revenue** sometimes in verse /ruh VEN y$\overline{oo}$/, but here as in mod. Eng. US /REV in $\overline{oo}$/; UK, SOUTH. US /-y$\overline{oo}$/.

Act 2 Scene 4

3. **remain** here with 1st syllable stress.

12. **throughly** archaic variant of *thoroughly*. /~~THR~~$\overline{OO}$ lee/ is the normal pronunciation on stage, but to enhance clarity a syncopated form of the modern pronunciation may be used: *thor'ghly*.

13. **th' arrearages** /ṭh^{y}uh REER ij iz/ debts.

16. **Statist** /STAYT ist/ statesman.

34. **thorough** archaic variant of *through,* which is often pronounced as mod. *thorough* in Shk, but here it should be one syllable, making **through** the better choice.

ă-bat, ăir-**marry**, air-**pair**, ạr-**far**, ĕr-**merry**, ĝ- get, ī-high, ĭr-**mirror**, ł-little, ṇ-listen, ŏ-hot, oh-go, $\overline{oo}$-**wood**, $\overline{oo}$-**moon**, oor-**tour**, ŏr- **or**, ow-**how**, ṭh-**that**, ~~th~~-**thin**, ŭ-but, UR-**fur**, ur-und**er**.   ( ) - suppress the syllable   see p. xiii for complete list.

36. **tenure** archaic variant of **tenor**, both /TEN ur/.

54. **wronger** US /RAWNG ur/; UK /RŎNG-/ someone who does wrong.

71. **Cydnus** /SID nus/.

88. ***cherubins** angels. US, CN /CHĔR uh binz/ [-yuh-]; UK uses both equally. /KĔR-/ not recommended.

98. **diamond** here should be /DĪ uh mund/, the standard UK form.

107. ***basilisk** legendary reptile whose glance was fatal. US /BĂSS ih lisk/ [BAZ ih lisk]; UK /BAZ-/ [BĂSS-]; CN both used equally.

127. ***cognizance** /CŎG nih zunss, -zn̩ss/; *rarely older* [CŎN ih-] badge.

Act 2 Scene 5

8. ***nonpareil** one without equal. /nŏn puh RELL/ is the oldest form, still common in the US, but now vanished from the UK and CN, where it has been replaced with /nŏn puh RAYL/ [-RAY], based on mod. Fr. /-RAY/ is also common in the US. /-RĪ, -RĪL/ are occasionally heard, but not recommended. Sometimes 1st syllable stress is used.

11. **pudency** /PYO͞OD n̩ see/ modesty.

13. **unsunn'd** here should be /UN sund/.

Act 3 Scene 1

5-41. **Cassibelan** /kass-, kuh SIB uh lun/ uncle of Cymbeline.

22. **topmast** /TŎP must/ is used by sailors; landsmen say US /TŎP măst/; UK, E.NEW ENG. /-mahst/.

31. **giglet** /ĜIG lit/ strumpet.

54, 58. **Mulmutius** /mŭl MYO͞O shus/.

72. **Behooves** /bih-. bee HO͞OVZ/ is necessary, proper for. UK prefers the spelling **Behoves** /bih HOHVZ/.

72. **perfect** here should be /PUR fict/ fully informed.

73. **Pannonians** /puh NOHN yunz/ inhabitants of present day Hungary.

74. **president** archaic variant of *__precedent__, both /PRESS ih dunt/. It is not clear whether /PREZ-/ was used in Shk's time.

Act 3 Scene 2

21. **feodary, fedarie** /FED (uh) ree/ accomplice. *Feodary* is usually a variant of *feudary* /FYŌŌD uh ree/ 'vassal,' which is incorrect here.

33. **med'cinable, medicinable** here /MED sin uh bł/ treatable.

43. **Cambria** /KAM bree uh/ Wales.

77. *__huswife__ /HUZ if/ is traditional, /HUSS wīf/ is a newer, spelling pronunciation. The former is the most common form in the UK, the latter in the US. In CN both are used equally. In North America /HUSS wif/ is also sometimes used. Some eds. prefer mod. **housewife**.

Act 3 Scene 3

6. **impious** /IM pyus/ profane.

6. **turbands** /TUR bundz/ archaic variant of **turbans**.

23. **bable** (*Babe* F1) presumably /BAB ł/, archaic variant of **bauble** /BAW bł/. Some eds. prefer **robe, bribe, badge**.

45. **usuries** /YŌŌ zhur eez/; UK *also* [-zhyoor eez, -zhoor eez] lending money for interest.

70. *__demesnes__ lands. US, CN /duh MAYNZ/ [-MEENZ]; UK uses both equally.

Act 3 Scene 4

36. **belie** /bih-, bee LĪ/ fill with lies.

58. **Aeneas** /ih NEE yus/; UK *also* /EE NEE yus/ Prince of Troy.

ă-bat, ăir-**marry**, air-**pair**, ạr-**far**, ĕr-**merry**, ĝ- **get**, ī-**high**, ĭr-**mirror**, ł-**little**, ṇ-**listen**, ŏ-**hot**, oh-**go**, ōŏ-**wood**, ōō-**moon**, oor-**tour**, ōr- **or**, ow-**how**, ţh-**that**, th-**thin**, ŭ-**but**, UR-**fur**, ur-**under**.　　　( ) - suppress the syllable　　　see p. xiii for complete list.

59. **Sinon's** traitor who caused Troy's fall. /SĪ nunz/, but /-nŏnz/ is becoming more common. See App. D *-on.*

62. **leaven** /LEV ṇ, -in/ sour-dough used to make bread rise, here alluding to its spoiling other dough.

78. **cravens** /CRAY vinz, -vṇz/ makes cowardly.

80. **scabbard** /SKAB urd/ sword sheath.

82. **heresy** /HĔR ih see/ dissent from the dominant thinking.

84. **stomachers** /STUM (uh) kurz/ ornamental chest covering.

85. **teachers**. Some eds. prefer **treachers** /TRETCH urz/ traitors.

103. **pretense** (UK **pretence**) here should be /prih TENSS/, the normal UK pronunciation, or /pree TENSS/ based on the most common US pronunciation /PREE tenss/.

105. **perturb'd** here should be /PUR turbd/.

123. ***courtezan** a rich man's whore. Some eds. prefer **courtesan**, both pronounced US /CORT ih zun, -zan/, *rarely* [cort ih ZAN];
CN /CORT ih zan/ [-zun], *rarely* [cort ih ZAN]; UK /CORT ih zan, cort ih ZAN/.

158. **gibes** /jībz/ sarcastic comments.

Act 3 Scene 5

17. **Severn** /SEV urn/.

46. **keeping close** /clohss/ hidden.

85. **Close** /clohss/ secretive.

Act 3 Scene 6

33. **savory** (UK **savoury**) /SAY v(ur) ree/ tasty, spicy.

34. ***sloth** US, CN /slawth/ [slohth]; UK /slohth/ [slŏth] laziness.

36. throughly archaic variant of *thoroughly*. /THROO lee/ is the normal pronunciation on stage, but to enhance clarity a syncopated form of the modern pronunciation may be used: *thor'ghly*.

40. victuals /VIT łz/ food.

43. *paragon US /PĂIR uh gŏn/ [-gun]; CN /-gŏn/; UK /-gun/ [-gn̩] most perfect example.

77. ballasting /BĂL ust ing/ possibly confused with *balancing*.

Act 3 Scene 7

3. Pannonians /puh NOHN yunz/ inhabitants of present day Hungary.

8. proconsul /proh CŎN sł/ Roman official.

8. *tribunes here should be /TRIB yōōnz/.

14. supplyant, suppliant /suh PLĪ unt/ supplementary.

Act 4 Scene 1

7. *vainglory pride. /VAYN glor ee/ [vayn GLOR ee]. The latter is older.

14. imperceiverant /im pur SEE vur unt/ unperceiving. Sometimes **imperceverant** /im pur SEV ur unt/.

Act 4 Scene 2

22. bier /beer/ coffin.

35. Th'imperious /ȶh^y im PEER yus/ imperial.

45. *huswife /HUZ if/ is traditional, /HUSS wīf/ is a newer, spelling pronunciation. The former is the most common form in the UK, the latter in the US. In CN both are used equally. In North America /HUSS wif/ is also sometimes used. Some eds. prefer mod. **housewife**.

ă-bat, ăir-marry, air-pair, ạr-far, ĕr-merry, ĝ- get, ī-high, ĭr-mirror, ł-little, n̩-listen, ŏ-hot, oh-go, ōō-wood, ōō-moon, oor-tour, ōr- or, ow-how, ȶh-that, ȶh-thin, Ŭ-but, UR-fur, ur-under.   ( ) - suppress the syllable   see p. xiii for complete list.

55. *commix mix. US /cuh MIKS/ [coh-], *rarely* [cŏm-];
UK /coh-/ [cŏm-, cuh-].

62, 63. runagates /RUN uh gayts/ fugitives, renegades.

71. mountainers. It is not certain whether Shk pronounced this
/MOWNT un urz, MOWNT ṇ urz/ or as in mod. mountaineers (used
elsewhere in this play) /mownt uh NEERZ, mownt ṇ-/.

73. slavish /SLAY vish/ slave-like.

111. defect here should be /dih-, dee FECT/.

118. I am perfect here should be /īm PUR fikt/ I know full well.

154. reak, reck /rek/ care.

170. divine here should be /DIV īn/.

170. thou blazon'st /BLAY zunst, -zṇst/ you display.

172. zephyrs /ZEF urz/ west winds.

174. enchaf'd /en CHAYFT/ heated.

177. instinct here should be /in STINCT/.

205. crare, crayer /crair/ small sailing boat.

214. clouted /CLOW tid/ hob-nailed.

214. brogues /brohgz/ shoes.

222. *azur'd blue. US /AZH oord/ [AZ yoord, AZH urd];
UK /AZH oord, AZ yoord/ [AY zyoord, -zhyoord]. Normal development would
favor /AZH urd, AY zhurd/.

223. *eglantine sweet-briar. /EGG lun tīn/ is older, /-teen/ is newer. The
former is by far the most common in the UK, the latter in the US.

224. raddock /RAD uk/ robin. Variant of ruddock /RUD uk/.

252. Thersites' /ṯhur SĪ teez/ mean-spirited Greek at Troy.

276. exorciser /EK sor sīz ur, EK sur-/ exorcist.

282. **obsequies** /ŎB suh kweez/ burial services.

310. ***Mercurial** fleet. US /mur KYUR ee ł, -KYOOR-/; CN /-KYOOR-/ [-KYUR-]; UK /MUR KYOOR ee ł/.

310. **Martial** /MAR shł/ like Mars, god of war.

313. **Hecuba** /HEK y(oo) buh/ Queen of Troy.

315. **irregulous** /ih REG y(oo) lus/; US *also* /ĭr-/ lawless.

324. **lucre** /LOO kur/ greed (for /lyoo-/ see App. D *lu*-).

327. **cordial** here 3 syllables US /COR jee ł/; UK /COR dee ył/ cheering.

337. **confiners** here /CŎN fīn urz/ inhabitants.

341. **Sienna's** /see EN uz/ the Duke of Sienna's.

349. **spungy** damp. Archaic variant of **spongy**, both pronounced /SPUN jee/.

372. **occident** /ŎK sih dunt/ west.

377. **Richard du Champ** the oldest angl. form is US /RICH urd doo CHAMP/; UK, SOUTH. US *also* /dyoo/. Other angl. forms are /-SHAMP, -SHAHM/. Fr. /ree shạr dừ SHAH[N]/.

385. **consul** /CŎN sł/ Roman official.

399. ***partisans** /PART ih zanz/ [-sanz, -zunz]; UK *also* /part ih ZANZ/ spears with a blade on the end.

Act 4 Scene 4

27. **aye** /ay/ ever. /ī/ is often used, but not recommended.

38. **bestrid** /bih-, bee STRID/ mounted.

39. **rowel** disc with points at the end of a spur. /ROW ł/ as in *how*.

ă-bat, ăir-**marry**, air-**pair**, ạr-**far**, ĕr-**merry**, ĝ- g**et**, ī-high, ĭr-m**irror**, ł-little, ṇ-liste**n**, ŏ-h**ot**, oh-g**o**, oo-w**ood**, ōō-m**oon**, oor-t**our**, ŏr- **or**, ow-h**ow**, ţh-**that**, th̲-**thin**, ŭ-b**ut**, UR-**fur**, ur-und**er**.   ( ) - suppress the syllable   see p. xiii for complete list.

Act 5 Scene 2

2. **belied** /bih-, bee LĪD/ slandered.

9. **lout** /lowt/ oaf.

Act 5 Scene 3 (*Complete Oxford* 5.5)

8. **Lolling** /LŎLL ing/ hanging out.

34. **distaff** cleft staff used in spinning thread. US /DIS stăf/;
E.NEW ENG., UK /DIS stahf/.

41. **rout** /rowt/ uproar.

72. **words.** Some eds. prefer **viands** /VĪ undz/ food. /VEE undz/ not
recommended.

77. **veriest** /VĔR yist/ most exceeding.

77. **hind** /hīnd/ menial laborer.

Act 5 Scene 4 (*Complete Oxford* continue this as 5.5—line nos. in parentheses)

6. (5.5.100) **perpetuity* eternity. /PUR puh TYŌŌ (ih) tee/; US *also* [-TŌŌ-].
/-CHŌŌ-/ is also used but is considered non-standard in the UK.

14. (5.5.108) **gyves** /jīvz/ chains, fetters.

43. (5.5.137) **Lucina** Roman goddess of childbirth. /lōō SĪ nuh/;
restored Latin /-SEE-/ (for /lyōō-/ see App. D *lu-*).

51. (5.5.145) **Sicilius'** /sih SILL yus/.

73. (5.5.167) **fealty** /FEEL tee/ faithfulness.

73. (5.5.167) **Tenantius'** /tuh NAN shus/.

80. (5.5.174) **dolors** (UK **dolours**) /DOH lurz/; UK *also* /DŎL urz/ pains. See
App. D *-or*.

89. (5.5.183) ***synod** US, CN /SIN ud/ [-ŏd]; UK /SIN ŏd/ [-ud] council of the
gods.

97. (5.5.191) ***Elysium** the realm of the blessed in the after-life.
US /ih LEEZH yum/ [-LIZ-, -LIZH-, -LEESS-, -LISS-]; UK /-LIZ-/; *also* /ee-/ in all countries. The oldest forms still in use are /-LIZ-/, /-LIZH-/. The historic form is /ih LIZH um/.

113. (5.5.207) ***crystalline** US, UK /CRISS tuh līn/ [-leen, -lin]; CN /-līn/ [-leen]. Here rhymes with *mine*.

168. (5.5.262) **debitor** /DEB ih tur/ archaic variant of *debtor*. See App. D *-or*.

199. (5.5.293) **gibbets** /JIB its/ posts from which they hung corpses after hanging.

200. (5.5.294) **verier** /VĔR ee ur/ more outrageous.

Act 5 Scene 5 (*Complete Oxford* 5.6)

5. **targes** light shields. Here should be one syllable /TARJ (i)z/ light shields. The /z/ can be attached to the following *of*.

17. **Cambria** /KAM br(ee) yuh/ Wales.

70. **ras'd** /rayst/ erased. Some eds. prefer **razed** /rayzd/ which could also mean 'erased' or 'cut, slashed.'

137. **diamond** here should be /DĪ uh mund/, the standard UK form.

142. **Which torments me to conceal. By what villainy . . .** *Torments* here should be /TOR ments/, followed by *me t' conceal* /cun SEEL/. Alternatively it could be scanned with an anapest in the first foot (see p. 19).

147. ***paragon** US /PĂIR uh gŏn/ [-gun]; CN /-gŏn/; UK /-gun/ [-gn̩] most perfect example.

156. **viands** /VĪ undz/ food. /VEE undz/ not recommended.

164. **straight-pight** /strayt pīt/ having a tall, erect figure. Some eds. prefer **straight-pitched**.

164. **Minerva** /mih NUR vuh/ goddess of wisdom.

177. **crak'd** /craykt/ boasted. Some eds. prefer **cracked**.

ă-bat, ăir-marry, air-pair, ar-far, ĕr-merry, ĝ- get, ī-high, ĭr-mirror, ł-little, n̩-listen, ŏ-hot, oh-go, o͞o-wood, o͞o-moon, oor-tour, ōr- or, ow-how, t̪h-that, t̶h̶-thin, ŭ-but, UR-fur, ur-under.　　　( ) - suppress the syllable　　　see p. xiii for complete list.

190. **Phoebus'** /FEE bus/ god of the sun.

200. **simular** /SIM y(uh) lur/ pretended.

203. **averring** /uh VUR ing/ citing.

211. **Egregious** /ih GREE jus/ notorious.

214. **justicer** /JUST ih sur/ judge.

247. **cordial** US /COR jł/; UK /COR dył/ restorative medicine.

249. ***importun'd** /im POR chund/ asked insistently. See App. D.

265. **dullard** /DULL urd/ stupid person.

284. **unchaste** here should be /UN chayst/.

323. **confiscate** here /cŏn FISS kayt, -ut/ confiscated.

364. **sanguine** /SANG gwin/ red.

381. **instinct** here /in STINCT/.

392. **interrogatories**, **inter'gatories** questions. Here US /in TUR guh tor eez/; UK /-tur eez/.

405. **forlorn** here /FOR lorn/.

422. **holp** /hohlp/ helped.

445. **Leo-natus** Ang.Lat. /LEE oh NAY tus/; Class.Lat. /LAY oh NAH to͞os/ born of a lion.

447. **mollis aer** Ang.Lat. /MŎL iss AY ur/; Class.Lat. /MŎL iss AH ayr/ gentle air.

448. **mulier** Ang.Lat. /MYO͞O lee ur/; Class.Lat. /Mo͞oL ee ĕr/ woman.

480. ***ensign** flag. US, CN /EN sn̩/, US *rarely* [-sīn]; UK /-sn̩, -sīn/.

Edward III

People in the Play

Audley /AWD lee/.

Artois /ahr TWAH/ or /AHR twah/ depending on meter.

Bohemia /boh HEEM (ee) yuh/ part of the present-day Czech Republic.
  Boheme /BOH heem/.
  Bohemian /boh HEEM yun/.

Copland /COHP lund/, /CŎP-/. Some eds. prefer **Copeland** /COHP-/.

Derby US /DUR bee/; UK /DAR bee/.

Gobin de Grey /GOH bin-, GŎB in duh GRAY/; Fr. /goh ba^n/.

Lodwick /LŎD wik, LOHD-/. Some eds. prefer **Lodowick** but at no point are 3 syllables needed.

Lorraine in some cases must have 1st syllable stress US /LŌR ayn/;
E.COAST US, UK *also* /LŎR-/. Sometimes may also be stressed on the 2nd syllable as in mod. Eng. /luh RAYN/.

Mountague /MOWNT uh gyōō/. Some eds. prefer **Montague**
/MŎNT uh gyōō/; *formerly also* [MUNT-].

Mountford /MOWNT furd/.

Philippe, Philip /FILL ip/. Some eds. prefer **Philippa**, which would have to be /FIL (ih) puh/.

A Polish Captain some eds. prefer **Polonian Captain** /puh LOH nee yun/.

Salisbury 2 or 3 syllables, depending on meter US /SAWLZ b(ĕ)r ee/;
UK /SAWLZ b(u)r ee/ [SĂLZ-].

Warwick US /WŌR ik/; E.COAST US, UK /WŎR-/. Place names in the US often have /-wik/ but this is not recommended for Shk.

ă-bat, ăir-marry, air-pair, ạr-far, ĕr-merry, ĝ- get, ī-high, ĭr-mirror, ł-little, ṇ-listen, ŏ-hot, oh-go, ōō-wood, ōō-moon, oor-tour, ŏr- or, ow-how, țh-that, th-thin, ŭ-but, UR-fur, ur-under.   ( ) - suppress the syllable   see p. xiii for complete list.

People in the Play (cont.)

Villiers today angl. /VILL urz, -yurz/, however in some instances 2nd syllable stress is indicated, in Shk's time /vill YEERZ/.

Places in the Play

Callice /KAL iss/ city on north. coast of France. Archaic variant of **Calais** which here should be /KAL ay/, the normal UK form; Fr. /KAH lay/.

Cressy /CRESS ee/. Some eds. prefer **Crécy**, anglicized the same way, or following Fr., /CRAY see/.

Act 1 Scene 1

3. **signiory, seignory** /SEEN yur ee/ rank.

6, 18. **le Beau** /luh BOH/, *Bew* (Q1) /BYOO/.

17. **rancor** (UK **rancour**) /RANK ur/ ill-will. See App. D -*or*.

18. **linage** /LĪN ij/ archaic variant of **lineage** /LIN (ee) yij/.

21, 37. **Valois** here should be /VAL wah/, the usual UK form; Fr. /VAHL wah/.

30. *****heinous** /HAYN us/ hateful. /HEEN us/ is non-standard though common in the UK.

40. **rebate** diminish. Here should be /rih-, ree BAYT/.

42. **fructful** /FRUCKT fł/ is older, /FROOKT-/ is newer. US has an additional newer form, /FROOKT-/. Archaic variant of **fruitful**.

59. **Guyenne** here should be /ĜEE en/.

60. *****homage** /HŎM ij/; US *also* /ŎM ij/ acknowledgement of allegience.

74. *****servilely** /SUR vīl ee/, *rarely* [SUR vł ee] in a slave-like manner.

77. *****vizard** /VIZ urd/ mask. /-ạrd/ not recommended.

79. **fealty** /FEE ł tee/ pledge of faithfulness to an overlord.

93. **scurrilous** coarse, vulgar. US /SKUR ih lus/;
E.COAST US, UK /SKUH rih lus/.

105. **Regenerate** /rih-, ree JEN (u)r ut, -ayt/. /-ut/ would be the usual form for
an adj. *Regenerate* means 'reborn, restored to a higher state,' so probably an
error for *degenerate*.

123. **dissever'd** /dih SEV urd/ severed.

128. **Berwick** /BĔR ik/.

128. **Newcastle** usually with 1st syllable stress today, but locally near
Newcastle, England, with 2nd syllable stress.

129. **begirt** /bih-, bee GURT/ surrounded.

130. **Roxborough** here 2nd syllable stress is indicated, though 1st syllable
stress is usual today: US /RŎCKS bur oh/; UK /-bur uh/.

133. **Britain, Brittaine** /BRIT ṇ/ Brittany. In Shk's time /-ayn/ was also used.

142. **shire** /shīr/ county.

148. **Hainault** in present day Belgium. US /HAY nawlt/;
UK /HAY nawt/ [-nawlt, -nŏlt]; Fr. /AY noh/.

150. **allies** here with 2nd syllable stress.

152. **Almaigne, Almaine** /AL mayn/ Germany.

159. **ure** /yoor/; US, CN *rarely* [yur] accustom.

161. ***tumult** turmoil. US /TŌŌM ult/; SOUTH.US *also* /TYŌŌM-/;
CN /TYŌŌM-/ [TŌŌM-]; UK /TYŌŌM-/. /CHŌŌM-/ considered non-standard
in the UK. A newer pronunciation /TUM ult/ is not recommended.

164. **Ave, Caesar!** Hail, Caesar! /AY vee SEE zur/ is the older, angl. form. The
newer /AH vay/ is much more common and based on Church Latin.

Act 1 Scene 2

2. **succor** (UK **succour**) /SUCK ur/ help. See App. D *-or*.

ă-bat, ăir-**marry**, air-**pair**, ạr-**far**, ĕr-**merry**, ĝ- g**et**, ī-high, ĭr-**mirror**, ł-**little**, ṇ-**listen**, ŏ-hot, oh-go, ōō-**wood**, ōō-**moon**, oor-**tour**, ōr- **or**, ow-**how**, ţh-**that**, th-**thin**, ŭ-**but**, UR-f**ur**, ur-**under**.   ( ) - suppress the syllable   see p. xiii for complete list.

21. **embassage** /EM buh sij/ ambassador's message.

22. *__parley__ /PAR lee/. Newer [-lay] not recommended.

29. **gymold, *gimmaled mail** chain mail. US /ĜIM łd/; UK /JIM łd/. The latter is the older form, the former a spelling pronunciation.

30. **staves** /stayvz/ staffs.

33. **whinyards** /WHIN yurdz/ short swords.

39. **acceptable** here should be /AK sep tuh bł/.

50. **descry** /dih SKRĪ/ see.

55. **hindmost** /HĪND mohst/ furthest behind.

122. **triumph** rejoice. Here should be /trī UMF/.

123. **niggard** /NIG urd/ give only a small amount to.

135. **Contemplative** here should be /cun TEMP luh tiv/ thoughtful.

147. *__Presageth__ foretells. Here /pree-, prih SAY jith/ would produce a normal line. However the foot may be inverted to allow /PRESS ij ith/, the most common UK, US form today.

151. **sere** /seer/ withered.

151. **fructless** /FRUCKT liss/ is older; /FRŏŏKT liss/ is newer. US has an additional newer form, /FRŌŌKT-/. Archaic variant of **fruitless**.

153. **parti-color'd** (UK **-colour'd**) /PART ee-/ with colors in splotches,

155. *__ordure__ manure. US /OR dyoor/ [-dyur, -joor, -jur]; CN /-dyur/ [-dyoor, -jur]; UK /OR dyoor/, *rarely* [-jur]. Normal development in the US would result in /-jur/. See App. D *-ure*.

164. **albeit** /awl BEE (i)t/ although.

Act 2 Scene 1

30. **epithetes** /EP ih thets, -thits/ expressions. Archaic variant of **epithets** pronounced the same way.

63. **conventicle** here should be /CŎN ven tih kł/ secret meeting.

65. **invocate** /IN voh kayt/ call upon.

71. **Tartar's** /TAR turz/ people of Central Asia, i.e., savages.

72. *****Scythian** /SITH yun/ [SIṬH yun] *Scythia* was north of the Black Sea. Some scholars prefer restored Latin /SK-/.

79. **humane** here should be /HYOO mayn/; US *sometimes* [YOO mayn]. Some eds. prefer **human.**

82. **abstract** /AB stract/ summary.

100. **requisite** /REK wiz it/ necessary.

110. **adulterate** /uh DULL trayt, -trut/ defiled with adultery. /-ut/ is more usual for an adj.

121. **descant** /DES kănt/ melody sung above the main tune.

146. **taper** /TAY pur/ slender candle.

177. **emured** (Q1) imprisoned. Archaic variant of **immured** both pronounced /ih MYOOR id/.

198. **solace** /SŎL us/ comfort.

231. *****solder'd** US /SŎD urd/; UK /SOHL durd/ [SŎL durd] welded.

254. **Sarah** wife of Abraham. Some eds. prefer **Sara,** pronounced as *Sarah,* or sometimes with a restored pronunciation, /SAH ruh/.

263. **progenitor** /proh-, pruh JEN ih tur/ ancestor. See App. D *-or.*

303. *****peise** weigh down. US /peez/, *sometimes* [payz]; UK /peez, payz/. Dialect evidence shows that /ee/ was the form found in southern Eng., and /ay/ in the North.

307. **charact'red** written down. Here /kăir AKT urd/.

322. **medicinable** treatable. Here should be /MED sin uh bł/.

ă-bat, ăir-m**a**rry, air-**pair**, a̧r-f**a**r, ĕr-m**e**rry, ĝ- get, ī-high, ĭr-mirror, ł-little, n̦-listen, ŏ-hot, oh-go, o͞o-wood, o͞o-moon, oor-**tour**, ōr- or, ow-how, ţh-**that**, th-**thin**, ŭ-but, UR-**fur**, ur-und**er**.   ( ) - suppress the syllable   see p. xiii for complete list.

325. **accompt** /uh COWNT/ archaic variant of Q2's **account**. See App. D.

333. **excommunicate** /eks kuh MY$\overline{OO}$N ih kut, -kayt/ excommunicated.

347. **detestable** here should be /DEE tess tuh bł/ or /DET es tuh bł/.

368. **embassage** /EM buh sij/ ambassador's message.

370. *****importune** /im POR chun/ ask insistently. See App. D.

373. **arrant** /ĂIR unt/, archaic variant of *errand*.

392. **Achilles'** /uh KILL eez/ Gk. hero.

402. **hugy, hugey** /HY$\overline{OO}$ jee/; US *sometimes* /Y$\overline{OO}$ jee/ huge.

402. **vastures** US, CN /VASS churz/; UK /VAHSS churz/ [-tyoorz] spaces.

414. **invir'd. envired** (*invierd* Q1) /in V$\overline{I}$RD/ surrounded, besieged.

Act 2 Scene 2

3. **fortnight** /FORT n$\overline{i}$t/; US *also* [FORT nit] two weeks. Virtually obsolete in the US.

12. **via!** /V$\overline{I}$ uh/ onward! /VEE uh/ is newer.

15. *****malcontent** displeased. US /mal cun TENT/ [MAL cun tent]; CN, UK /MAL cun tent/, *rarely* [mal cun TENT].

41. **imperator** emperor. /im puh RAYT ur/ is older; /im puh RAHT ur/ is newer. See App. D *-or*.

44. **Cleopatra's** US /clee oh PAT ruz/; UK *also* /-PAHT ruz/.

60. **resounds** /rih-, ree ZOWNDZ/ resonances.

80. **elsewhere** here with 2nd syllable stress, a form still used in the UK, but unknown in the US.

91. *****lanthorns** archaic variant of **lanterns**. Probably pronounced /LAN turnz/, but possibly /LANT hornz/ or /LAN ~~th~~urnz, -~~th~~ornz/.

106. **Dolphin** /DŎL fin/; US *also* /DAWL-/ angl. form of *Dauphin* 'the French heir to the throne.' In Shk's time /l/ in this position was often silent, so *dolphin* and *dauphin* were probably both /DAW fin/.

153. **Leander** /lee AN dur/ he swam the Hellespont to be with Hero.

154. **swom** (Q1). Most eds. prefer **swum** or **swam**. The meaning here is 'swam,' but in older forms of Eng. the past tense could be written all three ways. Whether *swom* was meant to indicate /swum/ or /swŏm/ is unclear. For simplicity use /swăm/; for an archaic flavor use /swum/, which is still used in dialects on both sides of the Atlantic.

155. **Hellespont** /HEL iss pŏnt/ the Dardenelles.

156. ***Sestos** US /SESS tus, -tŏs/; UK /-tŏs/ [-tus]. A newer pronunciation /-ohss/ is also used, especially in the US. Normal development would favor /-us/.

178. **lascivious** /luh SIV yus/ lustful.

204. **Newhaven** here 2nd syllable stress is indicated.

210. **martial** /MAR shł/ warlike.

Act 3 Scene 1

6. **martial** /MAR shł/ warlike.

6. **exploit** here should be /ek SPLOYT/.

9. **bruited** /BRO͞OT id/ told.

13. ***malcontents** /MAL cun tents/; CN, UK *rarely* [mal cun TENTS] discontented persons.

14. **Catilines** /KAT ł īnz/ conspirators.

25. **epicures** /EP ih kyoorz/; US *also* /-kyurz/ pleasure-seekers, those leading riotous lives.

34. **Polonian** /puh LOH nyun/ Pole.

45. **servitors** /SURV ih turz/ servants. See App. D *-or*.

ă-bat, äir-**marry**, air-**pair**, ạr-**far**, ĕr-**merry**, ĝ- **get**, ī-**high**, ĭr-**mirror**, ł-**little**, n̩-**listen**, ŏ-**hot**, oh-**go**, o͞o-**wood**, o͞o-**moon**, oor-**tour**, ŏr- **or**, ow-**how**, ţh-**that**, t̶h̶-**thin**, ŭ-**but**, UR-**fur**, ur-**under**.   ( ) - suppress the syllable   see p. xiii for complete list.

54. *puissant powerful. The traditional forms are /PWISS ṇt/, /PYŌŌ sṇt/ (see App. D).

55. *Agamemnon chief king of the Greeks at Troy. US, CN /ag uh MEM nŏn/; UK /-nŏn/ [-nun]. See App. D -on.

56. Xerxes /ZURK seez/ Persian conqueror.

58. Bayard-like *Bayard* was a magic horse, i.e., recklessly. /BAY urd/ or esp. UK, *newer* /-ahrd/.

59. *diadem /DĪ uh dem/ [-dum] crown.

62. descried /dih SKRĪD/ found out.

64. armado /arm AY doh/ archaic form of armada /arm AH duh/ fleet.

68. *ensigns flags. US, CN /EN sṇz/, US *rarely* [-sīnz]; UK /-sṇz, -sīnz/.

73. top-gallant mast above the mainmast. Sailors say /tuh GAL unt/, landsmen /tŏp GAL unt/.

78. amain /uh MAYN/ with full speed.

79. flower-de-luce (Q1) /FLOWR duh lŌŌss/ lily flower. Some eds. prefer fleure-de-luce /FLUR duh lŌŌss/ national emblem of France. For both these variants main stress may also fall on the 3rd syllable, the usual US form (for /lyŌŌ-/ see App. D *lu-*).

99. Muscovites /MUSK uh vīts/ soldiers from Moscow.

105. concept here final syllable stress is indicated in a refashioning of *conceit* 'thought.' It may have been pronounced /cun SEET/ (cf. *receipt*).

112. *conduit fountain. Here must be 2 syllables /CŎN dwit/; UK *also* [CUN dwit, CŎN dywit, CŎN dit, CUN dit].

124. cates /kayts/ food.

128. exhalations /eks huh LAY shunz, eks uh-/ [egz uh-] meteors.

131. rancor (UK rancour) /RANK ur/ ill-will. See App. D -or.

140. discomfiture /dis CUM fih chur/ defeat. See App. D -ure.

164. **cleftures** /CLEF churz/ places where splitting has occurred.

165. **dissever'd** /dih SEV urd/ severed.

177. **Nonpareille** one without equal. In this Fr. spelling /noh^n pah ray/. In its angl. version ***Nonpareil** /nŏn puh RELL/ is the oldest form, still common in the US, but now vanished from the UK and CN, where it has been replaced with /nŏn puh RAYL/ [-RAY], based on mod. Fr. /-RAY/ is also common in the US. /-RĪ, -RĪL/ are occasionally heard, but not recommended. Sometimes 1st syllable stress is used.

178. **Bullen** here 2nd syllable stress is indicated /bull EN/, though in H8, *Anne Bullen* is /BULL in/. Archaic variant of the Fr. city **Boulogne** angl. /bōō LOYN/; US *also* /-LOHN/; Fr. /bōō LŎN^y/.

Act 3 Scene 2

22. ***peradventure** perhaps. /PUR ad VEN chur/;
US *rarely* [PĔR-, PUR ad ven chur];
UK, CN *also* [PUR-, PĔR ad ven chur, pĕr ad VEN chur].

23. **throughly** archaic variant of *thoroughly*. /THRŌŌ lee/ is the normal pronunciation on stage, but to enhance clarity a syncopated form of the modern pronunciation may be used: *thor'ghly*.

28. **subjugate** /SUB juh gut, -gayt/ subjugated.

32. **Tush** /tŭsh/ expression of disdain.

37. **Valois** here should be /val WAH/, the usual US form; Fr. /vahl WAH/.

43. **flower-de-luce** (Q1) /FLOWR duh lōōss/ lily flower. Some eds. prefer **fleure-de-luce** /FLUR duh lōōss/ national emblem of France. For both these variants main stress may also fall on the 3rd syllable, the usual US form (for /lyōō-/ see App. D *lu-*).

Act 3 Scene 3

2. **Somme** /sŏm/; US *also* /sum/.

20. **Harflew** /HAR flōō/ archaic variant of **Harfleur** /HAR flur/; Fr. /AHR flör/.

ă-bat, äir-marry, air-pair, ạr-far, ĕr-merry, ĝ- get, ī-high, ĭr-mirror, ł-little, ṇ-listen, ŏ-hot, oh-go, ōō-wood, ōō-moon, oor-tour, ōr- or, ow-how, ţh-that, th-thin, ŭ-but, UR-fur, ur-under.   ( ) - suppress the syllable   see p. xiii for complete list.

20. **Lo** /loh/. Q1 has **Lie**.

20. **Crotaye, Crotay** 1st or 2nd syllable stress are possible /croh tay/.

20. **Carentigne** angl. /KAIR un teen/ or /kair un TEEN/; Fr. /kah rah[n] teen[y]/.

23. **progress** here 1st syllable stress is indicated.

31. **froward** /FROH wurd, FROH urd/ difficult to deal with.

51. **Upbraids** /up BRAYDZ/ insults. Some eds. prefer Q1's archaic variant **obraids** /uh BRAYDZ/.

84. **defects** here should be /dih-, dee FECTS/.

86. **timorous** /TIM uh rus/; US *also* /TIM ur us/ frightened.

93. **Valois** here should be /VAL wah/, the usual UK form; Fr. /VAHL wah/.

98. **execrations** /ek suh CRAY shunz/ curses.

111. **Valois** here should be /val WAH/, the usual US form; Fr. /vahl WAH/.

120. ***entrails** /EN traylz/; US *also* [-trĭz] guts.

126. **Upbraid'st thou him . . . ?** (Q2) /up BRAYDST/ Do you insult him . . . ? Some eds. prefer the archaic variant **Obraidst** (Q1) /uh BRAYDST/.

156. **lascivious** /luh SIV yus/ lustful.

165. **Vive le roi** /VEE vuh luh RWAH/ long live the king.

174. **martialists** /MAR shł ists/ military men.

178-198. **Plantagenet** /plan TAJ ih nit/.

189. **Bellona's** /buh LOHN uz/ goddess of war.

194. **brazen** /BRAY zun, -zn̩/ brass.

195. **stratagems** /STRAT uh jumz/ schemes.

200. ***Perseus'** he rode the winged horse, Pegasus. /PUR syus/ [-syo͞oss], US *rarely* [-so͞oss]. See App. D *-eus*.

209. ***good-presaging** here should be /pree-, prih SAY jing/ foretelling good.

210. **comfortable** here should be /CUM fur tuh bɫ/.

220. ***vaward** US /VAW wurd, VAY-/ [VOW-]; UK /VAW wurd/
[VAY-, VOW-, VAW WURD]. The vowel of *war* not recommended in the
second syllable. Archaic variant of **vanguard**. See App. D *-aun-*.

Act 3 Scene 4

3. **Genoaes** /JEN oh uz/ troops from Genoa. Some eds. prefer **Genoese**
/jen oh EEZ/, /JEN oh eez/.

12. **assay** /uh-, ass SAY/ attempt, test.

Act 3 Scene 5

19,34. **succor** (UK **succour**) /SUCK ur/ help. See App. D *-or*.

37. **Nestor's** /NEST urz/ oldest of the Greeks at Troy. See App. D *-or*.

38. **savor** (UK **savour**) /SAY vur/ taste, enjoy.

47. **haggard-like** /HAG urd/ like a wild hawk.

62. **Plantagenet** /plan TAJ ih nit/.

69. **travail's** here should be /TRAV aylz/ hard, painful work.

76. **glaives** /glayvz/ swords.

103. **Towards Poictiers** city in France. Here with 1st syllable stress, angl.
/POY teerz/. Archaic variant of **Poitiers** /PWAH tyay/. *Towards* must be one
syllable.

106. **begirt** /bih-, bee GURT/ surround.

113. **Sic et vos** Ang.Lat. US /SICK et VAWSS/; UK /-VŎSS/;
Class.Lat. /SEEK et VOHSS/ and so should you.

ă-bat, ăir-**marry**, air-**pair**, ạr-**far**, ĕr-**merry**, ĝ- get, ī-high, ĭr-mirror, ɫ-little, ṇ-listen,
ŏ-hot, oh-go, o͝o-**wood**, o͞o-**moon**, oor-**tour**, ŏr- or, ow-how, t̠h-**that**, t̵h̵-**thin**, ŭ-but,
UR-**fur**, ur-under.   ( ) - suppress the syllable   see p. xiii for complete list.

Act 4 Scene 1

2. **Blois** /blwah/ region in France.

4. **Britain's, Brittaine's** /BRIT n̦z/ Brittany's. In Shk's time /-ayn/ was also used.

7. **coronet** small crown. US /COR uh net, -nit/, /cor uh NET/;
E.COAST US /CŎR-, cŏr-/; UK /CŎR uh nit/ [-net, cŏr uh NET].

8. **Bear it unto him, and withal mine oath.** Here 2nd syllable stress is indicated for *unto*.

27. ***recourse** access. Here should be /rih CORSS/, the usual UK pronunciation; US *also* /ree-/.

Act 4 Scene 2

4-31. **victuals** /VIT łz/ food.

5. **succor** (UK **succour**) /SUCK ur/ help. See App. D -*or*.

38. ***vicegerent** /vīss JĔR unt/, *rarely older* [-JEER-] deputy ruler.

44. **travel**. Some eds. prefer ***travail** which here should be /TRAV ayl/ hard work. In Elizabethan Eng. both words were pronounced /TRAV ł/.

49. **An esquire** (*A esquire* Q1) here Q2's **A squire** fits the meter better.

54. ***pursuivant** herald. US /PUR swiv unt/ [PUR siv unt]; UK /PUR swiv unt/, *rarely* [PUR siv unt].

77. ***prostrate** /PRŎS trayt/, US *rarely* [-trut] lying face down.

Act 4 Scene 3

1.***importune** /im POR chun/ ask insistently. See App. D.

4. **advocate** /AD vuh kut/ someone who supports a person or cause.

11.***commix'd** mixed. US /cuh MIKST/ [coh-], *rarely* [cŏm-];
UK /coh-/ [cŏm-, cuh-].

21. **gin** /jin/ snare.

Act 4 Scene 4

5. **dissever'd** /dih SEV urd/ severed.

19. **bannerettes, bannerets** /ban ur ETS/, or, especially in the UK, /BAN ur ets/ small banners.

27. ***antique** ancient. Here /AN teek/, *rarely older* [AN tik].

29. **the Hesperides** normally /hess PĔR ih deez / the garden where golden apples grew. However, Shk did not necessarily pronounce the /h/ in this word, so *the* should be attached as /t̯hʸess PĔR ih deez/.

34,39. **Chatilion** here should be /shuh TILL ee un/.

63.***puissant** powerful. The traditional forms are /PWISS ṇt/, /PYŌŌ sṇt/ (see App. D).

78.***orisons** prayers. US, CN /OR ih zunz, -zṇz/ [-sunz, -sṇz]; E.COAST US /ŎR-/; UK /ŎR ih zunz, -zṇz/.

83.***burgonet** /BURG uh net/; US *also* /burg uh NET/ helmet.

90. **engirt with** /en GURT/ enclosed, surrounded.

91. **jennet** /JEN it/ Spanish horse.

108. **towards** /TOH wurdz/ heaven-ward.

115. **divine extemporal** /ek STEM p(ur) rł/ minister preaching without reading from a text.

129. **stratagems** /STRAT uh jumz/ schemes.

158. **halfpenny** here must be 3 syllables /HAY puh nee/.

Act 4 Scene 5

21.***presage** here should be /pree-, prih SAYJ/ foretell.

ă-bat, ăir-m**arry**, air-p**air**, ạr-f**ar**, ĕr-m**erry**, ĝ- g**et**, ī-h**igh**, ĭr-m**irror**, ł-l**ittle**, ṇ-l**isten**, ŏ-h**ot**, oh-g**o**, ŏ͞o-w**ood**, o͞o-m**oon**, oor-t**our**, ōr- **or**, ow-h**ow**, t̯h-t**hat**, t̶h̶-t**hin**, ŭ-b**ut**, UR-f**ur**, ur-**under**.   ( ) - suppress the syllable   see p. xiii for complete list.

25. **craven** /CRAY vin, -vn̦/ cowardly.

76. **Charact'red** written down. Here second syllable stress was probably intended, but the foot may be inverted to allow mod. first syllable stress.

103. **presidents** archaic variant of *precedents, both /PRESS ih dunts/. It is not clear whether /PREZ-/ was used in Shk's time.

115.*azure blue. US /AZH oor/ [AZ yoor, AZH ur]; UK /AZH oor, AZ yoor/ [AY zyoor, -zhyoor]. Normal development would favor /AZH ur, AY zhur/. See App. D -*ure*.

121. **amain** /uh MAYN/ with full speed.

Act 4 Scene 6

17. **prophesy** /PRŎF uh sī/ predict.

Act 4 Scene 7

5. **abject** /AB ject/ contemptible.

19. **Goliahs** /guh LĪ uz/ archaic variant of **Goliaths** /guh LĪ ut̶h̶s/.

21. *puissant powerful. The traditional forms are /PWISS n̦t/, /PYO͞O sn̦t/ (see App. D).

22. **in all accomplements** /uh CŎM pluh munts/ fully armed.

23. **Mordieu, mortdieu** angl. /mor DYO͞O/; UK *also* /-DYUR/; Fr. /mor dyö/ God's (i.e., Jesus') death!

23. **quoit at us** hurl stones at us. Q1-2 have the archaic variant **quait** /kwayt/.

32. **enow** /ih NOW/; US *also* /ee-/ archaic variant of *enough*.

Act 4 Scene 9

2.*ensigns flags. US, CN /EN sn̦z/, US *rarely* [-sīnz]; UK /-sn̦z, -sīnz/.

17. **low'ring** threatening. /LOWR ing/, with the vowel of *how*.

51, 57. **esquires** here *squires* fits the meter best.

Act 5 Scene 1

11.*__alarum__ US, CN /uh LAHR um/ [-LĂIR-]; UK /uh LĂIR um, uh LAHR um/
a call to arms.

15.*__respite__ interval. Here should be US /RESP it/, *rarely* [-īt];
CN /RESP it/ [-īt]; UK /RESP īt/ [-it]. /RESP it/ is older, but /-īt/ has been in use
since the 17th cent.

17. **tortering** (Q1) /TOR tring/ archaic variant of **torturing**.

22.*__peradventure__ perhaps. /PUR ad VEN chur/;
US *rarely* [PĚR-, PUR ad ven chur];
UK, CN *also* [PUR-, PĚR ad ven chur, pĕr ad VEN chur].

22.*__servile__ /SUR vīl/, *rarely* [SUR vł] slave-like.

23. **felonious** /fuh LOHN yus/ evil.

25. **Albeit** /awl BEE (i)t/ although.

25. **severity** /suh VĚR ih tee/.

65. **esquire of the north** *'squire o'th' north* /SKWĪR uth NORTH/ fits the
meter best.

67. **esquire** here *squire* fits the meter best.

74. **loth** /lohth/ variant of *loath* 'unwilling.'

92. *__recourse__ access. Here should be /rih CORSS/, the usual UK pronunciation;
US *also* /ree-/.

97. **Britain, Brittaine** /BRIT n/ Brittany. In Shk's time /-ayn/ was also used.

100. **coronet** small crown. US /COR uh net, -nit/, /cor uh NET/;
E.COAST US /CŎR-, cŏr-/; UK /CŎR uh nit/ [-net, cŏr uh NET].

107. **Poictiers** city in France. Here with 1st syllable stress, angl. /POY teerz/.
Archaic variant of **Poitiers** /PWAH tyay/.

ă-bat, ăir-marry, air-pair, ąr-far, ĕr-merry, ĝ- get, ī-high, ĭr-mirror, ł-little, ņ-listen,
ŏ-hot, oh-go, ōō-wood, ōō-moon, oor-tour, ōr- or, ow-how, ţh-that, th-thin, ŭ-but,
UR-fur, ur-under.   ( ) - suppress the syllable   see p. xiii for complete list.

111. **Dolphin's** /DŎL finz/; US *also* /DAWL-/ angl. form of *Dauphin's* 'the French heir to the throne.' In Shk's time /l/ in this position was often silent, so *dolphin* and *dauphin* were probably both /DAW fin/.

126. **wan** /wŏn/ pale.

131. **descry** /dih SKRĪ/ see.

134. **barricado's** barricade's. /băir ih KAY dohz/ is older, /-KAH dohz/ is newer.

135. **brazen** /BRAY zun, -zn̩/ brass.

135. **ordinance** artillery. Archaic spelling of **ordnance**. Both would have to be three syllables in this line, /OR dih nunss/.

149.*****clangor** (UK **clangour**) /CLANG ur/ [-gur] loud shrill noise.

169. **sere** /seer/ dried up.

173. **tapers** /TAY purz/ slender candles.

178. **servitor** /SURV ih tur/ servant. See App. D -*or*.

183.*****diadem** /DĪ uh dem/ [-dum] crown.

186. **Plantagenet** /plan TAJ ih nit/.

207. **irrevocable** here should be /ih REV uh kuh bł/; US *also* /ĭr-/.

215. **misconster** /mis CŎN stur/ misconstrue.

Hamlet

People in the Play

Claudius /CLAW dee yus/ his name is never spoken.

Cornelius /cor NEEL yus/.

***Fortinbras** US /FOR tin brahss/ [-brăss]; UK, CN use both with equal frequency.

Gonzago /gŏn-, gun ZAH goh/ character in the players' piece.

Guildenstern /ĜILL din sturn/.

Horatio /huh RAY shyoh/ [-shoh]; UK *also* [hŏ-].

***Laertes** /lay AIR teez/ is newer, /lay UR teez/ older. In the US, CN the former is more common, in the UK the latter. /LAY ur teez/ will not fit the meter.

Marcellus /mar SELL us/.

***Ophelia** US /oh FEEL yuh/ [uh-]; UK /oh-, ŏf-/ [uh-].

***Osric** /ŎZ rik/ [ŎSS-].

***The Polack(s)** US /POH lack, -lŏck/; CN, UK /POH lack/; US, CN *rarely* [-luck] Polish soldiers.

Polonius /puh LOHN yus/. In prose it may be /puh LOHN ee yus/.

Reynaldo (Q2) /ray-, rih NAL doh, -NAWL-, -NAHL-/. **Reynoldo** (F1) /-NAWL-, -NŎL-/.

Rosencrantz /ROH zin crănts/.

Voltemand (F1) /VŎL tih mund/. **Valtemand** (Q2) /VŎL-/ or /VAWL-/.

Places in the Play

***Elsinore** /EL sin or/.

ă-bat, ăir-m**a**rry, air-p**a**ir, ạr-f**a**r, ĕr-m**e**rry, ĝ- g**e**t, ī-high, ĭr-m**i**rror, ł-litt**le**, ṇ-liste**n**, ŏ-hot, oh-go, o͞o-wood, o͞o-moon, oor-t**our**, ŏr- **or**, ow-how, ţh-**th**at, t̶h̶-**th**in, ŭ-but, UR-f**ur**, ur-und**er**.   ( ) - suppress the syllable   see p. xiii for complete list.

Act 1 Scene 1

18. **Holla** /huh LAH/ a call to attract attention.

30. **Tush** /tŭsh/ expression of disdain.

57. **avouch** /uh VOWCH/ affirmation.

61. **combated** here should be /CŎM buh tid/.

62. **parle** /pạrl/ conference with an enemy. Some eds. prefer mod. *****parley**
/PAR lee/. Newer [-lay] not recommended.

66. **martial** /MAR shł/ warlike.

73. **brazen** /BRAY zun, -zņ/ brass.

75. **impress** here should be /im PRESS/ forcing into labor.

77. **toward** /TOH wurd, -urd/ about to take place.

83. **emulate** /EM y(uh) lut/ trying to surpass a rival.

86. **compact** here should be /cŏm-, cum PACT/ agreement.

90. **moi'ty, moiety** /MOY tee/ portion.

93. **Had he been vanquisher; as by the same comart** (Q2) /koh MART/
agreement. Some eds. prefer F1's **cov'nant** /KUV nunt/, in which case *by the*
should become one syllable, *by th'*.

103. **compulsatory** (Q2) by force. /cum PULS uh tree/ in a normal line, or
possibly US /-tor ee/; UK /-tur ee/ before a caesura. F1 has **compulsative**
/cum PULS uh tiv/.

107. **romage** intense activity. Archaic variant of **rummage**, both pronounced
/RUM ij/.

109. **portentous** /por TEN tuss/ prophetic. In Q2 but not F1.

116. *****gibber** /JIB ur/, *rarely* [ĜIB ur] chatter. In Q2 but not F1.

121. **precurse** /pree-, prih CURSS/ indication in advance. In Q2 but not F1.

122. **harbingers** /HAR bin jurz/ advance messengers. In Q2 but not F1.

125. **climatures** /CLĪ muh churz/ regions. Some eds. prefer **climature**. See App. D -*ure*. In Q2 but not F1.

140.***partisan** /PART ih zan/ [-san, -zun]; UK *also* /part ih ZAN/ a spear with a blade on the end.

155. **confine** /cŏn-, cun FĪN/ confines, limits of an area.

Act 1 Scene 2

12. **dirge** /durj/ funeral music.

21. **Co-leagued** (Q2) /coh LEEG id/ allied. **Colleagued** (F1) /cuh-, cŏl LEEG id/.

29. **bedred** (Q2) archaic variant of F1's **bedrid** 'bedridden.' Both pronounced /BED rid/.

38. **delated** (Q2) /dih-, dee LAYT id/ described in detail. Variant of F1's **dilated** /dih-, dī LAYT id/.

58. **H'ath** /hʸath/ he hath.

79. **suspiration** /suh spur RAY shun/ sigh.

87. **commendable** here should be /CŎM en duh bł/.

91. **filial obligation** /FIL ył/ a son's obligation.

92. **obsequious** /ŏb-, ub SEEK w(ee) yus/ dutifully mourning.

92. **persever** /pur SEV ur/ persevere.

93. **condolement** /cun DOHL munt/ mourning.

94. **impious** /IM pyus/ lacking in respect, profane.

113-168. **Wittenberg** angl. /WIT n̩ burg/; Germ. /VIT n̩ bĕrk/ city in Germany.

125.***jocund** /JŎCK und/; US, CN *rarely* [JOHK-] merry.

ă-bat, ăir-m**arr**y, air-**pair**, a̩r-**far**, ĕr-**merry**, ĝ- get, ī-high, ĭr-**mirror**, ł-little, n̩-listen, ŏ-hot, oh-**go**, ōō-wood, ōō-moon, oor-**tour**, ōr- or, ow-**how**, t̩h-that, t̶h̶-thin, Ŭ-but, UR-**fur**, ur-**under**.   ( ) - suppress the syllable   see p. xiii for complete list.

127. **the King's rouse** /rowz/ the King's bumper, deep drinking.

127. **bruit** /brōōt/ loudly declare.

140.***Hyperion** /hī PEER yun/ god of the sun. Sometimes newer /-PĔR-/ or
/-ŏn/ are used, but are not recommended.

140. ***satyr** US, CN /SAYT ur/, *rarely* [SAT ur]; UK /SAT ur/ [SAYT-]
lecherous, goat-like creature.

149. **Niobe** /NĪ uh bee, -oh bee/ she wept endlessly when her children were
killed.

157. **incestious** (Q2) /in SESS chus/ archaic variant of F1's **incestuous**
/in SESS chwus/; UK *also* /-tywus/.

177. **studient** (Q2) /STŌŌD yunt/; UK, SOUTH. US /STYŌŌD-/. Archaic variant
of F1's **student**.

193. **attent** /uh TENT/ attentive.

200. **cap-a-pe** from head to toe. Archaic variant of ***cap-à-pie**. Traditionally
/kap uh PEE/, still the most common form in the US, CN, and also used in the UK.
A newer form /-PAY/ is preferred in the UK and also used in the US. Stress may
also fall on the 1st syllable. A Frenchified version /kap uh pee AY/ is also
increasingly used. The spelling pronunciation /-PĪ/ is not recommended.

204. **truncheon's** /TRUN chunz/ short staff of office.

239. **grisl'd** (*grissl'd* Q2) graying. Archaic variant of **grizzled**, both pronounced
/GRIZ łd/. F1 has **grisly** (F1) /GRIZ lee/.

247. **tenable** /TEN (uh) bł/ held close. Q1 has **tenible** /TEN (ih) bł/.

Act 1 Scene 3

3. **convey** (*conuay* Q2) /CŎN vay/ transport. Some eds. prefer F1's **convoy**.

9. **suppliance** /suh PLĪ unss/ pastime.

12. ***thews** /thyōōz/; US, CN *also* [thōōz] muscles.

15. **cautel** /KAWT ł/ deceit.

21. **The safety and health of this whole state** (Q2) the meter calls for expansion to /SAYF uh tee/, though some eds. have emmended it to **safety and the health**. Other eds. prefer **sanity** or F1's **sanctity**.

30. **credent** /CREED ṇt/ trusting.

32. **importunity** /im por-, im pur TYO͞ON ih tee/; US *also* /-TO͞ON-/ insistent requests.

36. **chariest** /CHAIR yist/; E.COAST US *also* [CHĂIR-] most cautious, shyest.

38. **calumnious** /cuh LUM nyus/ slanderous.

49.***libertine** /LIB ur teen/, *rarely* [-tīn] person who acts without moral restraint.

50. **dalliance** /DAL yunss/ frivolity.

51. **reaks** /reks/ pays attention to. Most eds. prefer Q1's **recks**, pronounced the same way.

51. **rede** /reed/ advice.

59. **character** write down. Here with second syllable stress.

65. **courage** (Q2) brave fellow. Some eds. prefer F1's ***comrade**, here showing original 2nd syllable stress US, CN /cŏm RAD/, *rarely* [cum-]; UK /cŏm RAYD/, *rarely* [-RAD, cum-]. Others prefer **comrague** 'fellow rogue,' presumably pronounced /cŏm-, cum RAYG/. *Courage* would require an unusual inversion.

97. **behooves** (Q2) /bih-, bee HO͞OVZ/ is necessary, proper for. UK prefers the F1 spelling **behoves** /bih HOHVZ/.

110. ***importun'd** /im POR chund/ asked insistently. See App. D.

115. **springes** /SPRIN jiz/ snares.

123. **parle** /pạrl/ conference with an enemy. F1 has ***parley** /PAR lee/. Newer [-lay] not recommended.

125. **teder** (Q3-4) /TED ur/ archaic variant of F1's **tether**.

ă-bat, ăir-**marry**, air-**pair**, ạr-**far**, ĕr-**merry**, ĝ- get, ī-high, ĭr-mirror, ł-little, ṇ-listen, ŏ-hot, oh-go, o͞o-wood, ōͦo-moon, oor-tour, ōr- or, ow-how, ţh-that, th̶-thin, ŭ-but, UR-**fur**, ur-under.   ( ) - suppress the syllable   see p. xiii for complete list.

129. **implorators** (F1) /im PLOR (uh) turz/ those who ask passionately for something. Some eds. prefer **imploratators** (following Q2) /im PLOR uh tay turz/. See App. D *-or*.

Act 1 Scene 4

1. **shrowdly** (Q2) /SHROHD lee/ sharply. Archaic variant of F1's **shrewdly**.

8. **rouse** /rowz/ revels.

9. **Keeps *wassail** (Q1) festivities where much carousing occurs.
Here stressed on the 1st syllable US /WŎSS ł, -ayl/, *rarely* [WĂSS ł];
CN /WŎSS ayl/ [WŎSS ł]; UK /WĂSS ayl/ [WŎSS-]. Normal development
would favor /WŎSS-/. F1 has the plural form.

10. **draughts** US, CN /drăfts/; UK, EAST. N.ENG. /drahfts/ drinks.

10. **Rhenish** /REN ish/ Rhine wine.

---

lines 17-38 are found in Q2, but not in F1.

18. **traduc'd** slandered. /truh DYŌŌST/; US *also* /-DŌŌST/. /-JŌŌST/ is considered non-standard in the UK.

19. **clip** (Q2) call. Variant of Q5's **clepe** /cleep/.

29. **o'er-leavens** /or LEV ṇz, -inz/ having too much leaven (sour-dough used to make bread rise), i.e., takes over.

30. ***plausive** /PLAW ziv/ [-siv] pleasing.

31. **defect** here should be /dih-, dee FECT/.

36. **ev'l**. Some eds. prefer Q2's **eale** or **evil, e'il, ale**. Q3-4 have **ease**. If *evil*, it could have been pronounced /eel/ in Shk's time, but since the word occurs at the end of the line, it can be pronounced normally /EE vł/ [EE vil], creating a feminine ending.

37. **of a doubt** some eds. prefer **often dout** /dowt/ extinguish, banish. **Over-daub** has also been suggested.

---

47. **canoniz'd** here should be /kan ŎN īzd/ buried according to church rites.

48. ***cerements** waxed grave clothes. /SEER munts/ is older, but virtually extinct. Today the spelling pronunciation /SĔR (uh) munts/ is used, which, if three syllables, would force *sepulchre* to be stressed on the 2nd syllable.

48. **sepulchre** /SEP ł kur/ tomb.

50. **op'd** /ohpt/ opened.

52. **complete steel** here should be /CŎM pleet/ full armor.

61, 78. **waves** (Q2). F1 has ***wafts** US, CN /wŏfts/, SOUTH. US /wăfts/; UK /wŏfts/ [wăfts, wahfts] beckons. /wăfts/ is newer and considered non-standard by many.

77. **fadoms** /FAD umz/ archaic variant of **fathoms** /FĂṬH umz/. Omitted F1.

82.***artere** (*arture* Q2) artery. F1 has **artire**, Q3 has **artyre**. All are pronounced the same way US /ART ur, -eer/; UK /ART ur/ [-eer]. Some eds. substitute Q5's **artery**, which here would be /AR tree/.

83. **Nemean lion's** /NEE myun/ lion killed by Hercules.

Act 1 Scene 5

20. **porpentine** /POR pin tīn/ archaic variant of **porcupine**.

21. **blazon** /BLAY zun, -zṇ/ revealing of secrets.

33. **Lethe** /LEETH ee/ river of forgetfulness in Hades.

42. **adulterate** /uh DULL trayt, -trut/ adulterous. /-ut/ is more usual for an adj.

61. **secure** safe, leisure. Here 1st syllable stress is indicated.

62. **hebona** (Q2) /HEB (uh) nuh/ a poison plant, perhaps ebony. Some eds. prefer F1's **hebonon**, sometimes spelled **hebenon** /HEB (uh) nun/. *H* was often silent in Shk's time, and with raising of the final vowel to /ee/ (cf. *sirrah-sirry, Ursula-Ursley*) *hebona* and *ebony* would have been homonyms.

68. **posset** /PŎSS it/ curdle.

72. ***lazar-like** /LAY zur, LAZZ ur/ leper-like.

ă-bat, ăir-ma**rr**y, air-p**air**, ạr-**far**, ĕr-me**rr**y, ĝ- get, ī-high, ĭr-mi**rr**or, ł-little, ṇ-listen, ŏ-hot, oh-go, ōō-wood, ōō-moon, oor-**tour**, ōr- **or**, ow-how, ṭh-that, t̶h̶-thin, Ŭ-but, UR-**fur**, ur-und**er**.   ( ) - suppress the syllable   see p. xiii for complete list.

77. **Unhous'led** /un HOWZ ld/ without the eucharist.

77. **unanel'd** /un uh NEELD/ without extreme unction.

89. **matin** /MAT in, -ŋ/ morning.

90. **gins** /ĝinz/ begins.

94. **sinows** (Q2) /SIN ohz/. Archaic variant of F1's **sinews** /SIN yo͞oz/; US *also* [SIN o͞oz].

99. **records** here should be /rik-, rek ORDZ/.

102. **commandement** (Q2). Archaic variant of F1's **commandment**, originally with 4 syllables, /-uh munt/, but here the usual mod. 3-syllable pronunciation is required.

124. **arrant** /ĂIR unt/ thoroughgoing.

151. **cellarage** /SELL ur ij/ cellar.

156.   **Hic   et ubique**
Ang.Lat. /HICK et yo͞o BĪ kwee/
Class.Lat. /HEEK et o͞o BEE kway/
            'here and everywhere'

163. **pioner** soldier who dug trenches and planted mines. It is not certain whether Shk pronounced this /PĪ uh nur/ or as in mod. **pioneer** /pī uh NEER/.

Act 2 Scene 1

3. **marvell's** (*meruiles* Q2, *maruels* F1) marvellously. Some eds. prefer Q3-4's **marvellous**. In any event it should be two syllables, either /MARV lss/ or, as indicated in spellings elsewhere in Shk, /MARV lus/.

42. **converse** /cun VURSS/ conversation.

43. **prenominate** /prih-, pree NŎM (ih) nut, -ayt/ aforementioned. /-ut / is more usual for an adj.

56. **rouse** /rowz/ carousing.

59. *Videlicet namely (abbreviated *viz.*). The older, anglicized pronunciations are US /vih DELL ih sit/ [-DEEL-, vī-]; UK /vih DEEL ih sit/ [vī-, -DELL-]. Newer pronunciations mix in restored Latin syllables, for example, /-ket/ or /-DAYL-/. These are not recommended.

59. *brothel US, CN /BRŎ̵T̵H̵ ł/ [BRŎ̵T̵H̵ ł, BRAW̵T̵H̵ ł]; UK /BRŎ̵T̵H̵ ł/ whorehouse.

62. windlasses /WIND luss iz/ here means 'roundabout ways.'

62. assays /uh-, ass SAYZ/ attempts.

66. God buy ye (Q2) /gŏd BĪ yee/; US *also* /gawd-/ good bye. God buy you (F1). Some eds. substitute God bye ye, God b'wi' ye or some other variation of that phrase, however it would have to be reduced to something like /gŏd BWEE yee/ to fit the meter.

77. down-gyved /down JĪ vid/ hanging down like a prisoner's chains.

100. fordoes /for DUZ/ destroys.

110. beshrow /bih-, bee SHROH/ curse. Archaic variant of beshrew /-SHROO̅/ which some eds. prefer.

115. close /clohss/ secret.

Act 2 Scene 2

13. voutsafe your rest (Q2) allow yourself to rest. /vowt SAYF/ archaic variant of F1's vouchsafe /vowch SAYF/.

71. th' assay /t̥hʸ uh-, t̥hʸ ass SAY/. Some eds. prefer essay /es SAY/. Both mean 'test.'

86. expostulate /ek SPŎS chuh layt/; UK *also* /-tyoo layt/ discuss, object.

102. defect here should be /dih-, dee FECT/.

105. Perpend /pur PEND/ consider.

142. prescripts (Q2) /PREE scripts/ commands. F1 has precepts.

ă-bat, ăir-marry, air-pair, ạr-far, ĕr-merry, ĝ- get, ī-high, ĭr-mirror, ł-little, ṇ-listen, ŏ-hot, oh-go, o̅o̅-wood, o̅o̅-moon, oor-tour, ŏr- or, ow-how, t̥h-that, t̵h̵-thin, ŭ-but, UR-fur, ur-under.　　( ) - suppress the syllable　　see p. xiii for complete list.

163. **arras** /ĂIR us/ tapestry.

174, 189. ***fishmonger** fish seller. US /FISH mŏng gur/ or /-mawng-/ [-mung-]; CN /-mung gur, -mŏng gur/; UK /-mung gur/.

274. **halfpenny** /HAY puh nee, HAYP nee/.

283. ***conjure** entreat. US, CN /CŎN jur/, *rarely* [CUN-]; UK /CUN jur/ [CŎN-], *rarely* [cun JOOR]. The older pronunciation for this meaning is /cun JOOR/.

284. **consonancy** /CŎN suh nun see/ harmony.

307. ***paragon** US /PĂIR uh gŏn/ [-gun]; CN /-gŏn/; UK /-gun/ [-gṇ] most perfect example.

308. **quintessence** /kwin TESS unss, -ṇss/ the purest essence.

320. **adventerous** /ad VENT ur us/ archaic variant of **adventurous**.

322. ***gratis** unrewarded. US, UK /GRAHT iss/ [GRAT-], UK *rarely* [GRAYT-]; CN /GRAT-/ [GRAHT-].

324. **sere** archaic variant of **sear** catch of a gunlock. Both pronounced /seer/.

328. **tragedians** /truh JEE dee unz/ actors of tragedies.

339. ***aery, eyrie, aerie** high nest. /AIR ee, EER-/; E.COAST US *also* [ĂIR-]. /ĪR ee/ not recommended. /AIR ee/ is the oldest pronunciation.

339. **eyases** /Ī uh siz/ young hawks.

346. **escoted** /es SKŎT id/ financially supported.

353. **tarre, tar** /tar/ incite.

364. **mouths** (Q2). Some eds. prefer F1's ***mows** grimaces. /mohz/ and /mowz/ were both used in Shk's time and are still used today. Shk's rhymes elsewhere indicate /mohz/.

366. **'Sblood** (Q2) /zblud/ God's (i.e., Jesus') blood. Omitted F1.

383. **swaddling-clouts** (Q2) /SWŎD ling clowts/ swaddling clothes. F1 has **swathing clouts** /SWAYṬH ing/; US *also* /SWŎṬH ing/.

386. **prophesy** /PRŎF uh sī/ to predict the future.

391. ***Roscius** famous actor in ancient Rome. Normal development would favor /RŎSH us/. /RŎSH ee yus/ is also used, and restored Latin /RŌS kee yus/ is the most common in all countries.

399. **individable** /in dih VĪ duh bł/.

400. **Plautus** /PLAWT us/ Roman writer of comedies.

403-11. **Jephthah** one of the judges of Israel. Following the usual rules, /JEF t̶h̶uh/, but /JEP t̶h̶uh/ has also been used since Elizabethan times. Note /DIP t̶h̶ -/ for *diphth-* is the most common pronunciation today in *diphthong*, *diphtheria*.

419. **chanson** song. Angl. forms are US /SHAN sun, -sn̩, -sŏn/, /shahn SAWN, -SOHN/; UK /SHAH^N sah^n/ [SHŎN-, -sŏn]; Fr. /shah^n soh^n/. Normal development would give /SHAN sn̩, CHAN-/ (see App. D *-on*).

423. ***valanced** US /VAYL unst/ [VAL-]; UK /VAL-/ fringed, i.e., bearded. F1 has **valiant.**

425. **by' lady** (Q2) /bī-, buh LAY dee/ by Our Lady, a mild oath. F1 has **byrlady** /bīr-, bur LAY dee/.

427. ***chopine** US /CHŎP in/ [choh PEEN]; UK /choh PEEN/ [CHŎP in] thick-soled shoe.

437. ***caviary** /kav ee AIR ee/, /kav ee AHR ee/ archaic variant of **caviare, caviar** /KAV ee ahr/ [kav ee AHR]; the first syllable may sometimes also be /kah-/, especially in the US.

441. **sallets** /SAL its/ spicy herbs.

442. **savory** (UK **savoury**) /SAY vur ee/ tasty, spicy.

443. **indict** /in DĪT/ accuse.

446. **Aeneas'** /ih NEE yus/; UK *also* /EE NEE yus/ Prince of Troy.

446. **Dido** /DĪ doh/ Queen of Carthage.

ă-bat, ăir-**marry**, air-**pair**, ạr-**far**, ĕr-**merry**, ĝ- get, ī-high, ĭr-**mirror**, ł-little, n̩-listen, ŏ-hot, oh-go, o͞o-wood, o͞o-moon, oor-**tour**, ōr- or, ow-how, t̶h̶-**that**, t̶h̶-**thin**, ŭ-but, UR-**fur**, ur-und**er**.   ( ) - suppress the syllable   see p. xiii for complete list.

In the recitations by Hamlet and the Player, these names appear several times:

*__Priam__ King of Troy. US, CN /PRĪ um/ [-am]; UK /-am/, *rarely* [-um]. Normal development would favor /-um/.

__Pyrrhus__ /PĬR us/ Achilles' son.

---

450. __th' Hyrcanian__ normally /HUR KAYN yun/ of Hyrcania (in the Caucausus). However, Shk did not pronounce the /h/ in this word, so *th'* can be attached as /ṭhʸUR KAYN yun/.

457. __gules__ red. Here 2 syllables /GYOO̅ łz/ red.

459. __impasted__ /im PAY stid/ crusted.

462. __coagulate__ /coh AG y(uh) lut, -ayt/ coagulated, clotted.

469. *__antique__ ancient. Here /AN teek/, *rarely older* [AN tik].

474. __Ilium__ (F1) /ILL ee um/; UK *sometimes newer* [Ī lee um] the citadel of Troy. Omitted Q2.

490. __eterne__ /ih TURN/; US *also* /ee-/ eternal.

494. *__synod__ US, CN /SIN ud/ [-ŏd]; UK /SIN ŏd/ [-ud] council.

501. __Hecuba__ /HEK yoo buh/ Queen of Troy.

502-4. __mobled, mobbled__ /MŎB łd/ muffled.

506. __bisson__ /BISS ņ/ blinding.

506. __rheum__ /rōo̅m/ tears.

506. __clout__ /clowt/ cloth.

507. *__diadem__ /DĪ (uh) dem/ [-dum] crown.

509. __the alarm__ (Q2). Some eds. prefer F1's __th'Alarum__ which however here should be two syllables /ṭhʸuh LARM/.

517. __milch__ /milch/ milky.

524. __abstract__ /AB stract/ summary. F1 has __abstracts__.

549. **God buy to you** (Q2), **God buy'ye** (F1) see 2.1.66.

554. **wann'd** /wŏnd/ paled. F1 has **warm'd**.

558, 559. **Hecuba** /HEK yoo buh/ Queen of Troy.

580. **offal** /ŎF ł/; US *also* /AWF ł/ animal guts and remains after butchering.

581. **kindless** /KĪND liss/ unnatural.

587. **foh, faugh** indicates an expression of disgust made with the lips /pff/! or /pfuh/! Sometimes vocalized as /foh/ or /faw/.

592. **malefactions** /mal ih FAK shunz/ evil deeds.

599. **May be a dev'l, and the dev'l hath power** (*deale* Q2, *Diuell. . . Diuel* F1) the 1st instance should be two syllables /DEV ł/, the 2nd should be one /devl/, with /v/ and /l/ pronounced nearly simultaneously. The Q2 form /deel/ is found in Scot. and some northern Eng. dialects.

Act 3 Scene 1

13. **Niggard** /NIG urd/ miser or miserly.

14. **assay** /uh-, ass SAY/ attempt.

17. **o'erraught** here should be /OR rawt/ passed.

31. **espials** (F1) /ess SPĪ łz/ spies. Q2 and *Riverside* omit this word.

50. **harlot's** /HAR luts/ whore's.

70. ***contumely** insolence. Here should be stressed on the 1st syllable /CŎN tyoom lee, -tyum-/; US, CN *also* /-toom-, -tum-/. [-chum-, -choom-] are considered non-standard in the UK. The occasionally used US pronunciation [CŎN tuh mee lee, -too-] is also possible, producing a feminine ending. Often pronounced with 2nd syllable stress in mod. Eng.

71. **despis'd** here should be /DESS pīzd/. F1 has **dispriz'd** /DIS prīzd/ undervalued.

ă-bat, ăir-**marry**, air-**pair**, ar-**far**, ĕr-**merry**, ĝ- **get**, ī-**high**, ĭr-**mirror**, ł-**little**, n-**listen**, ŏ-**hot**, oh-**go**, ōō-**wood**, ōō-**moon**, oor-**tour**, ōr- **or**, ow-**how**, th-**that**, th-**thin**, ŭ-**but**, UR-**fur**, ur-**under**.   ( ) - suppress the syllable   see p. xiii for complete list.

74. *quietus final payment on a debt. /kwī EE tus/ is older and in the US more frequently used; /kwī AY tus, kwee AY tus/ are newer and in the UK more frequently used; in CN all three are equally used.

75. fardels /FAR dłz/ burdens.

78. *bourn /born, boorn/ boundary. North American [burn] not recommended. Normal development would favor /born/.

86. awry (Q2) /uh RĪ/ askew. F1 has away.

88. *orisons prayers. US, CN /OR ih zunz, -zṇz/ [-sunz, -sṇz]; E.COAST US /ŎR-/; UK /ŎR ih zunz, -zṇz/.

128. arrant /ĂIR unt/ thoroughgoing.

136. calumny /CAL um nee/ slander.

159. unmatch'd here should be /UN matcht/.

159. stature (Q2) /STATCH ur/. F1 has feature.

188. unwatch'd (F1) here with 1st syllable stress. Q2 has unmatched.

Act 3 Scene 2

3. as live as soon. May have been /liv/ in Shk's time. Variant of as lief /leef/. In the US lieve /leev/ is still found in some dialects and can also be used here.

9. robustious /roh BUS chus/ boisterous.

10. periwig-pated /PĔR ih wig PAYT id/; also /PĔR ee-/ wig-headed.

12. inexplicable /in eks PLICK uh bł/ [in EKS plick uh bł].

12. dumb shows /DUM shohz/ pantomime.

13. Termagant /TUR muh gunt/ a violent Saracen god.

14. out-Herods Herod /HĔR ud/ ranting villain in period plays.

32. pagan /PAYG un/ non-Christian.

58. revenue here should be /ruh VEN yōo/.

60. **absurd** here should be /AB surd/; US *sometimes* [-zurd], but this is considered non-standard in the UK.

65. **Sh'hath** /sh^ya~~th~~/. **S'hath** (Q2), **Hath** (F1).

67. **buffets** /BUFF its/ blows.

69. **co-meddled** (Q2) /coh MED łd/ mixed.   F1 has **co-mingled** /coh MING głd/ archaic variant of **commingled** US /cuh MING głd/ [coh-], *rarely* [cŏm-]; UK /coh-/ [cŏm-, cuh-].

80. **occulted** /uh CULT id/ [ŏ-] hidden.

84. **stithy** /STIṬH ee/; US *also* /STI~~TH~~ ee/ forge.

94. ***capons** US /KAY pŏnz, -punz/; CN, UK /KAY pŏnz/ [-punz] chickens.   See App. D -*on*.

133. **by'r lady** (F1) /bīr-, bur LAY dee/ by Our Lady, a mild oath.   Q2 has *ber lady*, pronounced the same way.

137. **this' miching mallecho** (**miching malicho** F1) 'this is sneaking mischief.' Often rendered as /MITCH ing MAL uh koh/, but the best choice is probably /MAL uh choh/, following the derivation from Sp. **malhecho** /mahl AY choh/ 'misdeed.' *Mitching,* or *meeching* 'cringing, slinking' (cf. *britches-breeches*) was still used in New Eng. in this century. Other eds. prefer **munching Mallico** (Q2). Note *Riverside* adds an apostrophe to *this* suggesting that *this is* was intended.

155. **Phoebus'** /FEE bus/ god of the sun.

156. **Tellus'** /TEL us/ goddess of the earth.

160. **comutual** /coh MYO͞OCH wo͞ol/; UK *also* [-MYO͞OT yo͞ol, -chł].   Archaic variant of **commutual** US /cum-/ [coh-], *rarely* [cŏm-]; UK /coh-/ [cŏm-, cum-].

174. **operant** /ŎP (ur) runt/ vital, active.

197. **enactures** /en AK churz/ fulfillments.

200. **for aye** /ay/ forever.   /ī/ is often used, but not recommended.

228. ***mischance** in verse normally with 2nd syllable stress.

ă-bat, ăir-**marry**, air-**pair**, ạr-**far**, ĕr-**merry**, ĝ- **get**, ī-**high**, ĭr-**mirror**, ł-**little**, ṇ-**listen**, ŏ-**hot**, oh-**go**, o͞o-**wood**, o͞o-**moon**, oor-**tour**, ōr- **or**, ow-**how**, ṭh-**that**, ~~th~~-**thin**, ŭ-**but**, UR-**fur**, ur-**under**.   ( ) - suppress the syllable   see p. xiii for complete list.

240. **Baptista** angl. /bap TISS tuh/, but is sometimes given the continental pronunciation /bahp TEES tah/, or a mix of the two /bap TEES tuh/, etc.

244. **Lucianus** /loō shee AYN us/, /loō see-/, are the oldest angl. forms. Normal development would favor the former. Another anglicization is /-ANN-/. Other choices based on Ital. and restored Latin are /-chee-, -AHN-/ (for /lyoō-/ see App. D *lu-*).

252. **mistake** here /mis TAYK/ to take wrongfully. The spelling **mis-take**, which some eds. prefer, reflects this pronunciation.

258. **Hecat's** /HEK uts/ goddess of witchcraft. /HEK uh tee/ is the usual non-Shakespearean pronunciation.

262. ***extant** still in existence. US /EK stunt/ [ek STĂNT]; UK /ek STĂNT/, *rarely* [EK stunt]; in CN both are used equally.

271. **strooken** (Q2) /STRoōK in/ or perhaps simply a variant spelling of F1's **strucken**. Some eds. prefer **stricken**.

276. **Provincial** /pruh VIN shł, -chł/. Some eds. substitute **Provencial** /proh VEN shł, -chł/. Both are archaic forms of **Provençal** /prŏv un SAHL, -ahⁿ-, -ŏn-/; US *also* /proh-/ of Provence, southern France.

281. **Damon** /DAY mun/. Sometimes newer /-ŏn/ is used. See App. D *-on*.

284. **pajock** some eds. believe this is a misprint for or variant of **peacock** still pronounced /PAY cŏck/ in some dialects. Others believe it is related to **patchock** /PATCH ŏck, -uck/ 'scoundrel,' which here would be pronounced /PAJ ŏck, -uck/.

294. **perdy, perdie** /PUR DEE/ 'by God, indeed.' Some eds. prefer the variant **pardie** /par DEE/.

296. **voutsafe** (Q2) /vowt SAYF/ grant. Archaic variant of F1's **vouchsafe** /vowch SAYF/.

316. **commandement.** Archaic variant of **commandment**, originally with 4 syllables, /-uh munt/, but in this prose passage the usual mod. 3-syllable pronunciation may be used.

328. **stonish** (Q2) /STŎN ish/ short form of F1's **astonish**.

369. **'Sblood** /zblud/ God's (i.e., Jesus') blood. F1 has **why**.

Act 3 Scene 3

14. **weal** /weel/ welfare.

20. **mortis'd** /MORT ist/ joined.

24. **viage** (Q2) /VĪ ij/ archaic variant of F1's **voyage**.

28. **arras** /ĂIR us/ tapestry.

37. **primal** /PRĪ mł/ original.

68. **limed** /LĪ mid/ caught in a trap made of lime paste.

69. **assay** /uh-, ass SAY/ attempt.

90. **th'incestious** (Q2) /t̩hʸin SESS chus/ archaic variant of F1's **th'incestuous**
/t̩hʸin SESS chwus/; UK *also* /-tywus/.

Act 3 Scene 4

14. **rood** /ro͞od/ cross.

18. **boudge** /BUJ/, or possibly /bo͞oj/. Archaic variant of **budge**.

38. ***bulwark** structure for defense. US, CN /BU̩LL wurk/ [BŬL wurk];
UK /BU̩LL WURK, -wurk/. The vowels /or/, /ahr/ not recommended in the final
syllable, and are non-standard in the UK.

54. **presentment** /pree-, prih ZENT munt/ likeness.

56. ***Hyperion's** /hī PEER yunz/ god of the sun. Sometimes newer /-PĔR-/ or
/-ŏn/ are used, but are not recommended.

67. ***moor** /moor/ [mor] swamp.

73. **apoplex'd** (Q2) /AP uh plekst/ paralyzed. Omitted F1.

79. **sans** (Q2) /sănz/ without. Omitted F1.

83. **mutine** /MYO͞OT in, -n̩/ to rebel.

ă-bat, ăir-marry, air-pair, a̩r-far, ĕr-merry, ĝ- get, ī-high, ĭr-mirror, ł-little, n̩-listen,
ŏ-hot, oh-go, o͞o-wood, o͞o-moon, oor-tour, ōr- or, ow-how, t̩h-that, t̶h̶-thin, ŭ-but,
UR-fur, ur-under.   ( ) - suppress the syllable   see p. xiii for complete list.

86. **ardure** warm emotion. Archaic variant of **ardor** (UK **ardour**), all pronounced /ARD ur/.

97. **tithe** /tīth/ tenth part.

98. **precedent** /prih-, pree SEED unt, -ņt/ preceding.

100. ***diadem** /DĪ (uh) dem/ [-dum] crown.

144. **gambol** /GAM bł/ frolic.

153. **pursy** /PUR see/ fat, short-winded.

168. **use** (Q2) /yo͞oss/ habit. Omitted F1.

175. **scourge** /SKURJ/ instrument of punishment.

184. **reechy** /REECH ee/ filthy.

190. **paddock** /PAD uk/ toad.

190. **gib** /ĝib/ a male cat.

---

lines 202-210 are found in Q2 but not in F1

206. **enginer** archaic variant of **engineer**. In Shk's time it may have been /EN jih nur/, or mod. /en jih NEER/.

207. **petar** /puh TAR/ archaic variant of **petard** /puh TARD/ bomb.

Act 4 Scene 1

1. **profound** here should be /PROH fownd/ deep.

2. **translate** here should be stressed on the 2nd syllable, the normal UK pronunciation US /trănss LAYT, trănz-/; UK /trănss LAYT/ [trănz-, trahnz-, trahnss-, trunss-, trunz-].

9. **arras** /ĂIR us/ tapestry.

Act 4 Scene 3

6. **scourge** /SKURJ/ severe punishment.

20. **politic** (Q2) /PŎL ih tik/ shrewd. Omitted F1.

27. **hath eat** /et/ dialect variant of **eaten**.

60. **cicatrice** /SIK uh triss/ scar.

62. ****homage** /HŎM ij/; US *also* /ŎM ij/ acknowledgement of allegience.

64. **congruing** (Q2) here should be /CŎN groo ing/ in agreement with. F1 has
****conjuring** solemnly charging. Here should be US, CN /CŎN jur ing/, *rarely*
[CUN-]; UK /CUN-/ [CŎN-]. However the older pronunciation for this meaning
is /cun JOOR ing/.

Act 4 Scene 4

---

lines 9-66 are found in Q2 but not in F1

16. **frontier** here should be /FRUN teer/ [FRŎN-].

27. **th'imposthume** /ţhʸim PŎS choōm/; UK *also* /-tyoōm, -tyoōm/ abcess.

30. **God buy you** see 2.1.66.

40. ****Bestial** beastlike. /BEST yŀ/; US *also* [-chŀ].   US, CN /BEES-/ not
recommended.

40. **craven** /CRAY vin, -vṇ/ cowardly.

Act 4 Scene 5

2. **importunate** /im POR chuh nut/; UK *also* /-tyoo nut/ insistant.

26. **shoon** /shoōn/ Scottish and Nth. English dialect form of *shoes*.

42. **God dild you** /gŏd ILD yoō/; US *also* /gawd/ God reward you, thank you.
Some eds. prefer **God 'ield you** /-EELD-, -ILD-/.

ă-bat, ăir-**marry**, air-**pair**, ạr-**far**, ĕr-**merry**, ĝ- **get**, ī-**high**, ĭr-**mirror**, ŀ-**little**, ṇ-**listen**,
ŏ-**hot**, oh-**go**, oō-**wood**, oō-**moon**, oor-**tour**, ōr- **or**, ow-**how**, ţh-**that**, t̶h̶-**thin**, Ŭ-**but**,
UR-**fur**, ur-**under**.   ( ) - suppress the syllable   see p. xiii for complete list.

---

52. **clo'es** /clohz/ a pronunciation of *clothes* which is still the most common in the US.

58. **Gis** /jiss/ Jesus.

119. **harlot** /HAR lut/ whore.

137. **throughly** archaic variant of *thoroughly*. /T̶H̶R̅O̅O̅ lee/ is the normal pronunciation on stage, but to enhance clarity a syncopated form of the modern pronunciation may be used: *thor'ghly*.

165. **bier** /beer/ coffin.

181. **columbines** /CŎL um bīnz/ a flower.

196. **pole** archaic spelling of **poll** /pohl/ 'head.'

199. **God 'a' mercy** (Q2) /uh/ God have mercy. F1 has **Gramercy** /gruh MUR see/ God grant mercy.

201. **God buy you** see 2.1.66. **God buy ye** (F1).

203. **commune** here should be /CŎM yōōn/ share.

207. **collateral** US /cuh LAT rł/; UK *also* [cŏ-] indirect.

214. **obscure** here should be /ŎB skyoor/; US *also* [-skyur].

Act 4 Scene 7

10. **unsinow'd** /un SIN ohd/ weak. Archaic variant of **unsinewed** which many eds. prefer /un SIN yōōd/; US *also* [-ōōd].

11. **th'are** (*tha'r* Q2), **they are** (F1). Should be one syllable /thair/ 'they're.'

21. **gyves** /jīvz/ chains, fetters. Some eds. substitute **guilts**.

40. **Claudio** /CLAW dyoh/.

64. **exploit** here should be /ek SPLOYT/.

77. **riband** (Q3) /RIB und/. Archaic variant of **ribbon**. Omitted F1.

87. ***demi-natur'd*** /DEM ee-/ i.e., become half man, half beast.

92. **Lamord** /luh MORD/. Some eds. prefer **Lamond** /luh MŎND/.

93. *****brooch** /brohch/ ornament. US [bro͞och] not recommended.

100. **scrimers** (Q2) /SKREEM urz/ fencers. Omitted F1.

117. **plurisy** archaic variant of **pleurisy** 'excess.' Both pronounced /PLO͞OR ih see/; US *also* /PLUR-/.

127. **sanctuarize** /SANK chwuh rīz/; UK *also* [-ty(oo)uh-] provide asylum to.

129. **close** /clohss/ confined.

141. **mountebank** /MOWNT uh bank/ quack doctor.

143. **cataplasm** /KAT uh plazm/ poultice.

152. **assay'd** /uh-, ass SAYD/. Some eds. prefer **essayed** /es SAYD/. Both mean 'attempted.'

160. **chalice** /CHAL iss/ goblet.

160. *****nonce** /nŏnss/ occasion. US, CN [nunss] not recommended.

166. **askaunt** (*ascaunt* Q2) at a sideways angle. Archaic variant of **askant** US /uh SKĂNT/; UK, E. NEW ENG. /uh SKAHNT/ [uh SKĂNT]. See App. D *aun* . Some eds. prefer F1's **aslant** /uh SLĂNT/.

172. **crownet** (*cronet* Q2) /CROWN it/. F1 has **coronet** which here should be US /COR (uh) net, -nit/; E.COAST US, UK /CŎR-/. Both mean 'small crown.'

177. **chaunted** archaic variant of **chanted** US, CN /CHĂNT id/; E. NEW ENG, UK /CHAHNT id/. See App. D *-aun-*.

179. *****indued** /in DYO͞OD/; US *also* [-DO͞OD] accustomed to. Some eds. prefer **endued** /en-/.

191. **drowns** (Q2). Some eds. prefer **douts** (following F1's *doubts*) /dowts/ extinguishes.

ă-bat, ăir-m**arry**, air-**pair**, ạr-**far**, ĕr-**merry**, ĝ- get, ī-high, ĭr-mirror, ł-little, ṇ-listen, ŏ-hot, oh-go, o͝o-wood, o͞o-moon, oor-**tour**, ōr- **or**, ow-how, t̬h-**that**, t̶h̶-thin, ŭ-but, UR-**fur**, ur-under.   ( ) - suppress the syllable   see p. xiii for complete list.

Act 5 Scene 1

4. **sate** archaic variant of **sat**. May have been /sayt/ or /sat/.

9. **se offendendo** (F1) gravedigger's mistake for *se defendendo* 'in self-defense.' The older anglicized form would be /see ŏff in DEN doh/; US *also* /-awf-/. The more common restored Latin form is /say-/. Q2 has **so offended**.

> 12-48. **argal** /A̧RG ł/ the gravedigger's mistake for *ergo /UR go/ is older, /E̛R go/ is newer. The former is more common in the UK, the latter in the US, CN.

14. **goodman** (F1) /Go͞oD mun/ title of a man under the rank of gentleman. Q2 has **good man**.

23. **an't, on't** /unt/ of it.

28. **even-Christen** (Q2) /CRISS ņ/ fellow-Christian. Archaic variant of F1's **Christian**.

60. **get thee in** (Q2). F1 has **get thee to Yaughan** /YAWN, YAW un/. Some eds. substitute **Johan,** /YOH hahn/ referring to a local innkeeper.

60. **sup** (*soope* Q2) mouthful. F1 has **stoup** /sto͞op/ tankard.

63. **contract** /cun TRACT/ shorten.

63. **behove** /bih-, bee HOHV/ advantage.

89. **mazzard, mazard** /MAZ urd/ head.

92. **loggats** /LŎG uts/; US *also* /LAWG uts/ a game where blocks of wood are thrown at a stake.

102. **sconce** /skŏnss/ head.

105. *****recognizances** /rih CŎG nih zun siz/; *rarely older* [rih CŎN ih-] pledges before a court to perform specific acts.

138. **equivocation** /ih kwiv uh KAY shun/; US *also* /ee-/ using vague or deceptive answers in an argument.

173. **lien** (*lyen* Q2) /līn/ past participle of *lie* in some dialects.   F1 has **lain**.

180. **flagon** /FLAG un/ drinking vessel.

180. **Rhenish** /REN ish/ Rhine wine.

181, 184. **Yorick('s)** /YOR ik/; E.COAST US, UK /YŎR ik/.

189. **gibes** /jībz/ sarcastic comments.

189. **gambols** /GAM błz/ leaps, frolics.

213. **Imperious** (Q2) /im PEER yus/ imperial. **Imperiall** (F1) /im PEER ył/.

221. **Foredo** /for DOO/ destroy.

226. **obsequies** /ŎB suh kweez/ burial services.

227. **warranty** (Q2) authorization. Some eds. prefer **warrantise, -ize** (*warrantis* F1) US /WŌR un tīz/; UK, E.COAST US /WŎR un tīz/.

232. **crants** (Q2) /crănts/ garland. F1 has **rites**.

237. ***requiem** /REK w(ee) yum/ funeral music.

253. **Pelion** /PEE lee un/ mountain in NE Greece. Sometimes newer /-ŏn/ is used, but is not recommended.

261. **splenitive, splenative** /SPLEN uh tiv/ impetuous, quick-tempered.

274. **thou't** (*th'owt* Q2) /thowt/ archaic variant of F1's **thou'lt** /thowlt/.

275-6. **Woo't** /woot/ variant of **wilt** in the sense 'wilt thou.'

276. ***eisel** US, CN /EE zł/ [AY zł]; UK /AY zł, EE zł/ vinegar. /ĪZ ł/ not recommended.

278. **outface** here should be /OWT fayss/ outdo.

283. **Ossa** /ŎSS uh/ Greek mountain.

Act 5 Scene 2

6. **mutines** /MYOOT inz, -n̩z/ mutineers.

ă-bat, ăir-m**a**rry, air-p**ai**r, a̯r-f**a**r, ĕr-m**e**rry, ĝ- g**e**t, ī-h**i**gh, ĭr-m**i**rror, ł-litt**le**, n̩-listen, ŏ-h**o**t, oh-g**o**, o͞o-w**oo**d, o͞o-m**oo**n, oor-t**our**, ōr- **or**, ow-h**ow**, th-**th**at, th-**th**in, ŭ-b**u**t, UR-f**ur**, ur-und**er**.   ( ) - suppress the syllable   see p. xiii for complete list.

6. **bilboes** (F1) /BIL bohz/ shackles attached to a heavy iron bar. **bilbo** (Q2).

29. **benetted** /bih-, bee NET id/ caught in a net.

33. **statists** /STAYT ists/ statesmen.

36. **yeman's service** (Q2) /YEE munz/ solid service. Archaic variant of F1's **yeoman's** /YOH munz/.

42. **amities** /AM ih teez/ friendships.

44. **That on the view and knowing of these contents.** Usually /cŏn TENTS/ in Shk, but if *knowing* is pronounced with two syllables, mod. /CŎN tents/ may be used.

48. **ordinant** (Q2) /OR dih nunt/ guiding. F1 has **ordinate** /OR dih nut/ orderly, ordered.

54. **sequent** /SEE kwunt/ referring to what followed.

78. **portraiture** /POR truh chur/; UK *also* /-tyoor/ picture. See App. D *-ure.*

87. **chough, chuff** /chuf/ jackdaw.

---

lines 106-143 are found in Q2 but not in F1

112. **perdition** /pur DISH un/; UK *also* [PUR DISH un] loss.

116. ***extolment** praise. /ek STOHL munt/; UK *sometimes* and US *rarely* [-STŎL-].

118. **semblable** /SEM bluh bł/ likeness, equal.

119. **umbrage** /UM brij/ shadow.

---

147. **Barbary, Barb'ry** /BAR buh ree, BAR bree/ region in North Africa.

148. **impawn'd** (Q2) /im PAWND/. F1 has **impon'd** /im POHND/. Both mean 'wagered.'

149. **poniards** /PŎN yurdz/; UK *also newer* [-yardz] daggers.

155. **margent** /MAR junt/ archaic variant of **margin**. Omitted F1.

158. **germane** US /jur MAYN/; UK /JUR MAYN/ [JUR mayn] pertinent.

189. **breed** (Q2). F1 has **bevy** /BEV ee/ company.

189. **drossy** /DRŎSS ee/; US *also* /DRAWSS ee/ worthless.

219. ***augury** /AWG yur ee/ [AWG ur ee]; UK *also* /AWG yoor ree/ prediction of the future.

249. **president** archaic variant of ***precedent**, both /PRESS ih dunt/. It is not clear whether /PREZ-/ was used in Shk's time.

267. **stoups** /stōōps/ tankards.

272, 326. **union** (F1) pearl. Q2c, Q3-4 have **onyx** /ŎN iks/, *rarely* [OHN iks].

306. **springe** /sprinj/ snare.

308. **sounds** archaic variant of **swoons**. In Shk's time the vowel could be either /ow/ or /ōō/.

325. **incestious** (Q2) /in SESS chus/ archaic variant of F1's **incestuous** /in SESS chwus/; UK *also* /-tywus/.

341. ***antique** ancient. Here /AN teek/, *rarely older* [AN tik].

347. **Absent** /ub-, ab SENT/ keep away from.

355. **prophesy** /PRŎF uh sī/ predict the future.

365. **toward** here should be one syllable /tord/ about to take place.

374. **commandement**. Archaic variant of **commandment**, originally with 4 syllables, /-uh munt/, but here the usual mod. 3-syllable pronunciation is required.

394. ***mischance** in verse normally with 2nd syllable stress.

ă-bat, ăir-m**arry**, air-p**air**, ạr-f**ar**, ĕr-m**erry**, ĝ- g**et**, ī-h**igh**, ĭr-m**irror**, ł-l**ittle**, ṇ-l**isten**, ŏ-h**ot**, oh-g**o**, ōō-w**ood**, ōō-m**oon**, oor-t**our**, ōr- **or**, ow-h**ow**, ţh-**that**, th-**thin**, ŭ-b**ut**, UR-f**ur**, ur-**under**.   ( ) - suppress the syllable   see p. xiii for complete list.

Henry IV part one

People in the Play

Bardolph /BAR dŏlf/; US *also* /-dawlf/. Some eds. prefer **Russell**.

Bullingbrook Shk also spelled this name **Bullinbrook, Bullingbrooke, Bullinbrooke**, and pronounced it /BULL in brŏŏk/. Pope was the first to change it to **Bolingbroke** in the early 18th century. Today pronounced US, CN /BOHL ing brŏŏk/ [BULL-, BŎL-]; UK /BŎL-/, *rarely* [BULL-].

Drawer /DRAW ur/ tapster, the person who draws the liquor at a tavern.

Falstaff US /FAWL stăff/; E. NEW ENG., UK /-stahff/. Some eds. prefer **Oldcastle**.

Gadshill /GADZ hill/.

Glendower, Owen /GLEN dowr, GLEN dow ur/ or /glen DOWR, -DOW ur/ depending on meter. Some eds. prefer Welsh **Owain Glyndûr**, normally /OH īn/ or /OH in glin DŌŌR/, but with stress shifts as needed in verse.

Lancaster US /LANG kăst ur, -kᵘss tur/;
UK /LANG kᵘss tur/ [-kahst ur, -kăst ur].

Northumberland /north UM bur lund/.

Ostler /ŎSS lur/.

Peto /PEET oh/. Some eds. prefer **Harvey**.

Poins /poynz/.

Scroop /skrŏŏp/. Some eds. prefer mod. **Scrope**, pronounced the same way.

Westmerland archaic variant of **Westmor(e)land**, all pronounced /WEST mur lund/ in the UK. US is usually /west MOR lund/ which will not fit the meter.

Worcester /WŏŏS tur/.

Places in the Play

Gadshill /GADZ hill/.

*Ravenspurgh here should be 3 syllables /RAV in SPURG, -SPUR/ or
/RAY vin-/. Sometimes spelled **Ravenspur** /-SPUR/.

Shrewsbury 3 syllables in verse US /SHRŌOZ bĕr ee/ [SHROHZ-];
UK /SHROHZ bur ee/ [SHRŌOZ-], or in prose /-bree/.

A recurring word in this play

'sblood (Q1) /zblud/ God's (i.e., Jesus') blood. Omitted F1.

Act 1 Scene 1

1. **wan** /wŏn/ pale.

4. **stronds** /strŏndz/ shores. Archaic variant of **strands**.

12. **intestine** /in TESS tin/; UK *also* [-teen] internal.

13. **close** /clohz/ hand-to-hand combat.

16. **allies** here with 2nd syllable stress.

19. **sepulchre** /SEP ł kur/ tomb.

24. **pagans** /PAY gunz/ non-Christians.

39. **Herfordshire, Herefordshire**. In the US both would be /HUR furd shur/.
In the UK the county is normally /HĔR ih furd shur/ [-sheer] which here should
be 3 syllables /HĔR furd shur, -sheer/.

55-70. **Holmedon('s)** /HOHM dun/ mod. *Homildon, Humbleton.*

67. **discomfited** /dis CUM fit id/ defeated.

71, 95. **Mordake** /MOR dayk, -duk/. Some eds. prefer **Murdoch** /MUR dŏck/.

---

72. **Athol, Atholl** /ATH ł/.

ă-bat, ăir-**marry**, air-**pair**, ạr-far, ĕr-**merry**, ĝ- get, ī-high, ĭr-mirror, ł-little, ṇ-listen,
ŏ-hot, oh-go, ōō-wood, ōō-moon, oor-**tour**, ōr- or, ow-how, ţh-that, ŧh-thin, ŭ-but,
UR-**fur**, ur-under.   ( ) - suppress the syllable   see p. xiii for complete list.

73. **Murray** US /MUR ee/; E.COAST US, UK /MUH ree/. Some eds. prefer **Moray**, which in this case is pronounced the same way.

73. **Menteith** /men TEE~~TH~~/.

89. **Plantagenet** /plan TAJ ih nit/.

97. **Malevolent** /muh LEV uh lunt/ hostile.

Act 1 Scene 2

7. *__capons__ US /KAY pŏnz, -punz/; CN, UK /KAY pŏnz/ [-punz] chickens. See App. D *-on.*

10. **taffata, taffeta** /TAF uh tuh/ a silk-like cloth.

15. **Phoebus** /FEE bus/ god of the sun.

34. **dissolutely** /DIS uh lo͞ot lee/ riotously (for /lyo͞o-/ see App. D *lu-*).

41. **Hybla** /HĪ bluh/ region of Sicily.

43. *__durance__ /DYOOR unss/; US *also* /Do͞oR-/ [DUR-] double meaning: durability, prison clothes.

74. **gib** /ĝib/ male cat.

76. **Lincolnshire** /LINK un shur/ [sheer].

78. **Moor-ditch** /MOOR ditch/ [MOR-].

90. **iteration** /it ur AY shun/ repetition (of scriptures).

109. **omnipotent** /ŏm NIP uh tunt/ all-powerful.

116. **Madeira** /muh DEER uh/ type of wine.

116. *__capon's__ US /KAY pŏnz, -punz/; CN, UK /KAY pŏnz/ [-punz] chicken's. See App. D *-on.*

128, 178. *__vizards__ /VIZ urdz/ masks. /-ạrdz/ not recommended. Some eds. prefer **visors**.

158. **All-hallown summer** /awl HAL ohn, -un/; US *also* /HŎL-/ Indian Summer.

172. **exploit** /ek SPLOYT/ in verse, but here may be mod. /EK sployt/.

179. **buckrom, buckram** /BUCK rum/ course linen cloth stiffened with paste.

180. ***nonce** /nŏnss/ occasion. US, CN [nunss] not recommended.

196. **unyok'd** here should be /UN yohkt/ undisciplined.

Act 1 Scene 3

11. **scourge** /SKURJ/ instrument of punishment.

13. **holp** /hohlp/ helped.

17. **peremptory** overbearing. Here stressed on the first syllable, either /PĔR um tur ee/; US *also* /-tor ee/, or /PĔR um tree/.

19. **frontier** here should be /FRUN teer/ [FRŎN-] i.e., forehead.

24. **Holmedon** /HOHM dun/ mod. *Homildon, Humbleton.*

27. **misprision** here expanded to /mis PRIZH ee un/ misunderstanding.

31. **extreme** here should be /EK streem/.

36. **mllllner** /MILL ih nur/ seller of fancy goods.

38. **pouncet-box** /POWN sit-/ perfume box.

43. **untaught** here should be /UN tawt/.

44. **slovenly** /SLUV un lee/ messy.

50. **popingay** /PŎP in gay/ parrot. Archaic variant of **popinjay**.

58. **parmaciti** fatty substance in whales, used as an ointment. A variant of **parmacity**, both pronounced /par muh SIT ee/. Other eds. prefer **parmaceti, parmacety** /par muh SET ee, -SEE tee/, mod. ***spermaceti** /SPURM uh SET ee, -SEE tee/.

60. ***saltpetre, -peter** a component of gunpowder. Here should be /sawlt PEET ur/, a pronunciation used with /SAWLT peet ur/ in all countries.

ă-bat, ăir-marry, air-pair, ạr-far, ĕr-merry, ĝ- get, ī-high, ĭr-mirror, ł-little, ṇ-listen, ŏ-hot, oh-go, ŏŏ-wood, ōō-moon, oor-tour, ōr- or, ow-how, ţh-that, ŧh-thin, ŭ-but, UR-fur, ur-under.   ( ) - suppress the syllable   see p. xiii for complete list.

78. **proviso** /pruh VĪ zoh/ stipulation.

98, 103. **Severn's** /SEV urnz/.

107. **combatants** here should be stressed on the first syllable as is usual in the UK /CŎM buh tunts/ [CUM-].

113. **belie him** /bih-, bee LĪ/ not tell the truth about him.

128. **Albeit** /awl BEE (i)t/ although.

137. **ingrate** here should be /in GRAYT/ ungrateful.

191. **adventerous** /ad VENT rus/ archaic variant of **adventurous**.

199. **exploit** here should be /ek SPLOYT/.

204. **fadom-line** /FAD um-/ archaic variant of **fathom-** /FĂTH um-/ rope used for measuring depth.

207. **corrival** /coh-, cuh RĪ vł/ rival.

222. **hollow, hollo** /HŎL uh, -oh/ call.

232. *****mischance** in verse normally with 2nd syllable stress.

234. **Farewell** /FAIR ee wel/ (from *Fare thee well*) may have been intended, though our usual pronunciation is possible in a headless line.

239. **scourg'd** /SKURJD/ harshly punished.

240. *****pismires** /PISS mīrz/; US *also* [PIZ mīrz] ants.

243. **Gloucestershire** /GLŎSS tur shur/ [-sheer]; US *also* /GLAWSS-/.

249. **Berkeley** US /BURK lee/; UK /BARK lee/.

262. *****divers** various. Here should be stressed on the first syllable US, CN /DĪ vurss, -vurz/; UK /DĪ vurss/ [-vurz].

267. **prelate** /PREL ut/ high-ranking churchman.

268. **The Archbishop** here should be /ARCH bish up/ if *the* is pronounced fully, or if compressed /ᵗh^yarch BISH up/ as in mod. Eng.

271. **Bristow** /BRIST oh/ archaic variant of **Bristol** /BRIST ł/.

Act 2 Scene 1

1. ***Heigh-ho!*** US /hay ho, hī-/; CN /hī-/, *rarely* [hay-]; UK /hay-/. Shk intended /hay/. Spoken with evenly stressed syllables or as if sighing, with 1st syllable stress.

17. **christen** /CRISS n̩/ archaic variant of **christian**.

24. **gammon of bacon** /GAM un/ ham.

25. **Charing Cross** US /chăir ing CRAWSS/; UK /-CRŎSS/ [chair-].

26. **pannier** /PAN ee ur, PAN yur/ large basket.

55. **Wild.** Some eds. prefer **Weald** /weeld/ a forest in SE Eng.

75. **mustachio** moustache. US /muh STASH ee oh/ [muh STASH oh, -STAHSH-]; UK /muh STAHSH ee yoh/ [-STASH-].

76. **burgomasters** US /BUR guh măss turz/; UK /-mahss turz/ mayors.

76. **great oney'rs** /WUN yurz/ great ones. Other suggestions include ***oyez-ers*** /OH yez urz/ [OH yay urz] 'court officials,' **moneyers** /MUN ee urz/ 'rich men,' **owners, mynheers** /mīn HEERZ, -HAIRZ/ 'gentlemen,' **wonners** /WUN urz/ or /WOHN urz/ 'dwellers,' **younkers** /YŬNG kurz/ 'young lords.'

Act 2 Scene 2

3-97. **Stand close** /clohss/ keep hidden.

12. **squier** /skwīr/ archaic variant of **square** 'carpenter's square.'

24. **veriest** /VĔR ee ist/ most exceeding.

36, 55. ***exchequer*** /eks CHEK ur/; US *rarely* [EKS chek ur] treasury.

42. **ostler** /ŎSS lur/ person who tends the horses.

ă-bat, ăir-**ma**rry, air-**pair**, a̦r-**far**, ĕr-**me**rry, ĝ- get, ī-high, ĭr-mirror, ł-**li**ttle, n̩-**li**sten, ŏ-hot, oh-go, o͝o-wood, o͞o-moon, oor-**tour**, ōr- **or**, ow-**how**, t̠h-**that**, t̶h̶-**thin**, ŭ-but, UR-**fur**, ur-**un**der.   ( ) - suppress the syllable   see p. xiii for complete list.

53. *vizards /VIZ urdz/ masks. /-ardz/ not recommended. Some eds. prefer visors.

67. Gaunt /gawnt/ Hal's grandfather.

The Complete Oxford begins 2.3 here (line nos. in parentheses).

100. (2.3.8) arrant /ĂIR unt/ thoroughgoing.

Act 2 Scene 3 (*Complete Oxford* 2.4)

stage direction: solus /SOH lŭss/ alone.

15. hind /hīnd/ menial laborer.

29. pagan /PAYG un/ non-Christian.

38. fortnight /FORT nīt/; US *also* [FORT nit] two weeks. Virtually obsolete in the US.

49. manage. Some eds. prefer manège US /mah NEZH, -NAYZH/; UK /man AYZH/ [-EZH, MAN ayzh]; Fr. /mah nezh/. Both words mean 'horsemanship.'

52. palisadoes defences made of stakes. /pal ih SAY dohz/ is older, but a newer spelling pronunciation /-SAH-/ is also used.

52. frontiers here with 1st syllable stress /FRUN teerz/ [FRŎN-] fortifications.

52. parapets /PĂIR uh pets, -pits/ walls of a fortification.

53. *basilisks canons. US /BĂSS ih lisks/ [BAZ ih lisks]; UK /BAZ-/ [BĂSS-]; CN both used equally.

53. culverin /CŬL vur in/ an early type of canon.

62. portents here should be /por TENTS/ omens.

65. Gilliams /ĜILL yumz/.

71. Esperance angl. /ES pur unss/; Fr. /es pĕr ah^{n}ss/ hope.

85. paraquito /păir uh KEE toh/ parakeet.

92. **mammets** /MAM its/ dolls. Variant of **maumets** /MAW mits/.

Act 2 Scene 4 (*Complete Oxford* 2.5)

7-91. **drawer(s)** /DRAW ur/ tapster, the person who draws the liquor at a
tavern.

8. **christen** /CRISS ṇ/ archaic variant of **Christian**.

23, 59. **pennyworth** the older form is /PEN urth/, but in these prose passages
the newer spelling pronunciation /PEN ee wurth, -WURTH/ may be used.

25. **sixpence** /SIKS punss, -pṇs/; US *also* /SIKS penss/.

33. **president** (F1) example. Archaic variant of *ᐧ**precedent**, both
/PRESS ih dunt/. It is not clear whether /PREZ-/ was used in Shk's time.

38. **Pomgarnet** /PUM-, PŎM gar nit/ room in the tavern. Archaic variant of
*ᐧ**Pomegranate** US, CN /PŎM uh gran it/; US *also* [PUM-, PŎM gran it,
PUM ih gran it]; UK /PŎM uh gran it/ [PŎM gran it].

45-424. **by'r lady** /bīr-, bur LAY dee/ by Our Lady (i.c., Mary).

54. **Michaelmas** /MIK ł mus/ Sept. 29.

70. **agate-ring** /AG ut/ a jewel.

70. **caddis-garter** /KAD iss/ worsted-taped garters.

75. **Barbary** /BAR buh ree/ region in North Africa.

93. **goodman** /GŌŌD mun/ title of a man under the rank of gentleman.

111. **Rivo!** /REE voh/ drink up!

119. *ᐧ**extant** in existence. US /EK stunt/ [ek STĂNT]; UK /ek STĂNT/, *rarely*
[EK stunt]; in CN both are used equally.

137. **lath** US /lăth/; UK, E. NEW ENG. /lahth/ [lăth] narrow strip of wood.

ă-bat, ăir-**marry**, air-**pair**, ạr-**far**, ĕr-**merry**, ĝ- **get**, ī-**high**, ĭr-**mirror**, ł-**little**, ṇ-**listen**,
ŏ-**hot**, oh-**go**, ōō-**wood**, ōō-**moon**, oor-**tour**, ōr- **or**, ow-**how**, ṭh-**that**, th-**thin**, Ŭ-**but**,
UR-**fur**, ur-**under**.   ( ) - suppress the syllable   see p. xiii for complete list.

169. **ecce signum** Ang.Lat. /EK see SIG num/; Class.Lat. /EK ay SIG nōōm/ behold the proof (or sign).

193-219. **buckrom, buckram** /BUCK rum/ course linen cloth stiffened with paste.

222-232. **Kendal green** /KEN dł/ named after a town in Westmoreland.

237. ***strappado** a type of torture. /struh PAH doh/; UK *rarely older* [struh PAY doh].

242. **sanguine** /SANG gwin/ red-faced.

280, 316. **extempore** /ek STEM pur ree/ on the spur of the moment.

320. **exhalations** /eks huh LAY shunz, eks uh-/ [egz uh-] meteors.

327. **bumbast** /BUM băst/ cotton stuffing. Variant of **bombast** formerly pronounced the same way, though now /BŎM băst/ is the only pronunciation used.

330. **talent** /TAL unt/ archaic variant of **talon**.

336. **Amamon** /uh MAY mun/ a devil. Sometimes newer /-mŏn/ is used. See App. D -*on*.

337. ***bastinado** beating with a stick. /bas tih NAH doh/; UK *rarely older* [bas tih NAY doh].

357. **Mordake** /MOR dayk, -duk/. Some eds. prefer **Murdoch** /MUR dŏck/.

362. **buffeting** /BUFF it ing/ fighting.

380. **join'd stool** /JOYND stōōl/ a well-crafted stool. Some eds. prefer **joint stool**.

387. **in King Cambyses' vein** /kam BĪ seez/ ranting. A newer pronunciation /-zeez/ is also used.

395. **harlotry** /HAR luh tree/ scoundrely.

400. ***camomile** /KAM uh mīl/; US, CN *also* /-meel/. /-īl/ is older.

408. **micher** /MITCH ur/ truant.

429. **peremptorily** /pur EM tur ih lee/ decisively.

437. **poulter's** /POHL turz/ seller of poultry.

451. **bombard** /BŎM bard/ leather bottle.   /BUM burd/ is an archaic variant.

456-535. ***capon** US /KAY pŏn, -pun/; CN, UK /KAY pŏn/ [-pun] chicken.   See App. D *-on*.

463. **Sathan** archaic form of **Satan**, both pronounced /SAYT n̩, -un/ the devil.

487. ***Heigh!** US /hay, hī/; CN /hī/, *rarely* [hay]; UK /hay/.   Shk intended /hay/.

500-528. **arras** /ĂIR us/ tapestry.

535-9. Falstaff's bill reads:
2s. 2d. *two shillings and tuppence* /TUP unss, -n̩ss/
4d. *fourpence* /FOR punss, -pn̩ss/
5s. 8d. *five shillings and eightpence* /AYT punss, -pn̩ss/
2s. 6d. *two shillings and sixpence* /SIKS punss, -pn̩ss/
ob. (*obulus* /ŎB uh lus/) stands for *ha'pence* /HAYP n̩ss, -unss/.
2s. 2d., etc. could also be read *two shillings tuppence* or *two and tuppence.*

538. **anchoves** archaic variant of ***anchovies.**   Shk probably said /AN chuh veez/, a pronunciation used today along with /AN choh veez/ or /an CHOH veez/ in all countries.

540. **half-pennyworth** /HAYP nee WUR̶T̶H̶/.

542. **keep close** /clohss/ keep secret.

Act 3 Scene 1

28. **colic** /CŎL ik/ stomach ache.

31. ***beldame** grandmother.   Some eds. prefer **beldam**, both pronounced the same US /BEL dam, -dum/; UK /BEL dam/, *rarely* [-dum].   /-daym/ is also used, but normal development would probably favor /-dam, -dum/.

33. ***grandam** /GRAN dam/; US *rarely* [-dum] grandmother.   Informally /GRAN um/.

ă-bat, ăir-marry, air-pair, ạr-far, ĕr-merry, ĝ- get, ī-high, ĭr-mirror, ł-little, n̩-listen, ŏ-hot, oh-go, ōō-wood, ōō-moon, oor-tour, ōr- or, ow-how, t̩h-that, t̶h̶-thin, ŭ-but, UR-fur, ur-under.   ( ) - suppress the syllable   see p. xiii for complete list.

40. **extraordinary** here main stress should fall on the third syllable US /ek struh OR dih něr ee/; UK /-dih nuh ree/, or reduced to /-dn̦ ree/.

64. **Wye** /wī/ river in Wales.

65-75. **Severn** /SEV urn/.

68. **agues** /AY gyо̄о̄z/ malarial fevers.

79. **tripartite** here should be /TRĪ par tīt/ in three parts.

95. **moi'ty, moiety** /MOY tee/ portion.

128. **ballet-mongers** sellers of songs. US /BAL ut mŏng gurz/ or /-mawng-/ [-mung-]; CN /-mung gurz, -mŏng gurz/; UK /-mung gurz/. *Ballet* is an archaic variant of **ballad**.

129. **brazen** /BRAY zun, -zn̦/ brass.

138. **cavil** /KAV ł/; UK *also* /KAV il/ quibble.

161. **cates** /kayts/ delicacies.

182. **Defect** here may be /DEE fect/ or /dih FECT/; US *also* /dee-/.

196. **harlotry** /HAR luh tree/ hussy.

201. *****parley** /PAR lee/ conference with an enemy. Newer [-lay] not recommended.

231. **By'r lady** /bīr-, bur LAY dee/ by Our Lady (i.e., Mary).

235. **brach** /bratch/ female dog.

248. **comfit-maker's** /CUM fit/ [CŎM fit] candy maker's.

251. **sarcenet, sarsenet** /SAR snit/ fine silk, hence 'flimsy.'

251. *****surety** guarantee. Here should be two syllables, though in mod. English, three syllables are more common, /SHUR (ih) tee, SHOOR-, SHOR-/ (see App. D).

252. **Finsbury** US /FINZ b(ě)r ee/; UK /-b(u)r ee/ North of London.

255. **protest** here 2nd syllable stress is indicated.

Act 3 Scene 2

7. **scourge** /SKURJ/ punishment.

25. **newsmongers** newspeddlers. US /-mŏng gurz/ or /-mawng-/ [-mung-];
CN /-mung gurz, -mŏng gurz/; UK /-mung gurz/.

59. **wan** possibly /wŏn/, archaic variant of **won**.

61. **bavin** /BAV in/ bundle of brushwood, kindling.

66. **gibing** /JĪ bing/ sarcastic.

69. ***Enfeoff'd** put a person in possession of lands, i.e., surrendered.
/en FEEFT/, UK *rarely older* [en FEFT].

78. **extraordinary** here main stress should fall on the third syllable
US /ek struh OR dih nĕr ee/; UK /-dih nuh ree/.

107. **renowmed** /rih-, ree NOW mid/ archaic variant of **renowned**
/rih-, ree NOWN id/.

112. **swathling** /SWŎṬH ling/ or /SWAYṬH ling/ archaic variant of **swaddling**
/SWŎD ling/.

114. **Discomfited** /dis CUM fit id/ defeated.

145. **northren** /NORṬH run/ archaic variant of **northern**.

155. ***salve** heal. US /salv/ [sav]; NEW ENG. *also* [sahv];
CN /salv/ [sahlv, sav, sahv]; UK /salv/. Normal development would favor
the *l*-less form (cf. *halve, calve*).

172. **advertisement** here should be /ad VURT iss munt, -iz-/ news.

175, 178. **Bridgenorth, Bridgnorth** /BRIJ north/.

176. **Gloucestershire** /GLŎSS tur shur/ [-sheer]; US *also* /GLAWSS-/.

ă-bat, ăir-ma**rr**y, air-pa**ir**, ạr-f**ar**, ĕr-me**rr**y, ĝ- g**e**t, ī-h**igh**, ĭr-mi**rr**or, ł-litt**le**, ṇ-liste**n**,
ŏ-h**o**t, oh-g**o**, o͞o-w**oo**d, o͞o-m**oo**n, oor-t**our**, ōr- **or**, ow-h**ow**, ṭh-**th**at, th-**th**in, ŭ-b**u**t,
UR-f**ur**, ur-und**er**.   ( ) - suppress the syllable   see p. xiii for complete list.

Act 3 Scene 3

30. **memento mori** Ang.Lat. /muh MEN toh MOR ī/;
Class.Lat. /mem EN toh MOR ee/ reminder of death.

32. **Dives** /DĪ veez/ rich man in the Bible.

39. **ignis fatuus** US /IG niss FATCH oo us/; UK /FAT yoo us/ will o' the wisp.

57. **tithe** /tīţh/ tenth part.

69. **Dowlas** /DOW lus/ course linen.

79. **denier** coin of little value. /duh NEER, DEN yur/ are older;
/DEN yay, den YAY/ are newer, based on Fr.

80. **younker** /YŬNG kur/ fashionable young man.

90. **Newgate** a London prison. /NYŌŌ gut/ is older and rarer, especially in
North America. The US variant is /NŌŌ-/. /-gayt/ is newer and more common.

98. **arras** /ĂIR us/ tapestry.

134. **ought** /awt/ archaic variant of **owed**.

159. **pennyworth** the older form is /PEN urţh/, but in this prose passage the
newer spelling pronunciation /PEN ee wurth, -WURŦH/ may be used.

172. **guesse** /ĜESS/ (*ghesse* Q1) archaic variant of F1's **guests**.

183. *****exchequer** /eks CHEK ur/; US *rarely* [EKS chek ur] treasury.

189. *****heinously** /HAYN us lee/ terribly. /HEEN us lee/ is non-standard though
common in the UK.

Act 4 Scene 1

18. **justling** /JUSS ling/ turbulent. Archaic variant of **jostling** /JŎS ling/.

36. **advertisement** here should be /ad VURT iss munt, -iz-/ advice.

46. **exact** here should be /EG zact/.

58. *****mischance** in verse normally with 2nd syllable stress.

70. **arbitrement, arbitrament** /ạr BIT ruh munt/ inspection.

96.*comrades here with 2nd syllable stress US, CN /cŏm RADZ/, *rarely* [cum-];
UK /cŏm RAYDZ/, *rarely* [-RADZ, cum-].

96. **daff'd** /dăft/ thrust aside. Archaic variant of **doffed** /dŏft/; US *also* /dawft/.

102. **midsummer** here should be /MID sum ur/.

105. **cushes** perhaps /KŏŏSH iz/ armor for thighs. Variant of **cuisses**
/KWISS iz/ which some eds prefer. Others prefer **cuishes** /KWISH iz/.

105. **gallantly** is in an inverted foot, pronounced as in mod. Eng. /GAL unt lee/.

109. **wind** /wīnd/ turn a horse.

112. **agues** /AY gyŏŏz/ malarial fevers.

125. **Worcester** /WŏŏS tur/.

Act 4 Scene 2

1, 39. **Coventry** US /KUV n̞ tree/; UK /KŎV n̞ tree/ [KUV-].

3. **Sutton Co'fil', Cophill** /SUT n̞ COH fil/ or /COH feel/ archaic variant of
mod. **Sutton Coldfield** /COHLD feeld/.

12. **sous'd** /sowst/ pickled.

12. **gurnet** /GUR nit/ type of fish.

15. **yeomen's** /YOH minz/ freemen who own small farms.

17. **banes** /baynz/ proclamation in church of an intended marriage. Archaic
variant of **banns** /banz/.

18. **as lieve** /leev/ 'as soon,' still used in some US dialects. Some eds. prefer **lief**
/leef/.

19. **caliver** /KAL ih vur/ light musket.

ă-bat, äir-**marry**, air-**pair**, ạr-**far**, ĕr-**merry**, ĝ- get, ī-high, ĭr-**mirror**, ł-little, n̞-listen, ŏ-hot, oh-go, ŏŏ-wood, ōō-moon, oor-**tour**, ōr- or, ow-how, ţh-that, ŧh-thin, ŭ-but, UR-**fur**, ur-**under**.   ( ) - suppress the syllable   see p. xiii for complete list.

24, 31. **ancient(s)** /AYN chunt/ archaic variant of the rank **ensign** US /EN sn̩/; UK /-sīn/.

25. **Lazarus** /LAZ uh russ/ beggar in Jesus' parable.

29. **ostlers** /ŎSS lurz/ innkeepers.

31. **feaz'd** /feezd/ frayed. Some eds. prefer **faced**.

35. **draff** /drăf/ pig swill.

37. **gibbets** /JIB its/ posts from which they hung corpses after hanging.

41. **gyves** /jīvz/ chains, fetters.

46. **Saint Albons** archaic variant of **St. Albans**. Both pronounced US /saynt AWL bunz/; UK /sint-, sn̩t-/.

47. **Daventry** /DAV in tree/, pronounced /DAYN tree/ locally.

51. **Warwickshire** US /WŌR ik shur/ [-sheer]; E.COAST US, UK /WŎR-/. Place names in the US often have /-wik-/ but this is not recommended for Shk.

67. **Tush** /tŭsh/ expression of disdain.

Act 4 Scene 3

69. **boroughs** towns. US /BUR ohz/ [-uz]; E.COAST US /BUH rohz/ [-ruz]; UK /BUH ruz/.

79. **edicts** /EE dicts/ decrees.

109. ***surety** guarantee. Here should be two syllables, though in mod. English, three syllables is more common, /SHUR (ih) tee, SHOOR-, SHOR-/ (see App. D).

Act 4 Scene 4

2. **Marshal** here an archaic form /MAR uh shł/ is indicated.

24. **Mordake** /MOR dayk, -duk/. Some eds. prefer **Murdoch** /MUR dŏck/.

31. **corrivals** (F1), **corivals** (Q1-6) /coh-, cuh RĪ vłz/ associates.

Act 5 Scene 1

3. **southren** /SUȚH run/ archaic variant of **southern**.

19. **exhal'd** here with 1st syllable stress, /EKS hayld/, the normal US form.

20. **portent** here should be /por TENT/ omen.

21. **unborn** here should be /UN born/.

29. **chewet** /CHŌŌ it/ jackdaw.

42, 58. **Doncaster** US /DŎNG kăss tur/ [DŎNG kᵘss tur];
UK /DŎNG kᵘss tur/ [-kahss tur, -kăss tur].

45. **Gaunt** /gawnt/ Hal's grandfather.

69. **unkind** here should be /UN kīnd/.

72. **articulate** /ạr TIK yuh layt, -lut/ articulated, i.e, stated in articles.

102. **Albeit** /awl BEE (i)t/ although.

123. **Colossus** /kuh LŎS us/ giant.

140. **scutcheon** /SKUTCH un/ escutcheon, heraldic device often shown at funerals.

141. **catechism** /KAT uh kiz um, -kizm/ series of questions and answers.

Act 5 Scene 2

39. **scourge** /SKURJ/ punish harshly.

49. **Monmouth** /MŎN muth/; UK *also* [MUN-].

61. **cital** /SĪT ł/ recital.

68. **misconstrued** here should be /mis CŎN strōōd/.

96. **Esperance** angl. /ES pur unss/; Fr. /es pĕr ahⁿss/ hope. The final *e* may have been sounded /uh/ to make the line scan correctly.

ă-bat, ăir-**marry**, air-**pair**, ạr-**far**, ĕr-**merry**, ĝ- **get**, ī-high, ĭr-**mirror**, ł-little, ṇ-listen,
ŏ-hot, oh-go, ōō-wood, ōō-moon, oor-**tour**, ōr- **or**, ow-how, țh-**that**, th-thin, ŭ-but,
UR-**fur**, ur-under.   ( ) - suppress the syllable   see p. xiii for complete list.

Act 5 Scene 3

14. **Holmedon** /HOHM dun/ mod. *Homildon, Humbleton.*

21. **Semblably** /SEM bluh blee/ similarly.

27. **wardrop** /WŌR drup/ or perhaps /-drŏp/, archaic variant of **wardrobe** which some eds. prefer.

stage direction after 28: **solus** /SOH lŭss/ alone.

58. ***carbonado** slashed meat. /car buh NAH doh/; UK *rarely older* [-NAY doh].

Act 5 Scene 4

23. **ungrown** here should be /UN grohn/.

34. **assay thee** /uh-, ass SAY/ make trial of thee.

45, 58. **Gawsey** /GAW zee, -see/.

45. **succor** (UK **succour**) /SUCK ur/ help. See App. D -*or.*

59. **Monmouth** /MŎN muth/; UK *also* [MUN-].

82. **survey** here should be /sur VAY/.

83. **prophesy** /PRŎF uh sī/ to predict the future.

100. **ignominy** /IG nuh min ee/ disgrace.

114. **termagant** /TUR muh gunt/ violent.

159. **retrait** /rih-, ree TRAYT/ archaic variant of **retreat**.

Act 5 Scene 5

37. **prelate** /PREL ut/ high-ranking churchman.

Henry IV part two

People in the Play

Ancient (Pistol) /AYN chunt/ is an archaic variant of the rank **Ensign** US /EN sn̩/; UK /-sīn/.

Archbishop (Scroop) usually /ARCH bish up/, but mod. /arch BISH up/ at 2.1.175 and in prose.

Bardolph /BAR dŏlf/; US *also* /-dawlf/.

Beadle /BEE dł/ this word is not spoken.

Bullingbrook Shk also spelled this name **Bullinbrook, Bullingbrooke, Bullinbrooke,** and pronounced it /BU̩LL in brōōk/. Pope was the first to change it to **Bolingbroke** in the early 18th century. Today pronounced US, CN /BOHL ing brōōk/ [BU̩LL-, BŎL-]; UK /BŎL-/, *rarely* [BU̩LL-].

Coleville /KOHL vil/ or /KOHL uh vil/ depending on meter.

Drawers /DRAW urz/ tapsters, the people who draw the liquor at a tavern.

Falstaff US /FAWL stăff/; E. NEW ENG., UK /-stahff/.

Gloucester /GLŎS tur/; US *also* /GLAWSS-/.

Gower /GOW ur/.

Harcourt /HAR cort/ [-curt].

Lancaster US /LANG kăst ur, -kᵘss tur/; UK /LANG kᵘss tur/ [-kahst ur, -kăst ur].

Monmouth (Prince Henry) /MŎN muth/; UK *also* [MUN-].

Mowbray, Mowbrey both pronounced /MOH bree/ [-bray]. The latter is the traditional form.

Northumberland /north UM bur lund/.

ă-bat, ăir-m**arry**, air-p**air**, a̩r-f**ar**, ĕr-m**erry**, ĝ- g**et**, ī-high, ĭr-m**irror**, ł-little, n̩-listen, ŏ-hot, oh-go, ōō-wood, ōō-moon, oor-t**our**, ōr- or, ow-how, t̪h-t**hat**, t̪h-t**hin**, ŭ-but, UR-f**ur**, ur-und**er**.   ( ) - suppress the syllable   see p. xiii for complete list.

People in the Play (cont.)

Peto /PEET oh/.

Pistol, Ancient see **Ancient**.

Poins /poynz/.

Scroop /skrōōp/. Some eds. prefer mod. **Scrope**, pronounced the same way.

Surrey US /SUR ee/; UK, E.COAST US /SUH ree/.

Tearsheet, Doll /TAIR sheet/ which means 'sheet of the finest quality.'

Warwick US /WŌR ik/; E.COAST US, UK /WŎR-/. Place names in the US often have /-wik/ but this is not recommended for Shk.

Westmerland archaic variant of **Westmor(e)land**, all pronounced /WEST mur lund/ in the UK. US is usually /west MOR lund/ which will not fit the meter.

Places in the Play

Shrewsbury 3 syllables in verse US /SHRŌŌZ bĕr ee/ [SHROHZ-]; UK /SHROHZ bur ee/ [SHRŌŌZ-], or in prose /-bree/.

Induction

9. *****covert** secret. Here should be stressed on the 1st syllable US, CN /KOHV urt/ [KUV-]; UK /KUV-/ [KOHV-], *rarely* [KŎV-].

21. **anatomize** /uh NAT uh mīz/ explain.

Act 1 Scene 1

8. **stratagem** /STRAT uh jum/ scheme.

32. **retail** repeat to others. Here should be /rih-, ree TAYL/.

34. **Umfrevile** here /um FREV il/ is indicated, though /UM frih vil/ is more usual. Some eds. prefer **Lord Bardolph** /BAR dŏlf/; US *also* /-dawlf/.

46. **rowel-head** disc with points at the end of a spur. /ROW ł/ as in *how*.

54. **barony** /BĂIR un ee/ lands of a baron.

57. **hilding** /HILL ding/ good-for-nothing.

59. **venter** /VEN tur/ archaic variant of **venture**.

62. **strond** /strŏnd/ shore. Archaic variant of **strand**.

62. **imperious** /im PEER yus/ imperial.

69. **arrand** /ĂIR und/ archaic variant of **errand**.

72, 74. ***Priam('s)** King of Troy. US, CN /PRĪ um/ [-am]; UK /-am/, *rarely* [-um]. Normal development would favor /-um/.

86. **instinct** here should be /in STINCT/.

91. ***gainsaid** /gayn SED/ [-SAYD] denied.

98. **belie** /bih-, bee LĪ/ lie.

103. **tolling** (Q). Some eds. prefer F1's **knolling** /NOHL ing/ with the same meaning.

114. **bruited** /BRŌOT id/ rumored.

125. **Worcester** /WŌoS tur/.

147. **coif** /coyf/ tight-fitting cap worn by the sick.

163. **complices** /CŎM pliss iz/ accomplices.

167. **the accompt** /thʸuh COWNT/ archaic variant of **account**. See App. D.

168. **presurmise** /pree sur MĪZ/ previously formed opinion.

191.***surety** pledge. Here should be two syllables, though in mod. English, three syllables is more common, /SHUR (ih) tee, SHOOR-, SHOR-/ (see App. D).

205. **Pomfret** US /PŎM frit/; UK /PUM frit/ [PŎM-].

ă-bat, ăir-ma**rr**y, air-**pair**, ạr-**far**, ĕr-me**rr**y, ĝ- get, ī-high, ĭr-mi**rr**or, ł-little, ṇ-listen, ŏ-hot, oh-go, ŏŏ-wood, ōō-moon, oor-**tour**, ōr- **or**, ow-how, ţh-that, t̶h̶-thin, ŭ-but, UR-**fur**, ur-und**er**.   ( ) - suppress the syllable   see p. xiii for complete list.

Act 1 Scene 2

16. **agot** a type of jewel. Archaic variant of **agate**, both pronounced /AG ut/.

19. **juvenal** /JOO vin ł/ youth.

25. **sixpence** /SIKS punss, -pn̩ss/; US *also* /SIKS penss/.

29. **Dommelton** (Q), **Dumbleton** /DUM ł tun/, **Dombledon** (F1) /DUM ł dun/ simpleton.

35. **Achitophel** /uh KIT uh fel/ Absalom's counsellor.

41. **as live** as soon. May have been /liv/ in Shk's time. Variant of **as lief** /leef/. In the US **lieve** /leev/ is still found in some dialects and can also be used here.

48. **lanthorn** archaic variant of **lantern**. Probably usually pronounced /LAN turn/, but possibly /LANT horn/ or /LAN ~~thurn~~, -thorn/. Here the /-horn/ pronunciation is necessary for a pun on a cuckold's horns.

57. **close** /clohss/ nearby.

90. **avaunt** /uh VAWNT/ begone!

98. **ague** (Q) /AY gyoo/ malarial fever. Some eds. prefer F1's **age.**

108, 111. **apoplexy** /AP uh plek see/ paralysis.

117. **Galen** /GAY lin/ Gk. doctor.

126. **Job** /johb/.

149. **exploit** /ek SPLOYT/ in verse, but here may be mod. /EK sployt/.

149. **Gadshill** /GADZ hill/; UK *sometimes* with equal stress.

158. ***wassail candle** large candle for feasts. US /WŎSS ł, wŏss AYL/ [WŎSS ayl], *rarely* [WĂSS ł]; CN /WŎSS ł, WŎSS ayl, wŏss AYL/; UK /WĂSS ayl/ [WŎSS ayl, wŏss AYL]. Normal development would favor /WŎSS-/.

169. **costermongers'** petty tradesman. US /CŎS tur mŏng gurz/ or /-mawng-/ [-mung-]; CN /-mung-, -mŏng-/; UK /-mung-/.

169. **berrord** (*Berod* Q) bearkeeper. Archaic variant of **bearward** or F1's **bearherd**. All were pronounced /BAIR urd/, but recent spelling pronunciations /BAIR hurd/, /-wârd/ (as in *war*) are also used today.

176. ***vaward*** US /VAW wurd, VAY-/ [VOW-]; UK /VAW wurd/ [VAY-, VOW-, VAW WURD]. The vowel of *war* not recommended in the second syllable. Archaic variant of **vanguard**. See App. D -*aun*-.

190. **hallowing, halloing** /HAL-, HŎL oh ing/ shouting to the hounds in hunting.

228. **fillip** /FILL ip/ strike smartly.

Act 1 Scene 3

9. ***puissance*** power (i.e., army). Here should be 2 syllables. The traditional forms are /PWISS nss/, /PYŌŌ snss/, but today /PWEE snss/ is most common (see App. D).

59. **thorough** archaic variant of *through*, pronounced as *thorough*. Used when the meter demands two syllables. Here at the end of a line some eds. prefer **through**, since the two-syllable form creates a superfluous feminine ending.

72. **Glendower** here should be /glen DOWR/ or /-DOW ur/. Some eds prefer Welsh **Glyndûr** /glin DŌŌR/.

73. **unfirm** here should be /UN furm/.

77. ***puissance*** strength. Here 3 syllables, traditionally /PYŌŌ ih snss/ (but see App. D).

Act 2 Scene 1

3. **yeoman** /YOH mun/ assistant.

18. **close** /clohz/ grapple.

28. **indited** /in DĪT id/ Mrs. Quickly's error for *invited*.

28. **Lumbert street** /LUM burt/ archaic variant of **Lombard** which in the UK is /LŎM burd/ [LUM-, -bard].

ă-bat, äir-marry, air-pair, ar-far, ĕr-merry, ĝ- get, ī-high, ĭr-mirror, ł-little, n̩-listen, ŏ-hot, oh-go, ŏŏ-wood, ōō-moon, oor-tour, ōr- or, ow-how, t̪h-that, th-thin, ŭ-but, UR-fur, ur-under.   ( ) - suppress the syllable   see p. xiii for complete list.

30. **exion** /EK shun/ Mrs. Quickly's version of *action.*

39. **arrant** /ĂIR unt/ thoroughgoing.

39. **malmsey-nose** i.e, drunkard. *Malmsey* is a sweet wine. /MAHM zee/ is the older pronunciation, but today the /l/ is sometimes pronounced. This however is considered non-standard in the UK.

47. **quean** /kween/ ill-behaved woman.

57. **wo't** (Q), **wot** /wōͤt/ variant of **wilt.**

58. **wo't ta, wot 'a, wot ta** wilt thou. All pronounced /WōͤT uh/, but /WILT ţhow/ may be substituted for greater clarity.

59. **rampallian, rampallion** /ram PAL yun/ ruffian.

60. **fustilarian** /fuss tih LAIR ee un/ fat, frowzy woman.

89. **Wheeson** (Q) /WHEE sn̩, WHISS n̩/ dialect variant of F1's **Whitson** /WHIT sn̩/ Pentecost, the seventh Sunday after Easter.

144. **drollery** /DROHL ur ee/ comic picture.

169. **Basingstoke** (F1) /BAY zing stohk/, *****Billingsgate** (Q) /BILL ingz gayt/; UK *also* [- ĝit].

Act 2 Scene 2

15. *viz.* /viz/ abbreviation for *****videlicet** 'namely.' The older, anglicized pronunciations are US /vih DELL ih sit/ [-DEEL-, vī-]; UK /vih DEEL ih sit/ [vī-, -DELL-]. Newer pronunciations mix in restored Latin syllables, for example, /-ket/ or /-DAYL-/. These are not recommended.

26. **kinreds** /KIN ridz/ archaic variant of **kindreds.**

40. **albeit** /awl BEE it/ although.

46. **obduracy** persistance in evil. /ŎB dyoor uh see, -dyur-/ [-jur-]; US *sometimes* [-dur-].

60. **accites** /ak SĪTS/ prompts.

63. **engraff'd** US /en GRĂFT/; E.NEW ENG., UK /-GRAHFT/ attached.

87, 89. **Althaea('s)** /al ~~THEE~~ uh(z)/ here confused with Hecuba, Queen of Troy.

95. **sixpence** /SIKS punss, -pn̪ss/; US *also* /SIKS penss/.

102. **martlemas** /MART ł muss/ Martinmas, Nov.11, i.e., fatted pig or ox.

118. **Japhet** /JAY fit/ one of Noah's sons.

150. ***Ephesians** /ih-, ee FEEZH unz/; *sometimes newer* /-ee unz/ old buddies.

154. **pagan** /PAYG un/ whore.

168. **Saint Albons** archaic variant of **St. Albans**, both pronounced US /saynt AWL bunz/; UK /sint-, sn̪t-/.

Act 2 Scene 3

20. **chevalry** /SHEV ł ree/ knights. Archaic variant of **chivalry** /SHIV ł ree/.

52. ***puissance** strength.   Here should be 2 syllables. The traditional forms are /PWISS n̪ss/, /PYŌŌ sn̪ss/, but today /PWEE sn̪ss/ is most common (see App. D).

Act 2 Scene 4

19. **old utis** /YŌŌ tiss/ a racket, a fine to-do.

 20. **stratagem** /STRAT uh jum/ scheme.

48. ***brooches** /BROH chiz/ ornament. US [BRŌŌCH-] not recommended.

48. ***ouches** /OW chiz/ jewelry.

53. **cunger** (Q) /KUNG gur/ type of eel. Archaic variant of **conger** /KŎNG gur/. Omitted F1.

57. **rheumatic** full of colds. Usually /rōō MAT ik/ today, but elsewhere in Shk /RŌŌM uh tik/. Mrs. Quickly's error for *splenetic*.

64. **Burdeaux** city in France (i.e., wine from that city), possibly /BUR dŏcks/ in Shk's time. Archaic variant of **Bordeaux, Bourdeaux** /bor DOH/.

ă-bat, ăir-marry, air-pair, a̧r-far, ĕr-merry, ĝ- get, ī-high, ĭr-mirror, ł-little, n̪-listen, ŏ-hot, oh-go, ōō-wood, ōō-moon, oor-tour, ōr- or, ow-how, t̪h-that, ~~th~~-thin, ŭ-but, UR-fur, ur-under.   ( ) - suppress the syllable   see p. xiii for complete list.

85. **Tisick** archaic variant of *phthisic 'a lung disease.' Shk's spelling reflects the traditional pronunciation /TIZ ik/. A variety of newer spelling pronunciations also exist of which /~~THIZ~~ ik/ is the most common, especially in CN, UK.

88. **Dumbe, Dumb** /dum/.

99. **Barbary** /BAR buh ree/ region in North Africa.

142. **truncheon** /TRUN chun/ cudgel.

147. **pruins** in Shk's time probably /PROO inz/, archaic and dialect variant of **prunes**.

157. **Erebus** /ĔR ih bus/ hell.

159. **faitors** (UK **faitours**) /FAYT urz/ scoundrels. Some eds. prefer **Fates**.

159-175. **Hiren** /HĪ run/ Pistol's name for his sword.

161. **Peesel** Mrs. Quickly's reference to Pistol probably was meant to be pronounced /PIZ ł/, possibly /PEE zł/. Some eds. respell it **Pizzle** /PIZ ł/ 'penis.'

168. **Cerberus** /SUR bur us/ three-headed dog of Hades.

179. **Then . . . Calipolis** /kuh LIP uh liss/ a quotation from a play.

181. **Si fortune   me tormente,   sperato   me contento** Ital. /see for TOO nay may tor MEN tay, spay RAH toh may kohn TEN toh/ 'if fortune torments me, hope contents me.'

186. **neaf** /neef/ fist.

189. *****fustian** pompous. /FUSS tee un/; US *also* /FUSS chun/. Normal development would favor the latter.

191. **Galloway** /GAL uh way/ region in Ireland.

199. **Untwind** /un TWĪND/ undo, destroy. Archaic variant of **Untwine**.

199. *****Atropos** one of the Fates. US /AT ruh pohss/ [-troh-, -pŏss], *rarely* [-pŭs]; UK /-pŏss/ [pŭs]. /-ohss/ is a newer pronunciation. Normal development would favor /-us/.

204. *****tumult** turmoil. US /TOOM ult/; SOUTH.US *also* /TYOOM-/;

CN /TYŌŌM-/ [TŌŌM-]; UK /TYŌŌM-/. /CHŌŌM-/ considered non-standard in the UK. A newer pronunciation /TUM ult/ is not recommended.

219. **Hector** /HEK tur/ Trojan hero. See App. D for *-or*.

220. ***Agamemnon** chief king of the Greeks at Troy. US, CN /ag uh MEM nŏn/; UK /-nŏn/ [-nun]. See App. D *-on*.

241. **Tewksbury** US /TŌŌKS bĕr ee/; SOUTH. US /TYŌŌKS bur ee/. UK /TYŌŌKS bur ee, -bree/. UK [CHŌŌKS-] is considered non-standard.

245. **cunger** /KUNG gur/ type of eel. Archaic variant of **conger** /KŎNG gur/.

247. **join'd stools** /JOYND stōōlz/ well-crafted stools. Some eds. prefer **joint stools**.

251. **gambol** /GAM bł/ sportive.

254. **haberdepois** weight. /HAB ur duh poiz/, or /h/ can be dropped as is often the case in Elizabethan Eng. Archaic variant of ***avoirdupois** which has many pronunciations, the most common being /av wah dyōō PWAH/. The older, angl. forms are /AV ur duh poiz/, /av ur duh POIZ/, which today are rarely used.

259. **pole** archaic variant of **poll** /pohl/ 'head.'

265. **Trigon** part of the Zodiac. /TRĪ gun/, but /-gŏn/ is becoming more common. See App. D *-on*.

268. **busses** /BŬS iz/ kisses.

274. **kirtle** /KURT ł/ long gown.

277, 278. **Thou't** (Q) /thowt/ variant of **Thou'lt**, or F1's **Thou wilt**.

307. **Gadshill** /GADZ hill/; UK *sometimes* with equal stress.

327. **close with** /clohz/ pacify.

343. **indictment** /in DĪT munt/ charge of wrongdoing.

346. **vict'lers** (*vitlors* Q), **victuallers** (F1) both pronounced /VIT lurz/ innkeepers.

ă-bat, ăir-m**arry**, air-**pair**, ạr-**far**, ĕr-m**erry**, ĝ- **get**, ī-**high**, ĭr-m**irror**, ł-**little**, ṇ-**listen**, ŏ-**hot**, oh-**go**, ōō-**wood**, ōō-**moon**, oor-**tour**, ōr- **or**, ow-**how**, ṭh-**that**, t̶h̶-**thin**, ŭ-**but**, UR-**fur**, ur-**under**.　　　( ) - suppress the syllable　　　see p. xiii for complete list.

355. **Westminster** here should be /WEST min stur/.

383. **peascod-time** /PEEZ cŏd-/ peapod.

Act 3 Scene 1

1. **Surrey** US /SUR ee/; UK, E.COAST US /SUH ree/.

17. * **'larum-bell** US, CN /LAHR um/ [-LĂIR-]; UK /LĂIR um, LAHR um/ bell
that calls men to arms.

20. **imperious** /im PEER yus/ imperial.

53. ***divers** various. Here should be stressed on the first syllable
US, CN /DĪ vurss, -vurz/; UK /DĪ vurss/ [-vurz].

66. **Nevil** /NEV ł/ [-il].

82. **prophesy** /PRŎF uh sī/ to predict the future.

103. **Glendower** here should be /glen DOWR/. Some eds prefer Welsh
Glyndŵr /glin DŌOR/.

104. **fortnight** /FORT nīt/; US *also* [FORT nit] two weeks. Virtually obsolete in
the US.

Act 3 Scene 2

3. **rood** /rōōd/ cross.

8. **woosel** (Q) /WŌOZ ł/ blackbird. Variant of F1's **ouzel** (or **ousel**) /ŌOZ ł/.

19. **Staffordshire** /STĂF urd shur/ [-sheer].

21. **Squele, Squeal** /skweel/.

21. **Cotsole** /CŎTS ł, -ohl/ local pronunciation of the **Cotswold** hills in
Gloucestershire, /CŎTS wohld/ [CŎTS ohld, -włd].

22. **swingebucklers** /SWINJ buck lurz/ swashbucklers.

23. **bona robas** /BOH nuh ROH buz/ whores.

24. **commandement**. Archaic variant of **commandment**, originally with 4 syllables, /-uh munt/, but in this prose passage the usual mod. 3-syllable pronunciation may be used.

26. **Mowbray, Mowbrey** both pronounced /MOH bree/ [-bray]. The latter is the traditional form.

26. **Norfolk** /NOR fᵘk/.

37. **saith** says. US /SAY ith/, *rarely* [seth]; UK /seth/ [sayth, SAY ith]. The older form is /seth/.

38. **bullocks** /BULL uks/ bulls or oxen. /-ŏks/ not recommended.

44. **Gaunt** /gawnt/ Hal's grandfather.

46. **clout** /clowt/ center of a target.

72. **accommodo** Ang.Lat. /uh CŎM uh doh/; Class.Lat. /ah CŎM ŏ doh/ 1st person sing. of Lat. *accommodare* 'to make comfortable.'

205. **bona roba** /BOH nuh ROH buh/ whore.

222. **as live** as soon. May have been /liv/ in Shk's time. Variant of **as lief** /leef/. In the US **lieve** /leev/ is still found in some dialects and can also be used here.

258. ˣ**thews** /thyooz/; US, CN *also* [thooz] muscles.

259. **stature** /STATCH ur/ size.

264. **gibbets** /JIB its/ hangs.

267. **retrait** /rih-, ree TRAYT/ archaic variant of **retreat**.

270, 273. **caliver** /KAL ih vur/ light musket.

272. *****traverse** US, CN /truh VURSS/ [TRAV urss];
UK /truh VURSS, TRAV urss/ [TRAV URSS] march or take aim.

272. **thas** (Q) Bardolph's pronunciation of **thus** (F1) as he shouts it as a command.

280. **Sir Dagonet** /DAG uh net, -nit/.

ă-bat, ăir-marry, air-pair, ạr-far, ĕr-merry, ĝ- get, ī-high, ĭr-mirror, ł-little, n̦-listen, ŏ-hot, oh-go, ōͦ-wood, ōō-moon, oor-tour, ŏr- or, ow-how, ţh-that, th-thin, ŭ-but, UR-fur, ur-under.   ( ) - suppress the syllable   see p. xiii for complete list.

287. **woll** /wōōl/ (*wooll* Q) variant of F1's **will**.

295. ***Peradventure** perhaps. /PUR ad VEN chur/;
US *rarely* [PĔR-, PUR ad ven chur];
UK, CN *also* [PUR-, PĔR ad ven chur, pĕr ad VEN chur].

307. **duer paid** /DYŌŌ ur/; US, CN *also* /DŌŌ ur/ paid more punctually.

311. **redish** /RED ish/ archaic variant of **radish**.

317. ***huswives** /HUZ ivz/ is traditional, /HUSS wīvz/ is a newer, spelling
pronunciation. The former is the most common form in the UK, the latter in the
US. In CN both are used equally. In North America /HUSS wivz/ is also
sometimes used. Here means 'hussies, whores.'

320, 324. **Gaunt** /gawnt/ Hal's grandfather.

326. **hoboy, hautboy** /HOH boy/ or /OH boy/ archaic variant of *oboe*.

Act 4 Scene 1

2. **Gaultree** /GAWL tree/.

9. **tenure** archaic variant of **tenor**, both /TEN ur/.

33. **abject** /AB ject/ contemptible.

33. **routs** /rowts/ mobs.

47. **translate** here should be stressed on the 2nd syllable, the normal UK
pronunciation. US /trănss LAYT, trănz-/; UK /trănss LAYT/ [trănz-, trahnz-,
trahnss-, trunss-, trunz-].

78. **access** here should be /ak SESS/.

90. **suborn'd** /sub ORND/ persuaded to do wrong.

after 93. a passage from one of the quartos which some eds. include contains
unhouseled /un HOWZ łd/ 'without the eucharist.' Omitted F1, *Riverside.*

109. **Norfolk's** /NOR fˀks/.

109. **signories** /SEEN yur eez/ domains.

117. **coursers** /COR surz/ warhorses.

118. **staves** /stayvz/ lances.

126. **indictment** /in DĪT munt/ charge of wrongdoing.

129, 136. **Herford, Hereford** in the US both would be /HUR furd/. In the UK the county is normally /HĔR ih furd/ which here should be 2 syllables /HĔR furd/.

133. **Coventry** US /KUV ṇ tree/; UK /KŎV ṇ tree/ [KUV-].

157. *****parley** /PAR lee/ conference with an enemy. Newer [-lay] not recommended.

170. **ensinewed to** /en SIN yōōd/; US *also* [en SIN ōōd] involved in.

215. *****chastisement** punishment. Here stress should be on 1st syllable /CHĂSS tiz munt/; US *also* /-tīz-/.

Act 4 Scene 2 (*Complete Oxford* continues this as 4.1—line no. given in parenthesis)

9. (4.1.235) **rout** /rowt/ mob.

Act 4 Scene 3 (*Complete Oxford* 4.2)

51. **twopences** /TUP ṇ siz, -un siz/.

69. *****gratis** (Q) at no cost. US, UK /GRAHT iss/ [GRAT-], UK *rarely* [GRAYT-]; CN /GRAT-/ [GRAHT-]. Omitted F1.

72. **Retrait** /rih-, ree TRAYT/ archaic variant of **retreat**.

82, 128. **Gloucestershire** /GLŎSS tur shur/ [-sheer]; US *also* /GLAWSS-/.

96-121. **sherris** /SHĔR iss, -eess/ archaic variant of **sherry** which some eds. prefer.

98. **crudy** /CRŌŌ dee/ curded.

ă-bat, ăir-**marry**, air-**pair**, ạr-**far**, ĕr-**merry**, ĝ- **get**, ī-**high**, ĭr-**mir**ror, ł-**little**, ṇ-**listen**, ŏ-**hot**, oh-**go**, ōō-**wood**, ōō-**moon**, oor-**tour**, ōr- **or**, ow-**how**, ṭh-**that**, ŧħ-**thin**, ŭ-**but**, UR-**fur**, ur-**under**.   ( ) - suppress the syllable   see p. xiii for complete list.

99. *environ /en VĪ run/; US *also* [-urn] surround.

105. *pusillanimity /pyōō sł uh NIM ih tee/ [pyōō zł-] cowardice.

107. inwards /IN wurdz/ internal parts. /IN urdz/ is still a dialect and colloquial form in the US.

112. retinue US /RET ih nōō/, /RET ṇ ōō/; UK, SOUTH. US /-nyōō/ band of followers.

124. potations /poh TAY shunz/ drinks.

Act 4 Scene 4 (*Complete Oxford* 4.3)

32. meting /MEET ing/ giving out.

48. aconitum /ak un NĪT um/ a poison.

77. mete /meet/ measure.

99. shrieve (Q) /shreev/ archaic variant of sheriff (*Sherife* F1) which should be one syllable /SHĔR (i)f/.

99. Yorkshire /YORK shur/ [-sheer].

119. mure /myoor/ wall.

130. apoplexy /AP uh plek see/ paralysis.

Act 4 Scene 5 (*Complete Oxford* continue this as 4.3—line nos. given in parentheses)

27. (4.3.158) biggen, biggin /BIG in/ nightcap.

36. (4.3.167) *rigol /RIG ohl/ [RĪ gł, RIG ł, RĪ gohl] circle, crown. The ending /-ohl/ is a newer, spelling pronunciation. /RĪ gł/ is recommended to avoid confusion with *wriggle*.

39. (4.3.170) filial tenderness /FILL ył/ a son's tenderness.

73. (4.3.203) martial /MAR shł/ warlike.

85. (4.3.214) *quaff'd /kwŏft/; UK *rarely* [kwahft] drink freely. /kwăft/ is also used but is not recommended.

148. (4.3.277) *prostrate /PRŎS trayt/, US *rarely* [-trut] lying face down.

161. (4.3.290) carat /KĂIR ut/ worth.

164. (4.3.293) eat /et/ dialect variant of eaten.

186. (4.3.215) sate archaic variant of sat. May have been /sayt/ or /sat/.

233. (4.3.362) swound archaic variant of swoon. In Shk's time the vowel could be either /ow/ or /ōō/.

236. (4.3.365) prophesied /PRŎF uh sīd/ predicted the future.

Act 5 Scene 1

28. kickshaws /KICK shawz/ fancy foods.

32, 41. arrant /ĂIR unt/ thoroughgoing.

35. marvail's (*maruailes* Q) archaic variant of F1's marvellous 'marvellously.' Short forms are /MARV łss/ or /MARV luss/ but in this prose section mod. /MARV ł us/ can be used.

39-41. Visor /VĪ zur/.

39. Woncote, Woncot, Wo'ncot /WUNG kut, WŎNG kut/.

39. Clement Perkes, Perks /CLEM unt PARKS/.

64. staves /stayvz/ staffs.

65. semblable coherence /SEM bluh bł/ similarity.

81. intervallums /in tur VAL umz/ intervals.

Act 5 Scene 2

48. *Amurath (Q) a Turkish sultan. The most common angl. pronunciation among scholars is /ah MŌO rahth/ which will not fit the meter. Here should be /AM oo rat, -rath/, /AHM oo raht, -rahth/. More rare is one of these pronunciations with stress on the final syllable. On stage sometimes /AM yoo răth/.

72. Lethe /LEETH ee/ river of forgetfulness in Hades.

127. rase out /rayss/ erase. Some eds. prefer raze /rayz/ which could mean 'erase' or 'cut, slash.'

141. accite /ak SĪT/ summon.

Act 5 Scene 3

3. graffing US /GRĂF ing/; E.NEW ENG., UK /GRAHF-/ archaic variant of grafting which some eds. prefer.

28. Proface! /proh FAYSS/ term of welcome.

33. shrows /shrohz/ archaic variant of shrews.

47. *leman sweetheart. US /LEE mun/ [LEM un, LAY mun]; CN /LAY mun/, sometimes [LEM un, LEE mun]; UK /LEM-/ [LEE mun], rarely [LAY mun]. /LAY mun/ is newer and not recommended.

59. cabileros (Q) angl. /kab ih LEER ohz/ gentlemen. Today sometimes /kah buh YAIR ohz/ after Sp., caballeros /kah bah YAY rohss/, especially in the US. Other eds. prefer cavalieros (Cauileroes F1) /kav ih LEER ohz/.

75. Samingo /suh MING goh/.

89. By'r lady (Q) /bīr-, bur LAY dee/ by Our Lady (i.e., Mary). Indeed (F1).

89. goodman /GŏoD mun/ title of a man under the rank of gentleman.

90. Barson /BAR sun, -sṇ/.

92. recreant /REK r(ee) yunt/ coward.

99, 115. foutre /FŌO truh, FŌO tur/ 'a fig for,' a term of contempt.

101. **Assyrian** /uh SĬR ee un/.

102. **Cophetua** /kuh FETCH oo wuh/; UK *also* /kuh FET yoo wuh/ subject of an old ballad.

104. **Helicons** /HEL ih cŏnz, -cunz/ i.e., poets. /-ŏn/ is usual in the US, /-un/ is more common in the UK.

113. **besonian, bezonian** /bih ZOHN ee un/ scoundrel.

137. **commandement**. Archaic variant of **commandment**, originally with 4 syllables, /-uh munt/, but in this prose passage the usual mod. 3-syllable pronunciation may be used.

Act 5 Scene 4

1. **arrant** /ĂIR unt/ thoroughgoing.

19, 21. **swing'd** /swinjd/ beat.

21. **half-kirtles** /-KURT łz/ short skirts.

22. **knight-arrant** /ĂIR unt/ wandering knight. Some eds. prefer **errant** /ĔR unt/.

28. **Goodman** /Go͞oD mun/ title of a man under the rank of gentleman.

29. **atomy** (Q) /AT uh mee/. Hostess' blunder for **anatomy** (F1) /uh NAT uh mee/ skeleton.

Act 5 Scene 5

28. **semper idem** always the same. Ang.Lat. /SEM pur Ī dum/; Class.Lat. /SEM pĕr EE dem/ or /ID em/.

28.   **obsque   hoc   nihil   est**
Ang.Lat.   /ŎB skwee   hŏk   NĪ hil   est/
Class.Lat. /ŎPS kway   hohk   NIH hil   est/
             'without this there is nothing'
Some eds. correct the mistake of *obsque* to **absque** Ang.Lat. /AB skwee/; Class.Lat. /AHPS kway/.

ă-bat, ăir-ma**rry**, air-**pair**, ạr-**far**, ĕr-**merry**, ĝ- **get**, ī-high, ĭr-**mir**ror, ł-li**ttle**, ṇ-lis**ten**, ŏ-hot, oh-go, o͞o-**wood**, o͞o-**moon**, oor-**tour**, ōr- **or**, ow-**how**, ʈh-**that**, t̶h̶-**thin**, ŭ-but, UR-**fur**, ur-**under**.   ( ) - suppress the syllable   see p. xiii for complete list.

34. ***durance** /DYOOR unss/; US *also* /DŌŌR-/ [DUR-] imprisonment.

37. **ebon** /EB un/ black.

37. **Alecto's** /uh LEK tohz/ one of the Furies.

40. **trumpet-*clangor** (UK **clangour**) /CLANG ur/ [-gur] loud shrill noise.

53. **gormandizing** /GOR mun dīz ing/ to eat like a glutton.

71. **tenure** archaic variant of **tenor**, both /TEN ur/.

96. **Si fortuna me tormenta, spero contenta** see 2.4.181. Some eds. add **me** after *spero*.

Henry V

People in the Play

Aunchient, Ancient (Pistol) both spellings pronounced /AYN chunt/. Archaic variant of the rank **ensign** US /EN sṇ/; UK /-sīn/.

Bardolph /BAR dŏlf/; US *also* /-dawlf/.

Beaumont /BOH mŏnt, -munt/. The latter is more common in the UK; Fr. /BOH mohⁿ/.

Berri, Berry /BĔR ee/.

Bourbon /BOOR bun/; *newer* /-bŏn/; Fr. /B$\overline{OO}$R bohⁿ/. See App. D -*on*.

Dolphin (Lewis) /DŎL fin/; US *also* /DAWL-/ angl. form of **Dauphin** 'the French heir to the throne' which here would be Fr. /DOH făⁿ/. In Shk's time /l/ in this position was often silent, so *dolphin* and *dauphin* were probably both /DAW fin/.

Ely /EE lee/ his name is not spoken.

Erpingham /UR ping um/, though in the US /UR ping ham/ would be usual.

Exeter /EK sih tur/.

Fluellen /fl$\overline{oo}$-, fl$\overline{oo}$ WEL un/. Some cds. prefer **Llewellyn** /l$\overline{oo}$-, l$\overline{oo}$ WEL in/.

Gloucester /GLŎS tur/; US *also* /GLAWSS-/.

Gower /GOW ur/.

Grandpré angl. /grand PRAY/; Fr. /grahⁿ PRAY/. An older angl. form /-PREE/ was used by Shk.

Jamy /JAY mee/.

Katherine /KA̶T̶H̶ rin/ or /KA̶T̶H̶ ur rin/ but should be 2 syllables in verse.

Lewis, Louis the meter calls for one syllable /L$\overline{OO}$ (i)ss/.

ă-bat, ăir-**marry**, air-**pair**, ạr-**far**, ĕr-**merry**, ĝ- **get**, ī-**high**, ĭr-**mirror**, ł-**little**, ṇ-**listen**, ŏ-**hot**, oh-**go**, $\overline{oo}$-**wood**, $\overline{oo}$-**moon**, oor-**tour**, ōr- **or**, ow-**how**, t̩h-**that**, t̶h̶-**thin**, ŭ-**but**, UR-**fur**, ur-**under**.   ( ) - suppress the syllable   see p. xiii for complete list.

People in the Play (cont.)

Monmouth (Henry) /MŎN muth/; UK *also* [MUN-].

Montjoy /MŎNT joy/ or /mŏnt JOY/ depending on meter. Some eds. prefer F1's **Mountjoy** /MOWNT-/.

Northumberland /north UM bur lund/.

Nym, Nim /nim/.

Orleance here should be /OR l(ee) yunss, OR leenss, or LEENSS/ depending on meter. Archaic variant of **Orleans** /OR l(ee) yunz, OR leenz, or LEENZ/. Other eds. prefer Fr. **Orléans** /or lay ah^n/.

Pistol, Aunchient see **Auncient.**

Rambures /ram BYOORZ/; Fr. /rah^n bür/.

Salisbury 2 or 3 syllables, depending on meter US /SAWLZ b(ĕ)r ee/; UK /SAWLZ b(u)r ee/ [SĂLZ-].

Scroop /skrōōp/. Some eds. prefer mod. **Scrope**, pronounced the same way.

Suffolk /SUFF ^{u}k/.

Warwick US /WŌR ik/; E.COAST US, UK /WŎR-/. Place names in the US often have /-wik/ but this is not recommended for Shk.

Westmerland archaic variant of **Westmor(e)land**, all pronounced /WEST mur lund/ in the UK. US is usually /west MOR lund/ which will not fit the meter.

Places in the Play

*****Agincourt** /AZH in cor/ [AJ-, -cort]. Sometimes Fr. /ah zha^n coor/ is used.

Callice, Callis /KAL iss/ city on north. coast of France. Both are archaic variants of **Calais** which here should be /KAL ay/, the normal UK form; Fr. /KAH lay/.

Harflew /HAR flōō/ archaic variant of **Harfleur** /HAR flur/; Fr. /AHR flör/.

Special note on the French Scenes

Henry V is unique in Shakespeare in that it contains several sections of extended French dialogue. No attempt is made to include a guide to the pronunciation of these scenes. A native speaker should be consulted for assistance wherever French is used.

Notes on Fluellen's Welsh accent

Shk indicates the Welsh accent with the following spelling substitutions: $k \Rightarrow g$ *(knock⇒knog), d ⇒ t (God⇒Got), b ⇒ p (by⇒py), v⇒f (valorous⇒falorous).* The reader should bear in mind that these substitutions are in no way sufficient to represent a true Welsh accent, which is best learned by listening to a native speaker. Seeing *by* spelled *py* does not mean the reader should simply use the English sound in *pie*. In Welsh /b, d, g/ may sometimes sound somewhat like /p, t, k/, but without the accompanying puff of air that characterizes /p, t, k/ in both Welsh and English. One way to think of it is, that in Welsh /b, d, g/ are half-way between the sounds of Eng. /p, t, k/ and Eng. /b, d, g/.

The *f* -*v* confusion should be ignored. It is not a characteristic of Welsh, but many English speakers believe it is because the Welsh spell /v/ with *f* (*Dafydd* /DAH vith/ 'David').

Shk's omission of the initial *w* in *woman, world* and *work*, is a widespread Welsh feature. Also a feature of North Wales is the lack of /z/ and /zh/ which are pronounced /ss/ and /sh/.

Prologue

13. **casques** /kăsks/; UK *also* [kahsks] helmets.

17. **accompt** /uh COWNT/ archaic variant of **account**. See App. D.

25. ***puissance** power (i.e., an army). Here 3 syllables, traditionally /PYOO ih snss/ (but see App. D).

Act 1 Scene 1

14. **esquires** here should be /ess KWĪRZ/, the usual UK form.

15. ***lazars** /LAY zurz, LAZZ urz/ lepers.

16. **indigent** /IN dih jint/ poor, needy.

ă-bat, ăir-**marry**, air-**pair**, ạr-**far**, ĕr-**merry**, ĝ- **get**, ī-high, ĭr-**mirror**, ł-**little**, ṇ-**listen**, ŏ-hot, oh-go, ŏŏ-wood, ōō-moon, oor-**tour**, ōr- **or**, ow-how, t͟h-**that**, t̶h̶-thin, ŭ-but, UR-**fur**, ur-**under**.   ( ) - suppress the syllable   see p. xiii for complete list.

17. **almshouses** poorhouses. /AHMZ-/ is older; /AHLMZ-, AWLMZ-/ are newer. In the UK the latter are non-standard.

40. **prelate** /PREL ut/ high-ranking churchman.

48. **charter'd *libertine** /LIB ur teen/, *rarely* [-tīn] licensed freeman.

52. **theoric** /THEE uh rik/ theory.

58. **sequestration** /see kwih STRAY shun/ [sek wih-] separation.

66. **crescive** /CRESS iv/ growing.

69. **perfected** here should be /PUR fikt id/ fully accomplished.

Act 1 Scene 2

14. **bow** /boh/ distort.

16. **miscreate** /MIS cree ut, -ayt/ miscreated, i.e., spurious.

In lines 37-91 these names appear several times:

*Capet first king of the French dynasty. Here should have 1st syllable stress. The most common pronunciations are /KAH pay, KAP et/; US *also* [KAY pet]. /KAY pet, KAP et/ are older, angl. forms, /KAH pay/ is based on Fr. Mixed forms like /KAP ay/ are also used.

Elbe /ELB/ German river.

Lewis, Louis the meter calls for one syllable /LOO (i)ss/.

Lorraine region on the French-German border. Here with 1st syllable stress US /LOR ayn/; E.COAST US, UK *also* /LŎR-/.

Pepin /PEP in/; Fr. **Pépin** /PAY pă^n/ father of Charlemagne.

Pharamond /FĂIR uh mund, -mŏnd/ legendary Frankish king.

Sala angl. /SAY luh/ one of the rivers at the mouth of the Rhine. Some eds. prefer Germ. **Saale** angl. /SAH luh/; Germ. /ZAH leh/. Others prefer **Saal**, however it should be 2 syllables.
   Salique, Salic /SAL ik/ [SAY lik].

38.   **In terram Salicam   mulieres   ne succedant**
Ang.Lat. /in TĚR um SAL ih kum   myōō LĪ uh reez nee suk SEE dṇt/
Class.Lat. /in TĚR ahm SAHL ih kahm Mōō LEE ĕr ayss nay sōōk KAY dahnt/
           'No woman shall succeed in Salique land.'

40. **gloze, glose** /glohz/ interpret. Some eds. prefer **gloss**.

53. **Meisen** /MĪ sṇ, -sun/ archaic variant of **Meissen**, pronounced the same way.

65. **Childeric** /CHIL dur ik/. Some eds. prefer Fr. **Childéric** /sheel day reek/.

67. **Blithild** /BLIṬH ild, BLIҬH ild/.

67. **Clothair** /CLOH ~~thair~~, -tair/ a Frankish king. Some eds. prefer **Clotaire**
/CLOH tair/.

74. **Lingare** /LING gar/ the mod. form is **Lingard** /LING gard/.

75. ***Charlemain, Charlemagne** US, CN /SHĄR luh mayn/,
rarely [shar luh MAYN]; UK /SHĄR luh mayn/ [shar luh MAYN].
/-mīn/ is a newer pronunciation, not recommended. Fr. /sharl mahnʸ/.

82. **Ermengare** /UR min gar/. The mod. form is **Ermengard** or **Ermingarde**
/UR min gard/.

91. **Howbeit** here should be /how BEE (i)t/ nevertheless.

95. **progenitors** /proh-, pruh JEN ih turz/ ancestors. See App. D *-or*.

116, 119. ***puissant** powerful. The traditional forms are /PWISS ṇt/,
/PYŌŌ sṇt/ (see App. D).

121. **exploits** here should be /ek SPLOYTS/.

132. **spiritualty** /SPĬR (ih) chōōl tee/ clergy.

143. **coursing** /COR sing/ hunting, running.

151. **assays** /uh-, ass SAYZ/ attacks.

154. **th'ill neighborhood** (F1). Some eds. prefer **the bruit thereof** (following
Q1-3) /brōōt/ report.

ă-bat, ăir-m**arry**, air-p**air**, ąr-f**ar**, ĕr-m**erry**, ĝ- g**et**, ī-h**igh**, ĭr-m**irror**, ł-li**tt**le, ṇ-li**sten**,
ŏ-h**ot**, oh-g**o**, ōō-w**ood**, ōō-m**oon**, oor-t**our**, ōr- **or**, ow-h**ow**, ṭh-**that**, ҭһ-**thin**, ŭ-b**ut**,
UR-f**ur**, ur-**under**.   ( ) - suppress the syllable   see p. xiii for complete list.

157. **chevalry** /SHEV ł ree/ body of knights. Archaic variant of **chivalry** /SHIV ł ree/.

182. **Congreeing** /cun-, cŏn GREE ing/ agreeing.

182. **close** /clohz/ cadence.

184. ***divers** various. US, CN /DĪ vurss, -vurz/; UK /DĪ vurss/ [-vurz]. Some eds. prefer **diverse**, which however should be stressed on the 1st syllable.

191. ***magistrates** /MAJ ih strayts/; US *also* [-struts].

192. **venter** /VEN tur/ archaic variant of **venture**.

203. **executors** here should be /EK suh kyōōt urz/ executioners. See App. D *-or*.

213. **defeat** (F1). Some eds prefer **defect** (Q1-3) here stress should fall on the 2nd syllable.

216. **Gallia** /GAL yuh/ France.

226. **empery** /EM pur ee/ imperial power.

248. ***predecessor** US /PRED ih sess ur/; UK /PREE dih sess ur/; in CN both /PREE-/ and /PRED-/ are used equally. Rarely with stress on the 3rd syllable. See App. D *-or*.

250, 295. **savor** (UK **savour**) /SAY vur/ have the characteristic of.

252. **galliard** /GAL yurd/; UK *also newer* /GAL yard/ a lively dance.

255. **in *lieu of** US, CN /lōō, lyoo/; UK /lyōō/ [lōō] in return for.

Act 2 prologue

2. **dalliance** /DAL yunss/ sportiveness.

10. **coronets** small crowns. US /COR uh nets, -nits/, /cor uh NETS/; E.COAST US /CŎR-, cŏr-/; UK /CŎR uh nits/ [-nets, cŏr uh NETS].

24. **Masham** /MASS um, MASH um/.

30-42. **Southampton** /sowth HAMP tun/ [-AMP-, suth-, suth-].

Act 2 Scene 1

30. **Gadslugs** (Q1-3) /gadz LUGZ/ God's ears. **This hand** (F1).

45-51. **solus** /SOH lus/ double meaning: unmarried, alone.

46. **egregious** /ih GREE jus/ notorious.

47. **mervailous** /mar VAY lus/ archaic variant of **marvellous**, which here would be /mar VEL us/. *-er-* was often pronounced /-ar-/ in Shk's time. Some eds. make this a prose passage which would allow 1st syllables stress.

49. **perdy, perdie** /PUR DEE/ 'by God, indeed.' Some eds. prefer the variant **pardie** /par DEE/.

54. **Barbason** /BAR buh sŏn, -sun, -sn̩/ a devil. /-ŏn/ is usual in the US and is increasingly common in the UK. See App. D *-on*.

62. **exhale** draw your sword. Here with 2nd syllable stress, /eks HAYL/, the normal UK form.

71. **Couple a gorge** in Pistol's bad Fr. it might be /COOP ł ah GORJ/, or Fr. /gorzh/, his mistake for *couper à gorge* or *coupez la gorge* /cōō pay/ cut the throat.

74. **spittle, Spital** /SPIT ł/ hospital in Spitalfields.

76. ***lazar** /LAY zur, LAZZ ur/ leper.

76. **Cressid's** /CRESS idz/ Cressida, a false lover.

77. **Tearsheet** /TAIR sheet/.

78. ***quondam** former. US /KWŎN dum/, *rarely* [-dam];
UK /-dam/, *rarely* [-dum]

79. **pauca** shortened form of *pauca verba* 'few words,' i.e., 'enough said.' Ang.Lat. /PAW kuh VUR buh/; Class.Lat. /POW kah WĔR bah/.

119. **quotidian** /kwoh TID ee un/; UK *also* [kwŏ TID ee un] type of fever.

119. **tertian** /TUR shun/ type of fever returning every 48 hrs.

ă-bat, ăir-**marry**, air-**pair**, ạr-**far**, ĕr-**merry**, ĝ- **get**, ī-**high**, ĭr-**mirror**, ł-**little**, n̩-**listen**, ŏ-**hot**, oh-**go**, ōō-**wood**, ōō-**moon**, oor-**tour**, ōr- **or**, ow-**how**, t̪h-**that**, t̪h-**thin**, ŭ-**but**, UR-**fur**, ur-**under**.   ( ) - suppress the syllable   see p. xiii for complete list.

119. ***lamentable** US /luh MEN tuh bł/ [LAM en tuh bł];
CN, UK /LAM un tuh bł/ [luh MEN-].

124. **corroborate** /kuh RŎB ur ut/ Pistol's mistake for *corrupted*.

127. **condole** /cun DOHL/ grieve with.

Act 2 Scene 2

4. **sate** archaic variant of **sat**. May have been /sayt/ or /sat/.

13-148. **Masham** /MASS um, MASH um/.

---

42. **excess** here should be /ek SESS/, the most common UK form.

53. ***orisons** prayers. US, CN /OR ih zunz, -zṇz/ [-sunz, -sṇz]; E.COAST US /ŎR-/;
UK /ŎR ih zunz, -zṇz/.

87. **appertinents, appurtenants** /uh PURT ih nunts/ fittings.

108. **hoop** /ho͞op, ho͝op/ variant of ***whoop** /who͞op/ [ho͞op, ho͝op, who͝op].

117. **glist'ring** /GLIS tring/ glistening.

123. **Tartar** /TAR tur/ Tartarus, hell.

127. **affiance** /uh FĪ unss/ trust.

139. ***indued** /in DYO͞OD/; US *also* [-DO͞OD] **endowed**.

190. ***puissance** power (i.e., army). Here 3 syllables, traditionally
/PYO͞O ih sṇss/ (but see App. D).

Act 2 Scene 3

2. **Staines** /staynz/ town west of London.

3, 6. **ern, erne** (F1) /urn/ mourn. Some eds. make the first instance **yearn** and
the second **earn**.

4. **blithe** /blīth/; US *also* /blīth/ merry.

5. **Falstaff** US /FAWL stäff/; E. NEW ENG., UK /-stahff/.

12. **christom** /CRISS um/ archaic variant of **chrisom** /CRIZ um/ child in its chrisom-cloth, i.e., newly christened.

25. **up'ard** /UP urd/. Some eds. prefer Q1-3's **upward**, or F1's **up-peer'd**.

32. **incarnate** /in CAR nit/ [-nayt] in the flesh. /-ut/ is usual for adjs.

38. **rheumatic** suffering from a cold. Usually /roo MAT ik/ today, but elsewhere in Shk /ROOM uh tik/ which fits better here since the hostess means *lunatic*.

46. **Southampton** /sowth HAMP tun/ [-AMP-, suth-, suth-].

48. **chattels** /CHAT łz/ property.

53. **Caveto** /kah VET oh/ beware. Pistol may mean *cavete*, Ital. 'be careful.'

62. ***huswifery** /HUZ if ree/ is traditional, /-wīf ree, -wiff ree/ are newer, based on spelling. Some eds. prefer **housewifery** /HOWSS-/.

62. **Keep close, I thee command** (F1) /clohss/ keep hidden. **Keepe fast thy buggle boe** (Q1-3) /BUG ł boh/ keep your hobgoblin secure, i.e., your privates.

Act 2 Scene 4

5. **Brabant** angl. /BRAB unt/; Dutch /BRAH bahnt/; Fr. /BRAH bah^n/ former duchy where Belgium is today.

25. **Whitsun** /WHIT sn/ Pentecost, the seventh Sunday after Easter.

39. ***ordure** manure. US /OR dyoor/ [-dyur, -joor, -jur]; CN /-dyur/ [-dyoor, -jur]; UK /OR dyoor/, *rarely* [-jur]. Normal development in the US would result in /-jur/. See App. D *-ure*.

46. **niggardly** /NIG urd lee/ miserly.

54. **Cressy** /CRESS ee/ angl. variant of Fr. **Crécy** /CRAY see/.

57. **mountain** (F1). Some eds. prefer **mountant** /MOWNT unt, -nt/ 'gaining the ascendency,' or **mounting**.

85. **sinister** illegitimate. Here should be /sin ISS tur/.

| ă-bat, äir-**marry**, air-**pair**, ar-**far**, ĕr-**merry**, ĝ- **get**, ī-**high**, ĭr-**mirror**, ł-little, ṇ-listen, |
| ŏ-hot, oh-go, oo-**wood**, oo-**moon**, oor-**tour**, ōr- **or**, ow-**how**, ţh-**that**, th-thin, ŭ-but, |
| UR-**fur**, ur-**under**.   ( ) - suppress the syllable   see p. xiii for complete list. |

89. **demonstrative** /duh MŎN struh tiv/.

108. **betrothed** /bih-, bee TROHṬH id/ engaged to be married.

109. **That shall be swallowed in this controversy.** Despite the spelling with -ed, *swallowed* is two syllables /SWŎL ohd/, followed by /CŎN truh vur see/, the normal US pronunciation.

124. **womby** /WŌŌM ee/ hollow.

126. **ordinance** artillery. Archaic spelling of **ordnance**. Both would have to be three syllables in this line, /OR dih nunss/.

132. **Louvre** palace of the Fr. kings. Here should be two syllables, angl. /LŌŌV ruh/ or /LŌŌV ur/. The former is common in the UK.

Act 3 Chorus

2. **celerity** /suh LĔR ih tee/ speed.

6. **Phoebus** /FEE bus/ god of the sun.

14. *****rivage** /RIV ij/ shore. [riv AHZH] is a new pronunciation based on Fr. and will not fit the meter. /RĪ vij/, mentioned in some dicts., is now obsolete.

21. *****puissance** power, Here the line allows a double or triple ending. The traditional forms are /PWISS ṇss/, /PYŌŌ (ih) sṇss/, but today /PWEE sṇss/ is most common (see App. D).

26. **ordinance** artillery. Archaic spelling of **ordnance**. Both should be three syllables in this line, /OR dih nunss/.

35. *****eche out** US /eech/ [etch]; UK /etch/ [eech]. Elsewhere rhymes with *speech*. Some eds. prefer **eke out** /eek/. Both mean 'increase.'

Act 3 Scene 1

25. **yeomen** /YOH mun/ freemen who own small farms.

Act 3 Scene 2

20. **Avaunt** /uh VAWNT/ be off!

20. **cullions** /CŬL yunz/ scoundrels, literally 'testicles.'

25. **lenity** /LEN ih tee/ leniency.

44. **half-pence** (F1), **hapence** (Q1-2) /HAYP n̦ss, -unss/.

48. **handkerchers** /HANK ur churz/ archaic variant of **handkerchiefs**.

> **Note on dialects:** Shk's spellings are not a reliable guide to the correct reproduction of the Scots, Irish, and Welsh dialects of Jamy, Macmorris and Fluellen in this scene. The notation of this guide is also ill-suited to help the reader understand the phonetic nuances of dialect speech. Jamy's *gud* 'good' for example represents a Scots sound that in some dialects is pronounced with the tongue forward from the usual English /o͞o/, somewhat like German *ü*; in other dialects it is /uh/. These accents are best learned by listening to native speakers.

> *The Complete Oxford* begins 3.3 here (line nos. in parentheses).

81. (3.3.26) *****pristine** US /priss TEEN/ [PRISS teen]; in the UK, CN both are used equally.

84. (3.3.29) **God-den** /gud-, go͞od EN/ good evening. Some eds. prefer **Good e'en**.

87. (3.3.31) **pioners** soldiers who dug trenches and planted mines. It is not certain whether Shk pronounced this /PĪ uh nurz/ or as in mod. **pioneers** /pī uh NEERZ/.

95. (3.3.39) **voutsafe** /vowt SAYF/ grant. Archaic variant of **vouchsafe** /vowch SAYF/.

110, 113. (3.3.54, 57) **God sa' me** /say/ God save me.

119. (3.3.63) **tway, twae** /tway/ Scots 'two.'

126. (3.3.70) *****peradventure** perhaps. /PUR ad VEN chur/;
US *rarely* [PĔR-, PUR ad ven chur];
UK, CN *also* [PUR-, PĔR ad ven chur, pĕr ad VEN chur].

137. *****parley** (3.3.79) /PAR lee/ conference with an enemy. Newer [-lay] not recommended.

> ă-b**at**, ăir-**marry**, air-**pair**, a̦r-**far**, ĕr-**merry**, ĝ- **get**, ī-**high**, ĭr-**mirror**, l̵-**little**, n̦-**listen**, ŏ-**hot**, oh-**go**, o͝o-**wood**, o͞o-**moon**, oor-**tour**, ŏr- **or**, ow-**how**, țh-**that**, t̶h̶-**thin**, ŭ-**but**, UR-**fur**, ur-**under**.　　　( ) - suppress the syllable　　　see p. xiii for complete list.

Act 3 Scene 3 (*Complete Oxford* continues this as 3.3 (line nos. in parentheses).

2. (3.3.85) **parle** /p̯arl/ conference with an enemy.

15. (3.3.98) **impious** /IM pyus/ lacking in respect, profane.

22. (3.3.105) **licentious** /lī SEN chus/ lustful.

26. (3.3.109) **precepts** here should be /prih-, pree SEPTS/.

26. (3.3.109) **leviathan** /luh VĪ uh ~~th~~un/ sea monster.

41. (3.3.124) **Herod's** /HĔR udz/ King in Judea in Jesus' lifetime.

45. (3.3.128) **succors** (UK **succours**) /SUCK urz/ help. See App. D -*or*.

Act 3 Scene 4

56. **Foh** indicates an expression of disgust made with the lips /pff/! or /pfuh/!
Sometimes vocalized as /foh/ or **faugh** /faw/.

Act 3 Scene 5

1. **Somme** /sŏm/; US *also* /sum/.

7. **scions** /SĪ unz/ living plants grafted onto root stock.

8. **Spirt up, Spurt up** /spurt/ sprout up.

14. **Albion** /AL bee un/ Britain.

33. **lavoltas** bounding dances. /luh VOHLT uz/ or older /luh VŎLT uz/.

33. ***corantos** courants, a type of dance. US /cuh-, coh RAHN tohz/ [-RAN-];
UK /-RAHN-, -RAN-/.

Some of the names in the list in lines 40-5 appear under "People in the Play."

40. **Charles Delabreth** /del uh BRET, -BRE~~TH~~/. Some eds. prefer **Delabret.**
1st syllable stress is also possible.

42. **Alanson** angl. /AL un sun, -sn̩/ or /uh LAN sun/; Fr. **Alençon** /ah lahⁿ sohⁿ/.
At 4.8.96 it has 1st syllable stress.

42. **Brabant** angl. /BRAB unt/; Dutch /BRAH bahnt/; Fr. /BRAH bah^n/ former duchy where Belgium is today.

43. **Jacques Chatillion, Rambures, Vaudemont** there are two possibilities for this line. *Jacques* should be two syllables, usually /JAY kweez/ (see *As You Like It* "People in the Play"), followed by /shuh TILL yun, RAM byoorz, VOH duh mŏnt/ or /shuh TILL ee yun, ram BYOORZ, vohd MŎNT/. Some eds. prefer **Chatillon** or **Châtillon**; Fr. /shah tee yoh^n, rah^n bür, voh duh moh^n/.

44. **Roussi** /R$\overline{OO}$ see, r$\overline{oo}$ SEE/ are both possible.

44. **Faulconbridge** /FAWL kun brij/ or the older pronunciation [FAW kun-], still used by some in the UK. Some eds. prefer **Falconbridge** which may also be /FAL-/; UK *also* [FŎL-]. Others prefer **Fauconbridge** /FAW kun-/, **Fauconberg** angl. /-burg/; Fr. /-bĕrg/.

45. **Foix** angl. /foyz/; Fr. /fwah/.

45. **Lestrake** /LESS strayk/. Some eds. prefer F1's **Lestrale** /LESS strahl/ or **Lestrelles** /LESS strel/.

45. **Bouciqualt, Boucicault** /B$\overline{OO}$ see koh/ (which is also the Fr. pronunciation); US *also* /B$\overline{OO}$ see kawlt/.

45. **Charolois** /SHĂIR uh loiz/ archaic variant of **Charolais** /shăir uh LAY/; US *also* /shahr-/; Fr. /shahr oh lay/.

49. **pennons** /PEN unz/ banners.

52. **rheum** /r$\overline{oo}$m/ spit, i.e., waters.

54, 64. **Roan** /rohn, ROH un/ archaic angl. variant of **Rouen** which here would be Fr. /rwah^n/ or /R$\overline{OO}$ ah^n/.

Act 3 Scene 6

7. *****Agamemnon** chief king of the Greeks at Troy. US, CN /ag uh MEM nŏn/; UK /-nŏn/ [-nun]. See App. D *-on*.

14. **Antony** /AN tuh nee/. Some eds. prefer F1's **Anthony** which in the UK is also usually pronounced with /t/.

ă-bat, ăir-ma**rry**, air-**pair**, ạr-**far**, ĕr-**merry**, ĝ- get, ī-high, ĭr-**mirror**, ł-li**ttle**, ṇ-**listen**, ŏ-hot, oh-go, o͞o-wood, o͞o-moon, oor-**tour**, ŏr- or, ow-how, ţh-**that**, ᵼh-**thin**, ŭ-but, UR-**fur**, ur-und**er**.   ( ) - suppress the syllable   see p. xiii for complete list.

36. *spherical US, CN /SFEER ih kł/ [SFĔR-]; UK /SFĔR ih kł/.

57. *figo /FEE goh/, /FIG oh/ an obscene gesture, also called the *fig of Spain.* Some eds. prefer the variant **fico** /FEE koh/.

61. arrant /ĂIR unt/ thoroughgoing.

70, 75. perfit(ly) /PUR fit (lee)/ archaic variant of **perfect(ly)**. Also /PAR fit/ in Shk's time.

72. sconce /skŏnss/ fortification.

98. perdition /pur DISH un/; UK *also* [PUR DISH un] losses.

102. bubukles, bubuckles /BYOO buck łz/ pimples. Some eds. prefer **bubuncles** /BYOO bunk łz/.

112. lenity /LEN ih tee/ leniency.

130. *exchequer /eks CHEK ur/; US *rarely* [EKS chek ur] treasury.

Act 3 Scene 7

12. pasterns /PĂSS turnz/ part of a horse's foot.

13. *entrails /EN traylz/; US *also* [-trłz] guts.

18. Hermes /HUR meez/ messenger of the gods.

21. *Perseus he rode the winged horse, Pegasus. /PUR see us/ [-syōōss], US *rarely* [-sōōss]. See App. D *-eus.*

27, 33. palfrey(s) /PAWL free(z)/; UK *also* [PŎL-] saddle horse.

29. *homage /HŎM ij/; US *also* /ŎM ij/ acknowledgement of allegience.

44. courser /COR sur/ warhorse.

53. kern /kurn/ Irish foot soldier.

54. strossers /STRŎSS urz/; US *also* /STRAWSS-/ archaic variant of *trousers.*

59. as live as soon. May have been /liv/ in Shk's time. Variant of **as lief** /leef/. In the US **lieve** /leev/ is still found in some dialects and can also be used here.

141, 148. **mastiffs** /MĂST ifs/; UK *sometimes* [MAHST-] powerful watchdogs.

148. **robustious** /roh BUS chus/ boisterous.

152. **shrowdly** /SHROHD lee/ badly. Archaic variant of **shrewdly**.

Act 4 Chorus

9. **umber'd** /UM burd/ darkened.

43. *****largess, largesse** generous gift. Here should have 1st syllable stress
US /LAR jess/ [-zhess]; CN, UK /LAR zhess/ [-jess]. Forms with /j/ are older.

Act 4 Scene 1

23. **slough** /sluff/ skin.

23. **legerity** /luh JĔR ih tee/ nimbleness.

40. *****puissant** powerful. The traditional forms are /PWISS nt/, /PYŌŌ snt/ (see
App. D).

60. *****figo** /FEE goh/, /FIG oh/ an obscene gesture, also called the *fig of Spain.*
Some eds. prefer the variant **fico** /FEE koh/.

67. **prerogatifes, prerogatifs**. Fluellen's version of **prerogatives** 'rights'
/pur RŎG uh tivz/ [prih-, pree-]. /pree-/ non-standard in the UK.

69, 71. **Pompey('s)** /PŎMP ee/ Roman general.

115. **Thames** /temz/ the major river of London.

160. **arbitrement, arbitrament** /ar BIT ruh munt/ settlement.

161. *****peradventure** perhaps. /PUR ad VEN chur/;
US *rarely* [PĔR-, PUR ad ven chur];
UK, CN *also* [PUR-, PĔR ad ven chur, pĕr ad VEN chur].

164. *****bulwark** structure for defense. US, CN /BULL wurk/ [BŬL wurk];
UK /BULL WURK, -wurk/. The vowels /or/, /ahr/ not recommended in the final
syllable, and are non-standard in the UK.

ă-bat, ăir-m**arry**, air-p**air**, ar-f**ar**, ĕr-m**erry**, ĝ- g**et**, ī-h**igh**, ĭr-m**irror**, ł-litt**le**, ṇ-**listen**,
ŏ-h**ot**, oh-g**o**, ōō-w**ood**, ōō-m**oon**, oor-t**our**, ōr- **or**, ow-h**ow**, ţh-**that**, ~~th~~-**thin**, ŭ-b**ut**,
UR-f**ur**, ur-und**er**.   ( ) - suppress the syllable   see p. xiii for complete list.

169. **beadle** /BEE dl/ local official in charge of whippings.

223. **enow** /ih NOW/; US *also* /ee-/ archaic variant of **enough**.

250. ***homage** /HŎM ij/; US *also* /ŎM ij/ acknowledgement of allegience.

255. **flexure** /FLEK shur/; UK *also* [-syoor] bowing. See App. D -*ure*.

273. **Phoebus** /FEE bus/ god of the sun.

274. ***Elysium** the realm of the blessed in the after-life. US /ih LEEZH yum/
[-LIZ-, -LIZH-, -LEESS-, -LISS-]; UK /-LIZ-/; *also* /ee-/ in all countries. The
oldest forms still in use are /-LIZ-/, /-LIZH-/. The historic form is
/ih LIZH um/.

275. ***Hyperion** /hī PEER yun/ god of the sun. Sometimes newer /-PĔR-/ or
/-ŏn/ are used, but are not recommended.

296. **contrite** here should be /CŎN trīt/ remorseful.

301. **chauntries** archaic variant of **chantries** US /CHĂNT reez/;
UK, E. NEW ENG. /CHAHN treez/ chapels. See App. D -*aun*-.

Act 4 Scene 2

2. **varlot** attendent.   Archaic variant of **varlet**, both pronounced /VAR lut/.

11. **dout** /dowt/ extinguish.

18. **shales** /shaylz/ archaic variant of **shells**.

28. **enow** /ih NOW/; US *also* /ee-/ archaic variant of **enough**.

29. **hilding** /HILL ding/ base.

35. **sonance** /SOH nunss/ sound.

43. ***bankrout** /BANK rowt/ [-rut] archaic variant of **bankrupt**.

46. **torch-staves** /stayvz/ staffs.

49. ***gimmal'd** hinged. US /ĜIM ld/; UK /JIM ld/, the latter is the older form, the
former a spelling pronunciation.   Some eds. prefer **gimmal** or **gemmelled**
/JEM ld/ 'having double rings.'

55. **liveless** /LĪV liss/ archaic variant of **lifeless**.

58. **provender** /PRŎV n̩ dur/ dry food for animals.

60. *__*guidon__ US /ĜĪ dn̩, -dun/ [-dŏn]; UK /-dŏn/ [-dn̩, -dun] standard. See App. D -*on*.

Act 4 Scene 3

6. **God buy you.** Some eds. substitute **God bye ye, God be wi' ye** or some other variation of that phrase, however it would have to be reduced to something like /gŏd BWEE yuh/ to fit the meter.

20. **enow** /ih NOW/; US *also* /ee-/ archaic variant of **enough**.

40-57. **Crispian** /CRISP ee un/.

54. **Talbot** US /TAL but/ [TAWL-]; UK /TAWL but/ [TŎL-, TAL-].

105. **bullet's crasing** (F1, Q1-3) variant of **crazing**, both pronounced /CRAY zing/ meaning 'breaking into pieces,' or 'ricocheting.' Some eds. prefer F2's **grasing**, variant of **grazing**, both pronounced /GRAY zing/ 'ricocheting.'

107. **relapse** here should be /REE laps/, the normal US form. The usual UK form is /rih LAPS/.

114. **slovenry** /SLUV un ree/ untidiness.

131. *__*vaward__ US /VAW wurd, VAY-/ [VOW-]; UK /VAW wurd/ [VAY-, VOW-, VAW WURD]. The vowel of *war* not recommended in the second syllable. Archaic variant of **vanguard**. See App. D -*aun*-.

Act 4 Scene 4

In this scene Pistol's prisoner speaks a dialect, or archaic form of French which is in some cases different from present day standard French. *Moi* is /moy/, which Pistol repeats. *Bras* is /brahss/.

8. **Perpend** /pur PEND/ consider.

ă-bat, ăir-**marry**, air-**pair**, ạr-**far**, ĕr-**merry**, ĝ- get, ī-**high**, ĭr-**mirror**, l̩-**little**, n̩-**listen**, ŏ-hot, oh-go, o͞o-**wood**, o͞o-**moon**, oor-**tour**, ŏr- **or**, ow-**how**, t̠h-**that**, t̶h̶-**thin**, ŭ-but, UR-**fur**, ur-under.   ( ) - suppress the syllable   see p. xiii for complete list.

8. **Dew** the soldier says *Dieu* /dyö/, which Pistol interprets as *dew*, which was /dih-o͞o/ in Shk's Eng.

11. **Egregious** /ih GREE jus/ extraordinary.

26-28. **Le Fer** /luh FAIR/.

28, 31. **firk** /furk/ beat.

37. **Owy, cuppele gorge, permafoy** Pistol is trying to say *Oui, couper la gorge, par ma foi* 'Yes, cut (your) throat, by my faith.' In French: /wee, ko͞o pay lah GORZH, par mah FWAH/.   *-er-* sometimes represented /ahr/ in Shk's English.

Act 4 Scene 5

7. *****perdurable** (F1) here should be /PUR dyur uh bł/; US *also* [-dur-] lasting. Omitted Q1-2.

14. **pander** (F1) /PAN dur/ pimp. Q1-2 have **leno** Latin 'pimp.' Ang.Lat. /LEE noh/; Class.Lat. /LAY noh/.

19. **enow** (F1) /ih NOW/; US *also* /ee-/ archaic variant of Q1-2's **enough**.

Act 4 Scene 6

21. **raught** /rawt/ reached.

35. *****alarum** US, CN /uh LAHR um/ [-LĂIR-]; UK /uh LĂIR um, uh LAHR um/ a call to arms.

Act 4 Scene 7

2. **arrant** /ĂIR unt/ thoroughgoing.

11-100. **Monmouth** /MŎN muth/; UK *also* [MUN-].

20-27. **Macedon** /MĂSS uh dun, -dŏn/. /-ŏn/ is usual in the US and is increasingly common in the UK. See App. D *-on*.

28, 106. **Wye** /wī/ river in Wales.

39-45. Clytus some eds. prefer **Cleitus** both pronounced /CLĪ tuss/ Alexander's friend.

49. gipes some eds. prefer **gypes**. Fluellen's version of **gibes** /jībz/ 'sarcastic comments' with the /b/ slightly *p*-like.

51. Falstaff US /FAWL stăff/; E. NEW ENG., UK /-stahff/.

61. skirr /skur/ scurry.

62. Assyrian /uh SĬR yun/.

80. Yerk /yurk/ kick.

91. Crispin Crispianus /CRISP in crisp ee AY nuss/; Class.Lat. /-AHN ōōs/.

103. Saint Tavy's Fluellen's version of **St. Davy's**. The use of the letter *T* is deceptive. The Welsh would use a /d/ more or less like that in Eng.

111. Jeshu (Q1-2) Fluellen's Welsh version of Q3's **Iesu** /JEE zōō, -zyōō/ (see p. 35, *Jesu*).

133. craven /CRAY vin, -vn̩/ coward.

138. Belzebub /BEL zih bub/ archaic variant of **Beelzebub** /bee EL zih bub/ a devil.

141. arrant /ĂIR unt/ thoroughgoing.

154, 157. Alanson angl. /AL un sun, -sn/, /uh LAN sun/; Fr. **Alençon** /ah lahⁿ sohⁿ/. At 4.8.96 with 1st syllable stress.

Act 4 Scene 8

4. *peradventure perhaps. /PUR ad VEN chur/;
US *rarely* [PĔR-, PUR ad ven chur];
UK, CN *also* [PUR-, PĔR ad ven chur, pĕr ad VEN chur].

9. 'Sblud, 'Sblood /zblud/ God's (i.e., Jesus') blood. Some eds. prefer **God's plood** (following Q1).

9, 34. arrant /ĂIR unt/ thoroughgoing.

ă-bat, ăir-marry, air-pair, ạr-far, ĕr-merry, ĝ- get, ī-high, ĭr-mirror, l-little, n̩-listen, ŏ-hot, oh-go, ōō-wood, ōō-moon, oor-tour, ŏr- or, ow-how, ṭh-that, th-thin, ŭ-but, UR-fur, ur-under.   ( ) - suppress the syllable   see p. xiii for complete list.

Some of the names listed in this scene appear in "People in the Play."

18-96. **Alanson ('s)** angl. /AL un sun/, /uh LAN sun, -sņ/; Fr. **Alençon**
/ah lah^n soh^n/. Line 96. must have 1st syllable stress (or possibly 3rd, if the Fr.
pronunciation is used).

36. **avouchment** /uh VOWCH munt/ affirmation.

44. **martial law** /MAR shł/ laws of war.

63. **twelvepence** /TWELV punss, -pņss/; US *also* /TWELV penss/.

77. **Bouciqualt, Boucicault** /BO͞O see koh/ (which is also the Fr.
pronunciation); US *also* /BO͞O see kawlt/.

84, 104. **esquire(s)** here should be /ess KWĪR(Z)/, the usual UK form.

92. **Charles Delabreth** /del uh BRET, -BRE̶T̶H̶/. Some eds. prefer **Delabret**.
1st syllable stress is also possible.

93. **Jacques of Chatillion** there are two possibilities: *Jacques* can be two
syllables, usually /JAY kweez/ (see AYL "People in the play") and *Chatillion*
angl. /SHAT ł yun, SHAT il yun/. Or *Jacques* can be one syllable /jayks/,
followed by /shuh TIL yun/. Some eds. prefer **Chatillon** or Fr. **Châtillon**
/shah tee yoh^n/. *Jacques* in Fr. is /zhahk/.

95. **Sir Guichard Dolphin** in Shk's time /GWITCH-, ĜITCH urd DŎL fin/;
which in the US today would have become /DAWL-/ in some areas;
Fr. /ĜEE shar/. Some eds. prefer **Guischard** /ĜISH urd/ or Fr. **Guiscard
Dauphin** angl. /ĜIS card DAW fin/; Fr. /ĜEES car DOH fă^n/.

96. **Anthony** US /AN t̶h̶uh nee/; UK /AN tuh nee/ [-t̶h̶uh nee]. Some eds. prefer
Antony.

96. **Brabant** angl. /BRAB unt/; Dutch /BRAH bahnt/; Fr. /BRAH bah^n/ former
duchy where Belgium is today.

98. **Edward** some eds. prefer Fr. **Édouard** /AY dwahr/.

99. **Roussi** /RO͞O see/.

99. **Faulconbridge** /FAWL kun brij/ or the older pronunciation [FAW kun-],
still used by some in the UK. Some eds. prefer **Falconbridge** which may also be

/FAL-/; UK *also* [FŎL-]. Others prefer **Fauconbridge** /FAW kun-/,
Fauconberg angl. /-burg/; Fr. /-bĕrg/.

99. **Foix** angl. /foyz/; Fr. /fwah/.

100. **Marle** /marl/.

100. **Vaudemont** here should be 3 syllables /VOH duh mŏnt/;
Fr. /voh duh moh^n/.

100. **Lestrake** /LESS strayk/. Some eds. prefer **Lestrale** /LESS strahl/,
Lestrelles /LESS strel/.

104. **Ketley** (F1) /KET lee/ archaic variant of **Keighley** /KEE̶T̶H̶ lee, KEE lee/.
Some eds. prefer **Kikely** /KĬK lee/.

104. **esquire** here should be /ess KWĪR/, the usual UK form.

108. **stratagem** /STRAT uh jum/ plan.

123. **Non nobis** Ang.Lat. /NŎN NOH bis/; Church Latin /NOHN NOH beess/
Psalm 115.

123. **Te Deum** Ang.Lat. /TEE DEE um/; Church Latin /TAY DAY ōōm/ hymn
of thanksgiving.

Act 5 Chorus

16. **Blackheath** /black HEE̶T̶H̶/, or with evenly stressed syllables.

21. **ostent** here should be /ŏ STENT/ display.

26. **th'*antique** ancient. Here /T̶H̶ ʸAN teek/, *rarely older* [AN tik].

27. **plebeians** /plih BEE unz/ common people.

Act 5 Scene 1

5-53. **scald** /skawld/ scabby.

ă-bat, ăir-m**arry**, air-p**air**, ạr-f**ar**, ĕr-m**erry**, ĝ- g**et**, ī-h**igh**, ĭr-m**irror**, ł-l**ittle**, ṇ-l**isten**,
ŏ-h**ot**, oh-g**o**, ōō-w**ood**, ōō-m**oon**, oor-t**our**, ōr- **or**, ow-h**ow**, ţh-t**hat**, t̶h̶-t**hin**, Ŭ-b**ut**,
UR-f**ur**, ur-u**nder**.   ( ) - suppress the syllable   see p. xiii for complete list.

19. **bedlam** /BED lum/ crazy.

20. **Parca's** /PAR kuz/ one of the Fates.

21. **qualmish** nauseated. /KWAHM ish/ is older; /KWAHL mish, KWAWL mish/ are newer. In UK the latter are non-standard.

28. **Cadwallader** /KAD wawl uh dur/ last of the Welsh kings.

34. **victuals** /VIT łz/ food.

65. **woodmonger** woodseller. US /Wo͞oD mŏng gur/ or /-mawng-/ [-mung-]; CN /-mung gur, -mŏng gur/; UK /-mung gur/.

66. **God buy you** (F1) good bye. Some eds. substitute **God b'wi' you** /gŏd BWEE yo͞o/ or some other variation of that phrase.

73. **avouch** /uh VOWCH/ uphold.

80. ***huswife** /HUZ if/ is traditional, /HUSS wīf/ is a newer, spelling pronunciation. The former is the most common form in the UK, the latter in the US. In CN both are used equally. In North America /HUSS wif/ is also sometimes used. Some eds. prefer mod. **housewife**. Here means **hussy**.

81. **spittle, Spital** /SPIT ł/ hosptial in Spitalfields.

89. **Gallia** /GAL yuh/ France.

Act 5 Scene 2

17. ***basilisks** canons. US /BĂSS ih lisks/ [BAZ ih lisks]; UK /BAZ-/ [BĂSS-]; CN both used equally.

31. **congreeted** /cun-, cŏn GREET id/ greeted each other.

44. **leas** /leez/ fields.

45. **darnel** /DAR nł/ a weed.

45. **femetary** a weed. Probably /FEM ih tuh ree, -tree/, variant of **fumitory** US /FYO͞OM ih tor ee/; UK /-tuh ree, -tree/.

46. **coulter** /KOHL tur/ cutting edge of a plow.

47. **deracinate** /dih-, dee RĂSS ih nayt/ wipe out.

48, 54. **mead(s)** /meedz/ meadows.

48. **erst** /urst/ formerly.

49. **cowslip** /COW slip/ a yellow flower.

49. **burnet** /BUR nit/ a flower. US *also* /bur NET/ which does not fit the meter.

72. **tenures** archaic variant of **tenors** 'general principles,' both /TEN urz/.

81. **re-survey** here should be /ree sur VAY/.

82. **peremptory** here should be /PĔR um tur ee/; US *also* /-tor ee/ final.

137. **vauting** (*vawting* F1) /VAWT ing/ archaic variant of **vaulting**.

140. **buffet** /BUFF it/ box.

142. **jack-an-apes** /JACK uh nayps/ monkey.

144. *****protestation** expressions of love. US /proh tess-, prŏt ess TAY shun/; CN /prŏt ess-/ [proh tess-]; UK /prŏt ess-/.

158. **prater** /PRAY tur/ chatterer.

183, 207. **Saint Denis** US /saynt DEN iss/; UK /sint-, sṇt-/ patron saint of France.

208. **Constantinople** /cŏn stan tih NOH pł/.

210. **flower-de-luce** /FLOWR duh lōōss/ lily flower, the national emblem of France. Main stress may also fall on the 3rd syllable, the usual US form (for /lyōō-/ see App. D *lu-*).

215. **moi'ty, moiety** /MOY tee, MOY uh tee/ portion.

235. **avouch** /uh VOWCH/ affirm.

240. **Plantagenet** /plan TAJ ih nit/.

ă-bat, ăir-**marry**, air-**pair**, ạr-**far**, ĕr-**merry**, ĝ- get, ī-**high**, ĭr-**mirror**, ł-**little**, ṇ-**listen**, ŏ-**hot**, oh-**go**, ōō-**wood**, ōō-**moon**, oor-**tour**, ōr- **or**, ow-**how**, ṭh-**that**, t̶h̶-**thin**, ŭ-**but**, UR-**fur**, ur-**under**.   ( ) - suppress the syllable   see p. xiii for complete list.

341-42.   **Praeclarissimus**   **filius**   **noster**   **Henricus,**
Ang.Lat. /pree clair ISS ih muss   FIL ee us   NŎST ur   hen RĪ k̇uss/
Class.Lat. /prī clah RISS ih mōōs   FEE lee ōōs   NŎST ĕr   hen REE kōōs/
          'Our most famous son, Henry,'

                Rex   Angliae,   **et   Heres**   **Franciae**
Ang.Lat. /reks   ANG lih ee   et   HEER eez   FRAN shih ee/
Class.Lat. /rayks AHNG glih ī   et   HAY rayss   FRAHN kih ī/
          'King of England and heir of France.'

Praeclarissimus is an error for **Praecarissimus** 'most dear':
Ang.Lat. /pree kair-/; Class.Lat. /prī kahr-/. Some eds. prefer the Latin variant
Haeres instead of *Heres*, which would be the same in Ang.Lat. and /HĪR ayss/
in Class.Lat.

362. **spousal** /SPOW zł/ union.

366. **incorporate** /in CORP rut, -rayt/ united. /-ut / is more usual for an adj.

372. ***surety** guarantee. Here should be two syllables, though in mod. English,
three syllables are more common, /SHUR (ih) tee, SHOOR-, SHOR-/ (see
App. D).

Henry VI part one

People in the Play

Aire (Joan) (F1) /air/. Most eds. prefer **Arc** /ark/.

Alanson /uh LAN sun, -sņ/. At 1.1.95 it should be /AL un sun/. Some eds. prefer Fr. **Alençon** /ah lah^n soh^n/.

Auvergne always 2 syllables. Angl. /oh VAIRN/ [-VURN]; Fr. /oh VĔRN ^{y}/.

Basset /BĂSS it/.

Beauford (F1) /BOH furd/. Some eds. prefer **Beaufort** /BOH furt/.

Cardinal (Henry Beauford) 2 or 3 syllables depending on meter /CARD ņ ł/, /CARD (ih) nł/. Two syllables is usual in the US, three syllables in the UK.

Dolphin /DŎL fin/; US *also* /DAWL-/ angl. form of **Dauphin** 'the French heir to the throne' which here would be Fr. /DOH fă^n/. In Shk's time /l/ in this position was often silent, so *dolphin* and *dauphin* were probably both /DAW fin/.

de la Pole (Suffolk) today pronounced /del uh POHL/ or /P$\overline{OO}$L/, the latter being older. The choice will depend on the interpretation of the pun at 2H6 4.1.70.

Exeter (Thomas Beauford) /EK sih tur/.

Falstaff US /FAWL stăff/; E. NEW ENG., UK /-stahff/. Some eds prefer **Fastolfe, Fastolf** /FĂSS tŏlf/.

Glansdale /GLĂNZ dayl, -dł/. Some eds. prefer **Glasdale** US /GLĂS dayl, GLĂZ-/; UK *also* /GLAHSS-, GLAHZ-/.

Gloucester /GLŎS tur/; US *also* /GLAWSS-/. At 1.3.6 and 62 expanded to 3 syllables /-uh tur/.

Henry 2 or 3 syllables depending on meter /HEN (ur) ree/.

Jailers some eds. prefer the UK spelling **Gaolers**, pronounced the same way.

ă-bat, ăir-**ma**rry, air-**pair**, ạr-**far**, ĕr-**merry**, ĝ- **get**, ī-**high**, ĭr-**mirror**, ł-**little**, ņ-**listen**, ŏ-**hot**, oh-**go**, $\overline{oo}$-**wood**, $\overline{oo}$-**moon**, oor-**tour**, ōr- **or**, ow-**how**, ţh-**that**, ŧħ-**thin**, ŭ-**but**, UR-**fur**, ur-**under**.   ( ) - suppress the syllable   see p. xiii for complete list.

People in the Play (cont.)

Joan de Pucelle the mod. angl. pronunciation would be /duh pyo͞o SELL/ but in Shk *Pucelle* should have first syllable stress in some verse, and lines which allow 2nd syllable stress were meant to be inverted. Shk's pronunciation was /PŬZZ ł/ or /PŬS ł/, see 1.4.107. Some eds. prefer **la Pucelle**, Fr. /lah pü sel/.

Lancaster US /LANG kăst ur, -kᵘss tur/;
UK /LANG kᵘss tur/ [-kahst ur, -kăst ur].

Margaret /MAR guh rit/ or /MAR grit/ depending on meter.

Orleance here should be /OR l(ee) yunss, OR leenss, or LEENSS/ depending on meter. Archaic variant of **Orleans** /OR l(ee) yunz, OR leenz, or LEENZ/. Other eds. prefer Fr. **Orléans** /or lay ahⁿ/.

Plantagenet /plan TAJ ih nit/.

Pole see **de la Pole**

Pucelle see **Joan**

Regent (Bedford) /REE junt/.

Reignier stressed on 1st or 2nd syllable depending on meter.
Angl. /RAY neer, ray NEER/ or quasi-Fr. /RAYN yay, rayn YAY/;
Fr. /ren yay/. Some eds. prefer **René** /REN ay, ren AY/. Note that when it occurs in the first foot, it may be inverted with first syllable stress.

Salisbury 2 or 3 syllables, depending on meter US /SAWLZ b(ĕ)r ee/;
UK /SAWLZ b(u)r ee/ [SĂLZ-].

Shrewsbury (Talbot) 3 syllables US /SHRO͞OZ bĕr ee/ [SHROHZ-];
UK /SHROHZ bur ee/ [SHRO͞OZ-].

Suffolk /SUFF ᵘk/.

Talbot US /TAL but/ [TAWL-]; UK /TAWL but/ [TŎL-, TAL-].

Warwick US /WŌR ik/; E.COAST US, UK /WŎR-/. Place names in the US often have /-wik/ but this is not recommended for Shk.

Winchester (Henry Beauford) /WIN chih stur/; US *also* /WIN chess tur/.

People in the Play (cont.)

Woodvile, Woodville /WŏŏD vil/.

Places in the Play

Orleance city in France. Here should be /OR l(ee) yunss, OR leenss, or LEENSS/ depending on meter. Archaic variant of **Orleans** /OR l(ee) yunz, OR leenz, or LEENZ/. Other eds. prefer Fr. **Orléans** /or lay ahⁿ/.

Poictiers angl. /poy TEERZ/ city in France. Archaic variant of **Poitiers** /pwah TYAY/.

Roan city in France. 1 or 2 syllables depending on meter /rohn, ROH un/. Archaic angl. variant of **Rouen** which here would be Fr. /rwahⁿ/ or /RŌŌ ahⁿ/.

Act 1 Scene 1

4. **scourge** /SKURJ/ whip.

23. **mishap** here should be /mis HAP/.

50. **nourish** US /NUR ish/; UK, E.COAST US /NUH rish/ archaic variant of **nurse**. Some eds. prefer **marish** /MĂIR ish/ marsh.

52. **invocate** /ĬN voh kayt/ call upon.

59. **discomfiture** /dis CUM fih chur/ defeat. See App. D -*ure*.

60. **Guienne, Guyenne** /ĝee ENN/.

60. **Champaigne** /sham PAYN/. Some eds. prefer **Compiègne** /kohⁿ PEN^Y/.

60, 92. **Rheims** angl. /reemz/; Fr. /răⁿss/ city in France.

---

61. **Guysors.** Mod. **Gisors** angl. /jee ZOR, -ZORZ/; Fr. /zhee ZOR/ but it may have been /g/ for Shk.

71. **maintain** here should be /MAYN tayn/.

79. ***sloth** US, CN /slawth/ [slohth]; UK /slohth/ [slŏth] laziness.

ă-bat, ăir-**marry**, air-**pair**, ạr-**far**, ĕr-**merry**, ĝ- get, ī-**high**, ĭr-**mirror**, ł-**little**, ṇ-**listen**, ŏ-**hot**, oh-**go**, ŏŏ-**wood**, ōō-**moon**, oor-**tour**, ŏr- **or**, ow-**how**, ṭh-**that**, th-**thin**, ŭ-**but**, UR-**fur**, ur-**under**.   ( ) - suppress the syllable   see p. xiii for complete list.

80. **flower-de-luces** /flowr duh L$\overline{OO}$S iz/ lily flowers. Main stress may also fall on the 1st syllable (for /ly$\overline{oo}$-/ see App. D *lu-*).

89. *****mischance** in verse normally with 2nd syllable stress.

94. **Anjou** angl. here /an J$\overline{OO}$/; Fr. /ah^n ZH$\overline{OO}$/.

126. **agaz'd** /uh GAYZD/ amazed.

128. **amain** /uh MAYN/ with full force.

132. *****vaward** US /VAW wurd, VAY-/ [VOW-]; UK /VAW wurd/ [VAY-, VOW-, VAW WURD]. The vowel of *war* not recommended in the second syllable. Archaic variant of **vanguard**. See App. D *-aun-*.

137. **Wallon** person from S. Belgium. Archaic variant of **Walloon** /wŏ-, wuh L$\overline{OO}$N/, probably pronounced the same; Fr. /vah loh^n/.

146. **Hungerford** /HUNG gur furd/.

170, 176. **Eltam** /EL tum/ variant of **Eltham** /EL thum/.

177. **weal** /weel/ welfare.

Act 1 Scene 2

11. **provender** /PRŎV ņ dur/ dry food for animals.

18. *****alarum** US, CN /uh LAHR um/ [-LĂIR-]; UK /uh LĂIR um, uh LAHR um/ a call to arms.

19. **forlorn** here should be /FOR lorn/.

The Complete Oxford begins 1.3 here (line nos. in parentheses).

29. (1.3.8) **Froissard** /FROY surd, -sard/. Some eds. prefer **Froissart** angl. /FROY surt, -sart/. Fr. for both forms is /frwah sahr/.

33. (1.3.12) **Goliases** /guh L$\overline{I}$ us iz/ archaic variant of **Goliaths** /guh L$\overline{I}$ uths/ which would not fit the meter.

41. (1.3.20) **gimmors**, **gimmers** /JIM urz/ part of a clock's works.

50. (1.3.29) **succor** (UK **succour**) /SUCK ur/ help. See App. D *-or*.

56. (1.3.35) **sibyls** /SIB łz/; UK *also* /SIB ilz/ prophetesses.

57. (1.3.36) **descry** /dih SKRĪ/ see.

78. (1.3.57) **deigned** /DAY nid/ thought it appropriate.

83. (1.3.62) **complete** here should be /CŎM pleet/.

84. (1.3.63) **swart** /swōrt/ black.

99. (1.3.78) **flower-de-luces** /flowr duh LOOS iz/ lily flowers (for /lyoo-/ see App. D *lu-*). Main stress may also fall on the 1st syllable.

100. (1.3.79) **Touraine** here should have 1st syllable stress /TOO rayn/, normally /too RAYN/; Fr. /too ren/.

105. (1.3.84) **Deborah** here should be 3 syllables /DEB uh ruh/.

117. (1.3.96) ***prostrate** /PRŎS trayt/, US *rarely* [-trut] lying face down.

126. (1.3.105) **recreants** /REK ree unts/ cowards.

129. (1.3.108) **scourge** /SKURJ/ instrument of punishment.

131. (1.3.110) **halcyons' days** calm weather. US /HAL see ŏnz/ [-unz]; UK /-unz/ [-ŏnz]. Some eds. prefer F1's **halcyon's**.

140. (1.3.119) **Mahomet** here should be /MAY uh met, -mit/ archaic variant of **Mohammed**, but 1st syllable stress is required.

142. (1.3.121) **Constantine** US /CŎN stun teen/ [-tīn]; UK /-tīn/ [-teen] Roman emperor.

Act 1 Scene 3 (*The Complete Oxford* 1.4)

5. **that knocks so imperiously** /im PEER yus lee/ imperially, arrogantly. Some eds. prefer **that knocketh** . . . to improve the line metrically.

13. **warrantize** authorization. US /WŌR un tīz/; UK, E.COAST US /WŎR un tīz/.

20. **commandement, commandment** here an archaic form with 4 syllables is indicated /-uh munt/.

ă-bat, äir-marry, air-pair, ạr-far, ĕr-merry, ĝ- get, ī-high, ĭr-mirror, ł-little, ṇ-listen, ŏ-hot, oh-go, oo-wood, oo-moon, oor-tour, ōr- or, ow-how, ţh-that, th-thin, ŭ-but, UR-fur, ur-under.   ( ) - suppress the syllable   see p. xiii for complete list.

23. **prelate** /PREL ut/ high-ranking churchman.

31. **proditor** /PRŎD ih tur/ traitor. See App. D *-or*.

57. **supreme** here should be US /SŌŌ preem/; UK, SOUTH. US *also* [SYŌŌ-].

57. *****magistrates** /MAJ ih strayts/; US *also* [-struts].

58. **contumeliously** disdainfully. /cŏn tyuh MEE lyus lee/; US *also* /cŏn tuh-/.
/cŏn chuh-/ considered non-standard in the UK.

70. *****tumultuous** full of turmoil. US /tōō MŬLL chwus/ [-tywus];
SOUTH. US *also* /tyōō-/; CN /tyōō-, tōō MUL chwus, -tywus/;
UK /tyōō MŬLL tywus/ [-chwus], *rarely* [tōō MŬLL-]. In the
UK /chōō MŬLL-/ is considered non-standard.

Act 1 Scene 4 (*The Complete Oxford* 1.5)

8. **Prince's espials** (F1) spies. /PRINSS ess SPĪ łz/ with the possessive *'s* not
pronounced as is usual in Shk. following /s/. Some eds. prefer **Prince's spials**
/PRINSS iz SPĪ łz/.

9. **close** /clohss/ tightly.

The Complete Oxford begins 1.6 here (line nos. in parentheses).

28. (1.6.6) **Ponton de Santrailles** angl. /PŎN tun duh san TRAYLZ/ or
/-TRAYL iz/; Fr. /POH^N toh^n duh sah^n TRĪ/.

39. (1.6.17) **contumelious** disdainful. /cŏn tyuh MEE lyus /; US *also* /cŏn tuh-/.
/cŏn chuh-/ considered non-standard in the UK.

52. (1.6.30) **adamant** /AD uh munt/ the hardest substance. /-mant/ not
recommended.

67. (1.6.45) *****bulwark** structure for defense. US, CN /BŲLL wurk/ [BŬL wurk];
UK /BŲLL WURK, -wurk/. The vowels /or/, /ahr/ not recommended in the final
syllable, and are non-standard in the UK.

74. (1.6.52) **martial** /MAR shł/ warlike.

98. (1.6.76) *****tumult's** turmoil's. US /TŌŌM ults/; SOUTH.US *also* /TYŌŌM-/;
CN /TYŌŌM-/ [TŌŌM-]; UK /TYŌŌM-/. /CHŌŌM-/ considered non-standard
in the UK. A newer pronunciation /TUM ult/ is not recommended.

99. (1.6.77) *alarum US, CN /uh LAHR um/ [-LĂIR-];
UK /uh LĂIR um, uh LAHR um/ a call to arms.

107. (1.6.85) **Pucelle or puzzel.** Other eds. offer a variety of readings: **Puzel or pucelle, Pucelle or pussel,** all based on F1's *Puzel or Pussel*. The wordplay in this line is founded on the double meaning of *pucelle* in Eliz. England: 'virgin,' and 'slut,' with the various eds. trying to indicate that there may have been a pronunciation difference between the two forms. Shk may have pronounced the words alike, or the second consonants may have been different as indicated in the F1 spellings. It is also difficult to determine whether the vowel was short or long, though F1 probably indicates /PŬZZ ł or PŬS ł/. The modern pronunciation of *pucelle* in Shk's verse would be /PYOO sł, -sel/, though here it could be /pyoo SELL/ in the first foot. *The Complete Oxford* has **Pucelle or pucelle,** which seems to indicate a Fr. pronunciation for the italicized first instance: /pü SEL or PYOO sł/.

109. (1.6.87) *quagmire bog. US, CN /KWĂG mīr/, US *rarely* [KWŎG-];
UK /KWŎG-/ [KWĂG-]. Normal development would favor /KWĂG-/.

Act 1 Scene 5 (*The Complete Oxford* 1.7)

12. *chastise punish. Here should be /CHĂSS tīz/, the usual US pronunciation, also used in CN; in the UK 2nd syllable stress is usual.

14. **victual** /VIT ł/ provide food for.

23. **noisome** /NOY sum/ disgusting.

31. **leopard** here 3 syllables are indicated, /LEE uh purd/ in Shk's time.

Act 1 Scene 6 (*The Complete Oxford* 1.8)

4. **creature** here 3 syllables are indicated /CREE uh chur/.

4. **Astraea's** /ass TREE uz/ goddess of justice.

6. *Adonis' US, CN /uh DŎN iss/, *rarely* [-DOHN-]; UK /uh DOHN iss/, *rarely* [-DŎN-] Venus' lover.

21. **pyramis** /PĬR uh mis/ archaic variant of **pyramid.**

ă-bat, ăir-**ma**rry, air-**pair**, ạr-**far**, ĕr-**merry**, ĝ- get, ī-**high**, ĭr-**mirror**, ł-**little**, ṇ-**listen**, ŏ-**hot**, oh-**go**, ōō-**wood**, ōō-**moon**, oor-**tour**, ōr- or, ow-**how**, ţh-**that**, th-**thin**, ŭ-**but**, UR-**fur**, ur-**under**.   ( ) - suppress the syllable   see p. xiii for complete list.

22. **Rhodope's** here should be /ROH doh peez/. /roh DOH pee/ is more usual today.

25. **Darius** /duh RĪ us/ Persian king.

28. **Saint Denis** US /saynt DEN iss/; UK /sint-, sṇt-/ patron saint of France.

Act 2 Scene 1

5. **servitors** /SURV ih turz/ servants. See App. D *-or*.

9. **Artois** /ahr TWAH/.

10. **Wallon** probably /wŏ-, wuh LO͞ON/ was intended; Fr. /vah loh^{n}/ present day *Wallonie*.

10. **Picardy** /PIK ur dee, -ahr-/ region in France.

21. **martial** /MAR shł/ warlike.

27. ***bulwarks** structures for defense. US, CN /BỤLL wurks/ [BŬL-]; UK /BỤLL WURKS, -wurks/. The vowels /or/, /ahr/ not recommended in the final syllable, and are non-standard in the UK.

41. ***trow** US, CN /troh, trow/; UK /trow/ [troh] trust. Shk's rhymes elsewhere indicate /-oh/.

42. ***alarums** US, CN /uh LAHR umz/ [-LĂIR-]; UK /uh LĂIR umz, uh LAHR umz/ calls to arms.

43. **exploits** here should be /ek SPLOYTS/.

68. **precinct** here should be /prih-, pree SINCT/.

Act 2 Scene 2

6. **centure** (F1) belt. /SEN chur/; UK *also* [-tyoor]. Archaic variant of **cincture** /SINK chur/. Some eds. prefer F2's **centre** (UK spelling of US **center**) 'enclosure, town square.' *Centure* could also have been pronounced /SEN tur/ in Shk's time. See App. D *-ure* and App. E.

Act 2 Scene 3

5. **exploit** here should be /ek SPLOYT/.

6. ***Scythian** /SI̶T̶H̶ yun/ [SIṬH yun] *Scythia* was north of the Black Sea. Some scholars prefer restored Latin /SK-/.

6. **Tomyris** /TŎM ih riss/ killed Cyrus in battle.

15. **scourge** /SKURJ/ instrument of punishment.

20. **Hector** /HEK tur/ Trojan hero. See App. D *-or.*

23. **writhled** /RIṬH ɫd/ shriveled.

42. **captivate** /KAP tih vayt, -ut/ taken prisoner. /-ut / is more usual for an adj.

47. **severity** /suh VĔR ih tee/.

57. ***nonce** /nŏnss/ occasion. US, CN [nunss] not recommended.

59. **contrarieties** /cŏn truh RĪ uh teez/ contradictions.

68. **bruited** /BRŌŌT id/ loudly declared.

73. **misconster** /mis CŎN stur/ misconstrue.

79. **cates** /kayts/ delicacies.

Act 2 Scene 4

17. **quillets** /KWIL its/ quibbles.

21. **purblind** /PUR blīnd/ blind or partly blind.

60. **scabbard** /SKAB urd/ sword sheath.

81-95. **yeoman, -men** /YOH mun, -min/ freeman who owns a small farm.

87. **craven** /CRAY vin, -vṇ/ cowardly.

102. **scourge** /SKURJ/ harshly punish.

| ă-bat, ăir-**marry**, air-**pair**, ạr-**far**, ĕr-**merry**, ĝ- **get**, ī-**high**, īr-**mirror**, ɫ-**little**, ṇ-**listen**, ŏ-**hot**, oh-**go**, ōō-**wood**, ōō-**moon**, oor-**tour**, ōr- **or**, ow-**how**, ṭh-**that**, t̶h̶-**thin**, ŭ-**but**, UR-**fur**, ur-**under**.   ( ) - suppress the syllable   see p. xiii for complete list. |

108. *cognizance /CŎG nih zunss, -zn̥ss/, *rarely older* [CŎN ih-] emblem.

124. prophesy /PRŎF uh sī/ to predict the future.

Act 2 Scene 5

5. *pursuivants heralds. US /PUR swiv unts/ [PUR siv unts];
UK /PUR swiv unts/, *rarely* [PUR siv unts].

6. Nestor-like /NEST ur/ oldest of the Greeks at Troy. See App. D -*or*.

9. exigent /EGZ-, EKS ih junt/ end.

23. Monmouth /MŎN muth/; UK *also* [MUN-].

25. sequestration /see kwih STRAY shun/ [sek wih-] seclusion.

49. obloquy /ŎB luh kwee/ insult.

77. Gaunt /gawnt/.

83. Bullingbrook Shk pronounced this name /BŲLL in brŏŏk/. Some eds.
prefer Bolingbroke, today pronounced US, CN /BOHL ing brŏŏk/ [BŲLL-,
BŎL-]; UK /BŎL-/, *rarely* [BŲLL-].

85. Langley /LANG lee/.

89. *diadem /DĪ uh dem/ [-dum] crown.

101. politic /PŎL ih tik/ cunning.

Act 3 Scene 1

6. extemporal /ek STEM p(ur) rł/ composed on the spur of the moment.

14-57. prelate /PREL ut/ high-ranking churchman.

15. pestiferous /pes TIF (uh) rus/ pestilential.

15. dissentious /dih SEN shus/ causing arguments.

17. usurer /YŌŌ zhur ur/; UK *also* [-zhyoor ur, -zhoor ur] someone who lends
money for interest.

18. **Froward** /FROH wurd, FROH urd/ difficult to deal with.

19. **Lascivious** /luh SIV yus/ lustful.

44. **imperious** /im PEER yus/ imperial.

66. **weal** /weel/ commonwealth.

74. ***tumult's** turmoil's. US /TOŌM ults/; SOUTH.US *also* /TYOŌM-/;
CN /TYOŌM-/ [TOŌM-]; UK /TYOŌM-/. /CHOŌM-/ considered non-standard
in the UK. A newer pronunciation /TUM ult/ is not recommended.

98. **commonweal** /CŎM un weel/ commonwealth.

143. **contract** here should be /cŏn TRACT/.

155. **Eltam** /EL tum/ variant of **Eltham** /EL t̶h̶um/.

169. **reguerdon** /ree-, rih GURD n̩/ reward.

197. **Monmouth** /MŎN mu̶t̶h̶/; UK *also* [MUN-].

Act 3 Scene 2

7. ***slothful** US, CN /SLAWT̶H̶ fu̩ll/ [SLOHT̶H̶-]; UK /SLOHT̶H̶-/ [SLŎT̶H̶-]
lazy.

13. **Qui là?** /kee lah/ who's there?

14. **Paysans, la pauvre gens de France** /pay zah[n], lah POHV r[uh] zhah[n] duh
FRAH[N]SS/ Peasants, the poor people of France. Some eds. prefer **gent** 'tribe'
instead of *gens*, pronounced the same way.

17. ***bulwarks** structures for defense. US, CN /BU̩LL wurks/ [BŬL-];
UK /BU̩LL WURKS, -wurks/. The vowels /or/, /ahr/ not recommended in the final
syllable, and are non-standard in the UK.

The Complete Oxford begins 3.3 here (line nos. in parentheses).

3.2.18. (3.3.1) **Saint Denis** US /saynt DEN iss/; UK /sint-, sn̩t-/ patron saint of
France.

ă-bat, ăir-marry, air-pair, a̩r-far, ĕr-merry, ĝ- get, ī-high, ĭr-mirror, l̵-little, n̩-listen,
ŏ-hot, oh-go, ōō-wood, ōō-moon, oor-tour, ōr- or, ow-how, t̩h-that, t̶h̶-thin, ŭ-but,
UR-fur, ur-under.   ( ) - suppress the syllable   see p. xiii for complete list.

3.2.18. (3.3.1) **stratagem** /STRAT uh jum/ scheme.

3.2.28. (3.3.11) **Talbonites** US /TAL bun īts/ [TAWL-];
UK /TAWL-/ [TŎL-, TAL-] followers of Talbot.

The Complete Oxford begins 3.5 here (line nos. in parentheses).

3.2.44. (3.5.4) **darnel** /DAR nł/ a weed.

3.2.45. (3.5.5) *__courtezan, courtesan__ a rich man's whore.
US /CORT ih zun, -zan/, *rarely* [cort ih ZAN]; CN /CORT ih zan/ [-zun], *rarely*
[cort ih ZAN]; UK /CORT ih zan, cort ih ZAN/.

3.2.53. (3.5.13) *__paramours__ US, CN /PĂIR uh moorz/ [-morz];
UK /-morz/ [-moorz] lovers.

3.2.64. (3.5.24) **Hecate** here, exceptionally in Shk, /HEK ut ee/ goddess of
witchcraft.

3.2.68. (3.5.27) **muleters** it is not certain whether Shk pronounced this
/MYOO lih turz/ or as in mod. **muleteers** /myoo lih TEERZ/.

3.2.73. (3.5.32) **God buy** some eds. substitute **Goodbye**, or **God b'uy** /-BĪ/.

3.2.83. (3.5.42) **Cordelion's** /cor duh LĪ unz/ Richard the Lionhearted. Angl.
variant of **Coeur de Lion's** US /cur de LĪ unz, -LEE unz/; UK prefers the
Fr. /CUR duh LEE ohⁿz/, or sometimes semi-angl. [-LEE ŏnz, -LEE unz].

3.2.92. (3.5.51) **weal** /weel/ welfare.

The Complete Oxford begins 3.6 here (line nos. in parentheses).

3.2.118. (3.6.4) **martial** /MAR shł/ warlike.

3.2.123. (3.6.9) **glikes** scoffs. Uncertain, may have been /glicks/ or /glīks/,
variant of **gleeks** /gleeks/.

3.2.124. (3.6.10) **amort** /uh MORT/ downcast.

3.2.133. (3.6.19) **exequies** /EKS ih kweez/ funeral rites.

3.2.136. (3.6.22) **potentates** /POHT n tayts/ rulers.

Act 3 Scene 3 (*Complete Oxford* 3.7)

3. **corrosive** here should be US /COR uh siv/; E.COAST US, UK /CŎR-/.

10. **diffidence** /DIF ih dunss/ distrust.

24. **extirped** /ek STUR pid/ rooted out.

30. **unto Paris-ward** /PĂIR iss wurd/ toward Paris.

35-37. *****parley** /PAR lee/ conference with an enemy. Newer [-lay] not recommended.

61. **progeny** descent. /PRŎJ ih nee/; UK *also* [PROH-], a newer form.

89. **coronet** small crown. US /COR uh net, -nit/, /cor uh NET/;
E.COAST US /CŎR-, cŏr-/; UK /CŎR uh nit/ [-net, cŏr uh NET].

Act 3 Scene 4 (*Complete Oxford* 3.8)

23. **reguerdon'd** /ree-, rih GURD n̩d/ rewarded.

44. **miscreant** /MIS cr(ee) yunt/ scoundrel.

Act 4 Scene 1

9, 170. **Callice, Callis** /KAL iss/ city on north. coast of France. Both are archaic variants of **Calais** which here should be /KAL ay/, the normal UK form; Fr. /KAH lay/.

15. **craven's** /CRAY vinz, -vn̩z/ coward's.

19. **Poictiers** city in France. Angl. /poy TEERZ/. Archaic variant of **Poitiers** /pwah TYAY/. Some eds. prefer **Patay** angl. /pă TAY/; Fr. /pah TAY/.

25. *****divers** various. Here should be stressed on the first syllable US, CN /DĪ vurss, -vurz/; UK /DĪ vurss/ [-vurz].

69. *****chastisement** punishment. Here stress should be on 1st syllable /CHĂSS tiz munt/; US *also* /-tīz-/.

ă-bat, ăir-m**arry**, air-p**air**, a̞r-f**ar**, ĕr-m**erry**, ĝ- g**et**, ī-h**igh**, ĭr-m**irror**, ł-li**ttle**, n̩-lis**ten**, ŏ-h**ot**, oh-g**o**, o͞o-w**ood**, o͞o-m**oon**, oor-t**our**, ŏr- **or**, ow-h**ow**, t̪h-t**hat**, t̪h-t**hin**, ŭ-b**ut**, UR-f**ur**, ur-**under**.   ( ) - suppress the syllable   see p. xiii for complete list.

92. **sanguine** /SANG gwin/ red.

94. **repugn** /ree-, rih PYŌON/ reject.

107. **Bewray'd** /bih RAYD/; US *also* /bee-/ showed.

126. **clamorous outrage** here should be /CLAM ur us owt RAYJ/.

134. **combatants** here should be stressed on the first syllable, as is usual in the UK, /CŎM buh tunts/ [CUM-].

151. **umpeer** (*Vmper* F1) /UM peer/ archaic variant of **umpire**.

166. **progenitors** /proh-, pruh JEN ih turz/ ancestors. See App. D -*or*.

170. *****respite** interval. Here should be US /RESP it/, *rarely* [-īt]; CN /RESP it/ [-īt]; UK /RESP īt/ [-it]. /RESP it/ is older, but /-īt/ has been in use since the 17th cent.

173. **rout** /rowt/ mob.

175. *****orator** US, CN /OR uh tur/; UK, E.COAST US /ŎR-/. Sometimes /OR ayt ur/ is used, but it is not recommended. See App. D -*or*.

178. **Tush** /tŭsh/ expression of disdain.

180. **I wist** (*I wish* F1) I know. Some eds prefer *****iwis** /ih WISS/; US, CN *also* /ee WISS/ indeed.

191. *****presage** here should be /pree-, prih SAYJ/ foretell.

Act 4 Scene 2

1. **Burdeaux** city in France, possibly pronounced /BUR dŏcks/ in Shk's time. Archaic variant of **Bordeaux**, **Bourdeaux** which here should be /BOR doh/.

7. *****homage** /HŎM ij/; US *also* /ŎM ij/ acknowledgement of allegience.

16. **scourge** /SKURJ/ punishment.

29. **rive** /rīv/ fire a gun. Other eds. prefer **fire, rove, drive, aim**.

40, 46. **timorous** /TIM (uh) rus/ frightened.

Act 4 Scene 3

4-22. **Burdeaux** city in France, possibly pronounced /BUR dŏcks/ in Shk's time.
Archaic variant of **Bordeaux**, **Bourdeaux** which here should be /BOR doh/.

6. **espials** /ess PĪ łz/ spies.

13. **louted** /LOWT id/ mocked.

14. **chevalier** angl. /shev uh LEER/; Fr. /shev ahl YAY/ knight.

25. **cornets** here should be /COR nits/ cavalry squadrons.

29. **remiss** here should be /REE miss/ negligent.

30. **succor** (UK **succour**) /SUCK ur/ help. See App. D -*or*.

30. **distressed** here 1st syllable stress is indicated.

45. **Maine** angl. /mayn/; Fr. /men/ region in France.

45. **Blois** /blwah/ region in France.

45. **Tours** /toor/ city in France.

Act 4 Scene 4

11. **oe'rmatch'd** here with 1st syllable stress.

23. **succors** (UK **succours**) /SUCK urz/ helps. See App. D -*or*.

Act 4 Scene 5

2. **stratagems** /STRAT uh jumz/ schemes.

27. **exploit** here should be /ek SPLOYT/.

Act 4 Scene 6

15. **Gallia** /GAL yuh/ France.

ă-bat, ăir-marry, air-pair, ạr-far, ĕr-merry, ĝ- get, ī-high, ĭr-mirror, ł-little, ṇ-listen,
ŏ-hot, oh-go, ōō-wood, ōō-moon, oor-tour, ōr- or, ow-how, ţh-that, ŧh-thin, ŭ-but,
UR-fur, ur-under.　　　( ) - suppress the syllable　　　see p. xiii for complete list.

45. **paltry** /PAWL tree/ worthless.

49. ***mischance** in verse normally with 2nd syllable stress.

55. ***Icarus** /IK uh rus/ Daedalus' son. UK /ĪK-/ not recommended.

57. **commendable** here should be /CŎM en duh bł/.

Act 4 Scene 7

9. **guardant** /GARD ṇt/ guard.

16. ***Icarus** /IK uh rus/ Daedalus' son. UK /ĪK-/ not recommended.

20. ***perpetuity** eternity. /PUR puh TY$\overline{OO}$ ih tee/; US *also* [-T$\overline{OO}$-].
/-CH$\overline{OO}$-/ is also used but is considered non-standard in the UK.

21. **lither** /LIH t̩hur/ yielding.

35. **wood** /wo͞od/ crazy, distraught. It was also /wo͞od, wohd/ in the dialects of
North. Eng.

41. **giglot wench** /ĜIG lit/ loose woman.

48. **Gallia's** /GAL yuz/ France's.

60. **Alcides** /al SĪ deez/ Hercules.

63. **Valence** /VAL unss/; Fr. /VAH lah^{n}ss/.

64. **Goodrig** /Go͞oD rig/ in an inverted foot. Some eds. prefer **Goodrich**.

64. **Urchinfield** /UR chin feeld/.

65. **Blackmere** /BLACK meer/.

65. **Verdon, Verdun** here with 2nd syllable stress, both pronounced /vur DUN/;
Fr. /vĕr DĂ^N/.

65. **Alton** /AWL tun, AWLT ṇ/; UK *also* [ŎL-].

66. **Cromwell** US /CRŎM wel/; UK /CRŎM wł/. Formerly /CRUM ł/.

66. **Furnival** /FUR nih vł/.

67. **Falconbridge** /FAWL-, FAL kun brij/; UK *also* [FŎL-], *rarely older* [FAW kun-].

70. **Great marshal to Henry the Sixt.** If there are five feet in this line, then *marshal* must be pronounced in its archaic form /MAR uh shł/ with *Henry* expanded to /HEN ur ree/. Some eds. prefer Fr. **Maréchal** /mar ay shahl/,

77. **scourge** /SKURJ/ instrument of punishment.

Act 5 Scene 1

2, 17. **Arminack** perhaps pronounced /ARM ih nack/. Archaic variant of **Armagnac** angl. /arm un YAK/, /ARM un yak/; Fr. /arm ahn yahk/.

10. **stablish** /STAB lish/ establish.

12. **impious** /IM pyus/ lacking in respect, profane.

13. **immanity** /ih MAN ih tee/ barbarity.

23. **dalliance** /DAL yunss/ sportiveness.

23. *****paramour** US, CN /PĂIR uh moor/ [-mor]; UK /-mor/ [-moor] lover.

27. **weal** /weel/ welfare.

31. **prophesy** /PRŎF uh sī/ to predict the future.

46. **contract** here should be /cŏn TRACT/.

51. **legate** /LEG ut/ churchman representing the pope.

56. *****trow** US, CN /troh, trow/; UK /trow/ [troh] trust. Shk's rhymes elsewhere indicate /-oh/.

Act 5 Scene 2

5. **dalliance** /DAL ee unss/ idle delay.

ă-bat, ăir-marry, air-pair, ạr-far, ĕr-merry, ĝ- get, ī-high, ĭr-mirror, ł-little, ṇ-listen, ŏ-hot, oh-go, ōō-wood, ōō-moon, oor-tour, ōr- or, ow-how, th-that, th-thin, ŭ-but, UR-fur, ur-under.   ( ) - suppress the syllable   see p. xiii for complete list.

Act 5 Scene 3

2. **periapts** /PĔR ee apts/ amulets.

<hr>

The Complete Oxford begins 5.4 here (line nos. in parentheses)

<hr>

5.3.35. (5.4.6) **Circe** /SUR see/ enchantress in the Odyssey.

5.3.44. (5.4.15) **miscreant** /MIS cree unt/ faithless person.

<hr>

Complete Oxford begins 5.5 here (line nos. in parentheses)

<hr>

5.3.55. (5.5.11) **allotted** /uh LŎT id/ fated.

5.3.56. (5.5.12) **cygnets** /SIG nits/ young swans.

5.3.58. (5.5.14) *__servile__ /SUR vīl/, *rarely* [SUR vł] slave-like.

5.3.82. (5.5.38) *__paramour__ US, CN /PĂIR uh moor/ [-mor]; UK /-mor/ [-moor] lover.

5.3.85. (5.5.41) **randon** /RAN dun/ archaic form of **random**.

5.3.89, 107. (5.5.45,63) **Tush** /tŭsh/ expression of disdain.

<hr>

5.3.95, 154. (5.5.51, 110) **Anjou** angl. /AN jōō/ or /an JŌŌ/ depending on meter; Fr. /ahⁿ zhōō/.

5.3.95, 154. (5.5.51, 110) **Maine** angl. /mayn/; Fr. /men/.

<hr>

5.3.107. (5.5.63) **captivate** /KAP tih vayt, -vut/ taken prisoner. /-ut / is more usual for an adj.

5.3.130. (5.5.86) *__parley__ /PAR lee/ conference with an enemy. Newer [-lay] not recommended.

5.3.151. (5.5.107) **deign** /dayn/ think it appropriate.

5.3.169. (5.5.125) **diamond** here should be /DĪ mund/, the most common form in the US.

5.3.189. (5.5.145) *__Minotaurs__ monsters. US /MIN uh torz/ [MĪN-]; CN, UK both used equally.

Act 5 Scene 4 (*Complete Oxford* 5.6)

18. **collop** /CŎL up/ small slice of meat.

21. **avaunt** /uh VAWNT/ begone!

21. **suborn'd** /sub ORND/ persuaded someone to do something wrong.

38. **progeny** children. /PRŎJ ih nee/; US *also* [PROH-], a newer form.

56. **enow** /ih NOW/; US *also* /ee-/ archaic variant of **enough**.

74. **Machevile** /MATCH uh vil, -vł/ a cunning, deceitful person. Archaic variant of **Machiavel** /MAK yuh vel/, /MAHK-/.

90. ***Environ** /en VĪ run/; US *also* [-urn] surround.

102. ***travail** here should be /TRAV ayl/ hard work.

110. **progenitors** /proh-, pruh JEN ih turz/ ancestors. See App. D *-or*.

114. **severe** here should be /SEV eer/.

125. **lenity** /LEN ih tee/ leniency.

134. **coronet** small crown. US /COR uh net, -nit/, /cor uh NET/; E.COAST US /CŎR-, cŏr-/; UK /CŎR uh nit/ [-net, cŏr uh NET].

139. **Gallian** /GAL yun/ French.

141. **lucre** /LOO kur/ gain (for /lyoo-/ see App. D *lu-*).

142. ***prerogative** /pur RŎG uh tiv/ [prih-, pree-] right. /pree-/ non-standard in the UK.

149. **compremise** archaic variant of **compromise**, both pronounced /CŎM pruh mīz/.

156. **cavil** /KAV ł/; UK *also* /KAV il/ quibble.

156. **contract** here should be /cŏn TRACT/.

174. ***ensigns** flags. US, CN /EN snz/, US *rarely* [-sīnz]; UK /-snz, -sīnz/.

ă-bat, ăir-marry, air-pair, ạr-far, ĕr-merry, ĝ- get, ī-high, ĭr-mirror, ł-little, n̦-listen, ŏ-hot, oh-go, ōō-wood, ōō-moon, oor-tour, ōr- or, ow-how, t̪h-that, t̪h-thin, Ŭ-but, UR-fur, ur-under.   ( ) - suppress the syllable   see p. xiii for complete list.

Act 5 Scene 5 (*Complete Oxford* 5.7)

10. **Tush** /tŭsh/ expression of disdain.

26. **betroth'd** /bih-, bee TROHTHD/ engaged to be married.

28. **contract** here should be /cŏn TRACT/.

44. **Arminack** perhaps pronounced /ARM ih nack/. Archaic variant of
Armagnac angl. /arm un YAK/, /ARM un yak/; Fr. /arm ahn yahk/.

49. **abject** /AB ject/ contemptible.

58. *****nuptial** wedding. US, UK /NUP chł/ [-shł]; in CN both are used equally.

85. *****alarums** US, CN /uh LAHR umz/ [-LĂIR-];
UK /uh LĂIR umz, uh LAHR umz/ calls to arms.

Henry VI part two
The Complete Oxford calls this *The First Part of the Contention*

People in the Play

Beadle /BEE dł/.

Beauford (F1) /BOH furd/. Some eds. prefer **Beaufort** /BOH furt/.

Bevis /BEV iss, BEEV iss/. This name is not spoken.

Bolingbrook, Roger (Bullingbrooke F1, Bullenbrooke Q1-3), Bolingbroke
US /BOHL ing brŏŏk/ [BULL-, BŎL-]; CN /BOHL-/, *rarely* [BŎL-, BULL-];
UK /BŎL-/ [BOHL-], *rarely* [BULL-]. Shk's pronunciation was
/BULL in brŏŏk/.

Buckingham /BUCK ing um/, though in the US /BUCK ing ham/ is common.

Cardinal (Beauford) 2 or 3 syllables depending on meter /CARD (ih) nł/,
/CARD ņ ł/. Two syllables is usual in the US, three syllables in the UK.

Chartam, Clerk of (F1) /CHART um/ modern **Chartham**. Other eds. prefer
Chatham /CHAT um/ (*Chattam* Q1-3).

de la Pole (Suffolk) today pronounced /del uh POHL/ or /P$\overline{OO}$L/. The latter is
older. The choice will depend on the interpretation of the pun at 2H6 4.1.70.

Eleanor 2 or 3 syllables depending on meter /EL (ih) nur/; US *also* /-nor/.

Gloucester /GLŎS tur/; US *also* /GLAWSS-/.

Goffe, Gough US /gawf/; UK /gŏf/.

Henry 2 or 3 syllables depending on meter /HEN (ur) ree/.

Hume /hy$\overline{oo}$m/.

Humphrey (Gloucester) 2 or 3 syllables depending on meter /HUM f(ur) ree/.

Iden /ĪD ņ/

ă-bat, ăir-m**arry**, air-p**air**, ạr-f**ar**, ĕr-m**erry**, ĝ- g**et**, ī-h**igh**, ĭr-m**irror**, ł-li**ttle**, ņ-li**sten**,
ŏ-h**ot**, oh-g**o**, $\overline{oo}$-w**ood**, $\overline{oo}$-m**oon**, oor-t**our**, ōr- **or**, ow-h**ow**, ţh-**that**, ₮**h**-**thin**, ŭ-b**ut**,
UR-f**ur**, ur-**under**.   ( ) - suppress the syllable   see p. xiii for complete list.

People in the Play (cont.)

Jordan, Margery /MARJ ree JOR dน̩/. Some eds. prefer **Margaret Jourdain**
or **Jordane** which in Shk's time could have indicated either /JOR dayn/ or
/JOR dน̩/, with **Margaret** 2 syllables.

Lancaster US /LANG kăst ur, -kᵘss tur/;
UK /LANG kᵘss tur/ [-kahst ur, -kăst ur].

Margaret /MAR guh rit/ or /MAR grit/ depending on meter.

Nevil /NEV ł/ [-il] family name of Warwick and Salisbury, used throughout.

Plantagenet /plan TAJ ih nit/.

Salisbury always 3 syllables /SAWLZ bĕr ee/; UK /SAWLZ bur ee/ [SĂLZ-].

Say, Saye /say/.

Simpcox /SIMP cŏcks/.

Southwell /SOW̶T̶H̶ wł, SOW̶T̶H̶ ł/.

Suffolk (de la Pole) /SUFF ᵘk/.

***Vaux** angl. /vawks, vŏks/; formerly /vawz/; Fr. /voh/.

Warwick US /WŌR ik/; E.COAST US, UK /WŎR-/. Place names in US often have
/-wik/ but this is not recommended for Shk.

Winchester (Beauford) /WIN chih stur/; US *also* /WIN chess tur/.

Places in the Play

Bury /BĔR ee/ Bury St. Edmonds.

Maine /mayn/; Fr. /men/.

Saint Albons archaic variant of **St. Albans.** Both pronounced
US /saynt AWL bunz/; UK /sint-, sน̩t-/.

Act 1 Scene 1

3. **procurator** /PRŎCK yur ayt ur/; UK *also* /-yoor-/ agent. See App. D -*or*.

5. **Tours** /toor/.

6. **Sicil** /SISS ł/ Sicily.

7. **Orleance** here should be /OR leenss/, /OR lyunss/, archaic variant of
Orleans /OR leenz/, /OR lyunz/ which some eds. prefer. Others prefer Fr.
Orléans /or lay ahⁿ/, which here should be compressed to 2 syllables.

7. **Calaber** /KAL uh bur/ or /KAL (uh) bur/ (see *Alanson* below) Calabria, in
southern Italy.

7. **Bretagne** Brittany. Here should be /BRET ahnʸ/ if *Calaber* is 2 syllables. If
Calaber is 3 syllables, then stress could fall on the first or second syllable. F1's
Britaigne was /BRIT ṇ/ or /-ayn/ in Shk's time.

7. **Alanson** /AL un sun/ if *Calaber* is three syllables, /uh LAN sun, -sṇ/ if
Calaber is two. Some eds. prefer Fr. **Alençon** /ah lahⁿ sohⁿ/.

15-63. **marquess** /MAR kwiss/. Some eds. prefer **marquis**, pronounced the
same way.

---

28. **alder-liefest** (F1) /AWL dur LEEF ist/ dearest of all. Sometimes written
alderlievest /AWL dur LEEV ist/. Omitted in Q.

33. **yclad** /ee-, ih CLAD/ archaic form of *clad*.

43. **Inprimis** /in PRĪ miss/ in the first place. Archaic variant of *imprimis
/im PRĪ miss/ (traditional), /im PREE miss/ (restored Latin). The latter is now
more common.

47, 111. **Reignier** the second occurrence is stressed on the second syllable, but
in prose (line 47) it may be stressed on the 1st or 2nd syllable.
Angl. /RAY neer, ray NEER/ or quasi-Fr. /RAYN yay, rayn YAY/;
Fr. /ren yay/. Some eds. prefer **René** /REN ay, ren AY/.

---

48. **Sicilia** /sih SILL yuh/ Sicily.

50-110. **duchy** /DUTCH ee/ lands of a duke.

ă-bat, ăir-marry, air-pair, ạr-far, ĕr-merry, ĝ- get, ī-high, ĭr-mirror, ł-little, ṇ-listen,
ŏ-hot, oh-go, o͞o-wood, o͞o-moon, oor-tour, ōr- or, ow-how, ţh-that, t̶h̶-thin, ŭ-but,
UR-fur, ur-under.   ( ) - suppress the syllable   see p. xiii for complete list.

51-236. **Anjou** stressed on 2nd syllable, but at the beginning of a line may be inverted, angl. /AN jo͞o/ or /an JO͞O/; Fr. /ah^n zho͞o/.

101. **Rasing** (*Racing* F1) /RAY sing/ erasing. Some eds. prefer **Razing** /RAY zing/ which can also mean 'erase.'

105. **peroration** /pĕr uh RAY shun/ flowery speech.

123. **Mort Dieu!** angl. /mor DYO͞O/; UK *also* /-DYUR/; Fr. /mor dyö/ God's (i.e., Jesus') death!

124. **suffocate** /SUFF uh kut, -kayt/ suffocated.

142. **Rancor** (UK **Rancour**) /RANK ur/ ill-will. See App. D *-or*.

142. **prelate** /PREL ut/ high-ranking churchman.

146. **prophesied** /PRŎF uh sīd/ predicted the future.

169. **hoise** /hoyz/ archaic variant of **hoist**.

182. **Behooves it us** /bih-, bee HO͞OVZ/ it is proper for us. UK prefers the spelling **Behoves** /bih HOHVZ/.

189. **commonweal** /CŎM un weel/ commonwealth.

196. **exploits** here should be /ek SPLOYTS/.

222. **pennyworths, penn'worths** bargains. Both pronounced /PEN ur̶t̶h̶s/.

223. ***courtezans, courtesans** rich men's whores. US /CORT ih zunz, -zanz/, *rarely* [cort ih ZANZ]; CN /CORT ih zanz/ [-zunz], *rarely* [cort ih ZANZ]; UK /CORT ih zanz, cort ih ZANZ/.

234. **Althaea** /al T̶HEE uh/ mother of Meleager of Calydon.

235. **Calydon** /KAL ih dun, -dŏn/. /-ŏn/ is usual in the US and is increasingly common in the UK. See App. D *-on*.

246. ***diadem** /DĪ uh dem/ [-dum] crown.

Act 1 Scene 2

2. **Ceres'** /SEER eez/ goddess of the harvest.

7, 40. ***diadem** /DĪ uh dem/ [-dum] crown.

9. ***grovel** US, CN /GRŎV ł, GRUV ł/; UK /GRŎV ł/ [GRUV ł].

36. **sate** archaic variant of **sat**. May have been /sayt/ or /sat/.

37. **Westminster** here should be /WEST min stur/.

75. **cunning witch** (F1). Q1-2 add **of Ely** /EE lee/, Q3 **of Rye**. Some eds. prefer **of Eye**.

106. **attainture** US /uh TAYN chur/; UK *also* /-tyoor/ conviction, stain. See App. D *-ure*.

Act 1 Scene 3

1. **stand close** /clohss/ keep hidden.

17. **Goodman** /GŌŌD mun/.

34. ***pursuivant** herald. US /PUR swiv unt/ [PUR siv unt]; UK /PUR swiv unt/, *rarely* [PUR siv unt].

40. **cullions** /CŬL yunz/ scoundrels, literally 'testicles.'

45. **Albion's** /AL byunz/ Britain's.

50. **Tours** /toor/.

56. **Ave-Maries** the prayer "Hail, Mary." /AY vee MAIR eez/ is the older, angl. form. The newer /AH vay MAIR eez/ is much more common and based on Church Latin.

60. **Are brazen images of canonized saints** may either be a hexameter with /KAN un ī zid/, or a regular pentameter line with *images* syncopated to /IM jiz/ followed by /kan ŎN īzd/ as elsewhere in Shk.

ă-bat, ăir-marry, air-pair, ạr-far, ĕr-merry, ĝ- get, ī-high, ĭr-mirror, ł-little, ṇ-listen, ŏ-hot, oh-go, ōō-wood, ōō-moon, oor-tour, ōr- or, ow-how, ţh-that, ţh-thin, ŭ-but, UR-fur, ur-under.   ( ) - suppress the syllable   see p. xiii for complete list.

60. **brazen** /BRAY zun, -zn̩/ brass.

69. **The imperious** /th̯ʸim PEER yus/ arrogant.

80. **revenues** here should be /ruh VEN yōōz/.

83. **callot, callet** /KAL ut/ whore.

88. **lim'd** /līmd/ coated with lime, i.e., paste.

104. **denay'd** (F1) /dih-, dee NAYD/ variant of F4's **denied**.

125. **Dolphin** /DŎL fin/; US *also* /DAWL-/ angl. form of **Dauphin** 'the French heir to the throne' which here would be Fr. /DOH fǎⁿ/. In Shk's time /l/ in this position was often silent, so *dolphin* and *dauphin* were probably both /DAW fin/.

142. **commandements**. Archaic variant of **commandments**, originally with 4 syllables, /-uh munts/, but here the usual mod. 3-syllable pronunciation is required.

146. *****breeches** /BRITCH iz/ is traditional, /BREECH iz/ is newer. The former pronunciation is more common in the UK, and the latter in the US, CN.

Act 1 Scene 4

10. *****prostrate** US /PRŎS trayt/, *rarely* [-trut]; CN /PRŎS trayt/; UK /PRŎS trayt/, *rarely* [prŏs TRAYT] lying face down.

11. *****grovel** US, CN /GRŎV ł, GRUV ł/; UK /GRŎV ł/ [GRUV ł].

---

after 16 Q1-3 have several lines omitted in F1 and Riverside.

Sosetus /suh SEE tus/.

Askalon /ĂSK uh lŏn, -lun/. /-ŏn/ is usual in the US and is increasingly common in the UK. See App. D *-on*.

Assenda /uh-, ǎ SEN duh/, /ASS en duh/.

---

stage direction after 22. **conjuro te** I conjure you.
Ang.Lat. /cun JOOR oh tee/; Class.Lat. /cŏn YŌŌ roh tay/. Some eds. prefer **coniuro te**, pronounced as in Class.Lat.

23. **Adsum** Ang.Lat. /AD sum/; Class.Lat. /AHD sōōm/ I am here.

24. **Asmath** /AZ măth/ perhaps a misprint for **Asnath** /AZ năth/ Satan.

39-40. **Dytas** (Q1-3) US /DĪ tuss/ [-tăss]; UK, CN /-tăss/ [-tus]. Normal development would favor /-tus/. Omitted *Riverside* and F1.

42. *****Beldam** old woman, hag. US /BEL dam, -dum/; UK /BEL dam/, *rarely* [-dum].

43. **commonweal** /CŎM un weel/ commonwealth.

46. **guerdon'd** /GURD ṇd/ rewarded.

50. **close** /clohss/ securely.

62.   **Aio   te, Aeacida,   Romanos   vincere   posse**
Ang.Lat. /AY yoh   tee ee ASS ih duh, roh MAY nohz VIN sur ee   PŎSS ee/
Class.Lat. /AH ee oh tay ī AH sid ah,   roh MAH nohss WINK ĕr ay PŎSS ay/
          'I say that you, descendent of Aeacus, the Romans conquer.'
Some eds. substitute **Aio Aecidam** Ang.Lat. /-dum/; Class.Lat. /-dahm/ for *Aio, te Aeacida.*

Act 2 Scene 1

22. **commonweal** /CŎM un weel/ commonwealth.

23. **peremptory** here should be /pur EM tur ee/ or /-tree/ overbearing.

24.   **Tantaene   animis   caelestibus   irae?**
Ang.Lat. /tan TEE nee AN ih miss   sel ESS tih bus Ī ree/
Class.Lat. /tahn TĪ nay   AHN ih meess kī LESS tih bōōs EE rī/
          'Is there such anger in heavenly minds?'
Some eds. prefer **coelestibus**, a medieval Lat. error, pronounced the same in Ang.Lat.

52. **Medice, teipsum** Ang.Lat. /MED ih see tee IP sum/;
Class.Lat. /MED ih kay tay IP sōōm/ doctor, heal thyself.

56. **compound** settle. Here should be /cŏm POWND/.

ă-bat, ăir-marry, air-pair, ạr-far, ĕr-merry, ĝ- get, ī-high, ĭr-mirror, ł-little, ṇ-listen, ŏ-hot, oh-go, ōō-wood, ōō-moon, oor-tour, ōr- or, ow-how, ṭh-that, ꞇh-thin, ŭ-but, UR-fur, ur-under.   ( ) - suppress the syllable   see p. xiii for complete list.

61-129. **Saint Albon('s)** archaic variant of **St.Alban**. Both pronounced
US /saynt AWL bun/; UK /sint-, snt-/.

81, 156. **Berwick** /BĔR ik/.

100. **damsons** a type of plum. /DAM zunz, -znz/ is older, /DAM sunz, -snz/
is newer.

134. **Beadles** /BEE dłz/ local officers in charge of whippings.

166. **rout** /rowt/ mob.

187. **commonweal** /CŎM un weel/ commonwealth.

Act 2 Scene 2

3. **close walk** /clohss/ private pathway.

14-54. **Gaunt** /gawnt/.

15, 46. **Langley** /LANG lee/.

21-39. **Bullingbrook** Shk pronounced this /BULL in brōōk/. Some eds. prefer
Bolingbroke, today pronounced US, CN /BOHL ing brōōk/ [BULL-, BŎL-];
UK /BŎL-/, *rarely* [BULL-].

26. **Pomfret** (Q3) US /PŎM frit/; UK /PUM frit/ [PŎM-]. *Pumfret* (F1).

35, 49. **Philippe** /FIL ip/ Philippa.

41. **Owen Glendower** here should be /OH in GLEN dowr/. Some eds. prefer
Welsh **Owain Glyndûr**, normally /OH īn/ or /OH in glin DŌŌR/, but here
/GLIN dōōr/.

76. **prophesy** /PRŎF uh sī/ to predict the future.

Act 2 Scene 3

1. **Cobham** /CŎB um/.

21. **solace** /SŎL us/ comfort.

25. **lanthorn** archaic variant of **lantern**. Probably pronounced /LAN turn/, but possibly /LANT horn/ or /LAN ~~thurn~~, -~~thorn~~/.

34. **ere** (F1, Q3). Some eds. prefer Q1-2's **erst** /urst/ formerly.

43. **raught** /rawt/ seized.

49, 57. **the appellant** / th{y}uh PELL unt/ challenger.

56. **bestead** /bih-, bee STED/ prepared.

63. **charneco** angl. /CHAHR nih koh/; newer is /shahr NAY koh/ sweet Portuguese wine.

after 69. **claret** (Q1) /CLĂIR it/ a red wine. Omitted F1 and *Riverside*.

73. **draught** US, CN /drăft/; UK, E.NEW ENG. /drahft/ drink.

75. **aporn** /AY purn/ archaic variant of **apron**.

---

after line 90 Q1-3 has a section not included in F1 containing these words:

Beuis (Bevis) /BEEV iss/, /BEV iss/ hero of a popular romance.

South-hampton (Southampton) /sow~~th~~ HAMP tun/ [-AMP-, suth-, suth-].

Askapart /ASK uh part/ giant conquered by Bevis.

---

92. ***alarum** US, CN /uh LAHR um/ [-LĂIR-]; UK /uh LĂIR um, uh LAHR um/ a call to arms.

92. **combatants** here should be stressed on the first syllable, as is usual in the UK, /CŎM buh tunts/ [CUM-].

Act 2 Scene 4

8. **Uneath** /un EE~~TH~~/ scarcely.

11. **abject** /AB ject/ common.

13. **erst** /urst/ formerly.

ă-bat, ăir-**marry**, air-**pair**, ạr-**far**, ĕr-**merry**, ĝ- get, ī-high, ĭr-mirror, l̵-little, n̩-listen, ŏ-hot, oh-go, o͞o-wood, o͞o-moon, oor-**tour**, ōr- **or**, ow-how, th-**that**, ~~th~~-**thin**, ŭ-but, UR-**fur**, ur-under.   ( ) - suppress the syllable   see p. xiii for complete list.

38. *Trowest thou do you think. Here one syllable US, CN /trohst, trowst/; UK /trowst/ [trohst]. Shk's rhymes elsewhere indicate /-oh/.

45. forlorn here should be /FOR lorn/.

53. impious /IM pyus/ profane.

54. lim'd /līmd/ coated with lime, i.e., paste.

58. awry /uh RĪ/ askew.

62. scathe /skayth̲/ harm.

73. close dealing /clohss/ secret, underhanded.

Act 3 Scene 1

2. hindmost /HĪND mohst/ furthest behind.

8. peremptory here should be /PĔR um tur ee/; US also /-tor ee/ dictatorial.

51. bedlam /BED lum/ crazy.

74. affiance /uh FĪ unss/ trust.

129. felonious /fuh LOHN yus/ evil.

130. condign here should be /CŎN dīn/ fitting.

144. rancor's (UK rancour's) /RANK urz/ ill-will's. See App. D -or.

164. liefest /LEEF ist/ dearest.

166. conventicles here should be /CŎN ven tih kłz/ secret meetings.

180. suborned /sub ORN id/ persuaded someone to do something wrong.

200. engirt /en GURT/ enclosed, surrounded.

206. low'ring (F1), louring threatening. /LOWR ing/, with the vowel of how.

214. lowing /LOH ing/ bleating.

229. slough /sluff/ skin.

261. **quillets** /KWIL its/ quibbles.

262. **gins** /jinz/ traps.

281. **impugns** /im PYŌŌNZ/ calls into question.

282. **amain** /uh MAYN/ with full speed.

285. **succors** (UK **succours**) /SUCK urz/ helps. See App. D *-or*.

300. **character'd** written. Here with second syllable stress.

310-361. **kern(s)** /kurnz/ Irish foot soldiers.

328. **Bristow** /BRIST oh/ archaic variant of **Bristol** /BRIST ł/.

341. **politicly** /PŎL ih tik lee/ shrewdly.

363. **porpentine** /POR pin tīn/ archaic variant of **porcupine**.

365. **Morisco** US /mor ISS koh/; UK, E.COAST US /mŏr-/ morris dance.

381. **rascal** (F1). Some eds. prefer Q1's **coistrel** /COY strł/ scoundrel.

Act 3 Scene 2

52. *****basilisk** legendary reptile whose glance was fatal. US /BĂSS ih lisk/ [BAZ ih lisk]; UK /BAZ-/ [BĂSS-]; CN both used equally.

77. **forlorn** here should be /FOR lorn/.

80. **statuë, statua** here should be three syllables /STATCH oo uh/; UK *also* /STAT yoo uh/.

87. **unkind** here should be /UN kīnd/.

89. **brazen** /BRAY zun, -zņ/ brass.

92. **Aeolus** /EE (uh) lus/ god of the winds.

ă-bat, ăir-marry, air-pair, ạr-far, ĕr-merry, ĝ- get, ī-high, ĭr-mirror, ł-little, ņ-listen, ŏ-hot, oh-go, ōō-wood, ōō-moon, oor-tour, ōr- or, ow-how, ţh-that, ŧħ-thin, ŭ-but, UR-fur, ur-under.   ( ) - suppress the syllable   see p. xiii for complete list.

107. **diamonds** here should be /DĪ uh mundz/, the standard pronunciation in the UK.

113. **Albion's** /AL byunz/ Britain's.

116. **Ascanius** /ass-, us KAYN yus/ son of Aeneas.

117. **Dido** /DĪ doh/ Queen of Carthage.

146. **obsequies** /ŎB suh kweez/ burial services.

151. **solace** /SŎL us/ comfort.

191. **puttock's** /PUTT uks/ a bird, the red kite.

196. **talons** (F1). Q1-3 have the archaic variant **talents** /TAL unts/.

201. **Warwickshire** US /WŌR ik shur/ [-sheer]; E.COAST US, UK /WŎR-/. Place names in the US often have /-wik-/ but this is not recommended for Shk.

204. **contumelious** disdainful. /cŏn tyuh MEE lyus/; US *also* /cŏn tuh-/. /cŏn chuh-/ considered non-standard in the UK.

224. *****homage** /HŎM ij/; US *also* /ŎM ij/ acknowledgement of allegience.

239. *****tumultuous** full of turmoil. US /tōō MŬLL chwus/ [-tywus]; SOUTH. US *also* /tyōō-/; CN /tyōō-, tōō MUL chwus, -tywus/; UK /tyōō MŬLL tywus/ [-chwus], *rarely* [tōō MŬLL-]. In the UK /chōō MŬLL-/ is considered non-standard.

250. **instinct** here should be /in STINCT/.

258. **edict** here should be /ee DICT/ decree.

271. **hinds** /hīndz/ menial laborers.

274. *****orator** US, CN /OR uh tur/; UK, E.COAST US /ŎR-/. Sometimes /OR ayt ur/ is used, but it is not recommended. See App. D -*or*.

283. **prophesy** /PRŎF uh sī/ to predict the future.

284, 300. *****Mischance** in verse normally with 2nd syllable stress, but in these instances inversion is possible, allowing the alternative mod. form with 1st syllable stress.

292, 385. **increase** here /in CREESS/. In the second instance the meaning is 'offspring, crops.'

294. **irrevocable** /ih REV uh kuh bł/; US *also* /ir-/.

305. **execrations** /ek suh CRAY shunz/ curses.

324. ***basilisks** canons. US /BĂSS ih lisks/ [BAZ -]; UK /BAZ-/ [BĂSS-]; CN both used equally.

327. **consort** /CŎN sort/ group of musicians.

372. **Blaspheming** speaking irreverently. 2nd syllable stress produces a regular line /blăss FEEM ing/; UK, E.NEW ENG. *also* [blahss-]. Here may also have 1st syllable stress, a pronunciation sometimes used in the US.

399. ***Elysium** the realm of the blessed in the after-life. US /ih LEEZH ee um/ [-LIZ-, -LIZH-, -LEESS-, -LISS-]; UK /-LIZ-/; *also* /ee-/ in all countries. The oldest forms still in use are /-LIZ-/, /-LIZH-/. The historic form is /ih LIZH um/, here expanded to 4 syllables /ih LIZH ee um/.

403. **corrosive** here should be US /COR uh siv/; E.COAST US, UK /CŎR-/.

Act 3 Scene 3

17. **the apothecary** druggist. US /thʸuh PŎTH uh kĕr ee/; UK /-kuh ree/.

Act 4 Scene 1

6. **Cleep, Clepe** /cleep/ variant of **Clip** embrace.

9. **pinnace** /PIN uss/ light sailing ship.

14-38. **Walter** in Shk's time pronounced without /l/ to make it more or less homonymous with *water*.

37, 38. **Gualtier** (F1) Fr. form of *Walter*. In Shk's time /GWAWT yur/, /GAWT yur/, or /GAWT ur/ (cf. *Gaulter* Q1-3). Some eds. prefer Fr. **Gaultier** /goh tyay/.

60. **allay** /uh LAY/ diminish.

ă-bat, ăir-ma**rry**, air-**pair**, ạr-**far**, ĕr-me**rry**, ĝ- g**et**, ī-h**igh**, ĭr-mi**rror**, ł-li**ttle**, ṇ-list**en**, ŏ-h**ot**, oh-g**o**, ōō-w**ood**, ōō-m**oon**, oor-**tour**, ōr- **or**, ow-h**ow**, ţh-**that**, th-**thin**, ŭ-b**ut**, UR-f**ur**, ur-und**er**.   ( ) - suppress the syllable   see p. xiii for complete list.

65. **forlorn** here should be /FOR lorn/.

70. **Poole** . . . This is either a pun on *poll* /pohl/ 'head' with the name pronounced /pohl/, or a pun on *pool*, hence *puddle,* etc., in which case the name would be /pōōl/. The historical pronunciation is /pōōl/.

80. **affy** /uh FĪ/ engage to marry.

82. ***diadem** /DĪ uh dem/ [-dum] crown.

84. **Sylla** /SILL uh/ Roman dictator. Variant of **Sulla** /SŬLL uh/.

86. **Anjou** here angl. /an JŌŌ/; Fr. /ahⁿ ZHŌŌ/.

87. **thorough** archaic variant of *through*, used when the meter demands two syllables. It is often pronounced as *thorough* on stage, but using /-rōō/ as the final syllable will bring it closer to mod. *through*.

88. **Picardy** /PIK ur dee, -ahr-/ region in France.

99. **Invitis nubibus** Ang.Lat. (US) /in VĪ tiss NŌŌ bih bus/; (UK /NYŌŌ-/); Class.Lat. /in WEE tōōs NŌŌ bih bōōs/ in spite of clouds.

105. **paltry** /PAWL tree/ worthless.

105. ***servile** /SUR vīl/, *rarely* [SUR vɫ] slave-like.

105. **abject** /AB ject/ contemptible.

107. **pinnace** /PIN uss/ light sailing ship.

108. **Bargulus** /BAR gyuh lus, BAR guh lus/.

108. **Illyrian** /ih LĬR yun/ of Illyria, the coast of Yugoslavia.

115, 116. ***waft** convey. US, CN /wŏft/; SOUTH. US /wăft/; UK /wŏft/ [wăft, wahft]. /wăft/ is newer and considered non-standard by many.

117.   **Pene   gelidus   timor   occupat   artus**
Ang.Lat. /PEE nee   JEL ih dus   TĪ mor   ŎK (y)uh pat   ART us/
Class.Lat. /PAY nay ĜEL ih dōōs   TIM or   ŎK ōō paht   ART tōōs/
          'Cold fear almost overpowers my limbs.'
Some eds. prefer the Latin variant **Paene**, pronounced the same in Ang.Lat.; Class.Lat. /PĪ nay/.

134. **besonians, bezonians** /bih ZOHN ee unz/ scoundrels.

136. **Tully** /TŬL ee/ executed by Antony's soldiers.

138. **Pompey** /PŎMP ee/.

142. **liveless** /LĪV liss/ archaic variant of **lifeless**.

Act 4 Scene 2

2. **lath** US /lă̵th̵/; UK, E. NEW ENG. /lah̵th̵/ [lă̵th̵] narrow strip of wood.

4. **clothier** /CLOH t̪hyur, -t̪hee ur/ someone engaged in the cloth trade.

17, 18.***magistrates** /MAJ ih strayts/; US *also* [-struts].

22. **Wingham** /WING um/.

29. **Argo** /A̤RG oh/. Archaic form of ***ergo** /UR go/ is older, /ĔR go/ is newer. The former is more common in the UK, the latter in the US, CN, but both forms appear in all countries.

66. **halfpenny** /HAY puh nee, HAYP nee/.

69. **palfrey** /PAWL free/; UK *also* [PŎL-] saddle horse.

78. ***lamentable** US /luh MEN tuh bł/ [LAM en tuh bł]; CN, UK /LAM un tuh bł/ [luh MEN-].

86. **accompt** /uh COWNT/ archaic variant of **account**. See App. D.

122. **hinds** /hīndz/ menial laborers.

133. **shearman** /SHEER mun/ someone who shears the nap of woolen cloth.

158. **span-counter** /SPAN cownt ur/ a tossing game.

163. **puissance** power, i.e., army. The traditional forms are /PWISS n̩ss/, /PYŌO sn̩ss/, but in this prose passage any of the current forms may be used (See App. D).

166. **eunuch** /YŌO nuk/ castrated man.

ă-bat, ăir-ma**rry**, air-**pair**, a̤r-**far**, ĕr-**merry**, ĝ- g**et**, ī-h**igh**, ĭr-**mirror**, ł-l**ittle**, n̩-l**isten**, ŏ-h**ot**, oh-g**o**, ōō-w**ood**, ōō-m**oon**, oor-**tour**, ōr- **or**, ow-h**ow**, t̪h-**that**, t̵h̵-**thin**, ŭ-b**ut**, UR-f**ur**, ur-**under**.   ( ) - suppress the syllable   see p. xiii for complete list.

185. **clouted** /CLOW tid/ hobnailed.

185. **shoon** /sho͞on/ Scottish and Nth. English dialect form of *shoes.*

Act 4 Scene 4

13. ***parley** /PAR lee/ negotiate. Newer [-lay] not recommended.

27. ***Southwark** /SUȚH urk/.   Sometimes [SOW~~TH~~ wurk] in the US, but not recommended.

31. **Westminster** here should be /WEST min stur/.

33. **hinds** /hīndz/ menial laborers.

55. **succor** (UK **succour**) /SUCK ur/ help. See App. D *-or.*

Act 4 Scene 5

8. **assay'd** /uh-, ass SAYD/. Some eds. prefer **essayed** /es SAYD/. Both mean 'attempted.'

Act 4 Scene 6

3. **pissing-*conduit** pipe or channel. /CŎN doo it/;
UK *also* [CUN doo it, CŎN dyoo it, CŎN dit, CUN dit].

4. **claret** /CLĂIR it/ a red wine.

Act 4 Scene 7

2. **Savoy** /suh VOY/ palace of the dukes of Lancaster.

25. **serge** /surj/ a type of cloth.

25. **buckram** /BUCK rum/ course linen cloth stiffened with paste.

28. **Mounsieur** /mown SEER, MOWN seer/ lower-class variant of **Monsieur.**

28. **Basimecu** /băss-, bayz-, baz ee mee KYO͞O/. Main stress may also fall on the first syllable. From Fr. *Baise mon cul* 'kiss my ass.' **Bus mine cue** (Q) /bus-/.

29. **Dolphin** /DŎL fin/; US *also* /DAWL-/ angl. form of **Dauphin** 'the French heir to the throne' which here would be Fr. /DOH fă͏ⁿ/. In Shk's time /l/ in this position was often silent, so *dolphin* and *dauphin* were both /DAW fin/.

31. **besom** /BEE zum/, *rarely* [BIZ um] broom.

56. **bona terra, mala gens**
Ang.Lat. /BOH nuh TĔR uh, MAY luh jenz/
Class.Lat. /BŎN ah TĔR ah, MAH lah gaynss/.
'good land, bad people.'

after 56. **Hough him** (Q1-3) /hŏck/ cut his hamstrings. Omitted F1 and *Riverside*.

77. *****parley'd** /PAR leed/ negotiated. Newer [-layd] not recommended.

78. **behoof** /bih-, bee HO͞OF/ profit, advantage.

90. **caudle** /KAW dł/ warm drink given to sick people.

93. **palsy** /PAWL zee/; UK *also* [PŎL-] a shaking disease.

111. **Cromer** /CROH mur/.

115. *****obdurate** unmoveable. Here should be stressed on the 2nd syllable /ŏb-, ub DYOOR it/; US *also* /-DYUR-/ [-DUR-]. 1st syllable stress is more usual today.

123. **in capite** Ang.Lat. /in KAP ih tee/; Class.Lat. /in KAHP ee tay/ as tenant in chief.

---

after 125 and 129 Q1 has several lines omitted in F1 and Riverside (*Complete Oxford* line nos. in parentheses).

(124) *****Billingsgate** /BILL ingz gayt/; UK *also* [- ĝit].

(139) **hough him** /hock/ cut his hamstrings.

(145) **kirtle** /KURT ł/ long gown.

ă-bat, ăir-marry, air-pair, a̱r-far, ĕr-merry, ĝ- get, ī-high, ĭr-mirror, ł-little, ṇ-listen, ŏ-hot, oh-go, o͞o-wood, o͞o-moon, oor-tour, ŏr- or, ow-how, t̠h-that, t̶h̶-thin, ŭ-but, UR-fur, ur-under.　　　( ) - suppress the syllable　　see p. xiii for complete list.

Act 4 Scene 8 (*Complete Oxford* continues this as 4.7—line nos. in parentheses).

3. (4.7.156) **Thames** /temz/ the major river of London.

4. (4.7.158) ***parley** /PAR lee/ conference with an enemy. Newer [-lay] not recommended.

25. (4.7.179) ***Southwark** /SUṬH urk/. Sometimes [SOW~~TH~~ wurk] in the US, but not recommended.

27. (4.7.181) **recreants** /REK ree unts/ cowards.

46. (4.7.201) **Villiago!** /vil ee YAH go/ scoundrel.

Act 4 Scene 9 (*Complete Oxford* 4.8)

stage direction: tarras /TĂIR us/ archaic variant of **terrace**.

23. **advertised** informed. Here should be /ad VUR tih zed, -sed/.

25. ***puissant** powerful. The traditional forms are /PWISS ṇt/, /PYOO sṇt/ (see App. D).

26. **kerns** /kurnz/ Irish foot soldiers.

47. **redound** /ree-, rih DOWND/ contribute.

Act 4 Scene 10 (*Complete Oxford* 4.9)

8-15. **sallet** /SAL it/ double meaning: archaic form of *salad* 'raw vegetables,' and 'helmet.'

16. **turmoiled** here should be /tur MOYL id/ agitated.

39. **eat** /et/ dialect variant of **eaten**.

43. **an esquire** here should be /ess KWĪR/, the usual UK form, in a hexameter, or *a 'squire* as elsewhere in Shk after an epic caesura.

44. **combat** here should be /CŎM bat/; UK *also* [CUM-].

49. **truncheon** /TRUN chun/ staff.

Act 5 Scene 1

5. **sancta majestas** Ang.Lat. /SANK tuh muh JESS tus/;
Class.Lat. /SAHNK tah mah YESS tahss/ holy majesty. Some eds. prefer
maiestas, pronounced as in Class.Lat.

11. **flow'r-de-luce** (following F3) /FLOWR duh lōōss/ lily flower, Some eds.
prefer F1's **fleure-de-luce** /FLUR duh lōōss/ or **fleur-de-lis** /FLUR duh lee/
national emblem of France. For all these variants main stress may also fall on
the 3rd syllable, the usual US form (for /lyōō-/ see App. D *lu-*).

25. **abject** /AB ject/ contemptible.

26. **Ajax Telamonius** /AY jacks tel uh MOHN ee us/ Gk. hero.

50. **fealty** /FEE ł tee/ faithfulness.

63. **discomfited** /dis CUM fit id/ defeated.

72. **I was** some eds. prefer *Iwis /ih WISS/; US, CN *also* /ee WISS/ indeed.

75. **esquire** here should be /ess KWĪR/, the usual UK form.

99. **engirt** /en GURT/ encircle.

100. **Achilles'** /uh KILL eez/ Gk. hero.

113. **enfranchisement** /en FRAN chiz munt/ liberty.

114. **amain** /uh MAYN/ with full speed.

116, 121. *surety guarantee, bail. Here should be two syllables, though in mod.
English, three syllables are more common, /SHUR (ih) tee, SHOOR-, SHOR-/
(see App. D).

117. **Neapolitan** /nee uh PŎL ih tun/ man from Naples.

118. **scourge** /SKURJ/ punishment.

131, 132. **Bedlam** /BED lum/ in 1st instance 'lunatic hospital', in 2nd 'lunatic.'

ă-bat, ăir-**marry**, air-**pair**, ạr-**far**, ĕr-**merry**, ĝ- get, ī-high, ĭr-mirror, ł-little, ṇ-listen,
ŏ-hot, oh-go, ōō-wood, ōō-moon, oor-tour, ōr- or, ow-how, ţh-that, th̶-thin, ŭ-but,
UR-**fur**, ur-**under**.   ( ) - suppress the syllable   see p. xiii for complete list.

149, 210. **bearard** bearkeeper. Archaic variant of **bearward** or **bearherd**. All were pronounced /BAIR urd/, but recent spelling pronunciations /BAIR wârd/ (as in *war*), /-hurd/, are also used today.

187. **reave** /reev/ bereave, rob.

191. **sophister** /SŎF ist ur/ someone skilled in arguing or equivocating.

200-8. *****burgonet** /BURG uh net/; US *also* /burg uh NET/ helmet.

212. **complices** /CŎMP lih siz/ accomplices.

215. **stigmatic** here should be /STIG muh tik/ a deformed person.

Act 5 Scene 2 (*Complete Oxford* 5.3)

3. *****alarum** US, CN /uh LAHR um/ [-LĂIR-]; UK /uh LĂIR um, uh LAHR um/ a call to arms.

19-60. In this section Q1-3 have several lines omitted in F1 and Riverside (*Complete Oxford* line nos. in parentheses).

(5.3.28) **sinows** (Q1) /SIN ohz/ archaic variant of Q2-3's **sinews** /SIN yooz/; US *also* [SIN o͞oz].

(5.3.29) *****grovelling** US, CN /GRŎV-, GRUV ł ing/; UK /GRŎV-/ [GRUV-].

28. **La fin couronne les oeuvres** Fr. /lah fă^n ko͞o rawn layz öv^{ruh}/ the end crowns the works. Omitted Q1-3.

31. **rout** /rowt/ retreat.

37. **dedicate** /DED ih kayt, -kut/ dedicated.

41. **premised** /prih MĪ zid/ preordained.

59. **Medea** /mih DEE uh/ enchantress who helped Jason.

59. **Absyrtus** /ub SUR tus/ brother of Medea, hacked to pieces by her.

62, 64. **Aeneas** /ih NEE yus/; UK *also* /EE NEE yus/ Prince of Troy.

62. *****Anchises** /an-, ang KĪ seez/; US *also newer* [-zeez] Aeneas' father.

67. **paltry** /PAWL tree/ worthless.

The Complete Oxford begins 5.4 here (line nos. given in parentheses).

---

85. (5.4.14) **blasphemy** /BLĂSS fuh mee/; UK, E. NEW ENG. *also* /BLAHSS-/ irreverent speech.

86. (5.4.15) **discomfit** /dis CUM fit/ defeat.

Act 5 Scene 3 (*Complete Oxford* 5.5)

8. **holp** /hohlp/ helped.

9. **bestrid** /bih-, bee STRID/ mounted.

31. **eterniz'd** /ih TURN īzd/; US *also* /ee-/ made eternal.

ă-bat, ăir-**marry**, air-**pair**, ạr-**far**, ĕr-**merry**, ĝ- **get**, ī-**high**, ĭr-**mirror**, ḷ-**little**, ṇ-**listen**, ŏ-**hot**, oh-**go**, ŏŏ-**wood**, ōō-**moon**, oor-**tour**, ōr- **or**, ow-**how**, t̪h-**that**, t̶h̶-**thin**, ŭ-**but**, UR-**fur**, ur-**under**.   ( ) - suppress the syllable   see p. xiii for complete list.

Henry VI part three
The Complete Oxford calls this *Richard Duke of York*

People in the Play

Bona /BOH nuh/.

Bourbon /BOOR bun/; *newer* /-bŏn/; Fr. /B͞OOR bohⁿ/. See App. D *-on*.
The Admiral in 3.3.

Exeter /EK sih tur/.

Gloucester (Richard) /GLŎS tur/; US *also* /GLAWSS-/.

Henry 2 or 3 syllables depending on meter /HEN (ur) ree/.

Lancaster US /LANG kăst ur, -kᵘss tur/;
UK /LANG kᵘss tur/ [-kahst ur, -kăst ur].

Lewis, Louis one syllable usually, but may be 2 depending on meter
/L͞OO (i)ss/.

Margaret /MAR guh rit/ or /MAR grit/ depending on meter.

Montague, Marquess of /MŎNT uh gy͞oo/; *formerly also* [MUNT-].
/MAR kwiss/. Some eds. prefer **Marquis**, pronounced the same way.

Montgomery 3 or 4 syllables depending on meter
US /munt-, mŏnt GUM (ur) ree/, UK *also* [-GŎM-].

Norfolk /NOR fᵘk/.

Northumberland /north UM bur lund/.

Pembroke US /PEM brohk/; UK /PEM br͞ook/ [-bruck, -brohk].

Plantagenet /plan TAJ ih nit/.

Somerville /SUM ur vil/.

People in the Play (cont.)

Warwick US /WŌR ik/; E.COAST US, UK /WŎR-/. Place names in the US often have /-wik/ but this is not recommended for Shk.

Westmerland archaic variant of **Westmor(e)land**, all pronounced /WEST mur lund/ in the UK. US is usually /west MOR lund/ which will not fit the meter.

Places in the Play

Saint Albons US /saynt AWL bunz/; UK /sint-, sn̩t-/. Archaic variant of **St. Albans**, pronounced the same way.

Act 1 Scene 1

10. **Buckingham** /BUCK ing um/, though in the US /BUCK ing ham/ is common.

14. **Wiltshire's** /WILT shurz/ [-sheerz].

19. **Gaunt** /gawnt/

62. **Patience is for poltroons** cowards. /PŎL trōōnz/, an archaic variant, in a headless line (or perhaps an inverted first foot with *Patience* expanded to 3 syllables). Today /pŏl TRŌŌNZ/ is more common.

108. **Dolphin** /DŎL fin/; US *also* /DAWL-/ angl. form of **Dauphin** 'the French heir to the throne' which here would be Fr. /DOH fã^n/. In Shk's time /l/ in this position was often silent, so *dolphin* and *dauphin* were probably both /DAW fin/.

117. **cavilling** here should be 2 syllables /KAV ling/ quibbling.

156. **Suffolk** /SUFF ^{u}k/.

211. **bewray** /bih-, bee RAY/ reveal.

231. **timorous** /TIM (uh) rus/ frightened.

236. **sepulchre** /SEP ł kur/ tomb.

ă-bat, ăir-**marry**, air-**pair**, ạr-**far**, ĕr-**merry**, ĝ- get, ī-high, ĭr-**mirror**, ł-little, n̩-listen, ŏ-hot, oh-go, ōō-wood, ōō-moon, oor-**tour**, ōr- or, ow-how, ţh-that, t̶h̶-thin, ŭ-but, UR-**fur**, ur-**under**.   ( ) - suppress the syllable   see p. xiii for complete list.

238. **Callice, Callis** /KAL iss/ city on north. coast of France. Both are archaic
variants of **Calais** which here should be /KAL ay/, the normal UK form;
Fr. /KAH lay/.

239. **Falconbridge** /FAWL-, FAL kun brij/; UK *also* [FŎL-],
rarely older [FAW kun-].

242. ***environed** /en VĪ rund/; US *also* [en VĪ urnd] surrounded.

Act 1 Scene 2

2. ***orator** US, CN /OR uh tur/; UK, E.COAST US /ŎR-/. Sometimes /OR ayt ur/ is
used, but it is not recommended. See App. D -*or*.

23. ***magistrate** /MAJ ih strayt/; US *also* [-strut].

30. ***Elysium** the realm of the blessed in the after-life.
US /ih LEEZH ee um/ [-LIZ-, -LIZH-, -LEESS-, -LISS-]; UK /-LIZ-/; *also* /ee-/
in all countries. The oldest forms still in use are /-LIZ-/, /-LIZH-/. The historic
form is /ih LIZH um/ here expanded to 4 syllables /ih LIZH ee um/.

39. **privily** /PRIV ih lee/ privately.

40, 56. **Cobham** /CŎB um/.

63. **Sandal** /SAN dł/.

Act 1 Scene 3

48.   **Dii   faciant   laudis**
Ang.Lat. /DĪ ī   FAY shunt   LAWD iss/
Class.Lat. /DIH ee FAHK ee ahnt LOW diss/ (/LOW-/ as in *how*)
                'The gods grant that this may be'

           summa   sit   ista   tuae
Ang.Lat. /SUM uh   sit   ISS tuh   TO͞O ee/ (UK /TYO͞O-/)
Class.Lat. /So͞oM ah sit   ISS tah   TO͞O ī/
                'the summit of thy glory.'
Some eds. prefer **Di** (Ang.Lat. /dī/; Class.Lat. /dee/) rather than *Dii*.

Act 1 Scene 4

12. ***falchion** type of sword. /FĂL chun/ [-shun]; *older* [FAWL chun].

17. **sepulchre** /SEP ł kur/ tomb.

33. **Phaëton** /FAY ih tun, -tŏn/ son of the sun god. /-ŏn/ is usual in the US and is increasingly common in the UK. Some eds. prefer **Phaëthon** /--thun, -thŏn/. See App. D -*on*.

61. **gin** /jin/ snare.

62. ***cony** rabbit. /KOH nee/, *rarely older* [KUN ee].

68. **raught** /rawt/ reached.

87. ***entrails** /EN traylz/; US *also* [-trłz] guts.

104. ***diadem** /DĪ uh dem/ [-dum] crown.

110. ***orisons** prayers. US, CN /OR ih zunz, -zṇz/ [-sunz, -sṇz]; E.COAST US /ŎR-/; UK /ŎR ih zunz, -zṇz/.

114. **Amazonian** /am uh ZOHN yun/ referring to a warlike woman.

116. ***vizard-like** /VIZ urd/ mask-like. /-ạrd/ not recommended.

118. **assay** /uh-, ass SAY/. Some eds. prefer **essay** /es SAY/. Both mean 'attempt.'

122. **Sicils** /SISS łz/ the kingdom of the two Sicilies.

123. **yeoman** /YOH mun/ freeman who owns a small farm.

135. **antipodes** /an TIP uh deez/ the opposite side of the world.

136. **septentrion** /sep TEN tree un/ north. Sometimes newer /-ŏn/ is used, but is not recommended.

142. ***obdurate** unmoveable. Here stressed on the 2nd syllable /ŏb-, ub DYOOR it/; US *also* /-DYUR-/ [-DUR-]. 1st syllable stress is more usual today.

ă-bat, ăir-**marry**, air-**pair**, ạr-**far**, ĕr-**merry**, ĝ- get, ī-high, ĭr-**mirror**, ł-little, ṇ-listen, ŏ-hot, oh-go, o͞o-**wood**, o͞o-**moon**, oor-**tour**, ōr- **or**, ow-how, th-**that**, th-**thin**, ŭ-but, UR-**fur**, ur-under.   ( ) - suppress the syllable   see p. xiii for complete list.

146. **allays** /uh LAYZ/ diminishes.

147. **obsequies** /ŎB suh kweez/ burial services.

154. **inexorable** /in EK sur uh bł/; US *also* /-EG zur-/ unyielding. May also be /-sruh bł/.

155. **Hyrcania** /HUR KAYN ee yuh/ region in the Caucausus.

Act 2 Scene 1

24. **younker** /YŬNG kur/ young lord.

30. **inviolable** /in VĪL uh bł/ unbreakable.

50. ***Environed** /en VĪ run ed/; US *also* [en VĪ urn ed] surrounded.

71. **chevalry** /SHEV ł ree/ knightly qualities. Archaic variant of **chivalry** /SHIV ł ree/.

96. **recompt** (F2) /ree-, rih COWNT/. Archaic variant of F3's **recount**. Q1-3 have **report**. See App. D *accompt*.

98. **poniards** /PŎN yurdz/; UK *also newer* [-yardz] daggers.

116. **advertised** warned. Here should be /ad VUR tih zed, -sed/.

153. ***diadem** /DĪ (uh) dem/ [-dum] crown.

162. **Ave-Maries** the prayer "Hail, Mary." /AY vee MAIR eez/ is the older, angl. form. The newer /AH vay MAIR eez/ is much more common and based on Church Latin.

182. **via** /VĪ uh/ onward! /VEE uh/ is newer.

195. **borough** town. US /BUR oh/ [-uh]; E.COAST US /BUH roh/ [-ruh]; UK /BUH ruh/.

207. ***puissant** powerful. The traditional forms are /PWISS ṇt/, /PYOO̅ sṇt/ (see App. D).

Act 2 Scene 2

9. **lenity** /LEN ih tee/ leniency.

33. **president** model. Archaic variant of **precedent**, both /PRESS ih dunt/. It is not clear whether /PREZ-/ was used in Shk's time.

43. *****orator** US, CN /OR uh tur/; UK, E.COAST US /ŎR-/. Sometimes /OR ayt ur/ is used, but it is not recommended. See App. D *-or*.

66. **toward** /TOH wurd, -urd/ bold.

72. **Darraign, Deraign** /duh RAYN/ draw up for battle.

82. *****diadem** /DĪ uh dem/ [-dum] crown.

110. *****parley** /PAR lee/ conference with an enemy. Newer [-lay] not recommended.

116. **sunset** here should be /sun SET/. Some eds. prefer **sun set**.

136. **stigmatic** here should be /STIG muh tik/ a deformed person.

145. **callet** /KAL ut/ whore.

147. **Menelaus** /men uh LAY us/ i.e., a cuckold.

148. *****Agamemnon's** US, CN /ag uh MEM nŏnz/; UK /-nŏnz/ [-nunz] brother of Menelaus. See App. D *-on*.

151. **Dolphin** /DŎL fin/; US *also* /DAWL-/ angl. form of **Dauphin** 'the French heir to the throne' which here would be Fr. /DOH fãⁿ/. In Shk's time /l/ in this position was often silent, so *dolphin* and *dauphin* were probably both /DAW fin/.

159. *****tumult** turmoil. US /TŌŌM ult/; SOUTH.US *also* /TYŌŌM-/; CN /TYŌŌM-/ [TŌŌM-]; UK /TYŌŌM-/. /CHŌŌM-/ considered non-standard in the UK. A newer pronunciation /TUM ult/ is not recommended.

164. **increase** here should be /in CREESS/ harvest.

ă-bat, ăir-**marry**, air-**pair**, ạr-**far**, ĕr-**merry**, ĝ- get, ī-high, ĭr-**mirror**, ł-little, ṇ-listen, ŏ-hot, oh-go, ōō-**wood**, ōō-**moon**, oor-**tour**, ōr- **or**, ow-**how**, ţh-**that**, t̶h̶-**thin**, ŭ-but, UR-**fur**, ur-**under**.   ( ) - suppress the syllable   see p. xiii for complete list.

Act 2 Scene 3

18. *clangor (UK clangour) /CLANG ur/ [-gur] loud shrill noise.

40. brazen /BRAY zun, -zn̩/ brass.

56. amain /uh MAYN/ with full speed.

Act 2 Scene 4

4. *environ'd /en VĪ rund/; US also [-urnd] surrounded.

4. brazen /BRAY zun, -zn̩/ brass.

Act 2 Scene 5

6. combat here should be /CŎM bat/; UK also [CUM-].

36. ean /een/ variant of yean /yeen/ give birth.

52. viands /VĪ undz/ food. /VEE undz/ not recommended.

89. stratagems /STRAT uh jumz/ schemes.

115. sepulchre /SEP l̩ kur/ tomb.

118. obsequious /ub-, ŏb SEE kw(ee) yus/ respectful to the dead.

120. *Priam King of Troy. US, CN /PRĪ um/ [-am]; UK /-am/, rarely [-um].
Normal development would favor /-um/.

126. chafed /CHAY fid/ enraged.

128. Berwick /BĔR ik/.

128, 133. amain /uh MAYN/ with full speed.

135. expostulate /ek SPŎS chuh layt/; UK also /-tyoo layt/ discuss, object.

Act 2 Scene 6

6. *commixtures (F1) i.e., alliances. US /cuh MIKS churz/ [coh-], *rarely* [cŏm-]; UK /coh-/ [cŏm-, cuh-]. Some eds. prefer Q's comixture /coh-, cuh-/.

7. misproud here should be /MIS prowd/ arrogant.

11. Phoebus /FEE bus/ god of the sun.

12. Phaëton /FAY ih tun, -tŏn/ son of the sun god. /-ŏn/ is usual in the US and is increasingly common in the UK. Some eds. prefer Phaëthon /--t̶h̶un, -t̶h̶ŏn/. See App. D -on.

22. lenity /LEN ih tee/ leniency.

36. argosy /A̧RG uh see/ large merchant ship.

83. *unstanched insatiable. Variant of unstaunched /un STAWN chid/. See App. D -aun-.

91. sinow /SIN oh/ tie. Archaic variant of F1's sinew /SIN yo͞o/; US *also* [SIN o͞o].

Act 3 Scene 1

2. laund /lawnd/ glade.

3. *covert hiding place. US, CN /KOHV urt/ [KUV-]; UK /KUV urt/ [KOHV urt], *rarely* [KUV ur], an older form.

23. *quondam US /KWŎN dum/, *rarely* [-dam]; UK /-dam/, *rarely* [-dum] former.

33. *orator US, CN /OR uh tur/; UK, E.COAST US /ŎR-/. Sometimes /OR ayt ur/ is used, but it is not recommended. See App. D -or.

41. brinish /BRĪ nish/ referring to salt water, i.e., tears.

63. diamonds here should be /DĪ uh mundz/, the standard pronunciation in the UK.

| ă-bat, äir-marry, air-pair, a̧r-far, ĕr-merry, ĝ- get, ī-high, ĭr-mirror, l̷-little, n̦-listen, ŏ-hot, oh-go, o͝o-wood, o͞o-moon, oor-tour, ŏr- or, ow-how, t̠h-that, t̶h-thin, ŭ-but, UR-fur, ur-under.   ( ) - suppress the syllable   see p. xiii for complete list. |

Act 3 Scene 2

85. **incomparable** /in CŎM pur uh bł/ or /in CŎMP ruh bł/.

99. **cavil** /KAV ł/; UK *also* /KAV il/ quibble.

108. **shriver** /SHRĪ vur/ priest who hears confession.

161. **unlick'd** here should be /UN lickt/.

170. **misshap'd** here should be /MIS shaypt/.

187. ***basilisk** legendary reptile whose glance was fatal. US /BĂSS ih lisk/ [BAZ ih lisk]; UK /BAZ-/ [BĂSS-]; CN both used equally.

188. ***orator** US, CN /OR uh tur/; UK, E.COAST US /ŎR-/. Sometimes /OR ayt ur/ is used, but it is not recommended. See App. D -*or.*

188. **Nestor** /NEST ur/ oldest of the Greeks at Troy. See App. D -*or.*

189. **Ulysses** /yōō LISS eez/; US *also* /yōō-/. The less common UK pronunciation /YŌŌ lih seez/ will not fit the meter.

190. **Sinon** traitor who caused Troy's fall. /SĪ nun/, but /-nŏn/ is becoming more common. See App. D -*on.*

192. ***Proteus** sea god who could change his shape. /PROH tyus/ [-tyōōss], US *rarely* [-tōōss]. See App. D -*eus.*

193. **Machevil** /MATCH uh vil, -vł/ a cunning, deceitful person. Archaic variant of **Machiavel** /MAK ee uh vel/, /MAHK-/.

Act 3 Scene 3

7, 49. **Albion ('s)** Britain. The first instance is /AL byunz/, the second /AL bee yun/.

8, 18. ***mischance** in verse normally with 2nd syllable stress.

41-207. **succor** (UK **succour**) /SUCK ur/ help. See App. D -*or.*

55. ***nuptial** wedding. US, UK /NUP chł/ [-shł]; in CN both are used equally.

81. **disannuls** /dis uh NŬLZ/ annuls.

81, 83. **Gaunt** /gawnt/.

97. **bewray** /bih-, bee RAY/ reveal.

102. **Aubrey Vere** /AW bree VEER/.

136. **jointure** /JOYN chur/ marriage settlement. See App. D -*ure*.

153. ***quondam*** US /KWŎN dum/, *rarely* [-dam]; UK /-dam/, *rarely* [-dum] former.

172. **unhop'd** here should be /UN hohpt/.

191. **guerdon'd** /GURD ṇd/ rewarded.

196. **servitor** /SURV ih tur/ servant. See App. D -*or*.

198. **replant** here with 1st syllable stress.

224. **masquers** performers in masked dances and pantomime. US /MĂSK urz/; UK, E. NEW ENG. /MAHSK-/ [MĂSK-].

247. **irrevocable** /ih REV uh kuh bł/; US *also* /ĭr-/.

253. ***waft*** convey. US, CN /wŏtt/; SOUTH. US /wăft/; UK /wŏft/ [wăft, wahft]. /wăft/ is newer and considered non-standard by many.

254. ***mischance*** in verse normally with 2nd syllable stress.

Act 4 Scene 1

10, 60. **malecontent** displeased. Archaic variant of ***malcontent***. Both pronounced US /mal cun TENT/ [MAL cun tent]; CN, UK /MAL cun tent/, *rarely* [mal cun TENT].

48. **Hungerford** /HUNG gur furd/.

58. **elsewhere** here with 2nd syllable stress, a form still used in the UK, but unknown in the US.

ă-bat, ăir-**marry**, air-**pair**, ạr-**far**, ĕr-**merry**, ĝ- **get**, ī-**high**, ĭr-**mirror**, ł-**little**, ṇ-**listen**, ŏ-**hot**, oh-**go**, ōō-**wood**, ōō-**moon**, oor-**tour**, ōr- **or**, ow-**how**, țh-**that**, ŧħ-**thin**, Ŭ-**but**, UR-**fur**, ur-**under**.   ( ) - suppress the syllable   see p. xiii for complete list.

94. **masquers** performers in masked dances and pantomime. US /MĂSK urz/; UK, E. NEW ENG. /MAHSK-/ [MĂSK-].

Act 4 Scene 2

19. **Ulysses** /yo͞o LISS eez/; US *also* /yo͞o-/. The less common UK pronunciation /YO͞O lih seez/ will not fit the meter.

19. **Diomede** /DĪ uh meed/. Some eds. prefer **Diomed** /DĪ uh med/ Gk. hero at Troy.

20. **sleight** /slīt/ cunning.

20. **Rhesus'** /REE sus/ King of Thrace.

21. **Thracian** /T̶H̶RAY shun/ from Thrace, in Greece.

Act 4 Scene 3

20. ***halberds** US, CN /HAL burdz, HAWL-/; UK /HAL-/ [HAWL-] spears with blades on the end.

The Complete Oxford begins 4.4 here (line nos. in parentheses)

---

32. (4.4.5) ***embassade** an ambassador's errand. /em buh SAYD/ is older; /-SAHD/ is newer and much more common. First syllable stress is also used today.

43. (4.4.16) ***mischance** in verse normally with 2nd syllable stress.

44. (4.4.17) **complices** /CŎMP lih siz/ accomplices.

53. (4.4.26) **Archbishop** here should be /ARCH bish up/.

Act 4 Scene 5 (*Complete Oxford* 4.6)

9. **advertis'd** informed. Here should be /ad VUR tisst/, /-tīzd/.

17. **close** /clohss/ hidden.

Act 4 Scene 6 (*Complete Oxford* 4.7)

55. **confiscate** here should be /cŏn FISS kayt, -ut/ confiscated.

88. *****salve** ointment. US /sav/ [salv]; NEW ENG. /sahv/; CN /sav, salv/ [sahlv]; UK /salv/. Normal development would favor the *l*-less form (cf. *halve, calve*).

92. *****presaging** here should be /pree-, prih SAY jing/ foretelling.

97-101. **Brittany** /BRIT n̩ ee/.

Act 4 Scene 7 (*Complete Oxford* 4.8)

8. *****Ravenspurgh haven** here should be 2 syllables /RAVN SPURG, -SPUR/ or /RAYVN-/. Sometimes spelled **Ravenspur** /-SPUR/. Note *haven* is also compressed.

13. **Tush** /tŭsh/ expression of disdain.

13. **abodements** /uh BOHD munts/ omens.

39. **deign** /dayn/ are willing.

56. **succor** (UK **succour**) /SUCK ur/ help. See App. D -*or*.

64. **bruit** /br͞o͞ot/ noise.

66. *****diadem** /DĪ uh dem/ [-dum] crown.

74. **gainsays** /gayn SEZ, -SAYZ/ denies.

81. **horizon** here should be US /HŌR ih zun/; UK, E.COAST US /HŎR-/.

84. **froward** /FROH wurd, FROH urd/ difficult to deal with.

Act 4 Scene 8 (*Complete Oxford* 4.9)

1. **Belgia** here should be 3 syllables /BEL jee uh/ Belgium.

4, 64. **amain** /uh MAYN/ with full speed.

ă-bat, ăir-marry, air-pair, ạr-far, ĕr-merry, ĝ- get, ī-high, ĭr-mirror, ł-little, n̩-listen, ŏ-hot, oh-go, o͞o-wood, o͞o-moon, oor-tour, ōr- or, ow-how, t̟h-that, th-thin, ŭ-but, UR-fur, ur-under.   ( ) - suppress the syllable   see p. xiii for complete list.

9. **Warwickshire** US /WŌR ik shur/ [-sheer]; E.COAST US, UK /WŎR-/. Place names in the US often have /-wik-/ but this is not recommended for Shk.

12. **Suffolk** /SUFF ᵘk/.

14. **Buckingham** /BUCK ing um/, though in the US /BUCK ing ham/ is common.

15. **Northampton** /nor ~~THAMP~~ tun/.

15. **Leicestershire** /LESS tur shur/ [-sheer].

18. **Oxfordshire** /ŎCKS furd shur/ [-sheer].

25. **Hector** /HEK tur/ Trojan hero. See App. D *-or*.

32. **Coventry** US /KUV ṇ tree/; UK /KŎV ṇ tree/ [KUV-].

The Complete Oxford begins 4.10 here (line nos. in parentheses).

4.8.42. (4.10.10) **allay'd** /uh LAYD/ diminished.

4,6,58, 64. (4.10.24, 30) **Coventry** US /KUV ṇ tree/; UK /KŎV ṇ tree/ [KUV-].

 4.8.59. (4.10.27) **peremptory** here should be /PĔR um tur ee/; US *also* /-tor ee/ overbearing.

Act 5 Scene 1

6. **Daintry, Da'ntry** /DAYN tree/ local form of *Daventry* /DAV in tree/ in Northamptonshire.

6. ***puissant** powerful. The traditional forms are /PWISS ṇt/, /PYŌŌ sṇt/ (see App. D).

9, 12. **Southam** /SOWṮH um/, an older pronunciation is /SUṮH um/.

16. **parle** /parl/ conference with an enemy.

18. **unbid** here should be /UN bid/ unbidden.

42. **forecast** here should be stressed on the 2nd syllable.

71. ***presageth** here should be /pree-, prih SAY jith/ has foreknowledge of.

after 79. **et tu Brute** (Q1,3) and you, Brutus. Ang.Lat. /et tōō BRŌŌ tee/, but now universally Class.Lat. /BRŌŌ tay/. Omitted F1 and *Riverside*.

85. ***trowest thou** US, CN /TROH ist, TROW-/; UK /TROW-/ [TROH-] do you think. Shk's rhymes elsewhere indicate /-oh/.

91. **Jephthah** one of the judges of Israel. Following the usual rules, /JEF thuh/, but /JEP thuh/ has also been used since Elizabethan times. Note /DIP th -/ for *diphth-* is the most common pronunciation today in *diphthong, diphtheria*. Some eds. prefer **Jephthah's**.

110. **Barnet** /BAR nit/.

Act 5 Scene 2

20. **sepulchres** /SEP ł kurz/ tombs.

31. ***puissant** powerful. The traditional forms are /PWISS nt/, /PYŌŌ snt/ (see App. D).

45. **mought** /mawt/ dialect variant of *might*.

after 50. **retrait** (Q1, 2) /rih-, ree TRAYT/ archaic variant of **retreat**. Omitted F1, *Riverside*.

Act 5 Scene 3

8. **Gallia** /GAL yuh/ France.

18. **advertis'd** informed. Here should be /ad VUR tisst/, /-tīzd/.

19. **Tewksbury** here 3 syllables US /TŌŌKS bĕr ee/; SOUTH. US /TYŌŌKS-/; UK /TYŌŌKS bur ee/. UK [CHŌŌKS-] is considered non-standard.

20. **Barnet** /BAR nit/.

Act 5 Scene 4

14. **topmast** /TŎP must/ is used by sailors; landsmen say US /TŎP măst/; UK, E.NEW ENG. /-mahst/.

ă-bat, ăir-**marry**, air-**pair**, ąr-**far**, ĕr-**merry**, ĝ- get, ī-high, ĭr-**mirror**, ł-**little**, ņ-**listen**, ŏ-hot, oh-go, ōō-**wood**, ōō-**moon**, oor-**tour**, ōr- or, ow-**how**, țh-**that**, th-**thin**, ŭ-but, UR-**fur**, ur-**under**.   ( ) - suppress the syllable   see p. xiii for complete list.

> Q1-3's version of lines 1-50 includes **timorous** /TIM uh rus/ frightened.
> Omitted *Riverside*.

Act 5 Scene 5

1. *****tumultuous** full of turmoil. US /tōō MŬLL chwus/ [-tywus];
SOUTH. US *also* /tyōō-/; CN /tyōō-, tōō MUL chwus, -tywus/;
UK /tyōō MŬLL tywus/ [-chwus], *rarely* [tōō MŬLL-]. In the
UK /chōō MŬLL-/ is considered non-standard.

24. *****breech** 'britches.' /breech/, but an older form /britch/ is still used in some
dialects (cf. *breeches* /BRITCH iz, BREECH iz/, the latter being a newer form).

32. *****malapert** /MAL uh purt/; US *also* [mal uh PURT] saucy.

34. **Lascivious** /luh SIV yus/ lustful.

45. **swoun** archaic variant of **swoon**. In Shk's time the vowel could be either
/ow/ or /ōō/.

79. **alms-deed** charitable gift. /AHMZ-/ is older; /AHLMZ-, AWLMZ-/ are
newer. In the UK the latter are non-standard.

Act 5 Scene 6

7. **reakless, reckless** /RECK liss/ heedless.

10. *****Roscius** famous actor in ancient Rome. Normal development would favor
/RŎSH us/. /RŎSH ee yus/ is also used, and restored Latin /RŎS kee yus/ is the
most common in all countries. Here must be 2 syllables.

13. **limed** /LĪ mid/ caught in a trap made of lime paste.

21. *****Daedalus** inventor in Gk. mythology. US, CN /DED uh lus/ [DEED-];
UK /DEED-, DĪD-/ [DED-]. Angl. /DED-, DEED-/ are oldest; /DĪD-/ is a
recent, restored pronunciation. /DAYD-/ is a recent spelling pronunciation, not
recommended.

21. *****Icarus** /IK uh rus/ Daedalus' son. UK /ĪK-/ not recommended.

22. *****Minos** king of Crete. US /MĪ nohss/ [-nŏs, -nus]; CN, UK /-nŏs/ [-us].
/-ohss/ is newer. Normal development would favor /-us/. Sometimes the
restored Gk. /MEE-/ is used.

37. **prophesy** /PRŎF uh sī/ to predict the future.

Act 5 Scene 7

9. **coursers** /COR surz/ warhorses.

38. **Reignier** the foot may be inverted, so stress may fall on the 1st or 2nd syllable. Angl. /RAY neer, ray NEER/ or partially Fr. /RAYN yay, rayn YAY/; Fr. /ren yay/. Some eds. prefer **René** /REN ay, ren AY/.

39. **Sicils** /SISS łz/ kingdom of the two Sicilies.

41. *****waft** convey. US, CN /wŏft/; SOUTH. US /wăft/; UK /wŏft/ [wăft, wahft]. /wăft/ is newer and considered non-standard by many.

ă-bat, ăir-ma**rry**, air-p**air**, ạr-f**ar**, ĕr-me**rry**, ĝ- g**et**, ī-high, ĭr-mi**rror**, ł-litt**le**, ṇ-liste**n**, ŏ-hot, oh-go, ŏŏ-wood, ōō-moon, oor-t**our**, ōr- **or**, ow-how, ţh-that, th̵-thin, ŭ-but, UR-f**ur**, ur-under.   ( ) - suppress the syllable   see p. xiii for complete list.

Henry VIII
The Complete Oxford calls this *All is True*

People in the Play

Aburgavenny, Abergavenny, Aburga'ny /ab ur GVEN ee/, /ab ur ĜEN ee/.

Archbishop (Cromwell) /ARCH bish up/ or /arch BISH up/ depending on meter.

Buckingham /BUCK ing um/, though in the US /BUCK ing ham/ is common.

Bullen /BU̦LL in/ was the older pronunciation. Some eds. prefer ***Boleyn** which today is usually /boh-, buh LIN/, but which here should be pronounced with 1st syllable stress.

Campeius /kam PEE yus/; restored Latin /kahm PAY ōŏs/.

Capuchius, Capuscius, Caputius /kuh PYOO shus/.

Cardinal (refers to both **Campeius** and **Wolsey**) 2 or 3 syllables depending on meter /CARD (ih) nł/, /CARD n̦ ł/. Two syllables is usual in the US, three syllables in the UK.

Cromwell US /CRŎM wel/; UK /CRŎM wł/. Formerly /CRUM ł/.

Denny, Sir Anthony US /AN ~~thuh~~ nee/; UK /AN tuh nee/ [-~~thuh~~ nee]. *Anthony* is not spoken.

Dorset, Marquess /DOR sit/. Some eds. prefer **Marquis**, both pronounced /MAR kwiss/. Appears in the coronation, 4.1.

Gardiner /GARD nur/.

Guilford /ĜIL furd/. Some eds. prefer **Guildford** /ĜILD furd/.

Katherine /KA̶T̶H̶ rin/ or /KA̶T̶H̶ ur rin/, but should be 2 syllables in verse.

Lovell /LUV ł/.

Norfolk /NOR fᵘk/.

People in the Play (cont.)

Pembroke,*Marchioness of (Anne Bullen) US /PEM brohk/; UK /PEM brŏŏk/ [-bruck, -brohk]. /MAR shuh niss, mar shuh NESS/.

Marquess, Marquis see **Dorset**.

Sands, Sandys (F1) /săndz/.

Suffolk /SUFF ᵘk/.

Surrey US /SUR ee/; UK, E.COAST US /SUH ree/.

*Vaux angl. /vawks, vŏks/; formerly /vawz/; Fr. /voh/.

Winchester (Gardiner) /WIN chih stur/; US *also* /WIN chess tur/.

Wolsey /WŏŏL zee/.

Prologue 16. **motley** /MŎT lee/ cloth of different colors worn by fools.

Act 1 Scene 1

4. **ague** /AY gyŏŏ/ malarial fever.

7. **Andren** /AN drun/. Some eds. prefer **Ardres** angl. /AHR druh/; Fr. /ahrd^ruh/.

7. **Guynes** archaic variant of Fr. **Guisnes** /ĝeen/.

7. **Arde** /ahrd/. Some eds. prefer **Ardres** angl. /AHR druh/; Fr. /ahrd^ruh/.

19. **clinquant** /CLINK unt/ ornate.

23. ***cherubins** angels. US, CN /CHĔR uh binz/ [-yuh-]; UK uses both equally. /KĔR-/ not recommended. Some eds. prefer mod. pl. **cherubim** /-bim/.

23. **madams** /MAD umz/. Some eds. prefer Fr. **mesdames** angl. /MAY dahmz/; Fr. /MAY dahm/.

26. **masque** US /măsk/; UK, E. NEW ENG. /mahsk/ [măsk] masked dancing and pantomime.

ă-bat, ăir-m**arry**, air-p**air**, ạr-f**ar**, ĕr-m**erry**, ĝ- g**et**, ī-h**igh**, ĭr-m**irror**, ł-litt**le**, ṇ-lis**ten**, ŏ-h**ot**, oh-g**o**, ŏŏ-w**ood**, ōō-m**oon**, oor-t**our**, ōr- **or**, ow-h**ow**, ṭh-t**hat**, ŧħ-**thin**, ŭ-b**ut**, UR-f**ur**, ur-**under**.   ( ) - suppress the syllable   see p. xiii for complete list.

27. **incomparable** here should be /in CŎMP ruh bł/.

38. **Bevis** /BEV iss, BEEV iss/ hero of a popular romance.

41. **discourser** here should be /dis CORSS ur/ talker.

48. **certes** certainly. Usually /SUR teez/, but here /surts/ is indicated.

60. **successors** here should be /SUCK sess urz/ descendants. See App. D *-or*.

61. **allied** here with 2nd syllable stress.

70. **niggard** /NIG urd/ miser.

74. **privity** /PRIV ih tee/ knowledge.

96. **Burdeaux** city in France, possibly pronounced /BUR dŏcks/ in Shk's time. Archaic variant of **Bordeaux, Bourdeaux** which here should be /BOR doh/.

123. **chaf'd** /chayft/ angry.

127. **abject** /AB ject/ contemptible.

135. **advise** here 1st syllable stress is indicated.

149. **allay** /uh LAY/ diminish.

153. **sincere** here should be /SIN seer/.

154. **July** here should be /JOO līi/.

177. **pretense** (UK **pretence**) here should be /prih TENSS/, the normal UK pronunciation or /pree TENSS/ based on the most common US pronunciation /PREE tenss/.

183. **privily** /PRIV ih lee/ privately.

184. ***trow** US, CN /troh, trow/; UK /trow/ [troh] believe. Shk's rhymes elsewhere indicate /-oh/.

200. **Herford** (*Hertford* F1), **Hereford** in the US both would be /HUR furd/. In the UK the county is normally /HĔR ih furd/ which here should be 2 syllables /HĔR furd/.

200. **Northampton** /nor THAMP tun/.

217. **Montacute** /MŎNT uh kyōōt/. Some eds. prefer **Montague**
/MŎNT uh gyōō/; *formerly also* [MUNT-].

218. **confessor** here should be /CŎN fess ur/. See App. D *-or*.

218. **de la Car** /duh luh CAR/.

219. **Perk, Perke** /park/.

221. **Chartreux** Carthusian. Here with 1st syllable stress, angl. /SHĄR trōō/;
Fr. /SHĄR trö/. Another angl. form in the UK is /SHĄR TRUR/.

222. **My** *surveyor* **is false** overseer, manager of a household. Here
/SUR vay ur/ is indicated.

Act 1 Scene 2

12. **moi'ty, moiety** /MOY tee/ portion.

31. **clothiers** /CLOH țhyurz/ those engaged in the cloth trade.

32. **many** (F1). Some eds. prefer **meiny** /MAYN ee/ common people.

59. **pretense** (UK **pretence**) here should be /prih TENSS/, the normal UK
pronunciation, or /pree TENSS/ based on the most common US pronunciation
/PREE tenss/.

72. **Traduc'd** slandered. /truh DYŌŌST/; US *also* /-DŌŌST/. /-JŌŌST/ is
considered non-standard in the UK.

91. **president** archaic variant of ***precedent**, both /PRESS ih dunt/. It is not
clear whether /PREZ-/ was used in Shk's time.

103. **shire** /shīr/ county.

118. **complete** accomplished. Here should be /CŎM pleet/.

148. **Chartreux** Carthusian. Here with 1st syllable stress, angl. /SHĄR trōō/;
Fr. /SHĄR trö/. Another angl. form in the UK is /SHĄR TRUR/.

149. **confessor** here should be /CŎN fess ur/. See App. D *-or*.

ă-bat, äir-**marry**, air-**pair**, ąr-**far**, ĕr-**merry**, ĝ- **get**, ī-**high**, ĭr-**mirror**, ł-**little**, n̦-**listen**,
ŏ-**hot**, oh-**go**, ōō-**wood**, ōō-**moon**, oor-**tour**, ōr- **or**, ow-**how**, țh-**that**, t̶h̶-**thin**, ŭ-**but**,
UR-**fur**, ur-**under**.   ( ) - suppress the syllable   see p. xiii for complete list.

153. **Poultney** /POHLT nee/ some eds. prefer **Poutney** /POHT nee/.

167. **demure** here with 1st syllable stress /DEEM-, DEM yoor/; US *also* [-yur] grave.

170. **commonalty** /CŎM un ł tee/ commoners.

182. **Tush** /tŭsh/ expression of disdain.

188. **Greenwich** /GREN ich/; UK *also* /GRIN-, -ij/.

190. **Bulmer** /BŲLL mur/. Some eds. prefer **Blomer** /BLOH mur/.

196. **Salisbury** here 3 syllables US /SAWLZ bĕr ee/; UK /SAWLZ bur ee/ [SĂLZ-].

Act 1 Scene 3

10. **Pepin** /PEP in/ father of Charlemagne. Fr. **Pépin** /PAY pă^n/.

10. *****Clotharius** US /cloh ~~THĄR~~ ee us/ [-~~THAIR~~-, -TAR-, -TAIR-]; UK /-TAR, - ~~THĄR~~-/ [-TAIR-] a Frankish king. It may also be 3 syllables /-yus/. /-AIR-/ is traditional,

12. **spavin** /SPAV in/ swelling of the hock.

14. **pagan** /PAY gun/ non-Christian.

23. **Louvre** here two syllables make the two short lines regular, /L$\overline{OO}$V ruh/ or /L$\overline{OO}$V ur/, the former being a common UK form. The usual US pronunciation /L$\overline{OO}$V/ may also be used with a missing syllable before the end of the first short line.

31. *****breeches** /BRITCH iz/ is traditional, /BREECH iz/ is newer. The former pronunciation is more common in the UK, and the latter in the US, CN.

34. **cum privilegio** with immunity. Ang.Lat. /kŭm priv ih LEE j(ee) oh/; Class.Lat. /k$\overline{oo}$m pree wih LAYG yoh/.

34. **oui** /wee/ Fr. yes.

46. **by'r lady** /bīr-, bur LAY dee/ by Our Lady (i.e., Mary).

67. *comptrollers keepers of accounts. US /cŏmp-, cump-, cun TROHL urz/; CN /cŏmp-/ [cun-, cump-]; UK /cŏmp-, cun-/. /cun-/ is the oldest pronunciation, the others are spelling pronunciations.

Act 1 Scene 4

stage direction: Hoboys, Hautboys /HOH boyz/ or /OH boyz/ archaic variant of *oboes.*

4. bevy /BEV ee/ company.

12-98. banket /BANK it/ light meal, often of fruit. Archaic variant of banquet.

93. Viscount /VĪ cownt/.

93. Rochford /RŎTCH furd/.

Act 2 Scene 1

17. *divers various. Here should be stressed on the first syllable US, CN /DĪ vurss, -vurz/; UK /DĪ vurss/ [-vurz].

18. *vivâ voce, viva voce in person. Ang.Lat. /VĪ vuh VOH see/; Class.Lat. /WEE wah WOH kay/; Church Latin /VEE vah VOH chay/. However the most common forms are US /VEE vuh VOH chee/; UK /VĪ vuh VOH chay/.

20. Perk, Perke /park/.

41. attendure /uh TEN dur/ dishonor. Archaic variant of attainder /uh TAYN dur/.

51. fadom /FAD um/ archaic variant of fathom /FĂTH um/.

55. stand close /clohss/ keep hidden.

103. Bohun /BOH un/; UK *also* /bōōn/.

109. succor (UK succour) /SUCK ur/ help. See App. D *-or.*

152. allay /uh LAY/ diminish.

ă-bat, ăir-marry, air-pair, ạr-far, ĕr-merry, ĝ- get, ī-high, ĭr-mirror, ł-little, ṇ-listen, ŏ-hot, oh-go, ōō-wood, ōō-moon, oor-tour, ōr- or, ow-how, ţh-that, th-thin, Ŭ-but, UR-fur, ur-under.   ( ) - suppress the syllable   see p. xiii for complete list.

Act 2 Scene 2

46. **imperious** /im PEER yus/ arrogant.

85. **president** example. Archaic variant of *****precedent**, both /PRESS ih dunt/.
It is not clear whether /PREZ-/ was used in Shk's time.

99. **conclave** /CŎNG-, CŎN clayv/ private meeting of cardinals.

Act 2 Scene 3

10. **give her the avaunt** /uh VAWNT/ tell her to begone.

21. **glist'ring** /GLIS tring/ glistening.

32. **cheveril** /SHEV rł/ kid leather, i.e., easily stretched.

36. **threepence** /T̶H̶REP unss, -n̥ss/ [T̶H̶RUP-, T̶H̶RIP-, T̶H̶Rōͦ P-].

36. **bow'd** /bohd/ bent, i.e., worthless.

48. **Carnarvonshire, Caernarvonshire** a county in Wales. Some eds. prefer
the Welsh spelling **Caernarfonshire**. All are pronounced
/cur-, car NA̧R vun shur/ [-sheer].

87. **compell'd** here should be /CŎM peld/.

Act 2 Scene 4

47. **unmatch'd** here should be /UN matcht/.

92-3. **consistory** here should be /CŎN sis tree, -tuh ree/; US *also* /-tor ee/ council
chamber.

96. **gainsay** /gayn SAY/ deny.

173. **Bayonne** US /bay OHN/; UK /bah YŎN/.

175. **Orleance** /OR leenss/ or /OR lyunss/. Archaic variant of **Orleans**
/OR lyunz, OR leenz/. Other eds. prefer Fr. **Orléans** /OR lay ah[n]/.

177. **determinate** /dih-, dee TUR m(ih) nut/ definitive.

178, 182. *respite interval. Here should be US /RESP it/, *rarely* [-īt];
CN /RESP it/ [-īt]; UK /RESP īt/ [-it]. /RESP it/ is older, but /-īt/ has been in use
since the 17th cent.

179. advertise inform. Here should be /ad VUR tiss, -tīz/.

181. dowager /DOW uh jur/ widow.

231. *paragon'd US /PĂIR uh gŏnd/ [-gund]; CN /-gŏnd/; UK /-gund/ [-gn̩d]
'treated as a perfect example.'

238. dilatory here should be 4 syllables US /DILL uh tor ee/;
UK /DILL uh tur ee/ slow.

238. *sloth US, CN /slawth/ [slohth]; UK /slohth/ [slŏth] laziness.

Act 3 Scene 1

3. *Orpheus here should be 2 syllables /OR fyus/ [-fyōōss]. See App. D -*eus*.

24. *huswife /HUZ if/ is traditional, /HUSS wīf/ is a newer, spelling
pronunciation. The former is the most common form in the UK, the latter in the
US. In CN both are used equally. In North America /HUSS wif/ is also
sometimes used. Some eds. prefer F1's housewife.

41.   **Tanta   est erga   te   mentis   integritas,**
Ang.Lat. /TAN tuh   est UR guh tee MEN tiss in TEG rih tuss/
Class.Lat. /TAHN tah est ĔR gah tay MEN tiss in TEG rih tahss/
           'so great is my integrity of mind toward you,'

           regina   serenissima
Ang.Lat. /ruh JĪ nuh   sĕr en ISS ih muh/
Class.Lat. /ray ĜEE nah sĕr en ISS ih mah/
           'most serene queen.'

106. cordial US /COR jł/; UK /COR dył/ healing medicine.

127. *vainglory pride. Here should be /vayn GLOR ee/. The more common
pronunciation today in all countries is /VAYN glor ee/.

ă-bat, ăir-marry, air-pair, ạr-far, ĕr-merry, ĝ- get, ī-high, ĭr-mirror, ł-little, n̩-listen,
ŏ-hot, oh-go, ōō-wood, ōō-moon, oor-tour, ōr- or, ow-how, t̩h-that, th-thin, ŭ-but,
UR-fur, ur-under.   ( ) - suppress the syllable   see p. xiii for complete list.

Act 3 Scene 2

17. **access** here should be /ak SESS/.

70. **Dowager** /DOW uh jur/ widow.

85. **Alanson** /uh LAN sun, -sn̩/. Some eds. prefer Fr. **Alençon** /ah LAH[N] soh[n]/.

102. **heretic** /HĔR ih tik/ a dissenter.

176. **allegiant** /uh LEE junt/ loyal.

206. **chafed** /CHAY fid/ enraged.

210. **th' accompt** /t͡h^{y}uh COWNT/ archaic variant of **account**. See App. D.

226. **exhalation** /eks huh LAY shun/ or /eks uh-/ [egz uh-] meteor.

250. ***letters-patents** US /PAT n̩ts/ [PAYT-]; UK /PAYT-/ [PAT-] documents conferring a right or power.

261. **succor** (UK **succour**) /SUCK ur/ help. See App. D -*or*.

295. **sacring bell** /SAY cring/ bell used in part of the mass.

311. **legate** /LEG ut/ churchman representing the pope.

314.   **Ego   et Rex   meus**
Ang.Lat. /EE goh   et reks   MEE us/
Class.Lat. /EGG oh   et rayks MEH o͞os/
            'my king and I.'

321. **Gregory de Cassado** /duh kuh SAH doh/.

323. **Ferrara** /fuh RAHR uh/.

339. **power legative** (F1) /LEG uh tiv/ power of a papal representative. Some eds. prefer ***legatine** /LEG uh teen/ [-tīn], or F4's **legantine** /-un-/, *both rarely older* [-tin].

340. **praemunire** /pree myo͞on Ī ree/ writ charging someone with advocating papal supremacy. There is also a newer pronunciation with /prī myo͞on EER ay/ based on Class.Lat.

343. **Chattels** /CHAT łz/ property.

399. **orphants'** (F1) /OR funts/ archaic variant of **orphans'**.

Act 4 Scene 1

23. **Dowager** /DOW uh jur/ widow.

27. **Dunstable** /DUN stuh bł/.

28. **Ampthill** /AMT il, -ł, /AMT hill/ is newer and more common in the UK.

34. **Kimmalton** /KIM ł tun/ archaic variant of **Kimbolton** /KIM bohl tun, -bł-/.

36. **stand close** /clohss/ stand aside.

---

stage direction after 36. **Hoboys, Hautboys** /HOH boyz/ or /OH boyz/ archaic variant of *oboes*. Not in *Riverside*.

quiristers /KWĬR ist urz/ archaic variant of **choristers**.

marquess /MAR kwiss/. Some eds. prefer **marquis**, pronounced the same way.

*__demi-coronal__ half-circlet, crown. /DEM ee-/; US /COR uh nł/;
E.COAST US, UK /CŎR-/.

---

49. **Cinque-Ports** /sink PORTS/ or with even stress. Five cities on the coast of
SE Eng.

54. **coronets** small crowns. Here should be US /COR (uh) nets, -nits/;
E.COAST US, UK /CŎR-/.

65. **sate** archaic variant of **sat**. May have been /sayt/ or /sat/.

92. **Te Deum** Ang.Lat. /TEE DEE um/; Class.Lat. /TAY DAY ōōm/ hymn of
thanksgiving.

97. **Whitehall** here should be /whĭt HAWL/, though in the UK it is more
commonly pronounced with stress on the 1st syllable.

ă-bat, ăir-marry, air-pair, ạr-far, ĕr-merry, ĝ- get, ī-high, ĭr-mirror, ł-little, ṇ-listen,
ŏ-hot, oh-go, ōō-wood, ōō-moon, oor-tour, ōr- or, ow-how, ţh-that, th-thin, ŭ-but,
UR-fur, ur-under.　　　( ) - suppress the syllable　　　see p. xiii for complete list.

Act 4 Scene 2

12. **Northumberland** /nor~~th~~ UM bur lund/.

17. **Leicester** /LESS tur/.

19. *covent US /KUV ṇt/ [KŎV-]; UK /KŎV ṇt/ [KUV-] archaic variant of **convent**. US /KOHV-/ not recommended.

36. *Simony US /SIM uh nee, SĪM-/; CN, UK /SĪM-/ [SIM-] buying and selling church offices.

38. **untruths** here /UN trōōths/ is indicated.

after 82 in the section called "The Vision" **congee** /CŎN jee/ or /cun-, cŏn JEE/ 'bow.' Some eds. prefer **congé** /CŎN zhay, -jay/ or /cŏn ZHAY/; Fr. /coh^n zhay/.

154. **contents** here should be /cŏn TENTS/.

Act 5 Scene 1

7. **primero** a card game. /prih MEER oh/ is older, /prih MAIR oh/ newer.

45. **arch-heretic** /ARCH HĔR ih tik/ worst of all dissenters.

52. **convented** /cun VENT tid/ summoned.

71. *travail here should be /TRAV ayl/ labor of birth.

110. **throughly** archaic variant of *thoroughly*. /~~THR~~OO lee/ is the normal pronunciation on stage, but to enhance clarity a syncopated form of the modern pronunciation may be used: *thor'ghly*.

112. **calumnious** /cuh LUM nyus/ slanderous.

116. **by my holidame** an oath referring to a 'holy object' or the 'holy lady,' i.e., Mary. Other variants are: **halidam, halidom, halidame, halidome, holidam**. Probably these were all variant spellings of /HAL ih dum, HŎL ih dum/ (note *hal-* can also be /HŎL-/ in the US in *Halloween*).

132. **corrupt** appears twice in this line; the first instance requires 1st syllable stress.

139. **precipit** (F1) /PRESS (ih) pit/ archaic variant of F2's **precipice**
/PRESS (ih) piss/.

Act 5 Scene 2

24. *****pursuivants** heralds, attendents. US /PUR swiv unts/ [PUR siv unts];
UK /PUR swiv unts/, *rarely* [PUR siv unts].

34. **close** /clohss/ securely.

53. *****Divers** various, i.e., perverse. Normally stressed on the first syllable in
Shk: US, CN /DĪ vurss, -vurz/; UK /DĪ vurss/ [-vurz]. Here stress may also fall on
the 2nd syllable.

53. **heresies** /HĔR ih seez/ dissent from the dominant thinking.

105. **sectary** /SEK tuh ree/; US *also* /SEK tair ee/ zealous member of a sect.

Act 5 Scene 3

8. **staves** /stayvz/ staffs.

16. **Powle's** /pohlz/ St. Paul's cathedral.   Dialect variant of F4's **Paul's**.

22. **Colbrand** /KOHL brand/ a Danish giant.

30. **keep the door close** /clohss/ shut tightly.

33. **Moorfields** /MOOR feeldz/ [MOR-].

41. **brazier** US /BRAY zhur/; UK /BRAY zee ur/ [-zhur, -zhee ur] brass worker.

48. **porringer** US /POR in jur/; E.COAST US, UK /PŎR-/ type of cap.

52. **truncheoners** /TRUN chun urz/ apprentices with clubs.

52. **succor** (UK **succour**) /SUCK ur/ help. See App. D *-or*.

53. **Strond** /strŏnd/ archaic variant of **Strand**, a London Street.

ă-bat, ăir-**marry**, air-**pair**, ạr-**far**, ĕr-**merry**, ĝ- get, ī-**high**, ĭr-**mirror**, ł-**little**, ņ-**listen**,
ŏ-hot, oh-go, ŏŏ-**wood**, ōō-**moon**, oor-**tour**, ōr- **or**, ow-**how**, ţh-**that**, ~~th~~-**thin**, ŭ-**but**,
UR-**fur**, ur-**under**.   ( ) - suppress the syllable   see p. xiii for complete list.

64. **Limbo Patrum** Ang.Lat. /LIM boh PAY trum/; Class.Lat. /PAH trōōm/ place where the souls of good men dwelt who died before Jesus lived.

66. **beadles** /BEE dłz/ local officers.

81. **bombards** /BŎM bardz/ leather bottles. /BUM burdz/ is an archaic variant.

86. **Marshalsea** /MAR shł see/ a prison.

88. **Stand close up** /clohss/ get back.

89. **chamblet** /CAM blit/ a type of rough cloth. Archaic variant of **camlet** /CAM lit/ which some eds. prefer.

Act 5 Scene 4

23. **Saba** /SAY buh/ archaic variant of *Sheba*.

Julius Caesar

People in the Play

Antony, Mark 2 or 3 syllables depending on meter /ANT (uh) nee/.
  Antonio 3 or 4 syllables depending on meter /an TOHN (ee) yoh/.
  Some eds. prefer **Antonius** /-yus/.

Artemidorus of Cnidos /art ih mih DOR us/; US /NĪ dus, -dŏs/;
UK /-dŏs/ [-dus]. A newer pronunciation /-ohss/ is also used, especially in
the US. Normal development would favor /-us/. Class.Lat. /K-NEE dŏs/.

Brutus /BRŌŌT us/.

*Caius (Cassius, Ligarius) US, CN /KĪ us/, *rarely* [KAY us];
UK /KĪ us, KAY us/. Ang.Lat. /KAY us/; Class.Lat. /KĪ ōōs/. Another
angl. form /keez/ is sometimes used, but doesn't fit the meter.

Calphurnia usually 3 syllables /cal FUR n(ee) yuh/. Some eds. prefer
Calpurnia /-PUR-/.

Casca /CĂSS kuh/.

*Cassius 2 or 3 syllables depending on meter /CĂSS (ee) yus/; US *also*
/CASH us/, /CASH ee yus/. Normal development would favor /CASH us/.

Cato /KAYT oh/.

Cicero 2 or 3 syllables depending on meter /SISS (uh) roh/.

Cinna /SIN uh/.

Claudio (F1) /CLAW dyoh/. Some eds. prefer **Claudius** /CLAW dyus/.

Clitus /CLĪ tus/.

Cnidos see **Artemidorus**.

Dardanius /dar DAYN yus/.

Decius Brutus /DEE shus BRŌŌT us/; sometimes newer /-syus/ is used.

ă-bat, ăir-marry, air-pair, ạr-far, ĕr-merry, ĝ- get, ī-high, ĭr-mirror, ł-little, ṇ-listen,
ŏ-hot, oh-go, ōō-wood, ōō-moon, oor-tour, ōr- or, ow-how, ṭh-that, th-thin, ŭ-but,
UR-fur, ur-under.   ( ) - suppress the syllable   see p. xiii for complete list.

People in the Play (cont.)

Flavius /FLAY vee yus/. Sometimes called **Flavio** /FLAY vee yoh/.

Lepidus, M. Aemilius /LEP ih dus/. *Aemilius* /ih MIL ee us/ is not spoken. At 3.2.264 /lep ID us/ is indicated.

Ligarius /lih GAIR yus/.

Lucilius, Lucillius 3 or 4 syllables depending on meter /l$\overline{oo}$ SILL (ee) yus/ (for /ly$\overline{oo}$-/ see App. D *lu-*).

Lucius /L$\overline{OO}$ shus, -syus/. The former is nearly universal in the US, the latter is most common in the UK. Normal development would favor /L$\overline{OO}$ shus/ (for /ly$\overline{oo}$-/ see App. D *lu-*).

Murellus (F1) /muh RELL us/. Some eds. prefer **Marullus** /muh RŬL us/.

Messala /muh SAY luh/; restored pronunciation /mess AH lah/.

Metellus Cimber /muh TEL us SIM bur/.

Octavius /ŏk TAY vyus/.

Pindarus /PIN dur us/.

Plebeians /plih BEE unz/ common people. This word is not spoken.

Pompey /PŎMP ee/.

Popilius Lena, Popillius Laena both pronounced /puh PILL yus LEE nuh/.

Portia /POR shuh/.

Publius 2 or 3 syllables depending on meter /PUB l(ee) yus/.

Strato /STRAYT oh/

Titinius /tī-, tih TIN yus/.

Trebonius /trih BOHN yus/.

Varrus (F1) /VĂIR us/. Some eds. prefer **Varro** /VĂIR oh/.

People in the Play (cont.)

Volumnius 3 or 4 syllables depending on meter /vuh LUM n(ee) yus/.

Places in the Play

Philippi /fih LIP ī/. Occasionally the Gk. form with 1st syllable stress is used in mod. Eng., but will not fit the meter in Shk.

Sardis /SAR diss/.

Tiber /TĪ bur/.

A frequently used phrase is:

the ides of March /īdz/ March 15.

Act 1 Scene 1

40. **sate** archaic variant of **sat**. May have been /sayt/ or /sat/.

41. *****livelong** US /LIV lŏng, -lawng/, *rarely* [LĪV-]; UK /LIV lŏng/ [LĪV-].

47. **concave** here should be /CŎN-, CŎNG kayv/.

67. *****Lupercal** the Roman protector of flocks. /LOOP ur kal/, *rarely* [-kł] (for /lyo͞o-/ see App. D *lu-*).

75. *****servile** /SUR vīl/, *rarely* [SUR vł] slave-like.

Act 1 Scene 2

45. **construe** here should be /CŎN stro͞o/.

50. **cogitations** /cŏj ih TAY shunz/ thoughts.

78. **rout** /rowt/ mob.

95. **as lief** /leef/ as soon.

101. **chafing** /CHAY fing/ raging.

ă-bat, ăir-marry, air-pair, ạr-far, ĕr-merry, ĝ- get, ī-high, ĭr-mirror, ł-little, n̦-listen, ŏ-hot, oh-go, o͞o-wood, o͞o-moon, oor-tour, ōr- or, ow-how, ţh-that, t̶h̶-thin, ŭ-but, UR-fur, ur-under.   ( ) - suppress the syllable   see p. xiii for complete list.

105. **Accoutred** /uh C$\overline{OO}$T urd/ clothed.

107. **buffet** /BUFF it/ fight.

109. **controversy** here should be /CŎN truh vur see/, the normal US pronunciation.

112. **Aeneas** /ih NEE yus/; UK *also* /EE NEE yus/ Prince of Troy.

114. *****Anchises** /an-, ang KĪ seez/; US *also newer* [-zeez] Aeneas' father.

136. **Colossus** /kuh LŎS us/ giant.

238. **coronets** small crowns. US /COR uh nets, -nits/, /cor uh NETS/; E.COAST US /CŎR-, cŏr-/; UK /CŎR uh nits/ [-nets, cŏr uh NETS].

244. **howted** /HOWT id/ archaic variant of **hooted**.

248, 251. **swound (ed)** archaic variant of **swoon**. In Shk's time the vowel could be either /ow/ or /$\overline{oo}$/.

Act 1 Scene 3

6. **riv'd** /rīvd/ split.

28. **Howting** /HOWT ing/ archaic variant of **Hooting**.

31. **portentous** /por TEN tuss/ prophetic.

34. **construe** here should be /CŎN str$\overline{oo}$/.

81. *****thews** /~~th~~y$\overline{oo}$z/; US, CN *also* [~~th~~$\overline{oo}$z] muscles.

106. **hinds** /hīndz/ double meaning: female deer, menial laborers.

109. **offal** /ŎF ł/; US *also* /AWF ł/ animal guts and remains after butchering.

131. **Stand close** /clohss/ keep hidden.

135. **incorporate** /in COR pur rut, -rayt/ a part of. /-ut / is more usual for an adj.

143. **praetor's** /PREE turz/ Roman official. See App. D *-or*.

159. **alchymy** /AL kuh mee/ the study of the transformation of base metals to gold. Archaic variant of **alchemy**, pronounced the same way.

Act 2 Scene 1

7, 35. **taper** /TAY pur/ slender candle.

33. **mischievous** here should be /MIS chiv us/. /mis CHEEV us/ is considered non-standard in all countries.

44. **exhalations** /eks huh LAY shunz, eks uh-/ [egz uh-] meteors.

54. **Tarquin** /TAR kwin/ king of Rome who raped Lucretia.

65. **phantasma** /fan TAZ muh/ evil vision.

84. **Erebus** /ĔR ih bus/ hell.

126. **palter** /PAWL tur/ shift position in an argument.

129. **cautelous** /KAWT uh lus/ deceitful.

200. *****augurers** /AWG yur urz/ [AWG ur urz]; UK *also* /-yoor-/ prophets.

227. **untir'd** here should be /UN tīrd/.

246.*****wafter** waving. US, CN /WŎFT ur/; SOUTH. US /WĂFT-/; UK /WŎFT-/ [WĂFT-, WAHFT-]. Variant of **wafture** /-chur/; UK *also* /-tyoor/. /WĂFT-/ is newer and considered non-standard by many. See App. D -*ure*.

266. **rheumy** /RŌŌM ee/ dank.

287. **harlot** /HAR lut/ whore.

307. **construe** here should be /CŎN strōō/ explain for legal purposes.

308. **charactery** /kuh RAK tur ee/ secret writing.

317, 318. **exploit** here should be /ek SPLOYT/.

ă-bat, ăir-**marry**, air-**pair**, ạr-**far**, ĕr-**merry**, ĝ- **get**, ī-**high**, ĭr-**mirror**, ł-**little**, ṇ-**listen**,
ŏ-**hot**, oh-**go**, ōō-**wood**, ōō-**moon**, oor-**tour**, ōr- **or**, ow-**how**, ṭh-**that**, t̶h̶-**thin**, ŭ-**but**,
UR-**fur**, ur-**under**.   ( ) - suppress the syllable   see p. xiii for complete list.

Act 2 Scene 2

37. ***augurers** /AWG yur urz/ [AWG ur urz]; UK *also* /-yoor-/ prophets.

39. ***entrails** /EN traylz/; US *also* [-trłz] guts.

76. **statuë, statua** here should be three syllables /STATCH oo uh/;
UK *also* /STAT yoo uh/.

80. **portents** here should be /por TENTS/ omens.

89. **relics, reliques** /REL iks/.

89. ***cognizance** /CŎG nih zunss, -zn̩ss/; *rarely older* [CŎN ih-] sign.

113. **ague** /AY gyo͞o/ malarial fever.

Act 2 Scene 4

35. **praetors** /PREE turz/ Roman officials. See App. D *-or*.

Act 3 Scene 1

33. ***puissant** powerful. The traditional forms are /PWISS n̩t/, /PYO͞O sn̩t/ (see
App. D).

57, 81. **enfranchisement** /en FRAN chiz munt/ liberty.

77. **Et tu, Brute** and you, Brutus. Ang.Lat. /et to͞o BRO͞O tee/, but now
universally Class.Lat. /BRO͞O tay/.

125. ***prostrate** /PRŎS trayt/, US *rarely* [-trut] lying face down.

136. **Thorough** archaic variant of *through*, used when the meter demands two
syllables. It is often pronounced as *thorough* on stage, but using /-o͞o/ in the
final syllable will bring it closer to mod. *through*.

136. **untrod** here should be /UN trŏd/.

202. **close** /clohz/ come to terms with.

206. **lethe** /LEE̶TH̶ ee/ stream of death.

209. **strooken** (*stroken* F1) /STRO�ther͞OK in/ or perhaps simply a variant spelling of **strucken**, **stricken** (F2).

215. **compact** here /cŏm-, cum PACT/ agreement.

259. **prophesy** /PRŎF uh sī/ to predict the future.

271. ***Ate** goddess of discord. /AYT ee/ is the older, angl. form; /AHT ay/ is the newer, restored form and much more common; /AHT ee/ is a mixed form, heard occasionally.

Act 3 Scene 2

95. ***Lupercal** the feast honoring the Roman protector of flocks. /LO͞OP ur kal/, *rarely* [-kł] (for /lyo͞o-/ see App. D *lu-*).

173. **Nervii** /NURV ee ī/ a Belgian tribe. Restored Latin /NĔRV-/.

188. **statuë, statua** here should be three syllables /STATCH oo uh/; UK *also* /STAT yoo uh/.

196. **vesture** /VES chur/ clothing, covering. See App. D *-ure*.

217. ***orator** US, CN /OR uh tur/; UK, E.COAST US /ŎR-/. Sometimes /OR ayt ur/ is used, but it is not recommended. See App. D *-or*.

242. **drachmaes** Gk. coins. Archaic pl. form /DRAK meez/. Some eds. prefer **drachmas** /DRAK muz/.

251. **recreate yourselves** /REK ree ayt/ refresh yourselves, amuse yourselves.

Act 4 Scene 1

20. ***divers** various. Here should be stressed on the first syllable US, CN /DĪ vurss, -vurz/; UK /DĪ vurss/ [-vurz].

30. **provender** /PRŎV n̩ dur/ dry food for animals.

32. **to wind** /wīnd/ turn a horse.

ă-bat, äir-**marry**, air-**pair**, a̩r-**far**, ĕr-**merry**, ĝ- **get**, ī-**high**, ĭr-**mirror**, ł-**little**, n̩-**listen**, ŏ-**hot**, oh-**go**, o͞o-**wood**, o͞o-**moon**, oor-**tour**, ōr- **or**, ow-**how**, th-**that**, t̶h̶-**thin**, ŭ-**but**, UR-**fur**, ur-**under**.   ( ) - suppress the syllable   see p. xiii for complete list.

46. *covert secret . Here should be stressed on the 1st syllable
US, CN /KOHV urt/ [KUV-]; UK /KUV-/ [KOHV-], *rarely* [KŎV-].

Act 4 Scene 3 (*Complete Oxford* continues this as 4.2—line nos. in parentheses)

2. (4.2.57) **Lucius Pella** US /LŌŌ shus PELL uh/, /-syus/. The former is nearly universal in the US, the latter is most common in the UK. Normal development would favor /LŌŌ shus/ (for /lyŌŌ-/ see App. D *lu-*).

3. (4.2.58) **Sardians** /SAR dee unz/.

16, 17 (4.2.70) *chastisement punishment. Here stress should be on 1st syllable /CHĂSS tiz munt/; US *also* /-tīz-/.

44. (4.2.100) **bouge** /BUJ/, or possibly /bŌŌj/. Archaic variant of **budge**.

73. (4.2.130) **drachmaes** Gk. coins. Archaic pl. form /DRAK meez/. Some eds. prefer **drachmas** /DRAK muz/.

85. (4.2.141) **riv'd** /rīvd/ split.

164. (4.2.218) **close** /clohss/ secretly.

164, 275. (4.2.218, 328) **taper** /TAY pur/ slender candle.

171. (4.2.225) **tenure** archaic variant of **tenor**, both /TEN ur/.

228. (4.2.282) **niggard** /NIG urd/ give a small amount to.

Act 5 Scene 1

19. **exigent** /EK sih junt, EG zih junt/ emergency.

21. *parley /PAR lee/ conference with an enemy. Newer [-lay] not recommended.

34. **Hybla** /HĪ bluh/ region of Sicily.

76. **Epicurus** /ep ih KYOOR us/; US *also* /-KYUR-/ Gk. philosopher.

78. *presage here should be /pree-, prih SAYJ/ foretell.

79. *ensign flag. US, CN /EN sṇ/, US *rarely* [-sīn]; UK /-sṇ, -sīn/.

82. **consorted** /cun SORT id/ accompanied.

109. **Thorough** archaic variant of *through*, used when the meter demands two syllables. It is often pronounced as *thorough* on stage, but using /-ōo/ in the final syllable will bring it closer to mod. *through*.

Act 5 Scene 3

3. *****ensign** standard-bearer. US, CN /EN sn̩/, US *rarely* [-sīn]; UK /-sn̩, -sīn/.

37. **Parthia** /PAR thyuh/ in NW Iran.

84. **misconstrued** here should be /mis CŎN strōod/.

96. *****entrails** /EN traylz/; US *also* [-trłz] guts.

104. *****Thasos, Thassos** island near Philippi. US /THASS ŏss, -us/ [THAHSS-, THAYSS-]; UK /THAYSS-, THASS ŏss/ [-us]. A newer pronunciation /-ohss/ is also used, especially in the US. /THAYSS us/ is the traditional anglicization. Some eds. prefer F1's **Tharsus** /TAR sus/,

108. **Labio** /LAY bee oh/ (F1) some eds. prefer **Labeo**, pronounced the same way.

Act 5 Scene 5

2. **Statilius** /stuh TIL yus/.

ă-bat, ăir-marry, air-pair, ạr-far, ĕr-merry, ĝ- get, ī-high, ĭr-mirror, ł-little, n̩-listen, ŏ-hot, oh-go, ŏŏ-wood, ōō-moon, oor-tour, ōr- or, ow-how, țh-that, th-thin, ŭ-but, UR-fur, ur-under.   ( ) - suppress the syllable   see p. xiii for complete list.

King John

People in the Play

Arthur of Britain /BRIT ņ/ Brittany. Some eds. prefer **Brittaine**, pronounced the same way, though in Shk's time /-ayn/ was also used. Other eds. prefer the mod. Fr. form **Bretagne**, which here should be /BRET ahn^y/. For clarity *Britt'ny* may be substituted.

Bigot /BIG ut/.

Cardinal 2 or 3 syllables depending on meter /CARD (ih) nł/, /CARD ņ ł/. Two syllables is usual in the US, three syllables in the UK.

Chatillion here stressed always on the 2nd syllable /shuh TIL yun/. Some eds. prefer Fr. **Chatillon** or **Châtillon** /shah TEE yoh^n/.

Cordelion Richard the Lionhearted. Angl. /cor duh LĪ un/; sometimes the semi-Fr. /-LEE un/ is used. Some eds. prefer French **Coeur de Lion**, anglicized as US /cur de LĪ un, -LEE un/; UK prefers the Fr. /CUR duh LEE oh^n/, or sometimes semi-angl. [-LEE ŏn, -LEE un].

de Burgh /duh BURG/.

Dolphin (Lewis) /DŎL fin/; US *also* /DAWL-/ angl. form of **Dauphin** 'the French heir to the throne' which here would be Fr. /DOH fä^n/. In Shk's time /l/ in this position was often silent, so *dolphin* and *dauphin* were probably both /DAW fin/.

Faulconbridge /FAWL kun brij/ or the older pronunciation [FAW kun-], still used by some in the UK. Some eds. prefer **Falconbridge** which may also be /FAL-/ or UK /FŎL-/.

Lewis, Louis one syllable is indicated /LOO (i)ss/.

Lymoges, Limoges /lee MOHZH/. 3.1.114 is either headless with /lee MOHZH/ or if the first foot is regular, /LIM uh jiz, -zhiz/.

Melune /muh LOON/. Some eds. prefer Fr. **Melun** /muh LÄ^N/.

Norfolk (Bigot) /NOR f^{u}k/. This name is not spoken.

People in the Play (cont.)

Pandulph /PAN dulf/. Some eds. prefer **Pandolf** /PAN dŏlf/; US *also* /-dawlf/.

Pembroke US /PEM brohk/; UK /PEM brŏŏk/ [-bruck, -brohk].

Plantagenet /plan TAJ ih nit/.

Salisbury 2 or 3 syllables, depending on meter US /SAWLZ b(ĕ)r ee/; UK /SAWLZ b(u)r ee/ [SĂLZ-].

A common word in the play

legate /LEG ut/ churchman representing the pope.

Act 1 Scene 1

11. **Poictiers** here with 1st syllable stress. Angl. /POY teerz/. Archaic variant of the city **Poitiers** /PWAH tyay/. Formerly the city was not distinguished from the surrounding province, **Poitou** /PWAH tŏŏ/.

11. **Anjou** here should have 1st syllable stress, angl. /AN jŏŏ/; Fr. /AH^N zhŏŏ/.

11. **Touraine** here with 1st syllable stress /TŌŌ rayn/, normally /tŏŏ RAYN/; Fr. /TŌŌ ren/.

11. **Maine** angl. /mayn/; Fr. /men/.

28. ***presage** here should be /PRESS ij/ omen.

44. **controversy** here should be /CŎN truh vur see/, the normal US pronunciation.

48. **priories** /PRĪ ur eez/ a type of religious home similar to an abbey.

51. **Northamptonshire** /nor ~~TH~~AMP tun shur/ [-sheer].

65. **diffidence** /DIF ih dunss/ mistrust.

103. ***sojourn'd** resided temporarily. Here stress should fall on the first syllable US, CN /SOH jurnd/; UK /SŎJ urnd/ [-URND, SOH-, SUJ-].

ă-bat, ăir-marry, air-**pair**, ạr-**far**, ĕr-**merry**, ĝ- **get**, ī-**high**, ĭr-**mirror**, ł-**little**, ṇ-**listen**, ŏ-**hot**, oh-**go**, ŏŏ-**wood**, ōō-**moon**, oor-**tour**, ōr- **or**, ow-**how**, ţh-**that**, ~~th~~-**thin**, ŭ-**but**, UR-**fur**, ur-**under**.   ( ) - suppress the syllable   see p. xiii for complete list.

153. **five pence** /FĪV punss, -pṇss/.

168. **grandame, *grandam** /GRAN dam/; US *rarely* [-dum] grandmother.
Informally /GRAN um/. /-daym/ may have been used, but /-dam, -dum/
probably reflect the normal development.

185. **Good den** /gōōd-, gud DEN/ good evening. Some eds. prefer **Good e'en**.

192. **catechize** /KAT uh kīz/ to instruct through a series of questions and
answers.

196. **Absey book** /AYB (ee) see, AB-/ a primer or "how-to" book.

202. **Apennines** /AP uh nīnz/ mountains in Italy.

203. **Pyrenean** /pĭr uh NEE un/ referring to mountains on Fr.-Sp. border.

211. **accoutrement** clothes. /uh COOT ruh munt, uh COOT ur munt/.

225. **Colbrand** /KOHL brand/ a Danish giant.

234. **eat** /et/ dialect variant of **eaten**.

240. **holp** /hohlp/ helped.

243. ***untoward** rude. Here must be /un TOH wurd, -urd/, though
/un tuh WÂRD/ (as in *war*) is the most common pronunciation in CN, UK.

244. ***Basilisco-like** a reference to a play. US /băss ih LISS koh/ [baz-];
UK /baz-/ [băss-]; CN both used equally.

Act 2 Scene 1

1-536. **Angiers** usually 1st syllable stress, angl. /AN jeerz/, but at 2.1.1
/an JEERZ/. Some eds. prefer Fr. **Angers** /ah[n] zhay/.

27. ***bulwark** structure for defense. US, CN /BULL wurk/ [BŬL wurk];
UK /BULL WURK, -wurk/. The vowels /or/, /ahr/ not recommended in the final
syllable, and are non-standard in the UK.

54. **paltry** /PAWL tree/ worthless.

63. *Ate goddess of discord. /AYT ee/ is the older, angl. form; /AHT ay/ is the newer, restored form and much more common; /AHT ee/ is a mixed form, heard occasionally.

73. *waft US, CN /wŏft/; SOUTH. US /wăft/; UK /wŏft/ [wăft, wahft]. Here past tense 'sailed lightly.' /wăft/ is newer and considered non-standard by many.

75. scathe /skayth̩/ harm. Variant of scath /skath/.

78. *parley /PAR lee/ negotiate. Newer [-lay] not recommended.

101. abstract /AB stract/ summary.

112. supernal /sōō PUR nł/; UK, SOUTH. US also [syōō-] heavenly.

117. *chastise punish. Here should be /CHĂSS tīz/, the usual US pronunciation, also used in CN; in the UK 2nd syllable stress is usual.

133-194. grandame, *grandam /GRAN dam/; US rarely [-dum] grandmother. Informally /GRAN um/. /-daym/ may have been used, but /-dam, -dum/ probably reflect the normal development.

144. Alcides' /al SĪ deez/ Hercules.

152-528. Anjou here with 1st syllable stress, angl. /AN jōō/; Fr. /AH^N zhōō/. At the beginning of a line the second syllable may be stressed instead.

Maine angl. /mayn/; Fr. /men/.

Touraine 1st or 2nd syllable stress depending on meter /TŌŌ rayn/, /tōō RAYN/; Fr. /tōō ren/.

---

183. Bedlam /BED lum/ a lunatic.

188. beadle /BEE dł/ local officer in charge of whippings.

205, 226. parle /pạrl/ conference with an enemy.

218. ordinance artillery. Archaic variant of ordnance. Here should be 3 syllables /OR dih nunss/.

244. hospitable here should be /HŎS pih tuh bł/.

ă-bat, ăir-marry, air-pair, ạr-far, ĕr-merry, ĝ- get, ī-high, ĭr-mirror, ł-little, n̩-listen, ŏ-hot, oh-go, ōō-wood, ōō-moon, oor-tour, ŏr- or, ow-how, t̲h-that, t̲h-thin, ŭ-but, UR-fur, ur-under.   ( ) - suppress the syllable   see p. xiii for complete list.

254. **unhack'd** here should be /UN hackt/.

259. **rounder** /ROWN dur/ roundness.   Variant of **roundure**
US, CN /-jur, -dyoor, -dyur/; UK /-dyoor/ [-dyur, -jur].   See App. D -*ure*.

262. **circumference** here should be 4 syllables /sur CUM fur unss/.

287. **chevaliers** angl. /shev uh LEERZ/; Fr. /shev ahl yayz/ horsemen.

288. **swing'd** /swinjd/ beat.

305. *****grovelling** US, CN /GRŎV-, GRUV ł ing/; UK /GRŎV-/ [GRUV-].

373. **scroyles** /skroylz/ scoundrels.

378. **mutines** /MYŌŌT inz, -ṇz/ mutineers.

388. **dissever** /dih SEV ur/ sever.

421. **Persever** /pur SEV ur/ persevere.

454. **peremptory** here should be /PĔR um tur ee/; US *also* /-tor ee/ determined.

463. *****bastinado** beating with a stick. /bas tih NAH doh/;
UK *rarely older* [bas tih NAY doh].

465. **buffets** /BUFF its/ boxes.

487, 528. **Poictiers** angl. /poy TEERZ/ or /POY teerz/ depending on meter. In
the first instance 2nd syllable stress is indicated; in the second, stress may fall on
either the 1st or 2nd syllable. Archaic variant of the city **Poitiers** /pwah TYAY,
PWAH tyay/. Formerly the city was not distinguished from the surrounding
province, **Poitou** /PWAH tōō, pwah TŌŌ/.

---

506. **espy** /ess SPĪ/ see.

509. **lout** /lowt/ oaf.

513. **translate** here should be stressed on the 2nd syllable, the normal UK
pronunciation US /trănss LAYT, trănz-/; UK /trănss LAYT/ [trănz-, trahnz-,
trahnss-, trunss-, trunz-].

527. **Volquessen** /vŏl KESS un, -ṇ/.

575. *peized, peised balanced. US /PEEZ id/, *sometimes* [PAYZ-];
UK /PEEZ-, PAYZ-/. Dialect evidence shows that /EE/ was the form found in
southern Eng., and /AY/ in the North.

Act 3 Scene 1((*The Complete Oxford* 2.2)

22. *lamentable here should be /LAM un tuh bł/ the usual UK pronunciation.

22. rheum /rōōm/ tears.

40. *heinous /HAYN us/ hateful. /HEEN us/ is non-standard though common
in the UK.

46. swart /swōrt/ black.

(*The Complete Oxford* begins 3.1 here (line nos. in parentheses).

78. (3.1.4) alchymist /AL kuh mist/ one who studies the transformation of base
metals to gold. Archaic variant of alchemist, pronounced the same way.

110. (3.1.36) sunset here should be /sun SET/. Some eds. prefer sun set.

129-199. (3.1.55-125) recreant /REK r(ee) yunt/ coward.

138. (3.1.64) Milan here should be /MILL un/.

143. (3.1.69) Archbishop here should be /ARCH bish up/.

147. (3.1.73) interrogatories /in tur RŎG uh treez/ produces a regular line.
Also possible is a feminine line US /-tor eez/; UK /-tur eez/.

154. (3.1.80) tithe /tīṭh/ collect money for the church.

155. (3.1.81) supreme here should be US /SŌŌ preem/;
UK, SOUTH. US *also* [SYŌŌ-].

161. (3.1.87) blaspheme here should be /blăss FEEM/;
UK, E.NEW ENG. *also* [blahss-] speak irreverently.

165. (3.1.91) dross /drŏss/; US *also* /drawss/ impure matter, rubbish.

ă-bat, ăir-marry, air-pair, ạr-far, ĕr-merry, ĝ- get, ī-high, ĭr-mirror, ł-little, ṇ-listen, ŏ-hot, oh-go, ōō-wood, ōō-moon, oor-tour, ōr- or, ow-how, ṭh-that, ŧ̶ħ̶-thin, ŭ-but, UR-fur, ur-under.   ( ) - suppress the syllable   see p. xiii for complete list.

169. (3.1.95) **revenue** here should be /ruh VEN yo͞o/.

173, 223. (3.1.99) **excommunicate** /eks kuh MYO͞ON ih kut, -kayt/
excommunicated.
---

175. (3.1.101) **heretic** /HĔR ih tik/ a dissenter.

177. (3.1.103) **Canonized** here /kan ŎN īz ed/ declared a saint.

192. (3.1.118) **arch-heretic** /ARCH HĔR ih tik/ worst of all dissenters.

201. (3.1.127) ***breeches** /BRITCH iz/ is traditional, /BREECH iz/ is newer.
The former pronunciation is more common in the UK, and the latter in the
US, CN.

220. (3.1.146) **lout** /lowt/ oaf.

282. (3.1.208) ***surety** guarantee, pledge. Here should be two syllables, though
in mod. English, three syllables are more common, /SHUR (ih) tee, SHOOR-,
SHOR-/ (see App. D).

334. (3.1.260) ***Grandam** /GRAN dam/; US *rarely* [-dum] grandmother.
Informally /GRAN um/.

339. (3.1.265) ***puissance** power (i.e., army). Here 3 syllables, traditionally
/PYO͞O ih sn̩ss/ (See App. D).

342. (3.1.268) **allay** /uh LAY/ diminish.

Act 3 Scene 2

2. **aery, airy** /AIR ee/ of the air.

Act 3 Scene 3

3, 14. **grandame, *grandam** /GRAN dam/; US *rarely* [-dum] grandmother.
Informally /GRAN um/. /-daym/ may have been used, but /-dam, -dum/
probably reflect the normal development.

36. **gawds, gauds** /gawdz/ toys.

38. **brazen** /BRAY zun, -zn̩/ brass.

73. **Callice, Callis** /KAL iss/ city on north. coast of France. Both are archaic variants of **Calais** which here should be /KAL ay/, the normal UK form; Fr. /KAH lay/.

Act 3 Scene 4

2. **armado** /arm AY doh/ archaic form of **armada** /arm AH duh/ fleet.

6. **Angiers** angl. /AN jeerz/. Some eds. prefer Fr. **Angers** /AH^N zhay/.

7. *****Divers** various. Here should be stressed on the first syllable US, CN /DĬ vurss, -vurz/; UK /DĬ vurss/ [-vurz].

26. **odoriferous** /oh dur RIF (uh) rus/ smelly.

29. **detestable** here should be /DEE tess tuh bł/ or /DET es tuh bł/.

32. *****fulsome** disgusting. /FŲLL sum/; US *rarely* [FŬL-].

35. **buss** /BŬS/ kiss.

44. **belie** /bih-, bee LĪ/ slander.

52. **canoniz'd** here should be /kan ŎN īzd/ declared a saint.

58. **babe of clouts** /clowts/ rag doll.

85. **ague's** /AY gyōōz/ malarial fever.

90. *****heinous** /HAYN us/ terrible. /HEEN us/ is non-standard though common in the UK.

133. **misplac'd** here should be /MIS playst/.

153. **exhalation** /eks huh LAY shun, eks uh-/ [egz uh-] meteor.

158. *****presages** here should be /PRESS ih jiz/ omens.

Act 4 Scene 1

2. **arras** /ĂIR us/ tapestry.

ă-bat, ăir-**marry**, air-**pair**, ạr-**far**, ĕr-**merry**, ĝ- **get**, ī-**high**, ĭr-**mirror**, ł-**little**, ṇ-**listen**, ŏ-**hot**, oh-**go**, ōō-**wood**, ōō-**moon**, oor-**tour**, ōr- **or**, ow-**how**, ţh-**that**, t̶h̶-**thin**, ŭ-**but**, UR-**fur**, ur-**under**.   ( ) - suppress the syllable   see p. xiii for complete list.

7. ***Uncleanly** /un CLEN lee/ or newer /un CLEEN lee/.

33. **rheum** /rōōm/ tears.

42. **handkercher** /HANK ur chur/ archaic variant of **handkerchief**.

50. **lien** (*lyen* F1) /līn/, archaic variant of **lain**.

116. **tarre, tar** /tar/ incite.

Act 4 Scene 2

14. **taper-light** /TAY pur/ slender candle.

16. **excess** here should be /ek SESS/, the most common UK form.

21. ***antique** ancient. Here /AN teek/, *rarely older* [AN tik].

43. ***indue** /in DYŌŌ/; US *also* [-DŌŌ] supply. Some eds. prefer **endue** /en-/.

52. **Th' enfranchisement** /ṭhʸen FRAN chiz munt/ liberty.

57. **mew up** /myōō/ cage.

65, 66. **weal** /weel/ welfare.

71. ***heinous** /HAYN us/ hateful. /HEEN us/ is non-standard though common in the UK.

72. **close aspect** /clohss ass SPECT/ furtive face.

92. **commandement.** Archaic variant of **commandment**, originally with 4 syllables, /-uh munt/, but here the usual mod. 3-syllable pronunciation is required.

148. **Pomfret** US /PŎM frit/; UK /PUM frit/ [PŎM-].

185. ***beldames** old women. Some eds. prefer **beldams**, both pronounced US /BEL damz, -dumz/; UK /BEL damz/, *rarely* [-dumz]. /-daymz/ is also used, but normal development would probably favor /-damz, -dumz/.

186. **prophesy** /PRŎF uh sī/ to predict the future.

200. **embattailed** drawn up for battle. Archaic variant of **embattled** /em BAT ł ed/ which in Shk's time could also be pronounced /em BAT ayl ed/,

201. **artificer** /ạr TIF ih sur/ craftsman.

216. **accompt** /uh COWNT/ archaic variant of **account**. See App. D.

234. **express** here should be /EK spress/.

238. ***parley** /PAR lee/ negotiate. Newer [-lay] not recommended.

246. **confine** /cŏn-, cun FĪN/ double meaning: region and prison.

247. ***tumult** turmoil. US /TO͞OM ult/; SOUTH.US *also* /TYO͞OM-/; CN /TYO͞OM-/ [TO͞OM-]; UK /TYO͞OM-/. /CHO͞OM-/ considered non-standard in the UK. A newer pronunciation /TUM ult/ is not recommended.

Act 4 Scene 3

11. **Saint Edmundsbury** US /saynt ED mundz bĕr ee/; UK /sint-, sṇt ED mundz bur ee/.

46. **heighth** /hīth/ or /hītth/ variants of **height**. /hītth/ is still used today, though non-standard.

56. ***heinous** /HAYN us/ hateful. /HEEN us/ is non-standard though common in the UK.

70. **conversant** here should be /CŎN vur sunt, -sṇt/ concerned with.

77. **Avaunt** /uh VAWNT/ begone!

108. **rheum** /ro͞om/ tears.

112. **Th' *uncleanly** /th͟ʸun CLEN lee/ or newer /-CLEEN lee/.

112. **savors** (UK **savours**) /SAY vurz/ smells.

114. **Bury** /bĕry/ Bury St. Edmonds.

147. **The unowed** here should be /th͟ee UN ohd/.

ă-bat, ăir-**ma**rry, air-**pair**, ạr-**far**, ĕr-**me**rry, ĝ- **g**et, ī-**high**, ĭr-**mi**rror, ł-**li**ttle, ṇ-**li**sten, ŏ-**hot**, oh-**go**, o͞o-**wood**, ō͞o-**moon**, oor-**tour**, ōr- **or**, ow-**how**, th͟-**that**, th-**thin**, ŭ-**but**, UR-**fur**, ur-**under**.   ( ) - suppress the syllable   see p. xiii for complete list.

155. **center** /SEN tur/ archaic variant of **centure, ceinture** /SEN chur/;
UK *also* /-tyoor/. Other eds. prefer **cincture** /SINK chur/. All mean 'belt.' See
App. D *-ure* and App. E.

Act 5 Scene 1

19. **convertite** /CŎN vur tīt/ a convert.

54. **glister** /GLIS tur/ **glisten**.

67. **compremise** archaic variant of **compromise**, both pronounced
/CŎM pruh mīz/.

68. *__parley__ /PAR lee/ conference with an enemy. Newer [-lay] not
recommended.

Act 5 Scene 2

3. **president** first draft . Archaic variant of **precedent**, both /PRESS (ih) dunt/.
It is not clear whether /PREZ-/ was used in Shk's time.

7. **inviolable** /in VĪL uh bł/ which cannot be broken.

9. **albeit** although. Here stressed on the 1st syllable /AWL bee it/.

10. **A voluntary zeal, and an unurg'd faith** may be a hexameter with *voluntary*
having four syllables and *unurged* /un UR jid/. It could also be scanned with
voluntary having four syllables, *zeal* two, and *unurg'd* stressed on the first
syllable, or with *voluntary* having three syllables with *unurg'd* /un URJ id/.

36. **pagan** /PAYG un/ non-Christian.

41. **wrastling** /RĂSS ling/ archaic variant of **wrestling**.

84. *__chastis'd__ punished. Here should be /CHĂSS tīzd/, the usual US
pronunciation, also used in CN; in the UK 2nd syllable stress is usual.

104. **Vive le roi** /VEE vuh luh RWAH/ long live the king.

120. **Milan** here should be /MILL un/.

132. **masque** US /mǎsk/; UK, E. NEW ENG. /mahsk/ [mǎsk] masked dancing and
pantomime.

133. **unhair'd** here should be /UN haird/ beardless, i.e., youthful.

147. ***chastisement** punishment. Here stress should be on 1st syllable /CHĂSS tiz munt/; US *also* /-tīz-/.

149. ***aery, eyrie, aerie** high nest. /AIR ee, EER-/; E.COAST US *also* [ĂIR-]. /ĪR ee/ not recommended. /AIR ee/ is the oldest pronunciation.

150. **souse** /sowss/ swoop down on.

151. **ingrate** ungrateful. Here should be /in GRAYT/ with *degenerate* /dee-, dih JEN (uh) rut/.

Act 5 Scene 3

8, 16. **Swinstead** /SWIN sted/. Some eds. prefer **Swineshead** /SWĪNZ hed/.

Act 5 Scene 4

18. **Saint Edmundsbury** US /saynt ED mundz bĕr ee/; UK /sint-, sṇt ED mundz bur ee/.

44. **In *lieu whereof** US, CN /lōō, lyoo/; UK /lyōō/ [lōō] in return for.

Act 5 Scene 6

16. **sans** /sănz/ without.

22. **swound** archaic variant of **swoon**. In Shk's time the vowel could be either /ow/ or /ōō/.

31. ***peradventure** perhaps. /PUR ad VEN chur/; US *rarely* [PĔR-, PUR ad ven chur]; UK, CN *also* [PUR-, PĔR ad ven chur, pĕr ad VEN chur].

Act 5 Scene 7

8. **allay** /uh LAY/ relieve.

ă-bat, ăir-**marry**, air-**pair**, ạr-**far**, ĕr-**merry**, ĝ- **get**, ī-**high**, ĭr-**mirror**, ł-little, ṇ-listen, ŏ-hot, oh-go, ōō-wood, ōō-moon, oor-**tour**, ōr- **or**, ow-**how**, ţh-**that**, th-**thin**, ŭ-**but**, UR-**fur**, ur-**under**.   ( ) - suppress the syllable   see p. xiii for complete list.

21. **cygnet** /SIG nit/ young swan.

22. **chaunts** archaic variant of **chants** /chănts/; E. NEW ENG, UK /chahnts/. See App. D -*aun*-.

26. **indigest** /IN dih jest/; US *also* /-dī-/ formless mass. The stress could also fall on the last syllable.

58. **module** /MŎD yo͞ol/; US *also* /MŎJ o͞ol/ image. *Module* was formerly confused with **model**. Both could be pronounced /MŎD ł/ in Shk's time.

68. *****surety** pledge, guarantee, stability. Here should be two syllables, though in mod. English, three syllables are more common, /SHUR (ih) tee, SHOOR-, SHOR-/ (see App. D).

99. **Worcester** /Wo͞oS tur/.

King Lear
The Complete Oxford line nos. are based on what it calls
The Tragedy of King Lear, the folio text.

People in the Play

*Albany US /AWL buh nee/, *rarely* [AL-]; CN, UK /AWL-/ [AL-].

Burgundy /BUR gun dee/.

Cordelia /cor DEEL yuh/.

Cornwall /CORN wawl/; UK *also* [-wł].

Curan US /CUR un/; UK, E.COAST US /CUH run/.

Gloucester /GLŎS tur/; US *also* /GLAWSS-/.

Goneril, Gonerill /GŎN ur il, -ł/.

Lear /leer/.

Oswald US /ŎZ wawld/; UK /-włd/.

Regan /REE gun/.

Act 1 Scene 1

7. **moi'ty** /MOY tee/ or **moiety** /MOY uh tee/ portion.

47. **amorous *sojourn** a temporary stay. If *amorous* is reduced to /AM russ/, then *sojourn* is stressed on the 1st syllable, the more usual pronunciation in all countries US, CN /SOH jurn/; UK /SŎJ urn/ [-URN, SOH jurn, SUJ urn]. If *amorous* is /AM ur us/, then *sojourn* is stressed on the 2nd syllable.

64. ***champains** (F1), **champaigns** open country. Here should have 1st syllable stress /SHAM paynz/; US *sometimes older* [CHAM paynz]. Omitted Q1.

65. **meads** /meedz/ meadows.

75. **felicitate** /fuh LISS ih tayt, -tut/ made happy. /-ut/ would be the usual adj. form.

ă-bat, äir-marry, air-pair, ạr-far, ĕr-merry, ĝ- get, ī-high, ĭr-mirror, ł-little, ṇ-listen, ŏ-hot, oh-go, o͝o-wood, o͞o-moon, oor-tour, ōr- or, ow-how, ţh-that, th̶-thin, ŭ-but, UR-fur, ur-under.　　　( ) - suppress the syllable　　　see p. xiii for complete list.

85. **be interess'd** (F1) /IN tur est/ establish a claim, be closely connected. Omitted Q1.

110. **Hecat, Hecate** /HEK ut/ goddess of witchcraft. /HEK uh tee/ is the usual non-Shakespearean pronunciation.

114. **Propinquity** /proh PINK wih tee/ kinship.

116. *****Scythian** /SITH yun/ [SITH yun] *Scythia* was north of the Black Sea. Some scholars prefer restored Latin /SK-/.

137. **revenue** here should be /ruh VEN yoo/.

139. **coronet** here should be US /COR (uh) net, -nit/; E.COAST US, UK /CŎR-/. Some eds. prefer **crownet** /CROWN it/. Both mean 'small crown.'

161. **miscreant** (F1) /MIS cree unt/ scoundrel. Q1 has **recreant** /REK ree yunt/ coward.

166. **recreant** may be a triple or double ending /REK r(ee) yunt/ traitor. Omitted Q1.

173. **allot** /uh LŎT/ grant.

228. **unchaste** (F1) here should be /UN chayst/. Q1 has **unclear** /UN cleer/.

240. **th' entire** may either be /TH^Y EN tir/, forming a five-foot line, or /thee en TĪ ur/ in a hexameter.

259. **unpriz'd** here should be /UN prīzd/.

265. *****benison** US, CN /BEN ih sun, -sṇ/ [-zun, -zṇ]; UK /-z-/ [-s-] blessing.

278. **alms** charity for the poor. /ahmz/ is older; /ahlmz, awlmz/ are newer. In the UK the latter are non-standard.

281. **covers.** Some eds. prefer *****covert** 'hidden,' here stressed on the 1st syllable US, CN /KOHV urt/ [KUV-]; UK /KUV-/ [KOHV-], *rarely* [KŎV-].

298. *****infirm** /in FURM/ sick.

Act 1 Scene 2

7. **compact** /cum-, cŏm PACT/ composed.

53-74. **revenue** sometimes in verse /ruh VEN yōō/, but in this prose passage may be mod. Eng. US /REV in ōō/; UK, SOUTH. US /-yōō/.

72. **perfect** (F1). Q1 has the archaic variant **perfit** /PUR fit/. Also /PAR fit/ in Shk's time.

92. **auricular assurance** /aw-, uh-, or RIK yuh lur/ proof one can hear.

98. **wind me** /wīnd/ worm your way in, insinuate yourself.

106. **scourg'd** /SKURJD/ harshly punished.

106. **sequent** /SEE kwunt/ following.

112. ***Machinations** (F1) plots. /mack ih NAY shunz/ is older, /mash-/ is a newer spelling pronunciation. The former is more common in the US, the latter in the UK, while in CN both are used equally. Omitted Q1.

123. **treachers** /TRETCH urz/ traitors.

123. ***spherical** (F1) US, CN /SFEER ih kł/ [SFĔR-]; UK /SFĔR ih kł/. Q1 has **spiritual**.

130. **Ursa Major** /UR suh MAY jur/ the Great Bear constellation.

131. **Fut** /fōōt/ God's foot!

132. **maidenl'est** /MAYD n̩ list/ in Shk's time, but in this prose passage **maidenliest** /-lee ist/ may be substituted.

136. **Tom o' Bedlam** (F1) /tŏm uh BED lum/ crazy beggar. Q1 has **them of Bedlam**.

---

lines 144-152 are in Q1, but omitted in F1

146. **maledictions** /mal uh DIK shunz/ curses.

147. **diffidences** /DIFF ih dunss iz/ suspicions.

148. ***nuptial** wedding. US, UK /NUP chł/ [-shł]; in CN both are used equally.

150. **sectary** /SEK tuh ree/; US *also* /SEK tair ee/ devotee.

ă-b**a**t, ăir-m**a**rry, air-p**ai**r, a̩r-f**a**r, ĕr-m**e**rry, ĝ- g**e**t, ī-h**i**gh, ĭr-m**i**rror, ł-litt**le**, n̩-list**en**, ŏ-h**o**t, oh-g**o**, ōō-w**oo**d, ōō-m**oo**n, oor-t**our**, ōr- **or**, ow-h**ow**, t̪h-t**h**at, t̲h̲-**th**in, ŭ-b**u**t, UR-f**ur**, ur-und**er**.   ( ) - suppress the syllable   see p. xiii for complete list.

164. **allay** /uh LAY/ diminish.

Act 1 Scene 4

49. **mungrel** /MUNG grł/ variant of **mongrel**, pronounced the same in the UK; US, CN *also* /MŎNG grł, MAWNG-/.

112. **Brach** /bratch/ female dog.

122. **thou *trowest** you believe. Here the rhymes demand /TROH ist/, though /TROW ist/ is also used in all countries, and is the dominant form in the UK.

---

lines 140-155 are in Q1, but omitted in F1

146. **motley** /MŎT lee/ the costume of different colored cloth worn by fools.

153. **an't, on't** /unt/ of it.

---

159. **eat** /et/ dialect variant of **ate**, which is also commonly /et/ in the UK.

174. ***breeches** /BRITCH iz/ is traditional, /BREECH iz/ is newer. The former pronunciation is more common in the UK, and the latter in the US, CN.

200. **sheal'd** /sheeld, shayld/ archaic variants of **shelled**.

200. **peascod** /PEEZ cŏd/ peapod.

202. **insolent *retinue*** band of followers. Here archaic /ruh TIN yōo/ seems called for, however if *insolent* is syncopated to *ins'lent*, then mod. US /RET ih nōo/, /RET n̩ ōo/; UK, SOUTH. US /-nyōo/.

211. **weal** /weel/ commonwealth.

214. **know** (F1). Q1 has ***trow** US, CN /troh, trow/; UK /trow/ [troh] 'know.' Shk's rhymes elsewhere indicate /-oh/.

225. ***Whoop!** /whōop/ [hōop, hŏop, whŏop].

237. **savor** (UK **savour**) /SAY vur/ character, style.

244. **Epicurism** riotous living. Here should be /ep IK yoor izm/, /-yur-/; 1st syllable stress is usual in mod. Eng.

245. *brothel US, CN /BRŎTH ł/ [BRŎTH ł, BRAWŦH ł]; UK /BRŎTH ł/ whorehouse.

251. besort /bih-, bee SORT/ befit.

279. organs of increase here /in CREESS/ reproductive organs.

280. derogate degraded. /DĔR (uh) gut/; UK also newer [DEER-].

285. cadent /KAY dunt, -dṇt/ falling.

293, 326. dotage /DOHT ij/ senility.

295. fortnight /FORT nīt/; US also [FORT nit] two weeks. Virtually obsolete in the US.

306. comfortable here may be 3 or 4 syllables /CUMF tur bł/, /CUM fur tuh bł/.

308. flea /flee/ archaic and dialect variant of flay /flay/ to skin.

323. politic (F1) /PŎL ih tik/ cunning. Omitted Q1.

339. compact /cum PACT/ confirm.

343. attax'd, ataxed /uh TAKST/. Others prefer F1's at task or Q1c's attask'd US /uh TĂSKT/; E.NEW ENG., UK /uh TAHSKT/ all mean 'blamed.'

Act 2 Scene 1

8. ear-bussing (Q1) /BŬS ing/ ear-kissing. F1 has ear-kissing.

10. toward /TOH wurd, -urd/ about to take place.

17. queasy question /KWEE zee/ i.e., delicate nature.

45. revengive (Q1) /ree-, rih VEN jiv/. F1 has revenging.

46. parricides /PĂIR ih sīdz/ father-killers.

53. *alarum'd US, CN /uh LAHR umd/ [-LĂIR-]; UK /uh LĂIR umd, uh LAHR umd/ called to arms.

ă-bat, ăir-marry, air-pair, ạr-far, ĕr-merry, ĝ- get, ī-high, ĭr-mirror, ł-little, ṇ-listen, ŏ-hot, oh-go, ŏŏ-wood, ōō-moon, oor-tour, ōr- or, ow-how, ṯh-that, ŧħ-thin, Ŭ-but, UR-fur, ur-under.   ( ) - suppress the syllable   see p. xiii for complete list.

55. **gasted, ghasted** US /GĂS tid/; UK, E.NEW ENG. /GAHSS tid/ frightened.

62. **coward** (F1). Q1 has **caitiff** /KAYT if/ scoundrel.

65. **pight** /pīt/ **pitched**.

74. **dullard** /DULL urd/ stupid person.

97. **consort** (F1) /CŎN sort/ group. Omitted Q1.

100. **revenues** here should be /ruh VEN yōōz/.

103. *****sojourn** reside temporarily. Here with 1st syllable stress
US, CN /SOH jurn/; UK /SŎJ urn/ [-URN, SOH-, SUJ-].

107. **bewray** (F1) /bih-, bee RAY/ reveal. Q1 has **betray**.

Act 2 Scene 2

19. **finical** /FIN ih kł/ finicky.

22. **pandar, pander** /PAN dur/ pimp.

22. **mungril** /MUNG grł/ variant of **mongrel**, pronounced the same in the UK;
US, CN *also* /MŎNG grł, MAWNG-/.

28. **brazen-faced** /BRAY zun-, -zṇ-/ shameless.

33. **cullionly** /CŬL yun lee/ rascally.

33. *****barber-monger** a fop, someone who constantly goes to the barber.
US /BAR bur mŏng gur/ or /-mawng-/ [-mung-]; CN /-mung-, -mŏng-/;
UK /-mung-/.

38. *****carbonado** slash. /car buh NAH doh/; UK *rarely older* [-NAY doh].

45. **goodman** /GŌŌD mun/ title of a man under the rank of gentleman.

75. **t'intrinse** /twin TRINSS, -TRINZ/ too intricate.   Some eds. prefer **intrince**
/in TRINSS/.

78. *****Renege** (Q1) deny. US /ree-, rih NEG, -NIG/ [-NEEG, -NAYG];
CN /-NEG, -NAYG/; UK /rih NAYG/ [-NEEG, -NEG, -NIG]. **Revenge** (F1).

78. **halcyon beaks** US /HAL see ŏn/ [-un]; UK /-un/ [-ŏn] kingfisher, i.e., weathervane.

83. **Sarum** /SAIR um/.

87. **contraries** /CŎN truh reez/ opposites.

103. **observants** /ŎB zur vunts/ attendants.

105. **sincere** here should be /SIN seer/.

108. **Phoebus'** /FEE bus/ god of the sun.

118. **compact** (F1) /cum-, cŏm PACT/ leagued with. Q1 has **conjunct** /cun JUNCT/ with the same meaning.

123. **exploit** here should be /ek SPLOYT/.

126. **ancient** (F1). Q1c, Q2 have **miscreant** /MIS cr(ee) yunt/ scoundrel.

164. **comfortable** here should be /CUM fur tuh bł/.

Act 2 Scene 3 (*The Complete Oxford* continues this as 2.2—line nos. in parentheses)

8. (2.2.171) **penury** /PEN yur ee/; UK *also* /PEN yoor ee/ poverty.

13. (2.2.176) **president** example. Archaic variant of *precedent, both /PRESS ih dunt/. It is not clear whether /PREZ-/ was used in Shk's time.

14. (2.2.177) **Bedlam** /BED lum/ crazy.

20. (2.2.183) **Turlygod** (F1, Q1c, Q2) /TUR lee gŏd/; US *also* /-gawd/, or **Tuelygod** (Q1u) perhaps US /TOO lee-/; UK, SOUTH. US /TYOO lee-/ unexplained.

Act 2 Scene 4 (*Complete Oxford* continues this as 2.2—line nos. in parentheses)

34. (2.2.210) **contents** here /cŏn TENTS/.

ă-bat, äir-**marry**, air-**pair**, ạr-**far**, ĕr-**merry**, ĝ- get, ī-high, ĭr-mirror, ł-little, ṇ-listen, ŏ-hot, oh-go, o͞o-wood, o͞o-moon, oor-**tour**, ōr- or, ow-how, t͟h-that, t͟h-thin, ŭ-but, UR-**fur**, ur-under.　　( ) - suppress the syllable　　see p. xiii for complete list.

35. (2.2.211) **meiny, meinie** (F1) /MAYN ee/ household servants.   Q1 has
men.

52. (2.2.227) **arrant** (F1) /ĂIR unt/ thoroughgoing.   Omitted Q1.

54. (2.2.229) **dolors** (F1) (UK **dolours**) /DOH lurz/; UK *also* /DŎL urz/ pains.
See App. D *-or.* Omitted Q1.

57. (2.2.232) **Hysterica passio, Histerica passio** Ang.Lat. /hih STĔR ih kuh
PĂSH oh/, /PĂSS ee yoh/, /PASH ee yoh/; Class.Lat. /hih STĔR ih kah
PAH see yoh/. Some eds. prefer **hysteria** /hih STEER ee uh/; US *also* /-STĔR-/.

85. (2.2.258) **perdie, perdy** 'by God, indeed.' Usually US /pur DEE/;
UK /PUR DEE/, but here rhymes with *fly.* Some eds. prefer the variant **pardie**
/par DEE/.

132. (2.2.304) **Sepulchring** entombing.   Here /suh-, sep PŬL cring/ is
indicated.

148. (2.2.321) **confine** confines, limits of an area.   Here /cŏn-, cun FĪN/.

197. (2.2.370) **dotage** /DOHT ij/ senility.

203. (2.2. 376) ***sojourn** reside temporarily.   Here with 1st syllable stress
US, CN /SOH jurn/; UK /SŎJ urn/ [-URN, SOH-, SUJ-].

208. (2.2.381) **abjure** /ab-, ub JOOR/; US *also* /-JUR/ renounce.

210. (2.2.383) ***comrade** US, CN /CŎM rad/, *rarely* [CUM-, CŎM rayd];
UK /CŎM rayd/, *rarely* [-rad, CUM-].

237. (2.2.410) **avouch** /uh VOWCH/ affirm.

Act 3 Scene 1

55. (33) **Holla** /huh LAH/ or /HŎL uh/ a call.

Act 3 Scene 2

2. ***hurricanoes** waterspouts. US /hur ih KAH nohz, -KAY-/;
E.COAST US /huh rih-/; CN /hur ih KAH nohz/ [-KAY nohz];
UK /huh rih KAY nohz/ [-KAH nohz]. The older pronunciation is /-KAY-/.

5. **Vaunt-*couriers** US /VAWNT CUR yurz/ [COOR-];
E.COAST US /CŬR-/ [COOR-]; UK /COOR-/ [CŬR-] forerunners. Main stress
may also fall on the 2nd syllable. A variant form is *vancouriers*. See
App. D *-aun-*.

8. **germains, germens** /JUR munz/ seeds.

20. ***infirm** /in FURM/ sick.

21. ***servile** /SUR vīl/, *rarely* [SUR vł] slave-like.

27. **house** /howz/ find a house.

29. **louse** /lowz/ become infested with lice.

50. **pudder** (F1) /PUD ur/ commotion. Archaic variant of **pother** /PŎTH ur/.
Q1's **powther** is meant to indicate /PUTH ur/. Q2 has **thundering**.

54. **simular** /SIM juh lur/ counterfeiter.

55. **incestuous** (F1) /in SESS chwus/; UK *also* /-tywus/. Q1 has an archaic
variant **incestious** /in SESS chus/.

55. **Caitiff** /KAYT if/ scoundrel.

56. ***covert** secret. Here stressed on the 1st syllable
US, CN /KOHV urt/ [KUV-]; UK /KUV-/ [KOHV-], *rarely* [KŎV-].

57. **Close** /clohss/ hidden.

61-78. ***hovel** poor cottage or shed. US /HUV ł/, *rarely* [HŎV ł];
CN /HUV-/ [HŎV-]; UK /HŎV-/ [HUV-].

75. ***heigh-ho!** (F1) US /hay ho, hī-/; CN /hī-/, *rarely* [hay-]; UK /hay-/. Shk
intended /hay/. Spoken with evenly stressed syllables or as if sighing, with 1st
syllable stress. Q1 has **hey ho**.

79. ***courtezan, courtesan** (F1) a rich man's whore. US /CORT ih zun, -zan/,
rarely [cort ih ZAN]; CN /CORT ih zan/ [-zun], *rarely* [cort ih ZAN];
UK /CORT ih zan, cort ih ZAN/. Omitted in Q1.

84. **heretics** (F1) /HĔR (ih) tiks/ dissenters. Omitted in Q1.

ă-bat, ăir-**marry**, air-**pair**, ạr-**far**, ĕr-**merry**, ĝ- **get**, ī-**high**, ĭr-**mirror**, ł-**little**, ṇ-**listen**,
ŏ-**hot**, oh-**go**, ōō-**wood**, ōō-**moon**, oor-**tour**, ōr- **or**, ow-**how**, ţh-**that**, t̶h̶-**thin**, ŭ-**but**,
UR-**fur**, ur-**under**.   ( ) - suppress the syllable   see p. xiii for complete list.

85. **Albion** (F1) /AL bee un/ Britain, here rhymes with *confusion* (4 syllables in this instance). Omitted in Q1.

91. **usurers** (F1) /Y$\overline{OO}$ zh(u)r urz/; UK *also* [-zh(yoo)r urz, -zh(oo)r urz] those who lend money for interest. Omitted in Q1.

Act 3 Scene 3

14. **privily** /PRIV ih lee/ privately.

19. **toward** /TOH wurd, -urd/ about to take place.

Act 3 Scene 4

14. **filial ingratitude** /FIL yl/ a child's ingratitude.

30. **unfed** here should be /UN fed/.

46. **Through** (Q2, F1). Some eds. make this a verse passage which calls for **Thorough** (Q1), used when the meter demands two syllables. It is often pronounced as *thorough* on stage, but using /-$\overline{oo}$/ in the final syllable will bring it closer to mod. *through*.

53. ***quagmire** bog.   US, CN /KWĂG mīr/, US *rarely* [KWŎG-]; UK /KWŎG-/ [KWĂG-].   Normal development would favor /KWĂG-/.

70. **subdu'd** here with 1st syllable stress.

71. **unkind** here should be /UN kīnd/.

76. **alow** (F1), **a lo** (Q1) /uh LOH/ 'below,' or perhaps a call like *halloo!* or the crow of a rooster.

91. ***out-paramour'd** US, CN /owt PǍIR uh moord/ [-mord]; UK /-mord/ [-moord] 'had more mistresses than.'

93. ***sloth** US, CN /slawth/ [slohth]; UK /slohth/ [slŏth] laziness.

96. ***brothels** US, CN /BRŎTH lz/ [BRŎṬH lz, BRAWTH lz]; UK /BRŎTH lz/ whorehouses.

99. **Dolphin** (F1) /DŎL fin/; US *also* /DAWL-/. Meaning unclear, but *Dolphin* is the angl. form for the French heir to the throne. The mod. form is **Dauphin** angl. /DAW fin/; Fr. /doh fä^n/.

99. **suum mun nonny** (F1) the noise of the wind. Q1 has **hay no nony** (*hay no on ny*).

100. **sessa** /SESS uh/ uncertain meaning, perhaps 'let it go!' or 'be quiet.' F1 has **sesey** /SESS ee/. Q2 has **cease**. Some eds. prefer Fr. **cessez** /sess ay/ 'stop.'

115. **Flibbertigibbet** (F1) /FLIB urt ee jib it/ a devil.

117. **squinies** /SKWIN eez/ archaic form of F1's **squints**.

120. **Swithold** /SWIŢH łd, SWIŦH łd/ St. Withold. Some eds. prefer **Swithin, Swithune**, both pronounced /SWIŢH in, -un/ or /SWIŦH -/.

120. **'old** /ohld/ an upland plain. Dialect variant of **wold** /wohld/.

124. **aroint, aroynt** /uh ROYNT/ begone.

132. **sallets** /SAL its/ 'spicy herbs,' or in other words, 'spicy jokes.' Some eds. prefer **salads**.

134. **tithing** /TĪ ţhing/ district.

140. **Smulkin** (F1) /SMŬL kin/ a devil. Some eds. prefer **Smolking** based on *Smolkin* from Q1's *snulbug*. /SMŬL kin/ or /SMŎL kin/ are probably indicated in this case (i.e., *Smolkin* is the same as *Smolkin'*, alternative form of *Smolking*).

143. **Modo** /MOH doh/ a devil.

144. **Mahu** /MAH hōō/ a devil. May have been /MAY-/ for Shk.

152. **ventured** (F1). Q1 has the archaic variant **ventered** /VEN turd/.

157. **learned Theban** /LURN id ŦHEE bun/ scholar.

161. *** Importune** /im POR chun/ ask insistently. See App. D.

174. *** hovel** poor cottage or shed. US /HUV ł/, *rarely* [HŎV ł]; CN /HUV-/ [HŎV-]; UK /HŎV-/ [HUV-].

ă-bat, ăir-m**a**rry, air-p**ai**r, ạr-f**a**r, ĕr-m**e**rry, ĝ- get, ī-high, ĭr-mirror, ł-little, ṇ-listen, ŏ-hot, oh-go, ōō-wood, ōō-moon, oor-t**ou**r, ōr- or, ow-how, ţh-that, ŧħ-thin, ŭ-but, UR-f**ur**, ur-under.   ( ) - suppress the syllable   see p. xiii for complete list.

180. **Athenian** /uh ~~THEEN~~ yun/.

182. **Rowland, Roland** /ROH lund/ in a line from a lost ballad.

Act 3 Scene 5

21. **persever** (F1), **persevere** (Q1) /pur SEV ur/ is normal in Shk's verse, but in this prose passage mod. /pur suh VEER/ may be used.

Act 3 Scene 6 (*Complete Oxford* line nos. in parentheses where they differ)

6. **Frateretto** /frat ur RET oh/ a devil.

10-13. **yeoman** /YOH mun/ freeman who owns a small farm.

---

lines 17-56 are contained in Q1, but omitted in F1

21, 56. **justicer** /JUST ih sur/ judge. Q1 has **justice**.

22. **sapient** /SAY pyunt/ wise.

25. **bourn** /born/ south. Engl. form of *burn* /burn/ stream. A more recent spelling pronunciation is /boorn/. Q has *broome*.

30. **Hoppedance, Hopdance** US /HŎP dănss/; UK /-dahnss/.

43. **minikin** /MIN ih kin/ dainty.

---

63. (21) **Trey, Tray** /tray/ name of a dog.

64. (22) **Avaunt** /uh VAWNT/ begone!

68. (26) **Mastiff** /MĂST tiff/; UK *sometimes* [MAHST-] powerful watchdog.

69. (27) **brach** /bratch/ female dog.

69. (27) **lym** bloodhound. Here the rhyme indicates /lim/. Some eds. prefer F1's, Q1's **him** 'male dog.' The more usual term for *bloodhound* was **lyam** /LĪ um/ or **lyme** /līm/.

74. (32) **Sessa** /SESS uh/ uncertain meaning, perhaps 'off you go.' F1's **sese** may indicate **cease** /seess/, **seize** /seez/, **cess** /sess/ (an archaic variant of *cease*

and *seize*), or **sessey** /SESS ee/ 'stop.' Some eds. prefer Fr. **cessez** /sess ay/ 'stop.' Omitted Q1.

76. (34) **anatomize** /uh NAT uh mīz/ dissect.

111. **bewray** (Q1) /bih-, bee RAY/ reveal. Omitted F1.

Act 3 Scene 7

10. **festinate** /FESS tih nayt, -nut/ hasty. /-ut/ would be the usual form for an adj.

40. **hospitable** here should be /HŎS pih tuh bł/ welcoming.

62. **holp** /hohlp/ helped.

63. *****dearn** (Q1), **dern** dread. Both pronounced /durn/. Some eds. prefer F1's **stern**.

103. **Bedlam** (Q1) /BED lum/ lunatic. Omitted F1.

Act 4 Scene 1

4. **esperance** (F1) /ES pur unss/ hope. Q1 has *experience.*

5. *****lamentable** here should be /LAM un tuh bł/ the usual UK pronunciation.

10. **parti-ey'd** (Q1c) /PAR tee-/ i.e., bleeding from the eyes. Some eds. prefer Q1u, F1's **poorly led** or **poorly eyed.**

20. **defects** here should be /dih-, dee FECTS/.

49. **'parel** /PĂIR ł/ apparel.

---

lines 58-63 are in Q1, but omitted in F1

59. **Obidicut** /oh BID ih kut/ a devil.

60. **Hobbididence** /hŏb ih DID ṇss/ a devil. Some eds. prefer **Hoberdidance** /hŏb ur-/.

ă-bat, ăir-ma**rry**, air-**pair**, ạr-**far**, ĕr-**merry**, ĝ- **get**, ī-high, ĭr-mirror, ł-little, ṇ-**listen**, ŏ-hot, oh-go, ō͞o-wood, o͞o-moon, oor-**tour**, ōr- **or**, ow-how, ţh-**that**, t̶h̶-thin, ŭ-but, UR-**fur**, ur-under.   ( ) - suppress the syllable   see p. xiii for complete list.

---

lines 58-63 are in Q1, but omitted in F1

60. **Mahu** /MAH hoo/ a devil. May have been /MAY-/ for Shk.

61. **Modo** /MOH doh/ a devil.

61. **Flibbertigibbet** /FLIB urt ee jib it/ a devil.

62. ***mowing** /MOH ing/ [MOW ing] grimacing. Both were used in Shk's time but his rhymes elsewhere indicate /moh/.

---

70. **excess** here should be /ek SESS/, the most common UK form.

Act 4 Scene 2 (*Complete Oxford* line nos. in parentheses)

17. **distaff** cleft staff used in spinning thread. US /DIS stăf/;
E.NEW ENG., UK /DIS stahf/.

---

lines 31-50, 62-8 are in Q1, but omitted in F1

39. **savor** (UK **savour**) /SAY vur/ smell.

63. **Bemonster** /bih-, bee MŎN stur/ make monsterous.

68. **mew** /myoo/ either means 'lock up' or indicates a derisive comment.

---

79. (47) **justicers** (Q1c) /JUST ih surz/, **justices** (Q1u, F1).

Act 4 Scene 3 (This scene contained in Q1 and *Riverside* is omitted in F1)

22. **diamonds** here should be /DĪ mundz/, the most common pronunciation in the US.

Act 4 Scene 4 (*Complete Oxford* 4.3)

3. **femiter** (Q1) /FEM ih tur/ a weed. F1 has **fenitar** /FEN ih tur/ which may be a misprint or an alternative form. Both are variants of **fumitory** which here would be /FYOOM ih tree/. Some eds. prefer **fumitor, fumiter**, both pronounced /FYOOM ih tur/.

4. **hardocks** /HARD ŏks/ another name for **burdocks**.

5. **Darnel** /DAR nl/ a weed.

17. **aidant** /AYD ̧nt/ helpful.

17. **remediate** /ree-, rih MEED ee ut/ medicinal.

26. ***importun'd** /im POR chund/ importunate, asking insistently. See App. D.

Act 4 Scene 5 (*Complete Oxford* 4.4)

13. **descry** /dih SKRĪ/ see.

25. **eliads** /ELL yudz/ flirting looks. Variant of ***oeillades** US, CN /ILL yudz/, CN *also* /AYL yudz/; UK *rarely* [ILL yudz]. The pronunciation based on Fr. /uh YAHDZ/, prefered in the UK, would have to have 1st syllable stress here.

Act 4 Scene 6 (*Complete Oxford* 4.5)

13. **choughs, chuffs** /chufs/ jackdaws.

15. **sampire** /SAM pīr/ an aromatic plant, eaten pickled. Archaic variant of **samphire** /SAM fīr/.

21. **chafes** /chayfs/ rages.

26. **th' extreme** here should be /ṬHᵞEK streem/.

49. **goss'mer** /GŎSS mur/ spider's thread.

57. ***bourn** /born, boorn/ boundary. North American [burn] not recommended. Normal development would favor /born/.

71. **welk'd** (Q1), **wealk'd** (F1) /welkt/ twisted. Some eds. prefer **whelked**.

88. **clothier's** /CLOH ̧thyurz, -̧thee urz/ one engaged in the cloth trade.

92. **clout** (F1) /clowt/ center of target. Q1 has **air**.

92. **hewgh** (F1), **hagh** (Q1) sound imitating an arrow in flight or whistling. Some eds. prefer **whew**.

ă-bat, ăir-**marry**, air-**pair**, ̧ar-**far**, ĕr-**merry**, ĝ- **get**, ī-**high**, ĭr-**mirror**, ł-**little**, ̧n-**listen**, ŏ-**hot**, oh-**go**, o͞o-**wood**, o͞o-**moon**, oor-**tour**, ōr- **or**, ow-**how**, ̧th-**that**, th-**thin**, ŭ-**but**, UR-**fur**, ur-**under**.　　　( ) - suppress the syllable　　　see p. xiii for complete list.

93. **marjorum** type of herb. Archaic variant of **marjoram**. Both pronounced /MAR jur rum/.

105. **ague-proof** (F1) /AY gyo͞o/ malarial fever.   Q1 has *argue-proofe.*

119. *****presages** (F1) here should be /pree-, prih SAY jiz/ foretells. Q1 has **presageth**.

122. **fitchew** /FITCH o͞o/ polecat, i.e., whore.

124. **Centaurs** /SEN torz/.

130. **civet** /SIV it/ a type of perfume.

130. **apothecary** US /uh PŎ̵T̵H̵ uh kĕr ee/; UK /-kuh ree/ druggist.

137. **squiny** /SKWIN ee/ archaic variant of **squint**.

160. **beadle** /BEE dł/ local officer in charge of whippings.

163. **usurer** /Y͞O͞O zh(u)r ur/; UK *also* [-zh(yoo)r ur, -zh(oo)r ur] someone who lends money for interest.

164. **Thorough** (F1) archaic variant of Q1's **Through**, which is often pronounced as mod. *thorough* in Shk, but here it should be one syllable, making *Through* the better choice.

180. **wawl, waul** (F1) /wawl/ yowl. Q1 has **wail**.

184. **stratagem** /STRAT uh jum/ scheme.

206. **redeems** here with 1st syllable stress.

209. **toward** /TOH wurd, -urd/ about to take place.

213. **descry** /dih SKRĪ/ sight.

225. *****benison** US, CN /BEN ih sun, -sn̩/ [-zun, -zn̩]; UK /-z-/ [-s-] blessing.

226. **proclaim'd** here should be /PROH claymd/.

Note on the dialect of Southwest England: Shk's spellings are not a reliable guide to the correct reproduction of the dialect in this scene. The notation of this guide is also ill-suited to help the reader understand the phonetic nuances of dialect speech. The correct representation of the dialect is best learned by listening to a native speaker   and imitating his or her speech.   There are however some general guidelines.   At the beginnings of words, and in the middle of words:

/s/ becomes /z/
/f/ becomes /v/
/th/ becomes /ṭh/
/sh/ becomes /zh/.

Further, /r/ is pronounced wherever it occurs with the sound of North American English.

235-244. **Chill** /chill, chł/ Somerset dialect for *ich will,* 'I will.'

235. **cagion** (Q1) /KAY jun/ occasion. Some eds. prefer F1's **'casion** /KAY zhun/.

238. **chud** /chud/ If I could.

239. **vortnight** SW Eng. dialect for **fortnight** /FORT nīt/; US *also* [FORT nit] two weeks. Virtually obsolete in the US.

240. **che vor'ye** /chuh VOR yih/ I warrant you.

241. **Ice** (F1), **I's, Ise** /īss/ dialect form for 'I'll,' today found only in NW Eng.

241. **costard** /CŎST urd/ head.

241. **ballow** (F1) /BAL oh/ cudgel. Some eds. prefer **baton** /BAT ṇ/.

275. **mature** here 1st syllable stress is indicated.

Act 4 Scene 7 (*Complete Oxford* 4.6)

34. ***perdu** (Q1) sentry. Here stress should fall on the first syllable. US /PĔR doo/ [PĔR dyoo, PUR doo, PUR dyoo]; UK /PUR dyoo, PĔR dyoo/ or /PUR DYOO/ with equal stress. The traditional form is /PUR-/. Omitted F1.

38. ***hovel** stay in a poor cottage. US /HUV ł/, *rarely* [HŎV-]; CN /HUV-/ [HŎV-]; UK /HŎV-/ [HUV-].

ă-bat, äir-**marry**, air-**pair**, ạr-**far**, ĕr-**merry**, ĝ- **get**, ī-**high**, ĭr-**mirror**, ł-**little**, ṇ-**listen**, ŏ-**hot**, oh-**go**, o͞o-**wood**, o͞o-**moon**, oor-**tour**, ŏr- **or**, ow-**how**, ṭh-**that**, th-**thin**, ŭ-**but**, UR-**fur**, ur-**under**.   ( ) - suppress the syllable   see p. xiii for complete list.

93. **arbiterment** (Q1) /ạr BIT ur munt/ decisive encounter. Archaic variant of **arbitrement, arbitrament** /ạr BIT ruh munt/. Omitted F1.

Act 5 Scene 1

12. **conjunct** (Q1) /cun JUNCT/ in league with. Omitted F1.

44. **avouched** /uh VOWCH id/ affirmed.

46. ***machination** plotting. US /mack ih NAY shun/ is older, /mash-/ is a newer spelling pronunciation. The former is more common in the US, the latter in the UK, while in CN both are used equally. Omitted Q1.

Act 5 Scene 3

50. **impress'd lances** here should be /IM prest/ drafted soldiers.

69. **compeers** /cum PEERZ/ equals.

71. **Holla** /huh LAH/ a call to attract attention.

87. **banes** /baynz/ proclamation in church of an intended marriage. Archaic variant of **banns** /banz/.

92. ***heinous** /HAYN us/ hateful. /HEEN us/ is non-standard though common in the UK.

132. **Maugre** /MAW gur/ in spite of.

136. **Conspirant** (F1) /cun SPĪ runt/ conspirator. Q1 has *Conspicuate*.

154. **unknown** here should be /UN nohn/.

156. **stopple** (Q1), **stople** /STŎP ł/ plug. F1 has **stop**.

176. **prophesy** /PRŎF uh sī/ predict the future.

217. ***puissant** (Q1) powerful. The traditional forms are /PWISS ṇt/, /PYOO sṇt/ (see App. D). Omitted F1.

236. **aye** /ay/ ever. /ī/ is often used, but not recommended.

277. ***falchion** type of sword. /FĂL chun/ [-shun]; *older* [FAWL chun].

284. ***Caius** US, CN /KĪ us/, *rarely* [KAY us]; UK /KĪ us, KAY us/. Ang.Lat. /KAY us/; Class.Lat. /KĪ o͞os/. Another angl. form /keez/ is also sometimes used, but not recommended.

ă-bat, âir-**marry**, air-**pair**, ạr-**far**, ĕr-**merry**, ĝ- **get**, ī-high, ĭr-**mirror**, ł-little, n̪-listen, ŏ-hot, oh-go, o͝o-**wood**, o͞o-**moon**, oor-**tour**, ōr- **or**, ow-how, t̪h-**that**, t̶h̶-thin, ŭ-but, UR-**fur**, ur-under.   ( ) - suppress the syllable   see p. xiii for complete list.

Love's Labor's Lost

People in the Play

Sometimes some of these names are given a French (or in Armado's case, Spanish) pronunciation in performance. These pronunciations are indicated as accurately as possible within the limits of this notation. Shakespeare, however, probably intended them to be anglicized.

Don Adriano de Armado usually in the semi-Sp. form /dŏn ay dree AH noh day arm AH doh/. F1sometimes has *Armatho* pointing to the Castilian Sp. pronunciation where *d* in some cases is almost like /t̠h/: /dohn ah t̠hree AH noh t̠hay arm AH t̠hoh/.

*__Berowne__ (F2) US /bih ROHN, -RO͞ON/ [-ROWN]; UK /bih ROHN/, *sometimes* [-RO͞ON, -ROWN]; in CN all three are used equally. Recommendation: /bih RO͞ON/ because it rhymes with *moon* at 4.3.230-2. This is the normal pronunciation of older words of this type loaned into Eng. from Fr. (cf. *dragoon, pontoon*). Some eds. prefer the spelling **Biron** (Qq, F1) which would favor the newer angl. form /-ROHN/; Fr. /bee ROH^N/. The choice of which pronunciation to use will depend on whether you view the name as sufficiently "English" to warrant the older anglicized pronunciation with /-O͞ON/ (just as we anglicize *Napoleon, Champlain*). If it seems to be a foreign name (like the city *Toulon*), then /-OHN/ or the Fr. pronunciation will be your choice. The degree of "foreignness" will affect your pronunciation of names like *Boyet, Dumaine, Maria, Longaville* as well.

Boyet /boy ETT/; Fr. /bwah YAY/. Rhymes with *debt* 5.2.333-4.

Costard /CŎST urd/.

Dull, Anthony US /AN t̶h̶uh nee/; UK /AN tuh nee/ [-t̶h̶uh nee].

Dumaine US /do͞o MAYN/; UK, SOUTH. US /dyo͞o-/; Fr. /dü MEN/.

Ferdinand /FUR dih nand/.

Holofernes /hŏl uh FUR neez/; US *also* [hohl-].

Jaquenetta /jack uh NET uh/ was probably Shk's pronunciation, but today /jack wuh-/ is also commonly used.

People in the Play (cont.)

Katherine /KA̶T̶H̶ ur rin/.

Longaville, *Longueville rhymes with *ill* 4.3.121, and with *mile, compile*
4.3.131, 5.2.53. US /LAWNG guh vil, -vīl/; UK /LŎNG guh vil, -vīl/;
Fr. /lohⁿ guh veel/. Sometimes a mixed form with Fr. ending /-veel/ is used,
and stress may also fall on the 3rd syllable.

Marcade /MAR kuh dee/. Some eds. prefer **Mercade** /MUR kuh dee/,
Fr. **Marcadé** /mar kah day/, or **Mercadé** /mĕr kah day/. In any case it should
be 3 syllables in its sole occurrence at 5.2.716.

***Maria** /muh RĪ uh/ is the older, angl. form, /muh REE uh/ is newer. In the US,
CN the latter is more often used for this character, in the UK both are used
equally. Some scholars pronounce this name differently from *Maria* in *Twelfth
Night,* where /muh RĪ uh/ is preferred.

Moth *th* was sometimes pronounced /t/ in Shk's time, leading some eds. to
conclude that he may have intended **Mote** /moht/ 'speck of dust.'

Navarre (Ferdinand) /nuh VAHR/; Fr. /nah vahr/.

***Rosaline** US /RŎZ uh linn, -līn/; CN, UK /RŎZ uh līn/ [-linn].
Recommendation: /-līn/ because of rhymes with *thine, mine.*

Act 1 Scene 1

2. **brazen** /BRAY zun, -zn̩/ brass.

4. ***cormorant** /COR m(uh) runt/; US *rarely* [-ant] a fishing bird, i.e., devouring.

11. **edict** decree. Here should be /ee DICT/.

12, 220. **Navarre** /nuh VAHR/; Fr. /nah vahr/.

---

13. **academe** /AK uh deem/ [ak uh DEEM] academy.

14. **contemplative** here should be /cun TEMP luh tiv/ thoughtful.

27.***bankrout** /BANK rowt/ [-rut] archaic variant of **bankrupt.**

ă-bat, ăir-marry, air-pair, a̧r-far, ĕr-merry, ĝ- get, ī-high, ĭr-mirror, l̩-little, n̩-listen,
ŏ-hot, oh-go, o͞o-wood, o͞o-moon, oor-tour, ôr- or, ow-how, t̪h-that, th-thin, ŭ-but,
UR-fur, ur-under.   ( ) - suppress the syllable   see p. xiii for complete list.

33. *protestation US /proh tess-, prŏt ess TAY shun/; CN /prŏt ess-/ [proh tess-]; UK /prŏt ess-/.

100. sneaping /SNEEP ing/ biting cold.

136. complete here should be /CŎM pleet/.

137. Aquitaine /AK wih tayn, ak wih TAYN/.

138. bedred (Q1) archaic variant of F1's bed-rid 'bedridden.' Both pronounced /BED rid/.

169. umpeer (Q1) /UM peer/ archaic variant of F1's umpire.

176. minstrelsy /MIN strł see/ group of minstrels.

184. farborough (Q1) US /FAR bur oh, -uh/; E. COAST US /-buh roh, -buh ruh/; UK /-buh ruh/. Dull's dialect pronunciation of tharborough (F1) /THĄR-/ which was a common variant of thirdborough /THURD-/, all meaning 'constable.'

187. Arme- Dull is trying to say Armado's name.

220.*vicegerent /vīss JĔR unt/, rarely older [-JEER-] deputy ruler.

240. ycliped /ih-, ee CLIPT/ called. Variant of ycleped /-CLEEPT/, yclept /-CLEPT/.

243. ebon-colored /EB un/ black-colored.

258. consorted /cun SORT id/ kept company with.

259. edict decree. In this prose passage mod. /EE dict/. Elsewhere in verse sometimes /ee DICT/.

290. damsel (Q1) /DAM złł/, damosel (F1) /DAM uh zel/, which in Shk's time was often syncopated to /DAM złł/.

Act 1 Scene 2

8-13. juvenal /JŌŌ vin ł/ youth.

14. epitheton epithet, an expression. /ih PITH ih tŏn, -tun]. /-ŏn/ is usual in the US and is increasingly common in the UK. See App. D -on.

16. **appertinent** /uh PURT ih nunt/ appropriate.

25. **condign praise** /cun DĪN/ [CŎN dīn] worthy.

44. **complete man** /cum PLEET/ or, as sometimes required in verse, /CŎM pleet/.

61. **reprobate** /REP ruh bayt, -but/ depraved. /-ut / is more usual for an adj.

92. **maculate** /MAK yuh lut/ defiled.

109, 111. **ballet** /BAL ut/ archaic variant of **ballad**.

117. **president** (F1) archaic variant of **precedent, both /PRESS ih dunt/. It is not clear whether /PREZ-/ was used in Shk's time.

118. **hind** /hīnd/ double meaning: peasant, deer.

131. **dey-woman** /DAY-/ dairymaid.

137. **situate US /SITCH (oo) wut/ [-wayt]; UK /-wayt/ situated.

174. **Salomon** archaic variant of **Solomon** /SŎL uh mun/. The spelling *Sal-* may also indicate /SŎL-/ (cf. *Halloween* with / HŎL-/ in the US).

178. **passado** /pah-, puh SΛH doh/ step and thrust in fencing.

179. **duello** /dōō EL oh/; UK, SOUTH. US *also* /dyōō-/ duelling code.

183. **extemporal** /ek STEM pur rł/ impromptu.

Act 2 Scene 1

5. **parley /PAR lee/ negotiate. Newer [-lay] not recommended.

> 7-248. **Navarre** /nuh VAHR/; Fr. /nah vahr/.
>
>   **Aquitaine** /AK wih tayn, ak wih TAYN/.

32. **Importunes /im POR chunz/ asks insistently. See App. D.

> ă-bat, ăir-marry, air-pair, ạr-far, ĕr-merry, ĝ- get, ī-high, ĭr-mirror, ł-little, ṇ-listen, ŏ-hot, oh-go, ōō-wood, ōō-moon, oor-tour, ōr- or, ow-how, ţh-that, ~~th-~~thin, ŭ-but, UR-fur, ur-under.   ( ) - suppress the syllable   see p. xiii for complete list.

37. **votaries** /VOHT uh reez/ persons who took a vow.

41. **Perigort** /PĔR (ih) gort/. Some eds. prefer Fr. **Périgort** /PAY r(ee) gor/.

42. *****Jaques** here should be 2 syllables. /JAY kweez/, *rarely*
US [-keez, -kiz, -kis]; UK [-kwis, -kwiz]. See AYL "People in the Play."

42, 205. **Falconbridge** /FAWL-, FAL kun brij/; UK *also* [FŎL-], *rarely older*
[FAW kun-]. Some eds. prefer **Fauconbridge** /FAW kun-/.

42. **solemnized** /suh LEM nīz ed/ in Shk's day, but here may be the modern
form /SŎL um nīzd/ in a broken-backed line.

61. **Duke Alanson's** here should be /uh LAN sunz, -sṇz/ archaic variant of
Alençon which has another angl. form /uh LEN sun/; Fr. here should be
/ah LAH^n soh^n/. See 2.1.195.

72. **expositor** /ek SPŎZ ih tur/ interpreter, commentator. See App. D *-or*.

76. **voluble** /VŎL yuh bł/ quick-witted.

114, 115. **Brabant** here should be stressed on 1st syllable; angl. /BRAB unt/;
Dutch /BRAH bahnt/; Fr. /BRAH bah^n/ former duchy where Belgium is today.

130. **entire** here should be /EN tīr/.

134. *****surety** collateral. Here should be two syllables, though in mod. English,
three syllables are more common, /SHUR (ih) tee, SHOOR-, SHOR-/ (see
App. D).

177. **consort** /cun SORT/ attend.

195. **Alanson** here should be /AL un sun, -sṇ/, archaic, angl. variant of
Alençon. Fr. here would be /AH lah^n soh^n/ or /ah lah^n SOH^N/. See 2.1.61.

235. **thorough** archaic variant of *through*, used when the meter demands two
syllables. It is often pronounced as *thorough* on stage, but using /-o͞o/ in the
final syllable will bring it closer to mod. *through*.

236. **agot** a type of jewel. Archaic variant of **agate**, both pronounced /AG ut/.

246. **margent** /MAR junt/ archaic variant of **margin**.

254. *****love-monger** love-seller. US /LUV mŏng gur/ or /-mawng-/ [-mung-];
CN /-mung-, -mŏng-/; UK /-mung-/.

Act 3 Scene 1

3. **Concolinel** probably the title of a lost song. Perhaps /cŏn CŎL ih nel, -nł/.

6. **festinately** /FES tin nayt lee, -nut lee/ quickly. /-ut/ would be the usual form for this type of adverb.

60. **Minime** Ang.Lat. /MIN ih mee/; Class.Lat. /MIN ih may/ by no means.

66. **juvenal** /JOO vin ł/ youth.

66. **volable** (Q1) /VŎL uh bł/ quick-witted.   Archaic variant of F1's **voluble** /VŎL yuh bł/.

In lines 71-122 the following words are used several times

*l'envoy concluding remarks of a play or poem. Normally *envoy* would be US, CN /AHN voy/ [EN voy]; UK /EN voy/. However Armado first uses the word with the French article *l'*, which may indicate that he is pronouncing it as in French /LAH^N vwah, lah^n VWAH/.

*salve ointment. US /sav/ [salv]; NEW ENG. /sahv/; CN /sav, salv/ [sahlv]; UK /salv/. Normal development would favor the *l*-less form (cf. *halve, calve*).

*plantan today spelled **plantain** a medicinal plant /PLĂNT ayn/ [-un]; UK *also* [PLAHNT ayn]. Variants with /-un/ are older.

---

82. **tofore** /too FOR/ previously.

82. **obscure** here should be /ŎB skyoor/; US *also* [-skyur].

82. **precedence** here should be /PRESS ih dunss/; UK *also* [PREE-] something said before.

84-95. **humble-bee** pronounced with the same stress as *bumble bee.*

102. **pennyworth, penn'worth** bargain. Both pronounced /PEN urth/.

124. **immured** /ih MYOORD/ imprisoned.

128.***durance** /DYOOR unss/; US *also* /DooR-/ [DUR-] imprisonment.

ă-bat, ăir-**marry**, air-**pair**, ar-**far**, ĕr-**merry**, ĝ- get, ī-high, ĭr-**mirror**, ł-little, n̩-listen, ŏ-hot, oh-go, oo-wood, oo-moon, oor-**tour**, ŏr- **or**, ow-**how**, t̩h-**that**, th-thin, ŭ-but, UR-**fur**, ur-**under**.   ( ) - suppress the syllable   see p. xiii for complete list.

129. **in *lieu thereof** US, CN /lo͞o, lyoo/; UK /lyo͞o/ [lo͞o] in return for.

131-72. **remuneration** /rih-, ree myo͞on ur RAY shun/ payment.

135. **incony** rare, pretty. Pronunciation uncertain: /INK (uh) nee/ seems called for in verse, but /in KUN ee/ has also been suggested.

148. **halfpenny** /HAY puh nee, HAYP nee/.

169-72. ***guerdon . . . Gardon** reward. Normally /GURD n̩/, but Costard's response to Berowne's pronunciation indicates that in Shk's time the pronunciation was /GARD n̩/. Spelling pronunciations /ĜER-, GWĔR-/ also are used, but not recommended. Some eds. substitute **guerdon** for Costard's *Gardon*.

175. **beadle** /BEE dł/ local officer in charge of whippings.

177. **pedant** /PED n̩t/ dull teacher.

179. **purblind** /PUR blīnd/ blind or partly blind.

183. **malecontents** discontented persons. Archaic variant of ***malcontents**. Both pronounced /MAL cun tents/; CN, UK *rarely* [mal cun TENTS].

185. **imperator** emperor. /im puh RAYT ur/ is older; /im puh RAHT ur/ is newer. Q1, F1 have **emperator** /em-/. See App. D -*or*.

186. **paritors** /PĂIR (ih) turz/ officers who summoned people to court. See App. D -*or*.

199. **Argus** /A̧RG us/ 100-eyed monster of Gk. mythology.

199. **eunuch** /Y͞OO nuk/ castrated man.

Act 4 Scene 1

9. **coppice** /CŎP iss/ grove.

22. **heresy** /HĔR ih see/ dissent from the dominant thinking.

42. **God dig-you-den all** /gŏd-, gud DIG yuh den AWL/ good evening.

56. ***capon** US /KAY pŏn, -pun/; CN, UK /KAY pŏn/ [-pun] chicken. See App. D -*on*.

64. **commiseration** /kuh miz ur RAY shun/ pity.

65.***illustrate** illustrious. US /ih LUST rut, -rayt/; UK /ih LUST rayt/ [-rut].
/-ut/ is more usual for an adj.

65. **King Cophetua** /kuh FETCH oo wuh/; UK *also* /kuh FET yoo wuh/ subject
of an old ballad.

66. **pernicious** /pur NISH us/ harmful. Some eds. prefer ***penurious**
/puh NYOOR ee us/; US *also* [-NOOR-, -NYUR-] poor.

66. **indubitate** US /in DŌŌB ih tut, -tayt/; UK, SOUTH.US /-DYŌŌB-/ undoubted.
/-ut / is more usual for an adj.

66. **Zenelophon** beggar woman in the ballad. /zen EL uh fŏn, -fun/. /-ŏn/ is
usual in the US and is increasingly common in the UK. See App. D *-on.*

67.   ***Veni,   vidi,   vici**
Ang.Lat.   /VEE nī,   VĪ dī,   VĪ sī/
Class.Lat.   /WAY nee, WEE dee, WEE kee/
Church Latin /VAYN ee, VEE dee, VEE chee/.
              'I came, I saw, I conquered.'
The older Ang.Lat. form is all but forgotten in all countries. In the US the
Class.Lat. and Church Latin forms are equally used. In CN and the UK the
Church Latin is prefered.

68. **annothanize** either an old spelling, perhaps with printer error, of *anatomize*
/uh NAT uh mīz/ 'explain,' or mock-Latin based on *annotate.* If the latter it
would be pronounced /uh NOHT uh nīz/.

69. ***videlicet** namely (abbreviated *viz.*). The older, anglicized pronunciations
are US /vih DELL ih sit/ [-DEEL-, vī-]; UK /vih DEEL ih sit/ [vī-, -DELL-].
Newer pronunciations mix in restored Latin syllables, for example, /-ket/ or
/-DAYL-/. These are not recommended.

77. ***nuptial** wedding. US, UK /NUP chł/ [-shł]; in CN both are used equally.

88. **Nemean lion** /NEE myun/ lion killed by Hercules.

94. **indited** /in DĪT id/ composed.

ă-**bat**, ăir-**marry**, air-**pair**, ạr-**far**, ĕr-**merry**, ĝ- **get**, ī-**high**, ĭr-**mirror**, ł-**little**, ṇ-**listen**,
ŏ-**hot**, oh-**go**, ōō-**wood**, ōō-**moon**, oor-**tour**, ōr- **or**, ow-**how**, ṭh-**that**, th̶-**thin**, ŭ-**but**,
UR-**fur**, ur-**under**.   ( ) - suppress the syllable   see p. xiii for complete list.

99. **phantasime** /FAN taz im/ someone full of fancies. Some eds. prefer
phantisim /FAN tih zim/.

99. **Monarcho** /MŎN ahr koh, -ur koh/ someone who thinks they are king of the
world.

120. **Pippen, Pippin** /PIP in/ father of Charlemagne. Some eds. prefer **Pepin**
/PEP in/ or Fr. **Pépin** /PAY pă^n/.

123. **Guinover** /GWIN uh vur, ĜIN-/ archaic variants of **Guinever**
/GWIN ih vur/ or **Guinevere** /GWIN ih veer/, which today is by far the most
common form.

132. **mete** /meet/ aim.

134. **clout** /clowt/ center of a target.

142. **incony** rare, pretty. Pronunciation uncertain: /INK (uh) nee/ seems called
for in verse, but /in KUN ee/ has also been suggested.

149. **Sola, sowla** (Q1, F1) /soh LAH/ a call to attract attention.

Act 4 Scene 2

3. **sanguis** Ang.Lat. /SANG gwiss/; Class.Lat. /SAHNG gwiss/ blood.

4. **pomewater** /PUM-, PŎM-/ a kind of apple.

5. **caelo** Ang.Lat. /SEE loh/; Class.Lat. /KĪ loh/ sky. Some eds. prefer **coelo**, a
medieval Lat. error whose angl. form is also /SEE loh/.

7. **terra** Ang.Lat. /TĔR uh/; Class.Lat. /TĔR ah/ earth.

8. **epithites** expressions. Perhaps /EP ih ~~th~~its/, archaic variant of **epithets**
/EP ih ~~th~~ets, -its/.

11-20. **haud credo** Ang.Lat. /hawd CREE doh/; Class.Lat. /howd CRAY doh/ I can't believe it.

12. **haud credo** Dull misunderstands *haud credo* as *old grey doe,* which some
eds. write as **auld grey doe**. A*uld* /awld/ represents a dialect form of *old*. It
could also be /l/-less.

14. **in via** Ang.Lat. /in VĪ uh/; Class.Lat. /in WEE uh/; Church Latin would be
/VEE ah/ in way.

15. **facere** Ang.Lat. /FASS ur ee/; Class.Lat. /FAHK ĕr ay/ to make.

15. **ostentare** Ang.Lat. /ŏst en TAIR ee/; Class.Lat. /ŏst en TAR ay/ to show.

22. **bis coctus** Ang.Lat. /biss CŎCK tus/; Class.Lat. /-tōōss/ twice boiled.

25. **eat** /et/ dialect variant of **eaten.**

29. **do fructify** are fruitful. /FRUCK tih fī/ is older, [FRōōK-] is newer. US has an additional newer pronunciation /FRŌŌK-/.

32. **omne bene** Ang.Lat. /ŎM nee BEE nee/; Class.Lat. /ŎM nay BEN ay/ all is well.

36. **goodman** /GōōD mun/ title of a man under the rank of gentleman.

36, 37. **Dictynna** /dik TIN uh/ the moon. Some eds. have Dull misunderstanding and replying **Dictima** (Q1, F1) /dik TIM uh/.

38. **Phoebe** /FEE bee/ the moon.

40. **raught** /rawt/ reached.

50. **extemporal** /ek STEM pur rł/ composed on the spur of the moment.

53. **Perge** Ang.Lat. /PURJ ee/; Class.Lat. /PĚR gay/ proceed.

54. **abrogate** /AB ruh gayt/ do away with.

54. **squirility** (Q1) possibly /skwur IL it ee/, the curate's error for **scurrility** /skur RIL ih tee/ 'coarse joking.' It could also simply be a variant spelling of *scurrility,* pronounced the same way.

58-60. **sorel** US /SŌR ł/; E.COAST US, UK /SŎR ł/ male fallow dear in its third year.

63, 64. **talent** /TAL unt/ the pun is built on this archaic variant of **talon.**

69.**pia mater** here, 'the brain.' Ang.Lat. /PĪ uh MAYT ur/ is older; Class.Lat. /PEE uh MAHT ur/ is newer and much more common. Forms that mix old and new are also used.

ă-bat, ăir-**marry**, air-**pair**, ạr-**far**, ĕr-**merry**, ĝ- **get**, ī-**high**, ĭr-**mirror**, ł-**little**, ṇ-**listen**, ŏ-**hot**, oh-**go**, ōō-**wood**, ōō-**moon**, oor-**tour**, ōr- **or**, ow-**how**, ţh-**that**, ᵺ-**thin**, ŭ-**but**, UR-**fur**, ur-**under**.   ( ) - suppress the syllable   see p. xiii for complete list.

78. **Mehercle** Ang.Lat. /mee HURK lee/; Class.Lat. /may HĔRK lay/ by Hercules.

80.   **vir sapit   qui   pauca   loquitur**
Ang.Lat.   /vur SAYP it kwee PAW kuh LŎCK wih tur/
Class.Lat. /wĭr SAHP it kwee POW kah LŎCK wih tōōr/
        'that man is wise who speaks little.'

83. **quasi** Ang.Lat. /KWAY zī/ [-sī]; Class.Lat. /KWAH see/ as if, that is. /KWAH zee, -zī/ are also commonly used today.

83. **pers-one.** Jacquenetta is probably saying **Master Person** (i.e., *Master Parson)* in her dialect as /PĔR sun/. Holofernes finds this pronunciation amusing because /pĕrss/ was one possible pronunciation of *pierce* in Elizabethan English. He imitates her pronunciation, saying **pers-one** (meaning 'pierce-one') with *one* pronounced either /ohn/ or /un/. Some eds. prefer the spelling **pierce-one**, which makes this clearer. In other words, Holofernes is saying, "It's as if she were saying *pierce-one.*" In other varieties of Elizabethan Eng. *parson, person,* and *pierce* were all pronounced with /ahr/.

93-4.   **Facile,**   **precor**   **gelida**   **quando**   **pecus**
Ang.Lat.   /FASS il ee   PREE cor   JEL ih duh KWAN doh   PEEK us
Class.Lat. /FAH kih lay   PREK or   ĜEL ih duh KWAHN doh   PEK ōōs

          omne **sub** **umbra**   **ruminat**
Ang.Lat.   /ŎM nee sub UM bruh RŌŌM ih nat/
Class.Lat. /ŎM naẙ sōōb ōōM brah RŌŌM ih naht/

Line from the poet Mantuan with one error: *Facile* should be **Fauste** Ang.Lat. /FAWS tee/; Class.Lat. /FOW stay/. The translation is: 'Faustus, while all the cattle chew their cuds in the cool shade.' Some eds. substitute **pecas** for *pecus,* pronounced the same in Ang.Lat.

95, 99. **Mantuan** US /MAN choo wun/; UK /MAN tyoo wun/ [MAN choo wun] a poet.

97. **Venechia, Venechia** (*Vemchie, vencha* F1, Q1) Venice. Perhaps the Q1 and F1 spellings indicate Shk's pronunciations /VEN chee, -chuh/, which *Riv.* tries to make /ven EE chuh/. The normal angl. form is **Venetia** /ven EE shuh/, or sometimes newer [-shee uh]. Some prefer Ital. **Venezia** /vay NAYT see ah/.

98. **Che non te vede,   che non te prechia**
      /kay nohn tay VAY day, kay nohn tay PRAY chah/.

Some eds. prefer the variant form:

Chi non ti vede, chi non ti pretia (prezia)
Ital. /kee nohn tee VAY day kee nohn tee PRAYT syah/.
'He who has not seen you cannot value you.'

100. **Ut** /ut, ōōt/ the lowest note in the scale, modern *do*.

104. **stanze** /STAN zee/. Archaic variant of **stanza**.

104. **lege, domine** Ang.Lat. /LEE jee DŎM in nee/;
Class.Lat. /LEG ay DŎM ih nay/ read, master.

108.*osiers US /OH zhurz/ [OH zyurz]; UK /OH zyurz/ willows.

119. **apostraphas, apostrophus** both pronounced /uh PŎS truh fuss/
apostrophe.

120. **canzonet** /kan zuh NET, -zoh-/ a light, graceful song.

122. *poesy US /POH ih see/ [-zee]; UK, CN /POH ih zee/ [-see] poetry.

123. **caret** Ang.Lat. /KAIR et/; Class.Lat. /KAHR et/ it is lacking.

123, 124. **Ovidius Naso** Ang.Lat. /oh VID ee us NAY zoh/;
Class.Lat. /oh WID ee ōōs NAH soh/ Ovid, Roman poet.

124. **odoriferous** /oh dur RIF ur us/ fragrant.

125. **Imitari** Ang.Lat. /im ih TAIR ī/; Class.Lat. /im ih TAH ree/ to imitate.

127. **damosella** /dam oh ZEL uh/ Holofernes' variation of *damosel* 'maiden.'
Some eds. prefer Ital. **domicella** /doh mee CHEL ah/.

137. **votaries** /VOHT uh reez/ persons devoted to something or someone.

138. **sequent** /SEE kwunt/ follower.

148, 161. **saith** says. US /SAY ith/, *rarely* [seth]; UK /seth/ [sayth, SAY ith].
The older form is /seth/.

157. **bien venuto** angl. /byen ven ŌŌ toh/; Fr. /byeh[n]/ welcome. Holofernes'
error for Ital. **ben venuto** /ben ven ŌŌ toh/.

ă-bat, ăir-marry, air-pair, ạr-far, ĕr-merry, ĝ- get, ī-high, ĭr-mirror, ł-little, ṇ-listen,
ŏ-hot, oh-go, ōō-wood, ōō-moon, oor-tour, ōr- or, ow-how, ţh-that, ŧħ-thin, ŭ-but,
UR-fur, ur-under.　　　( ) - suppress the syllable　　　see p. xiii for complete list.

163. **certes** /SUR teez/ certainly.

165. **pauca verba** 'few words,' i.e., 'enough said.'
Ang.Lat. /PAW kuh VUR buh/; Class.Lat. /POW kah WĔR bah/;
/VĔR bah/ is also used based on Church Latin.

Act 4 Scene 3

1. **coursing** /COR sing/ hunting, pursuing.

13, 14. **mallicholy** (F1), **mallicholie** (Q1) US /MAL ih cŏl ee/;
UK /MAL ih cuh lee/. Archaic variant of **melancholy**.

34. **triumphing** here should be /trī UM fing/.

51. **triumphery** either a mistake for or a variant of **triumviry** /trī UM vur ee/
'triumverate.'

52. **Tyburn** US /TĪ burn/; UK *also* /TĪ BURN/ site of public hangings in London.

68. **Exhal 'st** here with 2nd syllable stress, /eks HAYLST/, the normal UK form.

77. *****demigod** half-god. /DEM ee gŏd, DEM ih-/; US *also* /-gawd/.

96. **misprision** /mis PRIZH un, -ṇ/ mistake, misconduct.

116. **Ethiop** /EETH yŏp/ an Ethiopian.

156. **Tush** /tŭsh/ expression of disdain.

165. **gig** /ĝig/ top.

166. **profound** here should be /PROH fownd/.

166. **Salomon** archaic variant of **Solomon** /SŎL uh mun/. The spelling *Sal-*
may also indicate /SŎL-/ (cf. *Halloween* with / HŎL-/ in the US).

167. **Nestor** /NEST ur/ oldest of the Greeks at Troy. See App. D *-or.*

168. **Timon** Timon of Athens, famous for his hatred of mankind. /TĪ mun/, but
sometimes /-ŏn/ is used. See App. D *-on.*

172. **caudle** /KAW dł/ warm drink for the sick.

195. **Dun Adramadio** Costard mixes up or makes fun of Armado's name, perhaps /dun ay druh MAH dee oh/.

218. **Inde** India. Here should be /īnd/ to rhyme with *blind*.

220. **strooken** /STRo͞oK in/ or perhaps simply a variant spelling of **strucken**. Some eds. prefer **stricken**.

222. **peremptory** here should be /PĔR um tur ee/; US *also* /-tor ee/ determined.

263. **colliers** /CŎL yurz/ charcoal producers.

264. **Ethiops** /EETH yŏps/ Ethiopians. Some eds. prefer **Ethiopes** /EETH yohps/

284. **quillets** /KWIL its/ quibbles.

285. *__salve__ ointment. US /sav/ [salv]; NEW ENG. /sahv/; CN /sav, salv/ [sahlv]; UK /salv/. Normal development would favor the *l*-less form (cf. *halve*, *calve*).

299, 349. **academes** /AK uh deemz/ [ak uh DEEMZ] academics.

300-348. **Promethean** /proh-, pruh MEETH yun/ i.e., divine.

---

304. **sinowy** /SIN (oh) wee/ muscular. Archaic variant of **sinewy** /SIN y(oo) wee/.

325. **immured** /ih MYOOR id/ imprisoned.

336. *__Bacchus__ god of wine. US, CN /BAHK us/ [BACK us]; UK /BACK us/ [BAHK-]. /BAHK-/ is newer.

338. **Hesperides** /hess PĔR ih deez/ garden where golden apples grew.

367. **glozes, gloses** /GLOH ziz/ fancy words.

374. **solace** /SŎL us/ comfort.

380. **Allons** /ah LOH^N/ Fr. 'come on!'

ă-bat, ăir-m**arry**, air-p**air**, a̧r-f**ar**, ĕr-m**erry**, ĝ- g**et**, ī-high, ĭr-m**irror**, ł-little, n̩-listen, ŏ-hot, oh-go, o͝o-wood, o͞o-moon, oor-t**our**, ōr- **or**, ow-how, t̠h-that, t̶h̶-thin, ŭ-but, UR-f**ur**, ur-u**nder**. ( ) - suppress the syllable see p. xiii for complete list.

Act 5 Scene 1

1.   **Satis   quid sufficit**
Ang.Lat.   /SAYT iss   kwid SUFF ih sit/
Class.Lat. /SAHT iss   kwid So͞oF ih kit/
           'enough is as good as a feast.'
Some eds. add **est** /est/ after *Satis*.

4. **scurrility** /skur RIL ih tee/ coarse joking.

6. **heresy** /HĔR ih see/ dissent from the dominant thinking.

6. ***quondam** US /KWŎN dum/, *rarely* [-dam]; UK /-dam/, *rarely* [-dum]
former.

7. ***intituled** /in TIT yo͞old, -yłd/; US *also* [in TITCH o͞old, -łd] entitled.

9.   **Novi   hominem   tanquam   te**
Ang.Lat.   /NOH vī   HŎM ih nem   TANG kwam   tee/
Class.Lat. /NOH wee HŎM ih nem   TAHNG kwahm tay/
           'I know the man as well as I know you.'

10. **peremptory** US /pur REM tur ee/ [PĔR um tor ee, -tur ee];
UK /pur EM tur ee/ [PĔR um t(u)r ee] overbearing.

12. ***thrasonical** /t̶h̶ruh SŎN ih kł/ [t̶h̶ray SŎN ih kł] boastful.

14. **peregrinate** /PĔR ih grih nayt, -nut/ having the air of one who travels,
foreign. /-ut / is more usual for an adj.

15. **epithet** /EP ih t̶h̶et, -t̶h̶it/ expression.

17.***abhor** Holofernes would say /ab HOR/ not /ab OR/ (see *abhominable*
line 24).

18. **phantasimes** /FAN taz imz/ people full of fancies. Some eds. prefer
phantisims /FAN tih zimz/.

18. **point-devise, -device** /POYNT dih VĪSS/ fastidious.

19. **ortography** correct spelling. /or TŎG ruh fee/ archaic variant of
orthography /or T̶H̶ŎG ruh fee/.

20. **dout**, etc. Holofernes is saying that Armado uses the pronounciatons /dowt/,
/det/, but ought to say /dowbt/, /debt/ with the *b* pronounced. Shk. is making

fun of scholars who believed English words ought to be pronounced according to their Latin roots.

22. **clepeth** /CLEEP i~~th~~/ calls.

22. **cauf, hauf** again Holofernes believes these words should be pronounced as they are spelled: US /kălf, hălf/ or E.NEW ENG., UK /kahlf, hahlf/.

23. **vocatur** Ang.Lat. /vŏk AY tur/; Class.Lat. /vŏk AH tōōr/ is called.

23. **nebor . . . ne.** Around 1600 the Middle Eng. sound spelled -*gh* (pronounced as in Germ. *ich* or *Bach*) was in decline, but some scholars were arguing that correct pronunciation demanded it be retained. Holofernes is saying that the *gh* in *neighbor* and *neigh* should be pronounced with the German sound in *ich*.

24. **abhominable** Holofernes pronounces it /ab HŎM in uh bł/, or even /-ay bł/.

25. **insanie** /in SAYN ee/ insanity. Some eds. prefer **infamy** (*infamie* Q1, F1) /IN fuh mee/ evil deed. Other choices are **insanity**, or **insanire** 'to rave' Ang.Lat. /in san Ī ree/; Class.Lat. /in sahn EE ray/.

25.   **ne   intelligis,   domine?**
Ang.Lat. /nee   in TEL ih jiss   DŎM ih nee/
Class.Lat. /nay   in TEL ig iss   DŎM ih nay/
        'do you understand, master?'

27.   **Laus Deo,   bone   intelligo**
Ang.Lat. /lawss   DEE oh,   BOHN ee   in TEL ih goh/
Class.Lat. /lowss   DAY yoh, BŎN ay   in TEL ih goh/
        'God be praised, I understand well.'
Q1, F1 have the correct form **bene** (see line 28) but *bone* is required to make sense of the next line.

28. **Bone? bone for bene** Ang.Lat. /BOHN ee . . . BEEN ee/;
Class.Lat. /BŎN ay . . . BEN ay/ Holofernes is saying that the curate ought to have used *bene* 'well' instead of *bone* 'good.' Another interpretation is **Bone? Bon fort bon** /BOH nee? boh^n fawr boh^n/ i.e., he is adding in French that he did well to use *Bone*.

28. **Priscian** a Latin grammarian. /PRISH ee un/ is more common, but /PRISH un/ is the normal Ang.Lat. form.

ă-bat, ăir-**marry**, air-**pair**, ạr-**far**, ĕr-**merry**, ĝ- **get**, ī-**high**, ĭr-**mirror**, ł-**little**, n̦-**listen**,
ŏ-**hot**, oh-**go**, ōō-**wood**, ōō-**moon**, oor-**tour**, ōr- **or**, ow-**how**, țh-**that**, ~~th~~-**thin**, ŭ-**but**,
UR-**fur**, ur-**under**.   ( ) - suppress the syllable   see p. xiii for complete list.

30.   **Videsne   quis   venit**
Ang.Lat. /vid ESS nee   kwiss   VEE nit/
Class.Lat. /wid AYSS nay   kwiss   WEN it/
           'do you see who comes?'

31.   **Video,   et   gaudeo**
Ang.Lat. /VID ėe oh   et   GAW dee oh/
Class.Lat. /VID ay oh   et   GOW day oh/
           'I see and rejoice.'
Some eds. substitute **gaudio** for *gaudeo*, which would be the same in Ang.Lat.
but /GOW dee oh/ in Class.Lat.

32-3. **Chirrah** uncertain; perhaps Armado's attempt at Gk. *chaere* a salutation
'hail!' which young scholars used in their Greek classes: angl. /KEER ee/ (a final
-*a* or -*ah* spelling could sometimes indicate /-ee/). It may also be a variant of
sirrah /SĬR uh/ form of address to a servant or inferior.

33. **Quare** Ang.Lat. /KWAIR ee/; Class.Lat. /KWAH ray/ why.

38. **alms-basket** collection basket for the poor. /ahmz/ is older; /ahlmz, awlmz/
are newer. In the UK the latter are non-standard.

41. **honorificabilitudinitatibus** Costard would surely use an anglicized form of
this word /ŎN ur if ih KAB il ih T(Y)ŌŌD in ih TAT ih bus/ 'the state of being
loaded with honors.'

49. **pueritia** Ang.Lat. /pyōō ur RISH uh/; Class.Lat. /pŏō ĕr IT ee ah/
childishness, child.

52. **Quis** /kwiss/ who.

58. **Mediterraneum** Ang.Lat. /med ih tur AYN ee um/;
Class.Lat. /med ih tĕr AHN ay ōōm/. Some eds. prefer mod. **Mediterranean**.

59. **venue, venew** (F3-4) /VEN yōō/ a fencing thrust.

63. **wit-old** /WIT old/ pun on *wittol* /WIT ł/ 'cuckold.'

67, 69. **gig** /ĝig/ top.

69. **manu cita** Ang.Lat. /MAYN yōō SĪ tuh/; Class.Lat. /MAHN ōō KIT ah/
with ready hand. Some eds. prefer **circum circa** Ang.Lat. /SUR kum
SUR kuh/; Class.Lat. /KĬR kōōm KĬR kah/ around and around.

73. **remuneration** /rih-, ree myōōn ur RAY shun/ payment.

74. **halfpenny** /HAY puh nee, HAYP nee/.

77, 79. **ad dunghill, unguem** Ang.Lat. /ad UNG gwum/;
Class.Lat. /ahd o͞oNG gwem/ to the nail, i.e., perfectly.

81. **preambulate** /pree AM byoo layt/ walk ahead.

81. **singuled** archaic variant of **singled,** both pronounced /SING głd/ separated.

84. **mons** Ang.Lat. /mŏnz/; Class.Lat. /mohnss/ hill.

86. **sans** /sănz/ without.

99. **importunate** /im POR chuh nut/; UK *also* /-tyoo nut/ pressing.

104. **mustachio** US /muh STASH ee oh/ [muh STASH oh, -STAHSH-];
UK /muh STAHSH ee yoh/ [-STASH-] moustache.

110. **secrety** (*secretie* Q1) /SEE cruh tee/ archaic variant of **secrecy**
(*secrecie* F1).

113. **curate** /KYOOR ut/; US *also* /KYUR ut/ priest.

121.*****illustrate** US /ih LUST rut, -rayt/; UK /ih LUST rayt/ [-rut] illustrious.
/-ut / is more usual for an adj.

127. **Machabeus, Maccabeus** /mack uh BEE us/.

128. **Pompey** /PŎMP ee/.

149. **Via** /VĪ uh/ onward! /VEE uh/ is newer.

149. **goodman** /Go͞oD mun/ title of a man under the rank of gentleman.

152. **Allons** /ah LOH^N/ Fr. 'come on!'

154. **tabor** /TAY bur/ small drum. See App. D *-or.*

ă-bat, ăir-**marry**, air-**pair**, ạr-**far**, ĕr-**merry**, ĝ- **get**, ī-**high**, ĭr-**mirror**, ł-**little**, ṇ-**listen**,
ŏ-**hot**, oh-**go**, o͞o-**wood**, o͞o-**moon**, oor-**tour**, ōr- **or**, ow-**how**, ṭh-**that**, t̶h̶-**thin**, ŭ-**but**,
UR-**fur**, ur-**under**.   ( ) - suppress the syllable   see p. xiii for complete list.

Act 5 Scene 2

3. **diamonds** here should be /DĪ uh mundz/, the standard pronunciation in the UK.

8. **margent** /MAR junt/ archaic variant of **margin.**

12. **shrowd** /shrohd/ harsh. Archaic variant of **shrewd.**

17.***grandam** /GRAN dam/; US *rarely* [-dum] grandmother. Informally /GRAN um/.

44. **dominical** /duh MIN ih kł/ [doh-, dŏm-] letter to mark a calendar, here 'Sunday.'

46. **beshrow** /bih-, bee SHROH/ curse. Archaic variant of **beshrew** /-SHR͞OO/.

46. **shrows** /shrohz/ archaic variant of **shrews.**

67. **pair-taunt-like** a winning combination in cards. Some eds. prefer ***pursuivant-like** like an officer employed to make arrests /PUR sw(i)v unt/ [PURS (ih) vunt]; UK /PUR sw(i)v unt/, *rarely* [PURS (ih) vunt].

73. **excess** here should be /ek SESS/, the most common UK form.

87. **Saint Denis** US /saynt DEN iss/; UK /sint-, sṇt-/ patron saint of France.

98. **embassage** ambassador's message. Normally /EM buh sij/ but here rhymes with *page.*

112. **Via** /VĪ uh/ onward! /VEE uh/ is newer.

The following words are used several times between lines 121-404.

Muscovites (-vits) people from Moscow. Today usually /MUSK uh vīts/, but line 265 indicates Shk's pronunciation /-vits/ to rhyme with *wits.*

***vizard(s)** /VIZ urd(z)/ masks. /-ạrd/ not recommended. Some eds. prefer **vizor(s)** /VĪ zur(z)/.

---

122. ***parley** /PAR lee/ negotiate. Newer [-lay] not recommended.

159. **taffata, taffeta** /TAF uh tuh/ a silk-like cloth, here refers to masks.

171. **epithet** /EP ih thet, -thit/ expression.

200. **accompt** /uh COWNT/ archaic variant of **account**. See App. D.

206. **eyne** /īn/ dialect form of *eyes.*

232. **treys** /trayz/ threes.

233. **Metheglin** /muh ~~THEG~~ lin/ spiced drink of Wales.

233. **wort** /wurt/ sweet beer.

233. **malmsey** a sweet wine. /MAHM zee/ is the older pronunciation, but today the /l/ is sometimes pronounced. This, however is considered non-standard in the UK.

267. **Tapers** /TAY purz/ slender candles.

273.**lamentable** here should be /LAM un tuh bł/, the usual UK pronunciation, in a headless line.

279.**trow you** US, CN /troh, trow/; UK /trow/ [troh] would you believe. Shk's rhymes elsewhere indicate /-oh/.

296. **damask** /DAM usk/ pink or light red.

296.**commixture** mixture. US /cuh MIKS chur/ [coh-], *rarely* [cŏm-]; UK /coh-/ [cŏm-, cuh-].

298. **Avaunt** /uh VAWNT/ begone!

317. **retails** sells. Here should be /rih-, ree TAYLZ/.

318.**wassails** occasions of heaving drinking. Here stressed on the 1st syllable US /WŎSS łz, -aylz/, *rarely* [WĂSS łz]; CN /WŎSS aylz/ [WŎSS łz]; UK /WĂSS aylz/ [WŎSS-]. Normal development would favor /WŎSS-/.

332. **whalë's** walrus. Here the older genitive form /WHAYL iz/ is indicated.

341. **Conster** (*Consture* Q1) /CŎN stur/ explain the meaning of. **Construe** (F1) /cun STRŌŌ/.

389. **descried** /dih SKRĪD/ found out.

ă-bat, ăir-**marry**, air-**pair**, ạr-**far**, ĕr-**merry**, ĝ- get, ī-high, ĭr-mirror, ł-little, ṇ-listen, ŏ-hot, oh-go, ōō-wood, ōō-moon, oor-**tour**, ŏr- or, ow-how, ṭh-that, ~~th~~-thin, Ŭ-but, UR-**fur**, ur-under.   ( ) - suppress the syllable   see p. xiii for complete list.

392. **sound** archaic variant of **swoon**. In Shk's time the vowel could be either /ow/ or /o͞o/.

393. **Muscovy** /MUSK uh vee/ Moscow.

406. **Taffata, Taffeta** /TAF uh tuh/ a silk-like cloth.

407. **hyperboles** /hī PUR buh leez/ exaggerations.

408. **pedantical** /puh DANT ih kł/ learned by rote, without feeling.

413. **kersey** /KUR zee/ coarse woolen cloth.

415-16. **sans** /sănz/ without.

460. **an't, on't** /unt/ of it.

474. **squier** (Q1, F1) /skwīr/ archaic variant of F4's **square** 'carpenter's square.'

482. **manage**. Some eds. prefer **manège** which here has 1st syllable stress US /MAH nezh, -nayzh/; UK /MAN ayzh/ [-ezh]; Fr. /MAH nezh/. Both words mean 'horsemanship.'

487. **vara** very. Probably Shk's attempt to mark Costard as a rustic, dialect speaker. Readers should simply say *very* in whatever accent they are using.

501. **parfect** /PAR fikt/ perform. Archaic variant of **perfect** /PUR fikt, pur FEKT/.

502. **Pompion** /PUMP ee un, PUMP yun/ pumpkin. Costard's error for *Pompey*.

In this section these names are used several times:

Alisander US /al ih SAN dur/; UK /al ih SAHN dur/ [-SAN-] archaic variant of **Alexander**.

Hector /HEK tur/. See App. D for *-or*.

Judas Machabeus, Maccabeus /JO͞OD us mack uh BEE yus/.

Pompey /PŎMP ee/.

---

517. **Where zeal strives to content, and the contents**. *Content* /cun TENT/ means 'to please,' while *contents* refers to 'what is presented,' usually

/cŏn TENTS/ in Shk's verse but here may be mod. /CŎN tents/ in a broken-backed line.

530. **fortuna de la guerra** fortune of war. Armado would give this the Spanish pronunciation /for TŌON ah day lah GAYR rah/.

535. **curate** /KYOOR ut/; US *also* /KYUR ut/ priest.

536, 542. **pedant** /PED ṇt/ dull teacher.

544. **Abate** /uh BAYT/ unless.

544. **novum** /NOH vum/ a dice game.

546. **amain** /uh MAYN/ with full speed.

548. **libbard's** /LIB urdz/ archaic variant of **leopard's**.

550, 552. **surnam'd** here should be /sur NAYMD/.

553. **targe** /tarj/ light shield.

560. **halfpenny** /HAY puh nee, HAYP nee/.

564. **scutcheon** /SKUTCH un/ escutcheon, coat of arms.

577. ***close-stool** US /CLOHSS stōol, CLOHZ-/; UK /CLOHSS-/, *rarely* [CLOHZ-] chamber pot enclosed in a stool.

589. **Cerberus** /SUR bur us/ three-headed dog of Hades.

589. **canus** Ang.Lat. /KAYN us/. Error for *canis* Class.Lat. /KAHN iss/ dog.

591. **manus** Ang.Lat. /MAYN us/; Class.Lat. /MAHN ōos/ hands.

592. **Quoniam** Ang.Lat. /KWOHN ee um/; Class.Lat. /KWŎN ee ahm/ since.

593.***Ergo** /UR go/ is older, /ĔR go/ is newer. The former is more common in the UK, the latter in the US, CN, but both forms appear in all countries.

597. **Iscariot** /iss KĂIR ee ut/.

ă-bat, ăir-**marry**, air-**pair**, ạr-**far**, ĕr-**merry**, ĝ- **get**, ī-**high**, ĭr-**mirror**, ḷ-**little**, ṇ-**listen**, ŏ-**hot**, oh-**go**, ōō-**wood**, ōō-**moon**, oor-**tour**, ōr- **or**, ow-**how**, ṭh-**that**, ṭḥ-**thin**, ŭ-**but**, UR-**fur**, ur-**under**.   ( ) - suppress the syllable   see p. xiii for complete list.

598. **ycliped** /ih-, ee CLIP id/ called. Variant of **ycleped** /ih-, ee CLEEP id/, **yclept** /-CLEPT/. Here 2 syllables are indicated and /-CLIP-/ is necessary for the following line to make sense.

610. **cittern-head** /SIT urn/; UK *also* /SIT URN/ type of guitar.

614. **pommel** /PŎM ł, PUM ł/ the knob on the hilt of a sword.

614. ***falchion** type of sword. /FĂL chun/ [-shun]; *older* [FAWL chun].

616, 617.***brooch** /brohch/ ornament. US [br͞o͞och] not recommended.

618. **tooth-drawer** /DRAW ur/ tooth-puller.

628. **Jud-as** probably meant to be pronounced as *Jude- ass.*

632. **Achilles** /uh KILL eez/ Gk. hero.

641.***indu'd** /in DY͞O͞OD/; US *also* [-D͞O͞OD] endowed.

644, 651. **The armipotent** /ţhʸ ạr MIP (uh) tunt/ powerful in arms.

652. ***Ilion** Troy. /ILL ee un/; UK *sometimes newer* [Ī lee un], but here should rhyme with *pavilion,* which Armado would probably pronounce /puh VIL ee un/.

655. **columbine** /CŎL um bīn/ a flower.

678. **infamonize** /in FAM un īz/ variant of **infamize** /IN fuh mīz/ defame.

678. **potentates** /POHT ņ tayts/ rulers.

688. ***Ates** /AYT eez/ is the older, angl. form; /AHT ayz/ is the newer, restored form and much more common; /AHT eez/ is a mixed form, heard occasionally. *Ate* was the goddess of discord.

695. **Northren** /NOR ţhrun/ archaic variant of **northern**.

696. **bepray** /bih-, bee PRAY/ pray, beg.

711. **woolward** /W͞o͞oL wurd/ with the wool side next to the skin.

714. **dishclout** /DISH clowt/ dish cloth.

735. **converse** /cun-, cŏn VURSS/ conversation.

740. **extreme** here should be /EK streem/.

744. **progeny** children. /PRŎJ ih nee/; UK *also* [PROH-], a newer form.

748. **justle** /JUSS ł/ archaic variant of **jostle** /JŎS ł/.

766. **parti-coated** /PART ee-/ with colors in splotches, i.e., dressed like a fool.

781. **bombast** /BŎM băst/ cotton used as stuffing.   Formerly /BUM băst/.

847. **fructful** (Q1) fruitful. /FRUCKT fł/ is older, [FRo͞oKT-] is newer. US has an additional newer pronunciation /FRO͞OKT-/. F1 has **fruitfull**.

858. **gibing** /JĪ bing/ sarcastic.

875. **Gill** /jill/.

883. **votary** /VOHT uh ree/ someone who has taken a vow.

890. **Holla** /huh LAH/ a call to attract attention.

891. **Hiems** winter. Ang.Lat. /HĪ umz/; Class.Lat. /HIH emss/.

891, 893. **Ver** spring. Ang.Lat. /vur/; Class.Lat. /wayr/.

894. **pied** /pīd/ two or more colors in splotches.

ă-bat, ăir-**marry**, air-**pair**, ạr-**far**, ĕr-**merry**, ĝ- **get**, ī-**high**, ĭr-**mirror**, ł-**little**, n̩-**listen**, ŏ-**hot**, oh-**go**, o͝o-**wood**, o͞o-**moon**, oor-**tour**, ōr- **or**, ow-**how**, ţh-**that**, th-**thin**, Ŭ-**but**, UR-**fur**, ur-**under**.   ( ) - suppress the syllable   see p. xiii for complete list.

Macbeth

People in the Play

Banquo /BANG kwoh/.

Cathness, Caithness /KAY~~TH~~ ness, -niss/.

Donalbain /DŎN ł bayn/.

*Fleance US /FLEE ahnss/ [FLAY unss, FLEE-], *rarely* [FLAY ahnss];
CN /FLEE ahnss, FLAY unss/; UK /FLEE unss, FLAY-/ [FLEE ahnss],
rarely [FLAY ahnss]. Normal development would favor /FLEE unss/.

Hecat, Hecate /HEK ut/ goddess of witchcraft. /HEK uh tee/ is the usual non-
Shakespearean pronunciation.

Malcolm /MAL kum/.

Menteth, Menteith /men TEE~~TH~~/.

Rosse, Ross US /rawss/; UK /rŏss/. In CN /ŏ, aw/ are pronounced the same way.

Seyton /SEE tun, SEET n̥/.

*Siward US /SŌŌ wurd, SEE wurd/; CN /SEE wurd/; UK /SEE wurd/, *rarely*
[SYŌŌ-, SŌŌ-]. The older form is /S(Y)ŌŌ-/. /SEE-/ is a newer spelling
pronunciation. Some eds. prefer F1's **Seyward**, pronounced the same way.

Places in the Play

Birnan Wood /BURN un/. Some eds. prefer **Birnam** /BURN um/.

Cawdor /KAW dur/. Sometimes a spelling pronunciation /-dor/ is used (see
App. D *-or*).

*Dunsinane /DUN sih nayn/, *rarely* [dun sih NAYN]. At 4.1.93 2nd syllable
stress is indicated. Some eds. prefer mod. **Dunsinnan** /DUN sih nun/.

Glamis the 2 syllable pronunciation /GLAHM iss/ can be used in all instances.
Sometimes the meter also permits the mod., one syllable pronunciation
/glahmz/.

Special Words

thane /~~th~~ayn/ Scottish lord.

weïrd, weird having power to control men's fate. In verse it should be two syllables /WEE urd/, /WIH urd/. F1 spells it *wey(w)ard,* influenced by *wayward.*

Act 1 Scene 1

8. *****Graymalkin** gray cat. US /gray MAWL kin/, *rarely* [-MĂL-];
UK /-MĂL-/ [-MAWL-], *rarely* [-MAW kin-, -MŎL-]. Some eds. prefer
Grimalkin /grih-/. The Survey revealed a significant difference between this word and *****malkin** 'wench' in the UK: /MAW kin/ [MAWL-, MŎL-].

9. **Paddock** /PAD uk/ toad.

Act 1 Scene 2

9. **Macdonwald, Macdonald** both are /muk-, mack DŎN ld/.

13, 30. **kerns** /kurnz/ Irish foot soldiers.

25. **gins** /ĝinz/ begins.

31, 49. **Norweyan** /nor WAY un/ variant of **Norwegian.**

34. **captains** here /KAP ih tunz/ is indicated.

40. **Golgotha** here should be /GŎL guh ~~th~~uh/; US *also* /GAWL-/ hill where Jesus died.

54. **Bellona's** /buh LOHN uz/ goddess of war.

59. **Sweno** /SWEE noh/.

60. **deign** /dayn/ grant.

61. **Saint Colme's** /saynt COHL meez/; UK /sint-, sṇt-/. Some eds. prefer **Saint Colum's** /CŎL umz/.

ă-bat, ăir-m**a**rry, air-p**ai**r, ạr-f**a**r, ĕr-m**e**rry, ĝ- g**e**t, ī-h**igh**, ĭr-m**i**rror, l̶-l**i**ttle, ṇ-l**i**sten,
ŏ-h**o**t, oh-g**o**, ŏŏ-w**oo**d, ōō-m**oo**n, oor-t**ou**r, ōr- **o**r, ow-h**ow**, ţh-**th**at, ~~th~~-**th**in, ŭ-b**u**t,
UR-f**ur**, ur-und**er**.   ( ) - suppress the syllable   see p. xiii for complete list.

Act 1 Scene 3

4. **mounch'd** archaic variant of **munch'd**, both pronounced /muncht/.

6. **Aroint thee, Aroynt thee** /uh ROYNT/ begone.

6. **ronyon, runnion** /RUN yun/ scabby creature.

7. **Aleppo** /uh LEP oh/ city in present-day Syria.

8. **sieve** /siv/ strainer.

22. **sev'nnights** variant of **se'nnights** /SEN nits, -nīts/ 'weeks.'

39. **Forres** US /FŌR iss/; UK, E.COAST US /FŎR-/.

71. **Sinel's, Sinell's** /SĪN łz, SIN łz/ Macbeth's father.

84. **insane** here /IN sayn/ is indicated.

95. **Norweyan** /nor WAY un/ variant of **Norwegian**.

Act 1 Scene 4

42. **Enverness** /en vur NESS/ archaic variant of **Inverness** /in-/.

45. **harbinger** /HAR bin jur/ advance messenger.

Act 1 Scene 5

27. *****chastise** punish. Here should be /CHĂSS tīz/, the usual US pronunciation, also used in CN; in the UK 2nd syllable stress is usual.

39. **entrance** here /ENT ur unss/ is indicated.

44. **th' access** here should be /ŧhʸ ak SESS/.

Act 1 Scene 6

6. **frieze** /freez/ area between a door lintel and the cornice.

7. **coign** /coyn/ corner.

8. **procreant cradle** /PROH cr(ee) yunt/ bed for reproduction.

13. **God 'ield** /gŏd-, gud EELD us, -ILD-/; US *also* /gawd-/ thanks.

20. **ermites** /UR mits/ archaic variant of **hermits**, i.e., who will pray for you.

22. **purveyor** here should be /PUR vay ur/ someone who prepares the way for a king.

23. **holp** /hohlp/ helped.

26. **compt** /cownt/ archaic variant of **count** 'account.' See App. D *accompt.*

Act 1 Scene 7

3. **trammel up** /TRAM ł/ catch (in a net).

4. **surcease** /sur SEESS/ end, death.

11. **chalice** /CHAL iss/ goblet.

22. ***cherubin** angel. US, CN /CHĔR uh bin/ [-yuh-]; UK uses both equally. /KĔR-/ not recommended. Some eds. prefer **cherubins, cherubim**.

23. ***couriers** US /CUR yurz/ [COOR-]; E.COAST US /CŬR-/ [COOR-]; UK /COOR-/ [CŬR-].

54. **unmake** here with 1st syllable stress.

64. ***wassail** carousing. Here stressed on the 1st syllable US /WŎSS łz, -aylz/, *rarely* [WĂSS łz]; CN /WŎSS aylz/ [WŎSS łz]; UK /WĂSS aylz/ [WŎSS-]. Normal development would favor /WŎSS-/.

67. **limbeck** /LIM bek, -bik/ archaic variant of *alembic*, part of a distillery.

71. **spungy** archaic variant of **spongy**, both pronounced /SPUN jee/.

ă-bat, ăir-**marry**, air-**pair**, a̧r-**far**, ĕr-**merry**, ĝ- get, ī-**high**, ĭr-**mirror**, ł-**little**, n̦-**listen**, ŏ-**hot**, oh-**go**, ōō-**wood**, ōō-**moon**, oor-**tour**, ōr- **or**, ow-**how**, țh-**that**, t̶h̶-**thin**, ŭ-**but**, UR-**fur**, ur-**under**.　　　　( ) - suppress the syllable　　　see p. xiii for complete list.

Act 2 Scene 1

14. *largess, largesse generous gifts. Here should have 1st syllable stress
US /LAR jess/ [-zhess]; CN, UK /LAR zhess/ [-jess]. Forms with /j/ are older.

15. diamond here should be /DĪ uh mund/, the standard UK form.

18. defect here should be /dih-, dee FECT/.

46. dudgeon /DUJ un/ dagger handle.

46. gouts /gowts/ drops.

53. *Alarum'd US, CN /uh LAHR umd/ [-LĂIR-]; UK /uh LĂIR umd,
uh LAHR umd/ called to arms.

55. Tarquin's /TAR kwinz/ king of Rome who raped Lucretia.

Act 2 Scene 2

6. possets /PŎSS its/ spiced milk drinks.

49. *Infirm /in FURM/ irresolute.

59. multitudinous US /mŭl tih TŌŌD (ih) nus/; UK, SOUTH. US /-TYŌŌD-/ vast.

59. *incarnadine /in CAR nuh dīn/ [-deen] make red. The latter is newer, and
non-standard in UK.

Act 2 Scene 3

4. Belzebub /BEL zih bub/ a devil. Archaic variant of Beelzebub
/bee EL zih bub/.

6. enow /ih NOW/; US also /ee-/ archaic variant of enough.

8-35. equivocator, equivocates /ih KWIV uh kay tur/; US also /ee-/ an
equivocator is someone who uses vague or deceptive answers in an argument.
See App. D -or.

57. prophesying /PRŎF uh sī ing/ predicting the future.

59. obscure here should be /ŎB skyoor/; US also [-skyur].

60. ***livelong** US /LIV lŏng, -lawng/, *rarely* [LĪV-]; UK /LIV lŏng/ [LĪV-].

72. **Gorgon** /GOR gun/ Medusa, whose sight could kill.

74. ***alarum-bell** US, CN /uh LAHR um/ [-LĂIR-]; UK /uh LĂIR um, uh LAHR um/ bell that calls men to arms.

82. ***parley** /PAR lee/ conference with an enemy. Newer [-lay] not recommended.

116. ***breech'd** covered. /britcht/ is traditional, /breecht/ is newer. The former pronunciation is more common in the UK, and the latter in the US, CN.

131. **pretense** (UK **pretence**) intention, design. Here should be /prih TENSS/, the normal UK pronunciation, or /pree TENSS/ based on the most common US pronunciation /PREE tenss/.

135. **consort** /cun SORT/ keep company.

136. **unfelt** here should be /UN felt/.

Act 2 Scene 4

7. **travelling** (F3) /TRAV ling/. F1 has ***travailing** 'laboring,' which in Shk's time was also pronounced /TRAV ling/. Mod. pronunciations /truh VAYL ing, TRAV ayl ing/ will not fit the meter, and cannot be compressed.

18. **eat** /et/ dialect variant of **ate**, which is also commonly /et/ in the UK.

24. **suborned** /sub ORND/ bribed.

28. **ravin up** /RAV in/ devour. Some eds. prefer F1's **raven** pronounced the same way.

31, 35. ***Scone.** At 5.8.74-5 rhymes with *one* which in Shk's time was pronounced /ohn/. Today the Scots say /skōōn/, also used by a minority in England, but unknown in the US. In both the US and England /skohn/ is the usual pronunciation. US /skŏn, skun/ are not recommended.

33. **Colmekill** /KOHM kill/ Iona Island in W. Scotland.

ă-bat, ăir-**marry**, air-**pair**, ạr-**far**, ĕr-**merry**, ĝ- **get**, ī-**high**, ĭr-**mirror**, ł-**little**, n̩-**listen**, ŏ-**hot**, oh-**go**, ōō-**wood**, ōō-**moon**, oor-**tour**, ōr- **or**, ow-**how**, ţh-**that**, ŧħ-**thin**, ŭ-**but**, UR-**fur**, ur-**under**. ( ) - suppress the syllable see p. xiii for complete list.

34. *predecessors US /PRED ih sess urz/; UK /PREE dih sess urz/; in CN both /PREE-/ and /PRED-/ are used equally. Rarely with stress on the 3rd syllable. See App. D -or.

40. *benison US, CN /BEN ih sun, -sn̩/ [-zun, -zn̩]; UK /-z-/ [-s-] blessing.

Act 3 Scene 1

17. indissoluble that cannot be dissolved. Here should be /in DIS sŏl yuh bł/.

31. parricide /PĂIR ih sīd/ killing of a father.

56. Mark Antony's /ANT (uh) neez/. F1 has *Anthony's* which in the UK is also usually pronounced with /t/.

66. rancors (UK rancours) /RANK urz/ ill-will. See App. D -or.

92. mungrels /MUNG grłz/ variant of mongrels, pronounced the same in the UK; US, CN *also* /MŎNG grłz, MAWNG-/.

93. *Shoughs shaggy lap dogs. /shufs/, *rarely older* [shŏcks]. Sometimes spelled Shocks.

93. *demi-wolves /DEM ee-/ half-dog, half-wolf.

108. buffets /BUFF its/ knocks.

119. avouch /uh VOWCH/ justify.

Act 3 Scene 2

14. close /clohz/ heal.

33. lave /layv/ wash.

34. *vizards /VIZ urdz/ masks. /-ạrdz/ not recommended.

38. eterne /ih TURN/; US *also* /ee-/ eternal.

40. *jocund /JŎCK und/; US, CN *rarely* [JOHK-] merry.

Act 3 Scene 4

18. *nonpareil one without equal. /nŏn puh RELL/ is the oldest form, still common in the US, but now vanished from the UK and CN, where it has been replaced with /nŏn puh RAYL/ [-RAY], based on mod. Fr. /-RAY/ is also common in the US. /-RĪ, -RĪL/ are occasionally heard, but not recommended. Sometimes 1st syllable stress is used.

42. *mischance in verse normally with 2nd syllable stress.

65. Authoriz'd /aw ~~THOR~~ īzd/ is the older pronunciation, but here an inverted foot will allow the mod. pronunciation /AW ~~thur~~ īzd/.

65. *grandam /GRAN dam/; US rarely [-dum] grandmother. Informally /GRAN um/.

75. humane here should be /HYOO mayn/; US sometimes [YOO mayn].

75. weal /weel/ commonwealth.

92. Avaunt /uh VAWNT/ begone!

100. th' Hyrcan normally /HUR kun/ of Hyrcania (in the Caucausus). However, Shk did not pronounce the /h/ in this word, but attached th' as /ṬHᵞUR kun/.

123. *Augures, Augurs /AWG yurz/ [-urz]; UK also / yoorz/ auguries, prophecies.

124. choughs, chuffs /chufs/ jackdaws.

142. initiate fear /ih NISH yut, -yayt/ fear of a beginner. /-ut/ is more usual for an adj.

Act 3 Scene 5

2. *beldams hags. US /BEL damz, -dumz/; UK /BEL damz/, rarely [-dumz].

7. close /clohss/ hidden.

ă-bat, ăir-marry, air-pair, ar-far, ĕr-merry, ĝ- get, ī-high, ĭr-mirror, ł-little, ṇ-listen, ŏ-hot, oh-go, ōͦ-wood, ōō-moon, oor-tour, ōr- or, ow-how, ṭh-that, t̶h-thin, ŭ-but, UR-fur, ur-under.   ( ) - suppress the syllable   see p. xiii for complete list.

15. **Acheron** /AK ur ŏn, -un/ a river in Hades. /-ŏn/ is usual in the US and is increasingly common in the UK. See App. D -*on*.

26. **sleights** /slīts/ tricks.

Act 3 Scene 6

28. **malevolence** /muh LEV uh lunss/ ill-will.

31. **Northumberland** /north UM bur lund/.

36. ***homage** /HŎM ij/; US *also* /ŎM ij/ acknowledgement of allegience.

38. **exasperate** exasperated. /eg ZĂSS pur ayt, -ut/; UK *also* /-ZAHSS-/.

Act 4 Scene 1

1. **brinded** /BRIN did/ archaic variant of **brindled** /BRIND łd/ tawny with dark streaks.

5. ***entrails** /EN traylz/; US *also* [-trłz] guts.

12. **Fillet** /FILL it/ slice. This is the usual form in the UK; US /fill AY/ will not fit the meter.

17. **howlet's** /HOW lits/ young owl's. Variant of **owlet's**.

24. **ravin'd** /RAV ind/ glutted.

26. **blaspheming** here should be /blăss FEEM ing/; UK, E.NEW ENG. *also* [blahss-] speaking irreverently.

29. **Tartar's** /TAR turz/ people of Central Asia.

33. **chawdron, chaudron** /CHAW drun/ entrails.

34. **cau'dron** (*Cawdron* F1) /KAW drun/ archaic variant of **cauldron** /KAWL drun/.

37. **baboon's** here should be /BAB o͞onz/.

After line 43 some eds. add a song from another source, which contains lines with the words:

Liard /LĪ urd/ gray. In some cases it was written *Lyer* or *Liand,* which are probably errors.

younker /YŬNG kur/ young lord.

---

59. **germains, germens** /JUR munz/; **germain** (F1), **germen** 'seed' in the collective sense.

65. **sweaten** /SWET n̩/ sweated. In Shk's time *sweat* had the vowel of *sea,* hence the rhyme with *eaten.*

66. **gibbet** /JIB it/ post from which they hung corpses after hanging.

69. **unknown** here should be /UN nohn/.

91. **chafes** /chayfs/ is angry.

96. **bodements** /BOHD munts/ omens.

stage direction after 106: **Hoboys, Hautboys** /HOH boyz/ or /OH boyz/ archaic variant of *oboes.*

123. **blood-bolter'd** /BOHL turd/ matted with blood. Some eds. prefer **blood-balter'd** /BAWL turd/.

134. **aye** /ay/ ever. /ī/ is often used, but not recommended.

144. **exploits** here should be /ek SPLOYTS/.

Act 4 Scene 2

35. **gin** /jin/ snare.

57. **enow** /ih NOW/; US *also* /ee-/ archaic variant of **enough.**

ă-bat, ăir-**marry**, air-**pair**, ar̩-**far**, ĕr-**merry**, ĝ- **get**, ī-**high**, ĭr-**mirror**, l̩-**little**, n̩-**listen**, ŏ-**hot**, oh-**go**, o͞o-**wood**, o͞o-**moon**, oor-**tour**, ōr- **or**, ow-**how**, t̠h-**that**, th-**thin**, ŭ-**but**, UR-**fur**, ur-**under**.   ( ) - suppress the syllable   see p. xiii for complete list.

Act 4 Scene 3

8. **dolor** (UK **dolour**) /DOH lur/; UK *also* /DŎL ur/ pain. See App. D *-or*.

34. **affeer'd** /uh FEERD/ confirmed.

58. **avaricious** /av uh RISH us/ greedy.

63. **cestern** /SESS turn/ archaic variant of **cistern** /SISS turn/.

78. ***stanchless** insatiable. Variant of **staunchless** /STAWNCH liss/. See App. D *-aun-*.

78, 84. **avarice** /AV uh riss/ greed.

88. **foisons** /FOY zunz, -znz/ harvests, plenty.

93. **perseverance** here should be /pur SEV (uh) runss/.

108. **blaspheme** here should be /blăss FEEM/; UK, E.NEW ENG. *also* [blahss-] speak irreverently.

123. **abjure** /ab-, ub JOOR/; US *also* /-JUR/ renounce.

143. **assay** /uh-, ass SAY/. Some eds. prefer **essay** /es SAY/. Both mean 'attempt, test.'

180. **niggard** /NIG urd/ miser.

187. **create** here should be /CREE ayt/.

Act 5 Scene 1

20. **stand close** /clohss/ keep hidden.

39. **accompt** /uh COWNT/ archaic variant of **account**. See App. D.

Act 5 Scene 2

10. **unrough** here should be /UN ruff/ beardless.

18. **minutely** /MIN it lee/ occurring every minute.

27. **weal** /weel/ commonwealth.

Act 5 Scene 3

8. **epicures** /EP ih kyoorz/; US *also* /-kyurz/ pleasure-seekers, those leading riotous lives.

21. **disseat** (F1) /dis SEET/ dethrone.   F2 has **disease**.

35. **skirr** /skur/ scour.

52. *****pristine** here should be /PRISS teen/ perfect, as in its original state.

55. **cyme** (F1) /sīm/ tops of the colewort used as a purgative. Some eds. prefer F4's **senna** /SEN uh/ a type of tree whose leaves are a purgative.

55. **What rhubarb, *cyme*, or what purgative drug** some eds. prefer **senna** because it improves the meter, but *cyme* could also be considered two syllables, extended to /SAH eem/, (see MND 2.1.249). *Purgative* in either case is reduced to two syllables /PURG (uh) tiv/.

Act 5 Scene 4

19. **unsure** here with 1st syllable stress. Note 3 syllables are indicated for *speculative*.

Act 5 Scene 5

4. **ague** /AY gyo͞o/ malarial fever.

12. *****treatise** story. US /TREET iss/, *rarely* [-iz]; CN /-iss/; UK both /s/ and /z/ forms used equally.

42. **th'equivocation** /t̯hʸih kwiv uh KAY shun/; US *also* /ee-/ using vague or deceptive answers in an argument.

46. **avouches** /uh VOWCH iz/ affirms.

48. **gin** /ĝin/ begin.

50. *****alarum-bell** US, CN /uh LAHR um/ [-LĂIR-]; UK /uh LĂIR um, uh LAHR um/ bell calling men to arms.

ă-bat, ăir-**marry**, air-**pair**, a̯r-**far**, ĕr-**merry**, ĝ- **get**, ī-**high**, ĭr-**mirror**, l̯-**little**, n̯-**listen**, ŏ-**hot**, oh-**go**, o͞o-**wood**, o͞o-**moon**, oor-**tour**, ōr- **or**, ow-**how**, t̯h-**that**, t̶h̶-**thin**, ŭ-**but**, UR-**fur**, ur-**under**.   ( ) - suppress the syllable   see p. xiii for complete list.

Act 5 Scene 6

1. **leavy** /LEEV ee/ archaic variant of **leafy**.

10. **harbingers** /HAR bin jurz/ advance messengers.

Act 5 Scene 7 (*Complete Oxford* 5.8)

17. (5.8.4) **kerns** /kurnz/ Irish foot soldiers.

18. (5.8.5) **staves** /stayvz/ staffs.

22. (5.8.9) **bruited** /BRŌŌT id/ announced.

Act 5 Scene 8 (*Complete Oxford* 5.10)

20. **palter** /PAWL tur/ use vague or deceptive arguments.

Act 5 Scene 9 (*Complete Oxford* 5.11)

7. **prowess** here one syllable is indicated /PROW (i)ss/.

16. **knoll'd** /nohld/ rung. Archaic variant of **knell'd**.

41. ***Scone** here meant to rhyme with *one* which in Shk's time was pronounced /ohn/. Today the Scots say /skōōn/, also used by a minority in England, but unknown in the US. In both the US and England /skohn/ is the usual pronunciation. US /skŏn, skun/ are not recommended.

Measure for Measure

People in the Play
Abhorson /ub HOR sun, -sn̩/ [ub OR sun]. **Angelo** 2 or 3 syllables depending on meter /AN j(uh) loh/. **Barnardine** /BAR nur deen/. **Claudio** 2 or 3 syllables depending on meter /CLAW d(ee) yoh/. **Escalus** /ES kuh lus/. **Francisca** /fran SIS kuh/. **Juliet** /JŌOL yit, -yet/ or a triple ending /JŌOL ee yit, -yet/. If the meter allows it, the mod. variant /jōo lee ET/ may also be used. **Julietta** /jōol YET uh/. **Lodowick** 2 or 3 syllables depending on meter /LŎD (oh) wik, LOHD-, (-uh-)/. *__Lucio__ 2 or 3 syllables depending on meter /LŌOCH (ee) yoh/ is newer and more common, based on Ital. Older and less common are [LŌOS (ee) yoh], US *rarely* [LŌOSH (ee) yoh] (for /lyōo-/ see App. D *lu*-). **Mariana** /mair ee ANN uh/ is older, /-AHN uh/ is newer. **Pompey** /PŎM pee/. *__Provost__ US /PROH vohst/, *rarely* [PRŎV ohst, -ust]; UK /PRŎV ust/ [-ŏst]. **Varrius** /VĂIR yus/. **Vincentio (the Duke)** /vin SEN shee yoh/; It. /veen CHEN tsee oh/. His name is not spoken.

Act 1 Scene 1

41. **advertise** here should be /ad VUR tiss, -tīz/ make publicly known.

ă-bat, ăir-**marry**, air-**pair**, a̱r-**far**, ĕr-**merry**, ĝ- **get**, ī-**high**, ĭr-**mirror**, ł-li**ttle**, n̩-**listen**, ŏ-**hot**, oh-**go**, ōo-**wood**, ōo-**moon**, oor-**tour**, ōr- **or**, ow-**how**, t̟h-**that**, t̶h̶-**thin**, ŭ-**but**, UR-**fur**, ur-**under**.　　　( ) - suppress the syllable　　　see p. xiii for complete list.

51. **leaven'd** /LEV ṇd, -ind/ referring to the gradual rising of dough, i.e., thoughtful.

56. ***importune** /im POR chun/ urge. See App. D.

67. **privily** /PRIV ih lee/ privately.

70. **aves** hails. /AY veez/ is the older, angl. form. The newer /AH vayz/ is much more common and based on classical and church Latin.

Act 1 Scene 2

8, 12. **Commandement(s)**. Archaic variant of **commandment(s)**, originally with 4 syllables, /-uh munt/, but in this prose passage the usual mod. 3-syllable pronunciation may be used.

33. **as lief** /leef/ as soon.

33. **kersey** /KUR zee/ coarse woolen cloth.

50. **dolors** (UK **dolours**) /DOH lurz/; UK *also* /DŎL urz/ pains, with pun on *dollars*. See App. D *-or*.

59. **sciatica** /sī AT ih kuh/ pain in the lower back.

100. **burgher** /BURG ur/ citizen.

120. ***demigod** half-god. /DEM ee gŏd, DEM ih-/; US *also* /-gawd/.

129. **ravin down, raven down** /RAV in/ devour.

133. **as lief** /leef/ as soon.

145. **contract** here should be /cŏn TRACT/.

150. **propagation**. Some eds. prefer **procuration** /prŏck yur AY shun/ 'obtaining,' or **prorogation** /proh ruh GAY shun/; UK *also* [prŏ-] 'delay.'

167. **unscour'd** here should be /UN skowrd/.

181. **assay** /uh-, ass SAY/ attempt, test.

Act 1 Scene 3

3. **complete** here should be /CŎM pleet/ fully defended.

26. **use** here is the noun /yōōss/.

Act 1 Scene 4

5. **votarists** /VOHT (uh) rists/ those bound by vows to religious life.

11. **prioress** /PRĪ ur ess, -iss/ nun who is second in rank at a convent.

34. **enskied** /en SKĪD/ placed in the sky.

38. **blaspheme** here should be /blăss FEEM/; UK, E.NEW ENG. *also* [blahss-] speak irreverently.

43. **foison** /FOY zun, -zṇ/ harvest.

44. **tilth** /tilth/ plowing.

60. **rebate** blunt. Here should be /rih-, ree BAYT/.

62. **use** /yōōss/ custom.

76. **Assay** /uh-, ass SAY/ try, test.

Act 2 Scene 1

11. **coher'd** /koh HEERD/ agreed with.

35. **confessor** here should be /CŎN fess ur/. See App. D *-or*.

42. **commonweal** /CŎM un weel/ commonwealth.

52. *****malefactors** /MAL ih fak turz/, *rarely* [mal ih FAK turz] evil doers. See App. D *-or*.

55. **profanation** /prŏf uh NAY shun/ desecration.

ă-bat, ăir-marry, air-pair, ạr-far, ĕr-merry, ĝ- get, ī-high, ĭr-mirror, ł-little, ṇ-listen, ŏ-hot, oh-go, ōō-wood, ōō-moon, oor-tour, ōr- or, ow-how, ṭh-that, th-thin, ŭ-but, UR-fur, ur-under.   ( ) - suppress the syllable   see p. xiii for complete list.

90-107. **pruins** in Shk's time probably /PR$\overline{OO}$ inz/, archaic and dialect variant of **prunes**.

93-242. **threepence** /~~THREP~~ unss, -ņss/ [~~THRUP-~~, THRIP-, ~~THR$\overline{oo}$P-~~]. Some eds. prefer **three pence** which should be pronounced the same way.

124. *****Hallowmas** US /HŎL-, HAL oh muss/ [-mass]; UK /HAL oh mass/ [-muss]. All Saints Day, Nov. 1. The older form is /-muss/.

126. *****All-hallond eve** /awl HAL und/; US *also* /-HŎL-/ archaic variant of **All-Hallows eve** /awl HAL ohz/; US *also* /-HŎL-/. Some eds. prefer **All Hallow Eve**.

174, 184. **caitiff** /KAYT if/ scoundrel.

255. **carman** /CAR mun/ driver of a cart.

Act 2 Scene 2

19. **access** here should be /ak SESS/.

39. **cipher** /S$\overline{I}$ fur/ zero.

40. **record** here should be /rek-, rik ORD/.

41. **severe** here should be /SEV eer/.

60. **deputed** /duh PY$\overline{OO}$T id/ appointed.

61. **truncheon** /TRUN chun/ staff of office.

92. **th' edict** decree. Here should be /ţhee DICT/ in a headless line.

98. **successive** here should be /SUCK sess iv/.

128. **profanation** /prŏf uh NAY shun/ desecration.

131. **blasphemy** /BLĂSS fuh mee/; UK, E.NEW ENG. *also* /BLAHSS-/ irreverent speech.

132. **avis'd** /uh V$\overline{I}$ZD/ archaic variant of **advised**.

149. **sicles** /SIK łz/ type of coins. Archaic variant of **shekels** /SHEK łz/.

154. **dedicate** /DED ih kayt, -ut/ dedicated.

Act 2 Scene 3

39. **Benedicite** Ang.Lat. /ben uh DISS ih tee/;
Church Lat. /bay nay DEE chee tay/ bless you.

41. *****respites** reprieves. Here should be US /RESP its/, *rarely* [-īts];
CN /RESP its/ [-īts]; UK /RESP īts/ [-its]. /RESP it/ is older, but /-īt/ has
been in use since the 17th cent.

Act 2 Scene 4

9. **sere** /seer/ dry. Some eds. prefer **seared** /seerd/.

18. **access** here should be /ak SESS/.

24. **swounds** archaic variant of **swoons**. In Shk's time the vowel could be either
/ow/ or /o͞o/.

28. **obsequious** /ub-, ŏb SEE kw(ee) yus/ fawning.

29. **untaught** here should be /UN tawt/ ignorant.

57. **compell'd** here should be /CŎM peld/.

58. **accompt** /uh COWNT/ archaic variant of **account**. See App. D.

80. **enshield** /EN sheeld/ concealed, guarded. Some eds. prefer **enshell'd,
enshielded**.

111. **Ignomy** /IG nuh mee/ disgrace. Some eds. prefer **Ignominy**
/IG nuh min ee/ which will not fit the meter.

122. **fedary, feodary** (F2) /FED uh ree/ confederate. *Feodary* is usually a
variant of *feudary* /FYO͞OD uh ree/ 'vassal,' which is incorrect here.

155. **unsoil'd** here should be /UN soyld/.

159. **calumny** /CAL um nee/ slander.

ă-bat, ăir-**marry**, air-**pair**, ạr-**far**, ĕr-**merry**, ĝ- g**et**, ī-h**igh**, ĭr-m**irror**, ł-litt**le**, ṇ-liste**n**, ŏ-h**ot**, oh-g**o**, o͝o-w**ood**, o͞o-m**oon**, oor-t**our**, ŏr- **or**, ow-h**ow**, ţh-**that**, ŧħ-**thin**, ŭ-b**ut**, UR-f**ur**, ur-und**er**. ( ) - suppress the syllable see p. xiii for complete list.	

162. **prolixious** /proh LIK shus/ excessive.

Act 3 Scene 1

9. *****Servile** /SUR vīl/, *rarely* [SUR vł] slave-like.

26. **ingots** /ING guts/; UK *also* [-gŏts] gold or silver cast in bars.

31. **sapego** /suh PEE goh/ creeping skin disease. Variant of **serpigo**
/sur PEE goh, -PĪ-/ which some eds. prefer.

31. **the rheum** /ro͞om/ disease of the lungs.

35. *****alms** charity for the poor. /ahmz/ is older; /ahlmz, awlmz/ are newer.
In the UK the latter are non-standard.

36. **palsied** /PAWL zeed/; UK *also* [PŎL-].

58. **leiger** resident ambassador. Also written **leaguer, ledger, leger, legier,
lieger** and pronounced as /LEE gur, LEJ ur, LEE jur/.

66, 67. *****durance** /DYOOR unss/; US *also* /Do͞oR-/ [DUR-] imprisonment.

90. **enew** US /ih NO͞O/; SOUTH. US, UK /ih NYO͞O/ drive prey into the water
during a hunt.

93, 96. **prenzie** (F1) /PREN zee/ uncertain meaning. Some eds. prefer **precise**
which here should be /PREE sīss/, **puny, precious** or F2's **princely**.

114. **perdurably** here should be /PUR dyur uh blee/; US *also* [-dur-] eternally.

120. **delighted**. Some eds. prefer **dilated** /dih-, dī LAYT id/ expansive.

129. **penury** /PEN yur ee/; UK *also* /PEN yoor ee/ poverty.

162. **assay** test. Usually /uh-, ass SAY/ in Shk, but as a noun in this prose
passage, may be mod. /ASS ay/.

203. *****peradventure** perhaps. /PUR ad VEN chur/;
US *rarely* [PĔR-, PUR ad ven chur];
UK, CN *also* [PUR-, PĔR ad ven chur, pĕr ad VEN chur].

214. *****nuptial** wedding. US, UK /NUP chł/ [-shł]; in CN both are used equally.

214. **affianc'd** /uh FĪ unst/ engaged to be married.

222. **combinate-husband** /CŎM bih nut, -ayt/ the man sworn by oath to be her husband. /-ut / is more usual for an adj.

Act 3 Scene 2 (*The Complete Oxford* continues this as 3.1—line nos. in parentheses).

6. (3.1.275) **usuries** /YO͞O zhur eez/; UK *also* [-zhyoor eez, -zhoor eez] lending money for interest.

36. (3.1.304) ***whoremonger** pimp. US /HOR mŏng gur/, /-mawng-/ [-mung-]; CN /-mung gur, -mŏng gur/; UK /-mung gur/.

97. (3.1.363) **lenity** /LEN ih tee/ leniency.

99. (3.1.365) **severity** /suh VĔR ih tee/.

174. (3.1.433) **ungenitur'd** /un JEN ih churd/; UK *also* /-tyoord/ sexless.

175. (3.1.434) **continency** /CŎN tih nun see/ sexual self-restrained.

186. (3.1.445) **calumny** /CAL um nee/ slander.

279. (3.1.535) **betrothed** /bih-, bee TROHṬH id/ fiancée.

Act 4 Scene 1

28. **circummur'd** /sur kum MYO͞ORD/ surrounded by a wall.

30. **planched** made of boards. US /PLĂN chid/; E.NEW ENG., UK /PLAHN chid/. Some eds. prefer **plancked** /PLANK id/.

71. **pre-contract** /PREE cŏn TRACT/ a contract made in the past.

75. **tithe's** /tīṭhz/ tenth part due to the church. Some eds. prefer **tilth's** /tilṭhs/.

Act 4 Scene 2

11. **gyves** /jīvz/ chains, fetters.

ă-bat, äir-**marry**, air-**pair**, ạr-**far**, ĕr-**merry**, ĝ- get, ī-**high**, ĭr-**mirror**, ł-little, ṇ-listen, ŏ-hot, oh-go, o͞o-**wood**, o͞o-**moon**, oor-**tour**, ŏr- **or**, ow-**how**, ṭh-**that**, ŧh-**thin**, ŭ-but, UR-**fur**, ur-under.　　　( ) - suppress the syllable　　　see p. xiii for complete list.

58. ***yare** /yair/; US *also* /yạr/ ready.

67. **traveller's**. Some eds. prefer **travailer's** 'laborer's' which here should have 1st syllable stress /TRAV ayl urz/. In Shk's time both words were /TRAV ł urz/, and here should be compressed to two syllables.

89. ***postern** small back or side gate. US, CN /PŎST urn/ [POHST urn]; UK /PŎST urn/, *rarely* [POHST urn].

92, 97. ***countermand** US, CN /COWNT ur mănd/; UK /-mahnd/ the revoking of a command.

110. **celerity** /suh LĔR ih tee/ speed.

130. **Bohemian** /boh HEEM ee yun/ Czech.

143. **reakless, reckless** /REK liss/ heedless.

160. ***respite** reprieve. US /RESP it/, *rarely* [rih-, ree SPĪT]; CN /RESP it/ [RESP īt], [ree-, rih SPĪT]; UK /RESP īt/ [-it, rih SPĪT]. /RESP it/ is older, but /-īt/ has been in use since the 17th cent.

186. **avouch** /uh VOWCH/ affirm.

Act 4 Scene 3

55. **billets** /BILL its/ clubs.

71, 76. **Ragozine** /RAG uh zeen, -zin/.

74. **reprobate** /REP ruh bayt/ a depraved person.

79. **Prefix'd** appointed. Here may be /prih-, pree FIKST/ or with inverted foot, newer /PREE fikst/.

94. **contents** here should be /cŏn TENTS/.

100. **weal-balanc'd** /weel-/ balanced with regard to public welfare. Most eds. prefer **well-balanced.**

104. **commune** here should be /CŎM yo͞on/ speak intimately.

118. **close** /clohss/ silent.

128. *covent religious order. US /KUV ṇt/ [KŎV-]; UK /KŎV ṇt/ [KUV-].
US /KOHV-/ not recommended. Archaic variant of convent.

128. confessor here should be /CŎN fess ur/. See App. D -or.

141. perfect here should be /PUR fikt/ inform.

174. medlar /MED lur/ an apple-like fruit.

Act 4 Scene 4

26. credent bulk /CREED ṇt/ massive trust.

Act 4 Scene 5

6, Flavio's /FLAY vyohz/.

8. Valentius (Valencius F1) /vuh LEN shus/ does not fit the meter. Most eds.
prefer Valentinus /val en TĪ nus/.

8. Rowland /ROH lund/.

8. Crassus /CRĂSS us/.

10. Flavius' /FLAY vyus/.

Act 4 Scene 6

5. *peradventure perhaps. /PUR ad VEN chur/;
US rarely [PĔR-, PUR ad ven chur];
UK, CN also [PUR-, PĔR ad ven chur, pĕr ad VEN chur].

Act 5 Scene 1

10. *covert here should be stressed on the 1st syllable US, CN /KOHV urt/
[KUV-]; UK /KUV-/ [KOHV-], rarely [KŎV-] secret.

ă-bat, ăir-marry, air-pair, ạr-far, ĕr-merry, ĝ- get, ī-high, ĭr-mirror, ł-little, ṇ-listen,
ŏ-hot, oh-go, ōō-wood, ōō-moon, oor-tour, ōr- or, ow-how, ṭh-that, t̶h̶-thin, ŭ-but,
UR-fur, ur-under.   ( ) - suppress the syllable   see p. xiii for complete list.

13. ***razure, rasure** erasure, obliteration. US, CN /RAY shur/, US *rarely* [-zhur]; UK /-zhur/, *rarely* [shur]. /zh/ is more likely to be used if the *z* spelling is used. See App. D *-ure*.

53, 88. **caitiff** /KAYT if/ scoundrel.

56. **caracts, characts** /KĂIR ukts/ symbols of office.

98. **concupiscible** /cŏn KYOOP (ih) sih bł/ moved by strong sexual desire.

106, 306. **suborn'd** /sub ORND/ persuaded someone to do something wrong.

125-43. **Lodowick** /LŎD (oh) wick, LOHD-, (uh-)/.

130. **swing'd** /swinjd/ beat.

158. **convented** /cun VENT tid/ summoned.

209. **contract** here should be /cŏn TRACT/.

227. **affianc'd** /uh FĪ unst/ engaged to be married.

242. **Compact** /cum-, cŏm PACT/ in league with.

257. ***chastisement** punishment. Here stress should be on 1st syllable /CHĂSS tiz munt/; US *also* /- tīz-/.

259. **throughly** archaic variant of *thoroughly*. /T̶H̶ROO lee/ is the normal pronunciation on stage, but to enhance clarity a syncopated form of the modern pronunciation may be used: *thor'ghly*.

262.   **Cucullus   non   facit   monachum**
Ang.Lat. /kyōō KŬL us   nŏn   FAY sit MŎN uh kum/
Class.Lat. /kōō KōōL ōōs nŏn   FAH kit MŎN ah kōōm/.
             'the hood does not make the monk.'

311. **touze, touse** /towz/ pull roughly.

333. ***fleshmonger** flesh-seller, pimp. US /FLESH mŏng gur/ or /-mawng-/ [-mung-]; CN /-mung gur, -mŏng gur/; UK /-mung gur/.

342. **close** /clohz/ come to terms, finish.

347. **giglets** /ĜIG lits/ loose women.

351. **foh** indicates an expression of disgust made with the lips /pff/! or /pfuh/! Sometimes rendered as /foh/ or **faugh** /faw/.

373. **sequent** /SEE kwunt/ subsequent.

378. **consummate** /CŎN suh mut, -ayt/ completed.

383. ***Advertising** attentive. Here should be /ad VUR tih sing, -zing/.

387. **unknown** here should be /UN nohn/.

392. **remonstrance** /rih-, ree MŎN strunss/ grievance.

394. **celerity** /suh LĔR (ih) tee/ speed.

433. ***importune** /im POR chun/ ask insistently. See App. D.

503. ***extol** praise. /ek STOHL/; UK *sometimes* and US *rarely* [-STŎL].

512. ***nuptial** wedding. US, UK /NUP chł/ [-shł]; in CN both are used equally.

529. ***gratulate** gratifying. /GRATCH oo layt/ [-lut];
UK *also* /GRAT yoo-/. /-ut / is normally more usual for an adj.

533. **Ragozine** /RAG uh zeen, -zin/.

ă-bat, ăir-marry, air-pair, ạr-far, ĕr-merry, ĝ- get, ī-high, ĭr-mirror, ł-little, ṇ-listen, ŏ-hot, oh-go, o͝o-wood, o͞o-moon, oor-tour, ōr- or, ow-how, t̪h-that, th-thin, ŭ-but, UR-fur, ur-under.   ( ) - suppress the syllable   see p. xiii for complete list.

The Merchant of Venice

People in the Play

Sometimes some of these names are given an Italian (or, for *Arragon*, a Spanish) accent in performance. These pronunciations are indicated here as accurately as possible within the limits of this notation. Shakespeare, however, probably intended them to be anglicized.

Antonio 3 or 4 syllables depending on meter /an TOHN (ee) yoh/; Ital. /ahn-/.

*Arragon, Aragon US /ĂIR uh gŏn/, *rarely* [-gun]; UK /-gŏn/ [-gun]. Sp. /ah rah GOHN/. See App. D -*on*.

*Balthazar, Balthasar by far the most common pronunciation is /BAL thuh zar/. It is rarely /bal ~~thuh~~ ZAR/, which will also fit the verse, but another rare pronunciation /bal ~~THAZ~~ ur/ will not.

Bassanio 3 syllables in verse /buh SAH nyoh/; Ital. /bah-/. In prose it may be /-nee yoh/.

Bellario 3 or 4 syllables depending on meter /buh LAH r(ee) yoh/ Portia's assumed name.

Gobbo /GŎB oh/.

*Gratiano 3 or 4 syllables depending on meter US /grahsh (ee) YAH noh/ [grash-], *rarely* [graysh-]; CN /grahsh-/ [grash-]; UK /grash-/ [grahsh-]; Ital. **Graziano** /grah ts(ee) YAH noh/.

Launcelot 2 or 3 syllables depending on meter.
US /LAWNSS (uh) lŏt/ [LAHNSS-, LĂNSS-]; CN /LAWNSS-/ [LĂNSS]; UK /LAWNSS (uh) lut/ [LAHNSS-]. Archaic variant of **Lancelot**. Note that in CN and some parts of the US /LAWNSS-/ and /LAHNSS-/ are pronounced the same, and that in E. New Eng. and Standard Br., /LAHNSS-/ corresponds to US /LĂNSS-/ (cf. *dance, chance*). The usual UK pronunciation of *Lancelot* is with 2 syllables /LAHNSS lut/; the North American with 3 /LĂNSS uh lŏt/. See App. D -*aun*-.

Leonardo always 3 syllables /l(ee) yuh NAHR doh, l(ee) yoh-/; Ital. /lay oh-/.

Nerissa /nuh RISS uh/; Ital. /nay REESS ah/.

People in the Play (cont.)

Portia /POR shuh/ is the normal pronunciation, sometimes expanded to /POR shee uh/ to fit the meter.

Salarino /sal uh REE noh/; Ital. /sah lah REE noh/. In many editions, including *Riverside,* this character is left out, presumed to be the same as **Salerio.** In any case his name is not spoken.

Salerio always 3 syllables in verse. US, CN /suh LĔR yoh/, US *rarely* [-LEER-]; UK /-LĔR-/ [-LEER-]. /suh LEER yoh/ is the older angl. form, /suh LĔR yoh/ is newer, based on Ital. /sah LĔR yoh/.

Solanio /soh-, suh LAHN ee oh/. His name is not spoken.

Stephano the messenger in 5.1. /stef AH noh/ fits best, though in *The Tempest* stress is on the first syllable.

Tubal US /TO͞O bł/; UK, SOUTH. US /TYO͞O-/.

Places in the Play

*Padua 2 or 3 syllables depending on meter /PAD y(oo) wuh/ [PAJ (oo) wuh]. An Ital. vowel /PAHD-/ is not recommended, since the Ital. form is *Padova.*

Tripolis /TRIP uh lis/.

Act 1 Scene 1

9. **argosies** /ARG uh seez/ large merchant ships.

10. **burghers** /BURG urz/ citizens.

19. **Piring** /PĪ ring/ means **peering**.

23. **ague** /AY gyo͞o/ malarial fever.

50. **Janus** /JAY nus/ Roman two-faced god.

56. **Nestor** /NEST ur/ oldest of the Greeks at Troy. See App. D *-or.*

ă-bat, ăir-**marry**, air-pair, ar-**far**, ĕr-**merry**, ĝ- **get**, ī-**high**, ĭr-**mirror**, ł-**little**, n̦-**listen**, ŏ-hot, oh-go, o͞o-wood, o͞o-moon, oor-**tour**, ōr- **or**, ow-how, țh-**that**, t̶h̶-**thin**, ŭ-but, UR-**fur**, ur-**under.**   ( ) - suppress the syllable   see p. xiii for complete list.

84. **alablaster** a type of white rock. US /AL uh blăss tur/;
E. NEW ENG., UK /-blahss-/ [-blăss-]. Archaic variant of **alabaster**
/-băss-, -bahss-/.

85. **jaundies** /JAWN deez/ yellowing of the skin. Archaic variant of **jaundice**
/JAWN diss/.

102. **gudgeon** /GUJ in/ bait fish.

111. These are non-iambic lines, with **commendable** pronounced as in mod.
Eng. with stress on the 2nd syllable to rhyme with *vendible,* though elsewhere in
Shk stress falls on the first syllable.

166. **Cato's** /KAYT ohz/.

171. ***Colchis'** country where Jason won the Golden Fleece. US /KOHL kiss/
[KŎL-]; UK /KŎL kiss/. Normal development would favor /KŎL kiss/.
/KOHL chiss/ not recommended.

171. **strond** /strŏnd/ archaic variant of **strand** 'shore.'

175. ***presages** here should be /pree-, prih SAY jiz/ foretells.

Act 1 Scene 2

39, 58. **Neapolitan('s)** /nee uh PŎL ih tun/ of Naples.

45, 60. **Palentine** (Q1) /PAL in tīn/ archaic variant of Q2's **Palatine**
/PAL uh tīn/ region in Germany.

55. **le Bon** angl. /luh BŎN/; Fr. /luh BOH^N/.

60. **throstle** /~~THR~~ŎSS ł/ thrush.

66. **Falconbridge** /FAWL-, FAL kun brij/; UK *also* [FŎL-],
rarely older [FAW kun-].

71. **pennyworth** the older form is /PEN ur~~th~~/, but in this prose passage the
newer spelling pronunciation /PEN ee wur~~th~~, -WUR~~TH~~/ may be used.

73. **dumb show** /DUM shoh/ pantomime.

82. ***surety** pledge to repay something. Here may be 2 or 3 syllables
/SHUR (ih) tee, SHOOR-, SHOR-/ (see App. D).

96. **Rhenish** /REN ish/ Rhine wine.

106. **Sibylla** /sih BIL uh/ she was promised long life by Apollo.

114. **Marquis** angl. /MAR kwiss/; Fr. /MAR kee, mar KEE/.

114. **Montferrat** (Q1) angl. /mŏnt fuh RAT/; Fr. /moh^n fĕr AH/;
Mount- (F1) /mownt-/.

Act 1 Scene 3

18. **argosy** /ĄRG uh see/ large merchant ship.

19-107. **Rialto** /ree AL toh/ is older, /ree AHL toh/ is newer based on Ital.

34. **Nazarite** /NAZ uh rīt/ Jesus.

44. *****gratis** without cost. US, UK /GRAHT iss/ [GRAT-], UK *rarely* [GRAYT-];
CN /GRAT-/ [GRAHT-].

45-141. **usance(s)** /YŌŌ zn̩ss, -zunss/ interest on money.

61. **albeit** /awl BEE (i)t/ although.

62. **excess** here should be /ek SESS/, the most common UK form.

71-8. **Laban('s)** /LAY bun(z)/, but sometimes newer [-banz] is used.

72, 160. **Abram** /AY brum/ Abraham.

78. **compremis'd** agreed. Variant of **compromised**, both /CŎM pruh mīzd/.

79. **eanlings** /EEN lingz/ newborn lambs.

79. **pied** /pīd/ two or more colors in splotches.

86. *****fulsome** lustful. /FỤLL sum/; US *rarely* [FŬL-].

88. **parti-color'd** /PAR tee-/ with splotches of different colors.

ă-bat, ăir-marry, air-pair, ąr-far, ĕr-merry, ĝ- get, ī-high, ĭr-mirror, ł-little, n̩-listen, ŏ-hot, oh-go, ŏŏ-wood, ōō-moon, oor-tour, ōr- or, ow-how, ţh-that, th-thin, Ŭ-but, UR-fur, ur-under. ( ) - suppress the syllable   see p. xiii for complete list.

112. ***gaberdine** loose garment of course cloth. US /GAB ur deen/, *rarely* [gab ur DEEN]; UK /gab ur DEEN/ [GAB ur deen]; in CN both are used equally.

117. **rheum** /rōōm/ phlegm.

Act 2 Scene 1

5. **Phoebus'** /FEE bus/ god of the sun.

21. **comer** /KUM ur/ visitor.

24. ***scimitar** US /SIM ih tar/ [-tur]; CN /-tar/; UK /-tur/ [-tar] a curved sword.

25. **Sophy** /SOH fee/ Shah of Persia.

26. **Solyman** Turkish ruler. /SŎL-, SŬL ih mun/, or /SŎL ee-, SŬL ee-/. Archaic variant of ***Suleiman** /SŌŌ lay mahn, SŌŌ lih mahn/. Sometimes also with final syllable stress.

32. **Lichas** US /LĪ kus/ [-kăss]; UK, CN /-kăss/ [-kus] Hercules' servant. Normal development would favor /-kus/.

35. **Alcides** /al SĪ deez/ Hercules.

Act 2 Scene 2

11. **Fia!** /FĪ uh/ Launce's' version of **Via** /VĪ uh/ onward! /VEE uh/ is newer.

19-20. **bouge** /BUJ/, or possibly /bōōj/. Archaic variant of **budge**,

32. **commandement**. Archaic variant of **commandment**, originally with 4 syllables, /-uh munt/, but in this prose passage the usual mod. 3-syllable pronunciation may be used.

45. **Be God's sonties** /SŎNT eez/ 'By God's saints' or 'sanctities.' Some eds. prefer **By** . . . but the spelling *Be* indicates the unstressed form of *by*, pronounced /buh, bih/.

57, 60. ***ergo** therefore. /UR go/ is older, /ĔR go/ is newer. The former is more common in the UK, the latter in the US, CN, but both forms appear in all countries.

68. ***hovel-post** post supporting a shed. US /HUV ł/, *rarely* [HŎV ł]; CN /HUV-/ [HŎV-]; UK /HŎV-/ [HUV-].

89, 91. **Margery** /MARJ ur ee/.

121. **Gramercy** /gruh MUR see/ thanks.

131. **cater-cousins** /KAY tur KUZ inz/ intimate friends.

186. **To allay** /twuh LAY/ relieve.

188. **misconst'red** /mis CŎN sturd/ misconstrued.

196. **ostent** here should be /ŏ STENT/ appearance.

197. *****grandam** /GRAN dam/; US *rarely* [-dum] grandmother. Informally /GRAN um/.

Act 2 Scene 3

11. **pagan** /PAYG un/ non-Christian.

16. *****heinous** /HAYN us/ hateful. /HEEN us/ is non-standard though common in the UK.

Act 2 Scene 4

22. **masque** US /măsk/; UK, E. NEW ENG. /mahsk/ [măsk] masked dancing and pantomime.

Act 2 Scene 5

3. **gurmandize** /GUR-, GOOR mun dīz/ to eat like a glutton. Archaic variant of **gormandize** /GOR-/.

23-8. **masque(s)** US /măsk/; UK, E. NEW ENG. /mahsk/ [măsk] masked dancing and pantomime.

43. **Jewess' eye**. Some eds. prefer **Jewës eye** 'Jew's eye' indicating an older genitive form /JŌŌ iz/.

44. **Hagar's** /HAY garz, -gurz/ Abraham's non-Jewish wife.

ă-bat, äir-marry, air-pair, ar-far, ĕr-merry, ĝ- get, ī-high, ĭr-mirror, l-little, n-listen, ŏ-hot, oh-go, ōō-wood, ōō-moon, oor-tour, ōr- or, ow-how, ţh-that, th-thin, ŭ-but, UR-fur, ur-under.   ( ) - suppress the syllable   see p. xiii for complete list.

Act 2 Scene 6

14. **younger**. Some eds. prefer **younker** /YŬNG kur/ young lord.

27. **Albeit** /awl BEE (i)t/ although.

47. **close night** /clọhss/ secret night.

52. *__Beshrow__ **me** /bih-, bee SHROH/ damn me. Archaic variant of **Beshrew** /-SHRŌŌ/.

59, 64. **masque(-ing)** US /măsk/; UK, E. NEW ENG. /mahsk/ [măsk] masked dancing and pantomime.

Act 2 Scene 7

20. **dross** /drŏss/; US *also* /drawss/ impure matter, rubbish.

41. **The Hyrcanian** normally /HUR KAYN yun/ of Hyrcania (in the Caucausus). However, Shk did not pronounce the /h/ in this word, so *the* can be attached as /ţhᵞUR KAYN yun/.

51. **cerecloth** /SEER-/ shroud.

51. **obscure** here should be /ŎB skyoor/; US *also* [-skyur].

52. **immur'd** /ih MYOORD/ imprisoned.

65. **glisters** /GLIS turz/ glistens.

Act 2 Scene 8

8. **gondilo** Venetian boat. Archaic variant of **gondola**, both pronounced /GŎN duh luh/ (final *-o* could be /-uh/- or /-oh/).

44. **ostents** here should be /ŏ STENTS/ shows.

Act 2 Scene 9

6. *__nuptial__ wedding. US, UK /NUP chł/ [-shł]; in CN both are used equally.

28. **martlet** /MART lit/ a bird, the martin.

61. **distinct** here 1st syllable stress is indicated.

68. ***iwis** /ih WISS/; US, CN *also* /ee WISS/ indeed.

78. ***wroth** anger. US /raw~~th~~/; CN /raw~~th~~/ [roh~~th~~]; UK /rŏ~~th~~/ [roh~~th~~], *rarely* [raw~~th~~].

82. **heresy** /HĔR ih see/ dissent from the dominant thinking.

Act 3 Scene 1

1, 46. **Rialto** /ree AL toh/ is older, /ree AHL toh/ is newer based on Ital.

3. **lading** /LAYD ing/ cargo.

11. **prolixity** /proh LIK sih tee/ long-windedness.

42. **Rhenish** /REN ish/ Rhine wine.

44 ***bankrout** /BANK rowt/ [-rut] archaic variant of **bankrupt**.

48. **usurer** /YOO zhur ur/; UK *also* [-zhyoor ur, -zhoor ur] someone who lends money for interest.

79-108. **Genoa** /JEN oh uh/.

83. **diamond** in this prose passage may be either /DĪ uh mund/ or US *also* /DĪ mund/.

84. **Frankford** /FRANK furd/ archaic variant of **Frankfurt** /FRANK furt/.

100. **argosy** /ARG uh see/ large merchant ship.

113. ***divers** various. US, CN /DĪ vurss, -vurz/ [dī-, dih VURSS]; UK /DĪ vurss/ [-vurz, dī VURSS].

121. **turkis** (*Turkies* Q1, Q2, F1) /TUR kiss/ archaic variant of **turquoise** US /TUR kwoyz/ [-koyz]; UK /TUR kwoyz/ [-kwahz].

121. **Leah** /LEE uh/.

ă-bat, ăir-**marry**, air-**pair**, ạr-**far**, ĕr-**merry**, ĝ- **get**, ī-**high**, ĭr-**mirror**, ł-**little**, ṇ-**listen**, ŏ-**hot**, oh-**go**, o͞o-**wood**, o͞o-**moon**, oor-**tour**, ōr- **or**, ow-**how**, t͟h-**that**, ~~th~~-**thin**, ŭ-**but**, UR-**fur**, ur-**under**.   ( ) - suppress the syllable   see p. xiii for complete list.

126. **fortnight** /FORT nīt/; US *also* [FORT nit] two weeks. Virtually obsolete in the US.

Act 3 Scene 2

14. *****Beshrow** /bih-, bee SHROH/ curse. Archaic variant of **beshrew** /-SHR$\overline{OO}$/.

22. *****peize, peise** weigh down. US /peez/, *sometimes* [payz]; UK /peez, payz/. Dialect evidence shows that /ee/ was the form found in southern Eng., and /ay/ in the North. Some eds. prefer **piece** 'extend.'

23. *****eche** US /eech/ [etch]; UK /etch/ [eech]. Elsewhere it rhymes with *speech.* Some eds. prefer **eke** /eek/. Both mean 'increase.'

51. **dulcet** /DULL sit/ sweet.

55. **Alcides** /al SĪ deez/ Hercules.

58. **Dardanian** /dar DAYN yun/ Trojan.

60. **th' exploit** here should be /th^y ek SPLOYT/.

93. **gambols** /GAM błz/ frolics.

96. **sepulchre** /SEP ł kur/ tomb.

111. **allay** /uh LAY/ diminish.

112. **excess** here should be /ek SESS/, the most common UK form.

115. *****demigod** half-god. /DEM ee gŏd, DEM ih-/; US *also* /-gawd/.

173. *****presage** here should be /pree-, prih SAYJ/ foretell.

243. *****shrowd** /shrohd/ harsh, wicked. Archaic variant of **shrewd**.

243. **contents** here should be /cŏn TENTS/.

269. **Barbary** /BAR buh ree/ region in North Africa.

280. **magnificoes** /mag NIF ih kohz/ important people.

285. **Chus** /kŭss, kŏŏss, chŏŏz, kŏŏz/ have all been suggested.
Recommendation: /kŏŏss/ or **Cush** /kŭsh/, in order to avoid a homonym with *cuss*.

302. *****through** here should be 2 syllables /th^{uh} rŏŏ/. Some eds. prefer **thorough,** often used when the meter demands 2 syllables, pronounced as *thorough.*

Act 3 Scene 3

2. *****gratis** at no cost. US, UK /GRAHT iss/ [GRAT-], UK *rarely* [GRAYT-]; CN /GRAT-/ [GRAHT-].

Act 3 Scene 4

13. **egall** /EE gł/ archaic variant of **equal.**

15. **lineaments** /LIN yuh munts/ distinctive features.

53. **traject** (*Tranect* Q1,2, F1) /TRAJ ikt, -ekt/ ferry crossing.

63. **accoutered** /uh CŌŌT urd/ clothed.

Act 3 Scene 5

16. *****Scylla** /SILL uh/, restored Lat. [SKILL uh] a sea monster.

17. **Charybdis** /kuh RIB dis/ a whirlpool.

22. **enow** /ih NOW/; US *also* /ee-/ enough.

29. **jealious** (Q1) /JEL yus/ archaic variant of Q2's, F1's **jealous.**

39, 40. *****Moor** /moor/ [mor] black woman.

Act 4 Scene 1

8. *****obdurate** unmoveable. Here should be /ŏb-, ub DYOOR it/; US *also* /-DYUR-/ [-DUR-]. 1st syllable stress is more usual today.

ă-bat, ăir-**marry**, air-**pair**, a̦r-**far**, ĕr-**merry**, ĝ- **get**, ī-**high**, ĭr-**mirror**, ł-**little**, n̦-**listen**, ŏ-**hot**, oh-**go**, ŏŏ-**wood**, ōō-**moon**, oor-**tour**, ōr- **or**, ow-**how**, țh-**that**, t̶h̶-**thin**, ŭ-**but**, UR-**fur**, ur-**under**.　　　( ) - suppress the syllable　　　see p. xiii for complete list.

25. **humane** here should be /HYOO mayn/; US *sometimes* [YOO mayn]. Some eds. prefer **human**.

26. **moi'ty, moiety** /MOY tee/ portion.

29. **Enow** /ih NOW/; US *also* /ee-/ enough.

30. **commiseration** /kuh miz ur RAY shun/ pity.

32. **Tartars** /TAR turz/ fierce people of Central Asia.

36. **Sabaoth** (Q1) 'armies' commonly confused with Q2's, F1's **Sabbath**. In any case it should be pronounced with two syllables /SAB uth/.

46. **ban'd** /baynd/ poisoned.

92. **abject** /AB ject/ contemptible.

92. **slavish** /SLAY vish/ like a slave.

97. **viands** /VĪ undz/ food.   /VEE undz/ not recommended.

122. *****bankrout** /BANK rowt/ [-rut] archaic variant of **bankrupt.**

128. **inexecrable** (Q1, F1) /in EKS uh cruh bł/ something that cannot be cursed enough. Some eds. prefer F3's **inexorable** /in EK sur uh bł/; US *also* /-EG zur-/ unyielding.

131. *****Pythagoras** US /pih THAG uh rus/ [pī-]; UK /pī-/ Gk. philosopher.

160. *****importunity** /im por-, im pur TYOON ih tee/; US *also* /-TOON-/ insistent requests.

173. **throughly** archaic variant of *thoroughly.* /THROO lee/ is the normal pronunciation on stage, but to enhance clarity a syncopated form of the modern pronunciation may be used: *thor'ghly.*

179. **impugn** /im PYOON/ oppose.

220. *****precedent** /PRESS ih dunt/.

235. **tenure** archaic variant of **tenor**, both /TEN ur/.

296. **Barrabas** (F1) here should be /BĂIR uh bus/. The mod. form is **Barabbas** /buh RAB us/. Criminal at the time of Jesus' crucifixion.

298. **pursue** here with 1st syllable stress.

311, 332. **confiscate** /CŎN fiss kayt, -ut/ confiscated.

379. ***gratis** at no cost. US, UK /GRAHT iss/ [GRAT-], UK *rarely* [GRAYT-]; CN /GRAT-/ [GRAHT-].

410 ***lieu** US, CN /lōō, lyōō/; UK /lyōō/ [lōō] return.

444. **'scuse** /skyōōss/ excuse.

451. **commandement, commandment** here an archaic form in 4 syllables is indicated /-uh munt/.

Act 5 Scene 1

7. **Thisby, Thisbe** /THIZ bee/ she secretly met with her lover, Pyramus.

10. **Dido** /DĪ doh/ Queen of Carthage.

11. ***waft** beckoned. US, CN /wŏft/; SOUTH. US /wăft/; UK /wŏft/ [wăft, wahft]. /wăft/ is newer and considered non-standard by many.

12. **Carthage** /CAR thij/ ancient city in N. Africa.

13. **Medea** /mih DEE uh/ enchantress who helped Jason.

14. **Aeson** Jason's father. /EE sun, -sṇ/, but /-ŏn/ is becoming more common. See App. D *-on*.

16. **unthrift** here should be /UN thrift/ wasteful.

21. ***shrow** /shroh/ archaic variant of **shrew**, which here should rhyme with *so*.

39-44. **Sola!** /soh LAH/ a call to attract attention.

43. **hollowing** /HŎL uh wing/, /huh LOH ing/ calling. Variant of **hollering** which some eds. prefer.

59. **patens** /PAT ṇz, -inz/ plates, i.e., the stars.

ă-bat, ăir-marry, air-pair, ạr-far, ĕr-merry, ĝ- get, ī-high, ĭr-mirror, ł-little, ṇ-listen,
ŏ-hot, oh-go, ōō-wood, ōō-moon, oor-tour, ōr- or, ow-how, ţh-that, th-thin, ŭ-but,
UR-fur, ur-under.   ( ) - suppress the syllable   see p. xiii for complete list.

62. **quiring** archaic variant of **choiring**, both pronounced /KWĪR ing/.

62. ***cherubins** angels. US, CN /CHĔR uh binz/ [-yuh-]; UK uses both equally. /KĔR-/ not recommended.

64. **vesture** /VES chur/ covering. See App. D -*ure*.

80. ***Orpheus** here should be 2 syllables /OR fyus/ [-fyo͞oss]. See App. D -*eus*.

85. **stratagems** /STRAT uh jumz/ schemes.

87. **Erebus** /ĔR ih bus/ hell.

109. **Endymion** /en DIM ee un/ a shepherd loved by the moon. Sometimes newer /-ŏn/ is used, but is not recommended.

127. **Antipodes** /an TIP uh deez/ the opposite side of the world.

147. **paltry** /PAWL tree/ worthless.

175. **too unkind** here should be /twun KĪND/.

230. **Argus** /ARG us/ 100-eyed monster of Gk. mythology.

254. ***surety** guarantee, bail. Here should be two syllables, though in mod. English, three syllables are more common, /SHUR (ih) tee, SHOOR-, SHOR-/ (see App. D).

262. **In *lieu of** US, CN /lo͞o, lyo͞o/; UK /lyo͞o/ [lo͞o] in return for.

276. **argosies** /ARG uh seez/ large merchant ships.

298, 300. **inter'gatories, -y** /in TUR guh tree(z)/ questions under oath.

The Merry Wives of Windsor

People in the Play

Bardolph /BAR dŏlf/; US *also* /-dawlf/.

*Doctor Caius US /KAY us/ [KĪ us]; CN /KĪ us/ [KAY us, keez];
UK /KĪ us, KAY us/ [keez]. /KĪ ōōs/ is Class.Lat., /KAY us/ is Ang.Lat.
/keez/ is another angl. form sometimes used. It should be two syllables in the
only verse instance 4.6.28. Note the difference reported in the Survey between
this name and *Caius* in the Roman plays.

mine host de Jarteer /mīn OHST duh zhahr teer/. Dr. Caius' Fr.-accent
version of the **host of the Garter** (Fr. *jarretière* /zhahr tyĕr/).

Falstaff US /FAWL stăff/; E. NEW ENG., UK /-stahff/.

Fenton /FENT un, -ṇ/.

Herne /hurn/. The ghostly hunter, mentioned throughout.

Nym /nim/. Some eds. prefer **Nim**.

Places in the Play

Eton /EET un, -ṇ/.

Notes on Dr. Caius' French accent

The French of Dr. Caius, as well as his pronunciation of English words, is best
learned from a native French speaker. Shakespeare indicates the French accent
with the following spelling substitutions $w \Rightarrow v$, *th* $\Rightarrow$ *t* or *d*, *ch* $\Rightarrow$ *sh*, and the
addition of an extra syllable *-a* after some consonants: *peace-a, speak-a*. Today
Fr. speakers would not be likely to change /w/ to /v/, but would instead use /ōō/
(*where* would be /ōō AIR/).

ă-bat, ăir-**marry**, air-**pair**, ạr-**far**, ĕr-**merry**, ĝ- **get**, ī-**high**, ĭr-**mirror**, ł-**little**, ṇ-**listen**,
ŏ-**hot**, oh-**go**, ōō-**wood**, ōō-**moon**, oor-**tour**, ōr- **or**, ow-**how**, ţh-**that**, th-**thin**, ŭ-**but**,
UR-**fur**, ur-**under**.   ( ) - suppress the syllable   see p. xiii for complete list.

Notes on Evans' Welsh accent

Shk indicates the Welsh accent with the following spelling substitutions: $k \Rightarrow g$ (knock⇒knog), $d \Rightarrow t$ (God⇒Got), $b \Rightarrow p$ (by⇒py), $v \Rightarrow f$, and $\dot{f} \Rightarrow v$. The reader should bear in mind that these substitutions are in no way sufficient to represent a true Welsh accent, which is best learned by listening to a native speaker. Seeing *by* spelled *py* does not mean the reader should simply use the English sound in *pie*. In Welsh /b, d, g/ may sometimes sound somewhat like /p, t, k/, but without the accompanying puff of air that characterizes /p, t, k/ in both Welsh and English. One way to think of it is, that in Welsh /b, d, g/ are half-way between the sounds of Eng. /p, t, k/ and Eng. /b, d, g/.

The *f -v* confusion should be ignored. The Welsh have the /v/ sound, but many English speakers believe they substitute /f/ because in written Welsh the letter *f* stands for /v/ (*Dafydd* /DAH viṯh/ 'David').

Shk's omission of the initial *w* in *woman, world* and *work,* is a widespread Welsh feature. Also a feature of North Wales is the lack of /z/ and /zh/ which are pronounced /ss/ and /sh/.

Act 1 Scene 1

5. **Gloucester**/GLŎS tur/; US *also* /GLAWSS-/.

6. **Coram** /COR um/ Slender's pronunciation of *quorum,* 'a justice.'

7. **Custa-lorum** /cuss tuh LOR um/ Shallow means *custus rotulorum* /CUSS tus roht uh LOR um/, principal justice in the county.

8. **Rato-lorum** /rayt-, rat uh LOR um/ Slender means *rotulorum,* see line 7.

10-11. **Armigero** /ạr MIJ ur oh, ạr mih JEER oh, -JAIR oh/ esquire, one entitled to a coat of arms.

16. **luces** /L$\overline{OO}$S iz/ pike fish (for /ly$\overline{oo}$-/ see App. D *lu-*).

20. **passant** US /PĂSS ṇt/; UK /PAHSS ṇt/ Evans either means 'passing, exceedingly' or a heraldic term *passant* 'walking.'

28. **py'r lady** Evans' Welsh version of **by'r lady** /bīr-, bur LAY dee/ by Our Lady, a mild oath. F1's **per-lady** pronounced the same way.

33. **compremises** variant of **compromises**, both /CŎM pruh mīz iz/.

39. **vizaments, 'visaments** /VĪ zuh munts/ Evans' version of *advisements* 'considerations.'

44, 77. *peradventure(s) perhaps. /PUR ad VEN chur/;
US *rarely* [PĔR-, PUR ad ven chur];
UK, CN *also* [PUR-, PĔR ad ven chur, pĕr ad VEN chur].

90. Cotsall /CŎTS ł/ local pronunciation of the Cotswold hills in
Gloucestershire /CŎTS wohld/ [CŎTS ohld, -włd/.

107. saith says. US /SAY i̶t̶h̶/, *rarely* [se̶t̶h̶]; UK /se̶t̶h̶/ [sayt̶h̶, SAY i̶t̶h̶]. The
older form is /se̶t̶h̶/.

> 120, 132. Pauca verba 'few words,' i.e., 'enough has been said.'
> Ang.Lat. /PAW kuh VUR buh/; Class.Lat. /POW kah WĔR bah/; /VĔR bah/ is
> also used based on Church Latin.

120-1. worts Evans says *words* with Welsh accent /wurts/. Falstaff puns on
worts /wurts/ vegetables.

124. *cony-catching rabbit catching, i.e., deceitful. /KOH nee/, *rarely older*
[KUN ee].

128. Banbury US /BAN bĕr ee/; UK /-bur ee, -bree/.

130. Mephostophilus /mef uh STŎF ih lus/ Pistol's version of Mephistopholes
/mef ih STŎF uh leez/ the devil.

138, 139. *fid̶e̶l̶i̶c̶e̶t̶ Evans' version of *vid̶e̶l̶i̶c̶e̶t̶ namely (abbreviated *viz*.). /f/
would not normally be substituted for /v/ in Welsh, see above, "Notes on Evans'
Welsh accent." The older, anglicized pronunciations are US /vih DELL ih sit/
[-DEEL-, vī-]; UK /vih DEEL ih sit/ [vī-, -DELL-]. Newer pronunciations mix
in restored Latin syllables, for example, /-ket/ or /-DAYL-/. These are not
recommended.

157. two pence /TUP unss, -n̩ss/.

157. Yead, Yed /yed/ 'Ed' in Gloucestershire dialect.

162. latten /LAT n̩/ soft, brass-like metal.

163. labras angl. /LAB ruz/; Ital. /LAH brahss/ lips.

166. avis'd /uh VĪZD/ archaic variant of advised.

> ă-bat, äir-marry, air-pair, a̧r-far, ĕr-merry, ĝ- get, ī-high, ĭr-mirror, ł-little, n̩-listen,
> ŏ-hot, oh-go, o͞o-wood, o͞o-moon, oor-tour, ōr- or, ow-how, t̞h-that, t̶h̶-thin, ŭ-but,
> UR-fur, ur-under.   ( ) - suppress the syllable   see p. xiii for complete list.

195. *pasty meat pie. US /PĂSS tee, PAYSS-/; UK /PĂSS tee/ [PAYSS-].
/PAYSS-/ is newer.

204. *All-hallowmas US /awl HAL oh muss, -HŎL-/ [-măss];
UK /-măss/ [-muss] Nov. 1. The older form is /-muss/.

205. fortnight /FORT nīt/; US *also* [FORT nit] two weeks. Virtually obsolete in
the US.

205. Michaelmas /MIK ł mus/ Sept. 29.

229. *divers various. US, CN /DĪ vurss, -vurz/ [dī-, dih VURSS];
UK /DĪ vurss/ [-vurz, dī VURSS].

236. possitable, positible /PŎSS ih tuh bł/ Evans' version of *positively.*

252-4. dissolutely /DIS uh lōōt lee/ Evans means *resolutely* (for /lyōō-/ see
App. D *lu-*).

284. veneys /VEN eez/ bouts. Variant of venues /VEN yōōz/.

Act 1 Scene 3

9. Keiser /KĪ zur/ emperor. Some eds. prefer Kaiser, pronounced the same
way.

10. Pheazar /FEEZ ur/ perhaps the Host's version of *vizier.* Some eds. prefer
Feezer, Pheezer, pronounced the same way, from *feeze* 'to settle someone's
hash.'

11. Hector /HEK tur/. See App. D -*or.*

29. foh indicates an expression of disgust made with the lips /pff/! or /pfuh/!
Sometimes vocalized as /foh/ or *faugh* /faw/.

30. fico /FEE koh/ Ital. 'fig.' An obscene gesture.

33. *cony-catch rabbit catch, i.e., trick. /KOH nee/, *rarely older* [KUN ee].

61. *iliads (*illiads* F1) /ILL ee udz/ ogling. Variant of *oeillades
US, CN /ILL ee udz/ [uh YAHDZ]; CN *also* /AY lee udz/; UK as in
Fr. /uh YAHDZ/, *rarely* [ILL ee udz]. Q1-2 have eyes. Some actors use
eyelids as a substitute.

69. **Guiana** US /ĝee ANN uh, -AHN uh/; UK /ĝee AHN uh/ [-ANN-, ĝī-] in S.America.

71. ***exchequers** /eks CHEK urz/; US *rarely* [EKS chek urz] treasuries.

75. **Sir Pandarus** /PAN duh rus/ a pimp.

80. **pinnace** /PIN uss/ light sailing ship.

81. **avaunt** /uh VAWNT/ begone!

85. **fullam** loaded dice. Some eds. prefer **fulham** both pronounced /FỤLL um/.

88. **Phrygian Turk** /FRIJ un, -yun/ scoundrel. Normal development would favor the former.

96. **eke** /eek/ also.

104. **malecontents** discontented persons. Archaic variant of ***malcontents**. Both pronounced /MAL cun tents/; CN, UK *rarely* [mal cun TENTS].

Act 1 Scene 4

8. **posset** /PŎSS it/ spiced milk drink.

45. **une boîte en verd** /ün BWAHT ahⁿ VĔR/ a green box. Some eds. prefer **vert** instead of *verd* (both pronounced the same) or **un boîtier** /aⁿ bwah tyay/ a surgeon's box. Some also delete **en** which is better French.

51. **Fe** /fay/ an exclamation. It could also be interpreted as a sputtering series of /f/s.

51-2. ma foi,   il fait fort chaud. O, je   m'en vois
       /mah FWAH, eel fay for SHOH. oh, zhuh mahⁿ VWAH
       By my faith, it's extremely hot.   Oh, I'm going

       à la cour— la grande   affaire
       ah lah KOOR— lah GRAHND ah FĔR/
       to the court— the great business.

Some eds. prefer **vais** /vay/ 'going' or **vais voir** /vay vwahr/ 'going to see' instead of **vois**, which is surely an error.

ă-bat, ăir-**marry**, air-**pair**, ạr-**far**, ĕr-**merry**, ĝ- **get**, ī-**high**, ĭr-**mirror**, ł-**little**, ṇ-**listen**, ŏ-**hot**, oh-**go**, o͞o-**wood**, o͞o-**moon**, oor-**tour**, ôr- **or**, ow-**how**, ɫh-**that**, ᵺ-**thin**, ŭ-**but**, UR-**fur**, ur-**under**.   ( ) - suppress the syllable   see p. xiii for complete list.

54.   **Oui, mette le au mon   pocket,   dépêche.**
           /wee, met   luh oh moh^n / (*pocket* is English), /day PESH/
           yes, put it in my pocket, hurry.
Some eds. change **au** to **à** /ah/ and in addition have:
           Mettez- le   à ma pochette
           /MET tay luh ah mah pŏ shet/
           put it in my little pocket.
Some prefer the familiar form **Mets-le** /MAY luh/ instead of formal *Mettez-le.*

63. **Qu'ai-je oublie˙** What have I forgotten? Some eds. prefer **j'oublié**, both
/kay zhoo blee AY/.

67. **O diable!** /dee AH bl^{uh}/ the devil!

68. **laroon.** This is the Fr. word **larron** /lah roh^n/ 'robber.' The angl. form
would be /luh ROON/, but Caius is probably speaking Fr. here.

87. **baillez** Fr. /bah yay/ give. The *Complete Oxford* gives the familiar form
baile, which should be *baille* /bī^y/. The difficulty with *baille* is that audiences
will perceive it as Eng. *buy* in this context.

90. **throughly** archaic variant of *thoroughly.* /T̶H̶ROO lee/ is the normal
pronunciation on stage, but to enhance clarity a syncopated form of the modern
pronunciation may be used: *thor'ghly.*

100. **avis'd** /uh VĪZD/ archaic variant of **advised.**

107, 109. **jack'nape, jack-a-nape** /JACK (uh) nayp/ monkey, impertinent
fellow.

121. **what the good-jer** (*good-ier* F1) an oath derived from **what the good-
year**, which some eds. prefer. The F1 spelling may indicate it was reduced to
/GooD yur/, or as *Riverside* indicates /-jur, -jeer/ (cf. *soldier*).

132. ***trow** US, CN /troh, trow/; UK /trow/ [troh] wonder. Shk's rhymes
elsewhere indicate /-oh/.

154. **allicholy** US /AL ih cŏl ee/; UK /-cuh lee/ Mrs. Quickly's version of
melancholy.

Act 2 Scene 1

5. **precisian** /pree-, prih SIZH un/ strict spiritual guide. **Physician** has also been
suggested, as well as **precision.**

20. **Herod** /HĔR ud/ ranting villain in period plays.

25. **assay** /uh-, ass SAY/ attempt, test.

64. ***trow** US, CN /troh, trow/; UK /trow/ [troh] wonder. Shk's rhymes elsewhere indicate /-oh/.

80. **Pelion** /PEE lee un/ mountain in NE Greece. Sometimes newer /-ŏn/ is used, but is not recommended.

81. **lascivious** /luh SIV ee us/ lustful.

99. **chariness** /CHAIR ee ness/; E.COAST US *also* /CHĂIR-/ integrity.

103. **good man**. Some eds. prefer **goodman** /Go͞oD mun/ husband.

110. **curtal dog** /CURT ł/ dog with tail cut short.

115. **gallimaufry** /gal ih MAW free/ stew, hodgepodge, i.e. assortment.

115. **Perpend** /pur PEND/ consider.

118. ***Actaeon** hunter turned into a stag. Traditionally stressed on the second syllable US /ak TEE ŏn/ [-un]; UK /-un, -ŏn/. Normal development would favor /-un/. In this prose passage /AK tee ŏn/ may also be used, which is the most common US form today, also used in CN and the UK. See App. D *-on*.

134. **avouch** /uh VOWCH/ affirm.

144. **Cataian** /cat-, cuh TAY un/ scoundrel. Variant of **Cathayan** /cath͟ -, cuh ~~THAY~~ un/.

159. **paltry** /PAWL tree/ worthless.

194, 198. **Cavaleiro, Cavaliero** (*Caueleiro* F1*)* /kav uh LEER oh/. **Cavalera** (Q1-2) /kav uh LEER uh/ invented word for 'gentleman.'

220. **An-heires** (F1) uncertain. Most eds. prefer **Mynheers, Mijn'heers** /mīn HEERZ, -HAIRZ/ Dutch 'gentlemen.'

226. **stoccadoes, stoccados** /stuh KAH dohz/ thrusts with a rapier.

ă-bat, ăir-ma**rry**, air-**pair**, a̱r-**far**, ĕr-**merry**, ĝ- g**et**, ī-h**igh**, ĭr-m**irror**, ł-litt**le**, n̪-lis**ten**, ŏ-h**ot**, oh-g**o**, o͝o-w**ood**, o͞o-m**oon**, oor-t**our**, ōr- **or**, ow-h**ow**, t̪h-**that**, t͟h-**thin**, ŭ-b**ut**, UR-**fur**, ur-und**er**.   ( ) - suppress the syllable   see p. xiii for complete list.

Act 2 Scene 2

1. **equipage** /EK wih pij/ stolen goods.

9. **geminy** /JEM ih nee/ pair. Some eds. prefer **gemini** /JEM ih nī/.

16. ***gratis** without gaining something out of it, for free.
US, UK /GRAHT iss/ [GRAT-], UK *rarely* [GRAYT-]; CN /GRAT-/ [GRAHT-].

17. **gibbet** /JIB it/ post from which they hung corpses after hanging.

26. **ensconce** /en SKŎNSS/ to shelter.

68. **alligant, aligant** /AL ih gunt/ Mrs. Quickly's version of *elegant.*

90. **frampold** /FRAM pold, -płd/ disagreeable.

97. **fartuous** /FAR choo us/ *virtuous* in Mrs. Quickly's dialect.

147. **draught** US, CN /drăft/; UK, E.NEW ENG. /drahft/ drink.

153. **via** /VĪ uh/ onward! /VEE uh/ is newer.

159. **drawer** /DRAW ur/ tapster, the person who draws the liquor at a tavern.

197. **but niggardly** /NIG urd lee/ even in the slightest way.

212. ***importun'd** /im POR chund/ urged. See App. D.

265. **jealious** /JEL ee yus/ archaic variant of **jealous.**

272. **wittolly** /WIT ł ee/ cuckolded.

287. ***Epicurean** /ep ih kyŏŏ REE un/, /ep ih KYOOR ee un/;
US *also* /-KYUR-/ seeking the pleasures of the senses.

297. **Amaimon** /uh MAY mun/ a devil. Sometimes newer /-mŏn/ is used. See
App. D -*on.*

297. **Barbason** /BAR buh sŏn, -sun, -sṇ/ a devil. /-ŏn/ is usual in the US,
/-un, -sṇ/ is more common in the UK. See App. D -*on.*

299. **Wittol** /WIT ł/ cuckold.

304. ***aqua-vitae** distilled liquor, e.g., brandy. US /AHK-, AK wuh VEE tī/, *rarely* [-VĪ tee]; CN /AK wuh VEE tī/ [AHK-]; UK /AK wuh VEE tī/ [-VEE tuh]. /AK wuh VĪ tee/ is the oldest surviving form. /-VEE tay/ not recommended.

Act 2 Scene 3

25. ***traverse** shift from side-to-side in fencing. US, CN /truh VURSS/ [TRAV urss]; UK /truh VURSS, TRAV urss/ [TRAV URSS].

26. **puncto** (F1) a fencing thrust. /PUNK toh/ variant of Q's **punto** /PUN toh, P͞o͞oN toh/; Ital. /P͞O͞ON toh/.

27. **montant** /MŎNT unt/ an upward cut in fencing.

28. **Francisco** (F1) /fran SISS koh/, **Francoyes** (Q1-2) (i.e., *Francois*) /fran SWAH/ Frenchman.

29. ***Aesculapius** /es kuh-, es kyuh LAY pyus/; UK *also* /eess-/ Greek god of medicine.

29. **Galien** /GAY lee un/ Gk. doctor. The *-ien* ending could also be simply a spelling variant of the usual form **Galen** /GAY lun/ (cf. *Daniel* syncopated to *Dan'el*).

33. **Castalion** /kass-, kuh STAYL yun/ Host's version of **Castilian** /kass-, kuh STILL yun/ 'cowardly,' or perhaps 'courtier.' *Stale* meant 'urine.'

33. **King-*Urinal** doctor. US /YUR ih nł/ [YOOR-]; UK /YOOR ih nł, yo͞o RĪ nł/.

33. **Hector** /HEK tur/ hero of Troy. See App. D *-or*.

74. **eke** /eek/ also.

74. **Cavaleiro** (F1), **Cavaliero** /kav uh LEER oh/ invented word for 'gentleman.'

ă-bat, äir-m**arry**, air-p**air**, ạr-f**ar**, ĕr-m**erry**, ĝ- g**et**, ī-h**igh**, ĭr-m**irror**, ł-litt**le**, ṇ-list**en**, ŏ-h**ot**, oh-g**o**, o͞o-w**ood**, o͞o-m**oon**, oor-t**our**, ōr- **or**, ow-h**ow**, t̸h-t**hat**, t̶h̶-t**hin**, ŭ-b**ut**, UR-f**ur**, ur-und**er**.   ( ) - suppress the syllable   see p. xiii for complete list.

Act 3 Scene 1

5. **pittie-ward** /PIT ee wurd/ towards the Petty (Little) Park. Some eds. interpret this as **Petty Ward** /PET ee wârd/ (as in war) the Little Park.

5. **park-ward** /PARK wurd/ toward the Park. Some eds. prefer **Park Ward** /wârd/ (as in war) the ward of Windsor Great Park.

11. **Jeshu** (Q) /JEE shoō/ Evans' Welsh accent version of **Jesu** /JEE zoō, -zyoō/ (see p. 35). Omitted F1.

11. **chollors** Evans' version of *choler* 'anger,' which would be /CŎL urss/ with a Welsh accent.

14, 88. *****urinals** vessels to hold urine. US /YUR ih nłz/ [YOOR-]; UK /YOOR ih nłz, yoō RĪ nłz/. **Urinal** (F1) in line 88.

14. **costard** /CŎST urd/ head.

25. **vagram, vagrom** /VAY grum/ Evans' version of **vagrant**.

38. **studient** /STOōD yunt/; UK, SOUTH. US /STYOōD-/. Archaic variant of **student**.

47. **rheumatic** causing colds. /roō MAT ik/ is usual today, but elsewhere in Shk /ROōM uh tik/.

63. **as lief** /leef/ as soon.

65. **Hibocrates, Hibbocrates** Evans' version of **Hippocrates** /hih PŎK ruh teez/ Gk. doctor.

66. **Galen** /GAY lin/ Gk. doctor.

91. **Diable!** /dee AH bl^uh/ the devil!

97. **Gallia** /GAL ee yuh/ France.

97. **Gaul** /gawl/ France. The word should be **Wales**.

101. **politic** /PŎL ih tik/ shrewd.

101. **Machivel** (*Matchavil* Q), (*Machivell* F1) /MATCH uh vil, -vł, -vel/ a cunning, deceitful person. Archaic variant of **Machiavel** /MAK ee uh vel/, /MAHK-/.

117. **vlouting-stog** Evans' Welsh version of **flouting-stock** /FLOWT ing stŏck/ laughing stock. /f/ would not normally be substituted for /v/ in Welsh, see above, "Notes on Evans' Welsh accent."

120. **scall** /skawl/ scurvy creature. Variant of **scald, scalled** /skawld/.

Act 3 Scene 2

43. *****Actaeon** hunter turned into a stag. Traditionally stressed on the second syllable US /ak TEE ŏn/ [-un]; UK /-un, -ŏn/. Normal development would favor /-un/. In this prose passage /AK tee ŏn/ may also be used, which is the most common US form today, also used in CN and the UK. See App. D *-on*.

64. **be-gar** /buh GAR/ by God.

73. **Poins** /poynz/.

Act 3 Scene 3

15-148. **Datchet-mead** /DATCH it MEED/ Datchet meadow.

16. **Thames** /temz/.

22. **eyas-musket** /Ī us muss kit/ young hawk.

41. **pumpion** /PUMP yun/ archaic variant of *pumpkin.*

55. **diamond** in this prose passage may be either /DĪ uh mund/ or US *also* /DĪ mund/.

72. **Bucklersbury** US /BUCK lurz bĕr ee/; UK /-bur ee, -bree/ a street in London.

79. **lime-kill** /LĪM kill/ oven where lime is made from limestone. Some eds. prefer mod. **lime-kiln** now usually pronounced /kiln/, though /kill/ is older.

89. **ensconce** /en SKŎNSS/ take shelter.

90. **arras** /ĂIR us/ tapestry.

130. **stature** /STATCH ur/ size.

ă-bat, äir-**marry**, air-**pair**, a̱r-**far**, ĕr-**merry**, ĝ- g**et**, ī-**high**, ĭr-**mirror**, l̵-**little**, ṇ-**listen**, ŏ-**hot**, oh-**go**, o͞o-**wood**, o͞o-**moon**, oor-**tour**, ōr- **or**, ow-**how**, t̲h-**that**, t̵h̵-**thin**, ŭ-**but**, UR-**fur**, ur-**under**.   ( ) - suppress the syllable   see p. xiii for complete list.

191. **dissolute** /DIS uh lo͞ot/ immoral (for /lyo͞o-/ see App. D *lu-*).

213. **Be-gar** /buh GAR/ by God.

242. **gibes** /jībz/ sarcastic comments.

Act 3 Scene 4

13. **Albeit** /awl BEE (i)t/ although.

24. **'Slid** /zlid/ by God's eyelid.

44. **Gloucestershire** /-shur/ [-sheer].

49. **jointure** /JOYN chur/ marriage settlement. See App. D *-ure*.

108. **speciously** Mrs. Quickly's version of *specially* may be either /SPESH us lee/ or /SPEESH-/.

Act 3 Scene 5

5. **offal** /ŎF ł/; US *also* /AWF ł/ animal guts and remains after butchering.

6-127. **Thames** /temz/.

28. **chalices** /CHAL iss iz/ goblets.

70. **cornuto** /cor NO͞O toh/ Ital. 'horned one, cuckold.'

72. * **'larum** US, CN /LAHR um/ [-LĂIR-]; UK /LĂIR um, LAHR um/ call to arms.

98. **hinds** /hīndz/ menial laborers.

109. **jealious** /JEL yus/ archaic variant of **jealous**.

129. **ambassy** /AM buh see/ an ambassador's message. Archaic variant of **embassy** /EM-/.

146. **halfpenny purse** /HAY puh nee, HAYP nee/ tiny purse.

Act 4 Scene 1

24. **'Od's nouns** /ŏdz NOWNZ/ God's wounds.

27. **Pulcher** Ang.Lat. /PŬL kur/; Class.Lat. /PỤLL kĕr/ beautiful.

28, 29. **Poulcats** (F2), (*Powlcats* F1) /POHL cats/ whores. Archaic variant of **polecats**.

31-7. **lapis** Ang.Lat. /LAY pis/; Class.Lat. /LAHP iss/ stone.

41. **Singulariter** Ang.Lat. /sing gyuh LAIR ih tur/; Class.Lat. /sing gōō LAH rih tĕr/ singular.

41, 42. **nominativo** Ang.Lat. /nŏm ih nuh TĪ voh/; Class.Lat. /noh mih nah TEE woh/ nominative.

41-2. **hic, haec, hoc . . . hig, hag, hog.** They are repeating the forms of 'this' in Latin. The first speaker, William, says /hick, hack, hŏck/ which Evans repeats in his Welsh accent with /k/ sounding somewhat like /g/.

43. **genitivo hujus** (or **huius**) genitive. Ang.Lat. /jen ih TĪ voh/, /HYŌŌ jus/; Class.Lat. /ĝen ih TEE woh/, /HŌŌ yōōs/.

45-47. **Accusativo, hinc . . . hung, hang, hog** Ang.Lat. /uh kyōōz uh TĪ voh/; Class.Lat. /ah kōō sah TEE woh/ accusative. William gets this wrong, saying *hinc* /hink/, rather than *hunc, hanc, hoc.* Evans' Welsh accent again makes the final /k/ sound somewhat like /g/. The confusion is helped by the fact that in some Welsh dialects all words in final *-ng* are pronounced with a full /g/, as in *finger.*

51, 53. **focative** meant to indicate Evans' Welsh-accent version of **vocative** /VŎK uh tiv/.

52. **vocativo** Ang.Lat. /vŏk uh TĪ voh/; Class.Lat. /wŏk uh TEE woh/ vocative.

53. **caret** Ang.Lat. /KAIR et/; Class.Lat. /KAHR et/ is lacking, i.e., there is no vocative case of 'this.'

57, 59. **genitive** /JEN ih tiv/.

ă-bat, ăir-m**a**rry, air-**pair**, ạr-**far**, ĕr-**merry**, ĝ- g**e**t, ī-h**igh**, ĭr-m**i**rror, ł-l**i**ttle, ṇ-l**i**st**e**n, ŏ-h**o**t, oh-g**o**, ōō-w**oo**d, ōō-m**oo**n, oor-t**our**, ōr- **or**, ow-h**ow**, ţh-t**h**at, ŧh-**th**in, ʊ-b**u**t, UR-f**ur**, ur-und**er**.   ( ) - suppress the syllable   see p. xiii for complete list.

61. Genitivo, horum, harum, horum Ang.Lat. /jen ih TĪ voh, HOR um, HAIR um/; Class.Lat. /ĝen ih TEE woh, HOR ōōm, HAH rōōm/.   F1 has **Genitive** /JEN ih tiv/.

77-8. qui, quae, quod the forms for 'who, which.' Evans apparently does not use initial /kw-/ and uses the continental pronunciation /kee, kay, kŏd/, giving rise to the puns for **qui's, quae's, quod's** /keess, kayss, kŏdss/ as *keys, case* 'female genitals,' *cods* 'male genitals' (in Welsh the final /z/ is /s/). Ang.Lat. would be /kwī, kwee, kwŏd/. Some eds. prefer **que** instead of *quae,* pronounced the same in Ang.Lat.

79. preeches Evans' Welsh-accent version of *breeches meaning that William will be whipped. /BRITCH iz/ is traditional, /BREECH iz/ is newer. The former pronunciation is more common in the UK, and the latter in the US, CN.

82. sprag Evans' Welsh-accent version of **sprack** /sprack/ lively.

Act 4 Scene 2

2. obsequious /ub-, ŏb SEE kwee us/ dutiful.

5. accoustrement, accustrement (F1) /uh CUSS tur munt/ characteristics. Archaic variant of **accoutrement** /uh CŌŌT ruh munt, uh CŌŌT ur munt/.

22. lines (F1), Some eds. prefer **lunes** /lōōnz/ fits of madness (for /lyōō-/ see App. D, *lu-*). Q1-2 have *vaine.*

25. buffets /BUFF its/ strikes.

58. kill-hole oven hole. Some eds. prefer **kiln hole** now usually pronounced /kiln/, though /kill/ is older.

62. abstract /AB stract/ list.

107. draff /drăf/ pig swill. F1's **draugh** pronounced the same way. The standard pronunciation in the UK is also with /ă/, but here it rhymes with *laugh* (UK /ah/).

113. lief as /leef/ as soon.

118. ging /ĝing/ archaic variant of **gang**.

131. jealious /JEL ee yus/ archaic variant of **jealous**.

135. brazen-face /BRAY zun-, -zṇ-/ audacious woman.

164. *leman sweetheart. US /LEE mun/ [LEM un, LAY mun];
CN /LAY mun/ [LEM un, LEE mun]; UK /LEM-/ [LEE mun],
rarely [LAY mun]. /LAY mun/ is newer and not recommended.

172. quean /kween/ ill-behaved woman.

185. poulcat /POHL cat/ whore. Archaic variant of polecat.

185. runnion, runyon /RUN yun/ scabby creature.

Act 4 Scene 4

9. heretic /HĔR ih tik/ someone who believes in something contrary to
established opinion.

11. extreme here should be /EK streem/.

30. midnight here with 2nd syllable stress.

33. milch-kine /MILCH kīn/ milk cows.

50. *ouphes /o͞ofs/, *rarely* [owfs] elves. Some eds. prefer oafs.

51, 63. tapers /TAY purz/ slender candles.

69. taber Evans' version of *taper* /TAY pur/ candle.

70. *vizards /VIZ urdz/ masks. /-ardz/ not recommended. Some eds. prefer
vizors /VĪ zurz/.

Act 4 Scene 5

1. *boor US, CN /bo͞or/ [bor]; UK /bo͞or, bor/ peasant.

9. Anthropophaginian /an throh pŏf uh JIN ee un/ cannibal.

18. *Ephesian /ih-, ee FEEZH un/; *sometimes newer* /-ee un/ old buddy.

20. Bohemian-Tartar /boh HEEM ee yun TAR tur/ wild man.

ă-bat, ăir-marry, air-pair, a̧r-far, ĕr-merry, ĝ- get, ī-high, ĭr-mirror, ł-little, n̦-listen,
ŏ-hot, oh-go, o͞o-wood, o͞o-moon, oor-tour, ōr- or, ow-how, țh-that, th-thin, Ŭ-but,
UR-fur, ur-under.   ( ) - suppress the syllable   see p. xiii for complete list.

31. **thorough** archaic variant of *through*, used when the meter demands two syllables, and pronounced as mod. *thorough*.   In this prose passage *through* may be used.

65. **varletto** /vahr LET oh/ knave.

68. ***slough** bog. US, UK rhymes with *now*; US *also* [slo͞o]; CN /slo͞o/ [or rhymes with *now*].

70. **Faustuses** angl. /FAWSS tus iz/; based on Germ. *Faustus* /FOWSS to͞os/ scholar-magician of Germany.

77. **cozen-germans** (F1) /KUZ ṇ JUR munz/ deceiving Germans, with pun on *cousin german* 'close relative.' Some eds. prefer Q1-2's **cozen-garmombles** /GAR mŏm błz, -mum błz/ which may refer to Count Mömpelgard of Germany.

78. **Readins** /RED ṇz/ earlier form of **Reading** /RED ing/.

80. **gibes** /jībz/ sarcastic comments.

80. **vlouting-stocks** Evans' Welsh version of **flouting-stock** /FLOWT ing stŏck/ laughing stock. /f/ would not normally be substituted for /v/ in Welsh, see above, "Notes on Evans' Welsh accent."

102. **primero** a card game. /prih MEER oh/ is older, /prih MAIR oh/ newer.

111. **speciously** Mrs. Quickly's version of *specially* may be either /SPESH us lee/ or /SPEESH-/.

Act 4 Scene 6

13. **contents** here should be /cŏn TENTS/.

40. ***vizarded** /VIZ urd id/ masks. /-ạrd-/ not recommended. Some eds. prefer **visored** /VĪ zur id/.

42. **ribands** /RIB undz/ archaic variant of **ribbons**.

Act 5 Scene 1

22. **Goliah** /guh LĪ uh/ archaic variant of **Goliath** /guh LĪ uth/.

Act 5 Scene 5

3. **Europa** /yoor ROH puh/; US *also* /yur-/.

7. **Leda** /LEE duh/.

7. **omnipotent** /ŏm NIP uh tunt/ all-powerful.

20. **kissing-comfits** /CUM fits/ [CŎM fits] perfumed candies.

20. **eringoes** /ur RING gohz/ candied roots of sea-holly, an aphrodisiac.

41. ***Oyes, oyez** hear ye. Here should be stressed on the first syllable
/OH yez/ [-yay]; UK *also* [-yes].

42. **aery, airy** /AIR ee/ of the air.

49. **Bede** (F1), **Bead** both pronounced /beed/ (Q1-2 have *Pead,* Evans' Welsh-
accent version).

57. ***ouphes** /o͞ofs/, *rarely* [owfs] elves. Some eds. prefer **oafs**.

64. **blazon** /BLAY zun, -zn̩/ description of a coat of arms.

69. **Honi soit qui mal y pense** Fr. /oh nee swah kee mahl ee pah^{n}ss/ shame to
him who thinks evil of this. Mrs. Quickly pronounces *pense* with 2 syllables,
perhaps /PAH^N SS uh/, or angl. /PEN see/. She would very likely anglicize or
mangle the entire phrase.

73. **charactery** /kuh RAK tur ee/ writing.

78. ***lanthorns** archaic variant of **lanterns**. Probably pronounced /LAN turnz/,
but possibly /LANT hornz/ or /LAN ~~thurnz, -thornz~~/.

120. ***extant** in existence. US /EK stunt/ [ek STĂNT]; UK /ek STĂNT/, *rarely*
[EK stunt]; in CN both are used equally.

138. **frieze** /freez/ wool fabric.

153. ***entrails** /EN traylz/; US *also* [-trl̩z] guts.

155. **Sathan** archaic form of **Satan**, both pronounced /SAYT n̩, -un/ the devil.

ă-bat, ăir-**marry**, air-**pair**, ạr-**far**, ĕr-**merry**, ĝ- **get**, ī-**high**, ĭr-**mirror**, l̩-**little**, n̩-**listen**, ŏ-**hot**, oh-**go**, o͞o-**wood**, o͞o-**moon**, oor-**tour**, ōr- **or**, ow-**how**, t̠h-**that**, th-**thin**, ŭ-**but**, UR-**fur**, ur-**under**.   ( ) - suppress the syllable   see p. xiii for complete list.

159. **metheglins** /muh ~~THEG~~ linz/ spiced drinks of Wales.

171. **posset** /PŎSS it/ spiced milk drink, thickened with bread.

180. **Gloucestershire** /-shur/ [-sheer].

185, 186. **swing'd** /swinjd/ beat.

205. **oon garsoon** Caius is saying *one garçon,* i.e., 'a boy.' Some eds. prefer Fr. **un garçon** /ă^n gar soh^n/. Shk uses this spelling because the final Fr. vowel sounds somewhat like /$\overline{oo}$n/ in Eng. An archaic pronunciation of *one* in Shk's time was /ohn/, hence the spelling used here.

206. **oon pesant** (F1). Some eds. prefer Fr. **un paysan** /ă^n pay zah^n/ a peasant.

209. **be-gar** /buh GAR/ by God.

228. **evitate** /EV ih tayt/ avoid.

237. **eschew'd** /es CH$\overline{OO}$D/ avoided.

A Midsummer Night's Dream

People in the Play

Demetrius 3 or 4 syllables depending on meter /dih MEE tr(ee) yus/.

Egeus /ee-, ih JEE yus/.

Helena /HELL in uh/.

Hermia 2 or 3 syllables depending on meter /HUR m(ee) yuh/.

Hippolyta /hih PŎL ih tuh/.

Lysander /lī SAN dur/.

*Oberon /OH bur un/, /-ŏn/. The former is preferred in the UK, and the latter in the US. See App. D -*on*.

Philostrate /FILL uh strayt/.

Pyramus /PĬR uh mus/. In the play performed by Quince and company.

*Theseus 2 or 3 syllables depending on meter /THEE s(ee) yus/ [-syōōss], US *rarely* [-sōōss]. See App. D -*eus*.

Thisby, Thisbe /THIZ bee/. In the play performed by Quince and company.

*Titania 3 or 4 syllables depending on méter. Virtually all combinations of /tī-, tih-, -TAN-, -TAYN-, -TAHN-/ are found in all countries. The most common variants are: US /tih TAHN (ee) yuh, tī TAYN-/; CN /tih TAN (ee) yuh/; UK /tih TAHN (ee) yuh/. On historical principles the best choices are /tih-, tī TAYN ee yuh/.

Places in the Play

Athens /ATH inz/.
  Athenian /uh THEEN (ee) yun/. In verse it is always 3 syllables.

ă-bat, ăir-**marry**, air-**pair**, ạr-**far**, ĕr-**merry**, ĝ- get, ī-high, ĭr-mirror, ł-little, ṇ-listen, ŏ-hot, oh-go, ōō-wood, ōō-moon, oor-**tour**, ōr- or, ow-how, ṯh-that, ŧh-thin, ŭ-but, UR-**fur**, ur-un**der**.   ( ) - suppress the syllable   see p. xiii for complete list.

Act 1 Scene 1

1, 125. ***nuptial** wedding. US, UK /NUP chł/ [-shł]; in CN both afe used equally.

5. **dowager** /DOW uh jur/ widow.

6. **revenue** sometimes in verse /ruh VEN yo͞o/, but here as in mod. Eng.
US /REV in o͞o/; UK, SOUTH. US /-yo͞o/.

33. **gawds, gauds** /gawdz/ trinkets, toys.

65. **abjure** /ab-, ub JOOR/; US *also* /-JUR/ renounce.

71, 90. **aye** /ay/ ever. /ī/ is often used, but not recommended.

71. **mew'd** /myo͞od/ caged.

73. **Chaunting** archaic variant of **chanting** US /CHĂNT ing/;
E. NEW ENG, UK /CHAHNT ing/. See App. D *-aun-*.

80. **patent** US /PAT n̩t/; UK /PAYT n̩t/ [PAT-] privilege.

106. **avouch** /uh VOWCH/ affirm.

107. **Nedar's** /NEE durz/.

137. **misgraffed** mismatched. US /mis GRĂF id/;
E.NEW ENG., UK /mis GRAHF id/ archaic variant of **misgrafted**.

143. **momentany** (Q1) /MOH men tay nee, -tuh nee/ archaic variant of
momentary (F1).

145. **collied** /CŎL eed/ darkened.

151. **edict** decree. Here should be /ee DICT/.

157. **dowager** /DOW uh jur/ widow.

158. **revenue** here should be /ruh VEN yo͞o/.

173. **Carthage queen** /CAR thij/ Dido, ruler of Carthage in N. Africa.

183. **lodestars** /LOHD starz/ guiding stars.

191. **translated** here should be stressed on the 2nd syllable, the normal UK pronunciation. US /trănss LAYT id, trănz-/; UK /trănss-/ [trănz-, trahnz-, trahnss-, trunss-, trunz-].

209. **Phoebe** /FEE bee/ the moon.

212. **flights.** Some eds. prefer **sleights** /slīts/ tricks.

223. **midnight** here with 2nd syllable stress.

242. **eyne** /īn/ dialect form of *eyes*.

Act 1 Scene 2

11. *****lamentable** US /luh MEN tuh bł/ [LAM un tuh bł]; CN, UK /LAM un tuh bł/ [luh MEN-].

27. **condole** /cun DOHL/ grieve.

29, 40. **Ercles', 'erk'les** /URK leez/ Bottom's pronunciation of **Hercules'**.

35. **Phibbus'** /FIB us/ Bottom's pronunciation of **Phoebus'** /FEE bus/ the sun.

41. **condoling** /cun DOHL ing/ pathetic.

52. **Thisne** /THIZ nee/ Bottom's mistake for **Thisbe** /THIZ bee/.

68. **extempore** /ek STEM pur ree/ composed on the spur of the moment.

96, 109. **perfit** /PUR fit/ archaic variant of **perfect**. Also /PAR fit/ in Shk's time.

Act 2 Scene 1

3, 5. **Thorough** archaic variant of *through*, used when the meter demands two syllables. It is often pronounced as *thorough* on stage, but using /-o͞o/ in the final syllable will bring it closer to mod. *through*.

7. **moon's, moonës** here the older genitive /MO͞ON iz/ is indicated.

ă-bat, ăir-**marry**, air-**pair**, ạr-**far**, ĕr-**merry**, ĝ- get, ī-high, ĭr-mirror, ł-little, ṇ-listen, ŏ-hot, oh-go, o͞o-**wood**, o͞o-**moon**, oor-**tour**, ōr- or, ow-how, t̠h-that, t̶h̶-t̶h̶i̶n̶, ŭ-but, UR-**fur**, ur-**under**.   ( ) - suppress the syllable   see p. xiii for complete list.

10, 15. **cowslips** /COW slips/ a yellow flower.

13. **savors** (UK **savours**) /SAY vurz/ smells, perfumes.

20. **wrath.** Some eds. prefer *__wroth__ US /rawth/; CN /rawth/ [rohth]; UK /rŏth/ [rohth], *rarely* [rawth]. Both mean 'angry' here.

23. **changeling** here /CHAYNJ uh ling/ is indicated.

36. **quern** /kwurn/ a type of primitive grinder.

37. *__huswife__ /HUZ if/ is traditional, /HUSS wīf/ is a newer, spelling pronunciation. The former is the most common form in the UK, the latter in the US. In CN both are used equally. In North America /HUSS wif/ is also sometimes used. Some eds. prefer mod. **housewife.**

50. **dewlop** US /DŌŌ lŏp/; UK /DYŌŌ-/ archaic variant of **dewlap** /-lap/ 'loose skin of the throat.'

55. **quire** /kwīr/ archaic variant of **choir.**

55. **loff** /lŏf/ archaic variant of **laugh.**

66. **Corin** US /COR in/; E.COAST US, UK /CŎR in/ a shepherd.

68. **Phillida** /FILL ih duh/ a shepherdess.

71. **buskin'd** /BUSK ind/ wearing knee-length boots.

78. **Perigenia** (Q1), **Peregenia** (F1) /pĕr ih JEEN yuh/. Some eds. substitute *__Perigouna__ /pĕr ih GŌŌ nuh/ [-GOW-].

79. **Aegles** /EEG leez/. Some eds. substitute **Aegle** /EEG lee/, the correct form in Greek.

80. **Ariadne** /air ee AD nee/, E.COAST US *also* /ăir-/. /ăir ee AHD nee/ is a newer, partially restored Gk. pronunciation.

80. **Antiopa** /an TĪ oh puh, -uh puh/.

83. **mead** /meed/ meadow.

85. **margent** /MAR junt/ archaic variant of **margin.**

97. **murrion flock** flock dead of plague. Archaic spelling which may have had the ending /-yun/ or /-un/, but in any case was a variant of **murrain** US, CN /MUR in/; E.COAST US, UK /MUH rin/.

105. **rheumatic diseases** here should be /ROOM uh tik/ referring to colds, coughs, etc.

106. **thorough** archaic variant of *through*, used when the meter demands two syllables. It is often pronounced as *thorough* on stage, but using /-oo/ in the final syllable will bring it closer to mod. *through*.

109. **Hiems'** winter's. Ang.Lat. /HĪ umz/; Class.Lat. /HIH emss/.

110. **chaplet** /CHAP lit/ garland.

112. **childing** /CHĪLD ing/ fruitful.

114. **By their increase** here should be /in CREESS/ by what they produce.

115. **progeny** children. /PRŎJ ih nee/; UK *also* [PROH-], a newer form.

123, 163. **vot'ress** /VOHT riss/ female member of a religious group.

151. **dulcet** /DULL sit/ sweet.

174. **leviathan** /luh VĪ uh thun/ sea monster.

192. **wode within this wood.** *Wode* is a variant of **wood** /wŏōd/ 'furious, mad' which some eds. prefer. It was also /wŏōd, wohd/ in the dialects of North. Eng., and there may be a pun on *wooed within this wood*.

195. **adamant** /AD uh munt/ double meaning: magnet, the hardest substance. /-ant/ not recommended.

231. **Daphne** /DAFF nee/ nymph changed to a laurel tree.

232. **hind** /hīnd/ doe.

249. **I know a bank where the wild *thyme* blows.** Normally /tīm/, but here perhaps scanned as two syllables, /TAH eem/. Alternatively, *where* may be scanned as two syllables in an inverted foot.

ă-bat, ăir-marry, air-pair, ạr-far, ĕr-merry, ĝ- get, ī-high, ĭr-mirror, ḷ-little, ṇ-listen, ŏ-hot, oh-go, ŏō-wood, ōō-moon, oor-tour, ōr- or, ow-how, ṭh-that, t̸h-thin, ŭ-but, UR-fur, ur-under.　　　( ) - suppress the syllable　　　see p. xiii for complete list.

251. **woodbine** here 2nd syllable stress is indicated.

252. ***eglantine** sweet-briar. Here should be /EGG lun tīn/ for the rhyme, though /-teen/ is the most common form in the US and is also used in the UK.

262. **espies** /ess SPĪZ/ sees.

Act 2 Scene 2

1. **roundel** /ROWN dł/ circle dance.

4. **rere-mice** /REER-/ bats.

13, 24. **Philomele** /FILL uh meel, -oh-/ the nightingale. Variant of **Philomel** /-mel/.

30. **ounce** /ownss/ lynx.

57. **humane** courteous. Here should be /HYOO mayn/; US *sometimes* [YOO mayn].

99. **sphery** /SFEER ee/ like a sphere.

99. **eyne** /īn/ dialect form of *eyes*.

139-41. **heresies (-sy)** /HĚR ih seez/ dissent from the dominant thinking.

149. **eat** /et/ dialect variant of **ate**, which is also commonly /et/ in the UK.

150. **sate** archaic variant of **sat**. May have been /sayt/ or /sat/.

Act 3 Scene 1

2. **marvail's** (*maruailes* Q1; *maruailous* Q2, F1) archaic forms of **marvellous** 'marvellously.' Short forms are /MARV łss/ or /MARV luss/, but in this prose section mod. /MARV ł us/ can be used.

13. **By'r lakin** /bīr-, bur LAY kin/ by Our Lady (i.e., Mary).

13. **parlous** /PAR lus/ archaic variant of **perilous** which here would have to be /PĚR (ih) lus/.

79. **toward** /TOH wurd, -urd/ about to take place.

82, 84. **savors** (UK **savours**) /SAY vurz/ smells.

95. **juvenal** /JŌŌ vin ł/ youth. Some eds. substitute **juvenile** US /JŌŌ vin ł, -īl/;
UK /-īl/.

95. **eke** /eek/ also.

98. **Ninus'** /NĪ nus/ founder of Ninevah. Given the pun with *ninny,* Quince and
company probably pronounce it /NIN us/.

125. **woosel** /WŌŌZ ł/ black bird. Variant of **ouzel, ousel** both pronounced
/ŌŌZ ł/.

127. **throstle** /ŦHRŎSS ł/ thrush.

161. **aery** /AIR ee/ of the air. Some eds. prefer **airy**, pronounced the same way.

165. **gambol** /GAM bł/ frolic.

166. **apricocks** /AYP rih cŏcks/; US, CN *also* /AP-/ dialect variant of **apricots**.

168. **humble-bees** pronounced with the same stress as *bumble bees.*

169. **night-tapers** /TAY purz/ slender candles.

187. **Peascod** /PEEZ cŏd/ peapod.

Act 3 Scene 2

7. **close** /clohss/ hidden.

12. *****nuptial** wedding. US, UK /NUP chł/ [-shł]; in CN both are used equally.

21. **russet-pated** /RŬSS it PAY tid/ red-headed.

21. **choughs, chuffs** /chufs/ jackdaws.

32. **translated** transformed. Here should be stressed on the 2nd syllable, the
normal UK pronunciation. US /trănss LAYT id, trănz-/; UK /trănss-/
[trănz-, trahnz-, trahnss-, trunss-, trunz-].

ă-bat, ăir-**marry**, air-**pair**, ạr-**far**, ĕr-**merry**, ĝ- g**et**, ī-h**igh**, ĭr-**mirror**, ł-**little**, ṇ-**listen**,
ŏ-h**ot**, oh-g**o**, ŏŏ-**wood**, ōō-**moon**, oor-**tour**, ōr- **or**, ow-h**ow**, ţh-**that**, ŧh-**thin**, ŭ-b**ut**,
UR-**fur**, ur-**und**er.   ( ) - suppress the syllable   see p. xiii for complete list.

41. **Stand close** /clohss/ keep hidden.

55. **th'Antipodes** /th^{y}an TIP uh deez/ the opposite side of the world.

74. **mispris'd** here should be /MIS prīzd/ mistaken.

85. ***bankrout** /BANK rowt/ [-rut] archaic variant of **bankrupt.**

90. **misprision** /mis PRIZH un, -ṇ/ mistake.

101. **Tartar's** /TAR turz/ people of Central Asia.

105. **espy** /ess SPĪ/ see.

137. **perfect** here may be given its normal pronunciation in an inverted foot /PUR fikt/.

138. **eyne** /īn/ dialect form of *eyes.*

141. **Taurus'** /TOR us/ mountain range in Turkey.

157. **exploit** here should be /ek SPLOYT/.

171. ***sojourn'd** resided temporarily. Here stress should fall on the second syllable. US, CN /soh JURND/; US *rarely* [sŏ-]; UK /sŏ JURND/ [soh-], *rarely* [suh-].

175, 335. **aby** (Q1) /uh BĪ/ to pay for an offence. F1 has *abide.*

187. **engilds** /en ĜILDZ/ covers with gold.

188. **oes** variant spelling of **ohs, O's.**

208. **incorporate** /in COR pur rut, -rayt/ united in body. /-ut / is more usual for an adj.

234. **miserable** here should be /MIZ ur uh bł/.

237. **persever** /pur SEV ur/ persevere.

257. **Ethiop** /EE~~TH~~ yŏp/ Ethiopian.

263. **Tartar** /TAR tur/ member of a Central Asian tribe.

291. **statures** /STATCH urz/ sizes.

329. **minimus** /MIN ih mus/ small creature.

357. **Acheron** /AK ur ŏn, -un/ a river in Hades. /-ŏn/ is usual in the US and is increasingly common in the UK. See App. D -*on*.

380. **Aurora's** /uh ROR uz/; UK *also* [aw-] goddess of dawn.

380. **harbinger** /HAR bin jur/ advance messenger.

387. **aye** /ay/ ever. /ī/ is often used, but not recommended.

387. **consort** /cun SORT/ keep company.

409. **recreant** /REK r(ee) yunt/ coward.

433. **daylight** here with 2nd syllable stress.

Act 4 Scene 1

8-24. **Mounsieur** /mown SEER, MOWN seer/ lower-class variant of **Monsieur**.

12. **humble-bee** pronounced with the same stress as *bumble bee*.

19. **neaf** /neef/ fist.

23. **Cavalery, Cavallery** /kav uh LEER ee/ cavalier, form of address to a fashionable gentleman.

24. **marvail's** (*Maruailes* Q1) archaic form of F1's **marvellous** 'marvellously.' Short forms are /MARV łss/ or /MARV luss/, but in this prose section mod. /MARV ł us/ can be used.

31. **provender** /PRŎV n̩ dur/ dry food for animals.

47. **dotage** /DOHT ij/ blind love for someone.

52. **coronet** small crown. US /COR uh net, -nit/, /cor uh NET/;
E.COAST US /CŎR-, cŏr-/; UK /CŎR uh nit/ [-net, cŏr uh NET].

ă-bat, ăir-**marry**, air-**pair**, a̧r-**far**, ĕr-**merry**, ĝ- **get**, ī-**high**, ĭr-**mirror**, ł-**little**, n̩-**listen**, ŏ-**hot**, oh-**go**, o͞o-**wood**, o͞o-**moon**, oor-**tour**, ōr- **or**, ow-**how**, t̩h-**that**, ~~th~~-**thin**, ŭ-**but**, UR-**fur**, ur-**under**.　　　( ) - suppress the syllable　　see p. xiii for complete list.

55. **flouriets'** may have been /FLOWR yits/, but *-iet* could also be pronounced /-it/ in Shk's day making it the same as **flow'rets'** /FLOWR its/ (cf. *Daniel-Dan'el*).

96. **night's** (Q1), **nightës** here the older genitive /NĪT iz/ is indicated.   F1 has **the night's.**

105. ***vaward*** US /VAW wurd, VAY-/ [VOW-]; UK /VAW wurd/ [VAY-, VOW-, VAW WURD].   The vowel of *war* not recommended in the second syllable.   Archaic variant of **vanguard.**   See App. D *-aun-*.

122. **Thessalian** /t̶huh SAYL yun/ from Thessaly, a region in Greece.

125. **hollow'd, holla'd, holloed** /HŎL ud, -ohd/ given a hunting cry.

126. **Thessaly** /T̶HESS uh lee/ region in Greece.

130. **Nedar's** /NEE durz/.

167. **gaud** /gawd/ trinket, toy.

172. **betrothed** /bih-, bee TROHṬH id/ engaged to be married.

202. ***Heigh-ho!*** US /hay ho, hī-/; CN /hī-/, *rarely* [hay-]; UK /hay-/.   Shk intended /hay/.   Spoken with evenly stressed syllables or as if sighing, with 1st syllable stress.

215. **ballet** /BAL ut/ archaic variant of **ballad.**

218. ***Peradventure*** perhaps.   /PUR ad VEN chur/;
US *rarely* [PĔR-, PUR ad ven chur];
UK, CN *also* [PUR-, PĔR ad ven chur, pĕr ad VEN chur].

Act 4 Scene 2

12, 13. ***paramour*** US, CN /PĂIR uh moor/ [-mor]; UK /-mor/ [-moor] lover.

13. ***paragon*** US /PĂIR uh gŏn/ [-gun]; CN /-gŏn/; UK /-gun/ [-g̠n] most perfect example.

20-23. **sixpence** /SIKS punss, -p̣ss/; US *also* /SIKS penss/.

36. **ribands** /RIB undz/ archaic variant of **ribbons.**

Act 5 Scene 1

8. **compact** /cum-, cŏm PACT/ composed of.

16. **aery, airy** /AIR ee/ of the air.

32, 39. **masque(s)** US /măsk/; UK, E. NEW ENG. /mahsk/ [măsk] masked dancing and pantomime.

44. **Centaurs** /SEN torz/.

45. **eunuch** /Y͞OO nuk/ castrated man.

48. ***Bacchanals** orgiasitic followers of Bacchus. US /bahk uh NAHLZ/ [back uh NALZ, BACK uh nłz]; UK /BACK uh nalz/ [back uh NALZ, bahk uh NAHLZ]. The /ah/ vowel is newer.

49. **Thracian singer** /T̶H̶RAY shun/ Orpheus.

51. **Thebes** /t̶h̶eebz/ city in Greece.

55. ***nuptial** wedding. Here should be two syllables US, UK /NUP chł/ [-shł]; in CN both are used equally.

75. ***nuptial** wedding. Here should be three syllables. Shk probably intended /NUP shee ł/, but today /NUP chuh wł, NUP shuh wł/ are common, though considered non-standard in the UK.

130. **certain** here should be /sur TAYN/ to rhyme with *plain,* however final syllable stress was not usual for this word in Shk's time.

138. **Ninus'** /N͞I nus/ founder of Ninevah. Given the pun with *ninny* at 3.1.98 they probably pronounce it /NIN us/.

177. **eyne** /īn/ dialect form of *eyes.*

196. **Limander, Lemander** /lee MAN dur/ mistake for *Leander* /lee AN dur/.

198-9. **Shafalus, Shaphalus** /SHAF uh lus/ mistake for *Cephalus* /SEF uh lus/.

198-9. **Procrus** /PROHK rus, PRŎCK-/ mistake for *Procris* /PROH cris/.

ă-bat, ăir-marry, air-pair, a̧r-far, ĕr-merry, ĝ- get, ī-high, ĭr-mirror, ł-little, n̦-listen, ŏ-hot, oh-go, o͞o-wood, o͞o-moon, oor-tour, ŏr- or, ow-how, t̪h-that, t̶h̶-thin, ŭ-but, UR-fur, ur-under.   ( ) - suppress the syllable   see p. xiii for complete list.

239-60. lanthorn archaic variant of **lantern**. Probably pronounced /LAN turn/, but possibly /LANT horn/ or /LAN ~~thurn, -thorn~~/.

323. *videlicet namely (abbreviated *viz.*). The older, anglicized pronunciations are US /vih DELL ih sit/ [-DEEL-, vī-]; UK /vih DEEL ih sit/ [vī-, -DELL-]. Newer pronunciations mix in restored Latin syllables, for example, /-ket/ or /-DAYL-/. These are not recommended.

332. cowslip /COW slip/ a yellow flower.

353-61. Bergomask, bergamask US /BUR guh măsk/; UK, E.NEW ENG. /-mahsk/ [-măsk] country dance.

369. fortnight /FORT nīt/; US *also* [FORT nit] two weeks. Virtually obsolete in the US.

384. Hecat's, Hecate's /HEK uts/ goddess of witchcraft. /HEK uh tee/ is the usual non-Shakespearean pronunciation.

Much Ado About Nothing

People in the Play

Sometimes some of these names are given an Italian pronunciation in performance. These pronunciations are indicated here as accurately as possible within the limits of this notation. Shakespeare, however, probably intended them to be anglicized.

Antonio /an TOHN ee yoh/; Ital. /ahn-/. Occurs only once, in prose.
 Anthony US /AN ~~thuh~~ nee/; UK /AN tuh nee/ [-~~thuh~~ nee].

*****Balthasar** by far the most common pronunciation is /BAL thuh zar/. It is rarely /bal ~~thuh~~ ZAR/, which will also fit the verse, but another rare pronunciation /bal ~~THAZ~~ ur/ will not.

Beatrice 2 or 3 syllables depending on meter /BEE (uh) triss/.

Benedick /BEN ih dick/.

*****Borachio** US /bor AH chee yoh/ [bor AH kee oh]. In CN, UK the latter is rarely used. Shk. intended /ch/.

Claudio 2 or 3 syllables depending on meter /CLAW d(ee) yoh/.

Conrade, Conrad both pronounced /CŎN rad/.

Leonato /lee uh-, lee oh NAH toh/.

Margaret /MAR guh rit/ or /MAR grit/ depending on meter.

Don Pedro /dŏn PAY droh, PED-/. In the US the former is more common, in the UK the latter. /PEED-/ is an older, angl. form, now rare.

Seacole /SEE kohl/ one of the watch in 3.3, 3.5. Some eds. prefer **Seacoal**, pronounced the same way. This was the older name for what we now call simply *coal*.

Ursula US /UR suh luh/; UK /UR syoo luh, -syuh luh/. Three syllables in verse, but in one instance may be 2 or 3. Occurs once as **Ursley** /URS lee/.

ă-bat, ăir-**marry**, air-**pair**, ạr-**far**, ĕr-**merry**, ĝ- **get**, ī-**high**, ĭr-**mirror**, ł-**little**, ṇ-**listen**, ŏ-**hot**, oh-**go**, ŏŏ-**wood**, ōō-**moon**, oor-**tour**, ōr- **or**, ow-**how**, țh-**that**, ŧħ-**thin**, ŭ-**but**, UR-**fur**, ur-**under**.   ( ) - suppress the syllable   see p. xiii for complete list.

People in the Play (cont.)

Verges /VUR jiss, VUR jeez/.   Like *Jaques* the former is recommended by historians, but the latter is often used today (See AYL "People in the Play").

Places in the Play

Messina /muh SEE nuh/.

Act 1 Scene 1

2. ***Arragon, Aragon** US /ĂIR uh gŏn/, *rarely* [-gun]; UK /-gŏn/ [-gun]. Sp. /ah rah GOHN/ region of Spain. See App. D -*on.*

11. ***Florentine** US /FLŌR in teen/ [-tīn]; E.COAST US /FLŎR-/; UK /FLŎR in tīn/ [-teen].

30. **Mountanto** /mown TAN toh, -TAHN-/. Some eds. prefer **Montanto** /mŏn-/ a sarcastic comment based on the word for an upward thrust in fencing.

36. ***Padua** /PAD y(oo) wuh/ [PAJ (oo) wuh/. An Ital. vowel /PAHD-/ is not recommended, since the Ital. form is *Padova.*

50. **victual** /VIT ł/ food.

50. **holp** /hohlp/ helped.

134. **predestinate** /pree-, prih DESS tih nayt, -nut/ inevitable. /-ut/ would be more usual for an adj.

234. **heretic** /HĔR ih tik/ dissenter.

240. **rechate** /rih-, ree CHAYT/ notes on a horn to call hounds. Variant of **recheat** /rih-, ree CHEET/.

241. **winded** /WIN did/ blown.

242. **baldrick** /BAWL drik/ shoulder strap for a horn.

253. ***brothel-house** whorehouse. US, CN /BRŎTH ł/ [BRŎTH ł, BRAWTH ł]; UK /BRŎTH ł/.

280. **embassage** /EM buh sij/ ambassador's message.

287. **basted** /BAY stid/ loosely stitched.

315. **salv'd** softened. US /salvd/ [savd]; E. NEW ENG. [sahvd];
CN /salvd/ [sahlvd, savd, sahvd]; UK /salvd/. Normal development would favor
the *l*-less form (cf. *halve, calve*).

315. **treatise** narrative. US /TREET iss/, *rarely* [-iz]; CN /-iss/; UK both /s/ and
/z/ forms used equally.

Act 1 Scene 2

23. **peradventure** perhaps. /PUR ad VEN chur/;
US *rarely* [PĔR-, PUR ad ven chur];
UK, CN *also* [PUR-, PĔR ad ven chur, pĕr ad VEN chur].

Act 1 Scene 3

47. **betroths** /bih-, bee TROHŢHZ/ engages to be married.

61. **arras** /ĂIR us/ tapestry.

Act 2 Scene 1

40. **sixpence** /SIKS punss, -pṇss/; US *also* /SIKS penss/.

40. **berrord** bearkeeper. Archaic variant of **bearward** or **bearherd**. All were
pronounced /BAIR urd/, but recent spelling pronunciations /BAIR wârd/ (as in
war), /-hurd/ are also used today.

74, 79. **cinquepace** /SINK uh payss/, /SINK payss/ lively dance.

77. **ancientry** /AYN shun tree, -chun-/ ancient tradition.

96. **Philemon's** /fih LEE munz/ [fĭ-] he entertained Jupiter in his cottage.
Sometimes newer /-ŏn/ is used. See App. D -*on*.

139. **libertines** /LIB ur teenz/, *rarely* [-tīnz] people who act without moral
restraint.

ă-bat, ăir-marry, air-pair, ạr-far, ĕr-merry, ĝ- get, ī-high, ĭr-mirror, ł-little, ṇ-listen,
ŏ-hot, oh-go, ōō-wood, ōō-moon, oor-tour, ōr- or, ow-how, ţh-that, th-thin, Ŭ-but,
UR-fur, ur-under.   ( ) - suppress the syllable   see p. xiii for complete list.

147. *peradventure perhaps. /PUR ad VEN chur/;
US rarely [PĚR-, PUR ad ven chur];
UK, CN also [PUR-, PĚR ad ven chur, pĕr ad VEN chur].

189. usurer's /Y͞OO zhur urz; UK also [-zhyoor urz, -zhoor urz] someone who lends money for interest.

194. drovier /DROHV ee ur/ archaic variant of drover 'livestock dealer.' -ier could also be /-ur/ in Shk's day.

195. bullocks /BU̱LL uks/ bulls or oxen. /-ŏks/ not recommended.

247. poniards /PŎN yurdz/; UK also newer [-yardz] daggers.

256. *Ate goddess of discord. /AYT ee/ is the older, angl. form; /AHT ay/ is the newer, restored form and much more common; /AHT ee/ is a mixed form, heard occasionally.

264. arrand /ĂIR und/ archaic variant of errand.

265. Antipodes /an TIP uh deez/ the opposite side of the world.

269. Cham's /kamz/ ruler of China. Archaic variant of Khan's /kahnz/.

269. embassage /EM buh sij/ ambassador's message.

306. heralt /HĔR lt/ archaic variant of herald.

320. *Heigh-ho! US /hay ho, hī-/; CN /hī-/, rarely [hay-]; UK /hay-/. Shk intended /hay/. Spoken with evenly stressed syllables or as if sighing, with 1st syllable stress.

Act 2 Scene 2

5. med'cinable medicinal. Elsewhere in Shk's verse /MED sin uh bł/. Some eds. prefer medicinable, which in this prose passage may be /muh DISS nuh bł/.

9. *covertly secretly. US /koh VURT lee/ [KOH vurt lee, KUV urt lee], rarely [kuh VURT lee]; CN /koh VURT lee/ [KOH vurt lee]; UK /koh VURT lee/ [KUV urt lee, KOH vurt lee, kuh VURT lee], rarely [KŎV urt lee].

Act 2 Scene 3

14. **tabor** /TAY bur/ small drum. See App. D *-or*.

20. **ortography** /or TŎG ruh fee/ correct spelling. Archaic variant of
orthography /or ~~THŎG~~-/. Probably an error for *orthographer*
/or ~~THŎG~~ ruh fur/ someone who is a stickler for the correct use of words.

42. **with a pennyworth, penn'worth** with more than he bargained form. Both
pronounced /PEN ur~~th~~/.

73. **leavy** /LEEV ee/ archaic variant of **leafy**. Here supposed to rhyme with
heavy. In Shk's time the rhyme could have been /LEE vee : HEE vee/ or
/LEV ee : HEV ee/.

82. **as live** as soon. May have been /liv/ in Shk's time. Variant of **as lief** /leef/.
In the US **lieve** /leev/ is still found in some dialects and can also be used here.

140. **halfpence** /HAYP n̩ss, -unss/ here 'small bits.'

158.***alms** good deed. /ahmz/ is older; /ahlmz, awlmz/ are newer. In the UK the
latter are non-standard.

168, 216. **dotage** /DOHT ij/ love-sickness.

169. **daff'd** /dăft/ discarded. Archaic variant of **doffed** /dŏft/; US *also* /dawft/.

189. **Hector** /HEK tur/ Trojan hero. See App. D *-or*.

218. **dumb show** /DUM shoh/ pantomime.

Act 3 Scene 1

36. **haggards** /HAG urdz/ wild hawks.

38. **new-trothed** /-TROH t̩hid/ newly engaged.

42. **wrastle** /RĂSS l̩/ archaic variant of **wrestle**.

52. **Misprising, Misprizing** /mis PRĪZ ing/ undervaluing.

ă-bat, ăir-**marry**, air-**pair**, a̩r-**far**, ĕr-**merry**, ĝ- **get**, ī-**high**, ĭr-**mirror**, l̩-**little**, n̩-**listen**,
ŏ-**hot**, oh-**go**, o͞o-**wood**, o͞o-**moon**, oor-**tour**, ŏr- **or**, ow-**how**, t̩h-**that**, ~~th~~-**thin**, ŭ-**but**,
UR-**fur**, ur-**under**.   ( ) - suppress the syllable   see p. xiii for complete list.

65. **agot** a type of jewel. Archaic variant of **agate**, both pronounced /AG ut/.

71. **Sure, sure, such carping is not commendable** here, as elsewhere in Shk, /CŎM en duh bł/. However, if *is* is contracted (*carping's*) then the mod. form /cuh MEN duh bł/ can be used.

73. **As Beatrice is, cannot be commendable.** *Beatrice* should be 2 syllables with /CŎM en duh bł/ in a regular line, or mod. /cuh MEN duh bł/ in a broken-backed line.

104. **limed** here should be one syllable /līmd/ caught in a trap made of lime paste.

Act 3 Scene 2

2. **consummate** /CŎN suh mayt, -mut/ consummated.

2. ***Arragon, Aragon,** US /ĂIR uh gŏn/, *rarely* [-gun]; UK /-gŏn/ [-gun]; Sp. /ah rah GOHN/ region in Spain. See App. D *-on.*

50. **civet** /SIV it/ a type of perfume.

98. **holp** /hohlp/ helped.

131. ***untowardly** unluckily. US /un TORD lee, un tuh WÂRD lee/ (as in *war*); CN /un tuh WÂRD lee /; UK /un tuh WÂRD lee/ [un TWŌRD lee, -TORD-]. First syllable stress is also possible.

Act 3 Scene 3

9. **desartless** /dih ZART liss/ archaic variant of **desertless** /dih ZURT liss/ undeserving.

24. **lanthorn** archaic variant of **lantern.** Probably pronounced /LAN turn/, but possibly /LANT horn/ or /LAN t̶h̶urn, -t̶h̶orn/.

25. **vagrom** /VAY grum/ Dogberry's mistake for **vagrant.**

77, 83. ***by'r lady** /bīr-, bur LAY dee/ by Our Lady (i.e., Mary).

94. **vigitant** /VIJ ih tunt/ Dogberry's mistake for *vigilant.*

103. **close** /clohss/ hidden.

123. **Tush** /tŭsh/ expression of disdain.

134. **reechy** /REE chee/ grimy.

Act 3 Scene 4

6. ***rebato** a stiff ornamental collar. /ruh BAHT oh/; US *rarely older*
[ruh BAYT oh].

16. **Milan's** elsewhere in verse always /MILL unz/, but in this prose passage it
could be mod. /mih LAHNZ/.

54. ***Heigh-ho!** US /hay ho, hī-/; CN /hī-/, *rarely* [hay-]; UK /hay-/. Shk intended
/hay/. Spoken with evenly stressed syllables or as if sighing, with 1st syllable
stress.

59. ***trow** US, CN /troh, trow/; UK /trow/ [troh] I wonder. Shk's rhymes
elsewhere indicate /-oh/.

73-8. **carduus benedictus** /CAR dyoo us ben uh DIK tus/;
US *also* /CAR joo us/ blessed thistle, a medicinal herb.

82. **by'r Lady** /bīr-, bur LAY dee/ by Our Lady (i.e., Mary).

Act 3 Scene 5

9. **Goodman** /GŏŏD mun/ title of a man under the rank of gentleman.

16. **palabras** angl. /puh LAB ruz/; Sp. /pah LAHB rahss/ from *pocas palabras*
'few words,' i.e., 'best to say nothing.'

32. **arrant** /ĂIR unt/ thoroughgoing.

46. **aspicious** /uh SPISH us/ Dogberry's error for *suspicious*. Some eds. prefer
auspicious.

52. **suffigance** /suh FIJ unss/ Dogberry means *sufficient*.

ă-bat, ăir-**marry**, air-**pair**, ạr-**far**, ĕr-**merry**, ĝ- **get**, ī-**high**, ĭr-**mirror**, ł-**little**, ṇ-**listen**,
ŏ-**hot**, oh-**go**, ōō-**wood**, ōō-**moon**, oor-**tour**, ōr- **or**, ow-**how**, ţh-**that**, t̶h̶-**thin**, ŭ-**but**,
UR-**fur**, ur-**under**.   ( ) - suppress the syllable   see p. xiii for complete list.

Act 4 Scene 1

53. **show'd**. Q, F1 have the archaic variant **shew'd** which could be either /shōōd/ or /shohd/.

68. ***nuptial** wedding. US, UK /NUP chł/ [-shł]; in CN both are used equally.

78. **catechizing** /KAT uh kīz ing/ series of questions and answers.

104. **impious** /IM pyus/ profane.

135. **unknown** here should be /UN nohn/.

146. **belied** /bih-, bee LĪD/ slandered.

167. **tenure** archaic variant of **tenor**, both /TEN ur/.

185. **misprision** /mis PRIZH un, -ŋ/ misunderstanding.

194. **eat** /et/ dialect variant of **eaten**.

200. **throughly** archaic variant of *thoroughly*. /THROō lee/ is the normal pronunciation on stage, but to enhance clarity a syncopated form of the modern pronunciation may be used: *thor'ghly*.

213. ***travail** here should be /TRAV ayl/ double meaning: hard work, labor of childbirth.

306. **rancor** (UK **rancour**) /RANK ur/ ill-will. See App. D *-or*.

316. **Comfect** /CUM fect/ [CŎM fekt] variant of **Comfit** /CUM fit/ [CŎM fit] a candy.

Act 4 Scene 2

3. ***malefactors** /MAL ih fak turz/, *rarely* [mal ih FAK turz] evil doers. See App. D *-or*.

Act 5 Scene 1

5. **sieve** /siv/ strainer.

14. **lineament** /LIN yuh munt/ distinctive feature.

32. **advertisement** here should be /ad VURT iss munt, -iz-/ advice.

42-218. **belied** /bih-, bee LĪD/ slandered.

46. **Good den** /gōͦd-, guh DEN/ good evening. Some eds. prefer **Good e'en.**

58. **Tush** /tŭsh/ expression of disdain.

59. **dotard** /DOHT urd/ senile old man.

78. **daff** /dăf/ thrust aside. Archaic variant of **doff** /dŏf/; US *also* /dawf/.

94. **fashion-monging** foppish. US /FASH un mŏng ging, -ing/ or /-mawng-/ [-mung-]; CN /-mung-, -mŏng-/; UK /-mung-/.

125. **scabbard** /SKAB urd/ sword sheath.

262. **your wronger** US /RAWNG ur/; UK /RŎNG-/ someone who has done you wrong.

321. **arrant** /ĂIR unt/ thoroughgoing.

Act 5 Scene 2

30. **Leander** /lee AN dur/ he swam the Hellespont to be with Hero.

31. **pandars** /PAN durz/ pimps. Some eds. prefer **panders**, pronounced the same way.

32. ***quondam** US /KWŎN dum/, *rarely* [-dam]; UK /-dam/, *rarely* [-dum] former.

32. ***carpet-mongers** ladies' men. US /CAR pit mŏng gurz/ or /-mawng-/ [-mung-]; CN /-mung-, -mŏng-/; UK /-mung-/.

53. **noisome** /NOY sum/ disgusting.

63. **politic** /PŎL ih tik/ shrewdly managed.

ă-bat, ăir-marry, air-pair, ạr-far, ĕr-merry, ĝ- get, ī-high, ĭr-mirror, ł-little, ṇ-listen, ŏ-hot, oh-go, ōͦō-wood, ōō-moon, oor-tour, ōr- or, ow-how, ţh-that, ťh-thin, ŭ-but, UR-fur, ur-under.   ( ) - suppress the syllable   see p. xiii for complete list.

66. **epithite** /EP ih thit/ expression. Archaic variant of **epithet** /EP ih thet, -thit/.

83. **rheum** /room/ tears.

Act 5 Scene 3

5. *****guerdon** /GURD ŋ/ reward.

26. **Phoebus** /FEE bus/ god of the sun.

Act 5 Scene 4

17. **confirm'd** here should be /CŎN furmd/.

38. **Ethiope** /EE thee ohp/ person from Ethiopia.

44. **Tush** /tŭsh/ expression of disdain.

45, 46. **Europa** /yoor ROH puh/; US *also* /yur-/ the first instance is 'Europe,' the second refers to one of Jupiter's loves.

48. **low** soft mooing sound. Today /LOH/, but here an archaic variant rhyming with *cow* is indicated.

Othello

People in the Play

Sometimes some of these names are given an Italian pronunciation in performance. These pronunciations are indicated here as accurately as possible within the limits of this notation. Shakespeare, however, probably intended them to be anglicized.

Bianca US /bee AHNG kuh/ [bee ANG kuh]; UK /bee ANG kuh/, *rarely* [bee AHNG kuh]; CN both are used equally. Ital. /bee AHNG kah/.

Brabantio usually 3 syllables /bruh BAN sh(ee) yoh/, /-BAHN-/. Some eds. prefer Ital. **Brabanzio** /brah BAHN ts(ee) yoh/.

*Cassio 2 or 3 syllables depending on meter /KĂSS (ee) yoh/.

Desdemona /dez dih MOH nuh/.
  *Desdemon /DEZ dih mohn/ [-mŏn, -mun].

Emilia usually 3 syllables /ih MEEL (ee) yuh/. An older pronunciation /-MILL-/ is now rare.

*Gratiano 3 or 4 syllables depending on meter. US /grahsh (ee) YAH noh/ [grash-], *rarely* [graysh-]; CN /grahsh-/ [grash-]; UK /grash-/ [grahsh-]. Some eds. prefer Ital. **Graziano** /grah ts(ee) YAH noh/.

Iago /ee AH goh/, except at 5.2.154 where it is 2 syllables, /YAH goh/.

Lodovico /lohd-, lŏd uh VEE koh/; Ital. /loh doh VEE koh/.

Montano (F1) /mŏn TAN oh, -TAHN-/. **Mountanio** (Q1) /mown TAN yoh, -TAYN-, -TAHN-/.

*Othello /uh ~~THEL~~ oh/ [oh-]; UK, CN *also* /ŏ-/.

Roderigo 3 or 4 syllables depending on meter /rŏd ur REE goh/.

ă-bat, ăir-**ma**rry, air-**pair**, ạr-**far**, ĕr-**me**rry, ĝ- get, ī-**high**, ĭr-**mir**ror, l̩-**lit**tle, n̩-**lis**ten, ŏ-**hot**, oh-go, o͞o-**wood**, o͞o-**moon**, oor-**tour**, ōr- or, ow-**how**, t̬h-**that**, ~~th~~-**thin**, ŭ-**but**, UR-**fur**, ur-**un**der.   ( ) - suppress the syllable   see p. xiii for complete list.

Frequently Occurring Words in this Play

ancient /AYN chunt/ archaic variant of the rank **ensign** US /EN sṇ/; UK /-sīn/.

*moor, -ship /moor/ [mor] black man.

Act 1 Scene 1

1. **Tush** (Q1) /tŭsh/ expression of disdain. Omitted F1.

4. **'Sblood** /zblud/ God's (i.e., Jesus') blood. Omitted F1.

13. **bumbast circumstance** /BUM băst/ inflated style. Variant of **bombast** which formerly was pronounced the same way, though now /BŎM băst/ is the only pronunciation used.

14. **epithites** /EP ih ~~th~~its/ expressions. Archaic variant of **epithets** /EP ih ~~th~~ets, -~~th~~its/.

16. **Certes** /SUR teez/ certainly.

19. **arithmetician** /ăir-, uh ri~~th~~ muh TISH un/ one skilled in arithmetic.

20. ***Florentine** US /FLŌR in teen/ [-tīn]; E.COAST US /FLŎR-/; UK /FLŎR in tīn/ [-teen] person from Florence.

24. **theoric** /~~THEE~~ uh rik/ theory.

25. **toged, togaed** /TOH gud/ wearing togas.

25. **consuls** /CŎN słz/ senators.

30. **Christen'd** /CRISS ṇd/. Some eds. prefer **Christian**.

31. **debitor** /DEB ih tur/ archaic variant of *debtor*. See App. D *-or*.

39. **affin'd** (F1) /uh FĪND/ bound. Q1 has *assign'd*.

46. **obsequious** /ub-, ŏb SEE kw(ee) yus/ fawning.

48. **provender** /PRŎV ṇ dur/ dry food for animals.

54. ***homage** /HŎM ij/; US *also* /ŎM ij/ acknowledgement of allegience.

61. **demonstrate** here should be /dem ŎN strayt/.

63. **extern** /ek STURN/ external.

75. **timorous** /TIM (uh) rus/ terrifying.

99. **draughts** US, CN /drăfts/; UK, E.NEW ENG. /drahfts/ drinks.

111. **Barbary** /BAR buh ree/ region in North Africa.

113. **coursers** /COR surz/ warhorses.

113. **gennets, jennets** /JEN its/ Spanish horses.

116. **profane** if this line is iambic, /PROH fayn/ is demanded.

125. **gundolier** /gun duh LEER/ Venetian boatman. Archaic variant of **gondolier** /gŏn-/.

126. **lascivious** /luh SIV yus/ lustful.

141, 166. **taper(s)** /TAY pur/ slender candle.

152. **fadom** /FAD um/ depth, ability. Archaic variant of **fathom** /FĂTH um/.

158. **Sagittary** here should be /SAJ ih tree/ an inn.

Act 1 Scene 2

3. **contriv'd** here should be /CŎN trīvd/ premeditated.

5. **yerk'd** /yurkt/ stabbed.

12. **magnifico** /mag NIF ih koh/ important person.

18. **signiory, signory** /SEEN yur ee/ the Venetian government.

21. **provulgate** (Q1) /proh VŬL gayt/ make public. Some eds. prefer F1's
*promulgate** which here should be /prŏ MŬL gayt/ [proh-] rather than usual
/PRŎM ul gayt/.

33. **Janus** /JAY nus/ Roman two-faced god.

ă-bat, ăir-marry, air-pair, ạr-far, ĕr-merry, ĝ- get, ī-high, ĭr-mirror, ł-little, ṇ-listen,
ŏ-hot, oh-go, ōō-wood, ōō-moon, oor-tour, ōr- or, ow-how, ṭh-that, ᵵh-thin, ŭ-but,
UR-fur, ur-under.   ( ) - suppress the syllable   see p. xiii for complete list.

---

41. **sequent** (F1) /SEE kwunt/ successive. Q1 has **frequent**.

43. **consuls** /CŎN słz/ senators.

50. **carract** /KĂIR ukt/ a type of large merchant ship.   Archaič variant of **carrack** /KĂIR uk/.

56. **Holla** /huh LAH/ a call to attract attention.

70. **guardage** /GARD ij/ guardianship.

86. **direct** here should be /DĪ rect/ regular.

99. **pagans** /PAY gunz/ non-Christians.

Act 1 Scene 3

5. **accompt** (F1) /uh COWNT/ archaic variant of Q1's **account**. See App. D.

18. **assay** /uh-, ass SAY/ attempt.

23. *****facile** US /FASS ł/ [-īl]; CN /-īl/ [-ł]; UK /-īl/ easy.

33, 234. **the Ottomites** /ŎT uh mīts/ the Turks.

37. **restem** /ree-, rih STEM/ to retrace their passage.

40. **servitor** /SURV ih tur/ servant. See App. D -*or*.

44. **Marcus Luccicos** /lo͞o CHEE kohss/.

49. **Ottoman** /ŎT uh mun/ Turkish.

61. **mountebanks** /MOWNT uh banks/ quack doctors.

64. **Sans** /sănz/ without.

105. *****conjur'd** summoned by magic. Here with usual 1st syllable stress in an inverted foot; US, CN /CŎN jurd/, *rarely* [CUN-]; UK /CUN jurd/ [CŎN-].

115. **Sagittary** /SAJ ih tĕr ee/; UK /-tuh ree/ or /-tree/ an inn.

140. **antres** /ANT urz/ caves.

144. **Anthropophagi** /an throh PŎF uh jī/ cannibals. Sometimes /ĝī/ is used.

153. **dilate** /dih-, dī LAYT/ tell in detail.

189. **God be with you** (F1). Some eds. substitute **God b'wi' you**, or Q1's **God b'uy you** or some other variation. In any case it should be reduced to 3 syllables /gŏd BWEE yōō/, /gŏd BĪ yōō/; US *also* /gawd-/.

200. **grise** (F1) /grīss, grīz/ step. Variant of Q1's **greese** /greess, greez/. Other variants are **grece** /greess/, **grize** /grīz/, **grice** /grīss/.

217. **equivocal** /ih KWIV uh kł/; US *also* /ee-/ arguing both sides of an issue.

231. **agnize** /ag NĪZ/ recognize.

272. **housewives** (F1). Q1 has the archaic variant ***huswives** /HUZ ivz/ is traditional, /HUSS wīvz/ is a newer, spelling pronunciation. The former is the most common form in the UK, the latter in the US. In CN both are used equally. In North America /HUSS wivz/ is also sometimes used.

273. **indign** /in DĪN/ unworthy.

315. **guinea hen** /ĜIN ee/.

322. **hyssop** /HISS up/ a fragrant herb.

322. **tine** wild grasses. Some eds. prefer **thyme** (F1 *Time*) /tīm/ an herb.

325. **corrigible** US /COR ih jih bł/; E.COAST US, UK /CŎR-/ corrective.

327. **poise** counterbalance. Some eds. prefer **peise** with the same meaning. US /peez/, *sometimes* [payz]; UK /peez, payz/. Dialect evidence shows that /ee/ was the form found in southern Eng., and /ay/ in the North.

332. **scion** /SĪ un/ living plant grafted onto root stock.

338. *****perdurable** eternal. Elsewhere in Shk /PUR dyur uh bł/; US *also* [-dur-], but today usually /pur DYOOR uh bł/; US *also* [-DŌŌR-, -DUR-].

345. **sequestration** /see kwih STRAY shun/ [sek wih-] separation.

349. **acerb** (Q1) /uh SURB/ bitter. Some eds. prefer F1's **bitter**.

ă-bat, ăir-marry, air-pair, ạr-far, ĕr-merry, ĝ- get, ī-high, ĭr-mirror, ł-little, ṇ-listen, ŏ-hot,   oh-go,   ōō-wood, ōō-moon, oor-tour,   ōr- or, ow-how, ţh-that, th-thin, ŭ-but, UR-fur, ur-under.   ( ) - suppress the syllable   see p. xiii for complete list.

349. **coloquintida** /cŏl uh KWIN tih duh/ colocynth, used as a purgative.

371. ***Traverse** US, CN /truh VURSS/ [TRAV urss];
UK /truh VURSS, TRAV urss/ [TRAV URSS] forward.

390. ***surety** certainty. Here may be two or three syllables (the latter is more common in mod. English) /SHUR (ih) tee, SHOOR-, SHOR-/ (see App. D).

Act 2 Scene 1

4. **Descry** /dih SKRĪ/ see.

9. **hold the mortise** /MORT iss/ hold their joints together.

17. **enchafed** /en CHAYF id/ excited, stormy.

26. **Veronesa, Veronessa** /vĕr uh NESS uh/ ship from Verona, Italy.

39. **th' aerial blue** here should be /ȚH^Y AIR yɫ/ blue of the sky.

62. ***paragons** US /PĂIR uh gŏnz/ [-gunz]; CN /-gŏnz/; UK /-gunz/ [-gn̦z]
surpasses.

63. **blazoning** /BLAY z(uh) ning/ praising.

64. **vesture** /VES chur/ covering. See App. D -*ure*.

65. **ingener** (*Ingeniuer* F1) designer. Archaic variant of **engineer**. In Shk's time it may have been /IN jih nur/, or mod. /in jih NEER/. Q1 has *beare all excellency*.

73. **divine** here should be /DIV īn/.

77. **se'nnight's** /SEN its, -īts/ week's.

81. **renew'd** here should be US /REE nōōd/; UK, SOUTH.US /-nyōōd/.

112. ***huswifery** /HUZ if ree/ is traditional, /-wīf ree, -wiff ree/ are newer, based on spelling. Some eds. prefer **housewifery** /HOWSS-/.

112. ***huswives** /HUZ ivz/ is traditional, /HUSS wīvz/ is a newer, spelling pronunciation. The former is the most common form in the UK, the latter in the US. In CN both are used equally. In North America /HUSS wivz/ is also sometimes used. Here means **hussies**.

120. **assay** /uh-, ass SAY/ try. Some eds. prefer **essay** /es SAY/.

126. **frieze** /freez/ coarse wool cloth.

170. **gyve thee** (F2) /jīv/ trap thee. Q1 has **catch you**.

177. **clyster-pipes** /KLISS tur pīps/ enema pipes.

193. **unknown** here should be /UN nohn/.

228. **satiety** (F1) /suh TĪ uh tee/ fullness. Q1 has the archaic variant **saciety** /suh SĪ uh tee/.

238. **voluble** /VŎL yuh bł/ quick-witted.

238. **conscionable** /CŎN shun uh bł/ bound by conscience.

246. **requisites** /REK wih zits/ requirements.

263. **th'incorporate conclusion** /t͡h‌ʸin COR pur rut, -rayt/ i.e., sexual union. /-ut/ is more usual for an adj .

288. **howbeit** here should be /how BEE (i)t/ although.

292. **peradventure** perhaps. /PUR ad VEN chur/;
US *rarely* [PĔR-, PUR ad ven chur];
UK, CN *also* [PUR-, PĔR ad ven chur, pĕr ad VEN chur].

293. **accomptant** (F1) /uh COWNT unt, -ṇt/ accountable. Archaic variant of Q1's **accountant**. See App. D.

297. **inwards** /IN wurdz/ internal parts. /IN urdz/ is still a dialect form in the US.

309. **egregiously** /ih GREE jus lee/ notoriously.

Act 2 Scene 2

3. **perdition** /pur DISH un/; UK *also* [PUR DISH un] destruction.

7. ***nuptial** wedding. US, UK /NUP chł/ [-shł]; in CN both are used equally.

ă-bat, ăir-**marry**, air-**pair**, ạr-**far**, ĕr-**merry**, ĝ- get, ī-high, ĭr-**mirror**, ł-little, ṇ-listen,
ŏ-hot, oh-go, ōō-**wood**, ōō-**moon**, oor-**tour**, ōr- or, ow-how, t͡h-**that**, t̶h̶-**thin**, ŭ-but,
UR-**fur**, ur-und**er**.   ( ) - suppress the syllable   see p. xiii for complete list.

Act 2 Scene 3

23. *parley /PAR lee/ conference with an enemy. Newer [-lay] not recommended.

26. *alarum US, CN /uh LAHR um/ [-LĂIR-]; UK /uh LĂIR um, uh LAHR um/ a call to arms.

30. stope /stohp/ tankard. Archaic variant of stoup /sto͞op/.

54. Potations /poh TAY shunz/ drinks.

64. rouse /rowz/ drink.

69, 70. canakin, cannikin, canikin /KAN uh kin/ small drinking vessel.

83. Almain /AL mayn/ German.

90. *breeches /BRITCH iz/ is traditional, /BREECH iz/ is newer. The former pronunciation is more common in the UK, and the latter in the US, CN.

91. sixpence /SIKS punss, -pn̥ss/; US also /SIKS penss/.

92. lown /lown/ rogue.

96. auld /awld/ dialect variant of old.

124. *equinox /EK wih nŏks/ [EEK-] equal days and nights, i.e., exact counterpart. The latter pronunciation is older.

130. *horologe /HŌR uh lohj/ [-lŏj]; E.COAST US /HŎR-/; UK also /HŎR-/ early timekeeping device.

140. ingraft US /in GRĂFT/; E.NEW ENG., UK /-GRAHFT/ ingrained. Some eds. prefer engraffed /en-/.

154. mazzard, mazard /MAZ urd/ head.

161. Diablo /dee AHB loh/ devil.

171. the Ottomites /ŎT uh mīts/ the Turks.

176. propriety /pruh PRĪ (ih) tee/ own nature.

181. Devesting /duh VEST ing/ archaic variant of Divesting /dī-, dih-/ undressing.

206. **collied** /CŎL eed/ blackened.

207. **Assays** /uh-, ass SAYZ/ attempts. Some eds. prefer **Essays** /es SAYZ/.

210. **rout** /rowt/ riot.

218. **affin'd** /uh FĪND/ biased.

264. *__bestial__ beastlike. /BEST yɫ/; US *also* [-chɫ]. US, CN /BEES-/ not recommended.

275. **imperious** /im PEER yus/ imperial, proud.

280. *__fustian__ /FUSS tee un/; US *also* /FUSS chun/ nonsense. Normal development would favor the latter.

292. **pleasance** (F1) /PLEZ unss/ pleasantness, delight. Q1 has **pleasure**.

319. *__importune__ /im POR chun/ ask insistently. See App. D.

338. **Probal to thinking** /PROH bɫ/ reasonable.

373. **dilatory** here should be 4 syllables US /DILL uh tor ee/;
UK /DILL uh tur ee/ slow.

375. **cashier'd** here should be /KASH eerd/ dismissed.

380. **billeted** /BILL it id/ assigned quarters.

Act 3 Scene 1

23. **quillets** /KWIL its/ quibbles, puns and word play.

36. **access** here should be /ak SESS/.

38. **converse** /cun VURSS/ conversation.

40. *__Florentine__ US /FLŌR in teen/ [-tīn]; E.COAST US /FLŎR-/;
UK /FLŎR in tīn/ [-teen] person from Florence.

ă-bat, ăir-ma**rry**, air-**pair**, ạr-**far**, ĕr-**merry**, ĝ- **get**, ī-**high**, ĭr-**mirror**, ɫ-**little**, ṇ-**listen**,
ŏ-**hot**, oh-**go**, o͞o-**wood**, o͞o-**moon**, oor-**tour**, ŏr- **or**, ow-**how**, t̪h-**that**, t̶h̶-**thin**, ŭ-**but**,
UR-**fur**, ur-**under**.   ( ) - suppress the syllable   see p. xiii for complete list.

Act 3 Scene 3

13. **politic** /PŎL (ih) tik/ as policy demands.

74. **By'r lady** (Q1) /bīr-, bur LAY dee/ by Our Lady, a mild oath. **Trust me** (F1).

90. **Perdition** /pur DISH un/; UK *also* [PUR DISH un] damnation.

123. **close dilations** /clohss/ 'secret thoughts' or 'involuntary delays.'

139. ***uncleanly** /un CLEN lee/ or newer /-CLEEN lee/.

168. **wronger** US /RAWNG ur/; UK /RŎNG-/ someone who does someone wrong.

182. **exsufflicate** /ek SUFF lih kayt, -ut/ exaggerated. /-ut / is more usual for an adj.

183, 198. **jealious** (F1) /JEL yus/ archaic variant of Q1's **jealous**.

210. **close as oak** /clohss/ securely.

232. **Foh** indicates an expression of disgust made with the lips /pff/! or /pfuh/! Sometimes vocalized as /foh/ or **faugh** /faw/.

251. **importunity** /im por-, im pur TYOON ih tee/; US *also* /-TOON-/ insistent requests.

260. **haggard** /HAG urd/ wild hawk.

274. ***Prerogativ'd** privileged. US, UK /pur RŎG uh tiv/ [prih-]; CN /prih-/. /pree-/ is also sometimes used in the US and CN, but is considered non-standard in the UK.

294. ***conjur'd** solemnly entreated. Here should be /cun JOORD/, the older, now rare pronunciation.

319. **Be not acknown on't** /ak NOHN/ say you know nothing about it.

330. **mandragora** here should be /man DRAG uh ruh/ a narcotic.

335. **Avaunt** /uh VAWNT/ begone!

346. **Pioners** soldiers who dug trenches and planted mines. It is not certain whether Shk pronounced this /PĪ uh nurz/ or as in mod. **Pioneers** /pī uh NEERZ/.

360. **ocular** /ŎK y(uh) lur/ visual.

375. **God buy you** good bye. See 1.3.189.

431. **demonstrate** here should be /dem ŎN strayt/.

450. **aspics'** /ASS piks/ asps'.

453. **Pontic Sea** /PŎN tik/ Black Sea.

456. **Propontic** /proh-, pruh PŎN tik/ Sea of Marmora.

456. **Hellespont** /HEL iss pŏnt/ the Dardenelles.

Act 3 Scene 4

16. **catechize** (UK **catechise**) /KAT uh kīz/ to instruct through a series of questions and answers.

26. **crusadoes** /crōō SAY dohz/ coins.

28-185. **jealous** (F1) /JEL yus/ archaic variant of Q1's **jealous**.

40. **sequester** removal. Here 1st syllable stress is indicated.

51. **rheum** /rōōm/ tear.

67. **perdition** /pur DISH un/; UK *also* [PUR DISH un] loss.

70. **sibyl** /SIB ł/; UK *also* /SIB il/ prophetess.

108. *importune** /im POR chun/ ask insistently. See App. D.

117. *futurity** the future. US /fyōō TOOR ih tee, -CHOOR-/ [-TYOOR-, -TUR-, -CHUR-]; UK /-TYOOR-/ [-CHOOR-], however, the latter is considered non-standard in the UK.

ă-bat, ăir-**marry**, air-**pair**, ạr-**far**, ĕr-**merry**, ĝ- **get**, ī-**high**, ĭr-**mirror**, ł-**little**, ṇ-**listen**, ŏ-**hot**, oh-**go**, ōō-**wood**, ōō-**moon**, oor-**tour**, ōr- **or**, ow-**how**, ṭh-**that**, ŧh-**thin**, ŭ-**but**, UR-**fur**, ur-**under**. ( ) - suppress the syllable see p. xiii for complete list.

122. **alms** charity for the poor. /ahmz/ is older; /ahlmz, awlmz/ are newer. In the UK the latter are non-standard.

141. **unhatch'd** here should be /UN hatcht/.

142. **demonstrable** here should be /DEM un struh bł/, still common in the UK.

146. **endues** /en DYOOZ/; US *also* [-DŌŌZ] endows.

153. **suborn'd** /sub ORND/ pursuaded someone to give false evidence.

154. **indicted** /in DĪT id/ charged with wrongdoing.

178. **continuate** (F1) /cun TIN y(oo) wut/ uninterrupted. Q1 has **convenient** .

Act 4 Scene 1

2. **unauthorized** here /un aw ~~THOR~~ īzd/ is possible after an epic caesura, but the mod. pronunciation is also possible in the compressed form /un AW ~~thr~~īzd/.

9. **venial** /VEEN ył/ pardonable.

26. **importunate** /im POR chuh nut/; UK *also* /-tyoo nut/ insistant.

27. **dotage** /DOHT ij/ love-sickness.

36. **belie** /bih-, bee LĪ/ slander.

37. ***fulsome** revolting. /FU̯LL sum/; US *rarely* [FŬL-].

37. **Handkerchiefs** (F1). **Handkerchers** (Q1) /HANK ur churz/.

71. **secure** here 1st syllable stress is indicated.

79. **'scuses** /SKYŌŌ siz/ excuses.

82. **gibes** /jībz/ sarcastic comments.

94. ***huswife** /HUZ if/ is traditional, /HUSS wīf/ is a newer, spelling pronunciation. The former is the most common form in the UK, the latter in the US. In CN both are used equally. In North America /HUSS wif/ is also sometimes used. Here means **hussy**.

99. **excess** here should be /ek SESS/, the most common UK form.

101. **conster** /CŎN stur/ construe. Some eds. prefer **construe**, which here should be stressed on the first syllable.

108. **caitiff** /KAYT if/ scoundrel.

113. *****importunes** /im POR chunz/ asks insistently. See App. D.

139. **lolls** /lŏllz/ droops.

146. **fitchew** /FITCH o͞o/ polecat, i.e., whore.

198. **patent** US /PAT ņt/; UK /PAYT ņt/ [PAT-] license.

205. **expostulate** /ek SPŎS chuh layt/; UK *also* /-tyoo layt/ discuss, object.

225. **unkind** here should be /UN kīnd/.

260. **avaunt** /uh VAWNT/ begone!

Act 4 Scene 2

28. **procreants** /PROH cree unts/ people having sex.

61. **cestern** /SESS turn/ archaic variant of **cistern** /SISS turn/.

63. *****cherubin** angel. US, CN /CHER uh bin/ [-yuh-]; UK uses both equally. /KĔR-/ not recommended.

121. **callet** /KAL ut/ whore.

175. **thou daff'st** /dăfst/ archaic variant of **doffest** /DŎF ist/; US *also* /DAWF-/ you thrust aside.

187. **votarist** /VOHT uh rist/ nun.

221. **depute** /duh PYO͞oT/ appoint.

224. **Mauritania** /mor ih TAYN ee uh/.

227. **determinate** /dih-, dee TUR mih nut/ more to the purpose.

ă-bat, ăir-m**arry**, air-**pair**, aŗ-**far**, ĕr-m**erry**, ĝ- g**et**, ī-high, ĭr-m**irror**, ł-little, ņ-listen, ŏ-hot, oh-go, o͞o-wood, ō͞o-moon, oor-t**our**, ōr- **or**, ow-h**ow**, ţh-th**at**, t̶h̶-**thin**, ŭ-but, UR-**fur**, ur-und**er**.   ( ) - suppress the syllable   see p. xiii for complete list.

233. **harlotry** (F1) /HAR luh tree/, **harlot** (Q1) /HAR lut/ both mean 'whore.'

Act 4 Scene 3

26, 33. **Barbary** /BAR buh ree/.

75. **'ud's pity** (Q1) /udz/ reduced form of *God's*. F1 has **why**.

Act 5 Scene 1

11. **quat** (F1) /kwŏt/ pimple. Q1 has *gnat*.

38. *****mischance** in verse normally with 2nd syllable stress.

106. **gastness** US /GĂST niss/; UK, E.NEW ENG. /GAHST niss/ terror.

123. **Fough** (Q1). Some eds. prefer **Foh!** indicates an expression of disgust made with the lips /pff/! or /pfuh/! Sometimes rendered as /faw/ or /foh/.   Q2 has **now**. Omitted F1.

129. **foredoes me** /for DUZ/ ruins me.

Act 5 Scene 2

5. **alablaster** a type of white rock. US /AL uh blăss tur/; E. NEW ENG., UK /-blahss-/ [-blăss-]. Archaic variant of **alabaster** /-băss-, -bahss-/.

12. **Promethean** /proh-, pruh MEE~~TH~~ yun/ i.e., divine.

45. **portents** here should be /por TENTS/ omens.

133. **belie** /bih-, bee LĪ/ slander.

145. **chrysolite** /CRISS uh līt/ topaz.

150. **iterance** (F1) /IT (uh) runss/. Some eds prefer Q1's **iteration** /it ur AY shun/ both mean 'repetition.'

209. **reprobance** (F1) /REP ruh bunss/ state of damnation. Q1 has *reprobation*.

214. *****recognizance** /rih CŎG nih zunss, -zṇss/; *rarely older* [rih CŎN ih-] keepsake.

216. *antique ancient. Here /AN teek/, *rarely older* [AN tik].

273. compt (F1) /cownt/ accounting, i.e., Judgement Day. Variant of Q1's count which some eds. prefer. See App. D *accompt.*

301. *demi-devil /DEM ee-/ half-devil.

318. caitiff /KAYT if/ scoundrel.

335. close prisoner /clohss/ a securely kept prisoner.

345. jealious (F1) /JEL yus/ archaic variant of Q1's jealous.

348. subdu'd here should be stressed on the 1st syllable.

349. Albeit /awl BEE (i)t/ although.

351. medicinable (F1) here /MED sin uh bł/ medicinal.

352. Aleppo /uh LEP oh/ city in present-day Syria.

354. traduc'd slandered. /truh DYŌOST/; US *also* /-DŌOST/. /-JŌOST/ is considered non-standard in the UK.

ă-bat, ăir-marry, air-pair, ạr-far, ĕr-merry, ĝ- get, ī-high, ĭr-mirror, ł-little, ṇ-listen, ŏ-hot, oh-go, ŏŏ-wood, ōō-moon, oor-tour, ōr- or, ow-how, ţh-that, th-thin, ŭ-but, UR-fur, ur-under.   ( ) - suppress the syllable   see p. xiii for complete list.

Pericles

People in the Play

Antiochus 3 or 4 syllables depending on meter /an TĪ (uh) kus/.

Boult /bohlt/.

Cerimon /SĔR ih mŏn, -mun/. /-ŏn/ is usual in the US and is increasingly common in the UK. See App. D -on.

Cleon /CLEE ŏn/. /CLEE un/ is increasingly rare. See App. D -on.

Diana /dī AN uh/.
  Dian /DĪ un, -an/.

Dionyza (Q2), **Dioniza** (Q1) /dī uh NĪ zuh, dī oh-/.

Escanes, Aeschines /ES kuh neez/.

Gower /GOW ur/.

Helicanus /hel ih KAY nus/.
  Helicane /HEL ih kayn/.

Leonine 2 or 3 syllables depending on meter /LEE (uh) nīn, LEE (-oh-)/.

Lychorida, Lichorida /lī COR ih duh/.

Lysimachus /lī SIM uh kus/.

Marina /muh REE nuh/.

A Pander, Pandar /PAN dur/ pimp. This word is not spoken.

Pericles /PĔR ih cleez/.

Philemon /fih LEE mun/ [fī-]. Sometimes newer /-ŏn/ is used. See App. D -on.

Simonides /sī MŎN ih deez/.

People in the Play (cont.)

Thaisa /~~th~~ay ISS uh/ or /~~THAY~~ iss uh/ depending on meter. Sometimes restored /tah EE suh/ is used.

Thaliard 2 or 3 syllables depending on meter /~~THAL~~ (ee) yurd/; UK *also* /-yard/. Some eds. prefer Q1's **Thaliart** /-yurt/; UK *also* /-yart/. Normal development would favor /-urd, -urt/.

Places in the Play

Antioch 2 or 3 syllables depending on meter /AN t(ee) yŏck/.

Ephesus /EF ih sus/.

Metiline /met ih LEEN ee/. Some eds. prefer **Myteline**, or **Mytilene**, both pronounced /mit ih LEEN ee/. In some instances it is pronounced with three syllables, spelled **Metelin** /MET ih lin, -len/ to rhyme once with *din*, and once with *then*. For the spellings with **Myt-** this 3 syllable pronunciation would be /MIT uh lin, -len/.

Pentapolis /pen TAP uh liss/.

Tharsus, Tarsus both pronounced /TAR sus/.

Tyre /tīr/.
 Tyrian /TĬR yun/.
 Tyrus /TĪR us/.

Act 1 Chorus (*Complete Oxford* Scene 1)

10.	**Et**	**bonum**	**quo**	**antiquius,**		**eo**	**melius**
Ang.Lat.	/et	BOH num	kwoh	an TICK	wee us,	EE oh	MEE lee us/
Class.Lat.	/et	BŎN ōōm	kwoh	ahn TEE	kwih ōōs,	EH oh	MEL ee ōōs/

'and the older a good thing is the better it is.'

16. **taper-light** /TAY pur/ slender candle.

21. **peer** companion. Some eds. prefer **fere** /feer/ mate, wife.

ă-bat, ăir-**marry**, air-**pair**, ar̦-**far**, ĕr-**merry**, ĝ- get, ī-high, ĭr-**mirror**, l̄-little, n̦-**listen**, ŏ-hot, oh-go, ōō-**wood**, ōō-**moon**, oor-**tour**, ōr- **or**, ow-**how**, t̲h-**that**, ~~th~~-**thin**, ŭ-but, UR-**fur**, ur-**under**.   ( ) - suppress the syllable   see p. xiii for complete list.

23. **blithe** /blīth/; US *also* /blĭth/ merry.

Act 1 Scene 1 (*Complete Oxford* continues this as Scene 1—line nos. in parentheses)

8. (1.51) **Lucina** Roman goddess of childbirth. /loo SĪ nuh/; restored Latin /-SEE-/ (for /lyoo-/ see App. D *lu-*).

17. (1.60) **ras'd** /rayst/ erased. Some eds. prefer **razed** /rayzd/ which could also mean 'erase' or 'cut, slash.'

27. (1.70) **Hesperides** /hess PĔR ih deez/ garden where golden apples grew.

35. (1.78) **advent'rous** /ad VENT rus/ archaic variant of mod.
/ad VENCH russ/.

49. (1.92) **erst** /urst/ formerly.

81. (1.124) **viol** /VĪ ł/ six-stringed instrument.

110. (1.153) **gloze, glose** /glohz/ use deceptive language.

111. (1.154) **edict** here should be /ee DICT/ decree.

116. (1.159) *__respite__ grant a reprieve. Here should be US /RESP it/, *rarely* [-īt]; CN /RESP it/ [-īt]; UK /RESP īt/ [-it]. /RESP it/ is older, but /-īt/ has been in use since the 17th cent.

136. (1.179) **'schew** /ss-choo/ eschew, avoid. Some eds. prefer Q's **shew** /shoo/ 'shy,' others **shun**.

169. (1.213) **succor** (UK **succour**) /SUCK ur/ help. See App. D *-or*.

Act 1 Scene 2 (*Complete Oxford* Scene 2)

25. **th' ostent** here should be /ṭhʸŏ STENT/ display.

36. **comfortable** here may be 3 or 4 syllables /CUMF tur bł/, /CUM fur tuh bł/.

49. **lading's** /LAYD ingz/ cargo's.

89. **unlaid ope** here should be /UN layd OHP/ undisclosed.

91. **pretense** (UK **pretence**) pretext. Here should be /prih TENSS/, the normal UK pronunciation, or /pree TENSS/ based on the most common US pronunciation /PREE tenss/.

Act 1 Scene 3 (*Complete Oxford* Scene 3)

stage direction: solus /SOH lŭss/ alone.

34. **unknown** here should be /UN nohn/.

Act 1 Scene 4 (*Complete Oxford* Scene 4)

42. **nousle up** (*nouzell* Q1) /NUZ ł/. Some eds. prefer **nuzzle**, others **nurstle**. All mean 'nurture.'

60. **descried** /dih SKRĪD/ seen.

71. **semblance** here /SEM bł unss/ is indicated.

Act 2 Chorus (*Complete Oxford* Scene 5)

2. **I wis** /ī wiss/ I know. Some eds. prefer *iwis* /ih WISS/; US, CN *also* /ee WISS/ indeed.

3. **benign** here 1st syllable stress is indicated.

10. ***benison** US, CN /BEN ih sun, -sṇ/ [-zun, -zṇ]; UK /-z-/ [-s-] blessing.

12. **speken** a Middle Eng. form of the infinitive *speak*. Shk may have pronounced it something like /SPAY kun/, but the best choice is probably /SPEEK un/ today. Some eds. prefer Q1's **spoken**.

35. **perishen** /PĔR ish un/ archaic form of *perished*.

36. **Ne aught escapend** no one escaping. /nih-, nee AWT ess KAY pund/.

ă-bat, ăir-ma**rry**, air-**pair**, ạr-**far**, ĕr-**merry**, ĝ- **get**, ī-**high**, ĭr-**mirror**, ł-**little**, ṇ-**listen**, ŏ-**hot**, oh-**go**, o͞o-**wood**, o͞o-**moon**, oor-**tour**, ōr- **or**, ow-**how**, ṭh-**that**, t̶h̶-**thin**, ŭ-**but**, UR-**fur**, ur-und**er**.   ( ) - suppress the syllable   see p. xiii for complete list.

Act 2 Scene 1 (*Complete Oxford* continue this as Scene 5—line nos. in parentheses)

14. (5.55) **Patch-breech** /PATCH britch/ is traditional, /-breech/ is newer. The former pronunciation is more common in the UK, and the latter in the US, CN.

17. (5.58) **wanion** /WŎN yun/ vengeance.

24. (5.65) **porpas** /POR pus/ archaic variant of **porpoise**.

78. (5.119) **keth 'a** /kuth EE/ variant of **quotha** /kwohth EE/. This is the weak form of **quoth he** (spoken with the same stress as *says he* would be). For variation between unstressed /uh/ and /ee/ see p. 39 *'a.*

93. (5.134) **beadle** /BEE dł/ local officer in charge of whippings.

110. (5.152) **just** /just/ archaic variant of *joust US, CN /JOWST/, US rarely older [just]; UK /JOWST/, rarely [jōōst].*

110, 144. (5.152, 187) **tourney** perform in a tournament. US, CN /TUR nee/ [TOOR-]; parts of E.COAST US [TOR-]; UK /TOOR-/ [TOR-, TUR-].

146. (5.189) **d'ye, di'e** (Q1u) /dyih, dyee/ 'do ye,' i.e., 'go ahead.'

147. (5.190) **an't, on't** /unt/ of it.

150. (5.193) **condolements** /cun DOHL munts/ 'grievings,' but here the fisherman probably means *doles* 'shares.'

158. (5.201) **courser** /COR sur/ warhorse.

Act 2 Scene 2 (*Complete Oxford* Scene 6)

20. **Ethiope** /EETH yohp/ person from Ethiopia. Some eds. prefer **Ethiop** /EETH yŏp/.

21.   **Lux   tua   vita   mihi**
Ang.Lat.   /luks TŌŌ uh VĪ tuh   MĪ hee/   (UK, SOUTH. US /TYŌŌ uh/)
Class.Lat. /lōōks Tōō ah   WEE tah MIH hee/
                   'thy light is life to me.'

24. **Macedon** /MĂSS uh dun, -dŏn/. /-ŏn/ is usual in the US and is increasingly common in the UK. See App. D *-on.*

27. **Piu per dolcera que per força**. This phrase, 'more by gentleness than by force' is a mix of several languages, and has been rewritten by many eds. As given in *Riverside* it might be /pyōo pĕr dŏl CHĔR ah kay pĕr FOR sah/. Some eds. prefer the correct Ital.:

><u>Piùe</u>   per dolcezza   che per forza.
>/PYŌO ay pĕr dŏl CHET sah kay pĕr FORT sah/

Piùe is an archaic or poetic form.

30.   **Me pompae provexit   apex**
Ang.Lat. /mee PŎM pee proh VEK sit AY peks/
Class.Lat. /may PŎM pī   proh WEK sit AH peks/
            'the crown of triumph has led me on.'

33.   **Qui me alit,   me extinguit**
Ang.Lat. /kwee mee AY lit, mee ek STING gwit/
Class.Lat. /kwee may AH lit, may ek STING gwit/
            'who feeds me, extinguishes me.'

36. ***environed** /en VĪ run ed/; US *also* [en VĪ urn ed] surrounded.

38.   **Sic   spectanda   fides**
Ang.Lat. /sik   spek TAN duh   FĪ deez/
Class.Lat. /seek spek TAHN dah FID ess/
            'thus is faithfulness to be tried.'

44.   **In hac spe vivo**
Ang.Lat. /in hack spee VĪ voh/
Class.Lat. /in hahk spay WEE woh/
            'In this hope I live.'

Act 2 Scene 3 (*Complete Oxford* Scene 7)

29. **cates** /kayts/ delicacies.

31. **viands** /VĪ undz/ food.   /VEE undz/ not recommended.

36. **diamond** here should be /DĪ uh mund/, the standard pronunciation in the UK.

64. **entrance** here should be 3 syllables /EN tur unss/.

ă-bat, ăir-**marry**, air-**pair**, ạr-**far**, ĕr-**merry**, ĝ- get, ī-**high**, ĭr-**mirror**, ł-**little**, ṇ-**listen**, ŏ-**hot**, oh-go, ōō-**wood**, ōō-**moon**, oor-**tour**, ōr- or, ow-**how**, t̪h-**that**, t̶h̶-**thin**, ŭ-**but**, UR-**fur**, ur-**under**.   ( ) - suppress the syllable   see p. xiii for complete list.

Act 2 Scene 4 (*Complete Oxford* Scene 8)

5. **heinous* /HAYN us/ hateful. /HEEN us/ is non-standard though common in the UK.

53. **diamonds** here should be /DĪ mundz/, the most common pronunciation in the US.

Act 2 Scene 5 (*Complete Oxford* Scene 9)

7. **access** here should be /ak SESS/.

73. **peremptory** here should be /pur EM tur ee/ determined.

Act 3 Chorus (*Complete Oxford* Scene 10)

1. **yslacked** (Q1) /ih-, ee SLACK id/, **y-slaked** (Q2) /-SLAY kid/. Archaic forms of *slaked* 'quenched.'

1. **rout** /rowt/ crowd.

3. **oe'rfed** here should be /OR fed/.

5. **eyne** /īn/ dialect form of *eyes*.

8. **blither** /BLĪTH ur/; US *also* /BLĪTH -/ happier.

8. **drouth** /drowth/ dryness. Variant of **drought** /drowt/ still found in some dialects.

11. **attent** /uh TENT/ attentive.

13. **eche* augment. Here should be /eech/ to rhyme with *speech*.

15. **dern, dearn** /durn/ drear.

17. **coigns** /coynz/ corners.

35. **Yravished** /ih-, ee RAV ih shed/ enraptured.

47. **grisled, grizzled** /GRIZ łd/ grim, horrible.

52. **travail* here should be /TRAV ayl/ labor of childbirth.

Act 3 Scene 1 (*Complete Oxford* Scene 11)

10. **Lucina** Roman goddess of childbirth. /lōō SĪ nuh/; restored Latin /-SEE-/ (for /lyōō-/ see App. D *lu-*).

14. ***travails** here should be /TRAV aylz/ pains of childbirth.

43. **bolins** variant of **bowlines** ropes used to rig sails. Both pronounced /BOH linz/.

62. **e'er-remaining**. Some eds. prefer **aye-remaining** /ay/ ever. /ī/ is often used, but not recommended.

65. **Nestor** /NEST ur/. See App. D *-or*.

66. **Nicander** /nī KAN dur/.

71. **bitum'd** US /BIT ōōmd/; SOUTH. US, UK /-tyōōmd/ caulked with pitch.

Act 3 Scene 2 (*Complete Oxford* Scene 12)

9. **pothecary** US /PŎTH uh kĕr ee/; UK /-kuh ree/ apothecary, druggist.

25. **conversant** here should be /CŎN vur sunt, -sn̩t/ intimately acquainted with.

36. **vegetives** /VEJ ih tivz/ plants.

56. **close** /clohss/ tightly, securely.

56. **bitum'd** US /BIT ōōmd/; SOUTH. US, UK /-tyōōmd/ caulked with pitch. Q1 has **bottomed**.

67. **Apollo, perfect me in the characters** 'inform me what this writing means.' Shk intended /PUR fikt/ and /kuh RAK turz/.

71. **mundane** worldly. Here should be older /MUN dayn/, now very rare.

84. **oe'rpress'd spirits** here should be /OR prest/.

85. **lien** /līn/, archaic variant of **lain**. Some eds. omit this passage.

ă-bat, ăir-**marry**, air-**pair**, ạr-**far**, ĕr-**merry**, ĝ- get, ī-high, ĭr-**mirror**, ł-little, n̩-listen, ŏ-hot, oh-go, ōō-**wood**, ōō-**moon**, oor-**tour**, ōr- **or**, ow-how, ţh-**that**, ɬh-**thin**, ŭ-but, UR-**fur**, ur-under.   ( ) - suppress the syllable   see p. xiii for complete list.

94. **gins** /ĝinz/ begins.

100. **diamonds** here should be /DĪ uh mundz/, the standard pronunciation in the UK.

103. **creature** here an archaic form /CREE uh chur/ is indicated.

109. **relapse** here should be /rih-, ree LAPSS/ the usual stress in the UK.

110. *****Aesculapius** /es kuh-, es kyuh LAY pyus/; UK *also* /eess-/ Greek god of healing.

Act 3 Scene 3 (*Complete Oxford* Scene 13)

3. **litigious** /lih TIJ us/ full of disputes.

Act 3 Scene 4 (*Complete Oxford* Scene 14)

6. **eaning** /EEN ing/ birthing. Some eds. prefer the variant **yeaning** /YEEN ing/ or **yielding, bearing**.

Act 4 Chorus (*Complete Oxford* Scene 15)

4. **votaress** /VOHT uh riss, -ress/ female member of a religious group.

18-36. **Philoten** /FĪ loh tin, FIL oh tin/.

21. **sleided** /SLEED id/ separated into threads.   Q1 has **sleded,** pronounced the same way.

23. **needle** some eds. prefer the variant **nee'le** /neel/. One syllable is indicated here.

24. *****cambric** fine linen cloth.   /KAM brik/, or older [KAYM brik].

32. **Paphos** place on Cyprus sacred to Venus. US /PAY fus, -fŏs/;
UK /-fŏs/ [-fus]. A newer ending /-ohss/ is also used, especially in the US.
Normal development would favor /-us/. A more recent restored pronunciation with /PAH-/ is also used.

Act 4 Scene 1 (*Complete Oxford* continues this as Scene 15—line nos. in parentheses)

13. (15.65) **Tellus** /TEL us/ goddess of the earth.

14. (15.66) **strow** /stroh/ archaic variant of **strew**.

26. (15.78) **mar it**. Some eds. prefer **margent** /MAR junt/, archaic variant of **margin**.

35. (15.86) *****paragon** US /PĂIR uh gŏn/ [-gun]; CN /-gŏn/; UK /-gun/ [-gṇ] most perfect example.

61. (15.112) **wolt out** /wo͞olt/ archaic variant of **wilt** 'do you want?'

63. (15.114) **boatswain** /BOH sṇ/ is usual, though /BOHT swayn/ is sometimes used by landsmen.

96. (15.145) **Valdes** /VAL diss, -deez/.

Act 4 Scene 2 (*Complete Oxford* Scene 16)

26. **chequins** /chuh KEENZ/ gold coins.

52. **pieces**. Some eds. prefer **sesterces** /SESS TUR siz/ Roman coins.

88. **bow'd** /bohd/.

106. **Verollus** /vuh RŎL us/, /vuh ROH lus/. Some eds. prefer **Veroles, Verolles**, pronounced the same way, or /vuh ROH leez/.

138. **sojourner** temporary resident.   /soh-, suh JURN nur/, /SOH jurn ur/; UK *also* /SŎJ-/ [SUJ-].

140. *****paragon** US /PĂIR uh gŏn/ [-gun]; CN /-gŏn/; UK /-gun/ [-gṇ] most perfect example.

ă-bat, ăir-**ma**rry, air-**pair**, ạr-**far**, ĕr-**merry**, ĝ- **get**, ī-**high**, ĭr-**mir**ror, ł-**little**, ṇ-**listen**,
ŏ-**hot**, oh-**go**, o͞o-**wood**, o͞o-**moon**, oor-**tour**, ōr- **or**, ow-**how**, ţh-**that**, ŧħ-**thin**, ŭ-**but**,
UR-**fur**, ur-**under**.   ( ) - suppress the syllable   see p. xiii for complete list.

Act 4 Scene 3 (*Complete Oxford* Scene 17)

34. **mawkin** /MAW kin/ slut. Variant of *malkin US /MAWL kin/;
UK /MAW kin/ [MAWL-, MÖL-].

35. **thorough** archaic variant of *through*, pronounced as *thorough*. Used when
the meter demands two syllables. Here at the end of a line most eds. prefer
through, since the two-syllable form creates a superfluous feminine ending.

48. **talents** /TAL unts/ archaic variant of **talons**.

Act 4 Scene 4 (*Complete Oxford* Scene 18)

4. *bourn /born, boorn/ boundary. North American [burn] not recommended.
Normal development would favor /born/.

39, 41. *Thetis /T̶H̶EE tiss/, *sometimes newer* [T̶H̶ET iss] Achilles' mother.
Some eds. omit this passage.

Act 4 Scene 6 (*Complete Oxford* combines 4.5. and 4.6 into Scene 19—line nos.
in parentheses)

4. (19.12) **Priapus** /prī AYP us/ god of fertility.

12. (19.21) **cavalleria** /kav uh luh REE uh/ body of gentlemen. Some eds.
prefer **cavaliers**.

18. (19.26) **lown** /lown/ low-bred fellow. Some eds. prefer **loon** /lo͞on/.

24. (19.32) **resorters** /ree-, rih ZORT urz/ customers.

64. (19.68) **manage**. Some eds. prefer **manège** US /mah NEZH, -NAYZH/;
UK /man AYZH/ [-EZH]; Fr. /mah nezh/. Stress may also fall on the 1st
syllable. Both words mean 'horsemanship.'

after 105. (19.130) Some eds. add lines containing **laved** /LAY vid/ washed.

106. (19.134) **Persever** /pur SEV ur/ persevere.

110. (19.136) **savor** (UK **savour**) /SAY vur/ smell.

118. (19.144) **Avaunt** /uh VAWNT/ begone!

143. (19.168) **malleable** /MAL ee uh bł/ willing to be shaped to our will.

147. (19.172) *****conjures** 'entreats' or possibly 'summons by magic.'
US, CN /CŎN jurz/, *rarely* [CUN-]; UK /CUN jurz/ [CŎN-]. In the meaning
'entreats,' the older pronunciation /cun JOORZ/ is sometimes used.

166. (19.190) **Custrel** /CŬSS trł/ scoundrel. Variant of **Coistrel** /COY strł/.

175. (19.200) **Old receptacles** some have suggested /REE sep tuh kłz/ in verse,
or it could be a rare example of two weak stresses at the beginning of a line.

178. (19.203) **thou professest** you make your business. Here /PROH fess est/ is
indicated.

191. (19.214) **frequent** here should be /free-, frih KWENT/ visit.

Act 5 Chorus (*Complete Oxford* Scene 20)

1. *****brothel** US, CN /BRŎ̵T̵H̵ ł/ [BRŎ̵T̵H ł, BRAW̵T̵H̵ ł]; UK /BRŎ̵T̵H̵ ł/
whorehouse.

5. **neele** /neel/ archaic variant of **needle**.

18. **espies** /ess SPĪZ/ sees.

Act 5 Scene 1 (*Complete Oxford* Scene 21)

26. **prorogue** /pruh-, proh ROHG/ prolong.

51. **leavy** /LEEV ee/ archaic variant of **leafy**.

60. **graff** shoot grafted to another stem. US /grăf/; E.NEW ENG., UK /grahf/
archaic variant of **graft**.

109. **stature** /STATCH ur/ size.

121. **palace**. Another possible reading is Q1's *****Pallas** Athena, goddess of
wisdom. US /PAL us/ [-ăss]; UK, CN /-ăss/ [-us]. Normal development would
favor /-us/.

ă-bat, äir-**marry**, air-**pair**, ar̤-**far**, ĕr-**merry**, ĝ- **get**, ī-**high**, ĭr-**mirror**, ł-**little**, n̤-**listen**,
ŏ-**hot**, oh-**go**, o͞o-**wood**, o͞o-**moon**, oor-**tour**, ōr- **or**, ow-**how**, t̤h-**that**, t̵h̵-t̵h̵i̵n̵, ŭ-**but**,
UR-**fur**, ur-un**der**.   ( ) - suppress the syllable   see p. xiii for complete list.

177. **imposture** archaic variant of **impostor** 'swindler.' Both pronounced /im PŎS tur/ (see App. E).

206. **perfit** /PUR fit/ archaic variant of **perfect** /PUR fikt/ 'fully inform.' Also /PAR fit/ in Shk's time.

250. *****argentine** US, UK /AHR jin tīn/ [-teen]; CN /AHR jin teen, -tīn/ silvery.

255. **eftsoons** /eft SO͞ONZ/ soon, afterwards.

Act 5 Scene 2 (*Complete Oxford* Scene 22)

7. **minstrelsy** /MIN strł see/ playing and singing of minstrels.

Act 5 Scene 3 (*Complete Oxford* continues this as Scene 22—line nos. in parentheses)

23. (22.43) **op'd** /ohpt/ opened.

30. (22.50) **licentious** /lī SEN chus/ free of moral restraint, wild.

70. (22.93) **Night-oblations** /uh BLAY shunz/ [oh-, ŏb-] religious offerings. Some eds. prefer **Nightly-oblations**.

71. (22.94) **fair-betrothed** /bih-, bee TROHȚH id/ fiancée.

80. (22.103) *****nuptials** weddings. US, UK /NUP chłz/ [-shłz]; in CN both are used equally.

91. (22.114) **descry** /dih SKRĪ/ see.

94. (22.117) **aye** /ay/ ever. /ī/ is often used, but not recommended.

Richard II

People in the Play

Aumerle /oh MURL/.

Bagot /BAG ut/.

Berkeley US /BURK lee/; UK /BARK-/.

Bullingbrook Shk also spelled this name **Bullinbrook, Bullingbrooke, Bullinbrooke,** and pronounced it /BULL in brook/. Pope was the first to change it to **Bolingbroke** in the early 18th century. Today pronounced US, CN /BOHL ing brook/ [BULL-, BŎL-]; UK /BŎL-/, *rarely* [BULL-].

Bushy /BUSH ee/.

Carlisle /car LĪL/.

Exton, Sir Pierce of /EK stun/.

Fitzwater here should have 2nd syllable stress.

Gaunt /gawnt/.

Gloucester /GLŎS tur/; US *also* /GLAWSS-/.

Herford, Hereford (Bullingbrook) in the US both would be /HUR furd/. In the UK the county is normally /HĔR ih furd/ which in this play should be 2 syllables /HĔR furd/.

Lancaster US /LANG kăst ur, -k^{u}ss tur/; UK /LANG k^{u}ss tur/ [-kahst ur, -kăst ur].

Langley (York) /LANG lee/. This name is not spoken.

Mowbray, Mowbrey both pronounced /MOH bree/ [-bray]. The latter is the traditional form.

Norfolk (Mowbray) /NOR f^{u}k/.

ă-bat, ăir-m**arry**, air-**pair**, ạr-**far**, ĕr-m**erry**, ĝ- g**et**, ī-h**igh**, ĭr-m**irror**, ł-l**ittle**, ṇ-l**isten**, ŏ-h**ot**, oh-g**o**, o͞o-w**ood**, o͞o-m**oon**, oor-**tour**, ōr- **or**, ow-h**ow**, ţh-**that**, ŧh̵-**thin**, ŭ-b**ut**, UR-f**ur**, ur-und**er**.   ( ) - suppress the syllable   see p. xiii for complete list.

People in the Play (cont.)

Northumberland /nor~~th~~ UM bur lund/.

Salisbury 2 or 3 syllables, depending on meter US /SAWLZ b(ĕ)r ee/;
UK /SAWLZ b(u)r ee/ [SĂLZ-].

Scroop /skrōōp/. Some eds. prefer mod. **Scrope**, pronounced the same way.

Surrey US /SUR ee/; UK, E.COAST US /SUH ree/.

Westminster here should be /WEST min stur/.

Willoughby /WILL uh bee/.

Wiltshire /WILT shur/ [-sheer]. Mentioned throughout.

Places in the Play

Bristow /BRIST oh/ archaic variant of F1's **Bristol** /BRIST ł/.

***Ravenspurgh** here should be 3 syllables /RAV in SPURG, -SPUR/ or
/RAY vin-/. Sometimes spelled **Ravenspur** /-SPUR/.

Act 1 Scene 1

34. **appellant** /uh PELL unt/ challenger.

39. **miscreant** /MIS cree unt/ scoundrel.

70. **kinred** /KIN rid/ archaic variant of **kindred**.

93. **elsewhere** here with 1st syllable stress, the US form, also sometimes used in
the UK.

96. **Complotted** /cum PLŎT id/ plotted.

106. ***chastisement** punishment. Here stress should be on the 1st syllable
/CHĂSS tiz munt/; US *also* /-tīz-/.

126. **Callice, Callis** /KAL iss/ city on north. coast of France. Both are archaic
variants of **Calais** which here should be /KAL ay/, the normal UK form;
Fr. /KAH lay/.

143. **rancor** (UK **rancour**) /RANK ur/ ill-will. See App. D *-or*.

144. **recreant** /REK ree unt/ faithless.

192. ***parley** /PAR lee/ conference with an enemy. Newer [-lay] not recommended.

193. **slavish** /SLAY vish/ slave-like.

199. **Coventry** US /KUV ṇ tree/; UK /KŎV ṇ tree/ [KUV-].

Act 1 Scene 2

45, 56. **Coventry** US /KUV ṇ tree/; UK /KŎV ṇ tree/ [KUV-].

51. **courser's** /COR surz/ warhorse's.

53. **caitive** /KAYT iv/ base. Variant of **caitiff** /KAYT if/.

53. **recreant** /REK r(ee) yunt/ coward.

66. **Plashy** /PLASH ee/ modern **Pleshey** /PLUSH ee/.

Act 1 Scene 3

4, 52. **the appellant('s)** /ṭhʸuh PELL unt/ challenger.

28. **habiliments** /huh BIL ih munts/ equipment.

35-113. **Derby** US /DUR bee/; UK /DAR bee/.

70. **regenerate** reborn. /rih-, ree JEN ur ut, -ayt/. /-ut/ would be the usual form for an adj.

81. **casque** /kăsk/; UK *also* [kahsk] helmet.

90. **enfranchisement** /en FRAN chiz munt/ liberty.

95. ***jocund** /JŎCK und/; US, CN *rarely* [JOHK-] merry.

97. **espy** /ess SPĪ/ see.

ă-bat, ăir-marry, air-pair, ạr-far, ĕr-merry, ĝ- get, ī-high, ĭr-mirror, ł-little, ṇ-listen, ŏ-hot, oh-go, ŏŏ-wood, ōō-moon, oor-tour, ōr- or, ow-how, ṭh-that, ᵗh-thin, ŭ-but, UR-fur, ur-under.   ( ) - suppress the syllable   see p. xiii for complete list.

106, 111. **recreant** /REK ree unt/ cowardly or unfaithful.

117. **combatants** here should be stressed on the first syllable, as is usual in the UK, /CŎM buh tunts/ [CUM-].

134. **untun'd** here should be stressed on the first syllable.

138. **kinred's** /KIN ridz/ archaic variant of **kindred's**.

150. **determinate** /dih-, dee TUR mih nayt/ determine.

162. **viol** /VĪ ł/ six-stringed instrument.

167. **portcullis'd** /port CŬLL ist/ barred.

187. **low'ring, louring** threatening. /LOWR ing/, with the vowel of *how*.

189. **complot** here should be /CŎM plŏt/ plot.

196. **sepulchre** tomb. Here should be /suh-, sep PŬL kur/.

223. **taper** /TAY pur/ slender candle.

235. **low'r, lour** frown. /lowr/ with the vowel of *how*.

257. **dolor** (UK **dolour**) /DOH lur/; UK *also* /DŎL ur/ pain. See App. D *-or*.

262. **travel** /TRAV ł/ some eds. prefer *****travail** /TRAV ayl/ labor. In Shk's time *travail* was pronounced /TRAV ł/.

289. **strow'd** /strohd/ archaic variant of **strewed**.

295. **Caucasus** /KAW kuh suss/ Asian mountains.

Act 1 Scene 4

8. **rheum** /rōōm/ tears.

44. **liberal *largess, largesse** generous gift. Here should have 1st syllable stress after /LIB rł/: US /LAR jess/ [-zhess]; CN, UK /LAR zhess/ [-jess]. Forms with /j/ are older.

46. **revenue** sometimes in verse /ruh VEN yōō/, but here as in mod. Eng. US /REV in ōō/; UK, SOUTH. US /-yōō/.

58. **Ely** /EE lee/.

Act 2 Scene 1

2. **unstayed** here should be /UN stayd/ unchecked.

10. **glose, gloze** /glohz/ flatter.

19. **Lascivious** /luh SIV yus/ lustful.

38. **insatiate** /in SAYSH yut, -yayt/ never satisfied. /-ut/ is more usual for an adj.

38. ***cormorant** /COR m(uh) runt/; US *rarely* [-ant] a fishing bird, i.e., devouring.

42. ***demi-paradise** /DEM ee-/ half (i.e., nearly) paradise.

55. **sepulchre** /SEP ł kur/ tomb.

116. **ague's** /AY gyo͞oz/ malarial fever.

130. **president** example. Archaic variant of ***precedent**, both /PRESS ih dunt/. It is not clear whether /PREZ-/ was used in Shk's time.

151, 257. ***bankrout** /BANK rowt/ [-rut] archaic variant of **bankrupt.**

156. **kerns** /kurnz/ Irish foot soldiers.

161, 226. **revenues** sometimes in verse /ruh VEN yo͞oz/, but here as in mod. Eng. US /REV in o͞oz/; UK, SOUTH. US /-yo͞oz/.

182. **kinred** /KIN rid/ archaic variant of **kindred.**

202. ***letters-patents** US /PAT n̩ts/ [PAYT-]; UK /PAYT-/ [PAT-] documents conferring a right or power.

204. ***homage** /HŎM ij/; US *also* /ŎM ij/ acknowledgement of allegience.

216. **Ely** /EE lee/.

ă-bat, ăir-**marry**, air-**pair**, a̩r-**far**, ĕr-**merry**, ĝ- **get**, ī-high, ĭr-**mirror**, ł-little, n̩-listen, ŏ-hot, oh-**go**, o͞o-**wood**, o͞o-**moon**, oor-**tour**, ŏr- **or**, ow-**how**, t̩h-**that**, t̶h̶-**thin**, ŭ-but, UR-**fur**, ur-und**er**.   ( ) - suppress the syllable   see p. xiii for complete list.

218. ***trow** US, CN /troh, trow/; UK /trow/ [troh] believe. Shk's rhymes elsewhere indicate /-oh/.

277. **Le Port Blanc** (following Q1-5) angl. /luh port BLANK/; Fr. /luh por BLAH^N/. Some eds. prefer **Port le Blanc** (following F1) angl. /PORT luh BLANK/; Fr. /por luh BLAH^N/.

278, 285. **Britain, Brittaine** /BRIT n̩/ Brittany. In Shk's time /-ayn/ was also used. For clarity *Britt'ny* may be substituted.

279. **Rainold, Reinold** /REN łd/.

279. **Cobham** /CŎB um/.

280. **Arundel** /ĂIR un dł/.

281. **Exeter** /EK sih tur/.

283. **Erpingham** /UR ping um/, though in the US /UR ping ham/ would be usual.

291. **slavish** /SLAY vish/ referring to slaves.

Act 2 Scene 2

10. **unborn** here should be /UN born/.

18. **perspectives** here should be /PUR spek tivz/.

19, 21. **awry** /uh RĪ/ askew.

54. **Beaumond** /BOH mund/, older form of **Beamont** US /BOH mŏnt/; UK /-munt/ [mŏnt].

58. **Worcester** /W͞o͞oS tur/.

76. **comfortable** here /CUMF tur bł/ in an inverted foot is the best choice.

77. **belie** /bih-, bee LĪ/ show to be false.

90, 120. **Plashy** /PLASH ee/ modern **Pleshey** /PLUSH ee/.

115. **kinred** /KIN rid/ archaic variant of **kindred**.

119. **Berkeley** here 3 syllables are indicated US /BURK uh lee/; UK /BARK-/.

142. ***presages** here should be /pree-, prih SAY jiz/ intuitions.

Act 2 Scene 3

1-68. **Berkeley** US /BURK lee/; UK /BARK-/.

3. **Gloucestershire** /GLŎSS tur shur/ [-sheer]; US *also* /GLAWSS-/.

7. **delectable** here should be /DEE lek tuh bł/ or /DEL ek tuh bł/.

9. **Cotshall** /CŎTS ł/ local pronunciation of the **Cotswold** hills in Gloucestershire, /CŎTS wohld/ [CŎTS ohld, -włd].

22. **Worcester** /WŏŏS tur/.

56. ***estimate** US /ES tih mut/ [-mayt]; UK /-mayt/ [-mut] reputation.

61. **unfelt** here should be /UN felt/.

65. the ***exchequer** /ţhʸeks CHEK ur/ treasury.

75. **rase** /rayss/ erase. Some eds. prefer a variant **raze** /rayz/ which can also mean 'erase.'

104. **palsy** /PAWL zee/; UK *also* [PŎL-] paralysis or shaking.

104. ***chastise** punish. Here should be /CHĂSS tīz/, the usual US pronunciation, also used in CN; in the UK 2nd syllable stress is usual.

130. ***letters-patents** US /PAT ņts/ [PAYT-]; UK /PAYT-/ [PAT-] documents conferring a right or power.

165. **complices** /CŎMP lih siz/ accomplices.

Act 3 Scene 1

9. **lineaments** /LIN yuh munts/ distinctive features.

ă-bat, ăir-**marry**, air-**pair**, ạr-**far**, ĕr-**merry**, ĝ- **get**, ī-**high**, ĭr-**mirror**, ł-**little**, ņ-**listen**,
ŏ-**hot**, oh-**go**, ŏŏ-**wood**, ōō-**moon**, oor-**tour**, ōr- **or**, ow-**how**, ţh-**that**, t̶h̶-**thin**, ŭ-**but**,
UR-**fur**, ur-**under**.   ( ) - suppress the syllable   see p. xiii for complete list.

22. **signories** /SEEN yur eez/ domains.

25. **Ras'd out** (*rac't* Q1) /rayst/ erased. Some eds. prefer F1's **Razed** /rayzd/ which could mean 'erase' or 'cut, slash.' **Rac'd** /rayst/ from *arace* 'pluck off' is also possible.

25. **imprese** /IM preez/ heraldic device or devices. Variant of **impress** /IM press/.

43. **Glendower** here should be /GLEN dowr/. Some eds. prefer the Welsh **Glyndŵr**, normally /glin DŌŌR/, but here /GLIN dōōr/.

43. **complices** /CŎMP lih siz/ accomplices.

Act 3 Scene 2

1. **Barkloughly** /bark LECK lee/ or inversion is possible to allow 1st syllable stress. Based on Holinshed's error for *Hertlowli,* now **Harlech** (angl. /HAR leck/) in Wales. Some eds. prefer **Harlechly** /HAR leck lee/.

13. **comfort** here mod. /CUM furt/ is possible in an inverted foot.

32. **succors** (UK **succours**) /SUCK urz/ help. See App. D *-or.*

49. **the antipodes** (Q1) /thʸan TIP uh deez/ people on the opposite side of the world, i.e., Irish. Omitted F1.

118. **distaff-women** US /DIS stăf/; E.NEW ENG., UK /DIS stahff/ women who spin.

170. **thorough** (Q1) archaic variant of *through,* which is often pronounced as mod. *thorough* on stage, but here it should be one syllable, making F1's, Q2-5's **through** the better choice.

185. *****servile** /SUR vīl/, *rarely* [SUR vɫ] slave-like.

188. **chid'st** /chīdst/ chidest.

190. **ague** /AY gyōō/ malarial fever.

Act 3 Scene 3

18. **I know it, uncle, and oppose not myself** here 1st syllable stress for *oppose* is indicated.

33. **brazen** /BRAY zun, -zn̩/ brass.

33. ***parley** /PAR lee/ conference with an enemy. Newer [-lay] not recommended.

67. **occident** /ŎK sih dunt/ west.

85. **omnipotent** /ŏm NIP uh tunt/ all-powerful.

100. **pasters'** US /PĂSS turz/; UK, E.NEW ENG. /PAHSS turz/ archaic variant **pastures'**.

114. **Enfranchisement** /en FRAN chiz munt/ freedom from banishment.

149. **almsman's** poor person. /AHMZ munz/ is older; /AHLMZ-, AWLMZ-/ are newer. In the UK the latter are non-standard.

154. **obscure** here should be /ŎB skyoor/; US *also* [-skyur].

178. **glist'ring** /GLIS tring/ glistening.

178. **Phaëton** /FAY ih tun, -tŏn/ son of the sun god. /-ŏn/ is usual in the US and is increasingly common in the UK. Some eds. prefer **Phaëthon** /--thun, -thŏn/. See App. D *-on.*

Act 3 Scene 4

29. **apricocks** /AYP rih cŏcks/; US, CN *also* /AP-/ dialect variant of **apricots**.

38. **noisome** /NOY sum/ noxious, disagreeable.

63. **Superfluous** here a normal line requires US /soo͞ pur FLOO͞ us/; UK, SOUTH. US *also* [syoo͞-], rather than the usual mod. pronunciation with 2nd syllable stress.

92. ***mischance** here with 2nd syllable stress.

93. **embassage** /EM buh sij/ ambassador's message.

ă-bat, ăir-**marry**, air-**pair**, ạr-**far**, ĕr-**merry**, ĝ- get, ī-high, ĭr-mirror, ł-**little**, n̩-**listen**, ŏ-hot, oh-go, o͞o-wood, ōō-moon, oor-**tour**, ōr- or, ow-how, ţh-**that**, th-**thin**, ŭ-but, UR-**fur**, ur-**under**.   ( ) - suppress the syllable   see p. xiii for complete list.

Act 4 Scene 1

13, 82. **Callice, Callis** /KAL iss/ city on north. coast of France. Both are archaic variants of **Calais** which here should be /KAL ay/, the normal UK form; Fr. /KAH lay/.

---

22. *****chastisement** punishment. Here stress should be on 1st syllable /CHĂSS tiz munt/; US *also* /-tīz-/.

33. **valure** archaic variant of **valor** (UK **valour**) all pronounced /VAL ur/.

54. **hollowed** (Q1), **holloa'd** /HŎL ud, -ohd/ cried out, as in a hunt. Omitted F1.

89. **signories** /SEEN yur eez/ domains.

94. *****ensign** flag. US, CN /EN sṇ/, US *rarely* [-sīn]; UK /-sṇ, -sīn/.

95. **pagans** /PAYG unz/ non-Christians.

95. **Saracens** /SĂIR uh sṇz, -sunz/ Muslims.

104. **appellants** /uh PELL unts/ accusers.

119. **noblesse** /noh BLESS/ nobility.

131, 233. *****heinous** /HAYN us/ hateful. /HEEN us/ is non-standard though common in the UK.

---

136. **prophesy** /PRŎF uh sī/ to predict the future.

140. *****tumultuous** full of turmoil. US /tōō MŬLL chwus/ [-tywus]; SOUTH. US *also* /tyōō-/; CN /tyōō-, tōō MUL chwus, -tywus/; UK /tyōō MŬLL tywus/ [-chwus], *rarely* [tōō MŬLL-]. In the UK /chōō MŬLL-/ is considered non-standard.

144. **Golgotha** here should be /GŎL guh ~~th~~huh/; US *also* /GAWL-/ hill where Jesus died.

159. *****sureties** bails, pledges. Here should be two syllables, though in mod. English, three syllables are more common, /SHUR (ih) teez, SHOOR-, SHOR-/ (see App. D).

212. **revenues** here should be /ruh VEN yōōz/.

220. **unking'd** here should be /UN kingd/.

230. **record** here should be /rek-, rik ORD/.

239, 240. **Pilate(s)** /PĪ lut(s)/ Roman governor of Palestine.

267. ***bankrout** (Q4-5) /BANK rowt/ [-rut] archaic variant of F1's **bankrupt**.

297. **unseen** here should be /UN seen/.

Act 5 Scene 1

25. **Which our *profane* hours here have thrown down.** Scans as a headless line with /PROH fayn/. Some eds. replace **thrown** with **stricken** which produces a normal line with usual mod. /proh FAYN/.

42. **betid** /bih-, bee TID/ happened, past tense of *betide.*

44. ***lamentable** here should be /LAM un tuh bł/ the usual UK pronunciation.

52. **Pomfret** US /PŎM frit/; UK /PUM frit/ [PŎM-].

80. **Hollowmas** US /HŎL oh muss/ [-mass]; UK /-mass/ [-muss] variant of ***Hallowmas** US /HŎL-, HAL oh muss/ [-mass]; UK /HAL oh mass/ [-muss]. All Saints Day, Nov. 1. The older form is /-muss/.

Act 5 Scene 2

32. **combating** here should be /CŎM buh ting/; UK *also* [CUM-].

40. **aye** /ay/ ever. /ī/ is often used, but not recommended.

45. **fealty** /FEEL tee/ faithfulness.

49. **as lief** /leef/ as soon.

52. **justs** /justs/ archaic variant of ***jousts**, now /jowsts/ in all countries; but US *rarely* [justs]; UK *rarely* [jo͞osts], The oldest form is /justs/, the newest /jowsts/.

79, 102. **appeach** /uh PEECH/ inform against.

ă-bat, ăir-**marry**, air-**pair**, ạr-**far**, ĕr-**merry**, ĝ- **get**, ī-**high**, ĭr-**mirror**, ł-**little**, ṇ-**listen**, ŏ-**hot**, oh-**go**, o͞o-**wood**, o͞o-**moon**, oor-**tour**, ŏr- **or**, ow-**how**, t̪h-**that**, t̲h̲-**thin**, ŭ-**but**, UR-**fur**, ur-**under**.   ( ) - suppress the syllable   see p. xiii for complete list.

Act 5 Scene 3

6. **frequent** here should be /free-, frih KWENT/ visit.

12, 20. **dissolute** /DIS uh lōōt/ lacking moral restraint (for /lyōō-/ see App. D *lu-*).

34, 59. *****heinous** /HAYN us/ hateful. /HEEN us/ is non-standard though common in the UK.

75. **suppliant** /SUP lyunt/ someone who asks humbly for something.

119. **pardonne-moy** Fr. /par DUN uh MWAH/ excuse me. Some eds. prefer **pardonnez-moi** /par DUN ay MWAH/.

138. **consorted** /cun SORT id/ assembled.

Act 5 Scene 4

10. **Pomfret** US /PŎM frit/; UK /PUM frit/ [PŎM-].

Act 5 Scene 5

17. *****postern** small back or side gate. US, CN /PŎST urn/ [POHST urn]; UK /PŎST urn/, *rarely* [POHST urn].

20. **thorough** archaic variant of *through,* which is often pronounced as mod. *thorough* in Shk, but here it should be one syllable, making **through** the better choice.

26. **refuge** following the iambic beat would give /ref-, rih FYŌŌJ/, but the foot may be inverted to allow /REF yōōj/.

34. **penury** /PEN yur ee/; UK *also* /PEN yoor ee/ poverty.

62. **holp** /hohlp/ helped.

66. *****brooch** /brohch/ ornament. US [brōōch] not recommended.

76. **ern'd** /urnd/ grieved.

78, 81. **Barbary** /BAR buh ree/ horse from North Africa. Line 81 would be /BAR bree/.

79. bestrid /bih-, bee STRID/ mounted.

85. eat /et/ dialect variant of **eaten**.

94. jauncing /JAWN sing/ prancing.

113. valure archaic variant of **valor** (UK **valour**) all pronounced /VAL ur/.

Act 5 Scene 6

3. Ciceter, Ci'cester /SIS ih tur/ older form of *Cirencester*, still occasionally used.

3. Gloucestershire /GLŎSS tur shur/ [-sheer]; US *also* /GLAWSS-/.

14. Brocas, Broccas /BRŎCK us, BROH kus/.

15. consorted /cun SORT id/ plotting.

33. Burdeaux city in France, possibly pronounced /BUR dŏcks/ in Shk's time. Archaic variant of **Bordeaux, Bourdeaux** which here should be /BOR doh/.

43. *thorough* **shades** archaic variant of *through*, used when the meter demands two syllables. It is often pronounced as *thorough* on stage, but using /-o͞o/ in the final syllable will bring it closer to mod. *through*. Some eds. prefer Q1's **through shades**, though it should still be two syllables. Others prefer Q2-5's, F1's **through the shades**.

52. bier /beer/ coffin.

ă-bat, ăir-marry, air-pair, ạr-far, ĕr-merry, ĝ- get, ī-high, ĭr-mirror, l-little, ṇ-listen, ŏ-hot, oh-go, o͝o-wood, o͞o-moon, oor-tour, ōr- or, ow-how, ţh-that, t͟h-thin, ŭ-but, UR-fur, ur-under.   ( ) - suppress the syllable   see p. xiii for complete list.

Richard III

People in the Play

Berkeley US /BURK lee/; UK /BARK lee/.

Bourchier /BOW chur/ his name is not spoken.

Bra(c)kenbury US /BRACK in bĕr ee/; UK /BRACK in bur ee/ or /-bree/.

Breton see **Britan**, "Places in the Play."

Buckingham /BUCK ing um/, though in the US /BUCK ing ham/ is common.

Cardinal (Bourchier) 2 or 3 syllables depending on meter /CARD (ih) nł/, /CARD n̩ ł/. Two syllables is usual in the US, three syllables in the UK.

Catesby 2 or 3 syllables depending on meter /KAYTS bee, KAY tiz bee/.

Derby (Stanley) US /DUR bee/; UK /DAR bee/.

Dorset /DOR sit/.

Ely /EE lee/.

Gloucester (Richard) /GLŎS tur/; US *also* /GLAWSS-/. At 3.4.46 expanded to 3 syllables /-uh tur/.

Henry 2 or 3 syllables depending on meter /HEN (ur) ree/.

Lancaster US /LANG kăst ur, -kᵘss tur/;
UK /LANG kᵘss tur/ [-kahst ur, -kăst ur].

Lovel, Lovell /LUV ł/.

Margaret /MAR guh rit/ or /MAR grit/ depending on meter.

Marquess (Dorset) some eds. prefer **Marquis**, both pronounced /MAR kwiss/.

Norfolk /NOR fᵘk/.

People in the Play (cont.)

Plantagenet /plan TAJ ih nit/.

Rotherham /RŎTH ur um/ his name is not spoken.

Scrivener /SKRIV nur/ notary. This word is not spoken.

Surrey US /SUR ee/; UK, E.COAST US /SUH ree/.

Tressel /TRESS ł/.

Tyrrel, Tirrel /TĬR ł/.

Urswick /URZ ik, URZ wik/ his name is not spoken.

Vaughan always 2 syllables /VAW un/.

Warwick US /WŌR ik/; E.COAST US, UK /WŌR-/. Place names in the US often have /-wik/ but this is not recommended for Shk. Mentioned throughout the play.

Wiltshire, Sheriff of /WILT shur/ [-sheer] not spoken.

Woodvil(l)e, Anthony (Rivers) /WŏŏD vil/. US /AN thuh nee/; UK /AN tuh nee/ [-thuh nee].

Places in the Play

Britain /BRIT n̩/ Brittany. In Shk's time /-ayn/ was also used. Some eds. prefer **Bretagne** which here should be /BRET ahnʸ/. For clarity *Britt'ny* may be substituted. This word is also used for 'person from Brittany,' in which meaning some eds. prefer mod. **Breton** US /BRET n̩/; UK /BRET ŏn/ [-n̩, -un]. Sometimes the Fr. ending /-ohⁿ/ is used in the UK.

Pomfret US /PŎM frit/; UK /PUM frit/ [PŎM-].

Tewksbury here 3 syllables US /TŌŌKS bĕr ee/; SOUTH. US /TYŌŌKS-/; UK /TYŌŌKS bur ee/. UK [CHŌŌKS-] is considered non-standard.

ă-bat, ăir-**marry**, air-**pair**, a̩r-**far**, ĕr-**merry**, ĝ- **get**, ī-**high**, ĭr-**mirror**, ł-**little**, n̩-**listen**, ŏ-**hot**, oh-**go**, ōō-**wood**, ōō-**moon**, oor-**tour**, ōr- **or**, ow-**how**, t̩h-**that**, th-**thin**, ŭ-**but**, UR-**fur**, ur-**under**.   ( ) - suppress the syllable   see p. xiii for complete list.

Act 1 Scene 1

stage direction: solus /SOH lŭss/ alone.

3. **low'r'd, loured** frowned. /lowrd/ with the vowel of *how*.

7. ***alarums** US, CN /uh LAHR umz/ [-LĂIR-];
UK /uh LĂIR umz, uh LAHR umz/ calls to arms.

13. **lascivious** /luh SIV yus/ lustful.

18. **curtail'd** here should be /CUR tayld/ cut short.

27. **descant** here should be /DES kănt/ comment on.

38, 132. **mew'd** /my$\overline{oo}$d/ caged.

74. **suppliant** /SUP lee unt/ someone who asks humbly for something.

92. **jealious** (F1) /JELL ee yus/ archaic variant of (Q1-6's) **jealous**, but here 3 syllables are needed for a regular line.

106. **abjects** /ab JECTS/ miserable subjects.

158. **close** /clohss/ hidden.

Act 1 Scene 2

3. **obsequiously** /ub-, ŏb SEE kw(ee) yus lee/ mournfully.

8. **invocate** /IN voh kayt/ call upon.

29-225. **Chertsey** /CHUR see/ a monastery.

40. ***halberd** US, CN /HAL burd, HAWL-/; UK /HAL-/ [HAWL-] spear with blades on the end.

46. **Avaunt** /uh VAWNT/ begone!

53. ***heinous** /HAYN us/ hateful. /HEEN us/ is non-standard though common in the UK.

56. **Open their congeal'd mouths** here should be /CŎN jeeld/. Some eds. prefer **Ope their congealed** /cun JEEL id/.

58, 165. **exhale(s)** here with 2nd syllable stress, /eks HAYL/, the normal UK form.

84. **excuse** here should be /EK skyōōss/.

94. *__falchion__ type of sword. /FĂL chun/ [-shun]; *older* [FAWL chun].

107. **holp** /hohlp/ helped.

150. *__basilisks__ legendary reptiles whose glance was fatal. US /BĂSS ih lisks/ [BAZ ih lisks]; UK /BAZ-/ [BĂSS-]; CN both used equally.

187. **Tush** (Q1-6) /tŭsh/ expression of disdain. Omitted F1 and *Riverside.*

191. **accessary** here US /AK sess ĕr ee/; UK /-uh ree/ or /AK sess ree/.

217. *__divers__ various. Should be stressed on the first syllable US, CN /DĪ vurss, -vurz/; UK /DĪ vurss/ [-vurz].

217. **unknown** here should be /UN nohn/.

249. **moi'ty, moiety** /MOY tee/ or /MOY ih tee/ portion.

251. **denier** coin of little value. Here should have 2nd syllable stress /duh NEER/ is older; /den YAY/ is newer, based on Fr.

254. **marv'llous** (F1), **marv'lous**, **marvellous** (*merueilous* Q1, *maruailous* Q2-6) 'marvellously.' Here should be two syllables, either /MARV łss/ or /MARV lus/.

Act 1 Scene 3

46. **dissentious** /dih SEN shus/ causing arguments.

67. **children** (F1). Q2-5 have **kinred** /KIN rid/ archaic variant of Q1's **kindred**.

86. **advocate** /AD vuh kut/ someone who supports a person or cause.

88. **suspects** /suh SPECTS/ suspicions.

ă-bat, ăir-**marry**, air-**pair**, ạr-**far**, ĕr-**merry**, ĝ- get, ī-high, ĭr-mirror, ł-**little**, ṇ-**listen**, ŏ-hot, oh-go, ōō-**wood**, ōō-**moon**, oor-**tour**, ōr- **or**, ow-**how**, ţh-**that**, t̶h̶-**thin**, ŭ-**but**, UR-**fur**, ur-und**er**.   ( ) - suppress the syllable   see p. xiii for complete list.

101. *Iwis /ih WISS/; US, CN *also* /ee WISS/ indeed.

101. *grandam (F1) /GRAN dam/; US *rarely* [-dum] grandmother. This spelling could also be pronounced as indicated in Q1-6's granam /GRAN um/ (cf. *grandma* /GRAM uh/).

114. avouch't /uh VOWCHT/ affirm it.

129. Saint Albons archaic variant of St. Albans, both pronounced US /saynt AWL bunz/; UK /sint-, snt-/.

138. mewed up /myo͞od/ caged.

143. cacodemon evil spirit. /kack uh DEE mun/, /KACK uh dee mun/.

185. prophesied /PRŎF uh sīd/ predicted the future.

186. Northumberland /north UM bur lund/.

213. unlook'd /UN lo͞okt/.

254. *malapert /MAL uh purt/; US *also* [mal uh PURT] saucy.

263-69. *aery('s), eyrie, aerie high nest. /AIR ee, EER-/; E.COAST US *also* [ĂIR-]. /ĪR ee/ not recommended. /AIR ee/ is the oldest pronunciation.

316. scathe (Q1-5) /skayth/ harm. Variant of F1, Q6's scath /skath/.

329. allies here with 2nd syllable stress.

346. *obdurate unmoveable. Here should have 2nd syllable stress /ŏb-, ub DYOOR it/; US *also* /-DYUR-/ [-DUR-]. 1st syllable stress is more usual today.

349. Tut, tut (F1) some eds. prefer Q1-6's Tush /tŭsh/ expression of disdain.

Act 1 Scene 4

26. anchors. Some eds. substitute *ouches /OW chiz/ 'jewelry,' or ingots /ING guts/.

49. renowned (F1) /rih-, ree NOWN id/. Q1-5 have the archaic variant renowmed /rih-, ree NOW mid/.

50. scourge /SKURJ/ punishment.

59. *Environ'd /en VĪ rund/; US *also* [-urnd] surrounded.

154. costard /CŎST urd/ head.

> 155, 270. malmsey-butt cask of Malmsey, a sweet wine. /MAHM zee/ is the older pronunciation, but today the /l/ is sometimes pronounced. This, however is considered non-standard in the UK.

187. convict /cun VICT/ convicted.

198. edict /EE dict/ decree.

207. Unrip'st /un RIPST/, Unripped'st /un RIPTST/.

272. Pilate /PĪ lut/ Roman governor of Palestine.

Act 2 Scene 1

3. embassage /EM buh sij/ ambassador's message.

13. supreme here should be US /SOO preem/; UK, SOUTH. US *also* [SYOO-].

27. inviolable /in VĪL uh bł/ unbreakable.

30. allies here with 2nd syllable stress.

41. cordial US /COR jł/; UK /COR dył/ restorative medicine.

90. *countermand US, CN /COWNT ur mănd/; UK /-mahnd/ the revoking of a command.

Act 2 Scene 2

1-31. *grandam (F1) /GRAN dam/; US *rarely* [-dum] grandmother. This spelling could also be pronounced as indicated in Q1-6's granam /GRAN um/ (cf. *grandma* /GRAM uh/).

14. *importune /im POR chun/ ask insistently. See App. D.

28. visor (F1). Q1-6 have *vizard /VIZ urd/ mask. /-ard/ not recommended.

> ă-bat, ăir-marry, air-pair, ąr-far, ĕr-merry, ĝ- get, ī-high, ĭr-mirror, ł-little, ņ-listen, ŏ-hot, oh-go, ōō-wood, ōō-moon, oor-tour, ōr- or, ow-how, ţh-that, ᵵh-thin, ŭ-but, UR-fur, ur-under.   ( ) - suppress the syllable   see p. xiii for complete list.

60. **moi'ty, moiety** /MOY tee/ portion.

65. **widow-dolor** (UK **dolour**) /DOH lur/; UK *also* /DŎL ur/ pain. Q1-6 have *widdowes dolours*. See App. D *-or*.

117. **rancor** (UK **rancour**) /RANK ur/ ill-will. See App. D *-or*.

121-54. **Ludlow** /LUD loh/.

133. **compact** here should be /cŏm-, cum PACT/ agreement.

151. **consistory** here should be /CŎN sis tree, -tuh ree/; US *also* /-tor ee/ council chamber, i.e., source of wisdom.

Act 2 Scene 3

4. **by'r lady** /bīr-, bur LAY dee/ by Our Lady (i.e., Mary).

13. ***nonage** /NŎN ij/; US, UK *rarely older* [NOH nij]; UK *rarely* [NUN ij] minority, period of youth.

20. **politic** /PŎL ih tik/ cunning.

30. **solace** /SŎL us/ comfort.

42. **instinct** here /in STINCT/.

Act 2 Scene 4

2. **Northampton** /nor ~~TH~~AMP tun/.

10-32. ***Grandam** (F1) /GRAN dam/; US *rarely* [-dum] grandmother. This spelling could also be pronounced as indicated in Q1-6's **Granam** /GRAN um/ (cf. *grandma* /GRAM uh/).

35. **parlous** (F1) /PAR lus/ clever. Archaic variant of Q1-6's **perilous** which here would have to be /PĔR (ih) lus/.

50. **hind** /hīnd/ doe.

Act 3 Scene 1

39. ***obdurate** unmoveable. Here should be /ŏb-, ub DYOOR ut/;
US *also* /-DYUR-/ [-DUR-]. 1st syllable stress is more usual today.

62. ***sojourn** reside temporarily. Here stress should fall on the first syllable.
US, CN /SOH jurn/; UK /SŎJ urn/ [-URN, SOH-, SUJ-].

72, 74. **record** here should be /rek-, rik ORD/.

77. **retail'd** passed on. Here should be /rih-, ree TAYLD/.

81. **characters** 'written records' or 'moral qualtities.' Here with 2nd syllable stress.

86. **valure** (Q1) archaic variant of **valor** (UK **valour** Q 3-6, F1), all pronounced /VAL ur/.

145. ***grandam** (F1) /GRAN dam/; US *rarely* [-dum] grandmother. This spelling could also be pronounced as indicated in Q1-6's **granam** /GRAN um/ (cf. *grandma* /GRAM uh/).

154. **perilous** (Q1-6, F1) /PĔR (ih) lus/. Q7, F4 have the archaic variant **parlous** /PAR lus/. Here should be disyllabic.

192, 200. **complots** plots. The first instance should be /cum PLŎTS/, the second /CŎM plŏts/.

195. **Herford, Hereford.** In the US both would be /HUR furd/. In the UK the county is normally /HĔR ih furd/ which here should be 2 syllables /HĔR furd/.

Act 3 Scene 2

11. **rased, razed off** /RAY zid/ torn, cut off. **Raced** /RAY sid/ from *arace* 'pluck off' is also possible.

60. **fortnight** /FORT nīt/; US *also* [FORT nit] two weeks. Virtually obsolete in the US.

75. **rood** /rōōd/ cross.

ă-bat, äir-**marry**, air-**pair**, ạr-**far**, ĕr-**merry**, ĝ- get, ī-high, ĭr-**mirror**, ḷ-little, ṇ-listen, ŏ-hot, oh-go, ōō-**wood**, ōō-**moon**, oor-**tour**, ōr- **or**, ow-how, ṯh-that, ~~th~~-**thin**, ŭ-but, UR-**fur**, ur-under.   ( ) - suppress the syllable   see p. xiii for complete list.

84. ***jocund** /JŎCK und/; US, CN *rarely* [JOHK-] merry.

87. **rancor** (UK **rancour**) /RANK ur/ ill-will. See App. D *-or.*

stage direction after 94. ***Pursuivant** herald, attendant. US /PUR swiv unt/ [PUR siv unt]; UK /PUR swiv unt/, *rarely* [PUR siv unt].

101. **allies** here with 2nd syllable stress.

106. **Gramercy** /gruh MUR see/ thanks.

Act 3 Scene 3

24. **expiate** /EK spee ut, -ayt/ arrived.

Act 3 Scene 4

31. **Holborn** US /HOHL burn/; UK /HOH burn/ [HOHL-] Ely's home district in London.

71. **Consorted** /cun SORT id/ kept company with.

71. **harlot** /HAR lut/ whore.

82. **rase, raze** /rayz/ tear, cut off. **Race** /rayss/ from *arace* 'pluck off' is also possible.

88. ***pursuivant** herald, attendant. US /PUR swiv unt/ [PUR siv unt]; UK /PUR swiv unt/, *rarely* [PUR siv unt].

89. **triumphing** here should be /trī UM fing/.

104. **prophesy** /PRŎF uh sī/ predict the future.

Act 3 Scene 5

5. **tragedian** /truh JEE dee un/ or /-dyun/ tragic actor.

11. **stratagems** /STRAT uh jumz/ schemes.

32. **suspects** /suh SPECTS/ suspicions.

33. **covert'st** most secret.   US, CN /KOHV urtst/ [KUV-];
UK /KUV-/ [KOHV-], *rarely* [KŎV-].

44. **extreme** here should be /EK streem/.

57. **timorously** /TIM (uh) rus lee/ in a frightened manner.

61. **Misconster** /mis CŎN stur/ misconstrue.

81. **bestial** beastlike. /BEST yl̸/; US *also* [-chl̸].   US, CN /BEES-/ not
recommended.

87. **insatiate** /in SAYSH yut, -yayt/ never satisfied. /-ut/ is more usual for an
adj.

91. **lineaments** /LIN yuh munts/ distinctive features.

95. **orator** US, CN /OR uh tur/; UK, E.COAST US /ŎR-/. Sometimes /OR ayt ur/
is used, but it is not recommended.   See App. D *-or*.

98, 105. **Baynard's Castle** /BAY nurdz/ Richard's London home.

109. **recourse** access. Here should be /rih CORSS/, the usual UK
pronunciation; US *also* /ree-/.

Act 3 Scene 6

1. **the indictment** /th^yin DĪT munt/ charge of wrongdoing.

7. **precedent** (F1) /PRESS ih dunt/. Q1-6's **president** is an archaic variant,
pronounced the same way, or possibly /PREZ-/.

Act 3 Scene 7

5, 6. **contract** engagement. Here should be /cŏn TRACT/.

7. **Th'unsatiate** (Q1-6) /th^yun SAYSH yut, -yayt/ never satisfied. Some eds.
prefer F1's **insatiate** /in-/. /-ut/ is more usual for an adj.

12. **lineaments** /LIN yuh munts/ distinctive features.

| ă-bat, ăir-**marry**, air-**pair**, ạr-**far**, ĕr-**merry**, ĝ- **get**, ī-**high**, ĭr-**mirror**, l̸-**little**, ṇ-**listen**, ŏ-**hot**, oh-**go**, ōō-**wood**, ōō-**moon**, oor-**tour**, ŏr- **or**, ow-**how**, ţh-**that**, t̶h̶-**thin**, ŭ-**but**, UR-**fur**, ur-**under**.   ( ) - suppress the syllable   see p. xiii for complete list. |

25. **statuës**, (**statuas** F1, Q1-6) here should be three syllables /STATCH oo uz/; UK *also* /STAT yoo uz/.

30. **Recorder** here should be /REK ur dur/ a city official.

32. **saith** says. Here should be one syllable US /sayth̸/, *rarely* [seth̸]; UK /seth̸/ [sayth̸]. The older form is /seth̸/.

49. **descant** /DES kănt/ melody sung above the main tune.

55. **leads** /ledz/ roof.

72. **lulling** /LŬLL ing/ archaic variant of **lolling** /LŎL ing/.

74. ***courtezans, courtesans** rich men's whores. US /CORT ih zunz, -zanz/, *rarely* [cort ih ZANZ]; CN /CORT ih zanz/ [-zunz], *rarely* [cort ih ZANZ]; UK /CORT ih zanz, cort ih ZANZ/.

90. **perfit** (Q1-6) /PUR fit/ archaic variant of F1's **perfect**. It could also be /PAR fit/ in Shk's time.

118. **supreme** here should be US /SO͞O preem/; UK, SOUTH. US *also* [SYO͞O-].

130. **recure** cure. /ree-, rih KYOOR/; US *also* [-KYUR].

136. **empery** /EM pur ee/ status as emperor.

137. **consorted** /cun SORT id/ in company with.

158. **revenue** sometimes in verse /ruh VEN yo͞o/, but here as in mod. Eng. US /REV in o͞o/; UK, SOUTH. US /-yo͞o/.

160. **defects** here should be /dih-, dee FECTS/.

179. **contract** /cun TRACT/ engaged to be married.

181. **betroth'd** /bih-, bee TROH̤THD/ engaged to be married.

192. **expostulate** /ek SPŎS chuh layt/; UK *also* /-tyoo layt/ discuss, object.

213. **egally** /EE guh lee/ archaic variant of **equally**.

226. **Albeit** /awl BEE (i)t/ although.

234. **impure** here should be /IM pyoor/.

Act 4 Scene 1

31. **Westminster** here should be /WEST min stur/.

54. *****cockatrice** /CŎCK uh triss, -trīss/ a monster whose gaze kills.

84. **timorous** /TIM (uh) rus/ frightened.

Act 4 Scene 2

35. **close** /clohss/ secret.

35. **exploit** here should be /ek SPLOYT/.

38. *****orators** US, CN /OR uh turz/; UK, E.COAST US /ŎR-/. Sometimes
/OR ayt urz/ is used, but it is not recommended.   See App. D *-or.*

52. **keeping close** /clohss/ keeping hidden, imprisoned.

90. **Herford, Hereford** in the US both would be /HUR furd/. In the UK the
county is normally /HĔR ih furd/ which here should be 2 syllables /HĔR furd/.

96. **prophesy** /PRŎF uh sī/ predict the future.

103. **Exeter** /EK sih tur/.

105. **Rouge-mount** /RŌOZH mownt/. Some eds. prefer **Rougemont,
Ruge-mont** /RŌOZH mŏnt/ red mountain.

122. **Brecknock** /BRECK nuk/. Some eds. prefer **Brecon** /BRECK un/.

Act 4 Scene 3

4-17. **Dighton** /DĪT ṇ/.

4. **suborn** /sub ORN/ bribe.

6. **Albeit** /awl BEE (i)t/ although.

ă-bat, ăir-**marry**, air-**pair**, ạr-**far**, ĕr-**merry**, ĝ- **get**, ī-**high**, ĭr-**mirror**, ł-**little**, ṇ-**listen**, ŏ-**hot**, oh-**go**, ōō-**wood**, ōō-**moon**, oor-**tour**, ŏr- **or**, ow-**how**, ṭh-**that**, t̶h̶-**thin**, ŭ-**but**, UR-**fur**, ur-**under**.   ( ) - suppress the syllable   see p. xiii for complete list.

11. **alablaster** a type of white rock. US /AL uh blăss tur/;
E. NEW ENG., UK /-blahss-/ [-blăss-]. Archaic variant of **alabaster**
/-băss-, -bahss-/.

36. **close** /clohss/ securely.

38. **Abraham's** here should be /AY brumz/.

40. **Britain** /BRIT ṇ/ from Brittany. In Shk's time /-ayn/ was also used. Some
eds. prefer mod. **Breton** US /BRET ṇ/; UK /BRET ŏn/ [-ṇ, -un]. Sometimes the
Fr. ending /-ohⁿ/ is used in the UK.

52. **servitor** /SURV ih tur/ servant. See App. D -*or*.

Act 4 Scene 4

10. **unblown** here should be /UN blohn/.

13, 128. **aery, airy** /AIR ee/ of the air.

23. ***entrails** /EN traylz/; US *also* [-trĭz] guts.

28. **abstract** /AB stract/ summary.

28. **record** here should be /rek-, rik ORD/.

36. **seniory** /SEEN yur ee/ seniority.

45. **holp'st** /hohlpst/ helped.

69. **Th' adulterate** /t͜hʸuh DULL trayt, -trut/ adulterous. /-ut/ would be usual
for an adj.

79. **prophesy** /PRŎF uh sī/ predict the future.

101. **caitiff** /KAYT if/ scoundrel.

114. ***mischance** in verse normally with 2nd syllable stress.

128. ***intestate** (Q1-6) /in TESS tayt/; US *also* /-tut/ dead with nothing to
bequeath. F1 has **intestine** /in TESS tin/; UK *also* [-teen] internal.

129. ***orators** US, CN /OR uh turz/; UK, E.COAST US /ŎR-/. Sometimes
/OR ayt urz/ is used, but it is not recommended. See App. D -*or*.

149. ***alarum** US, CN /uh LAHR um/ [-LĂIR-]; UK /uh LĂIR um, uh LAHR um/ a call to arms.

166. **rood** /rōōd/ cross.

174. **comfortable hour** here should be /CUM fur tuh bł OW ur/.

186. **extreme** here should be /EK streem/.

190. **complete armor** here should be /CŎM pleet/ full armor.

229. ***entrails** /EN traylz/; US *also* [-trłz] guts.

251. **Lethe** /LEE~~TH~~ ee/ river of forgetfulness in Hades.

276. **handkercher** (Q1-6) /HANK ur chur/. Archaic variant of F1's **handkerchief** which some eds. prefer.

297. **increase** here should be /in CREESS/ offspring.

331. ***chastised** punished. Here should be /CHĂSS tīz ed/. The usual US pronunciation, also used in CN, has 1st syllable stress; in the UK 2nd syllable stress is usual.

335. **retail** pass on. Here should be /rih-, ree TAYL/.

434. ***puissant** powerful. The traditional forms are /PWISS n̩t/, /PYŌŌ sn̩t/ (see App. D).

444-538. **Salisbury** 2 or 3 syllables, depending on meter US /SAWLZ b(ĕ)r ee/; UK /SAWLZ b(u)r ee/ [SĂLZ-].

---

464. **runagate** /RUN uh gayt/ fugitive. Some eds. prefer **renegade**.

482. **Safe-conducting** /sayf CŎN duct ing/.

498. **Devonshire** /DEV un shur/ [-sheer].

499. **advertised** informed. Here should be /ad VUR tih zed, -sed/.

500. **Courtney, Courtenay** /CORT nee/.

ă-bat, ăir-**marry**, air-**pair**, a̱r-**far**, ĕr-**merry**, ĝ- get, ī-high, ĭr-**mirror**, ł-little, n̩-listen, ŏ-hot, oh-go, ōō-wood, ōō-moon, oor-**tour**, ōr- or, ow-how, t̪h-**that**, ~~th~~-**thin**, ŭ-but, UR-**fur**, ur-und**er**.   ( ) - suppress the syllable   see p. xiii for complete list.

500. **prelate** /PREL ut/ high-ranking churchman.

501. **Exeter** /EK sih tur/.

519. **Yorkshire** /YORK shur/ [-sheer].

521. **Britain** /BRIT n̩/ from Brittany. In Shk's time /-ayn/ was also used. Some eds. prefer mod. **Breton** US /BRET n̩/; UK /BRET ŏn/ [-n̩, -un]. Sometimes the Fr. ending /-oh^n/ is used in the UK.

522. **Dorsetshire** /DOR sit shur/ [-sheer].

527. **Hois'd** /hoyzd/ archaic variant of *hoisted.* *S*ome eds. prefer **Hoist.**

Act 4 Scene 5

10, 13. **Pembroke** US /PEM brohk/; UK /PEM br͞o͞ok/ [-bruck, -brohk].

10. **Ha'rford-west** /HAR furd WEST/. Variant form of **Haverford-west** /HAV (ur) furd WEST/ which here should be 3 syllables.

13. **Talbot** US /TAL but/ [TAWL-]; UK /TAWL but/ [TŎL-, TAL-].

15. **Rice ap Thomas** /RĪSS ap-/. Some eds. prefer Welsh **Rhys-ap-Thomas** /REES ahp-/.

Act 5 Scene 1

15. **allies** here with 2nd syllable stress.

19. ***respite** day to which something is postponed. Here should be US /RESP it/, *rarely* [-īt]; CN /RESP it/ [-īt]; UK /RESP īt/ [-it]. /RESP it/ is older, but /-īt/ has been in use since the 17th cent.

Act 5 Scene 2

11. **centry** (F1) /SEN tree/ an archic variant of Q1-6's **center** (UK **centre**).

12. **Leicester** /LESS tur/ .

13. **Tamworth** /TAM WURTH/ [-wurth]. /TAM uth/ is non-standard in the UK.

Act 5 Scene 3

9. **descried** /dih SKRĪD/ found out.

11. **battalia** order of battle. /buh TAYL yuh/ is older; /buh TAHL yuh/ is newer.

The Complete Oxford begins 5.4 here (line nos. in parentheses).

5.3.29. (5.4.5) **Pembroke** US /PEM brohk/; UK /PEM brōōk/ [-bruck, -brohk].

The Complete Oxford begins 5.5 here (line nos. in parentheses).

5.3.59. (5.5.12) ***pursuivant-at-arms** herald. US /PUR swiv unt/ [PUR siv unt]; UK /PUR swiv unt/, *rarely* [PUR siv unt].

5.3.65. (5.5.18) **staves** /stayvz/ staffs.

5.3.68, 271 (5.5.21, 225) **Northumberland** /north UM bur lund/.

5.3.89. (5.5.42) **the arbitrement, arbitrament** /thʸahr BIT ruh munt/ settlement.

5.3.105. (5.5.58) ***peize, peise** weigh. US /peez/, *sometimes* [payz]; UK /peez, payz/. Dialect evidence shows that /ee/ was the form found in southern Eng., and /ay/ in the North.

5.3.129. (5.5.83) **prophesied** /PRŎF uh sīd/ predicted the future.

5.3.132. (5.5.86) ***fulsome** cloying, offensive. /FULL sum/; US *rarely* [FŬL-].

5.3.180. (5.5.138) **midnight** here with 2nd syllable stress.

5.3.232. (5.5.186) ***jocund** /JŎCK und/; US, CN *rarely* [JOHK-] merry.

5.3.242. (5.5.196) ***bulwarks** structures for defense. US, CN /BULL wurks/ [BŬL-]; UK /BULL WURKS, -wurks/. The vowels /or/, /ahr/ not recommended in the final syllable, and are non-standard in the UK.

5.3.258. (5.5.212) **fat shall pay**. Some eds. substitute **foison pays** /FOY zun, -zn̩/ harvest, plenty.

ă-bat, ăir-**marry**, air-**pair**, ar-**far**, ĕr-**merry**, ĝ- g**et**, ī-h**igh**, ĭr-m**irror**, l̩-litt**le**, n̩-liste**n**, ŏ-h**ot**, oh-g**o**, ōō-w**ood**, ōō-m**oon**, oor-t**our**, ōr- **or**, ow-h**ow**, th-**that**, th-**thin**, ŭ-b**ut**, UR-f**ur**, ur-und**er**.   ( ) - suppress the syllable   see p. xiii for complete list.

> *The Complete Oxford* begins 5.6 here (line nos. in parentheses).

5.3.283. (5.6.13) **low'r, lour** threaten. /lowr/ with the vowel of *how*.

5.3.289. (5.6.19) **Caparison** /kuh PĂIR ih sn̩/ cover with an ornamental cloth.

5.3.299. (5.6.29) **In the main battle, whose ****puissance* **on either side** power (i.e., army). After the epic caesura *puissance* may be two syllables if *either* is pronounced as a single syllable, or if *either* is two syllables, *puissance* should be three in a six-foot line. In both cases it must be stressed on the 1st syllable. The traditional forms are /PWISS n̩ss/, /PYO͞O (ih) sn̩ss/ (see App. D).

5.3.305. (5.6.35) **Dickon** /DICK un/.

5.3.317, 333. (5.6.47, 63) **Britains** /BRIT n̩z/ men from Brittany. Some eds. prefer mod. **Bretons** US /BRET n̩z/; UK /BRET ŏnz/ [-n̩z, -unz]. Sometimes the Fr. ending /-ohⁿz/ is used in the UK.

5.3.323. (5.6.53) **paltry** /PAWL tree/ worthless.

5.3.330. (5.6.60) **exploit** here should be /ek SPLOYT/.

5.3.335. (5.6.65) **record** here should be /rek-, rik ORD/.

5.3.338. (5.6.68) **yeomen** /YOH min/ freemen who own small farms.

5.3.341. (5.6.71) **staves** /stayvz/ staffs.

Act 5 Scene 5 (*Complete Oxford* 5.7)

10. **Leicester** /LESS tur/.

13. **Ferrers** /FĔR urz/.

38. **increase** here should be /in CREESS/ harvest.

Romeo and Juliet

People in the Play

Abram /AY brum/ his name is not spoken. Some eds. prefer **Abraham**.

Apothecary US /uh PŎTH uh kĕr ee/; UK /-kuh ree/ druggist.

***Balthasar** (Q1, 4) /BAL thuh zar/, *rarely* /bal thuh ZAR, bal THAZ ur/. His
name is not spoken. Some eds. prefer Q2-3, F1's **Peter**.

Benvolio 3 or 4 syllables depending on meter /ben VOHL (ee) yoh/.

Capulet 2 or 3 syllables depending on meter /KAP y(uh) let, -lit/.
  Capels /KAP lz/.

Escalus (Prince) /ES kuh lus/ his name is not spoken.

Juliet /JOOL yit, -yet/ or a triple ending /JOOL ee yit, -yet/. If the meter allows
it, the mod. variant /joo lee ET/ may also be used.

Lawrence, Laurence US /LOR unss/; E.COAST US /LAH runss/;
UK /LOR runss/.

Mercutio 3 or 4 syllables depending on meter /MUR KYOO sh(ee) yoh/.

Montague /MŎNT uh gyoo/. /MUNT-/ is an older pronunciation, now
obsolete.

***Petruchio** /puh TROOK (ee) yoh/ is preferred over /puh TROOCH (ee) yoh/
in all countries. Some eds. prefer the Ital. spelling **Petruccio**
/pay TROOCH oh/. His name is not spoken.

Romeo 2 or 3 syllables depending on meter /ROHM (ee) yoh/.

***Rosaline** US /RŎZ uh linn, -līn/; CN, UK /RŎZ uh līn/ [-linn]. Mentioned
throughout.

Tybalt /TIB lt/.

ă-bat, ăir-**marry**, air-**pair**, ạr-**far**, ĕr-**merry**, ĝ- get, ī-high, ĭr-**mirror**, l-little, ṇ-listen,
ŏ-hot, oh-go, ōō-**wood**, ōō-**moon**, oor-**tour**, ōr- or, ow-**how**, ṭh-**that**, th-**thin**, ŭ-but,
UR-**fur**, ur-**under**.   ( ) - suppress the syllable   see p. xiii for complete list.

Places in the Play

Mantua 2 or 3 syllables depending on meter US /MAN ch(oo) wuh/;
UK /MAN ty(oo) wuh/ [MAN ch(oo) wuh].

Verona /vĕr-, vur ROH nuh/.

Act 1 Scene 1

2. **colliers** /CŎL yurz/; UK *also* /CŎL ee yurz/ charcoal producers.

66. **hinds** /hīndz/ menial laborers.

73, 94. *****partisans** /PART ih zanz/ [-sanz, -zunz]; UK *also* /part ih ZANZ/ a
spear with a blade on the end.

120. **drive** archaic past tense pronounced /driv/ in the dialects. Some eds. prefer
drove.

125. *****covert** hiding place. US, CN /KOHV urt/ [KUV-];
UK /KUV urt/ [KOHV urt], *rarely* [KUV ur], an older form.

136. **Aurora's** /uh ROR uz/; UK *also* [aw-] goddess of dawn.

145. *****importun'd** /im POR chund/ asked insistently. See App. D.

149. **close** /clohss/ secret.

219. **severity** /suh VĔR ih tee/.

232. **strooken** /STRᴏᴏK in/ or perhaps simply a variant spelling of **strucken**.

Act 1 Scene 2

47. **holp** /hohlp/ helped.

51. *****plantan** today spelled **plantain** a medicinal plant. /PLĂNT ayn/ [-un];
UK *also* [PLAHNT ayn]. Variants with /-un/ are older.

56. **God-den** /gud-, gᴏᴏd EN/ good evening. Some eds. prefer **Good e'en**.

57. **God gi' god-den** /gŏd-, gud gih gud EN/ or /gᴏᴏd EN/ good evening. Some
eds. prefer **God gi' good e'en**.

64. **Martino** /mar TEE noh/.

65. **Anselme** /AN selm/.

66. **Vitruvio** /vih TR$\overline{OO}$V ee oh/.

66. **Placentio** /pluh SEN shee yoh/; Ital. /plah CHEN tsee oh/.

66. **Valentine** /VAL in tīn/.

69. **Livia** /LIV ee uh/.

69. **Valentio** /vuh LEN shee yoh/; Ital. /vah LEN tsee oh/.

70. *****Lucio** /L$\overline{OO}$CH ee yoh/ is newer and much more common, based on Ital. Older and less common are angl. [L$\overline{OO}$S-], US *rarely* [L$\overline{OO}$SH-] (for /ly$\overline{oo}$-/ see App. D *lu-*).

70. **Helena** /HELL in uh/.

91. **heretics** /HĔR ih tiks/ dissenters.

Act 1 Scene 3

9. **thou s'hear** a north. Eng., and Scot. dialect form of *shall* is *sall*, which in its weak form reduces to *s'*. It is doubtful that Shk. intended this. The reader may meet the metrical demands by saying *thou sh't hear* /thowsht HEER/.

15, 21. **Lammas-tide, -eve** /LAM us/ Aug. 1st.

15. **fortnight** /FORT nīt/; US *also* [FORT nit] two weeks. Virtually obsolete in the US.

32. **teachy** /TETCH ee/ fretful. Still common in the UK as **tetchy**.

33. *****trow** US, CN /troh, trow/; UK /trow/ [troh] trust. Shk's rhymes elsewhere indicate /-oh/.

36. **rood** /r$\overline{oo}$d/ cross.

ă-bat, ăir-m**a**rry, air-**pair**, ạr-**far**, ĕr-**merry**, ĝ- g**e**t, ī-high, ĭr-m**i**rror, ł-little, ṇ-lis**ten**, ŏ-hot, oh-g**o**, $\overline{oo}$-wood, $\overline{oo}$-moon, oor-**tour**, ŏr- **or**, ow-h**ow**, ţh-**that**, ᵵħ-**thin**, ŭ-but, UR-**fur**, ur-und**er**.   ( ) - suppress the syllable   see p. xiii for complete list.

43. **by my holidam** an oath referring to a 'holy object' or the 'holy lady,' i.e., Mary. Other variants are: **halidam, halidom, halidame, halidome, holidame.** Probably these were all variant spellings of /HAL ih dum, HŎL ih dum/ (note *hal-* can also be /HŎL-/ in the US in *Halloween*).

53. **cock'rel's** /CŎCK rłz/ young cock's.

83. **lineament** /LIN yuh munt/ distinctive feature.

86. **margent** /MAR junt/ archaic variant of **margin.**

Act 1 Scene 4

3. **prolixity** /proh LIK sih tee/ long-windedness.

5. **Tartar's** /TAR turz/ people of Central Asia.

5. **lath** US /lăth/; UK, E. NEW ENG. /lahth/ [lăth] narrow strip of wood.

8. **entrance** here /ENT ur unss/ is indicated.

55. **agot-stone** a type of jewel. Archaic variant of **agate,** both pronounced /AG ut/.

57. **atomi** (Q1) tiny creatures. /AT uh mī/, the plural of Lat. *atomus.* Some eds. prefer **atomy,** which could be /AT uh mee/, or **atomies** (Q3-4, F1) /AT uh meez/.

79. **tithe-pig's** /tīṭh/ pig paid as part of the parish dues.

81. **benefice** /BEN ih fiss/ the living of a churchman.

84. **ambuscadoes** /am buh SKAY dohz/ archaic variant of *ambuscades* 'ambushes.'

85. **fadom** /FAD um/ archaic variant of **fathom** /FĂṬH um/.

89. **plats** /plats/ braids. Variant form of **plaits** /plats/; US *also* /playts/.

Act 1 Scene 5

33. **By'r lady** (F4) /bīr-, bur LAY dee/ by Our Lady, a mild oath. **Berlady** (Q2-4, F1), is pronounced the same way. **By Lady** (Q1) /bī-, buh-/.

35. ***nuptial** wedding. US, UK /NUP chł/ [-shł]; in CN both are used equally.

35. **Lucentio** /loo SEN shee yoh/; Ital. /loo CHEN tsee oh/ (for /lyoo-/ see App. D *lu-*).

36. **Pentecost** /PEN tih cŏst/; US *also* /-cawst/ seventh Sunday after Easter.

46. **Ethiop's** /EE̶T̶H̶ yŏps/ some eds. prefer **Ethiope's** /EE̶T̶H̶ yohps/ person from Ethiopia.

56. **antic face** /AN tik/ grotesque mask. Q3-4, F1's *antique* does not mean 'ancient' here.

77. **goodman** /G͞o͞oD mun/ title of a man under the rank of gentleman.

84. **scath** /skat̶h̶/ harm. Variant of **scathe** /skayt̯h/.

86. **princox** /PRIN cŏcks, PRING-/ insolent boy.

122. **towards** /TOH wurdz, -urdz/ about to take place.

129. **Tiberio** /tī BEER ee yoh/.

Act 2 pr.

9. **access** here should be /ak SESS/.

14. **extreme** here should be /EK streem/.

Act 2 Scene 1

12. **purblind** /PUR blīnd/ blind or partly blind.

13. **Abraham** here should be /AY brum/.

14. **Cophetua** /kuh FETCH (oo) wuh/; UK *also* /kuh FET y(oo) wuh/ subject of an old ballad.

20. ***demesnes** parklands. US, CN /duh MAYNZ/ [-MEENZ]; UK uses both equally.

ă-bat, ăir-**marry**, air-**pair**, a̯r-**far**, ĕr-**merry**, ĝ- **get**, ī-**high**, ĭr-**mirror**, ł-**little**, n̯-**listen**, ŏ-**hot**, oh-**go**, o͞o-**wood**, o͞o-**moon**, oor-**tour**, ōr- **or**, ow-**how**, t̯h-**that**, t̶h̶-**thin**, ʊ-**but**, UR-**fur**, ur-**under**.   ( ) - suppress the syllable   see p. xiii for complete list.

31. **consorted with** /cun SORT id/ in fellowship with.

34, 36. **medlar(s)** /MED lur/ an apple-like fruit.

38. **open-arse** /OHP in ạrss/ which in the US would be **open-ass** /OHP in ăss/, slang for *medlar*. Q2-3, F1 have *open, or*; Q1 has *open Et caetera*.

38. **pop'rin pear, popp'rin** /PŎP rin/ type of pear from Flanders.

Act 2 Scene 2 (*The Complete Oxford* continues this as 2.1 (line nos. in parentheses).

78. (2.1.120) **prorogued** /pruh-, proh ROHG id/ postponed.

117. (2.1.159) **contract** here should be /cŏn TRACT/.

158. (2.1.203) **falc'ner's** US /FĂLK nurz/ [FAWLK-]; CN /FAWLK-/; UK /FAWLK-, FĂLK-/ [FŎLK-].

167. (2.1.212) **My niesse, niësse, nyas** (*Neece* Q2-3, F1) nestling hawk. All are pronounced /NĪ uss/. **My deer** (Q4), **My sweete** (F2), **Madame** (Q1).

179. (2.1.224) **gyves** /jīvz/ chains, fetters.

188. (2.1.233) **sire's close cell** (F1, Q2-3) /clohss/ hidden, secluded. Q1 has **father's cell**.

Act 2 Scene 3 (*Complete Oxford* 2.2)

7. *****osier** US /OH zhur/ [OH zyur]; UK /OH zyur/ willow.

11. *****divers** various. Here should be stressed on the first syllable US, CN /DĪ vurss, -vurz/; UK /DĪ vurss/ [-vurz].

31. **Benedicite** Ang.Lat. /ben uh DISS ih tee/; Church Lat. /bay nay DEE chee tay/ bless you.

37. **unstuff'd** here should be /UN stuft/.

69. *****Maria** /muh RĪ uh/ is the older, angl. form, /muh REE uh/ is newer.

83. **badst** /badst/ 2nd person sing. past tense of *bid* 'asked.' See *bade* p. 33.

92. **rancor** (UK **rancour**) /RANK ur/ ill-will. See App. D *-or*.

Act 2 Scene 4 (*Complete Oxford* 2.3)

22. **minim rests** /MIN im/ the shortest rests in music.

26. **passado** /puh SAH doh/ step and thrust in fencing.

26. **punto reverso** angl. /P͞OON toh/ or /PUN toh rih VUR soh/;
Ital. /P͞OON toh ray VĚR soh/ back handed stroke in fencing.

26. **hay** /hay/ cry when scoring a hit in fencing. Some eds. prefer **hai** which
could also be /hī/.

28. **antic** /AN tik/. Q1-4, F1's *antique* does not mean 'ancient' here.

29. **phantasimes, phantasims** (*phantacies* Q2-4, F1) /FAN taz imz/ affected
young gentlemen. Some eds. prefer Q1's **fantasticoes** /fan TASS tih kohz/.

31. *****lamentable** US /luh MEN tuh bł/ [LAM en tuh bł]; CN, UK /LAM un tuh bł/
[luh MEN-].

33. *****fashion-mongers** fops. US /FASH un mŏng gurz/ or /-mawng-/ [-mung-];
CN /-mung-, -mŏng-/; UK /-mung-/.

39. *****Petrarch** /PET rahrk/; US *also* [PEET-] Italian poet.

41. **Dido** /DĪ doh/ Queen of Carthage.

41. **dowdy** /DOW dee/ shabby looking woman.

41. **Cleopatra** US /clee oh PAT ruh/; UK *also* /-PAHT ruh/.

42. **hildings** /HILL dingz/ good-for-nothings.

42. **harlots** /HAR luts/ whores.

42. **Thisby, Thisbe** /T͟HIZ bee/ in Gk. myth. the beloved of Pyramus.

44. **bon jour** angl. /bohn ZHOOR, -JOOR/; Fr. /boh^n zhoor/ good day.

53. **bow** /bow/.

ă-bat, ăir-**marry**, air-**pair**, a̧r-**far**, ĕr-**merry**, ĝ- get, ī-high, ĭr-**mirror**, ł-little, n̦-listen,
ŏ-hot, oh-go, o͞o-**wood**, o͞o-**moon**, oor-**tour**, ōr- or, ow-how, t͟h-**that**, t̶h̶-**thin**, ŭ-but,
UR-**fur**, ur-**under**.   ( ) - suppress the syllable   see p. xiii for complete list.

83. **cheverel** /SHEV ur ɫ/ kid leather, i.e., easily stretched. Archaic variant of **cheveril**, pronounced the same way.

92. **lolling** /LŎLL ing/ with tongue hanging out.

93. **bable** presumably /BAB ɫ/ a fool's short stick, i.e., penis. Archaic variant of **bauble** /BAW bɫ/.

129. **indite** /in DĪT/ invite.

153. **flirt-gills, flirt-jills** /FLURT jilz/ loose women.

154. **skains-mates** /SKAYNZ mayts/ companions. Some eds. prefer the variant **skeans-** /SKEENZ-/.

190. **top-gallant** mast above the mainmast. Sailors say /tuh GAL unt/, landsmen /tŏp GAL unt/.

203. **as lieve** /leev/ 'as soon,' still used in some US dialects. Some eds. prefer **lief** /leef/.

206. **clout** /clowt/ cloth.

206. **versal** /VUR sɫ/ universal.

Act 2 Scene 5 (*The Complete Oxford* 2.4)

6. **low'ring, louring** frowning. /LOWR ing/, with the vowel of *how*.

26, 52. **jaunce(-ing)** /jawnss/ jolting journey.

62. **I *trow** US, CN /troh, trow/; UK /trow/ [troh] I daresay. Shk's rhymes elsewhere indicate /-oh/.

63. **poultice** /POHL tiss/ cloth with medicine on it.

Act 2 Scene 6 (*The Complete Oxford* 2.5)

18. ***gossamers** /GŎSS uh murz/ spiders' threads.

21. **confessor** here should be /CŎN fess ur/. See App. D *-or*.

26. **blazon** /BLAY zun, -zn̩/ proclaim.

33. **excess** here should be /ek SESS/, the most common UK form.

Act 3 Scene 1

9. **drawer** /DRAW ur/ tapster, the person who draws the liquor at a tavern.

29. **riband** /RIB und/ archaic variant of **ribbon**.

45-130. **consort(est)** /cun SORT/ double meaning: 'keep company with' and 'play music with.'

74. **Alla stoccato** /ah lah stuh KAH toh/, or angl. /al uh-/. Ital. is *stoccata* 'at the thrust.' Some eds. prefer **stoccado** /stuh KAH doh/.

80. **pilcher** /PIL chur/ scabbard.

85. **passado** /puh SAH doh/ step and thrust in fencing.

123. **lenity** /LEN ih tee/ leniency.

161. **martial** /MAR shł/ warlike.

190. **amerce** /uh MURSS/ lay a heavy fine.

Act 3 Scene 2

2. **Phoebus'** /FEE bus/ god of the sun.

3. **Phaëton** /FAY ih tun, -tŏn/ son of the sun god. /-ŏn/ is usual in the US and is increasingly common in the UK. Some eds. prefer **Phaëthon** /--thun, -thŏn/. See App. D *-on*.

5. **close curtain** /clohss/ concealing curtain.

37. **weraday** (Q2) /WĚR uh day/ alas. Some eds. prefer Q3-4's, F1's **weladay** /WEL uh day/, Q1's **alack the day**.

47. ***cockatrice** /CŎCK uh triss, -trīss/ a monster whose gaze kills.

ă-bat, ăir-**marry**, air-**pair**, ạr-**far**, ĕr-**merry**, ĝ- **get**, ī-high, ĭr-mirror, ł-little, ṇ-listen, ŏ-hot, oh-go, ōō-wood, ōō-moon, oor-**tour**, ōr- **or**, ow-how, ţh-that, th-thin, ŭ-but, UR-fur, ur-under.   ( ) - suppress the syllable   see p. xiii for complete list.

51. **weal** /weel/ welfare.

56. **sounded** archaic variant of **swooned**. In Shk's time either /SOWN did/ or /SO͞ON did/.

57. *****bankrout** /BANK rowt/ [-rut] archaic variant of **bankrupt**.

60. **bier** /beer/ coffin.

76. **ravening** /RAV (i)n ing/ devouring.

88. *****aqua-vitae** distilled liquor, e.g., brandy.   US /AHK-, AK wuh VEE tī/, *rarely* [-VĪ tee]; CN /AK wuh VEE tī/ [AHK-]; UK /AK wuh VEE tī/ [-VEE tuh]. /AK wuh VĪ tee/ is the oldest surviving form. /-VEE tay/ not recommended.

Act 3 Scene 3

49. **confessor** here should be /CŎN fess ur/. See App. D -*or*.

70. **unmade** here should be /UN mayd/.

79. **errant** /ĔR unt/ archaic variant of **errand**.

98. **conceal'd** here should be /CŎN seeld/.

123. **usurer** /YO͞O zhur ur/; UK *also* [-zhyoor ur, -zhoor ur] someone who lends money for interest.

143. **mishaved** /MISS hay vid/ **misbehaved**.

Act 3 Scene 4

11. **mewed up** /myo͞od/ caged.

Act 3 Scene 5

4. *****pomegranate** today given a variety of pronunciations:
US, CN /PŎM uh gran it/; US *also* [PUM-, PŎM gran it, PUM ih gran it];
UK /PŎM uh gran it/ [PŎM gran it]. Here, however, it should be 3 syllables.

9. *****jocund** /JŎCK und/; US, CN *rarely* [JOHK-] merry.

13. **exhal'd** here with 2nd syllable stress, /eks HAYLD/, the normal UK form. Q3-4, F1 have **exhales**.

20. **reflex** here should be /ree-, rih FLEKS/ reflection.

62. **renowm'd** /rih-, ree NOWMD/ archaic variant of **renowned** /rih-, ree NOWND/.

89. **runagate** /RUN uh gayt/ fugitive.

129. ***conduit** fountain. Here must be 2 syllables /CŎN dwit/; UK *also* [CUN dwit, CŎN dywit, CŎN dit, CUN dit].

168. **hilding** /HILL ding/ good-for-nothing.

172. **God-i-goden** (F1), *Godigeden* (Q2-4), *goddegodden* (Q1) /gŏd-, gud ee guh DEN/. Some eds. prefer **God-'i-good e'en**. Here perhaps rather than the usual 'good evening' it means 'for God's sake.'

180. ***demesnes** estates. US, CN /duh MAYNZ/ [-MEENZ]; UK uses both equally.

180. **nobly lien'd** (*liand* Q2) well-connected. The Q2 spelling indicates 2 syllables, angl. /LĪ und/; or following Fr., /LEE und/. Q3-4, F1's **allied** would have to be compressed with *nobly* /NOH bl'uh LĪD/. Q1 has **trained**. Other eds. prefer **lined, 'lianc'd** /LĪ unst/ 'allianced,' **limb'd, ligned** angl. /līnd/; Fr. /leend/.

183. **puling** /PYO͞OL ing/ whining.

209. **stratagems** /STRAT uh jumz/ schemes.

219. **dishclout** /DISH clowt/ dish cloth.

221. **Beshrow** /bih-, bee SHROH/ curse. Archaic variant of **beshrew** /-SHRO͞O/.

Act 4 Scene 1

48. **prorogue** /pruh-, proh ROHG/ postpone.

ă-bat, ăir-ma**rry**, air-**pair**, a̦r-**far**, ĕr-**merry**, ĝ- get, ī-high, ĭr-mirror, l̩-little, n̩-listen, ŏ-hot, oh-go, o͝o-wood, o͞o-moon, oor-**tour**, ŏr- or, ow-how, t̪h-that, t̪h̶-thin, ŭ-but, UR-**fur**, ur-und**er**.   ( ) - suppress the syllable   see p. xiii for complete list.

63. **umpeer** /UM peer/ archaic variant of **umpire**.

88. **unstain'd** here should be /UN staynd/.

97. **surcease** /sur SEESS/ cease.

100. **wanny** /WŎN ee/ pale. Other choices are **paly** (Q4), **many** (Q2-3, F1).

110. **bier** /beer/ coffin.

Act 4 Scene 2

14. **harlotry** /HAR luh tree/ whore.

20. ***prostrate** /PRŎS trayt/; US *rarely* [-trut] lying face down.

39. **Tush** /tŭsh/ expression of disdain.

43. ***huswife** /HUZ if/ is traditional, /HUSS wīf/ is a newer, spelling pronunciation. The former is the most common form in the UK, the latter in the US. In CN both are used equally. In North America /HUSS wif/ is also sometimes used. Some eds. prefer mod. **housewife**.

Act 4 Scene 3

3. ***orisons** prayers. US, CN /OR ih zunz, -zn̩z/ [-sunz, -sn̩z]; E.COAST US /ŎR-/; UK /ŎR ih zunz, -zn̩z/.

8. **behoofeful** /bih-, bee HO͞OF fu̹ll/ needful. Variant of **behoveful** /-HOHV-/, **behooveful** /-HO͞OV-/.

39. **receptacle** here should be /REE sep tuh kɫ/.

50. ***Environed** /en VĪ run ed/; US *also* [en VĪ urn ed] surrounded.

Act 4 Scene 4

6. **cot-quean** /CŎT kween/ man who acts as housewife.

Act 4 Scene 5 (*Complete Oxford* 4.4)

4. (4.4.31) **pennyworths, penn'worths** bargains. Both pronounced
/PEN urths/.

15. (4.4.42) **weraday** /WĔR uh day/ alas. Some eds. prefer **weladay**
/WEL uh day/.

16. (4.4.43) *****aqua-vitae** distilled liquor, e.g., brandy.
US /AHK-, AK wuh VEE tī/, *rarely* [-VĪ tee]; CN /AK wuh VEE tī/ [AHK-];
UK /AK wuh VEE tī/ [-VEE tuh]. /AK wuh VĪ tee/ is the oldest surviving form.
/-VEE tay/ not recommended.

17-50. (4.4.44-81) *****lamentable** here should be /LAM un tuh bł/ the usual UK
pronunciation.

47. (4.4.78) **solace** /SŎL us/ comfort.

56. (4.4.71 [sic]) **detestable** here should be /DEE tess tuh bł/ or /DET es tuh bł/.

88. (4.4.115) **dirges** /DUR jiz/ funeral songs.

94. (4.4.121) **low'r, lour** frown. /lowr/ with the vowel of *how*.

133. (4.4.159) **Rebeck, Rebec** /REE beck/ a 3 stringed fiddle.

Act 5 Scene 1

2. *****presage** here should be /pree-, prih SAYJ/ foretell.

29. **Tush** /tŭsh/ expression of disdain.

49. **penury** /PEN yur ee/; UK *also* /PEN yoor ee/ poverty.

52. **caitiff wretch** /KAYT if/ scoundrel.

85. **cordial** US /COR jł/; UK /COR dył/ healing medicine.

ă-bat, ăir-ma**rry**, air-p**air**, a̧r-f**ar**, ĕr-me**rry**, ĝ- g**et**, ī-h**igh**, ĭr-m**irror**, ł-litt**le**, n̩-list**en**,
ŏ-h**ot**, oh-g**o**, o͞o-w**ood**, o͞o-m**oon**, oor-t**our**, ōr- **or**, ow-h**ow**, ṯh-**that**, t̶h̶-**thin**, ŭ-b**ut**,
UR-f**ur**, ur-und**er**.   ( ) - suppress the syllable   see p. xiii for complete list.

Act 5 Scene 3

16, 20. **obsequies** /ŎB suh kweez/ burial services.

22. **mattock** /MAT uk/ digging tool.

38. **inexorable** /in EK sur uh bł/; US *also* /-EG zur-/ unyielding.

45. **detestable** here should be /DEE tess tuh bł/ or /DET es tuh bł/.

68. **conjuration** (following Q1) /cŏn jur RAY shun/ [cun-] solemn entreaty. Q3, F1 have **commiseration** /kuh miz ur RAY shun/ pity.

84. **lanthorn** archaic variant of **lantern**. Probably pronounced /LAN turn/, but possibly /LANT horn/ or /LAN ~~th~~urn, -~~th~~orn/.

94. *****ensign** emblem. US, CN /EN sn̩/, US *rarely* [-sīn]; UK /-sn̩, -sīn/.

105. *****paramour** US, CN /PĂIR uh moor/ [-mor]; UK /-mor/ [-moor] lover.

141, 207. **sepulchre** /SEP ł kur/ tomb.

145. **unkind** here should be /UN kīnd/.

146. *****lamentable** here should be /LAM un tuh bł/ the usual UK pronunciation.

148. **comfortable** here should be /CUM fur tuh bł/ giving comfort.

181. **descry** /dih SKRĪ/ see.

185. **mattock** /MAT uk/ digging tool.

221. *****mischance** in verse normally with 2nd syllable stress.

238. **Betroth'd** /bih-, bee TROHTHD/ engaged to be married.

253. **prefixed** here should be /pree-, prih FIK sid/ appointed.

289. **pothecary** US /PŎ~~TH~~ uh kĕr ee/; UK /-kuh ree/ apothecary, druggist.

292. **scourge** /SKURJ/ severe punishment.

297. **jointure** /JOYN chur/ marriage settlement. See App. D *-ure.*

The Taming of the Shrew

People in the Play

Sometimes some of these names are given an Italian pronunciation in performance. These pronunciations are indicated here as accurately as possible within the limits of this notation. Shakespeare, however, probably intended them to be anglicized. The *-tio, -sio, -cio* endings in Shk's day represented /-s(ee) yoh/ or /-sh(ee) yoh/, or simply /-shoh/ (*Hortensio, Litio, Lisio, Licio, Lucentio, Vincentio*).

Baptista Minola /bap TISS tuh MIN uh luh/;
Ital. /bahp TEES tah MEEN oh lah/.

*****Bianca** 2 or 3 syllables depending on meter US /bee AHNG kuh/
[bee ANG kuh]; UK /bee ANG kuh/, *rarely* [bee AHNG kuh]; CN both are used equally; Ital. /bee AHNG kah/. If two syllables /BYAHNG kuh/ or /BYANG kuh/.

Biondello 3 or 4 syllables depending on meter /b(ee) yun DEL oh/;
Ital. /bee yohn DEL loh/.

Cambio assumed name of Lucentio. 2 or 3 syllables depending on meter:
/KAM b(ee) yoh/; Ital. /KAHM-/.

Christophero see **Sly**.

*****Gremio** 2 or 3 syllables depending on meter /GREEM (ee) yoh/ is the older angl. form, /GREM (ee) yoh/ is a newer angl. form. The former is preferred in the UK, the latter in the US. Ital. /GRAYM-/ is also sometimes used.

Grumio 2 or 3 syllables depending on meter /GRŌŌM (ee) yoh/.

*****Hortensio** 3 or 4 syllables depending on meter /hor TEN s(ee) yoh/;
US, CN *rarely* [-sh(ee) yoh]; Ital. /or TEN see yoh/. Normal development would favor /-sh-/.

*****Katherina** 3 or 4 syllables depending on meter US /kat-, kath (ur) REEN uh/, /kuh TREEN uh/; CN /kat-/, *rarely* [kath -]; UK /kat-/ [kath-];
Ital. /kaht (ay) REE nah/. (F1 has **Katerina**, occasionally).
   Katherine 2 or 3 syllables depending on meter /KATH (u)r in/, /KAT-/.

People in the Play (cont.)

*__Litio__ (F1) assumed name of Hortensio. 2 or 3 syllables depending on meter
US, CN /LISH (ee) yoh/; UK /LISH-, LISS-/; Ital. forms are also used:
[LITS-, LEETS-]. Some eds. prefer **Lisio** (which also appears in F1) or
Licio (F2), both anglicized as /LISS-, LISH-/. *Licio* would be
Ital. /LITCH-, LEECH-/.

Lucentio 3 or 4 syllables depending on meter /lo͞o SEN sh(ee) yoh/;
Ital. /lo͞o CHEN ts(ee) yoh/ (for /lyo͞o-/ see App. D *lu-*).

Minola see **Baptista**.

*__Petruchio__ 3 or 4 syllables depending on meter /puh TRO͞OK (ee) yoh/ is
preferred over /puh TRO͞OCH (ee) yoh/ in all countries. Some eds. prefer the
Ital. spelling **Petruccio** /pay TRO͞OCH oh/.   Shk probably meant to indicate the
pronunciation /ch/, not /k/ (cf. *Machiavel* sometimes spelled *Match-*).

Sly, Christopher sometimes referred to as **Christophero** /crih STŎF (ur) roh/.
See Induction 2.73.

*__Tranio__ 2 or 3 syllables depending on meter. The Ital. pronunciation is
more common than the angl. form US, CN /TRAH n(ee) yoh/ [TRAY-];
UK /TRAH-/, *rarely* [TRAY-].

Vincentio 3 or 4 syllables depending on meter: /vin SEN sh(ee) yoh/;
Ital. /veen CHEN ts(ee) yoh/.

Places in the Play

*__Padua__ 2 or 3 syllables depending on meter /PAD y(oo) wuh/ [PAJ (oo) wuh].
An Ital. vowel /PAHD-/ is not recommended, since the Ital. form is *Padova*.

Pisa /PEE zuh/.

Induction Scene 1

5. **paucas pallabris** angl. /PAW kus puh LAB riss, -riz/. Sly's confusion of Sp.
pocas palabras /POH kahss pah LAH brahss/ and Lat. *pauca verba*
Ang.Lat. /PAW kuh VUR buh/; Class.Lat. /POW kah WĔR bah/. Both mean
'few words,' i.e., 'enough said.'

6. **Sessa** /SESS uh/ uncertain meaning, perhaps 'hurry,' 'let it go,' 'cease.'

9. **denier** coin of little value. /duh NEER, DEN yur/ are older;
/DEN yay, den YAY/ are newer, based on Fr.

9. **Saint Jeronimy** /jur RŎN ih mee/.

12. **thirdborough** constable. US /THURD bur oh, -uh/;
E.COAST US /-buh roh, -buh ruh/; UK /-buh ruh/. F1 has **headborough**.

13. **borough** town. US /BUR oh/ [-uh]; E.COAST US /BUH roh/ [-ruh];
UK /BUH ruh/.

17, 18. **Brach** /bratch/ female dog. Some eds. prefer **Breathe** in line 17.

18. **Clowder** /CLOW dur/ name of a dog.

51. **dulcet** /DULL sit/ sweet.

57. **ewer** /YOO̅ ur/ pitcher.

101. **veriest** /VĔR yist/ most exceeding.

105. **Barthol'mew** here should be stressed /BAR ~~thl~~ myoo̅/, or as in Shk's time
/BAR tl myoo̅/.

108.***obeisance** /oh BAY sn̩ss/; US *also* [-BEE-] curtsy.

127. **close** /clohss/ secretly.

135. ***homage** /HŎM ij/; US *also* /ŎM ij/ acknowledgement of service to a lord.

Induction Scene 2

20. **bear-herd** /BAIR urd/ bearkeeper. A more recent spelling pronunciation
/BAIR hurd/, is also used.

22. **Wincot** /WINK ut/.

32. **abject** /AB ject/ contemptible.

39. **Semiramis** /suh MĬR uh miss/ lusty queen of Assyria.

ă-bat, ăir-**marry**, air-**pair**, ar̩-**far**, ĕr-**merry**, ĝ- get, ī-high, ĭr-mirror, ł-little, n̩-listen,
ŏ-hot, oh-go, oo̅-wood, oo̅-moon, oor-**tour**, ŏr- **or**, ow-how, ţh-**that**, ~~th~~-**thin**, ŭ-but,
UR-**fur**, ur-under.   ( ) - suppress the syllable   see p. xiii for complete list.

40. **bestrow** /bih-, bee STROH/ archaic variant of **bestrew** /-STROO/.

50. ***Adonis** US, CN /uh DŎN iss/, *rarely* [-DOHN-]; UK /uh DOHN iss/, *rarely* [-DŎN-] Venus' lover.

51. **Cytherea** /si̶t̶h̶ uh REE uh/ Venus.

54. **Io** /Ī oh/ maiden loved by Jupiter.

57. **Daphne** /DAFF nee/ nymph changed to a laurel tree.

71. **savors** (UK **savours**) /SAY vurz/ smells.

73. **Christopher** (F1) does not fit the meter. **Christophero** (F2) /cris TŎF (ur) roh/.

105. **goodman** /GŌOD mun/ husband.

110. **Al'ce** /ălss/ variant of **Alice**.

123. **absent** /ub-, ab SENT/ keep away from.

138. **comonty** /CŎM un tee/ Sly's error for **comedy**. Some eds. prefer **commodity**.

138. **gambold** /GAM błd/ frisk. Archaic variant of **gambol** /GAM bł/.

Act 1 Scene 1

3. ***Lombardy** /LŎM bar dee/ [LUM-] region in N. Italy.

13. **Bentivolii** /ben tih VOH lee ī/ a 15th century family.

24. **saciety** /suh SĪ (uh) tee/ fullness. Archaic variant of **satiety** /suh TĪ (uh) tee/.

25. **Mi perdonato** /mee pĕr doh NAH toh/ Ital. 'pardon me.' Some eds. substitute **Mi perdonate** /mee pĕr doh NAH tay/.

31. **Stoics** /STOH iks/ philosophers who showed no emotion.

33. **Ovid** /ŎV id/ Roman poet.

33. **abjur'd** /ab-, ub JOORD/; US *also* /-JURD/ renounced.

36. ***poesy** US /POH (ih) see/ [-zee]; UK, CN /- zee/ [-see] poetry.

41. **Gramercies** /gruh MUR seez/ thanks.

48. ***importune** /im POR chun/ ask insistently. See App. D.

62. ***Iwis** /ih WISS/; US, CN *also* /ee WISS/ indeed.

68. **Husht, master, here's some good pastime toward** /TOH wurd, -urd/ about to take place.

69. **That wench is stark mad or wonderful froward** /FROH wurd, FROH urd/ difficult to deal with. Both 68 and 69 are four foot lines with epic caesuras after *master* and *mad*. *Wonderful* is syncopated to /WUND (ur) fł/.

84. **Minerva** /mih NUR vuh/ goddess of wisdom.

87. **mew** /my$\overline{oo}$/ cage.

101. **commune** here should be /CŎM y$\overline{oo}$n/ speak intimately.

115. **parle** /pạrl/ conference with an enemy.

126. **Tush** /tŭsh/ expression of disdain.

127. ***alarums** US, CN /uh LAHR umz/ [-LĂIR-];
UK /uh LĂIR umz, uh LAHR umz/ calls to arms.

131. **as lief** /leef/ as soon.

154. **queen of Carthage** /CAR thij/ Dido, ruler of Carthage in N. Africa.

162.   **Redime   te captum   quam queas   minimo**
Ang.Lat. /RED ih mee tee KAP tum   kwam   KWEE ass MIN ih moh/
Class.Lat. /RED ih may   tay KAHP t$\overline{oo}$m kwahm KWAY ahs MIN ih moh/
          'Ransom yourself from captivity as cheaply as you can.'

163. **Gramercies** /gruh MUR seez/ thanks.

168. **Agenor** /uh JEE nur/ Europa's father. See App. D *-or*.

169. **Cretan** /CREET ṇ, -un/ of Crete.

ă-bat, ăir-marry, air-pair, ạr-far, ĕr-merry, ĝ- get, ī-high, ĭr-mirror, ł-little, ṇ-listen,
ŏ-hot, oh-go, $\overline{oo}$-wood, $\overline{oo}$-moon, oor-tour, ōr- or, ow-how, ţh-that, th-thin, ŭ-but,
UR-fur, ur-under.   ( ) - suppress the syllable   see p. xiii for complete list.

169. **strond** /strŏnd/ shore. Archaic variant of **strand**. Here rhymes with *hand*.

183. **mew'd** /myо̄о̄d/ caged.

198. **Basta** angl. /BAS tuh/; Ital. /BAH stah/ enough.

204. ***Florentine** US /FLŌR in teen/ [-tīn]; E.COAST US /FLŎR-/;
UK /FLŎR in tīn/ [-teen] person from Florence.

205. **Neapolitan** /nee uh PŎL ih tun/ man from Naples.

232. **descried** /dih SKRĪD/ found out.

Act 1 Scene 2

1-190. **Verona** /vĕr-, vur ROH nuh/.
---

4. ***trow** US, CN /troh, trow/; UK /trow/ [troh] trust. Shk's rhymes elsewhere
indicate /-oh/.

24. **Con tutto   il core,   ben trovato**
    /cŏn TŌŌ toh eel COR ay ben troh VAH toh/
    'with all my heart, well met.'
Some eds. substitute **cuore** /KWOR ay/ for *core*.

25. **Alla   nostra   casa   ben venuto,   molto   honorato**
    /ah lah NŎS trah KAH sah ben ven ŌŌ toh, MŎL toh ŏn or AH toh

    signor   mio   Petrucio
    SEEN yor MEE oh pay TRŌŌCH oh, -yoh/
    'welcome to my house, my most honored Signor Petrucio.'

28. **'leges** /LEJ iz/ alleges.

69. **Florentius'** /fluh REN shus/ he married an ugly wife.

70. **Sibyl** /SIB ł/; UK *also* /SIB il/ prophetess in Gk mythology.

70, 90. **shrowd** /shrohd/ sharp-tongued. Archaic variant of **shrewd**.
---

71. **Xantippe** /zan TIP ee/ wife of Socrates noted for her nagging. Some eds.
prefer the spelling **Xanthippe** also /zan TIP ee/, but now sometimes given a
spelling pronunciation /-T̶H̶I̶P̶-/. /gzan-/ not recommended.

79. **aglet-baby** /AG lit/ small figure on a lacing cord.

90. **froward** /FROH wurd, FROH urd/ difficult to deal with.

124. **defects** here should be /dih-, dee FECTS/.

127. **access** here should be /ak SESS/.

150. ***largess, largesse** generous gift. Here should have 1st syllable stress US /LAR jess/ [-zhess]; CN, UK /LAR zhess/ [-jess]. Forms with /j/ are older.

164. ***Trow you** US, CN /troh, trow/; UK /trow/ [troh] know. Shk's rhymes elsewhere indicate /-oh/.

190. **Antonio's** /an TOHN yohz/; Ital. /ahn-/.

202. **chafed** /CHAY fid/ enraged.

206. *** 'larums** US, CN /LAHR umz/ [-LĂIR-]; UK /LĂIR umz, LAHR umz/ calls to arms.

210. **Tush** /tŭsh/ expression of disdain.

242. **Leda's** /LEE duz/ mother of Helen of Troy.

256. **Alcides'** /al SĪ deez/ Hercules'.

259, 267. **access** here should be /ak SESS/.

268. **ingrate** here should be /in GRAYT/ ungrateful.

275. ***quaff** /kwŏf/; UK *rarely* [kwahf] drink freely. /kwăf/ is also used, but is not recommended.

280. **your ben venuto** /ben ven OO toh/ your welcome, i.e., 'host.'

Act 2 Scene 1

3. **gawds, gauds** /gawdz/ trinkets. Some eds. prefer F1's **goods**.

18. **envy** here with 2nd syllable stress /en VEE/.

ă-bat, ăir-ma**rry**, air-**pair**, a̯r-**far**, ĕr-**merry**, ĝ- g**et**, ī-**high**, ĭr-**mirror**, ł-**little**, ṇ-**listen**, ŏ-**hot**, oh-**go**, ŏŏ-**wood**, o̅o̅-**moon**, oor-**tour**, ŏr- **or**, ow-**how**, t̯h-**that**, t̶h̶-**thin**, ŭ-**but**, UR-**fur**, ur-**under**.   ( ) - suppress the syllable   see p. xiii for complete list.

26. **hilding** /HILL ding/ good-for-nothing.

47. **a gentleman of Verona** here *gentlemen* is compressed to 2 syllables and *Verona* is pronounced normally /vĕr-, vur ROH nuh/; but if *gentlemen* is 3 syllables, then *Verona* could be reduced to /VROH nuh/.

60. **Mantua** US /MAN choo wuh/; UK /MAN tyoo wuh/ [MAN choo wuh].

68. **Antonio's** /an TOHN yohz/; Ital. /ahn-/.

73. **Backare, Bacare** (F1), **Baccare** (F2) fake Latin for 'back off!' Accent could be on the 2nd or 1st syllable. Angl. /BACK uh ree/, /back AIR ee/ or with Ital. or Lat. ending /BACK ah ray/, /back AH ray/.

80. **Rheims** angl. /reemz/; Fr. /rǎ^{n}ss/ city in France.

97. **access** here should be /ak SESS/.

108. **Holla** /huh LAH/ a call to attract attention.

131. **I am as** *peremptory* **as she proud-minded** 'insisting on obedience.' If contracted to *I'm*, then /pur EM tur ee/ which is more common today. If *I am* is spoken as two words then /PĔR um tree/, which is also used today. Both forms appear elsewhere in Shk.

135. **extreme** here should be /EK streem/.

150. **bow'd** /bohd/ bent.

163. **discomfited** /dis CUM fit id/ defeated.

175. **volubility** /vŏl yuh BIL ih tee/ ability to talk easily, with quick-wit.

180. **banes** /baynz/ proclamation in church of an intended marriage. Archaic variant of **banns** /banz/.

198. **join'd stool** /JOYND sto͞ol/ a well-crafted stool. Some eds. prefer **joint stool**.

227. **craven** /CRAY vin, -vn̩/ coward.

247. **askaunce** at a sideways angle. Archaic variant of **askance** US /uh SKĂNSS/; UK, E. NEW ENG. /uh SKAHNSS/ [uh SKĂNSS]. See App. D *-aun-*.

263. **extempore** /ek STEM p(uh) ree/ composed on the spur of the moment.

293. **froward** difficult to deal with. /FROH wurd, FROH urd/ before an epic caesura.

295. **Grissel** /GRISS ł/ Griselda, a submissive wife.

296. **Lucrece** Lucretia, Roman who commited suicide after being raped. Here should be /LOO creess/ (for /lyoo-/ see App. D *lu-*).

313. **meacock** /MEE cŏck/ milksop.

348. **ewers** here should be one syllable /yoorz/ pitchers.

348. **lave** /layv/ wash.

349. **Tyrian** /TĬR yun/ purple, dark red.

351. **arras** /ĂIR us/ tapestry.

354. **Valens** archaic variant of **valence** short draperies edging a bed canopy. US /VAYL unss/ [VAL-]; UK /VAL unss].

357. **milch-kine** /MILCH kīn/ milk cows.

370. **jointer** /JOYNT ur/ marriage settlement. Archaic variant of **jointure** /JOYN chur/. See App. D *-ure* and App. E.

374-8. **argosy, -ies** /ĄRG uh see/ large merchant ship.

375. **Marsellis** /mar SELL iss/ archaic variant of **Marseilles**. The usual mod. pronunciation /mar SAY/ will not fit, but another modern variant from the UK will: [mar SAY łz].

378. ***galliasses** /GAL ee us iz/ [GAL ee ass iz] large galley ships.

390. **cavil** /KAV ł/; UK *also* /KAV il/ quibble.

Act 3 Scene 1

4-87. **pedant** /PED ṇt/ dull teacher.

ă-bat, ăir-**marry**, air-**pair**, ạr-**far**, ĕr-**merry**, ĝ- get, ī-high, ĭr-mirror, ł-**little**, ṇ-**listen**, ŏ-hot, oh-go, ōō-**wood**, ōō-**moon**, oor-**tour**, ōr- or, ow-how, ṭh-**that**, th-**thin**, ŭ-**but**, UR-**fur**, ur-**under**.   ( ) - suppress the syllable   see p. xiii for complete list.

6. *__prerogative__ /pur RŎG uh tiv/ [prih-, pree-] precedence. /pree-/ non-standard in the UK.

18. *__breeching scholar__ a still-whipable schoolboy. /BRITCH ing/ is traditional, /BREECH ing/ is newer. The former pronunciation is more common in the UK, and the latter in the US, CN.

28-29. | **Hic** | **ibat** | **Simois;** | **hic** | **est** | **Sigeia** | **tellus;** |
|---|---|---|---|---|---|---|
| Ang.Lat. | /hick | Ī bat | SIM oh iss | hick | est | sī JEE yuh | TEL us; |
| Class.Lat. | /heek | IB aht | SIM oh iss | heek | est | see GAY ih ah | TEL o͞os |

'Here flowed the Simois; here is the Sigeian land'

	Hic	**steterat**	**Priami**	**regia**	**celsa**	**senis**
Ang.Lat.	/hick	STET ur at	PRĪ am ī	REE jee uh	SEL suh	SEEN iss/
Class.Lat.	/heek	STET ĕr aht	PREE ah mee	RAY ĝee ah	KEL sah	SEN iss/

'Here stood the lofty palace of old Priam.'

30, 41. __Conster__ /CŎN stur/ explain the meaning. Some eds. prefer __construe__ which here should be /CŎN stro͞o/.

37. *__pantaloon__ foolish old man. US, UK /PANT uh lo͞on/ [pant uh LO͞ON]; CN /pant uh LOON/ [PANT uh lo͞on].

50. __Pedascule__ Ang.Lat. /puh DASS kyoo lee/; Class.Lat. /ped AHSS ko͞o lay/ tutor.

52. __Aeacides__ /ee ASS ih deez/ descendent of Aeacus.

67-79. __gamouth__ musical scale. Archaic variant of __gamut__, both pronounced /GAM ut/, or the former possibly /GAM uth/.

76. __ut__ /ut, o͞ot/ the lowest note on the scale, modern *do*.

Act 3 Scene 2

10. __rudesby__ /RO͞ODZ bee/ rude person.

16. __banes__ /baynz/ proclamation in church of an intended marriage. Archaic variant of __banns__ /banz/.

44. *__breeches__ /BRITCH iz/ is traditional, /BREECH iz/ is newer. The former pronunciation is more common in the UK, and the latter in the US, CN.

48. __chapeless__ /CHAYP liss/; US *also* /CHAP liss/ without a metal tip on the sheath.

51. **mose** /mohz/ uncertain, perhaps a discharge from the nostrils.

51. **lampass, lampas** /LAMP us/; UK *also* /LAMP uz/ swelling of the gums.

53. **spavins** /SPAV inz/ swelling of the hock.

65. **caparison'd** /kuh PĂIR ih sn̩d/ covered with an ornamental cloth.

67. **kersey** /KUR zee/ coarse woolen cloth.

119. **accoutrements** /uh COOT ruh munts, uh COOT ur munts/ furnishings, i.e., clothes.

The *Complete Oxford* begins Scene 3.3 here (line nos. in parentheses).

---

160. (3.3.33) **gogs-wouns** /gŏgz WOONZ/ God's (i.e., Jesus') wounds.

172. (3.3.45)***quaff'd** /kwŏft/; UK *rarely* [kwahft] drank freely. /kwăft/ is also used, but is not recommended.

172. (3.3.45) **muscadel** /muss kuh DEL/ strong sweet wine. Some eds. prefer **muscatel** /muss kuh TEL/.

181. (3.3.54) **rout** /rowt/ crowd of guests.

230. (3.3.102) **chattels** /CHAT l̩z/ property.

Act 4 Scene 1

11. **Holla** /huh LAH/ a call to attract attention.

43. ***cony-catching** rabbit catching, i.e., trickery. /KOH nee/, *rarely older* [KUN ee].

47. ***fustian** /FUSS tee un/; US *also* /FUSS chun/ coarse cloth of cotton and linen. Normal development would favor the latter.

50. **Gills, Jills** /jilz/ i.e., girls.

ă-bat, ăir-**marry**, air-**pair**, a̧r-**far**, ĕr-**merry**, ĝ- **get**, ī-**high**, ĭr-**mirror**, l̩-**little**, n̩-**listen**, ŏ-**hot**, oh-**go**, ōō-**wood**, ōō-**moon**, oor-**tour**, ōr- **or**, ow-**how**, t̪h-**that**, t̶h̶-**thin**, ŭ-**but**, UR-**fur**, ur-**under**.   ( ) - suppress the syllable   see p. xiii for complete list.

66. **Inprimis** /in PRĪ miss/ in the first place. Archaic variant of ***imprimis**
/im PRĪ miss/ (traditional), /im PREE miss/ (restored Latin). The latter is now
more common.

133. **Gabr'el's** /GAYB rłz/ variant of *Gabriel's,* still current today.

142. **Soud** uncertain, perhaps indicates Petruchio's humming. Some eds. prefer
Food.

147. **awry** /uh RĪ/ askew.

182. **continency** /CŎN tih nun see/ sexual self-restraint.

188. **politicly** /PŎL (ih) tik lee/ shrewdly.

193. **haggard** /HAG urd/ wild hawk.

197. **eat** appears twice in this line. The first is /et/, a dialect variant of **ate,**
which is also commonly /et/ in the UK.

211. **shew** archaic variant of **show.** Here meant to rhyme with *shrew,* but *shew*
and *shrew* each had variants with /o͞o/ and /oh/ in Elizabethan English.

Act 4 Scene 2

20. **cullion** 'scoundrel,' literally 'testicle.' Normally /CŬL yun/, here expanded
to /CŬL ee yun/.

39. **haggard** /HAG urd/ wild hawk.

63. **mercantant** merchant. /MUR kun tunt/ in a broken-backed line. F1 has the
variant **marcantant** /MAR-/. Some eds. prefer the Ital. form **mercatante**
angl. /mur kuh TAN tee/; Ital. /měr kah TAHN tay/.

63. **pedant** /PED ņt/ teacher.

76. **Tripoli** /TRIP (uh) lee/ city in N. Africa.

77-81. **Mantua** 2 or 3 syllables depending on meter US /MAN ch(oo) wuh/;
UK /MAN ty(oo) wuh/ [MAN ch(oo) wuh].

98. **incomparable** here should be /in CŎM pur ruh bł/.

Act 4 Scene 3

5. **alms** charity for the poor. /ahmz/ is older; /ahlmz, awlmz/ are newer. In the UK the latter are non-standard.

6. **elsewhere** a normal line demands 2nd syllable stress, a form still used in the UK, but unknown in the US. The foot may, however, be inverted to allow 1st syllable stress.

36. **amort** /uh MORT/ downcast.

56. **fardingales** /FAR ding gaylz/ hooped petticoats. Archaic variant of **farthingales** /FAR ͭhing gaylz/.

64. **porringer** US /PŌR in jur/; E.COAST US, UK /PŎR-/ a dish for porridge.

81. **paltry** /PAWL tree/ worthless.

87. **masquing** US /MĂSK ing/; UK, E. NEW ENG. /MAHSK-/ [MĂSK-] fit only for a masked dance or pantomime.

88. *****demi-canon** /DEM ee-/ large canon.

102. **nor more commendable** here /CŎM en duh bɫ/ in a regular line, or mod. /cuh MEN duh bɫ/ after an epic caesura.

110. **skein** /skayn/ loose coil.

112. **bemete** /bih-, bee MEET/ measure, i.e., beat.

127. *****Ergo** /UR go/ is older, /ĔR go/ is newer. The former is more common in the UK, the latter in the US, CN, but both forms appear in all countries.

134. **Inprimis** /in PRĪ miss/ in the first place. Archaic variant of *****Imprimis** /im PRĪ miss/ (traditional), /im PREE miss/ (restored Latin). The latter is now more common.

152. **mete-yard** /MEET yard/ measuring stick.

170. **habiliments** /huh BILL ih munts/ clothes.

ă-bat, ăir-marry, air-pair, ar-far, ĕr-merry, ĝ- get, ī-high, ĭr-mirror, ɫ-little, ṇ-listen, ŏ-hot, oh-go, ōō-wood, ōō-moon, oor-tour, ōr- or, ow-how, ͭh-that, ͭh-thin, ŭ-but, UR-fur, ur-under.   ( ) - suppress the syllable   see p. xiii for complete list.

Act 4 Scene 4

4. **Genoa** /JEN oh uh/ Italian city.

11. **throughly** archaic variant of *thoroughly.* /T̶H̶R̄OO lee/ is the normal
pronunciation on stage, but to enhance clarity a syncopated form of the modern
pronunciation may be used: *thor'ghly.*

49. **affied** /uh FĪD/ betrothed.

59. **scrivener** /SKRIV nur/ notary.

The *Complete Oxford* begins Scene 4.5 here (line nos. in parentheses).

---

93. (4.5.19) **cum   privilegio   ad   imprimendum   solum**
Ang.Lat.   /kŭm   priv ih LEE j(ee) oh   ad   im prim EN dum   SOH lum/
Class.Lat.   /kōōm pree wih LAYG ee yoh ahd im prim EN dōōm SOH lōōm/
                'with exclusive rights to print.'

Act 4 Scene 5 (*Complete Oxford* 4.6)

41. **Allots** /uh LŎTS/ gives.

78. **froward** /FROH wurd, FROH urd/ difficult to deal with.

79. ***untoward** unmannerly. Here should be /un TOH wurd, -urd/ to rhyme
with *froward,* though the most common pronunciation in CN, UK is
/un tuh WÂRD/ (as in *war*).

Act 5 Scene 1

13. **toward** /TOH wurd, -urd/ about to take place.

67. **copatain hat** hat shaped like a sugar loaf. This unusual word is usually
/CŎP uh tayn/ today, but normal development would yield the ending /-tin/
(cf. *captain*). Some eds. prefer the variant **copintank** /CŎP in tank/.

75. **'cerns** /surnz/ concerns.

78. **Bergamo** angl. /BUR guh moh/; Ital. /BĔR gah moh/ city in Italy.

99. ***cony-catch'd** i.e., tricked. /KOH nee/, *rarely older* [KUN ee].

106. **dotard** /DOHT urd/ senile old man.

117. **eyne** /īn/ dialect form of *eyes*.

Act 5 Scene 2

9. **banket** /BANK it/ light meal, often of fruit. Archaic variant of **banquet**.

64. **veriest** /VĔR yist/ most exceeding.

99. **by my holidam** an oath referring to a 'holy object' or the 'holy lady,' i.e.,
Mary. Other variants are: **halidam, halidom, halidame, halidome, holidame**.
Probably these were all variant spellings of /HAL ih dum, HŎL ih dum/ (Note
hal- can also be /HŎL-/ in *Halloween*.)

104. **Swinge** /swinj/ beat.

119-183. **froward** /FROH wurd, FROH urd/ difficult to deal with.

122. **bable** presumably /BAB ł/, archaic variant of **bauble** /BAW bł/.

136. **unkind** here should be /UN kīnd/.

139. **meads** /meedz/ meadows.

145. **deign** /dayn/ think it appropriate.

182. **toward** /TOH wurd, -urd/ obedient.

182-3 are four-beat lines in a dactylic form (a strong beat followed by two weak
ones).

188. **shrow** /shroh/ archaic variant of **shrew**, which here should rhyme with *so*.

ă-bat, ăir-**marry**, air-**pair**, ạr-**far**, ĕr-**merry**, ĝ- get, ī-high, ĭr-**mirror**, ł-**little**, ṇ-**listen**,
ŏ-hot, oh-go, ōō-**wood**, ōō-**moon**, oor-**tour**, ōr- **or**, ow-**how**, ţh-**that**, th-**thin**, ŭ-**but**,
UR-**fur**, ur-under.   ( ) - suppress the syllable   see p. xiii for complete list.

The Tempest

People in the Play

Alonso /uh LŎN zoh/.

Antonio 3 or 4 syllables depending on meter /an TOHN (ee) yoh/; Ital. /ahn-/.

Ariel 2 or 3 syllables depending on meter /AIR (ee) yɫ/; E.COAST US *sometimes* [ĂIR-]. /-el/ is newer.

Boatswain /BOH sn̩/ is usual, though /BOHT swayn/ is sometimes used by landsmen.

Caliban /KAL ih ban/.

Gonzalo /gŏn-, gun ZAH loh/.

Miranda /mih RAN duh/; US *also* /mur-/.

Prospero /PRŎS pur oh/ or /PRŎS proh/ depending on meter.
  Prosper /PRŎS pur/.

Sebastian US /suh BĂS chun/; UK /suh BĂST yun/.

Stephano, Stefano /STEF uh noh/.

Trinculo /TRINK yoo loh, -yuh-/.

Places in the Play

Milan here should be /MILL un/.

Act 1 Scene 1

4-34. *****yare(ly)** /yair/; US *also* /yạr/ quickly, smartly.

---

5. *****Heigh**! US /hay, hī/; CN /hī/, *rarely* [hay]; UK /hay/. Shk intended /hay/.

6. **topsail** sailors use /TŎP sɫ/; landsmen /TŎP sayl/.

25. *****mischance** 2nd syllable stress in verse, but in this prose passage, the alternative modern pronunciation with 1st syllable stress is possible.

34. **topmast** /TŎP must/ is used by sailors; landsmen say US /TŎP măst/; UK, E.NEW ENG. /-mahst/.

40. **blasphemous** /BLĂSS fuh mus/; UK, E.NEW ENG. *also* [BLAHSS-] speaking irreverently.

48. ***unstanch'd** unsatisfied. Variant of **unstaunched** /un STAWNCHT/. See App. D *-aun-*.

Act 1 Scene 2

2. **allay** /uh LAY/ calm.

30. **perdition** /pur DISH un/; UK *also* [PUR DISH un] loss.

31. **Betid** /bih TID/; US *also* /bee-/ happened, past tense of *betide.*

50. **abysm** /uh BIZM/ variant of **abyss** /uh BISS/ which some eds prefer.

63. **holp** /hohlp/ helped.

71. **signories** /SEEN yur eez/ lands.

79. **Being once perfected how to grant suits** *Being* has two syllables, and *perfected* is /PUR fik tid/ expert in.

87. ***verdure** vigor. US, CN /VUR jur, -dyoor, -dyur/; UK /-dyoor/ [-dyur, -jur]. See App. D *-ure.*

97. **sans** /sănz/ without.

98. **revenue** here should be /ruh VEN yo͞o/.

105. ***prerogative** /pur RŎG uh tiv/ [prih-, pree-] rights. /pree-/ non-standard in the UK.

113, 124. ***homage** /HŎM ij/; US *also* /ŎM ij/ acknowledgement of allegience.

---

114. **coronet** small crown. Here should be US /COR (uh) net, -nit/; E.COAST US, UK /CŎR-/.

ă-b**a**t, ăir-m**a**rry, air-p**ai**r, ạr-f**a**r, ĕr-m**e**rry, ĝ- g**e**t, ī-h**i**gh, ĭr-m**i**rror, ł-litt**l**e, ṇ-liste**n**, ŏ-h**o**t, oh-g**o**, o͝o-w**oo**d, o͞o-m**oo**n, oor-t**our**, ōr- **or**, ow-h**ow**, ţh-**th**at, th̶-**th**in, ŭ-b**u**t, UR-f**ur**, ur-und**er**.   ( ) - suppress the syllable   see p. xiii for complete list.

---

123. **in *lieu o'** US, CN /lо̄о̄, lyо̄о̄/; UK /lyо̄о̄/ [lо̄о̄] in return for.

125. **extirpate** here /ek STUR payt/ drive off.

128. **midnight** here with 2nd syllable stress.

152. ***cherubin** angel. US, CN /CHĔR uh bin/ [-yuh-]; UK uses both equally. /KĔR-/ not recommended.

161. **Neapolitan** /nee uh PŎL ih tun/ man from Naples.

180. ***prescience** foreknowledge. Here 3 syllables /PRESS ee unss/. /PRESH unss/ is sometimes used, especially in the US, but would have to be /PRESH ee unss/ to fit the meter.

199. **topmast** /TŎP must/ is used by sailors; landsmen say US /TŎP măst/; UK, E.NEW ENG. /-mahst/.

200. **boresprit** /BOR sprit/ archaic variant of ***bowsprit** US /BOW sprit/ [BOH-]; UK /BOH sprit/ the spar jutting forward from the bow of a ship to carry forward sail.

219. **thou badst** /badst/ 2nd person sing. past tense of *bid* 'asked.'

229. **Bermoothes** /bur MŌŌTH uz/ archaic variant of **Bermudas**.

258-340. Sycorax /SIK ur racks/.

261, 265. **Argier** /ahr JEER/, archaic variant of **Algiers** /al JEERZ/.

276. **unmitigable** /un MIT ih guh bł/ that cannot be softened.

295. ***entrails** /EN traylz/; US *also* [-trłz] guts.

370. **aches** Shk pronounced this with two syllables /AY chiz/.

373. **Setebos** US /SET uh bohss, -bŏs/, *rarely* [-bŭs]; UK /-bŏss/ [-bŭs, -bohss]. Normal development would favor /-us/. /-ohss/ is a newer pronunciation.

386. ***chanticleer** a rooster. US /CHĂNT-, SHĂNT ih cleer/; UK /CHĂNT-/, *rarely* [CHAHNT-, SHAHNT-]; *rarely* with 3rd syllable stress in both countries.

393. **Allaying** /uh LAY ing/ diminishing.

397. **fadom** /FAD um/ archaic variant of **fathom** /FĂTH um/.

476. *surety guarantee. Here should be two syllables, though in mod. English, three syllables is more common, /SHUR (ih) tee, SHOOR-, SHOR-/ (see App. D).

478. advocate /AD vuh kut/ someone who supports a person or cause.

Act 2 Scene 1

19. Dolor (UK Dolour) /DOH lur/; UK also /DŎL ur/ pain. See App. D -or.

31. cock'rel /CŎCK rł/ young cock.

71-258. Claribel /CLĂIR ih bel/.

72-259. Tunis US /TO͞O niss/; UK, SOUTH. US /TYO͞O-/. /CHO͞O-/ non-standard in the UK.

76. *paragon US /PĂIR uh gŏn/ [-gun]; CN /-gŏn/; UK /-gun/ [-gn̩] most perfect example.

77-102 . Dido('s) /DĪ doh/ Queen of Carthage.

80. Aeneas /ih NEE yus/; UK also /EE NEE yus/ Prince of Troy.

83-86. Carthage /CAR thij/ ancient city in N. Africa.

129. *importun'd /im POR chund/ urged. See App. D.

141. chirurgeonly /kī RUR jun lee/ in a surgeon-like manner.

148. contraries /CŎN truh reez/ the opposite of what is usual.

150. *magistrate /MAJ ih strayt/; US also [-strut].

152. contract here Shk may have intended /cŏn TRACT/, but the foot may be inverted to allow mod. /CŎN tract/.

153. *Bourn /born, boorn/ boundary. North American [burn] not recommended. Borne (F1). Normal development would favor /born/.

ă-bat, ăir-marry, air-pair, ạr-far, ĕr-merry, ĝ- get, ī-high, ĭr-mirror, ł-little, ṇ-listen, ŏ-hot, oh-go, o͞o-wood, o͞o-moon, oor-tour, ōr- or, ow-how, ţh-that, ŧħ-thin, ŭ-but, UR-fur, ur-under.   ( ) - suppress the syllable   see p. xiii for complete list.

153. **tilth** /tilth/ plowland.

164. **foison** /FOY zun, -zṇ/ plenty.

223, 228. ***sloth** US, CN /slawth/ [slohth]; UK /slohth/ [slŏth] laziness.

257. **cubit** /KYOO̅ bit/ about 20 inches.

266. **chough, chuff** /chuf/ jackdaw.

285. **aye** /ay/ ever. /ī/ is often used, but not recommended.

291. **president** archaic variant of ***precedent**, both /PRESS ih dunt/. It is not clear whether /PREZ-/ was used in Shk's time.

Act 2 Scene 2

9. ***mow** /moh/ [mow] grimace. Both were used in Shk's time, but his rhymes elsewhere indicate /moh/.

21. **bumbard** /BUM burd/ leather bottle. Archaic variant of **bombard**, formerly pronounced the same way, but usually /BŎM bard/ today.

38, 111. ***gaberdine** loose garment of course cloth. US /GAB ur deen/, *rarely* [gab ur DEEN]; UK /gab ur DEEN/ [GAB ur deen]; in CN both are used equally.

48. **Mall** /mawl/ is the usual pronunciation for this spelling, but here probably /mŏll/, as in *Molly*. Some eds. prefer **Moll** /mŏll/.

48. **Margery** /MARJ ur ee/.

52. **savor** (UK **savour**) /SAY vur/ smell.

58. **salvages** archaic variant of **savages**. May have been /SAL vuh jiz/ for some, but it was more likely only another way of spelling /SAV ij iz/ (cf. *halve* which had already lost its Middle English /l/ to become /hav/).

58. **Inde, Ind** the Indies. Shk's rhymes indicate /īnd/ elsewhere, but perhaps /ind/ is the better choice here, being closer to *India*.

66-136. **ague** /AY gyoo̅/ malarial fever.

113. **Neapolitans** /nee uh PŎL ih tunz/ men from Naples.

128. **Swom** most eds. prefer **Swum** or **Swam**. The meaning here is 'swam,' but in older forms of Eng. the past tense could be written all three ways. Whether *swom* was meant to indicate /swum/ or /swŏm/ is unclear. For simplicity use /swăm/; for an archaic flavor use /swum/ which is still used iň dialects on both sides of the Atlantic.

170. **marmazet** /MAR muh zet/ small monkey. Archaic variant of **marmoset**, pronounced the same way, as well as /MAR muh set/ [mar muh ZET, -SET].

172. **scamels** /SKAY młz, SKAM łz/ perhaps an error. May be a type of shellfish or seabird. Some eds. prefer **seamews** /SEE my͞oz/ or **seamels** /SEE młz/, both 'seagulls.' Others suggest **staniels** /STAN yłz/ inferior hawks.

Act 3 Scene 1

44. **defect** here should be /dih-, dee FECT/.

Act 3 Scene 2

26. **justle** /JUSS ł/ archaic variant of **jostle** /JŎS ł/.

63. **pied** /pīd/ having two or more colors in splotches.

80. **murrain** US, CN /MUR in/; E.COAST US, UK /MUH rin/ plague.

91. **wezand, weasand** /WEE zṇd/ wind pipe.

96. **utensils** here should be /Y͞OO ten słz/.

100. *****nonpareil** one without equal. /nŏn puh RELL/ is the oldest form, still common in the US, but now vanished from the UK and CN, where it has been replaced with /nŏn puh RAYL/ [-RAY], based on mod. French. /-RAYL/ is also common in the US. /-RĪ, -RĪL/ are occasionally heard, but not recommended. Sometimes 1st syllable stress is used.

101, 102. **Sycorax** /SIK ur racks/.

117. *****jocund** /JŎCK und/; US, CN *rarely* [JOHK-] merry.

ă-bat, ăir-**marry**, air-**pair**, ạr-**far**, ĕr-**merry**, ĝ- get, ī-high, ĭr-**mirror**, ł-little, ṇ-listen, ŏ-hot, oh-go, o͞o-wood, o͞o-moon, oor-**tour**, ōr- or, ow-how, ţh-**that**, ŧh-**thin**, ŭ-but, UR-**fur**, ur-under.　　( ) - suppress the syllable　　see p. xiii for complete list.

121. **scout** jeer at. Some eds. prefer F1's **cout** /kowt, koht/ as a dialect form of *colt* 'cheat.'

151. **taborer** /TAY bur ur/ player of a small drum. See App. D *-or*.

Act 3 Scene 3

1. **By'r lakin** /bīr-, bur LAY kin/ by Our Lady (i.e., Mary).

3. **forth-rights** here should be /FOR~~TH~~ rīts/ straight paths.

10. **frustrate** /FRUSS trayt, -trut/ frustrated.

14. **throughly** archaic variant of *thoroughly*. /~~TH~~RŌO lee/ is the normal pronunciation on stage, but to enhance clarity a syncopated form of the modern pronunciation may be used: *thor'ghly*.

15 *****travail** here should be /TRAV ayl/ hard work. Some eds. prefer **travel**. In Shk's time both were pronounced /TRAV ł/.

21. **drollery** /DROHL (uh) ree/ a puppet show, or comic play.

30. **certes** /SUR teez/ certainly.

41. **viands** /VĪ (u)ndz/ food. /VEE undz/ not recommended.

65. **dowle, dowl** /dowl/ small feather.

77. **perdition** /pur DISH un/; UK *also* [PUR DISH un] destruction.

stage direction after 82. *****mows** grimaces. /mohz/ and /mowz/ were both used in Shk's time and are still used today. Shk's rhymes elsewhere indicate /mohz/.

106. **gins** /ĝinz/ begins.

Act 4 Scene 1

26. *****opportune** here 2nd syllable stress is indicated /ŏp POR tyōōn/; US *also* /-tōōn/.

30. **Phoebus'** /FEE bus/ god of the sun.

47. *****mow** grimace. Here should be /moh/ for the rhyme, though /mow/ was also used in Shk's time and is still sometimes used today.

51. **dalliance** /DAL ee unss/ sportiveness.

53. **abstenious** /ab STEEN ee us/ archaic variant of **abstemious**
/ab STEEM ee us/.

56. **ardor** (UK **ardour**) /ARD ur/ warm emotion.

57. **Now come, my Ariel, bring a** *corollary* 'one too many.' If *Ariel* is three
syllables, then /cuh RŎL (uh) ree/, the normal UK form. If *Ariel* is two syllables,
then the US form /COR uh lĕr ee/ fits. Note E.COAST US also has /CŎR-/.

60-167. **Ceres** /SEER eez/ goddess of the harvest.

---

60. **leas** /leez/ meadows.

63. **meads** /meedz/ meadows.

63. **stover** /STOH vur/ hay for winter use.

64. **pioned** /PĪ un ed/ perhaps 'dug out.' Some eds. prefer **peonied**
/PEE uh need/ 'full of peonies.'

65. **spungy** archaic variant of **spongy**, both pronounced /SPUN jee/.

74. **amain** /uh MAYN/ with full speed.

78. **saffron** /SAFF run/ yellow.

89. **Dis** /dis/ Pluto.

93. **Paphos** place on Cyprus sacred to Venus. US /PAY fus, -fŏs/;
UK /-fŏs/ [-fus]. Normal development would favor /-us/. A newer ending
/-ohss/ is also used, especially in the US. A more recent restored pronunciation
with /PAH-/ is also used.

110. **Earth's increase** Earth's offspring, the harvest. Here /in CREESS/, used
elsewhere, is possible, but produces the only broken-backed line in this song.
Using the older genitive form /UR thiz IN creess/ is also possible.

110. **foison** /FOY zun, -zn/ harvest.

121. **confines** here should be /cŏn-, cun FĪNZ/.

ă-bat, ăir-**marry**, air-**pair**, ar-**far**, ĕr-**merry**, ĝ- **get**, ī-**high**, ĭr-**mirror**, l-**little**, n-**listen**,
ŏ-**hot**, oh-**go**, o͞o-**wood**, o͞o-**moon**, oor-**tour**, ōr- **or**, ow-**how**, th-**that**, th-**thin**, Ŭ-**but**,
UR-**fur**, ur-**under**.   ( ) - suppress the syllable   see p. xiii for complete list.

128. **Naiades** Shk's variant of *Naiads /NĪ adz/ [NAY-] river nymphs. Normal development would favor /NAY udz/.

128. **windring** /WĪND ring/ 'winding, wandering.' Some eds. prefer **wand'ring, winding**.

170. **varlots** attendents. Archaic variant of **varlets**, both pronounced /VAR luts/.

175. **tabor** /TAY bur/ small drum. See App. D -*or*.

176. **unback'd** here should be /UN backt/ never having had a rider.

179. **lowing** /LOH ing/ bleating.

180. **goss** /gŏss/; US *also* /gawss/ variant of **gorse**.

206. ***mischance** in verse normally with 2nd syllable stress.

219. **aye** /ay/ ever. /ī/ is often used, but not recommended.

Act 5 Scene 1

11. **boudge** /BUJ/, or possibly /bo͞oj/. Archaic variant of **budge**.

36. ***demi-puppets** /DEM ee-/ meaning either 'partially subject to Prospero's will' or 'small dolls.'

39. **mushrumps** (F1) /MUSH rumps/. Some eds. prefer **mushrooms**.

43. ***azur'd** blue. US /AZH oord/ [AZ yoord, AZH urd];
UK /AZH oord, AZ yoord/ [AY zyoord, -zhyoord]. Normal development would favor /AZH urd, AY zhurd/.

49. **op'd** /ohpt/ opened.

51. **abjure** /ab-, ub JOOR/; US *also* /-JUR/ renounce.

55. **fadoms** /FAD umz/ archaic variant of **fathoms** /FĂ<u>TH</u> umz/.

89. **cowslip's** /COW slips/ a yellow flower.

140. **Irreperable** here /ih REP ur uh bł/; US *also* /ĭr-/.

145. **supportable** here should be /SUP ort uh bł/.

158. **justled** /JUSS łd/ archaic variant of **jostled** /JŎS łd/.

209. **Claribel** /CLĂIR ih bel/.

209. **Tunis** US /TŌŌ niss/; UK, SOUTH. US /TYŌŌ-/. /CHŌŌ-/ non-standard in the UK.

217. **prophesied** /PRŎF uh sīd/ predicted the future.

218. **blasphemy** /BLĂSS fuh mee/; UK, E.NEW ENG. *also* /BLAHSS-/ irreverent speech.

224. ***yare** /yair/; US *also* /yạr/ ready, smart.

257, 258. **coraggio** /koh RAH joh/ or /-jee oh/ Ital. 'courage.'

261. **Setebos** the evil god of Caliban's mother. US /SET uh bohss, -bŏs/, *rarely* [-bus]; UK /-bŏss/ [-bus, -bohss]. Normal development would favor /-us/. /-ohss/ is a newer pronunciation.

263. ***chastise** punish. Here /chăss TĪZ/, the usual UK pronunciation, produces a regular iambic rhythm. In the US 1st syllable stress is usual.

272. ***demi-devil** /DEM ee-/ half-devil.

309. ***nuptial** wedding. Here should be three syllables. Shk probably intended /NUP shee ł/, but today /NUP chuh wł, NUP shuh wł/ are common, though considered non-standard in the UK.

310. **Of these our dear-belov'd** *solemnized.* /suh LEM nīz ed/ in Shk's day, which would mean *beloved* has 2 syllables. A better choice may be /bee-, bih LUV id/ and /SŎL um nīzd/.

ă-bat, ăir-m**a**rry, air-**pair**, ạr-**far**, ĕr-m**e**rry, ĝ- g**e**t, ī-h**igh**, ĭr-m**i**rror, ł-little, ṇ-listen, ŏ-hot, oh-go, ōō-wood, ōō-moon, oor-tour, ōr- or, ow-how, ţh-that, t̶h̶-thin, ŭ-but, UR-fur, ur-under.   ( ) - suppress the syllable   see p. xiii for complete list.

Timon of Athens

People in the Play
Alcibiades 4 or 5 syllables depending on meter /al sih BĪ (uh) deez/. **Apemantus** /ap ih MAN tus/. **Athenian(s)** always 3 syllables in verse /uh ~~THEEN~~ (ee) yun/. **Caphis** /KAY fiss/. **Flaminius** /fluh MIN ee yus/. **Flavius** /FLAY vee yus/. **Hortensius** /hor TEN shus, -see us/. Normal development would favor /-shus/. **Hostilius (2nd stranger)** 3 or 4 syllables /hŏs STILL (ee) yus/. Appears in 3.2. ***Isidore** /ĪZ ih dor/ [ISS-]. **Lucilius** /lōō SILL ee yus/ (for /lyōō-/ see App. D *lu-*). **Lucius** 2 or 3 syllables depending on meter /LŌŌ shus, -shee us/; /LŌŌ s(ee) yus/. The former is nearly universal in the US, the latter is the most common form in the UK. Normal development would favor /LŌŌ shus/ (for /lyōō-/ see App. D *lu-*). **Lucullus** /lōō CŬL us/ (for /lyōō-/ see App. D *lu-*). **Philotus** /fī-, fih LOH tus/. **Phrynia** (*Phrinia* F2) /FRIN ee uh/. *Phrinica* (F1). **Sempronius** 3 syllables in verse, but may be 4 in prose /sem PROH n(ee) yus/. **Servilius** 3 or 4 syllables depending on meter /sur VIL (ee) yus/. **Timandra** /tih MAN druh/.

People in the Play (cont.)

Timon /TĪ mun/, but sometimes /-ŏn/ is used. See App. D -*on.*

Varro /VĂIR oh/.

Ventidius (F4) 3 or 4 syllables depending on meter
/ven TID (ee) yus, -TIJ (ee) yus/. Shk seems to have preferred the latter form.

Act 1 Scene 1

5. **record** here should be /rek-, rik ORD/.

10. **incomparable** here should be /in CŎM pur ruh bł/.

11. **continuate** /cun TIN y(oo) wut/ continuous.

14. ***estimate** US /ES tih mut/ [-mayt]; UK /-mayt/ [-mut] price.

21. ***poesy** US /POH ih see/ [-zee]; UK, CN /POH ih zee/ [-see] poetry.

27. **my presentment** /pree-, prih ZENT munt/ my presenting (the poem).

54. **austere** here should be /AW steer/.

70. ***wafts** beckons. US, CN /wŏfts/; SOUTH. US /wăfts/; UK /wŏfts/
[wăfts, wahfts]. /wăfts/ is newer and considered non-standard by many.

72. **Translates** transforms. Here may be stressed on either the 1st or 2nd
syllables. The former is the usual US pronunciation and the latter is the most
common in the UK. US /trănss-, trănz-/; UK /trănss-/ [trănz-, trahnz-, trahnss-,
trunss-, trunz-].

91. **demonstrate** here should be /dem ŎN strayt/.

117. **frequents** here /free-, frih KWENTS/ visits.

133. **precedent** /prih-, pree SEED unt, -ṇt/ preceding, older.

166. **saciety** /suh SĪ uh tee/ fullness. Archaic variant of **satiety** /suh TĪ uh tee/.

ă-bat, ăir-**marry**, air-**pair**, ạr-**far**, ĕr-**merry**, ĝ- **get**, ī-**high**, ĭr-**mirror**, ł-**little**, ṇ-**listen**,
ŏ-**hot**, oh-**go**, ōō-**wood**, ōō-**moon**, oor-**tour**, ōr- **or**, ow-**how**, ṭh-**that**, th-**thin**, ŭ-**but**,
UR-**fur**, ur-**under**.   ( ) - suppress the syllable   see p. xiii for complete list.

167. ***extoll'd** praised. /ek STOHLD/; UK *sometimes* and US *rarely* [-STŎLD].

168. **unclew** /un CLO͞O/ undo.

208. **lascivious** /luh SIV yus/ lustful.

234. **angry wit.** Some eds. prefer **so hungry a wit.** Others ***augury**
/AWG yur ee/ [AWG ur ee]; UK *also* /AWG yoor ree/ prediction of the future.

248. **Aches** pronounced /AY chiz/ in Shk's time.

276. **Plutus** /PLO͞OT us/ god of riches.

Act 1 Scene 2

8. **deriv'd** here with 1st syllable stress.

28.   **Ira   furor   brevis   est**
Ang.Lat.   /Ī ruh   FYO͞O ror   BREE viss   est/
Class.Lat. /EE rah Fo͞o ror   BREV iss   est/
            'anger is a brief madness.'

33. **apperil** /uh PĔR il, -ł/ risk.

48. **draught** US, CN /drăft/; UK, E.NEW ENG. /drahft/ drink.

66. **harlot** /HAR lut/ whore.

72. **dich** /dich/ may it do. Some eds prefer **do't.**

211. **courser** /COR sur/ warhorse.

243. ***vainglories** /VAYN glor eez/ [vayn GLOR eez] boastings.

Act 2 Scene 1

16. ***Importune** /im POR chun/ ask insistently. See App. D.

28. **importunate** /im POR chuh nut/; UK *also* /-tyoo nut/ insistantly asking.

Act 2 Scene 2

3, 133. **accompt(s)** /uh COWNT(S)/ archaic variant of **account(s).** See App. D.

41. **importunacy** /im por-, im pur TYŌŌN (uh) see/; US *also* /-TŌŌN-/ insistent requests.

60-98. **usurer, -s'** /YŌŌ zhur ur/; UK *also* [-zhyoor ur, -zhoor ur] someone who lends money for interest.

67, 71. **Gramercies, -cy** /gruh MUR seez/ thanks.

70. **Corinth** US, CN /COR inth/; UK, E.COAST US /CŎR-/ prostitution district.

84. **thou't** /thowt/ variant of **thou'lt, thou wilt.**

151. **Lacedaemon** /lass ih DEE mun/ Sparta. Sometimes newer /-ŏn/ is used. See App. D *-on.*

161. **minstrelsy** /MIN strl see/ playing and singing of minstrels.

Act 3 Scene 1

7. **ew'r, ewer** pitcher. Prose, so may be /yoor/, or /YŌŌ ur/.

34. **towardly** /TOH wurd lee, -urd lee/ willing.

43. **solidares** /SŎL ih dairz/ coins.

53. **disease** here 1st syllable stress is indicated.

63. **expel** here should be /EK spel/.

Act 3 Scene 3

29, 34. **politic** /PŎL ih tik/ shrewd, cunning.

Act 3 Scene 4

50. **eat** /et/ dialect variant of **ate**, which is also commonly /et/ in the UK.

ă-bat, ăir-marry, air-pair, ạr-far, ĕr-merry, ĝ- get, ī-high, ĭr-mirror, l-little, n-listen, ŏ-hot, oh-go, ŏŏ-wood, ōō-moon, oor-tour, ōr- or, ow-how, th-that, th-thin, ŭ-but, UR-fur, ur-under.　　( ) - suppress the syllable　　see p. xiii for complete list.

The Complete Oxford begins 3.5 here (line no. in parentheses).

111. (3.5.8) **Sempronius—all** (F2), (*Sempronius Vllorxa: All* F1). Some eds. prefer **all luxors, all** /LUKS urz/ lechers. See App. D *-or*.

Act 3 Scene 5 (*Complete Oxford* 3.6)

22. **behoove** /bih-, bee HOOV/. UK prefers the spelling **behove** /bih HOHV/. Some eds. prefer **behave**. All mean 'control, manage.'

53. **condemn** here with 1st syllable stress.

57. **angry** here /ANG gur ree/ is indicated.

60. **Lacedaemon** /lass ih DEE mun/ Sparta. Sometimes newer /-ŏn/ is used. See App. D *-on*.

60. *****Byzantium** US /bih ZAN shee um, -tee um/; UK /-tee um/ [-shee um, bī-]. Normal development would favor /-shum/.

71. **commit** here 1st syllable stress is indicated.

98. **dotage** /DOHT ij/ feeble-mindedness.

98. **usury** /YOO zhur ee/; UK *also* [-zhyoor ee, -zhoor ee] lending money for interest.

109. **balsom** healing ointment. Archaic variant of **balsam**, both pronounced /BAWL sum/; UK *also* [BŎL sum].

109. **usuring** /YOO zh(u)ring/; UK *also* [-zh(yoo)r ing, -zh(oo)r ing] lending money for interest.

Act 3 Scene 6 (*Complete Oxford* 3.7)

11. *****conjur'd** entreated. US, CN /CŎN jurd/, *rarely* [CUN-, cun JOORD]; UK /CUN jurd/ [CŎN-], *rarely* [cun JOORD]. The older pronunciation for this meaning is /cun JOORD/.

13. **importunate** /im POR chuh nut/; UK *also* /-tyoo nut/ pressing.

60. **toward** /TOH wurd, -urd/ about to take place

120. **diamonds** here should be /DĪ mundz/, the most common pronunciation in the US.

Act 4 Scene 1

13. *****brothel** US, CN /BRŎ̵T̵H̵ ł/ [BRŎ̵T̵H ł, BRAW̵T̵H̵ ł]; UK /BRŎ̵T̵H̵ ł/ whorehouse.

20. **contraries** /CŎN truh reez/ things opposite to what is customary.

23. **sciatica** /sī AT ih kuh/ pain in the lower back.

30. **infect** here should be /IN fect/.

33. **detestable** here should be /DEE tess tuh bł/ or /DET es tuh bł/.

Act 4 Scene 2

4. **recorded** here should be stressed on the 1st syllable.

Act 4 Scene 3

5. **dividant** /dih VĪD ṇt/ able to be distinguished.

9. **deny't** (F1). Some eds. prefer **denude, deject, deknight,** or **demit** /dee-, dih MIT/ 'humble.'

12. **paster** US /PĂSS tur/; UK, E.NEW ENG. /PAHSS tur/ archaic variant **pasture.**

16. **grize** /grīz/ step, degree. Variant of **grise** /grīss, grīz/, **grece** /greess/, **grice** /grīss/.

18. **obliquy** /ŎB lih kwee/ immorality.

20. **direct** here should be /DĪ rect/.

22. **semblable** /SEM bluh bł/ his fellow man.

25. **operant** /ŎP (ur) runt/ powerful.

ă-bat, ăir-marry, air-pair, ạr-far, ĕr-merry, ĝ- get, ī-high, ĭr-mirror, ł-little, ṇ-listen, ŏ-hot, oh-go, o͝o-wood, o͞o-moon, oor-tour, ŏr- or, ow-how, t̲h-that, t̵h̵-thin, ŭ-but, UR-fur, ur-under.　　　( ) - suppress the syllable　　　see p. xiii for complete list.

27. **votarist** /VOHT uh rist/ someone who has taken a vow.

39. **wappen'd** /WŎP ṇd/ some eds. prefer **wappered** /WŎP urd/ both mean 'tired out' or 'worn out sexually.'

40. **spittle-house, spital-house** /SPIT ł/ hospital.

44. **rout** /rowt/ rabble, crowd.

46. **thou't** /ṭhowt/ variant of **thou'lt, thou wilt.**

54. **Misanthropos** hater of mankind. US /mis-, miz AN ~~throh~~ pŏss, -pŭs/; UK /-pŏs/ [-pus]. Normal development would favor /-us/. A newer pronunciation /-ohss/ is also used, especially in the US.

60. **gules, gules** /GY$\overline{OO}$ łz/ red. Each instance of *gules* comprises a foot.

64. ***cherubin** angelic. US, CN /CHĔR uh bin/ [-yuh-]; UK uses both equally. /KĔR-/ not recommended.

80. **harlots** /HAR luts/ whores.

93. ***penurious** /puh NYOOR ee us/; US *also* [-NOOR-, -NYUR-] poor, stingy.

104. **conquest** here /cŏn KWEST/ is indicated.

113. **usurer** /Y$\overline{OO}$ zhur ur/; UK *also* [-zhyoor ur, -zhoor ur] someone who lends money for interest.

116. **trenchant** /TRENCH unt/ keen.

123. **sans** /sănz/ without.

136. **mountant** /MOWNT ṇt, -unt/ raised.

138. **agues** /AY gy$\overline{oo}$z/ malarial fever.

143. **close** /clohss/ hidden.

155. **quillets** /KWIL its/ quibbles.

155. **flamen** /FLAY mun/ priest.

160. **weal** /weel/ welfare.

161. **unscarr'd** here should be /UN skahrd/.

184.*Hyperion's /hī PEER yunz/ god of the sun. Sometimes newer /-PĔR-/ or /-ŏn/ are used, but are not recommended.

187. Ensear /en SEER/ dry up.

193. leas /leez/ fields.

194. draughts US, CN /drăfts/; UK, E.NEW ENG. /drahfts/ drinks.

226. caudle /KAW dł/ provide a warm drink.

227. o'ernight's here should be /OR nīts/.

229. wreakful /REEK fu̯ll/ revengeful.

235. caitiff /KAYT if/ scoundrel.

252. *swath swaddling clothes. /swŏ̶t̶h̶/; UK also [swayt̶h̶, swaht̶h̶, swawt̶h̶]. /swăt̶h̶/ not recommended. The oldest forms are with /ŏ/ or UK /aw/. Some eds. prefer swathe /swayt̶h̶/.

304, 307. medlar /MED lur/ an apple-like fruit.

331. peradventure perhaps. /PUR ad VEN chur/; US rarely [PĔR-, PUR ad ven chur]; UK, CN also [PUR-, PĔR ad vcn chur, pĕr ad VEN chur].

340. germane US /jur MAYN/; UK /JUR MAYN/ [JUR mayn]. Some eds. prefer the form german /JUR mun/. Both mean 'related to'.

368. swound archaic variant of F1's swoon. In Shk's time the vowel could be either /ow/ or /o͞o/.

387. *sold'rest US /SŎD rist/; UK /SOHL drist/ [SŎL drist] solder, join metal together.

387. close /clohss/ tightly.

403. assay test. Usually /uh-, ass SAY/ in Shk, but as a noun in this prose passage, may be mod. /ASS ay/.

420. *huswife /HUZ if/ is traditional, /HUSS wīf/ is a newer, spelling pronunciation. The former is the most common form in the UK, the latter in the

ă-bat, ăir-marry, air-pair, a̯r-far, ĕr-merry, ĝ- get, ī-high, ĭr-mirror, ł-little, n̯-listen, ŏ-hot, oh-go, o͞o-wood, o͞o-moon, oor-tour, ŏr- or, ow-how, t̯h-that, t̶h̶-thin, Ŭ-but, UR-fur, ur-under.   ( ) - suppress the syllable   see p. xiii for complete list.

US. In CN both are used equally. In North America /HUSS wif/ is also sometimes used. Some eds. prefer mod. **housewife**.

437. **arrant** /ĂIR unt/ thoroughgoing.

441. **composture** /cum PŎS chur/; UK *also* /-tyoor/ compost, manure. See App. D *-ure*.

444. **uncheck'd theft** /UN chekt/ unlimited power to thieve.

485. **thorough** archaic variant of *through*, used when the meter demands two syllables. It is often pronounced as *thorough* on stage, but using /-o͞o/ in the final syllable will bring it closer to mod. *through*.

491. **comfortable** here may be 3 or 4 syllables /CUMF tur bł/, /CUM fur tuh bł/.

509. **usuring** /YO͞O zh(u)ring/; UK *also* [-zh(yoo)r ing, -zh(oo)r ing] lending money for interest.

522. **requite** pay back. Here stressed on the 1st syllable.

Act 5 Scene 1

15, 70. ***travail ('d)** here should be /TRAV ayl/ labor. In line 70 some eds. prefer **travelled**, which in Shk's time was pronounced the same as *travailed* /TRAV łd/.

---

37. **opulency** /ŎP y(uh) lun see/ wealth.

52. **aye** /ay/ ever. /ī/ is often used, but not recommended.

102. **draught** US, CN /drăft/; UK, E.NEW ENG. /drahft/ latrine.

114. **alcumist** one who studies the transformation of base metals to gold. Archaic variant of **alchemist**, both pronounced /AL kuh mist/.

The Complete Oxford begins 5.2 here (line nos. in parentheses).

---

133. (5.2.18) **cantherizing** (F1) possibly an error for **cauterizing** /KAW tur īz ing/. If it is not an error, it would have been /KAN tur īz ing/ in Shk's time, with the same meaning, 'searing a wound.'

174. (5.2.59) **contumelious** disdainful. /cŏn tyuh MEE lyus /; US *also* /cŏn tuh-/. /cŏn chuh-/ considered non-standard in the UK.

193. (5.2.78) **bruit** /br$\overline{oo}$t/ report.

195. (5.2.80) **thorough** archaic variant of *through*, pronounced as *thorough*. Here, however, the meter demands one syllable, making **through** the better choice.

196. (5.2.81) **triumphers** here should be /tr$\overline{i}$ UMF urz/.

199. (5.3.84) **aches** pronounced /AY chiz/ in Shk's time.

205. (5.2.90) **close** /clohss/ enclosure.

Act 5 Scene 2 (*Complete Oxford* 5.3)

6. *__courier__ US /CUR yur/ [COOR-]; E.COAST US /C$\breve{U}$R-/ [COOR-]; UK /COOR-/ [C$\breve{U}$R-].

Act 5 Scene 4 (*Complete Oxford* 5.5)

1. **lascivious** /luh SIV yus/ lustful.

4. **licentious** /l$\overline{i}$ SEN chus/ lustful, lacking moral restraint.

7. *__travers'd arms__ here should be /TRAV URST/ folded arms.

12. **pursy** /PUR see/ fat, short-winded.

28. **excess** here should be /ek SESS/, the most common UK form.

31. **tithed death** /T$\overline{I}$ thid/ the killing of one person in ten.

47. **rampir'd** /RAM p$\overline{i}$rd/ strengthened by ramparts.

67. **insculpture** /in SK$\breve{U}$LP chur/ inscription. See App. D *-ure*.

71. **caitiffs** /KAYT ifs/ scoundrels.

77. **niggard** /NIG urd/ miserly.

78. **aye** /ay/ ever. /$\overline{i}$/ is often used, but not recommended.

ă-bat, ăir-**marry**, air-**pair**, ạr-**far**, ĕr-**merry**, ĝ- **get**, ī-**high**, ĭr-**mirror**, ł-**little**, ṇ-**listen**, ŏ-**hot**, oh-**go**, $\overline{oo}$-**wood**, $\overline{oo}$-**moon**, oor-**tour**, ōr- **or**, ow-**how**, ţh-**that**, ~~th~~-**thin**, ŭ-**but**, UR-**fur**, ur-**under**.　　　( ) - suppress the syllable　　　see p. xiii for complete list.

Titus Andronicus

People in the Play

Aaron /AIR un/. A more recent pronunciation in the UK and E.COAST US is /ĂIR-/.

Aemilius normally /ee MIL ee yus/, but in verse sometimes should be 3 syllables /ee MIL yus/. A newer pronunciation /-MEEL-/ is also used.

Alarbus /uh LAHR bus/.

Andronicus /an DRŎN ih kus/.
 Andronici /an DRŎN ih sī/.

Bassianus /băss ee AY nus/; restored pronunciation /-AH nus/.

*****Caius** US, CN /KĪ us/, *rarely* [KAY us]; UK /KĪ us, KAY us/.
Ang.Lat. /KAY us/; Class.Lat. /KĪ ōōs/. Another angl. form /keez/ is sometimes used, but doesn't fit the meter.

Chiron /KĪ run/, but /-rŏn/ is also used. See App. D *-on.*

Demetrius 3 or 4 syllables depending on meter /dih MEE tr(ee) yus/.

Lavinia 3 or 4 syllables depending on meter /luh VIN (ee) yuh/.

Lucius 2 or 3 syllables depending on meter /LŌO shus, -shee us/;
/LŌO s(ee) yus/. The former is nearly universal in the US, the latter is the most common form in the UK. Normal development would favor /LŌO shus/ (for /lyōō-/ see App. D *lu-*).

Martius /MAR shus/. His name is not spoken.

Mutius 2 or 3 syllables depending on meter /MYŌO shus, -shee us/.

Philomela /fill oh MEE luh, fill uh-/ she was transformed to the nightingale. Referred to throughout the play.
 Philomel /FILL oh mel, -uh mel/.

Publius 2 or 3 syllables depending on meter /PUB l(ee) yus/.

People in the Play (cont.)

Quintus /KWIN tus/.

Saturninus /sat ur NĪ nus/.
  Saturnine /SAT ur nīn/.

Sempronius /sem PROH nyus/.

Tamora 2 or 3 syllables depending on meter /TAM (uh) ruh/.

Titus /TĪT us/.

*****Tribune** here always with stress on 1st syllable /TRIB yōōn/. At the beginning
of a line stress could also fall on the second syllable, a mod. Eng. pronunciation,
but in these cases an inverted foot also allows Shk's regular form with 1st
syllable stress.

A frequently occurring word in this play is

*****Moor** (referring to **Aaron**) /moor/ [mor] a black man.

Act 1 Scene 1

6. **ware** /wair/ archaic variant of **wore**.

6. ***diadem** /DĪ uh dem/ [-dum] crown.

14. **consecrate** /CŎN suh crut, -crayt/ consecrated.

19, 22. **empery** /EM pur ee/ status as emperor.

23. **surnamed** here should be /sur NAYM id/.

23. **Pius** /PĪ us/.

27. **accited** /ak SĪT id/ summoned.

32. ***chastised** punished. Here should be /CHĂSS tīz ed/. The usual US
pronunciation, also used in CN, has 1st syllable stress; in the UK 2nd syllable
stress is usual.

ă-bat, ăir-**marry**, air-**pair**, a̧r-**far**, ĕr-**merry**, ĝ- get, ī-high, ĭr-**mirror**, ł-little, n̦-listen,
ŏ-hot, oh-go, ōō-wood, ōō-moon, oor-**tour**, ōr- or, ow-how, țh-that, t̶h̶-thin, ŭ-but,
UR-**fur**, ur-**under**.   ( ) - suppress the syllable   see p. xiii for complete list.

After 35 Q1 has **expiation** /eks pee AY shun/ atonement. Omitted in Q2-3, F1, and *Riverside*.

47. **affy** /uh FĪ/ trust.

72. **lading** /LAYD ing/ cargo.

80. ***Priam** King of Troy. US, CN /PRĪ um/ [-am]; UK /-am/, *rarely* [-um].
Normal development would favor /-um/.

88. **Styx** /stiks/ river of Hades.

92. **receptacle** here /REE sep tuh kł/ is indicated.

98.	**Ad**	**manes**	**fratrum**
Ang.Lat.	/ad	MAY neez	FRAY trum/;
Class.Lat.	/ahd	MAHN ayss	FRAH trōōm/

'to the shades of our brothers.'

114-247. **commonweal** /CŎM un weel/ commonwealth.

131, 132. ***Scythia** /SITH yuh/ [SIṬH yuh] region north of Black Sea. Some
scholars prefer Class.Lat. /SK-/.

138. **Thracian tyrant** /THRAY shun/ Polymnestor, king of Thrace.

144. ***entrails** /EN traylz/; US *also* [-trłz] guts.

147. * **'larums** US, CN /LAHR umz/ [LĂIR-]; UK /LĂIR umz, LAHR umz/ calls
to arms.

152. **mishaps** here should be /mis HAPS/.

160. **obsequies** /ŎB suh kweez/ burial services.

166. **cordial** US /COR jł/; UK /COR dył/ comfort.

170. **triumpher** here should be /trī UM fur/.

177. ***Solon's happiness** i.e., 'death.' /SOH lŏnz/ [-lunz]. Normal development
would favor /SOH lunz/. See App. D *-on*.

182. **palliament** /PAL yuh munt/ white robe.

185. **candidatus** Ang.Lat. /kan dih DAY tus/; Class.Lat. /kahn dih DAH tōōs/
clad in a white robe.

201. **empery** /EM pur ee/ status as emperor.

208. **interrupter** here /in t(uh) RUP tur/.

231. **plebeians** /plih BEE unz/ common people.

242, 333. *****Pantheon** temple of the gods. US /PAN ᵗʰyŏn/, *rarely* [-un]; in the UK both are used equally. In the second instance an obsolete pronunciation /pan ̶T̶H̶E̶E̶ un/ is indicated. See App. D -*on*.

250. **imperious** /im PEER yus/ imperial.

252. *****ensigns** emblems. US, CN /EN sṇz/, US *rarely* [-sīnz]; UK /-sṇz, -sīnz/.

257. **fealty** /FEE ł tee/ faithfulness.

280. **Suum cuique** Ang.Lat. (US) /SOO um kyōō Ī kwee/; (UK, SOUTH. US) /SYOO-/; Class.Lat. /Soō ōōm KWIH kway/ to each his own.

283. **avaunt** /uh VAWNT/ begone.

286. **betroth'd** /bih-, bee TROHṬHD/ fiancée.

316. **Phoebe** /FEE bee/ the moon, Diana.

324. **tapers** /TAY purz/ slender candles.

325. **Hymenaeus** /hī mun EE yus/ God of marriage.

337. **consummate** /CŎN suh mayt/ fulfill.

337. **spousal** /SPOW zł/ marriage.

352. **servitors** /SURV ih turz/ servants. See App. D -*or*.

373. **renowmed** /rih-, ree NOW mid/ archaic variant of **renowned** /rih-, ree NOWN id/.

380. *****Laertes'** Father of Ulysses. /lay AIR teez/ is newer, /lay UR teez/ older. In the US, CN the former is more frequent, in the UK the latter. /LAY ur teez/ will not fit the meter.

ă-bat, ăir-marry, air-pair, ạr-far, ĕr-merry, ĝ- get, ī-high, ĭr-mirror, ł-little, ṇ-listen, ŏ-hot, oh-go, ōō-wood, ōō-moon, oor-tour, ōr- or, ow-how, ṭh-that, t̶h̶-thin, ŭ-but, UR-fur, ur-under.   ( ) - suppress the syllable   see p. xiii for complete list.

398. **remunerate** (F1) /rih-, ree MY$\overline{OO}$N ur ayt/ pay. Omitted Q.

406. **betrothed love** /bih-, bee TROHṬH id/ fiancée.

446. **survey** considering of the facts. Here should be /sur VAY/.

448, 484. ***heinous** /HAYN us/ hateful. /HEEN us/ is non-standard though common in the UK.

---

451. **rase** /rayss/ erase. Some eds. prefer **raze** (also spelled **rase**) /rayz/ 'demolish.' **Race** (*race* Q1), a short form of *arace* 'root out,' has also been suggested.

462. **I am incorporate in Rome** I have become one of the Romans. /in COR pur rut, -rayt/. /-ut / is more usual for an adj.

494. **bon jour** angl. /bohn ZHOOR, -JOOR/; Fr. /boh^n ZHOOR/ good day.

495. **gramercy** /gruh MUR see/ thanks.

Act 2 Scene 1

7. **glistering** /GLIS tring/ glistening.

17. ***Prometheus** /proh MEE ~~th~~yus/ [-~~th~~y$\overline{oo}$ss], US *rarely* [-~~th~~$\overline{oo}$ss]. See App. D -*eus*.

17. **Caucasus** /KAW kuh suss/ Asian mountains.

18. **slavish weeds** /SLAY vish/ clothes of a slave.

18. ***servile** /SUR vīl/, *rarely* [SUR vł] slave-like.

22. **Semiramis** /suh MĬR uh miss/ lusty queen of Assyria.

24. **commonweal's** /CŎM un weelz/ commonwealth's.

25. **Hollo** (Q1), **Holloa** /huh LOH/. Some eds. prefer **Holla** /huh LAH/.

41. **lath** US /lă~~th~~/; UK, E. NEW ENG. /lah~~th~~/ [lă~~th~~] narrow strip of wood.

47. **maintain** here should be /MAYN tayn/.

104. **stratagem** /STRAT uh jum/ scheme.

108. **Lucrece** Lucretia, Roman who commited suicide after being raped. Here exceptionally the usual mod. form /lōō CREESS/ will fit the meter. However Shk's usual form with 1st syllable stress is also possible in an inverted foot (for /lyōō-/ see App. D *lu-*).

115. **unfrequented plots** here should be /un free KWEN tid/ 'lonely spots.'

121. **consecrate** /CŎN suh crut, -crayt/ consecrated.

133.   **Sit fas   aut   nefas**
Ang.Lat. /sit fass   awt NEE fass/
Class.Lat. /sit FAHS owt NEF ahss/
         'be it right or wrong.'

135.   **Per Stygia,   per manes   vehor**
Ang.Lat. /pur STIJ ee uh, pur MAY neez VEE hor/
Class.Lat. /pĕr STIG ee ah, pĕr MAHN ayss WEH hor/
         'I am borne through the Stygian regions, through the shades.'
Some eds. prefer **Styga** /STIG uh/.

Act 2 Scene 3

4. **abjectly** here should be /AB ject lee/ contemptibly.

5. **stratagem** /STRAT uh jum/ scheme.

9. **alms** charity for the poor. /ahmz/ is older; /ahlmz, awlmz/ are newer. In the UK the latter are non-standard.

12. **chaunt** archaic variant of **chant** US /chănt/; E. NEW ENG, UK /chahnt/. See App. D *-aun-*.

22. **Dido** /DĪ doh/ Queen of Carthage.

48. **espied** /ess SPĪD/ seen.

63. *****Actaeon's** hunter turned into a stag. Here should be stressed on the second syllable US /ak TEE ŏnz/ [-unz]; UK /-unz, -ŏnz/. Normal development would favor /ak TEE unz/. See App. D *-on.*

ă-bat, ăir-ma**rry**, air-**pair**, ạr-**far**, ĕr-**merry**, ĝ- get, ī-high, ĭr-**mirror**, ł-little, ṇ-listen, ŏ-hot, oh-go, ōō-wood, ōō-moon, oor-**tour**, ōr- or, ow-how, ţh-that, t̶h̶-thin, ŭ-but, UR-fur, ur-und**er**.   ( ) - suppress the syllable   see p. xiii for complete list.

72. **swart** /swōrt/ black. Some eds. prefer **swarthy** (*swartie* Q1), though it does not fit the meter.

72. **Cimmerian** /sih MEER ee un/ i.e., black person.

75. **sequest'red** secluded. Here 1st syllable stress is indicated.

77. **obscure** here should be /ŎB skyoor/; US *also* [-skyur].

90. **wan** /wŏn/ pale.

110. **Lascivious** /luh SIV yus/ lustful.

110. **Goth** /gŏth/; US *also* /gawth/. Shk pronounced it /goht/ or /gŏt/, producing a pun with *goat*.

118. **Semiramis** /suh MĬR uh miss/ lusty queen of Assyria.

120. **poniard** /PŎN yurd/; UK *also newer* [-yard] dagger.

125. *nuptial wedding. US, UK /NUP chł/ [-shł]; in CN both are used equally.

128. **eunuch** /YOO nuk/ castrated man.

153. **forlorn** here should be /FOR lorn/.

160. *obdurate unmoveable. Here with 2nd syllable stress /ŏb-, ub DYOOR it/; US *also* /-DYUR-/ [-DUR-]. 1st syllable stress is more usual today.

180. **satisfice** (Q1) /SAT is fĭss/ archaic variant of Q2's **satisfy**.

194. **espied** /ess SPĪD/ saw.

211. **uncouth** here should be /UN cooth/ strange.

222. **beray'd in blood** /bih-, bee RAYD/ defiled. Q1 has *bereavd in blood*, Q2-3, F1 have *embrewed heere*.

228. **taper** /TAY pur/ slender candle.

230. *entrails /EN traylz/; US *also* [-trłz] guts, interior.

231. **Pyramus** /PĬR uh mus/.

235. **devouring receptacle** here Shk. intended 1st syllable stress, but making *devouring* 4 syllables will allow our mod. pronunciation with 2nd syllable stress.

236. **Cocytus'** /kuh SĪ tus/ river in Hades.

265. **complot** here should be /CŎM plŏt/ plot.

285. **tortering** /TOR tring/ archaic variant of **torturing**.

Act 2 Scene 4

3. **bewray** /bih-, bee RAY/ reveal.

5. **scrowl** /skrohl/ archaic variant of *scroll* 'write.'

26, 41. **Tereus** he raped Philomel. /TEER yus/ [-yo͞oss]. See App. D *-eus*.

30. *****conduit** fountain. Here must be 2 syllables /CŎN dwit/; UK *also* [CUN dwit, CŎN dywit, CŎN dit, CUN dit].

51. **Cerberus** /SUR b(uh) rus/ three-headed dog of Hades.

51. **Thracian poet's** /THRAY shun/ Orpheus.

54. **meads** /meedz/ meadows.

Act 3 Scene 1

13. **languor** /LANG gur/; US *also* [LANG ur] grief. See App. D *-or*.

26. *****orators** US, CN /OR uh turz/; UK, E.COAST US /ŎR-/. Sometimes /OR ayt urz/ is used, but it is not recommended. See App. D *-or*.

71. **Nilus** /NĪL us/ the Nile.

90. **unrecuring** /un ree KYOOR ing/, /un rih-/; US *also* /-KYUR-/ incurable.

94. *****Environ'd** /en VĪ rund/; US *also* [-urnd] surrounded.

ă-bat, ăir-marry, air-pair, ạr-far, ĕr-merry, ĝ- get, ī-high, ĭr-mirror, ł-little, n̦-listen, ŏ-hot, oh-go, o͞o-wood, o͞o-moon, oor-tour, ŏr- or, ow-how, ţh-that, t̶h̶-thin, ŭ-but, UR-fur, ur-under.　　　　( ) - suppress the syllable　　　see p. xiii for complete list.

97. **brinish** /BRĪ nish/ referring to salt water.

146. **bewet** /bee-, bih WET/ made wet.

241. **Aetna, Etna** /ET nuh/ volcano in Sicily.

293. **tofore** /tōō FOR/ previously.

298. **Tarquin** /TAR kwin/ king of Rome who raped Lucretia.

Act 3 Scene 2

6. **passionate** /PASH uh nayt/ passionately express.

27. **Aeneas** /ih NEE yus/; UK *also* /EE NEE yus/ Prince of Troy.

Act 4 Scene 1

12. **Cornelia** /cor NEEL yuh/ mother of the Gracchi, political reformers.

14. **Tully's** /TŬL eez/.

14. *__Orator__ a work by Cicero. US, CN /OR uh tur/; UK, E.COAST US /ŎR-/. Sometimes /OR ayt ur/ is used, but it is not recommended.   See App. D -*or*.

20. **Hecuba** /HEK yoo buh/ Queen of Troy.

42. **Ovid's** /ŎV idz/ Roman poet.

48. **Tereus'** he raped Philomel. /TEER yus/ [-yōōss]. See App. D -*eus*.

63. **Tarquin** /TAR kwin/ king of Rome who raped Lucretia.

63. **erst** /urst/ formerly.

64, 91. **Lucrece'** here should be /LŌŌ creess/ (for /lyōō-/ see App. D *lu*-). Lucretia, Roman who commited suicide after being raped.

66. *__Pallas__ Athena. US /PAL us/ [-ăss]; UK, CN /-ăss/ [-us]. Normal development would favor /-us/.

78. **Stuprum** rape. Ang.Lat. US /STŌŌP rum/; SOUTH. US, UK /STYŌŌP rum/; Class.Lat. /STŏŏP rŏŏm/.

80. *heinous /HAYN us/ hateful. /HEEN us/ is non-standard though common in the UK.

81. **Magni   Dominator   poli,**
Ang.Lat. /MAG nī   dŏm ih NAY tur POH lī/
Class.Lat. /MAHG nee dŏm ih NAH tor PŎL ee/
        'Ruler of the great heavens,'

      Tam lentus   audis   scelera?   tam   lentus   vides?
Ang.Lat. /tam   LEN tus   AWD iss   SEL ur ruh   tam   LEN tus   VĪ deez/
Class.Lat. /tahm   LEN tōōs   OW deess SKEL ĕr ah   tahm   LEN tōōs WID ayss/
        'art thou so slow to hear crimes?   so slow to see them?'

88. **Hector's** /HEK turz/ Trojan hero. See App. D -or.

89. **fere** /feer/ mate, husband.

97. **wind** /wind/ scent.

105. **Sibyl's** /SIB łz/; UK *also* /SIB ilz/ prophetess in Gk mythology.

Act 4 Scene 2

7. **Gramercy** /gruh MUR see/ thanks.

20. **Integer   vitae,   scelerisque   purus,**
Ang.Lat. /IN tuh jur   VĪ tee,   sel ur ISS kwee   PYŌŌ rus/
Class.Lat. /IN teg ur   WEE tī   skel ĕr ISS kway   PŌŌ rōōss/
        'The man who is of pure life and free from crime'

      Non eget   Mauri   jaculis,   nec   arcu.
Ang.Lat. /nŏn   EE jet   MAW rī   JAK (y)uh liss, nek ARK yōō/
Class.Lat. /nŏn   EGG et   MOW ree   YAHK ōō leess nek ARK ōō/
        'does not need the arrows or the bow of the Moor.'
Some eds. prefer **iaculis** instead of **jaculis**, pronounced as in Class.Lat.
R. Whitney Tucker has pointed out that this quote from Horace's *Odes* I.22 is
Mauris jaculis 'Moorish arrows' in the oldest Latin manuscripts,
Ang.Lat. /MAW riss/; Class.Lat. /MOW reess/.

72. **blowse, blowze** /blowz/ a fat-faced wench.

ă-bat, äir-**ma**rry, air-**pair**, ạr-**far**, ĕr-**me**rry, ĝ- get, ī-high, ĭr-**mi**rror, ł-little, ṇ-listen,
ŏ-hot, oh-go, ōō-wood, ōō-moon, oor-**tour**, ōr- or, ow-how, ţh-that, ŧ̶ŧ̶-thin, Ŭ-but,
UR-**fur**, ur-**un**der.   ( ) - suppress the syllable   see p. xiii for complete list.

89. **tapers** /TAY purz/ slender candles.

91. ***scimitar's** US /SIM ih tarz/ [-turz]; CN /-tarz/; UK /-turz/ [-tarz] a curved sword.

93. **Enceladus** /en SEL uh dus/ one of the Titans.

94. ***Typhon's** giant with 100 hands. /TĪ fŏnz/ [-funz, -fohnz]. Normal development would favor /-funz/. See App. D -on.

95. **Alcides** /al SĪ deez/ Hercules.

97. **sanguine** /SANG gwin/ red-faced.

103. **lave** /layv/ wash.

110. **maugre** /MAW gur/ in spite of.

115. **ignomy** /IG nuh mee/ disgrace.

118. **close** /clohss/ secret.

138. **chafed** /CHAY fid/ enraged.

141. **Cornelia** /cor NEEL ee yuh/.

152. **Muliteus** (F1) /myo͞o lih TEE yus, MYO͞O lit yo͞os/. If the former, an epic caesura follows, if the latter it is a normal line. Some eds prefer the reading **Muli lives** /MYO͞O lee/.

Act 4 Scene 3

4.   **Terras   Astraea   reliquit**
Ang.Lat. /TĔR us   ass TREE uh   rel Ī kwit/
Class.Lat. /TĔR ahss ahss TRĪ uh   rel EE kwit/
            'Astraea (goddess of justice) has left the earth.'

11. **mattock** /MAT uk/ digging tool.

34, 52. **wreak** /reek/ vengence.

45. **Acheron** /AK ur ŏn, -un/ a river in Hades. /-ŏn/ is usual in the US and is increasingly common in the UK. See App. D -on.

54. **Ad Jovem** Ang.Lat. /ad JOH vem/; Class.Lat. /ahd YŎ wem/ to Jupiter. Some eds. prefer **Iovem** pronounced as in Class.Lat.

54. **Ad Apollinem** Ang.Lat. /ad uh PŎL ih nem/; Class.Lat. /ahd ah PŎL ih nem/ to Apollo.

55. **Ad Martem** Ang.Lat. /ad MAR tem/; Class.Lat. /ahd-/ to Mars.

56, 65. ***Pallas** Athena. US /PAL us/ [-ăss]; UK, CN /-ăss/ [-us]. Normal development would favor /-us/.

65. **Virgo's** /VUR gohz/.

72. **Aries** /AIR eez/; E.COAST US *also* [ĂIR eez] the ram.

81. **gibbet-maker** /JIB it/ post from which they hung corpses after hanging.

93. ***tribunal plebs** /trīb YŌON ł/ [trib-]; /plebz/ with an older pronunication /pleebz/ now virtually extinct. Here means 'plebeians.' This is an error for *tribunis plebis* /trib YŌO niss PLEEB iss/ 'tribune of the plebs.'

117. **suppliant** the line may end in a feminine or a triple ending /SUP l(ee) yunt/ someone who asks humbly for something.

Act 4 Scene 4

4. **egall** /EE gł/ archaic variant of **equal**.

11. **wreaks** /reeks/ revenge.

18. **blazoning** /BLAY z(uh) ning/ proclaiming.

35. **gloze** (Q1), **glose** (F1) /glohz/ use fair words.

43. **god-den** /gud-, gŏŏd EN/ good evening. Some eds. prefer **Good e'en**.

48. **by' lady** /bī-, buh LAY dee/ by Our Lady (i.e., Mary).

59. **holp'st** /hohlpst/ helped.

65. **amain** /uh MAYN/ with full speed.

ă-bat, ăir-marry, air-pair, ar-far, ĕr-merry, ĝ- get, ī-high, ĭr-mirror, ł-little, n̩-listen, ŏ-hot, oh-go, ŏŏ-wood, ōō-moon, oor-tour, ōr- or, ow-how, t̩h-that, th-thin, ŭ-but, UR-fur, ur-under.   ( ) - suppress the syllable   see p. xiii for complete list.

65. **conduct** here should be /cun-, cŏn DUCT/.

68. **Coriolanus** here 4 syllables /cor yuh LAY nus/; restored Latin [-LAHN-] Roman who joined his enemies to revenge himself on Rome.

80. **succor** (UK **succour**) /SUCK ur/ help. See App. D -*or*.

81. **imperious** /im PEER yus/ imperial.

101. ***parley** /PAR lee/ conference with an enemy. Newer [-lay] not recommended.

111. **blithe** /blīþ/; US *also* /blīth/ merry.

Act 5 Scene 1

6. **Imperious** /im PEER yus/ imperial.

7. **scath** /skăth/ harm.

11. **exploits** here should be /ek SPLOYTS/.

17. **saith** says. US /SAY ith/, *rarely* [seth]; UK /seth/ [SAY ith]. The older form is /seth/. Here one syllable produces a regular line, but an epic caesura also allows the 2 syllable form.

20. **Renowmed** /rih-, ree NOW mid/ archaic variant of **renowned** /rih-, ree NOWN id/.

28. **bewray** /bih-, bee RAY/ reveal.

40. **the incarnate** /th^yin CAR nit/ [-nayt] in the flesh. /-ut/ is usual for adjs.

65. **Complots** here may be either /CŎM plŏts/ or /cum PLŎTS/ plots. Both occur elsewhere in Shk.

88. **insatiate** /in SAYSH yut, -yayt/ never satisfied. /-ut/ is more usual for an adj.

94. **detestable** here should be /DEE tess tuh bł/ or /DET es tuh bł/.

113. **extreme** here should be /EK streem/.

119. **sounded** archaic variant of **swooned**. In Shk's time the vowel could be either /ow/ or /o͞o/.

123. ***heinous** /HAYN us/ hateful. /HEEN us/ is non-standard though common in the UK.

159. ***parley** /PAR lee/ conference with an enemy. Newer [-lay] not recommended.

Act 5 Scene 2

1. **habiliment** /huh BILL ih munt/ clothing.   F3 has **habiliments** /huh BILL ih munts/ clothes.

4. ***heinous** /HAYN us/ hateful. /HEEN us/ is non-standard though common in the UK.

32. **wreakful** /REEK fṳll/ revengeful.

46. **surance** /SHOOR unss/; US *also* /SHUR unss/ assurance.

50. **palfreys** /PAWL freez/; UK *also* [PŎL-] saddle horses.

55. ***servile** /SUR vīl/, *rarely* [SUR vł] slave-like.

56. ***Hyperion's** /hī PEER yunz/ god of the sun. Sometimes newer /-PĔR-/ or /-ŏn/ are used, but are not recommended.

59-103. ***Rapine** plundering, rape. US /RAYP īn/ [RAYP in, RAP in];
CN /RAYP in/ [RAP in]; UK /RAP īn/ [RAYP īn, RAP in]. /RAP in/ is the oldest pronunciation. The others are based on spelling and on analogy with *rape*.

72. **maintain** here should be /MAYN tayn/.

76-202. **banket** /BANK it/ light meal, often of fruit. Archaic variant of **banquet.**

147. **complot** here should be /CŎM plŏt/ plot.

151, 158. **Valentine** /VAL in tīn/.

189. ***pasties** US /PĂSS teez, PAYSS-/; UK /PĂSS teez/ [PAYSS-] meat pies.

ă-bat, ăir-marry, air-pair, a̤r-far, ĕr-merry, ĝ- get, ī-high, ĭr-mirror, ł-little, n̤-listen, ŏ-hot, oh-go, ŏŏ-wood, ōō-moon, oor-tour, ŏr- or, ow-how, t̤h-that, t̶h̶-thin, ŭ-but, UR-fur, ur-under.   ( ) - suppress the syllable   see p. xiii for complete list.

191. **increase** here should be /in CREESS/ offspring.

195. **Progne** /PRŎG nee/ sister of Philomel. Some eds. prefer **Procne** /PRŎCK nee/.

203. **Centaurs'** /SEN torz/.

Act 5 Scene 3

19. **parle** /pạrl/ conference with an enemy.

22. **ordain'd** here should be /OR daynd/.

36, 50. **Virginius** in the first instance is /vur JIN ee us/, in the second /vur JIN yus/. He killed his daughter to keep her from being raped—in other words the playwright has it mixed up.

43. **effectual** here 1st syllable stress is indicated, and it may be pronounced with 3 or 4 syllables.

44. **president** example. Archaic variant of **precedent**, both /PRESS ih dunt/. It is not clear whether /PREZ-/ was used in Shk's time.

80. **erst** /urst/ formerly.

82. **Dido's** /DĪ dohz/ Queen of Carthage.

84. *****Priam's** King of Troy. US, CN /PRĪ um/ [-am]; UK /-am/, *rarely* [-um]. Normal development would favor /-um/.

85. **Sinon** traitor who caused Troy's fall. /SĪ nun/, but /-ŏn/ is becoming more common. See App. D *-on*.

88. **compact** /cum PACT/ made up of.

93. **commiseration** /kuh miz ur RAY shun/ pity.

108. **op'd** /ohpt/ opened.

112. **advent'rous** /ad VENT rus/ archaic variant of mod. /ad VENCH rus/.

152. **obsequious** /ub-, ŏb SEE kw(ee) yus/ mournful.

177. **execrable** /EK suh cruh bł/ damnable.

195. **ravenous** (Q1) /RAV (uh) nus/. Some eds. prefer Q2-3, F1's ***heinous**
/HAYN us/ hateful. /HEEN us/ is non-standard though common in the UK.

ă-bat, ăir-ma**rry**, air-p**air**, ạr-f**ar**, ĕr-me**rry**, ĝ- **g**et, ī-h**igh**, ĭr-mi**rror**, ł-li**ttle**, ṇ-lis**ten**,
ŏ-h**ot**, oh-g**o**, o͞o-w**ood**, o͞o-m**oon**, oor-t**our**, ŏr- **or**, ow-h**ow**, ṭh-**th**at, t̶h̶-**th**in, ŭ-b**ut**,
UR-f**ur**, ur-un**der**.   ( ) - suppress the syllable   see p. xiii for complete list.

Troilus and Cressida

People in the Play

Achilles /uh KILL eez/.

Aeneas /ih NEE yus/; UK *also* /EE NEE yus/.

*****Agamemnon** US, CN /ag uh MEM nŏn/; UK /-nŏn/ [-nun]. See App. D *-on.*

Ajax /AY jacks/.

Andromache 3 or 4 syllables depending on meter /an DRŎM (uh) kee/.

Antenor /an TEE nur/. See App. D *-or.*

Calchas US /KAL kus/ [-kăss]; UK, CN /-kăss/ [-kus]. Normal development would favor /-kus/.

Cassandra /kuh SAN druh/.

Cressida /CRESS ih duh/.
  Cressid /CRESS id/.

Deiphobus /dee IF uh bus/.

Diomedes 3 or 4 syllables depending on meter /dī (uh) MEE deez/.
  Diomed 2 or 3 syllables depending on meter /DĪ (uh) med/,
  Diomede /-meed/.

Hector /HEK tur/. See App. D *-or.*

Hecuba /HEK yoo buh/ mentioned throughout.

Helenus /HELL in us/.

Margarelon 3 syllables /mar GAIR (uh) lŏn, -lun/. Some eds. prefer
Margareton /mar GAIR (uh) tŏn, -tun/. /-ŏn/ endings are usual in the US
and are increasingly common in the UK. See App. D *-on.*

Menelaus /men uh LAY us/.

People in the Play (cont.)

Myrmidons /MUR mih dunz, -dŏnz/; /-ŏn/ is usual in the US, /-un/ is more common in the UK.   See App. D -on.

Nestor /NEST ur/ oldest of the Greeks at Troy. See App. D -or.

Pandarus /PAN duh rus/.
  Pandar /PAN dur/.

*****Patroclus** US, CN /puh TROH cluss, puh TRŎCK luss/; UK /-TRŎCK-/. The common pronunciation /PAT ruh cluss/ will not fit the meter of the verse.

*****Priam** US, CN /PRĪ um/ [-am]; UK /-am/, *rarely* [-um]. Normal development would favor /-um/. May be one syllable at Prologue. 15.
  Priamus /PRĪ um us/; Class.Lat. /PRIH ah mōōs/.

Thersites /thur SĪ teez/.

Troilus /TROY lus/.   3 syllables at 5.2.161 /TROH ee lus/, or in some dialects /TRAW ee lus/.

Ulysses /yōō LISS eez/; US *also* /yōō-/. The less common UK form /YŌŌ lih seez/ cannot be used in verse.

Places in the Play

*****Ilion** 2 or 3 syllables depending on meter /ILL (ee) yun/;
UK *also newer* [Ī l(ee) yun].

Ilium 2 or 3 syllables depending on meter /ILL (ee) yum/;
UK *also newer* [Ī l(ee) yum].

Phrygia 2 or 3 syllables depending on meter /FRIJ uh, FRIJ (ee) yuh/.
  Phrygian /FRIJ un, -yun/. Normal development would favor the former.

Prologue

2. *****orgillous** /ORG ih lus/ proud. Variant of *****orgulous** US /ORG yuh lus/ [ORG uh lus]; in the UK both are used equally.

ă-bat, ăir-**marry**, air-**pair**, ar̤-**far**, ĕr-**merry**, ĝ- **get**, ī-**high**, ĭr-**mirror**, l̩-**little**, n̩-**listen**, ŏ-**hot**, oh-**go**, ōō-**wood**, ōō-**moon**, oor-**tour**, ōr- **or**, ow-**how**, t̲h-**that**, th-**thin**, ŭ-**but**, UR-**fur**, ur-**under**.   ( ) - suppress the syllable   see p. xiii for complete list.

2. **chaf'd** /chayft/ enraged.

6. **crownets** /CROWN its/ small crowns.

8. **immures** /ih MYOORZ/ walls.

11. **Tenedos** island near Troy. US /TEN uh dus, -dŏs/; UK /-dŏs/ [-dus]. Normal development would favor /-us/. A newer pronunciation /-ohss/ is also used, especially in the US.

13. **fraughtage** /FRAWT ij/ cargo. Some eds. prefer **freightage**.

13, 16. **Dardan** /DĄR dun/ Trojan.

16. **Timbria** /TIM br(ee) yuh/.

16. **Helias** US /HEELyus/. Some eds. prefer **Hellas** /HEL us/.

16. **Chetas** US /KEE tus/ [-tăss]; UK, CN /-tăss/ [-tus]. Normal development would favor /-tus/.

16. **Troien** /TROY un/.

17. **Antenorides** /an tuh NOR ih deez/.

19. **Sperr up** /SPUR/ bolt, bar. Variant of **Spar up**.

Act 1 Scene 1

17, 20. **bolting, boulting** /BOLT ing/ sifting.

20, 23. **leavening** /LEV ņ ing/ fermenting.

37. **a-scorn.** Some eds. prefer **a storm**, or **askance** 'at a sideways angle' US /uh SKĂNSS/; UK, E. NEW ENG. /-SKAHNSS/ [-SKĂNSS]. See App. D *-aun-*.

50. **fadoms** /FAD umz/ archaic variant of **fathoms** /FĄTH umz/.

58. **cygnet's** /SIG nits/ young swan's.

70. *****travail** hard work. In Shk's verse 1st syllable stress is usually indicated, today usually /truh VAYL/.

77. **blackamoor** /BLACK uh moor/ [-mor] a black.

96. **teachy** /TETCH ee/ fretful. Still common in the UK as **tetchy**.

98. **Daphne's** /DAFF neez/ nymph changed to a laurel tree.

Act 1 Scene 2

15. **per se** Ang.Lat. /PUR SEE/, today nearly always /PUR SAY/ 'unique.'

29. **Briareus** /brī AIR ee us/ [-yōōss] giant with 100 hands.

29. **purblind** (Q) /PUR blīnd/ blind or partly blind. F1 has **purblinded** /PUR blīn did/.

29. **Argus** /ĄRG us/ 100-eyed monster.

104. **as lieve** /leev/ 'as soon,' still used in some US dialects. Some eds. prefer **lief** /leef/.

136. *****marvell's** means 'marvellously' or **marvellous**, which some eds. prefer. In any event it should be two syllables, either /MARV ĭss/ or, as indicated in spellings elsewhere in Shk, /MARV lus/.

166. **chaf'd** /chayft/ enraged.

190. *****shrowd** /shrohd/ sharp. Archaic variant of **shrewd**.

249. **drayman** /DRAY mun/ driver of a brewer's cart.

294. **content** (Q) here /cŏn TENT/. Some eds. prefer F1's **contents**, here /cŏn TENTS/.

Act 1 Scene 3

2. **these jaundies** yellowing of the skin. Here considered a plural /JAWN deez/. Archaic variant of **the jaundice** /JAWN diss/.

7. **conflux** flowing together. Here should be /cŏn-, cun FLUCKS/.

9. **errant** /ĔR unt/ wandering.

ă-bat, ăir-**marry**, air-**pair**, ąr-**far**, ĕr-**merry**, ĝ- **get**, ī-**high**, ĭr-**mirror**, ł-**little**, ṇ-**listen**, ŏ-**hot**, oh-**go**, ōō-**wood**, ōō-**moon**, oor-**tour**, ōr- **or**, ow-**how**, ţh-**that**, t̶h̶-**thin**, ŭ-**but**, UR-**fur**, ur-**under**.   ( ) - suppress the syllable   see p. xiii for complete list.

14. **record** here should be /rek-, rik ORD/.

25. **affin'd** /uh FĪND/ closely related.

38. **Boreas** US /BOR yus/ [-yăss]; UK, CN /-yăss/ [-yus] northwind. Normal development would favor /-yus/.

39. *****Thetis** /~~THEE~~ tiss/; *sometimes newer* [~~THET~~ iss] Achilles' mother.

42. *****Perseus'** /PUR syus/ [-syo͞oss], US *rarely* [-so͞oss]. See App. D *-eus.*

44. **Corrivall'd** (Q) /coh-, cuh RĪ vłd/ vied with. Some eds. prefer F1's **Co-rivalled** /coh-/.

48. **breeze, breese** /breez/ gadfly.

70. **Ithaca** /~~ITH~~ uh kuh/ Ulysses' home.

73. **mastic** /MĂST ik/ 'abusive' or 'gummy.'

83. *****vizarded** /VIZ urd id/ masked. /-ạrd-/ not recommended.

84. **mask.** Some eds. prefer **masque** US /măsk/; UK, E. NEW ENG. /mahsk/ [măsk] masked dancing and pantomime.

87. **Insisture** /in SISS chur/ steady persistence. Some eds. prefer **Infixture** /in FIKS chur/ the state of being fixed in place. See App. D *-ure.*

89. *****Sol** the sun. US /sawl, sohl/ [sŏl]; CN /sŏl/ [sohl]; UK /sŏl/. /sŏl/ is older. In some parts of the US and virtually all of Canada /ŏ/ and /aw/ are pronounced alike, especially before /l/.

91. **med'cinable, medicinable** here /MED sin uh bł/ medicinal.

94. **Sans** /sănz/ without.

96. **portents** here should be /por TENTS/ omens.

99. **deracinate** /dih-, dee RĂSS ih nayt/ uproot.

101. **fixure** /FIK shur/; UK *also* /-syoor/ fixedness. Some eds. prefer **fixture**. See App. D *-ure.*

105. **Peaceful commerce from dividable shores** Shk probably intended *commerce* /cŏm MURSS/ and *dividable* with 1st syllable stress, but it is also possible to use mod. /CŎM urss/ and /dih VĪD (uh) bł/ in a headless line.

106. **primogenity** (Q) /prī moh JEN ih tee/, **primogenitive** (F1)
/prī moh JEN ih tiv/. Some eds. prefer **primogeniture** /prī moh JEN ih chur/;
UK *also* /-tyoor/. All mean 'the right of the firstborn.' See App. D -*ure.*

107. *Prerogative /pur RŎG uh tiv/ [prih-, pree-] privilege, right. /pree-/ non-
standard in the UK.

111. **oppugnancy** /uh PUG nun see/ hostility.

125. **suffocate** /SUF uh kut, -kayt/ suffocated.

143. **sinow** (Q) /SIN oh/ archaic variant of F1's **sinew** /SIN yōō/;
US *also* [SIN ōō].

147. *livelong US /LIV lŏng, -lawng/, *rarely* [LĪV-]; UK /LIV lŏng/ [LĪV-].

148. **scurril** using vulgar language. US /SKUR ł/; E.COAST US, UK /SKUH rł/.
Some eds. prefer **scurrile**, pronounced the same way, or, esp. in the UK, CN /-īl/.

156. **scaffolage** /SKAF ł ij/ boards of the stage. Variant of **scaffoldage**
/SKAF łd ij/ which some eds. prefer.

160. *Typhon giant with 100 hands. /TĪ fŏn/ [-fun, -fohn]. Normal
development would favor /-fun/. See App. D -*on.*

161. **hyperboles** /hī PUR buh leez/ extravant exaggeration.

162. **lolling** /LŎLL ing/ lying lazily.

172. **defects** here should be /dih-, dee FECTS/.

174. **palsy** /PAWL zee/; UK *also* [PŎL-] shaky.

174. **gorget** /GOR jit/ armor protecting the throat.

199. *prescience foreknowledge. Here should be the archaic form
/prih SĪ unss/ if the line is regular. The more usual forms are
US /PRESS ee unss/ [PRESH unss]; CN, UK /PRESS ee unss/,
rarely [PRESH unss].

207. **swinge** /swinj/ sweeping motion.

ă-bat, ăir-marry, air-pair, a̦r-far, ĕr-merry, ĝ- get, ī-high, ĭr-mirror, ł-little, n̦-listen,
ŏ-hot, oh-go, ōō-wood, ōō-moon, oor-tour, ōr- or, ow-how, țh-that, t̶h̶-thin, Ŭ-but,
UR-fur, ur-under.   ( ) - suppress the syllable   see p. xiii for complete list.

212. ***Thetis'** /~~THEE~~ tiss/; *sometimes newer* [~~THET~~ iss] Achilles' mother.

220. ***surety** guarantee. Here should be two syllables, though in mod. English, three syllables are more common, /SHUR (ih) tee, SHOOR-, SHOR-/ (see App. D).

230. **Phoebus** /FEE bus/ god of the sun.

287. **recreant** /REK r(ee) yunt/ coward.

297. **vambrace** (Q) /VAM brayss/ variant of F1's **vantbrace** /VĂNT brayss/ armor for the front part of the arm.

299. ***grandam** /GRAN dam/; US *rarely* [-dum] grandmother. Informally /GRAN um/.

330. **celerity** /suh LĔR ih tee/ speed.

343. **indexes** /IN deck siz/. Some eds. prefer **indices** /IN dih seez/.

344. **To their *subsequent* volumes there is seen** /sub SEE kwunt/ would be the pronunciation in a regular line.

390. **tarre, tar** /tar/ incite.

390. **mastiffs** /MĂST ifs/; UK *sometimes* [MAHST-] powerful watchdogs.

Act 2 Scene 1

14. **whinid'st** (F1) /WHIN idst/ mouldiest. Variant of **finewed'st** /FIN yo͞odst/, or in dialect form /FIN idst/; also **vinewed'st** /VIN yo͞odst/ which in dialect form is /VIN idst/. Q has **unsalted**. Some eds. prefer **unsifted**.

14. **leaven** /LEV ṇ, -in/ sour-dough used to make bread rise.

19. **murrion** plague. Archaic spelling which may have had the ending /-yun/ or /-un/, but in any case was a variant of **murrain** US, CN /MUR in/; E.COAST US, UK /MUH rin/.

26. **porpentine** /POR pin tīn/ archaic variant of **porcupine**.

34. **Cerberus** /SUR bur us/ three-headed dog of Hades.

34. **Proserpina's** /proh-, pruh SUR pih nuz/.

44. **asinico** /ăss ih NEE koh/ little ass, blockhead. Other variants are **asnego** /ăss NEE goh/, or Sp. **asnico** angl. /ăss NEE koh/.

71. ***pia mater** here 'the brain.' Ang.Lat. /PĪ uh MAYT ur/ is older; Class.Lat. /PEE uh MAHT ur/ is newer and much more common. Forms that mix old and new are also used.

97. **under an impress** drafted. Normally in Shk the noun is /im PRESS/, but in this prose passage it may be mod. /IM press/.

106. **draught-oxen** US, CN /drăft/; UK, E.NEW ENG. /drahft/.

114. **brach** /bratch/ female dog.

Act 2 Scene 2

4. ***travail** hard work. Here /truh VAYL/ makes the line regular, but the foot may be inverted to allow /TRAV ayl/. Both forms are used today, but the former is more common.

6. ***cormorant** /COR m(uh) runt/; US *rarely* [-ant] a fishing bird, i.e., devouring.

12. **spungy** archaic variant of **spongy**, both pronounced /SPUN jee/.

14, 15. ***surety** (F1) security. The second instance should be two syllables, though in mod. English, three syllables are more common. The first instance may be a triple ending /SHUR (ih) tee, SHOOR-, SHOR-/ (see App. D). Q has **surely**.

19. **tithe** /tīth/ tenth.

19. **dismes, dimes** /dīmz/ one-tenth of the men sacrificed.

28. **compters** (Q) /COWNT urz/ archaic variant of F1's **counters**. See App. D *accompt*.

54. ***estimate** US /ES tih mut/ [-mayt]; UK /-mayt/ [-mut] reputation.

70. **viands** /VĪ undz/ food. /VEE undz/ not recommended.

71. **sieve** /siv/ scrap-pot. Some eds. prefer **sewer**.

ă-bat, ăir-**marry**, air-**pair**, ạr-**far**, ĕr-**merry**, ĝ- get, ī-high, ĭr-**mirror**, ł-little, ṇ-**listen**, ŏ-hot, oh-go, ōō-**wood**, ōō-**moon**, oor-**tour**, ōr- **or**, ow-**how**, ţh-**that**, th-thin, ŭ-but, UR-**fur**, ur-und**er**.   ( ) - suppress the syllable   see p. xiii for complete list.

84. **avouch** /uh VOWCH/ accept.

107. **moi'ty, moiety** /MOY tee/ portion.

136. **propugnation** /proh pug NAY shun/ defense.

165. **gloz'd** /glohzd/ commented. Some eds. prefer **glossed**.

202. **canonize** here should be /kan ŎN īz/ glorify.

206. **revenue** here should be /ruh VEN yōō/.

211. *****advertis'd** informed. Here should be /ad VUR tisst/, /-tīzd/.

Act 2 Scene 3

stage direction: solus /SOH lŭss/ alone.

7. **execrations** /ek suh CRAY shunz/ curses.

8. **enginer** digging soldier. Archaic variant of **engineer**. In Shk's time it may have been /EN jih nur/, or mod. /en jih NEER/.

12. *****serpentine** snakelike. US /SUR pin tīn/ [-teen]; UK /SUR pin tīn/, *rarely* [-teen]. /-teen/ is newer.

12. **caduceus** Mercury's staff. Normal development would favor /kuh DYŌŌ shus/, with a US variant /-DŌŌ-/, and a UK variant /-JŌŌ-/. The newer, more common form has the ending /-see us/.

18. **Neapolitan** /nee uh PŎL ih tun/ of Naples.

29. **revenue** sometimes in verse /ruh VEN yōō/, but in this prose passage may be mod. Eng. US /REV in ōō/; UK, SOUTH. US /-yōō/.

33. *****lazars** /LAY zurz, LAZZ urz/ lepers.

73. **emulous** /EM yoo lus/ jealous.

74. **suppeago** /suh PEE goh/ a creeping skin disease. Variant of **serpigo** /sur PEE goh, -PĪ-/.

91. *****inveigled** /in VAYG łd/, *rarely* [-VEEG-] acquired by flattery.

106. **flexure** (Q) /FLEK shur/; UK *also* [-syoor]. See App. D -*ure*. F1 has **flight**.

130. **lines** (F1), **time** (Q). Some eds. prefer **lunes** /lo͞onz/ fits of madness (for /lyo͞o-/ see App. D *lu*-).

177. **plaguy, plaguey** /PLAYG ee/ confoundedly.

185. **bastes** /baysts/ sews on loosely.

192. **assubjugate** /uh SUB juh gayt/ debase.

197. *****Hyperion** /hī PEER yun/ god of the sun. Sometimes newer /-PĔR-/ or /-ŏn/ are used, but are not recommended.

205. **pheese, feeze** /feez/ settle, fix.

208. **paltry** /PAWL tree/ worthless.

231. **emulous** /EM y(o͞o) lus/ jealous.

233. **palter** /PAWL tur/ trifle.

243. *****erudition** /ĕr yuh DISH un/ [ĕr uh-] learning. The 2nd syllable may also have the vowel /o͞o/ or /o͝o/.

247. **Milo** /MĪ loh/ Gk. athelete.

248. **sinowy** /SIN (oh) wee/ muscular. Archaic variant of **sinewy** /SIN y(oo) wee/; US *also* [SIN (oo) wee].

249. *****bourn** /born, boorn/ boundary. North American [burn] not recommended. Normal development would favor /born/.

250. **dilated** /dih-, dī LAYT id/ extensive.

251. **antiquary** US /AN tih kwĕr ee/; UK /-kwuh ree/ ancient.

Act 3 Scene 1

81. **exploit's** /ek SPLOYTS/ in verse, but here may be mod. /EK sployts/.

ă-b**at**, ă**ir**-m**arry**, **air**-p**air**, a̧r-f**ar**, ĕr-m**erry**, ĝ- g**et**, ī-h**igh**, ĭr-m**irror**, l̩-l**ittle**, n̩-l**isten**, ŏ-h**ot**, oh-g**o**, o͞o-w**ood**, o͞o-m**oon**, oor-t**our**, ōr- **or**, ow-h**ow**, t̩h-t**hat**, t̶h̶-t̶**hin**, ŭ-b**ut**, UR-f**ur**, ur-und**er**.　　　( ) - suppress the syllable　　　see p. xiii for complete list.

Act 3 Scene 2

9. *__Stygian__ referring to the River Styx, the border of Hades. /STIJ yun/, *rarely* [STIJ un].

10. *__waftage__ passage. US /WŎFT ij/; SOUTH. US /WĂFT ij/; UK /WŎFT ij/ [WĂFT ij, WAHFT ij]. /WĂFT-/ is newer and considered non-standard by many.

10. *__Charon__ normal development would favor /CAIR un/; /-ŏn/ is newer. Both are used equally in the US. [CĂIR-] is a newer E.COAST US pronunciation. UK /CAIR ŏn/ [-un]. Restored Gk. /CAR-/ is also used with increasing frequency in all countries. See App. D *-on*.

22. __thrice-repured__ /ree-, rih PYOOR id/; US, CN *also* /-PYUR id/ purified three times. /ree-/ non-standard in the UK.

38. __vassalage__ /VĂSS ł ij/ vassals, i.e., people of humble birth.

46. __fills__ /filz/ variant of __thills__ /t̶h̶ilz/ shafts of a cart.

49. __close__ /clohz/ double meaning: settle the deal, come together.

52. __tercel__ /TUR sł/ variant of __tiercel__ /TEER sł/ a kind of hawk.

65. __espies__ /ess SPĪZ/ sees.

69. *__cherubins__ angels. US, CN /CHĔR uh binz/ [-yuh-]; UK uses both equally. /KĔR-/ not recommended. Some eds. prefer __cherubims__, both archaic plurals of *cherub*.

94. __desert__ /dih ZURT/ deserving.

134. __albeit__ /awl BEE (i)t/ although.

160. __aye__ /ay/ ever. /ī/ is often used, but not recommended.

175. __protest__ protestations of love. Here should be /proh TEST/.

176. __iteration__ /it ur RAY shun/ repetition.

177. __plantage__ US /PLĂN tij/; UK, E. NEW ENG. /PLAHNT-/ vegetation.

179. __adamant__ /AD uh munt/ lodestone, or the hardest substance. /-ant/ not recommended.

188. *characterless** without leaving any sign or mark. Here with second
syllable stress.

194. **hind** /hīnd/ doe.

Act 3 Scene 3

43. **unplausive** /un PLAW ziv/ [-siv] disapproving.

44. **medicinable** here /MED sin uh bł/ medicinal.

94. *Thetis'** /~~THEE~~ tiss/; *sometimes newer* [~~THET~~ iss] Achilles' mother.

125. **Th' unknown** (Q) here should be /ţhee UN nohn/ with *Th'* pronounced
fully, as in F1's **The unknown**.

128, 162. **abject** /AB ject/ contemptible.

146. *alms** charity for the poor. /ahmz/ is older; /ahlmz, awlmz/ are newer. In
the UK the latter are non-standard.

150. **Perseverance** here should be /pur SEV (uh) runss/.

158. **forthright** here should be /for~~th~~ RĪT/ straight path.

160. **hindmost** (F1) /HĪND mohst/ furthest behind.

164. **o'ertop** here should be /OR tŏp/.

168. **comer** /KUM ur/ the one who is arriving.

170. **Remuneration** /rih-, ree myōōn ur RAY shun/ payment.

174. **calumniating** /cuh LUM nee ayt ing/ slandering.

176. **gawds** /gawdz/ trinkets.

181. **complete** here should be /CŎM pleet/.

189. **emulous** /EM y(oo) lus/ zealous.

ă-bat, ăir-marry, air-pair, ạr-far, ĕr-merry, ĝ- get, ī-high, ĭr-mirror, ł-little, ņ-listen,
ŏ-hot, oh-go, ŏŏ-wood, ōō-moon, oor-tour, ōr- or, ow-how, ţh-that, ~~th~~-thin, ŭ-but,
UR-fur, ur-under.   ( ) - suppress the syllable   see p. xiii for complete list.

205. **commerce** here should be /cŏm URSS/ dealings.

208. **Polyxena** /puh-, pŏ LIK sin uh/.

209. **Pyrrhus** /PĬR us/ Achilles' son.

228. ***shrowdly** /SHROHD lee/ badly. Archaic variant of **shrewdly**.

232. **ague** /AY gyo͞o/ malarial fever.

254. **politic regard** /PŎL ih tik/ appearance of fairness.

259. ***vainglory** pride. /VAYN glor ee/ [vayn GLOR ee]. The latter is older.

293. **God buy you** good bye. Some eds. substitute **God b'wi' you**
/gŏd BWEE yo͞o/ or some other variation of that phrase.

Act 4 Scene 1

21. **humane** here should be /HYO͞O mayn/; US *sometimes* [YO͞O mayn].

22. ***Anchises'** /an-, ang KĪ seez/; US *also newer* [-zeez] Aeneas' father.

28. **complete** here should be /CŎM pleet/.

29. **emulous** /EM y(oo) lus/ jealous.

62. **puling** /PYO͞OL ing/ whining.

Act 4 Scene 2

9. ***ribald** bawdy, vulgar. US, UK /RIB łd/ [-awld], *rarely* [RĪ-]; CN /RĪ bawld/
[-błd, RIB łd, RIB awld]. /RIB łd/ is the traditional pronunciation.

31. **capocchia** angl. /kuh POH kee uh/; Ital. /kah POH kyah/ an innocent,
a simpleton.

73. **taciturnity** /tass ih TURN ih tee/ silence.

The *Complete Oxford* begins Scene 4.3 here (line nos. in parentheses).

97. (4.3.23) **consanguinity** /cŏn sang GWIN ih tee/ blood relationship.

Act 4 Scene 3 (*Complete Oxford* 4.4)

1. **prefix'd** here should be /pree-, prih FIKST/ appointed.

Act 4 Scene 4 (*Complete Oxford* 4.5)

8. **allayment** /uh LAY munt/ calming.

9. **dross** /drŏss/; US *also* /drawss/ impure matter.

34. **justles** /JUSS łz/ archaic variant of **jostles** /JŎS łz/.

36. **rejoindure** /ree-, rih JOYN dyur, -dyoor/ reunion.   Normal development would also produce /-jur/, especially in the US (see App. D -*ure*).

37. **embrasures** embraces. US, CN /em BRAY shurz/; US *rarely* [-zhurz]; UK /-zhurz/, *rarely* [-shurz]. See App. D -*ure*.

45. **distinct** here 1st syllable stress is indicated.

45. **consign'd** here should be /CŎN sīnd/.

60. **expostulation** US /ek spŏs chuh LAY shun/; UK *also* /-tyoo-/ protest.

64. **maculation** /mack yuh LAY shun/ stain.

66. **sequent** /SEE kwunt/ following.

66. ***protestation** US /proh tess-, prŏt ess TAY shun/; CN /prŏt ess-/ [proh tess-]; UK /prŏt ess-/.

86. **lavolt** a type of bounding dance. /luh VOHLT/ or older /luh VŎLT/.

Act 4 Scene 5 (*Complete Oxford* 4.6)

5, 92. **combatant(s)** here should be stressed on the first syllable, as is usual in the UK, /CŎM buh tunt/ [CUM-].

7. **brazen** /BRAY zun, -zṇ/ brass.

ă-bat, ăir-m**a**rry, air-**pair**, ạr-f**ar**, ĕr-m**e**rry, ĝ- g**e**t, ī-high, ĭr-m**i**rror, ł-little, ṇ-listen, ŏ-hot, oh-go, ōō-wood, ōō-moon, oor-**tour**, ōr- or, ow-how, ţh-**that**, th-**thin**, ŭ-but, UR-f**ur**, ur-und**er**.   ( ) - suppress the syllable   see p. xiii for complete list.

9. **colic** /CŎL ik/ swollen belly from indigestion.

9. **Aquilon** /AK wih lŏn, -lun/ north wind. /-ŏn/ is usual in the US and is increasingly common in the UK. See App. D -on.

45. **fillip me** /FILL ip/ strike me smartly, i.e, twit me.

74. **misprising, misprizing** /mis PRĪZ ing/ undervaluing.

103. **impare** (Q), **impaire** (F1) here should be /IM pair/. Sometimes written **impar** /IM par/. May mean 'unworthy', 'unconsidered,' or 'injurious.'

112. **translate** interpret. Here should be stressed on the 2nd syllable, the normal UK pronunciation. US /trănss LAYT, trănz-/; UK /trănss LAYT/ [trănz-, trahnz-, trahnss-, trunss-, trunz-].

The Complete Oxford begins Scene 4.7 here (line nos. in parentheses).

---

124. (8) *****commixtion** (Q) mixture. US /cuh MIKS shun/ [coh-], *rarely* [cŏm-]; UK /coh-/ [cŏm-, cuh-]. Variant of F1's **commixion** /-MIK shun/.

128. (12) **sinister** here should be /sin ISS tur/ left.

129. (13) **multipotent** /mŭl TIP uh tunt/ having power to do many things.

132. (16) **gainsay** here should be /gayn SAY/ forbid.

142. (26) **Neoptolemus** /nee up TŎL ih mus/, /nee ŏp-/ Achilles.

142. (26) **mirable** /MĪ ruh bł/ worthy of admiration.

143. (27) *****Oyes, Oyez** Hear ye. If preceding *loud'st* is one syllable, the *Oyes* is stressed on the 2nd syllable /oh YEZ/ [-YAY]; UK *also* [-YES]. If *loud'st* has two syllables, then *Oyes* is stressed on the 1st syllable as elsewhere in Shk, and most commonly today.

168. (52) *****extant** existing, present. Here stressed on the 1st syllable US /EK stunt/ [-stănt]; UK /-stănt/, *rarely* [-stunt]; in CN both are used equally. In the UK /ek STĂNT/ is usual.

172. (56) **imperious** /im PEER yus/ imperial.

179. (63) *****quondam** US /KWŎN dum/, *rarely* [-dam]; UK /-dam/, *rarely* [-dum] former.

186. (70) *****Perseus** /PUR syus/ [-syōōss], US *rarely* [-sōōss]. See App. D -eus.

194. (78) **wrastling** /RĂSS ling/ archaic variant of **wrestling**.

220. (103) **buss** /bŭS/ kiss.

232. (115) **exact** here should be /EG zact/.

255. (139) **stithied** /STIṬH eed/; US *also* /STIT̶H̶ eed/ forged.

275. (159) **taborins, tabourins** (F1) /TAB ur inz/ small drums. Omitted Q. See App. D *-or*.

Act 5 Scene 1

2. ***scimitar** US /SIM ih tar/ [-tur]; CN /-tar/; UK /-tur/ [-tar] a curved sword.

15, 16. **varlot** attendant. Archaic variant of **varlet**, both pronounced /VAR lut/.

19. **catarrhs** /kuh TAHRZ/ colds.

20. **cold palsies** /PAWL zeez/; UK *also* [PŎL-] paralysis.

21. **imposthume** (Q) /im PŎS chōōm/; UK *also* /-tyōōm, tyōōm/ abcess. Omitted F1.

21. **sciaticas** (Q) /sī AT ih kuz/ pains in the lower back. Omitted F1.

21. **lime-kills** (Q) /kilz/ psoriasis. Some eds. prefer mod. **lime kilns,** now usually pronounced /kilnz/, though /kilz/ is older. Omitted F1.

22. **rivell'd** (Q) /RIV łd/ wrinkled. Omitted F1.

30. **exasperate** exasperated. /eg ZĂSS pur ayt, -ut/; UK *also* /-ZAHSS-/.

31. **skein** /skayn/ loosely coiled yarn.

31. **sleave-silk** (Q) /SLEEV silk/ unfinished, soft silk. Variant of F1's **sleyd silk** /sleed/ which is derived from **sleaved** /sleevd/ **silk**. Some sources give /slayd/ based on a dialect variant.

31. **sarcenet, sarsenet** /SAR snit/ 'fine silk,' hence 'flimsy.'

ă-bat, ăir-**marry**, air-**pair**, a̯r-**far**, ĕr-**merry**, ĝ- **get**, ī-**high**, ĭr-**mirror**, ł-**little**, ṇ-**listen**, ŏ-**hot**, oh-**go**, ōō-**wood**, ōō-**moon**, oor-**tour**, ōr- **or**, ow-**how**, t̲h-**that**, t̶h̶-**thin**, ŭ-**but**, UR-**fur**, ur-**under**.   ( ) - suppress the syllable   see p. xiii for complete list.

32. **tossel** (F2) /TŎS ł/ archaic variant of **tassel** (F1).

61. **moile** /moyl/ archaic variant of **mule**.

61. **fitchook** (*Fichooke* Q) /FITCH o͞ok/ variant of F1's **fitchew** /FITCH o͞o/ polecat.

61. **lezard** /LEZ urd/ the original form of **lizard**.

62. **puttock** /PUTT uk/ a bird, the red kite.

65. ***lazar** /LAY zur, LAZZ ur/ leper.

75. **draught** US, CN /drăft/; UK, E.NEW ENG. /drahft/ latrine.

98. **varlots** 'scoundrels,' with play on *harlots* 'whores.' Archaic variant of **varlets**, both pronounced /VAR luts/.

Act 5 Scene 2

48. **palter** /PAWL tur/ use vague answers.

60. ***surety** guarantee, pledge. Here should be two syllables, though in mod. English, three syllables are more common, /SHUR (ih) tee, SHOOR-, SHOR-/ (see App. D).

120. **credence** /CREED n̩ss/ trust.

121. **esperance** /ES pur unss/ hope.

124. **calumniate** /cuh LUM nee ayt/ slander.

145. **perdition** /pur DISH un/; UK *also* [PUR DISH un] destruction.

151. **orifex** US /OR ih fecks/; E.COAST US, UK /ŎR ih fecks/ orifice.

152. **Ariachne's** /ăir ee AK neez/ should be **Arachne's** /uh RAK neez/ expert weaver in Gk. myth. Perhaps Shk. added the extra syllable in order to make the line scan correctly, or confused it with *Ariadne*.

159. **relics** (Q), **reliques** (F1) /REL iks/ remains.

170. **casque** /kăsk/; UK *also* [kahsk] helmet.

172. ***hurricano** waterspout. US /hur ih KAH noh, -KAY-/;
E.COAST US /huh rih-/; CN /hur ih KAH noh/ [-KAY-]; UK /huh rih KAY noh/
[-KAH-]. The older pronunciation is /-KAY-/.

173. **Constring'd** /cun STRINJD/ compressed.

177. **concupy** /CŎN kyoo pee/ Shk's invention meaning 'concubine.'

194. **commodious** /kuh MOH dee us/ accomodating.

Act 5 Scene 3

9. **Consort with me** /cun SORT/ join me.

53. **truncheon** /TRUN chun/ staff of office.

55. **recourse** repeatedly flowing. Here should be /rih CORSS/; US *also* /ree-/.

80. **bodements** /BOHD munts/ omens.

84. **dolors** (Q) (F1 has UK spelling **dolours**) /DOH lurz/; UK *also* /DŎL urz/
griefs. See App. D *-or*.

101. **tisick** archaic variant of ***phthisic** 'a lung disease, asthma.' Shk's spelling
reflects the traditional pronunciation /TIZ ik/. A variety of newer spelling
pronunciations also exist of which /THIZ ik/ is the most common, especially in
CN, UK.

104. **rheum** /rōōm/ tears.

Act 5 Scene 4

9. **arrant** /ĂIR unt/ archaic variant of **errand**.

19. **Styx** /stiks/ river of Hades.

ă-bat, ăir-marry, air-**pair**, ạr-**far**, ĕr-**merry**, ĝ- **get**, ī-**high**, ĭr-mirror, ł-little, ṇ-listen,
ŏ-hot, oh-go, ŏŏ-wood, ōō-moon, oor-tour, ōr- **or**, ow-how, ṭh-**that**, th-**thin**, ŭ-**but**,
UR-**fur**, ur-under.   ( ) - suppress the syllable   see p. xiii for complete list.

Act 5 Scene 5

4. *chastis'd punished. Here should be /chăss TĪZD/, the usual UK pronunciation, also used in North America. The usual US form has 1st syllable stress.

6. the fierce Polydamas if *fierce* is two syllables then /pŏl ih DAM us/; if *fierce* is one syllable then /puh LID uh mus/. The original Gk. had the former accentuation.

7. Menon /MEE nun/, but /-ŏn/ is becoming more common. See App. D *-on*.

8. Doreus /DOR yus/ [-yōōss]. See App. D *-eus*.

9. Colossus-wise /kuh LŎS us/ like a giant.

11. Epistrophus /ih PIS truh fus/.

11. Cedius /SEE dyus/.

11. Polyxenes, Polixenes /puh LIK sih neez/.

12. Amphimachus /am FIM uh kus/.

12. Thoas US /T̶H̶OH us/ [-ăss]; UK, CN /-ăss/ [-us]. Normal development would favor /-us/.

13. Palamedes /pal uh MEED eez/.

14. Sagittary US /SAJ ih tĕr ee/; UK /-tuh ree/ or /-tree/ half-man, half-horse.

20. Galathe /GAL uh t̶h̶e̶e̶/.

22. sculls /skullz/ archaic variant of schools (of fish).

25. *swath row of mown grass or grain. /swŏt̶h̶/;
UK *also* [swayt̶h̶, swaht̶h̶, swawt̶h̶]. /swăt̶h̶/ not recommended. The oldest forms are with /ŏ/ or UK /aw/. Some eds. prefer swathe /swayt̶h̶/.

Act 5 Scene 6

26. reak, reck /rek/ care.

Act 5 Scene 7 (*Complete Oxford* 5.8)

10, 11. (5.8. 2,3) **'Loo** (F4) /loo/, **Lowe** (Q, F1) /loh/. Both are cries to attract attention.

Act 5 Scene 8 (*The Complete Oxford* 5.9)

1. **putrefied** /PYOO͞ trih fī id/ rotted.

13. **amain** /uh MAYN/ with full force.

Act 5 Scene 9 (*The Complete Oxford* 5.10)

4. **bruit** /broo͞t/ noise.

Act 5 Scene 10 (*The Complete Oxford* 5.11)

16, 34. **aye** /ay/ always. /ī/ is often used, but not recommended.

19. **Niobes** /NĪ (uh) beez, -(oh) beez/ Niobe wept endlessly when her children were killed.

24. **pight** (F1) /pīt/. Q has **pitched** (*pitcht*).

33. **Ignominy** (Q) /IG nuh min ee/ disgrace. **Ignomy and** (F1) /IG nuh mee/.

41. **humble-bee** pronounced with the same stress as *bumble bee*.

54. **Winchester** /WIN chih stur/; US *also* /WIN chess tur/.

ă-bat, ăir-**marry**, air-**pair**, ạr-**far**, ĕr-**merry**, ĝ- **get**, ī-**high**, ĭr-**mirror**, ł-**little**, ṇ-**listen**, ŏ-**hot**, oh-**go**, o͝o-**wood**, o͞o-**moon**, oor-**tour**, ōr- **or**, ow-**how**, ţh-**that**, th-**thin**, ŭ-**but**, UR-**fur**, ur-**under**.   ( ) - suppress the syllable   see p. xiii for complete list.

Twelfth Night

People in the Play

Sometimes some of these names are given an Italian pronunciation in performance. These pronunciations are indicated here as accurately as possible within the limits of this notation. Shakespeare, however, probably intended them to be anglicized.

Sir Andrew Aguecheek /AY gy$\overline{oo}$ cheek/.

Antonio 3 or 4 syllables depending on meter /an TOHN (ee) yoh/; Ital. /ahn-/.

Cesario 3 or 4 syllables depending on meter /suh ZAH r(ee) yoh/; Ital. /chay-/.

Curio /KYUR ee yoh, KYOOR-/; Ital. /K$\overline{OO}$R-/.

Fabian occurs in verse once and should be 2 syllables. /FAY b(ee) yun/. In prose it may be 3.

Feste /FESS tee/.

***Jaques** usually /JAY kweez/ in Shk. His name is not spoken. See *As You Like It,* "People in the Play."

Malvolio in verse always 3 syllables /mal VOH l(ee) yoh/.

***Maria** /muh R$\overline{I}$ uh/ is the older, angl. form, /muh REE uh/ is newer. In CN the latter is more frequent, in the UK, US both are used equally. Note that some scholars prefer the form /muh R$\overline{I}$ uh/ in this play, but /muh REE uh/ for the character in LLL.

Olivia always 3 syllables in verse /uh-, oh LIV (ee) yuh/.

Orsino /or SEE noh/.

Sebastian US /suh B$\breve{A}$S chun/; UK /suh B$\breve{A}$ST yun/.

Valentine /VAL in t$\overline{i}$n/.

People in the Play (cont.)

*Viola angl. /VĪ uh luh/ is more common than [VEE oh luh] based on Ital.

Places in the Play

Illyria 3 or 4 syllables depending on meter /ih LĬR (ee) yuh/.

Act 1 Scene 1

2. **excess** here should be /ek SESS/, the most common UK form.

Act 1 Scene 2

4. ***Elysium** the realm of the blessed in the after-life. US /ih LEEZH ee um/ [-LIZ-, -LIZH-, -LEESS-, -LISS-]; UK /-LIZ-/; *also* /ee-/ in all countries. The oldest forms still in use are /-LIZ-/, /-LIZH-/. The historic form is /ih LIZH um/ here expanded to 4 syllables /ih LIZH ee um/.

15. **Arion** /uh RĪ un/ Gk. poet. Sometimes newer /-ŏn/ is used, but is not recommended. See App. D *-on*.

40. **abjur'd** /ab-, ub JOORD/; US *also* /-JURD/ renounced.

56, 62. **eunuch** /YOO nuk/ castrated male.

Act 1 Scene 3

14. ***quaffing** /KWŎF ing/; UK *rarely* [KWAHF-] drinking freely. /KWĂF-/ is also used, but is not recommended.

26. **viol-de-gamboys** a cello-like instrument. An unusual variant of *viol-de-gamba* /VĪ ł duh GAM buh/, or with the Italian vowel, /GAHM buh/. The ending *-oys* may have been just an alternative way of spelling the sound /-uz/, i.e., /GAM buz/.

31. **allay** /uh LAY/ put to rest.

40. **coystrill, coistrel** /COY strł/ knave.

ă-bat, ăir-marry, air-pair, ạr-far, ĕr-merry, ĝ- get, ī-high, ĭr-mirror, ł-little, ṇ-listen, ŏ-hot, oh-go, ŏŏ-wood, ōō-moon, oor-tour, ōr- or, ow-how, ţh-that, ŧh-thin, ŭ-but, UR-fur, ur-under.　　　　( ) - suppress the syllable　　　see p. xiii for complete list.

42. **Castiliano vulgo** /kas til YAN oh VUL goh/, /-YAHN oh/ meaning uncertain, perhaps 'speak of the devil.'

90, 91. **Pourquoi** /po͞or KWAH/ Fr. 'why.'

102. **distaff** cleft staff used in spinning thread. US /DIS stăf/; E.NEW ENG., UK /DIS stahf/.

103. ***huswife** hussy. /HUZ if/ is traditional, /HUSS wīf/ is a newer, spelling pronunciation. The former is the most common form in the UK, the latter in the US. In CN both are used equally. In North America /HUSS wif/ is also sometimes used. Some eds. prefer **housewife**.

113. **masques** US /măsks/; UK, E. NEW ENG. /mahsks/ [măsks] masked dancing and pantomime.

115. **kickshawses** /KICK shaw ziz/ gew-gaws.

120-33. **galliard** /GAL yurd/; UK *also newer* /GAL ee ard/ a lively dance.

127. **Mistress Mall's** /mawlz/ would be the usual pronunciation with this spelling, but here probably /mŏllz/, as in *Molly.*

129. ***coranto** courant, a type of dance. US /coh-, cuh RAHN toh/ [-RAN-]; UK /cŏr AHN toh, -AN toh/.

130. **sink-a-pace** some eds. prefer **cinquepace** 'lively dance,' both pronounced /SINK uh payss/ or sometimes /SINK payss/.

135. **dun-color'd.** Some eds. prefer ***divers-coloured** various-colored. US, CN /DĪ vurss, -vurz/ [dī-, dih VURSS]; UK /DĪ vurss/ [-vurz, dī VURSS].

Act 1 Scene 4

16. **access** here should be /ak SESS/.

28. ***nuntio's, nuncio's** messenger's. US /NO͞ON see ohz/ [NUN-]; UK /NUN see ohz/, *rarely* [NO͞ON see ohz]. Normal development would favor [NUN shohz], now rare.

30. **belie** /bih-, bee LĪ/ misrepresent.

32. **rubious** /RO͞OB yus/ ruby-red.

34. **semblative** /SEM bluh tiv/ resembling.

Act 1 Scene 5

35. **Quinapalus** /kwin AP uh lus/ name made up by Feste.

50. **syllogism** /SIL uh jizm/ a framework for logically analyzing an argument.

55. **Misprision** /mis PRIZH un, -n̥/ misunderstanding.

56.   **Cucullus   non   facit   monachum**
Ang.Lat. /kyo͞o KŬL us   nŏn   FAY sit MŎN uh kum/
Class.Lat. /ko͞o Ko͞oL o͞os   nŏn   FAH kit MŎN ah ko͞om/.
         'the hood does not make the monk.'

57. **motley** /MŎT lee/ costume of different colored cloth worn by fools.

62. **catechize** /KAT uh kīz/ to instruct through a series of questions and answers.

81. **twopence** /TUP n̥ss, -unss/.

97. ***indue** /in DYO͞O/; US *also* [-DO͞O] endow. Some eds. prefer **endue** /en-/.

97. **leasing** /LEE zing/ lying.

115. ***pia mater** here 'the brain.' Ang.Lat. /PĪ uh MAYT ur/ is older; Class.Lat. /PEE uh MAHT ur/ is newer and much more common. Forms that mix old and new are also used.

132. **draught** US, CN /drăft/; UK, E.NEW ENG. /drahft/ drink.

157. **peascod** /PEEZ cŏd/ peapod.

175. **comptible** /COWNT ih bł/ sensitive to. Some eds. prefer **'countable**. See App. D *accompt*.

209. ***homage** /HŎM ij/; US *also* /ŎM ij/ dues due a superior lord.

217. **profanation** /prŏf uh NAY shun/ desecration.

228. **heresy** /HĔR ih see/ dissent from the dominant thinking.

ă-b**at**, ăir-m**arry**, air-p**air**, a̧r-f**ar**, ĕr-m**erry**, ĝ- g**et**, ī-h**igh**, ïr-m**irror**, ł-litt**le**, n̥-list**en**, ŏ-h**ot**, oh-g**o**, o͞o-w**ood**, o͞o-m**oon**, oor-t**our**, ōr- **or**, ow-h**ow**, t̪h-t**hat**, th-t**hin**, Ŭ-b**ut**, UR-f**ur**, ur-und**er**.   ( ) - suppress the syllable   see p. xiii for complete list.

245. ***divers** various. US, CN /DĪ vurss, -vurz/ [dī-, dih VURSS];
UK /DĪ vurss/ [-vurz, dī VURSS].

254. ***nonpareil** one without equal. /nŏn puh RELL/ is the oldest form, still
common in the US, but now vanished from the UK and CN, where it has been
replaced with /nŏn puh RAYL/ [-RAY], based on mod. Fr. /-RAY/ is also
common in the US. /-RĪ, -RĪL/ are occasionally heard, but not recommended.
Sometimes 1st syllable stress is used.

270. **cantons** /KANT unz/ songs. Archaic variant of **cantos**.

272. **Hallow** /huh LOH/ or /HAL-, HŎL oh/ shout. Some eds. prefer **Halloo**
/huh LOO/.

272. **reverberate** /ree-, rih VUR bur ut, -ayt/ echoing. /-ut/ is more usual for an
adj.

293. **blazon** /BLAY zun, -zṇ/ description of a coat of arms, i.e., praise.

Act 2 Scene 1

11. **determinate** /dih-, dee TUR mih nut/ intended.

17. **Rodorigo, Roderigo** /rŏd ur REE goh/.

18. **Messaline** /MESS uh leen/.

Act 2 Scene 3

2. **deliculo surgere** Ang.Lat. /dih LICK yuh loh   SUR jur ee/ abbreviated form
of a proverb 'to get up at dawn is very healthful.' *Deliculo* is either Tobey's or
Shk's error for **diluculo** Ang.Lat. /dih LUCK yuh loh/;
Class.Lat. /dee LOO koo loh SOOR ĝer ay/.

14. **stoup** /stoop/ tankard.

23. **Pigrogromitus** name made up by Feste. /pī groh-, pig roh GRŎM ih tus/,
/pig roh groh MĪ tus/.

23. **Vapians** /VAY pee unz/.

24. **equinoctial** /ek wih NŎK shł/ [eek-] equator.

24. **Queubus** /KYOO bus/.

25, 31. **sixpence** /SIKS punss, -pṇss/; US *also* /SIKS penss/.

25. ***leman** sweetheart. US /LEE mun/ [LEM un, LAY mun]; CN /LAY mun/, *sometimes* [LEM un, LEE mun]; UK /LEM-/ [LEE mun], *rarely* [LAY mun]. /LAY mun/ is newer and not recommended.

26. **impeticos** /im PET ee kohz/ or /im PET ih kohz/ comic word meaning 'to pocket.'

26. **gratillity, gratility** /gruh TIL ih tee/ an invented variant of *gratuity*.

28. **Mermidons** a tavern. /MUR mih dunz, -dŏnz/; /-ŏn/ is usual in the US, /-un/ is more common in the UK. Archaic variant of **Myrmidons**, pronounced the same way. See App. D *-on*.

33. **testril** /TEST rł/ sixpence.

53. **mellifluous** /muh LIF loo us/ sweetly flowing.

56. **dulcet** /DULL sit/ sweet.

62. ***By'r lady** /bīr-, bur LAY dee/ by Our Lady (i.e., Mary).

72. **caterwauling** /KAT ur wawl ing/ yowling.

75. **Cataian** /cat-, cuh TAY un/ a person from China, i.e., scoundrel. Variant of **Cathayan** /cath-, cuh THAY un/ which some eds. prefer. Others suggest **Catharan** /CATH uh run, cuh THAIR un/ puritan.

76. **Peg a' Ramsey, Peg o' Ramsey** a term of contempt. *a'* and *o'* are /uh/ 'of.'

77. **consanguineous** /cŏn sang GWIN ee us/ related by blood.

90. **coziers'** US /KOH zhurz/ [KOH zyurz/; UK /KOH zyurz/ cobblers'.

120. **stope** /stohp/ tankard. Archaic variant of **stoup** /sto͞op/.

135. **an ayword** /AY wurd/ byword. Most eds. prefer **nayword** /NAY wurd/. Notice that *an ayword* would be pronounced nearly the same as *a nayword*.

ă-bat, ăir-marry, air-pair, ạr-far, ĕr-merry, ĝ- get, ī-high, ĭr-mirror, ł-little, ṇ-listen, ŏ-hot, oh-go, o͝o-wood, o͞o-moon, oor-tour, ōr- or, ow-how, ṭh-that, t̲h̲-thin, ŭ-but, UR-fur, ur-under.   ( ) - suppress the syllable   see p. xiii for complete list.

150. **swarths** /swōrt̶h̶s̶/ archaic and dialect variant of ***swaths** 'rows of mowed grass or grain, i.e., large amounts.'   /swŏt̶h̶s̶/; UK *also* [swayt̶h̶s̶, swaht̶h̶s̶, swawt̶h̶s̶]. /swăt̶h̶s̶/ not recommended. The oldest forms are with /ŏ/ or UK /aw/. Some eds. prefer **swathes** /swayt̲hz/.

155. **epistles** /ih-, ee PISS l̶z/ letters. /ee-/ non-standard in the UK.

177. **Penthesilea** queen of the Amazons. /pen t̶h̶uh sih LEE uh/ is older; /-LAY uh/ is the restored pronunciation.

Act 2 Sceen 4

3. **antique** ancient. Here /AN teek/, *rarely older* [AN tik]. Some eds. prefer **antic** /AN tik/ quaint.

46. **chaunt** archaic variant of **chant** US /chănt/; E. NEW ENG, UK /chahnt/. See App. D -*aun*-.

60. **strown** /strohn/ archaic variant of F1's **strewn**, here rhymes with *thrown*.

74, **taffata, taffeta** /TAF uh tuh/ a silk-like cloth.

112. **damask** /DAM usk/ pink or light red.

114. **sate** archaic variant of **sat**. May have been /sayt/ or /sat/.

124. **denay** /dee-, dih NAY/ archaic variant of *denial.*

Act 2 Scene 5

5. **niggardly** /NIG urd lee/ miserly.

19. **contemplative** daydreaming. In verse always /cun TEMP luh tiv/. but in this prose passage may be /CŎN tem play tiv/.

20. **Close** /clohss/ keep hidden.

33. **'Slight** /zlīt/ by God's light.

40. **Strachy, Strachey** /STRAY chee/.

40. **yeoman** /YOH mun/ an attendant.

70. ***prerogative** /pur RŎG uh tiv/ [prih-, pree-] right, privilege. /pree-/ non-standard in the UK.

83. **gin** /jin/ snare.

92, 105. **Lucrece** Lucretia, Roman who commited suicide after being raped. The second instance should be /LŌŌ creess/, the first is prose and may be the usual mod. /lōō CREESS/ (for /lyōō-/ see App. D *lu-*).

108. ***fustian** /FUSS tee un/; US *also* /FUSS chun/ nonsensical. Normal development would favor the latter.

113. **staniel** /STAN yl̸/ inferior hawk, i.e., useless person. Some eds. prefer F1's **stallion**.

123. **Sowter** /SOWT ur/ hound's name.

129. **consonancy** /CŎN suh nun see/ agreement.

148. ***inure** /in YOOR/; US *also* [in OOR], US, CN *rarely* [in YUR] accustom.

149. **slough** /sluff/ skin.

160. **champian** /CHAM pee un/ open country. Variant of ***champaign** /sham PAYN/ [SHAM payn]; US *sometimes* [CHAM payn]. The latter form is the oldest.

161. **politic** /PŎL ih tik/ shrewd.

163. **point-devise, -device** /POYNT dih VĪSS/ fastidious.

181. **Sophy** /SOH fee/ Shah of Persia.

196. ***aqua-vitae** distilled liquor, e.g., brandy. US /AHK-, AK wuh VEE tī/, *rarely* [-VĪ tee]; CN /AK wuh VEE tī/ [AHK-]; UK /AK wuh VEE tī/ [-VEE tuh]. /AK wuh VĪ tee/ is the oldest surviving form. /-VEE tay/ not recommended.

205. **Tartar** /TAR tur/ hell.

ă-bat, ăir-m**a**rry, air-p**ai**r, ar-f**a**r, ĕr-m**e**rry, ĝ- g**e**t, ī-h**i**gh, ĭr-m**i**rror, l̸-litt**le**, n̩-list**en**, ŏ-h**o**t, oh-g**o**, ōō-w**oo**d, ōō-m**oo**n, oor-t**our**, ōr- **or**, ow-h**ow**, th-**th**at, t̶h̶-**th**in, ŭ-b**u**t, UR-f**ur**, ur-und**er**.　　( ) - suppress the syllable　　see p. xiii for complete list.

Act 3 Scene 1

2,10. **tabor** /TAY bur/ small drum. See App. D -*or*.

12. **chev'ril, cheveril** /SHEV rł/ or /SHEV ur rł/ kidskin, i.e., pliable.

34. **pilchers** /PIL churz/ sardines. Archaic variant of **pilchards** /PIL churdz/.

51. **Pandarus** /PAN duh rus/ a pimp.

51. **Phrygia** /FRIJ uh, FRIJ ee uh/. Normal development would favor the former.

52, 55. **Cressida** /CRESS ih duh/.

56. **conster** /CŎN stur/ explain.

64. **haggard** /HAG urd/ wild hawk.

71. **Dieu vous garde, monsieur** /dyö vōō GARD mö syö/ Fr.: God save you, sir.

72. **Et vous aussi, votre serviteur** /ay vōōz oh SEE, voht ᵘʰ sĕr vee tör/ Fr.: And you too, your servant.

124. ***grize** /grīz/ step, degree. Variant of **grise** /grīss, grīz/, **grece** /greess/, **grice** /grīss/.

151. **maugre** /MAW gur/ in spite of.

Act 3 Scene 2

13. **'Slight** /zlīt/ by God's light.

31. **as lief** /leef/ as soon.

42. **martial** /MAR shł/ warlike.

47. **bed of Ware** /wair/ famous large bedstead.

52. **cubiculo** /kyōō BIK yuh loh/ from Ital. 'little bedchamber.'

65. ***presage** indication. US, UK /PRESS ij/ [pree-, prih SAYJ]; CN /pree-, prih SAYJ/ [PRESS ij].

70. **renegado** renouncer of his religion. /ren uh GAY doh/ is older, /-GAH doh/ is newer.

75. **pedant** /PED ṇt/ dull teacher.

Act 3 Scene 3

18. **reliques, relics** /REL iks/ ancient monuments.

31. **Albeit** /awl BEE (i)t/ although.

Act 3 Scene 4

68. **slough** /sluff/ skin.

74. **lim'd** /līmd/ caught in a trap made of lime paste.

116. **Sathan** archaic form of **Satan**, both pronounced /SAYT ṇ, -un/ the devil.

117. **collier** /CŎL yur/; UK *also* /CŎL ee yur/ coal miner.

196. *****cockatrices** /CŎCK uh triss iz, -trĭss iz/ monsters whose gaze kills.

202. **unchary** /un CHAIR ee/; E.COAST US *also* /-CHĂIR-/ carelessly.

224. *****yare** /yair/; US *also* /yạr/ prompt.

238. *****implacable** /im PLAK uh bł/ cannot be appeased.

240. **sepulchre** /SEP ł kur/ tomb.

261. **mortal arbitrement, arbitrament** /ạr BIT ruh munt/ trial by combat to the death.

274. **firago** /fih RAH goh, -RAY-/ female warrior. Variant of *****virago** /vih RAH goh/; US *also older* [-RAY-]. US, CN [VĬR uh goh] not recommended.

275. **scabbard** /SKAB urd/ sword sheath.

279. **Sophy** /SOH fee/ Shah of Persia.

ă-bat, ăir-**ma**rry, air-**pair**, ạr-**far**, ĕr-**merry**, ĝ- **get**, ī-**high**, ĭr-**mir**ror, ł-**little**, ṇ-**listen**, ŏ-**hot**, oh-**go**, o͞o-**wood**, o͞o-**moon**, oor-**tour**, ōr- **or**, ow-**how**, ţh-**that**, ŧh-**thin**, ŭ-**but**, UR-**fur**, ur-un**der**.   ( ) - suppress the syllable   see p. xiii for complete list.

287. **Capilet** /KAP ih let/. Some eds. prefer **Capulet** /-yuh-, -uh-/.

289. **perdition** /pur DISH un/; UK *also* [PUR-] destruction.

307. **duello** /dōō EL oh/; UK, SOUTH. US *also* /dyōō-/ duelling code.

385. **paltry** /PAWL tree/ worthless.

391. **'Slid** /zlid/ by God's eyelid.

Act 4 Scene 1

31. **twopence** /TUP n̩ss, -unss/.

44. ***malapert** here should have 1st syllable stress /MAL uh purt/ saucy.

51. **Rudesby** /RŌŌDZ bee/ rude person.

62. **Lethe** /LEE̶T̶H̶ ee/ river of forgetfulness in Hades.

Act 4 Scene 2

2-101. **Sir Topas** probably an older spelling of **Topaz**, both pronounced /TOH paz/. Sometimes a spelling pronunciation /TOH păss/ is used, but this is not recommended.

2, 21. **curate** /KYOOR ut/; US *also* /KYUR ut/ priest.

8. **studient** /STŌŌD yunt/; UK, SOUTH. US /STYŌŌD-/. Archaic variant of **student**.

12. **Bonos dies** angl. /BOH nohss/ or /BOH nus DĪ eez/ Feste's version of Lat. *Bonus dies*, Class.Lat. /BŎN ōōs DIH ess/ or Sp. *Buenos días* /BWAY nohss DEE ahss/ 'good day.'

13. **Prague** /prahg/.

14. **King Gorboduc** /GOR buh duck/ legendary king of England.

25. **hyperbolical** /hī pur BŎL ih kł/ raving.

31. **Sathan** archaic form of **Satan**, both pronounced /SAYT n̩, -un/ the devil.

37. **barricadoes** /băir ih KAY dohz/ is older, /-KAH dohz/ is newer. Archaic variant of *barricades.*

37. **clerestories** /CLEER stor eez/ windows in upper wall.

42. **thou errest** /UR ist, ĔR ist/. The former is older.

50, 58. ***Pythagoras** US /pih THAG uh rus/ [pī-]; UK /pī-/ Gk. philosopher.

52, 60. ***grandam** /GRAN dam/; US *rarely* [-dum] grandmother. Informally /GRAN um/.

75. ***perdie, perdy** /PUR DEE/ 'by God, indeed.' Some eds. prefer the variant **pardie** /par DEE/.

100. **God buy you** good bye. Some eds. substitute **God b'wi' you** /gŏd BWEE yōō/ or some other variation of that phrase.

126. **lath** US /lăth/; UK, E. NEW ENG. /lahth/ [lăth] narrow strip of wood.

131. **goodman** /GŌoD mun/ title of a man under the rank of gentleman.

Act 4 Scene 3

24. **chantry** US /CHĂNT ree/; UK, E. NEW ENG. /CHAHN tree/ chapel.

27. **jealious** /JEL yus/ archaic variant of **jealous**.

Act 5 Scene 1

36. **Primo, secundo, tertio** firstly, secondly, thirdly. Perhaps part of a child's game or dice game. Ang.Lat. /PRĪ moh, suh KUN doh, TUR shee oh/ or /-shoh/; restored Latin /PREE moh, sek KŌoN doh, TĔR shee oh/.

55. **draught** US, CN /drăft/; UK, E.NEW ENG. /drahft/ depth of water needed by a ship to float.

56. **scathful** /SKATH full/ harmful. Variant of **scatheful** /SKAYTH-/.

109. ***fulsome** distasteful. /FULL sum/; US *rarely* [FŬL-].

ă-bat, ăir-marry, air-pair, ar-far, ĕr-merry, ĝ- get, ī-high, ĭr-mirror, l-little, n-listen, ŏ-hot, oh-go, ōō-wood, ōō-moon, oor-tour, ōr- or, ow-how, th-that, th-thin, ŭ-but, UR-fur, ur-under.   ( ) - suppress the syllable   see p. xiii for complete list.

113. **ingrate** here should be /in GRAYT/ ungrateful.

120. **savors nobly** (UK **savours**) /SAY vurz/ has the characteristics of nobility.

132. *__jocund__ /JŎCK und/; US, CN *rarely* [JOHK-] merry.

147. **propriety** /pruh PRĪ ih tee/ identity.

182. **incardinate** /in CAR dih nut, -ayt/ Aguecheek's mistake for **incarnate** /in CAR nut/ [-nayt] 'in the flesh.' /-ut/ is usual for adjs.

200-1. **passy-measures pavin** /PĂSS ee-/, /PAV in/ slow, stately dance. Archaic variant of *__pavan__ US /puh VAHN/ [-VAN]; UK /-VAHN, -VAN/.

217. **natural perspective** Shk probably intended /NATCH rł PUR spek tiv/, but it could also be /NATCH ur ł pur SPEK tiv/ with an epic caesura.

232. **Messaline** /MESS uh leen/.

246. **record** here should be /rek-, rik ORD/.

263. **betroth'd** /bih-, bee TROHT̞HD/ engaged to be married.

276. *__durance__ /DYOOR unss/; US *also* /Do͞oR-/ [DUR-] imprisonment.

284. **Belzebub** /BEL zih bub/ a devil. Archaic variant of **Beelzebub** /bee EL zih bub/.

285. **stave's** /stayvz/ staff's.

287. **epistles** /ih-, ee PISS łz/ letters. /ee-/ non-standard in the UK.

296. **vox** /vŏks/ voice, dramatic reading.

299. **perpend** /pur PEND/ consider.

314. **savors** (UK **savours**) /SAY vurz/ has the characteristic of.

372. **Sir Topas** probably an older spelling of **Topaz**, both pronounced /TOH paz/. Sometimes a spelling pronunciation /TOH păss/ is used, but this is not recommended.

376. **whirligig** /WHUR lee ĝig/ spinning top.

382. **convents** /cun VENTS/ suits.

The Two Gentlemen of Verona

People in the Play

Sometimes some of these names are given an Italian pronunciation in performance. These pronunciations are indicated here as accurately as possible within the limits of this notation. Shakespeare, however, probably intended them to be anglicized.

Antonio /an TOH nyoh/; Ital. /ahn-/. **Anthonio** (F1) pronounced the same way.

*Eglamour US, CN /EG luh moor/ [-mor]; UK /-mor/ [-moor].

*Launce US /lawnss/ [lahnss, lănss]; CN /lawnss/ [lănss]; UK /lawnss/ [lahnss]. Note that in CN and some parts of US /aw/ and /ah/ are pronounced the same, and that in Standard British and E.New Eng. /lahnss/ corresponds to US /lănss/ (see also App. D -aun-). The mod. spelling of this name is **Lance** /lănss, lahnss/ which some eds. prefer.

Lucetta /lōō SET uh/; Ital. /lōō CHET tah/ (for /lyōō-/ see App. D lu-).

Milan, Duke of /MILL un/ this name is not spoken.

Panthino /pan THEE noh/; Ital. /pahn TEE noh/.

*Proteus 2 or 3 syllables depending on meter /PROH t(ee) yus/; UK, CN also [-tyōōss]. See App. D -eus.

*Thurio in verse always 2 syllables. US /THOOR (ee) yoh/ [THUR-], rarely [THYOOR-]; CN /THUR ee oh/ [THOOR-]; UK /THUR-, THOOR-/ [THYOOR-]; Ital. /TOOR ree yoh/.

Ursula 2 syllables, /URSS luh/, in its sole appearance, 4.4.117.

Valentine /VAL in tīn/. 1.2.38 **Valentine's** is two syllables /VAL (i)n tīnz/. **Valentinus** /val en TĪ nus/.

ă-bat, ăir-ma**rry**, air-p**air**, ạr-f**ar**, ĕr-me**rry**, ĝ- g**et**, ī-h**igh**, ĭr-mi**rror**, ł-li**ttle**, ṇ-li**sten**, ŏ-h**ot**, oh-g**o**, ōō-w**ood**, ōō-m**oon**, oor-t**our**, ōr- **or**, ow-h**ow**, ţh-th**at**, th-th**in**, ŭ-b**ut**, UR-f**ur**, ur-und**er**.   ( ) - suppress the syllable   see p. xiii for complete list.

Places in the Play

Mantua here 2 syllables US /MAN chwuh/; UK /MAN tywuh/ [MAN chwuh].

Milan here should be /MILL un/.
  Milano angl. /mih LAN oh/; Ital. /mee LAHN oh/.

Verona /vĕr-, vur ROH nuh/.

Act 1 Scene 1

16. *****environ** /en VĪ run/; US *also* [-urn] surround.

22. **Leander** /lee AN dur/ he swam the Hellespont to be with Hero.

22. **Hellespont** /HEL iss pŏnt/ the Dardenelles.

26. **swom** most eds. prefer **swum** or **swam**. The meaning here is 'swam,' but in older forms of Eng. the past tense could be written all three ways. Whether *swom* was meant to indicate /swum/ or /swŏm/ is unclear. For simplicity use /swăm/; for an archaic flavor use /swum/, which is still used in dialects on both sides of the Atlantic.

38. **cavil** /KAV ł/; UK *also* /KAV il/ quibble.

49. *****verdure** freshness. US, CN /VUR jur, -dyoor, -dyur/;
UK /-dyoor/ [-dyur, -jur]. See App. D -*ure*.

52. **votary** /VOHT uh ree/ someone devoted to something or someone.

112. **Nod-ay . . . noddy** /nŏd ī . . . NŎD ee/ *noddy* 'simpleton.'

145. **testern'd** /TEST urnd/ gave someone a *tester* (sixpence).

152. **deign** /dayn/ accept.

Act 1 Scene 2

5. **parle** /pạrl/ talk.

12. **Mercatio** /mur KAY shee yoh/.

36. **contents** here /cŏn TENTS/.

56. **the profferer construe "ay"** here *profferer* should be *proff'rer*, and *construe* /CŎN strōō/.

80. **Light o' love** /uh/ of.

91. **descant** /DES kănt/ melody sung above the main tune.

96. ***protestation*** US /proh tess-, prŏt ess TAY shun/; CN /prŏt ess-/ [proh tess-]; UK /prŏt ess-/.

106. **Unkind** here should be /UN kīnd/.

112. **throughly** archaic variant of *thoroughly.* /T̶H̶RŌŌ lee/ is the normal pronunciation on stage, but to enhance clarity a syncopated form of the modern pronunciation may used: *thor'ghly.*

121. **forlorn** here should be /FOR lorn/.

134. **month's mind** strong desire. Here an older form /MUN̶T̶H̶ iz/ is indicated.

Act 1 Scene 3

13, 17. ***importune*** /im POR chun/ ask insistently. See App. D.

23. **perfected** here should be /PUR fikt id/ fully informed.

39. **Don Alphonso** /dŏn al FŎN zoh/ [-soh].

71. **Excuse it not, for I am peremptory** 'resolved.' If *I am* is contracted to *I'm,* then /pur EM tur ee/ which is more common today. If *I am* is spoken as two words then /PĔR um tree/ which is also used today. Both appear elsewhere in Shk.

Act 2 Scene 1

20. **malecontent** discontented person. Archaic variant of ***malcontent***, both pronounced /MAL cun tent/; CN, UK *rarely* [mal cun TENT].

24. ***grandam*** /GRAN dam/; US *rarely* [-dum] grandmother. Informally /GRAN um/.

ă-bat, ăir-**marry**, air-**pair**, ạr-**far**, ĕr-**merry**, ĝ- **get**, ī-**high**, ĭr-**mirror**, ł-**little**, ṇ-**listen**, ŏ-**hot**, oh-**go**, ōō-**wood**, ōō-**moon**, oor-**tour**, ōr- **or**, ow-**how**, ţh-**that**, t̶h̶-**thin**, ŭ-**but**, UR-**fur**, ur-**under**.   ( ) - suppress the syllable   see p. xiii for complete list.

25. **puling** /PY$\overline{OO}$L ing/ whining.

26. ***Hallowmas** All Saints Day, Nov. 1. US /HŎL-, HAL oh muss/ [-măss];
UK /HAL oh măss/ [-muss]. The older form is /-muss/.

39. ***urinal** US /YUR ih nł/ [YOOR-]; UK /YOOR ih nł, y$\overline{oo}$ RĪ nł/ vessel to hold
urine.

82. **swing'd** /swinjd/ beat.

174. **victuals** /VIT łz/ food.

Act 2 Scene 2

11. ***mischance** in verse normally with 2nd syllable stress.

Act 2 Scene 3

12. ***grandam** /GRAN dam/; US *rarely* [-dum] grandmother. Informally
/GRAN um/.

27. **wood woman** /w$\overline{oo}$d/ 'crazy, distraught' with a pun on 'wooden.' It was also
/w$\overline{oo}$d, wohd/ in the dialects of North. Eng. Some eds. prefer **moved**.

Act 2 Scene 4

43. ***exchequer** /eks CHEK ur/; US *rarely* [EKS chek ur] treasury.

79. **potentates** /POHT n tayts/ rulers.

91. **fealty** /FEE ł tee/ faithfulness.

130. **imperious** /im PEER yus/ imperial.

146. ***paragon** US /PĂIR uh gŏn/ [-gun]; CN /-gŏn/; UK /-gun/ [-gn̩] most perfect
example.

160. **vesture** /VES chur/ clothing. See App. D *-ure.*

164. **braggadism** /BRAG ud izm/ boastfulness. Archaic variant of **braggartism**
/BRAG urt izm/ or **braggardism** /-urd-/.

179. **betroth'd** /bih-, bee TROHṬHD/ engaged to be married.

Act 2 Scene 5

9. **five pence** /FĪV punss, -pṇss/; US *also* /-penss/.

Act 2 Scene 6

stage direction: solus /SOH lŭss/ alone.

26. **Ethiope** /EE ~~thee~~ ohp/ person from Ethiopia.

Act 2 Scene 7

2. **And ev'n in kind love I do *conjure thee** entreat. If *ev'n* is spoken as one syllable then *conjure* is stressed on the first syllable, the most common pronunciation today, US, CN /CŎN jur/, *rarely* [CUN-]; UK /CUN jur/ [CŎN-]. But if *ev'n* is two syllables, then older /cun JOOR/ is required, now a rare pronunciation.

4. **character'd** written down. Here with second syllable stress.

22. **extreme** here should be /EK streem/.

37. **turmoil** here should be /tur MOIL/.

38. ***Elysium** the realm of the blessed in the after-life. US /el-, il LEEZH ee um/ [-LIZ-, -LIZH-, -LEESS-, -LISS-]; UK /-LIZ-/; *also* /ee-/ in all countries. The oldest forms still in use are /-LIZ-/, /-LIZH-/. The historic form is /ih LIZH um/ here expanded to 4 syllables /ih LIZH ee um/.

41. **lascivious** /luh SIV yus/ lustful.

49. ***breeches** /BRITCH iz/ is traditional, /BREECH iz/ is newer. The former pronunciation is more common in the UK, and the latter in the US, CN.

88. **in *lieu thereof** US, CN /loo, lyoo/; UK /lyoo/ [loo] in return for.

ă-bat, ăir-**marry**, air-**pair**, ạr-**far**, ĕr-**merry**, ĝ- get, ī-**high**, ĭr-**mirror**, ł-**little**, ṇ-**listen**, ŏ-**hot**, oh-go, o͞o-**wood**, o͞o-**moon**, oor-**tour**, ōr- or, ow-**how**, ţh-**that**, ŧħ-**thin**, ŭ-**but**, UR-**fur**, ur-**under**.   ( ) - suppress the syllable   see p. xiii for complete list.

Act 3 Scene 1

47. **pretense** (UK **pretence**) design. Here should be /prih TENSS/, the normal UK pronunciation, or /pree TENSS/ based on the most common US pronunciation /PREE tenss/.

56. **tenure** archaic variant of **tenor**, both /TEN ur/.

68. **froward** /FROH wurd, FROH urd/ difficult to deal with.

102. *__extol__ praise. /ek STOHL/; UK *sometimes* and US *rarely* [-STŎL].

109. **access** here should be /ak SESS/.

112. *__recourse__ access. Here should be /rih CORSS/, the usual UK pronunciation; US *also* /ree-/.

120. **Leander** /lee AN dur/ he swam the Hellespont to be with Hero.

145. *__importune__ /im POR chun/ urge, order. See App. D.

153. **Phaëton** /FAY ih tun, -tŏn/ son of the sun god. /-ŏn/ is usual in the US and is increasingly common in the UK. Some eds. prefer **Phaëthon** /-t̶h̶un, -t̶h̶ŏn/. See App. D *-on.*

153. **Merops'** /MEE rŏps, MEER ŏps/ are older; /MĔR ŏps/ is the restored pronunciation. Phaëton's step-father.

189. **Soho** /soh HOH/ a call.

222. **excess** here should be /ek SESS/, the usual UK form.

235. **chaf'd** /chayft/ enraged.

236. **suppliant** /SUP lee unt/ begging.

237. **close prison** /clohss/ tightly shut.

242. **dolor** (UK **dolour**) /DOH lur/; UK *also* /DŎL ur/ pain. See App. D *-or.*

253. **expostulate** /ek SPŎS chuh layt/; UK *also* /-tyuh layt/ discuss, object.

274. **cate-log** may indicate /KAYT lŏg/; US *also* /-lawg/ for *catelog.*

275, 301. **Inprimis** /in PRĪ miss/ in the first place. Archaic variant of *imprimis /im PRĪ miss/ (traditional), /im PREE miss/ (restored Latin). The latter is now more common.

382. **swing'd** /swinjd/ beaten.

Act 3 Scene 2

6. **impress** impression. Here should be /im PRESS/.

28. **persevers** /pur SEV urz/ perseveres.

58. **votary** /VOHT uh ree/ someone devoted to something or someone.

60. **access** here should be /ak SESS/.

71. ***poesy** US /POH ih see/ [-zee]; UK, CN /POH ih zee/ [-see] poetry.

77. ***Orpheus'** here should be 2 syllables /OR fyus/ [-fyōōss]. See App. D -eus.

79. **leviathans** /luh VĪ uh ~~th~~unz/ sea monsters.

81. **elegies** /EL uh jeez/ sorrowful poems.

83. **consort** /CŎN sort/ company of musicians. May have been /-surt/, making it equivalent to its mod. variant **concert**.

Act 4 Scene 1

13. **habiliments** /huh BILL ih munts/ clothes.

20. ***sojourn'd** resided temporarily. Here stress should fall on the first syllable. US, CN /SOH jurnd/; UK /SŎJ urnd/ [SŎJ URND, SOH-, SUJ-].

47. **allied** here with 2nd syllable stress.

58. ***parley** /PAR lee/ negotiate. Newer [-lay] not recommended.

62. **consort** here should be /cŏn-, cun SORT/ group, band.

ă-bat, äir-**marry**, air-**pair**, är-**far**, ĕr-**merry**, ĝ- **get**, ī-**high**, ĭr-**mirror**, ł-**little**, ņ-**listen**, ŏ-**hot**, oh-**go**, ōō-**wood**, ōō-**moon**, oor-**tour**, ōr- **or**, ow-**how**, ţh-**that**, ~~th~~-**thin**, ŭ-**but**, UR-**fur**, ur-**under**.   ( ) - suppress the syllable   see p. xiii for complete list.

64. *homage /HŎM ij/; US *also* /ŎM ij/ acknowledgement of allegience.

Act 4 Scene 2

4. access here should be /ak SESS/.

27. allycholly US /AL ih cŏl ee/; UK /-cuh lee/ Host's mistake for *melancholy.*

110. betroth'd /bih-, bee TROHȚHD/ engaged to be married.

111. importunacy /im por-, im pur TYŌŌN uh see/; US *also* /-TŌŌN-/ insistent requests.

117. sepulchre entomb. Here should be /suh-, sep PŬL kur/.

119 *obdurate unmoveable. Here the usual mod. form with 1st syllable stress /ŎB dyoor ut, -dyur-/ [-jur-]; US *sometimes* [-dur-]. Elsewhere 2nd syllable stress is required.

135. by my halidom an oath referring to a 'holy object' or the 'holy lady,' i.e., Mary. Other variants are: halidam, holidam, halidame, halidome, holidame. Probably these were all variant spellings of /HAL ih dum, HŎL ih dum/ (note *hal-* can also be /HŎL-/ in the US in *Halloween*).

Act 4 Scene 3

40. Reaking, recking /REK ing/ caring.

Act 4 Scene 4

9. *capon's US /KAY pŏnz, -punz/; CN, UK /KAY pŏnz/ [-punz] chicken's. See App. D *-on.*

40, 63. Sebastian US /suh BĂS chun/; UK /suh BĂST yun/.

66. lout /lowt/ oaf.

68.*augury /AWG yur ee/ [AWG ur ee]; UK *also* /AWG yoor ree/ prediction.

129. *protestations US /proh tess-, prŏt ess TAY shunz/;
CN /prŏt ess-/ [proh tess-]; UK /prŏt ess-/.

158. stature /STATCH ur/ size.

158. **Pentecost** /PEN tih cŏst/; US *also* /-cawst/ seventh Sunday after Easter.

166.*****lamentable** here should be /LAM un tuh bł/ the usual UK pronunciation.

167. **Ariadne** /ăir ee AD nee/ maiden deserted by Theseus. /ăir ee AHD nee/ is a newer, partially restored Gk. pronunciation.

168. *****Theseus'** here should be 2 syllables /T̶H̶E̶E̶ syus/ [-syo͞oss], US *rarely* [-so͞oss]. See App. D *-eus*.

168. **unjust** here should be /UN just/.

191. **periwig** /PĔR ee wig/ *also* /PĔR ih-/ wig.

Act 5 Scene 1

9. *****postern** small back or side gate. US, CN /PŎST urn/ [POHST urn]; UK /PŎST urn/, *rarely* [POHST urn].

Act 5 Scene 2

37. **Laurence** US /LŌR unss/; E.COAST US /LAH runss/; UK /LŌR runss/.

Act 5 Scene 3

3. *****mischances** in verse normally with 2nd syllable stress.

8. **Moyses** /MOY ziss/. Variation of *****Moses** /MOH ziss/; UK *also* [-ziz].

8. **Valerius** Ang.Lat. /vuh LEER yus/; restored Latin /-LĔR-/.

Act 5 Scene 4

2. **unfrequented** not often visited. Here should be /un free KWEN tid/ or /un frih-/.

12. **forlorn** here should be /FOR lorn/.

ă-b**a**t, ăir-m**a**rry, air-p**ai**r, ạr-f**a**r, ĕr-m**e**rry, ĝ- g**e**t, ī-h**igh**, ĭr-m**i**rror, ł-litt**le**, ṇ-list**en**, ŏ-h**o**t, oh-g**o**, o͞o-w**oo**d, o͞o-m**oo**n, oor-t**our**, ōr- **or**, ow-h**ow**, t̲h-**th**at, t̶h̶-**th**in, ŭ-b**u**t, UR-f**ur**, ur-und**er**.   ( ) - suppress the syllable   see p. xiii for complete list.

13. **hallowing, halloing** shouting. Here should be 2 syllables
/HAL-, HŎL (oh) wing/.

54. **Who respects friend?** here 1st syllable stress seems to be indicated for
respect, but with inversion of the 1st foot, *who* and *friend* are strongly stressed,
and both syllables of *respects* are relatively weak.

117. **close** /clohz/ union.

153. **endu'd** /en DYO͞OD/; US *also* [-DO͞OD] endowed.

The Two Noble Kinsmen

People in the Play

Arcite /AHR sīt/.

Artesius /ahr TEE zhus,- zyus/. Normal development would favor the former.

*Creon /CREE ŏn/ king of Thebes, mentioned throughout. /CREE un/ is increasingly rare. See App. D -*on*.

Emilia usually 3 syllables /ih MEEL (ee) yuh/. An older pronunciation /-MILL-/ is now rare.

Gerrold, Gerald /JĔR łd/ a schoolmaster.
  Geraldo, Giraldo /jur RAL doh, -RAHL-, -RAWL-/.

Hippolyta /hih PŎL ih tuh/.

Palamon /PAL uh mun, -mŏn/. /-ŏn/ is usual in the US and is increasingly common in the UK. See App. D -*on*.

Pirithous /pī RITH oh us/ or /PĪ rih thōōss/ depending on meter.

*Theseus 2 or 3 syllables depending on meter /THEE s(ee) yus/ [-syōōss], US *rarely* [-sōōss]. See App. D -*eus*.

Valerius /vuh LEER yus/; /-LĔR-/ is restored Latin.

Places in the Play

Thebes /theebz/ city in Greece.

Prologue

2. **gi'n** given. Here rhymes with *akin*. See p. 22 for deletion of *v* between vowels.

29. ***travail** here should be /TRAV ayl/ labor, with pun on *travel*. In Shk's time both pronounced /TRAV ł/.

ă-bat, ăir-marry, air-pair, ạr-far, ĕr-merry, ĝ- get, ī-high, ĭr-mirror, ł-little, ṇ-listen, ŏ-hot, oh-go, ōō-wood, ōō-moon, oor-tour, ŏr- or, ow-how, ţh-that, th-thin, ŭ-but, UR-fur, ur-under.   ( ) - suppress the syllable   see p. xiii for complete list.

Act 1 Scene 1

6. **thyme** /tīm/ an herb.

7. **Ver** spring. Ang.Lat. /vur/; Class.Lat. /wayr/. Here rhymes with *harbinger*.

8. **harbinger** /HAR bin jur/ advance messenger.

20. **chough, chuff** /chuf/ jackdaw.

31. **advocate** /AD vuh kut/ someone who supports a person or cause.

41. **talents** /TAL unts/ archaic variant of **talons**.

46. **Phoebus** /FEE bus/ god of the sun.

59. **Capaneus** /kap uh NEE us/.

68. **Nemean hide** /NEE myun/ skin of the lion killed by Hercules.

75. **Bellona** /buh LOHN uh/ goddess of war.

78. **Amazonian** /am uh ZOHN yun/ of the Amazons.

102. **as lief** /leef/ as soon.

127. **make a counter-reflect** /COWN tur REE flect/ be reflected from me.

133. **suppliants'** /SUP lyunts/ those who ask humbly for something.

134. **Knolls** /nohlz/ archaic variant of *knells* tolls.

138. **asprays** presumably /ASS prayz/, archaic variant of **ospreys** /ŎS prayz, -preez/; US *also* /AWSS-/ a type of fishing bird.

144. **humane** here should be /HYOO mayn/; US *sometimes* [YOO mayn].

155. **your *puissance** your powerful self. Here 3 syllables, traditionally /PYOO ih snss/ (but see App. D).

156. **Wrinching** /RINCH ing/ variant of **Rinsing**.

159. ***sloth** US, CN /slawth/ [slohth]; UK /slohth/ [slŏth] laziness.

161. **prim'st** /prīmst/ best.

165. **Dowagers** /DOW uh jurz/ widows.

169. **unpang'd** here with 1st syllable stress.

176. ***synod** US, CN /SIN ud/ [-ŏd]; UK /SIN ŏd/ [-ud] council of the gods.

177. **corslet** /CORSS lit/ body armor, i.e., embrace.

186. **banket** /BANK it/ light meal, often of fruit. Archaic variant of **banquet**.

195. **aye** /ay/ ever. /ī/ is often used, but not recommended.

196. **Prorogue** /pruh-, proh ROHG/ postpone.

202. **celerity** /suh LĔR ih tee/ speed.

209. **success** here 1st syllable stress is indicated.

212. **Aulis** /AW liss/.

214. **moi'ty, moiety** /MOY tee/ portion.

223. **Boudge** /BUJ/, or possibly /bōōj/. Archaic variant of **Budge**.

Act 1 Scene 2

16. **martialist** /MAR shł ist/ military man.

17. **ingots** /ING guts/; UK *also* [-gŏts] gold or silver cast in bars.

20. **To Mars's so scorn'd altar?** normally in Shk *Mars's* would be one syllable /marz/, in which case *scorn'd* would be /SCORN id/.

24. **repletion** /rih-, ree PLEE shun/ excesses.

60. **sequent** /SEE kwunt/ following.

61. **plantin** a medicinal plant. Today spelled ***plantain** /PLĂNT ayn/ [-in]; UK *also* [PLAHNT ayn]. /-in/ is older.

67. **Voluble** /VŎL yuh bł/ fickle.

ă-bat, ăir-**marry**, air-**pair**, ạr-**far**, ĕr-**merry**, ĝ- **get**, ī-high, ir-mirror, ł-little, ṇ-listen, ŏ-hot, oh-go, ōō-wood, ōō-moon, oor-**tour**, ōr- **or**, ow-how, ᶵh-that, ᵺ-thin, ŭ-but, UR-**fur**, ur-under.   ( ) - suppress the syllable   see p. xiii for complete list.

67. **attributes** here should be /AT rih by͞o͞ots/.

85. **Phoebus** /FEE bus/ god of the sun.

Act 1 Scene 3

3. **timorous** /TIM (uh) rus/ frightened.

4. **Excess** usually /ek SESS/ in verse, the most common UK form, but here the foot may be inverted allowing /EK sess/, the usual US form, also used in the UK.

5. **dure** /dyoor/; US *also* [do͞or] endure.

13. **Bellona** /buh LOHN uh/ goddess of war.

14. **terrene** /TĔR een/ earthly.

21. **eat** /et/ dialect variant of *eaten*.

54, 84. **Flavina** /fluh VEE nuh/.

63. **operance** /ŎP (ur) runss/ workings.

77. ***sojourn** reside temporarily. Here stress should fall on the second syllable. US, CN /soh JURN/; US *rarely* [sŏ-]; UK /sŏ JURN/ [soh-], *rarely* [suh-].

82. **in sex dividual** /dih VIJ oo l̸/ between persons of different sex.

Act 1 Scene 4

6. ***chastise** punish. Here should be /chăss TĪZ/, the usual UK pronunciation, also sometimes used in North America. The usual US pronunciation has 1st syllable stress.

10. **depute** /duh PY͞O͞OT/ appoint.

31. **Convent** /cun VENT/ convene.

31. **in their behoof** /bih-, bee H͞O͞OF/ to their advantage.

32. **niggard** /NIG urd/ spend grudgingly.

Act 1 Scene 5

9,10. **convent** /cun VENT/ summon.

Act 2 Scene 1

28. **grise** /grīss, grīz/ step. Variant of **grece** /greess/, **grize** /grīz/, **grice** /grīss/.

Act 2 Scene 2

21. **ware** /wair/ archaic variant of **wore**.

46. **Theban** /THEE bun/ from Thebes.

50. **Parthian** /PAR thyun/ of *Parthia*, in present-day Iran.

112. **record** here should be /rek-, rik ORD/.

138. **gently** here 3 syllables /JEN tł ee/ is indicated.

147. *****extant** in existence. Here stressed on the 1st syllable
US /EK stunt/ [-stănt]; UK /-stănt/, *rarely* [-stunt]; in CN both are used equally.
In the UK /ek STĂNT/ is usual.

197. **combat** here should be /CŎM bat/; UK *also* [CUM-].

236. **apricock** /AYP rih cŏck/; US, CN *also* /AP-/ dialect variant of **apricot**.

Act 2 Scene 3

34. **fescue** /FESS kyōō/ teacher's pointer.

37. **Arcas** US /ARK us/ [-ăss]; UK, CN /-ăss/ [-us]. Normal development would favor /-us/.

37. **Sennois** /SEN oyz/.

38. **Rycas** US /RĪ kus/ [-kăss]; UK, CN /-kăss/ [-kus]. Normal development would favor /-kus/.

ă-bat, äir-ma**rry**, air-**pair**, ạr-**far**, ĕr-me**rry**, ĝ- **get**, ī-**high**, ĭr-**mirror**, ł-**little**, ṇ-**listen**, ŏ-**hot**, oh-**go**, ōō-**wood**, ōō-**moon**, oor-**tour**, ōr- **or**, ow-**how**, ţh-**that**, ₵ħ-**thin**, ʊ-**but**, UR-**fur**, ur-**under**. ( ) - suppress the syllable see p. xiii for complete list.

40. ***domine, dominie** schoolmaster. /DŎM ih nee/ is older, /DOH-/ is a newer, spelling pronunciation. The latter is the most common in the US, but is unknown in the UK.

47. **breech** backside. /breech/, but an older form /britch/ is still used in some dialects (cf. *breeches* /BRITCH iz, BREECH iz/, the latter being a newer form).

49. ***heigh** US /hay, hī/; CN /hī/, *rarely* [hay]; UK /hay/. Some eds. prefer **hey** /hay/, the sound Shk intended to convey.

53. **parlously** /PAR lus lee/ cleverly.

67, 73. **Wrastle (-ing)** /RĂSS ł/ archaic variant of **wrestle**.

Act 2 Scene 5

3. **wrastle** /RĂSS ł/ archaic variant of **wrestle**.

11. **hollow'd** here /HŎL ud, -ohd/ given a hunting cry. Variant of **holler**.

22. **illustrate** here should be /ih LUST rayt/.

Act 2 Scene 6

6. **keep close** /clohss/ stay hidden.

15. **dirge** /durj/ funeral song.

35. **whoobub** archaic variant of **hubbub** /HUB ub/, very likely pronounced the same way.

Act 3 Scene 1

2. **land.** Some eds. prefer **laund** /lawnd/ glade.

3. **Athenians** /uh ~~THEEN~~ yunz/.

7. **mead** /meed/ meadow.

12. **eftsoons** here should be /EFT sōōnz/ soon. Elsewhere with 2nd syllable stress.

19. **prim'st** /prīmst/ best.

35. **confess'd** here should be /CŎN fest/.

47. **blazon** /BLAY zun, -zn̩/ description.

53, **maintain** here should be /MAYN tayn/.

58. **advertis'd** informed. Here should be /ad VUR tisst/, /-tīzd/.

68. **compell'd** here /CŎM peld/.

72. **gyves** /jīvz/ chains, fetters.

84. **viands** /VĪ undz/ food. /VEE undz/ not recommended.

97. **musit, muset** /MYŌŌ zit/ gap in a hedge.

109. **banket** /BANK it/ light meal, often of fruit. Archaic variant of **banquet**.

Act 3 Scene 2

7. **reak, reck** /rek/ care.

8, 9. **hallow ('d)** /HAL-, HŎL ohd/ cried out. Some eds. prefer **holler**.

9. *****whoop'd** /whōōpt/ [hōōpt, hŏŏpt, whŏŏpt].

12. *****livelong** US /LIV lŏng, -lawng/, *rarely* [LĪV-]; UK /LIV lŏng/ [LĪV-].

14. **gyves** /jīvz/ chains, fetters.

21. **char'd** /chaird/ done.

34. **errant step** /ĔR unt/ step from the correct path.

Act 3 Scene 3

10. *****parleys** /PAR leez/ conferences with an enemy. Newer [-layz] not recommended.

17, 19. **draught** US, CN /drăft/; UK, E.NEW ENG. /drahft/ drink.

| ă-bat, äir-**marry**, air-**pair**, ạr-**far**, ĕr-**merry**, ĝ- **get**, ī-**high**, ĭr-**mirror**, ł-**little**, ṇ-**listen**, |
| ŏ-**hot**, oh-**go**, ōō-**wood**, ōō-**moon**, oor-**tour**, ōr- **or**, ow-**how**, ţh-**that**, t̶h̶-**thin**, Ŭ-**but**, |
| UR-**fur**, ur-**under**.   ( ) - suppress the syllable   see p. xiii for complete list. |

24. **victuals** /VIT łz/ food.

34. **virginals** /VUR jin łz/ a keyboard instrument.

42. *__Heigh-ho!__ US /hay ho, hī-/; CN /hī-/, *rarely* [hay-]; UK /hay-/. Shk intended /hay/. Spoken with evenly stressed syllables or as if sighing, with 1st syllable stress.

Act 3 Scene 4

2. **aglets** /AG lits/ spangles.

14. **carreck, carrack** /KĂIR uk/ a type of large merchant ship.

20. **e'e** /ee/ dialect variant of **eye**.

22. **He s' buy** a north. Eng., and Scot. dialect form of *shall* is *sall*, which in its weak form reduces to *s.'*

Act 3 Scene 5

stage direction at beginning of scene: **Bavian** /BAY vee un/, **Babion** /BAY bee un/ dancer in an ape costume.

2. **disensanity, disinsanity** /dis in SAN ih tee/ utter folly.

8. **frieze** /freez/ wool fabric.

8. **jane** /jayn/ cheap cotton cloth. Archaic variant of **jean**.

11.   **Proh Deum,   medius   fidius**
Ang.Lat. /proh DEE um,   MEE dee us FID ee us/;
Class.Lat. /proh   DAY ōōm, MED ee ōōs FID ee ōōs/
            'O God! so help me heaven.'

13. **Close** /clohss/ hidden.

18. *__Meleager__ Gk. warrior. /mel ee AY gur/ [-jur]. The latter is older.

23. **taborer** /TAY bur ur/ player of a small drum. See App. D *-or*.

25. **Maudline, Maudlin** /MAWD lin/. Some eds. prefer **Madeline** /MAD (uh) lin/.

26. **Barbary** /BAR buh ree/ variant of **Barbara**.

28. **ribands** /RIB undz/ archaic variant of **ribbons**.

33. **Bavian** /BAY vee un/, **Babion** /BAY bee un/ dancer in an ape costume.

38.   **Quo   usque   tandem**
Ang.Lat.   /kwoh US kwee   TAN dum/
Class.Lat. /kwoh o͞oS kway TAHN dem/
            'how long then.'
Some eds. prefer to write **Quousque**.

41. **fatuus** US /FATCH oo wus/; UK /FAT yoo wus/ foolish.

42. **hilding** /HILL ding/ good-for-nothing.

44. **Cicely** /SIS uh lee/ with a weak stress missing preceding it.

44. **sempster's** /SEMP sturz/ variant of **seamster's** /SEM sturz/, which is mod.
seamstress' US /SEEM striss/; UK /SEM striss/ [SEEM-].

46. **Arcas** US /ARK us/ [-ăss]; UK, CN /-ăss/ [-us]. Normal development would
favor /-us/.

57. **frampal** /FRAM pł/ disagreeable, high-spirited. Variant of **frampold**
/FRAM pold, -płd/.

59. **George Alow** /uh LOH/ name of a ship.

60. **Barbary-a** /BAR buh ree uh/ region in North Africa.

67. **an howlet** /HOW lit/ young owl. In Shk's time *h* was sometimes silent so it
may be the same word as **owlet**.

75. **gambols** /GAM błz/ frolics.

83. **Dii boni!** Ang.Lat. /DĬ ī BOH nī/; Class.Lat. /DIH ee BŎN ee/ Good Gods!

86. **Qui passa** angl. /kwee/ or /kee PASS uh/ a popular tune.

ă-bat, ăir-**marry**, air-**pair**, ạr-**far**, ĕr-**merry**, ĝ- get, ī-high, ĭr-**mirror**, ł-little, ṇ-listen,
ŏ-hot, oh-go, o͞o-wood, o͞o-moon, oor-**tour**, ŏr- or, ow-how, ţh-that, ŧh-thin, ŭ-but,
UR-**fur**, ur-**under**.   ( ) - suppress the syllable   see p. xiii for complete list.

88.   **Et opus   exegi,   quod nec Jovis   ira,   nec ignis**
Ang.Lat. /et OH pus eks EE jī,   kwŏd nek JOH viss Ī ruh,   nek   IG niss/
Class.Lat. /et ŎP ōōs   eks AYG ee, kwŏd nek YŎ wiss EE rah, nek   IG niss/.
            'And I have completed a work which neither the anger of Jove nor fire
            [shall hinder].'
Some eds. prefer **Iovis** instead of **Jovis**, pronounced as in Class.Lat.

94. *****Pallas** Athena. US /PAL us/ [-ăss]; UK, CN /-ăss/ [-us]. Normal
development would favor /-us/.

100, 114. **doughty** /DOWT ee/ brave, strong.

106, 147. **rout** /rowt/ crowd.

---

107. **choris** /COR iss/ archaic variant of **chorus**.

110. **paedagogus** Ang.Lat. /pee duh GOH gus/; Class.Lat. /pī dah GOH gōōs/
schoolmaster.

111. *****breeches** /BRITCH iz/ is traditional, /BREECH iz/ is newer. The former
pronunciation is more common in the UK, and the latter in the US, CN.

112.*****ferula** cane. US /FĔR yuh luh, FĔR yoo luh/ [FĔR uh luh];
UK /FĔR uh luh/ [-yuh-, -yoo-].

113. **machine** device. Here /MASH een/ is indicated.

115. **Dis** /dis/ Pluto.

115. *****Daedalus** inventor in Gk. mythology. US /DED uh lus/, *rarely* [DEED-];
CN /DED-/ [DEED-]; UK /DEED-, DĪD-/ [DED-]. Angl. /DED-, DEED-/ are
oldest, /DĪD-/ is a recent, restored pronunciation. /DAYD-/ is a recent spelling
pronunciation, not recommended.

118. **Morr** /mor/. Some eds. prefer **Moor** /mor/ [moor] black man.

132. **Bavian** /BAY vyun/, **Babion** /BAY byun/ dancer in an ape costume.

132. **eke** /eek/ also.

133.   **Cum   multis   aliis**
Ang.Lat. /kŭm   MŬLT iss   AY lee iss/
ClassLat. /kōōm   MŌŌL teess AHL ih eess/
            'with many others.'

135, 148. *domine, dominie schoolmaster. /DŎM ih nee/ is older, /DOH-/ is a newer, spelling pronunciation. The latter is more common in the US, but is unknown in the UK.

157. dowsets /DOW sits/ testicles of a deer. Sometimes spelled doucets, pronounced /DŌŌ sits/.

158.　　Dii　　deaeque　　omnes
Ang.Lat.　/DĪ ī　dee EE kwee　ŎM neez/
Class.Lat. /DIH ee　day Ī kway　ŎM nayss/
　　　　'all you gods and goddesses.'

Act 3 Scene 6

10. out-dure here /OWT dyoor/; US also [-dōōr] outlast.

32. obbraidings either a spelling variant of abraidings /uh BRAYD ingz/ 'shouting,' or of upbraidings /up-/ 'insults.'

57. close /clohss/ securely.

62. casque /kăsk/; UK also [kahsk] helmet.

136. By Castor /KĂS tur/ a Roman oath. See App. D -or.

145,168. edict here /ee DICT/ decree.

304. prefix'd here should be /pree-, prih FIKST/ appointed.

308. bier /beer/ coffin.

Act 4 Scene 1

71. bevy /BEV ee/ large group.

73. chaplets /CHAP lits/ garlands.

74. damask /DAM usk/ pink or light red.

84. bulrush /BULL rush/ type of reed.

ă-bat, ăir-marry, air-pair, ạr-far, ĕr-merry, ĝ- get, ī-high, ĭr-mirror, ł-little, ṇ-listen, ŏ-hot, oh-go, ōō-wood, ōō-moon, oor-tour, ōr- or, ow-how, ṯh-that, ŧh-thin, Ŭ-but, UR-fur, ur-under.　　　( ) - suppress the syllable　　　see p. xiii for complete list.

130, 131. **keep close** /clohss/ keep silent.

147. **Owgh** grunts of men hauling up the anchor or the wind in the sails. Some eds. prefer **Uff**.

148. **bowling** variant of **bowline** rope used to rig sails. Both pronounced /BOH lin/.

148. **mainsail** sailors use /MAYN sł/; landsmen /-sayl/.

Act 4 Scene 2

15. *__Ganymede__ /GAN ih meed/; *also* /GAN ee-/ pretty youth.

21. **Pelops' son** /PEE lŏps/ he had an ivory shoulder.

27. **swarth** /swōrt/ dark-complexioned. Archaic variant of **swart** (*th* was often /t/ in Eliz. Eng.).

53. **gauds** /gawdz/ toys.

86. **baldrick** /BAWL drik/ shoulder strap for a horn or sword.

113. **lineaments** /LIN yuh munts/ distinctive features.

125. **aborn** /AY burn/ variant of *abran* /AY brun/ 'light yellow.' Later confused with **auburn** /AW burn/ 'reddish brown.'

Act 4 Scene 3

15. **Dido** /DĪ doh/ Queen of Carthage.

16. **Aeneas** /ih NEE yus/; UK *also* /EE NEE yus/ Prince of Troy.

25. **Proserpine** /PRŎSS ur pīn/ variant of *Proserpina* /proh-, pruh SUR pih nuh/ she was abducted by Pluto.

34. **shrowd** /shrohd/ harsh. Archaic variant of **shrewd**.

37. **usurers'** /YOO zhur urz/; UK *also* [-zhyoor urz, -zhoor urz] those who lend money for interest.

38. **gammon of bacon** /GAM un/ ham.

49. **engraff'd madness** implanted. In verse *engraff'd* would have 1st syllable stress in this position before a noun, but in this prose passage the normal 2nd syllable stress may be used US /en GRĂFT/; E.NEW ENG., UK /-GRAHFT/. Some eds. prefer **engrafted**.

55. **arras** /ĂIR us/ tapestry.

67. **penn'worth, penn'orth** /PEN urth/ bargain.

73. *****vagary** wandering. US /VAY guh ree/, *rarely* [vuh GAIR ee, -GĂIR-]; CN /VAY guh ree/; UK /VAY guh ree/ [vuh GAIR ee].

91. **play-feres** /feerz/ playmates.

Act 5 Scene 1

9. **germane** here should be /JUR mayn/ related.

46. **cestron** /SESS trun/ archaic variant of **cistern** /SISS turn/.

53. **Ceres'** /SEER eez/ goddess of the harvest.

53. **foison** /FOY zun, -zn̩/ harvest.

54. **armipotent** /ar MIP uh tunt/ powerful in arms.

66. **plurisy** archaic variant of **pleurisy** 'excess.' Both pronounced /PLo͞oR ih see/; US *also* /PLUR-/.

The Complete Oxford begins 5.2 here (line nos. in parentheses).

---

69. (5.2.1) **glister** /GLIS tur/. Some eds. prefer **glisten**.

85. (5.2.17) **poll'd** /pohld/ bald.

90. (5.2.22) **Phoebus** /FEE bus/ god of the sun.

99. (5.2.31) **reveal'd** here 1st syllable stress is indicated.

116. (5.2.48) **fere** /feer/ mate.

ă-bat, ăir-**marry**, air-**pair**, ạr-**far**, ĕr-**merry**, ĝ- get, ī-high, ĭr-mirror, l̵-little, n̩-listen, ŏ-hot, oh-go, o͞o-**wood**, o͞o-**moon**, oor-**tour**, ōr- or, ow-how, th-**that**, t̵h-**thin**, ŭ-but, UR-**fur**, ur-**under**.   ( ) - suppress the syllable   see p. xiii for complete list.

122. (5.2.54) **close** /clohss/ secret.

The Complete Oxford begins 5.3 here.
---

138. (5.3.2) **contemplative** here should be /cun TEMP luh tiv/ thoughtful.

145. (5.3.9) **maculate** /MAK yuh lut/ defiled.

147. (5.3.11) **scurril** vulgar. US /SKUR ł/; E.COAST US, UK /SKUH rł/. Some eds. prefer **scurrile**, pronounced the same way, or, esp. in the UK, CN /-īl/.

Act 5 Scene 2 (*Complete Oxford* 5.4)

35. *****Videlicet** namely (abbreviated *viz.*). The older, anglicized pronunciations are US /vih DELL ih sit/ [-DEEL-, vī-]; UK /vih DEEL ih sit/ [vī-, -DELL-]. Newer pronunciations mix in restored Latin syllables, for example, /-ket/ or /-DAYL-/. These are not recommended.

37. **ipso facto** /IP soh FAK toh/ by the very act.

54. **Light a' Love, Light o' Love** an inconstant lover, from a ballad. In either case /uh/ for *of* is intended.

59. **provender** /PRŎV ṇ dur/ dry food for animals.

59. *****hostler** US, CN /HŎSS lur, ŎSS-/; UK /ŎSS-/ [HŎSS-] innkeeper.

Act 5 Scene 3 (*Complete Oxford* 5.5)

70. **prim'st** /prīmst/ best.

76. **sinister** here should be /sin ISS tur/ left.

83. **titlers** /TĪT lurz/ contestants.

107. **arbitrement, arbitrament** /ạr BIT ruh munt/ power to decide.

119. **Alcides** /al SĪ deez/ Hercules.

120. **sow** heavy metal mass. /sow/ as in *how*.

124. **emulous** /EM y(oo) lus/ rival.

124. **Philomels** /FILL oh melz, -uh-/ nightingales.

130. **girlond** /ĜEER lund/ archaic variant of **garland** /GAR lund/.

Act 5 Scene 4 (*Complete Oxford* 5.6)

8. **rheum** /rōōm/ lung disease.

10. **unwapper'd** /un WŎP urd/ not worn out, fresh.

22. **banket** /BANK it/ light meal, often of fruit. Archaic variant of **banquet**.

55. **calkins** /KAWK inz, KAL kinz/ the turned down ends of a horseshoe.

63. **malevolent** /muh LEV uh lunt/ hurtful.

70. **rowel** disc with points at the end of a spur. /ROW ł/ as in *how*.

72. **jad'ry** /JAYD ree/ tricks of a jade (ill-tempered horse).

72. **disseat** /dis SEET/ throw-off.

95. ***Elysium** the realm of the blessed in the after-life. US /ih LEEZH ee um/ [-LIZ-, -LIZH-, -LEESS-, -LISS-]; UK /-LIZ-/; *also* /ee-/ in all countries. The oldest forms still in use are /-LIZ-/, /-LIZH-/. The historic form is /ih LIZH um/.

ă-bat, ăir-ma**rry**, air-**pair**, ặr-**far**, ĕr-me**rry**, ĝ- **get**, ī-high, ĭr-m**irror**, ł-little, ṇ-listen, ŏ-hot, oh-**go**, ōō-**wood**, ōō-**moon**, oor-**tour**, ōr- **or**, ow-**how**, ţh-**that**, ŧħ-**thin**, ŭ-but, UR-**fur**, ur-und**er**.   ( ) - suppress the syllable   see p. xiii for complete list.

The Winter's Tale

People in the Play

Antigonus /an TIG uh nus/.

Archidamus /ark ih DAY mus/ this name is not spoken.

Autolycus /aw TŎL ih kus/.

Camillo /kuh MILL oh/.

Cleomines, Cleomenes /clee ŎM ih neez/.

Dion /DĪ un/ is traditional, but sometimes newer pronunciations /DĪ ŏn/ or /DEE ŏn, -un/ are used. See App. D *-on.*

Dorcas /DOR kus/.

Emilia usually 3 syllables /ih MEEL (ee) yuh/. An older pronunciation /-MILL-/ is now rare.

Florizel US /FLŌR ih zel/; E.COAST US, UK /FLŎR-/.

Hermione 3 or 4 syllables depending on meter /hur MĪ (uh) nee/.

Jailer, (UK Gaoler) both /JAY lur/.

Leontes /lee ŎN teez/.

Mamillius 3 or 4 syllables depending on meter /muh MILL (ee) yus/.

Mopsa /MŎP suh/.

Paulina /paw LĪ nuh/ but sometimes newer /-LEE-/ is used.

Perdita /PUR dit uh/.

Polixenes 3 or 4 syllables depending on meter /puh LICKS (ih) neez/.

Places in the Play

Bohemia /boh HEEM (ee) yuh/ part of the present day Czech Republic.

*Delphos where the sacred oracle lies. US /DEL fohss/ [-fŏss, -fus];
UK /-fŏss/ [-fohss, -fus]. Normal development would favor /-us/. /-ohss/ is a
newer pronunciation.

Sicilia /sih SILL (ee) yuh/. 4.4.589 *And shall appear in Sicilia* points to
/SISS ł yuh/ or /sih sih LEE uh/.

Act 1 Scene 1

15. **insufficience** /in suh FISH unss/.

Act 1 Scene 2

5. ***perpetuity** eternity. /PUR puh TY$\overline{OO}$ ih tee/; US *also* [-T$\overline{OO}$-].
/-CH$\overline{OO}$-/ is also used but is considered non-standard in the UK.

13. **sneaping** /SNEEP ing/ biting cold.

17. **sev'nnight** variant of *se'nnight* /SEN nit, -nīt/ 'week.'

19. **gainsaying** /gayn SAY ing/ denying.

37. **distaffs** cleft staff used in spinning thread. US /DIS stăfs/;
E.NEW ENG., UK /DIS stahfs/.

41. **gest** /jest/ stage of a royal journey.

42. **Prefix'd** appointed. Here may be /prih-, pree FIKST/ or with inverted foot,
newer /PREE fikst/.

66. **verier** /VĔR yur/ more outrageous.

110. **tremor cordis** fluttering of the heart. Ang.Lat. /TREE mur COR diss/;
restored Latin /TREM ur COR diss/. The latter is more common today.

125. **virginalling** /VUR jin ł ing/ playing, fingering.

ă-bat, ăir-marry, air-pair, ạr-far, ĕr-merry, ĝ- get, ī-high, ĭr-mirror, ł-little, ṇ-listen,
ŏ-hot, oh-go, ōō-wood, ōō-moon, oor-tour, ōr- or, ow-how, ţh-that, ᵺ-thin, ŭ-but,
UR-fur, ur-under.   ( ) - suppress the syllable   see p. xiii for complete list.

134. *bourn /born, boorn/ boundary. North American [burn] not recommended. Normal development would favor /born/.

137. collop /CŎL up/ small slice of meat; here, part of my own flesh.

142. credent /CREED ṇt/ believable.

155. *unbreech'd not old enough for men's clothes. /un BRITCHT/ is traditional, /-BREECHT/ is newer. The former pronunciation is more common in the UK, and the latter in the US, CN.

169. July's here should be /JOO līz/.

204. barricado fortification. /băir ih KAY doh/ is older, /-KAH doh/ is newer.

227. extraordinary here US /ek struh OR dih něr ee/; UK /-dih nuh ree/.

228. purblind /PUR blīnd/ blind or partly blind.

244. hoxes /HŎK siz/ hamstrings.

271. cogitation /cŏj ih TAY shun/ thought.

301. lout /lowt/ oaf.

316. bespice /bih-, bee SPĪSS/ to spice.

318. draught US, CN /drăft/; UK, E.NEW ENG. /drahft/ drink.

318. cordial US /COR jł/; UK /COR dył/ healing medicine.

339. allied here with 2nd syllable stress.

372. *Wafting his eyes shifting his eyes. US, CN /WŎFT ing/; SOUTH. US /WĂFT-/; UK /WŎFT-/ [WĂFT-, WAHFT-]. /WĂFT/ is newer and considered non-standard by many.

388. *basilisk legendary reptile whose glance was fatal. US /BĂSS ih lisk/ [BAZ ih lisk]; UK /BAZ-/ [BĂSS-]; CN both used equally.

395. does behove /bih-, bee HOHV/ is an advantage to.

421. savor (UK savour) /SAY vur/ smell.

438, 464. *posterns small back or side gates. US, CN /PŎST urnz/ [POHST-]; UK /PŎST-/, rarely [POHST-].

Act 2 Scene 1

46. **pandar, pander** /PAN dur/ pimp.

52. ***posterns** small back or side gates. US, CN /PŎST urnz/ [POHST urnz];
UK /PŎST urnz/, *rarely* [POHST urnz].

72, 73. **calumny** /CAL um nee/ slander.

84. ***precedent** /PRESS ih dunt/ example.

90. **federary** confederate. Before an epic caesura US /FED uh rĕr ree/;
UK /-ruh ree/, but it may also be syncopated to *feder'ry* /FED uh ree/
(cf. UK *secret'ry*).

99. **throughly** archaic variant of *thoroughly*. /T̶H̶R̶OO̅ lee/ is the normal
pronunciation on stage, but to enhance clarity a syncopated form of the modern
pronunciation may be used: *thor'ghly*.

120. **deserv'd** here with 1st syllable stress.

157. **dungy** /DUNG ee/ filthy.

162. **Commune** speak intimately. Here may be the usual mod. /cuh MYOO̅N/,
or if the foot is inverted /CŎM yoo̅n/, found elsewhere in Shk.

163. ***prerogative** /pur RŎG uh tiv/ [prih-, pree-] right. /pree-/ non-standard in
the UK.

192. ***credulity** gullibility. /cruh DYOO̅ lih tee/; US *also* /-DOO̅-/; /-JOO̅-/ is
considered non-standard in the UK.

Act 2 Scene 2

10. **th' access** here should be /t̬hʸ ak SESS/.

28. **unsafe** here should be /UN sayf/.

28. **lunes** /loo̅nz/ fits of madness (for /lyoo̅-/ see App. D *lu-*).

37. **advocate** /AD vuh kut/ someone who supports a person.

ă-bat,	ăir-**marry**,	air-**pair**,	ạr-**far**, ĕr-**merry**, ĝ- get, ī-high, ĭr-**mirror**, ł-little, ṇ-listen,
ŏ-hot,	oh-go,	oo̅-wood,	oo̅-moon, oor-**tour**, ŏr- or, ow-how, t̬h-**that**, t̶h-**thin**, ŭ-but,
UR-**fur**,	ur-**under**.	( ) - suppress the syllable	see p. xiii for complete list.

Act 2 Scene 3

4. **harlot** /HAR lut/ whorish.

8. **moi'ty, moiety** /MOY tee/ portion.

37. **medicinal** here should be /MED sin ł/.

56. **Less *appear* so, in comforting your evils.** Here 1st syllable stress is indicated for *appear*. Possibly two weak stresses were intended in the first foot with *-pear* scanned as two syllables (see p. 33).

75. **dotard** /DOHT urd/ senile old man.

91. **callat, callet** /KAL ut/ whore.

109. ***lozel, losel** /LOH zł/ [LŎZ ł] scoundrel.

115. **heretic** /HĔR ih tik/ dissenter.

119. **savors** (UK **savours**) /SAY vurz/ smacks of, smells of.

160. **Margery** /MARJ ur ee/ a hen-like woman.

198. **accompt** /uh COWNT/ archaic variant of **account**. See App. D.

Act 3 Scene 1

20. **contents** here should be /cŏn TENTS/.

Act 3 Scene 2

11. **indictment** /in DĪT munt/ charge of wrongdoing.

37. **spectators** here should be /spek TAY turz/, a common UK pronunciation, virtually unknown in the US.

39. **moi'ty, moiety** /MOY tee/ portion.

56. **gainsay** /GAYN say/ deny.

170. **glisters** /GLIS turz/ glistens.

Act 3 Scene 3

62. **ancientry** /AYN shun tree/ old people.

70. **barne** /barn/ archaic dialect form meaning 'child.' Some eds. prefer **bairn** /bairn/ which today is a Scottish form.

77. **hallow'd** /HAL-, HŎL ohd/ or /huh LOHD/ shouted. Some eds. prefer **halloo'd** /huh LO͞OD/.

79. **Hilloa, loa** /hih LOH, LOH/ a call to attract attention.

88. **chafes** /chayfs/ rages.

92. **mainmast** /MAYN mᵘst/ is used by sailors; landsmen say US, CN /-măst/; UK, E.NEW ENG. /-mahst/.

124. **close** /clohss/ secret.

Act 4 Scene 1

2. **unfolds** here with 1st syllable stress.

9. **oe'rwhelm** here should be /OR whelm/.

14. **glistering** /GLIS tring/ glistening.

20. **spectators** here should be /spek TAY turz/, a common UK pronunciation, virtually unknown in the US.

26. **prophesy** /PRŎF uh sī/ to predict the future.

Act 4 Scene 2

1. **importunate** /im POR chuh nut/; UK *also* /-tyoo nut/ insistant.

8. **allay** /uh LAY/ relief.

ă-bat, ăir-**marry**, air-**pair**, ạr-**far**, ĕr-**merry**, ĝ- **get**, ī-**high**, ĭr-**mirror**, l̶-**little**, ṇ-**listen**, ŏ-**hot**, oh-**go**, o͞o-**wood**, o͞o-**moon**, oor-**tour**, ōr- **or**, ow-**how**, ţh-**that**, t̶h̶-**thin**, ŭ-**but**, UR-**fur**, ur-**under**.   ( ) - suppress the syllable   see p. xiii for complete list.

Act 4 Scene 3

2, 10. *heigh! US /hay, hī/; CN /hī/, *rarely* [hay]; UK /hay/. Here /hay/ was intended as indicated in F1, line 6 *hey,* and also the internal rhyme with *jay* in line 10.

2. doxy /DŎK see/ loose wench.

9. chaunts archaic variant of chants US /chănts/; E. NEW ENG, UK /chahnts/. See App. D *-aun-.*

20. bouget may have been /BOW jit/ to rhyme with *avouch it.* Archaic variant of budget /BUJ it/ leather bag.

22. avouch /uh VOWCH/ affirm.

27. caparison /kuh PĂIR ih sņ/ ornamental cloth covering for a horse.

27. revenue sometimes in verse /ruh VEN yōō/, but in this prose passage may be mod. Eng. US /REV in ōō/; UK, SOUTH. US /-yōō/.

35. springe /sprinj/ snare.

36. compters /COWNT urz/ archaic variant of counters 'discs to help calculate.' See App. D *accompt.*

45. saffron /SAFF run/ yellow food coloring used in baking.

48. pruins in Shk's time probably /PRŌŌ inz/, archaic and dialect variant of prunes.

Act 4 Scene 4

50. *nuptial wedding. US, UK /NUP chł/ [-shł]; in CN both are used equally.

65. unknown here should be /UN nohn/.

75. savor (UK savour) /SAY vur/ smell.

82, 98. gillyvors /JIL ee vurz/ dialect form of gillyflowers /JIL ee flow urz/ carnations.

87. piedness /PĪD niss/ having many colors.

93. scion /SĪ un/ living plant grafted onto root stock.

104. **savory** (UK **savoury**) /SAY v(uh) ree/ a type of herb.

104. **marjorum** type of herb. Archaic variant of **marjoram**, both pronounced /MAR jur rum/.

116. **Proserpina** /proh-, pruh SUR pih nuh/ abducted by Pluto.

118. **Dis's** god of the underworld. Here exceptionally the possessive form is two syllables after /s/, /DIS iz/.

122. **Cytherea's** /si̶t̶h̶ uh REE uz/ Venus'.

122. **primeroses** may have been pronounced /PRĪM roh ziz/ or as its mod. variant **primroses** /PRIM roh ziz/.

124. **Phoebus** /FEE bus/ god of the sun.

127. **flow'r-de-luce** /FLOWR duh lo͞oss/ lily flower. Main stress may also fall on the 3rd syllable, the usual US form (for /lyo͞o-/ see App. D *lu-*).

134. **Whitsun** /WHIT sn̩/ Pentecost, the seventh Sunday after Easter.

138. **alms** charity for the poor. /ahmz/ is older; /ahlmz, awlmz/ are newer. In the UK the latter are non-standard.

146-78. **Doricles** US /DŌR ih cleez/; E.COAST US, UK /DŎR-/.

149. **unstain'd** here should be /UN staynd/.

157. **green-sord** /sord/ archaic variant of **sward** /swōrd/.

182. **tabor** /TAY bur/ small drum. See App. D *-or*.

190. *****lamentably** US /luh MEN tuh blee/ [LAM en-]; CN, UK /LAM un tuh blee/ [luh MEN-].

192. **milliner** /MILL ih nur/ seller of fancy goods.

198, 200. *****Whoop** /who͞op/ [ho͞op, ho͝op, who͝op].

207. **caddises, caddisses** /KAD iss iz/ ribbons for garters.

ă-bat, ăir-m**a**rry, air-pair, a̱r-far, ĕr-m**e**rry, ĝ- g**e**t, ī-high, ĭr-m**i**rror, l̵-little, n̩-listen, ŏ-hot, oh-go, o͝o-wood, o͞o-moon, oor-t**ou**r, ȯr- **o**r, ow-how, t̤h-that, t̶h̶-thin, Ŭ-but, UR-f**u**r, ur-und**e**r.   ( ) - suppress the syllable   see p. xiii for complete list.

207. ***cambrics** fine linen cloths. /KAM briks/, or older [KAYM briks].

209. **chaunts** archaic variant of **chants** US /chănts/; E. NEW ENG, UK /chahnts/. See App. D -*aun*-.

213. **scurrilous** US /SKUR ih lus/; E.COAST US, UK /SKUH rih lus/ vulgar.

220. **damask** /DAM usk/ pink or light red.

224. **quoifs** tight-fitting caps. Variant of **coifs**, both pronounced /coyfs/.

224. **stomachers** ornamental chest covering. Mod. /STUM uh kurz/. In Shk's time /STUM uh cheerz/, rhyming with *dears,* though the rhyme could also have been based on variant pronunciations /-kairz/-/dairz/.

245. **kill-hole** oven hole. Some eds. prefer **kiln hole** now usually pronounced /kiln/, though /kill/ is older.

254. **behooves** /bih-, bee H$\overline{OO}$VZ/ is necessary, proper for. UK prefers the spelling **behoves** /bih HOHVZ/.

260. **ballet** /BAL ut/ archaic variant of **ballad.**

263, 268. **usurer('s)** /Y$\overline{OO}$ zhur urz/; UK *also* [-zhyoor urz, -zhoor urz] someone who lends money for interest.

265. ***carbonado'd** slashed for roasting. /car buh NAH dohd/; UK *rarely older* [-NAY dohd].

277. **fadom** /FAD um/ archaic variant of **fathom** /FĂŢH um/.

323. **ware-a** /WAIR uh/ referring to 'wares.' *Dear-a* could also have /air/ in Shk's time.

327. **Saltiers** uncertain. Perhaps confused with ***satyrs** US, CN /SAYT urz/, *rarely* [SAT urz]; UK /SAT urz/ [SAYT-] 'lusty goat-like creatures.' It may also show confusion with **saltiers** (also spelled **saltires**) /SAL-, SAWL teerz, -tīrz/ 'heraldic crosses.' Other eds. suggest that it may be **saultiers** 'leapers,' which could have been /SAWL teerz, -turz/ or /SAWT-/.

328. **gallimaufry** /gal ih MAW free/ stew, hodgepodge.

328. **gambols** /GAM błz/ frolics.

339. **by th' squier** /skwīr/ archaic variant of **square** 'carpenter's square,' i.e., 'precisely.'

368. ***protestation** US /proh tess-, prŏt ess TAY shun/;
CN /prŏt ess-/ [proh tess-]; UK /prŏt ess-/.

378. **perdition** /pur DISH un/; UK *also* [PUR DISH un] destruction.

395. ***nuptial** wedding. US, UK /NUP chł/ [-shł]; in CN both are used equally.

399. **rheums** /rōōmz/ diseases.

406. **unfilial** /un FIL ee ł/ contrary to the duty of a child.

417. **contract** here should be /cŏn TRACT/.

424. **thou cop'st with** /cohpst/ thou hast to do with.

431. **Farre** /far/ archaic variant of **far**, here 'farther.'

431. **Deucalion** father of the human race. /dyōō KAY lee un/; US *also* /dōō-/.
Sometimes newer /-ŏn/ is used, but is not recommended.

490. **close** /clohss/ hidden.

491. **unknown** here should be /UN nohn/.

491. **fadoms** /FAD umz/ archaic variant of **fathoms** /FĂTH umz/.

500. ***opportune** here should be /ŏp POR tyōōn/; US *also* /-tōōn/.

567. **unpath'd** here with 1st syllable stress.

567. **undream'd** here with 1st syllables stress.

597. **trompery, trumpery** /TRUMP ur ee/ worthless stuff.

598. ***pomander** scent ball. US /POH man dur/ [PŎM un dur, poh MAN dur];
CN /poh MAN dur/ [POH man dur, PŎM un dur, poh MAHN dur];
UK /poh MAN dur/. All the variants have existed for centuries, but
etymolgically the best choice is /PŎM un dur/ (from Fr. *pomme d'ambre*,
cf. *pomegranate* from Fr. *pomme granate*).

598. ***brooch** /brohch/ ornament. US [brōōch] not recommended.

ă-bat, ăir-ma**rr**y, air-pa**ir**, ạr-far, ĕr-me**rr**y, ĝ- get, ī-high, ĭr-mi**rr**or, ł-little, ṇ-listen,
ŏ-hot, oh-go, ōō-wood, ōō-moon, oor-tour, ōr- or, ow-how, ţh-that, th-thin, ŭ-but,
UR-fur, ur-und**er**.   ( ) - suppress the syllable   see p. xiii for complete list.

607. **pettitoes** /PET ee tohz/ trotters of a pig.

616. **whoobub** archaic variant of **hubbub** /HUB ub/, very likely pronounced the same way.

617. **choughs, chuffs** /chufs/ jackdaws.

635. **pennyworth** bargain. The older form is /PEN urth/, but in this prose passage the newer spelling pronunciation /PEN ee wurth, -WURTH/ may be used.

641. **flea'd** /fleed/ archaic and dialect variant of **flayed** /flayd/ skinned.

650. ***covert** hiding place. US, CN /KOHV urt/ [KUV-];
UK /KUV urt/ [KOHV urt], *rarely* [KUV ur], an older form.

655. **undescried** /un dih SKRĪD/ unseen.

672. **requisite** /REK wiz it/ required.

677. **extempore** /ek STEM pur ree/ on the spur of the moment.

708-56. **farthel** /FAR thl/ bundle. Variant of **fardel** /FAR dl/.

736. **cap-a-pe** from head to toe. Archaic variant of ***cap-à-pie**. Traditionally /kap uh PEE/, still the most common form in the US, CN, and also used in the UK. A newer form /-PAY/ is preferred in the UK and also used in the US. Stress may also fall on the 1st syllable. A Frenchified version /kap uh pee AY/ is also increasingly used. The spelling pronunciation /-PĪ/ is not recommended.

740, 742. **advocate('s)** /AD vuh kut/ someone who supports a person.

773. **germane** US /jur MAYN/; UK /JUR MAYN/ [JUR mayn] related to.

786. ***aqua-vitae** distilled liquor, e.g., brandy. US /AHK-, AK wuh VEE tī/, *rarely* [-VĪ tee]; CN /AK wuh VEE tī/ [AHK-]; UK /AK wuh VEE tī/ [-VEE tuh]. /AK wuh VĪ tee/ is the oldest surviving form. /-VEE tay/ not recommended.

788. **prognostication** a prediction. US /prŏg nŏss tih KAY shun/; UK /prug-/ [prŏg-].

800. **Close with him** /clohz/ make the deal.

812. **moi'ty, moiety** /MOY tee, MOY uh tee/ portion.

Act 5 Scene 1

4. **More penitence than done trespass**. *Penitence* was meant to be syncopated /PEN (ih) tunss/ and *trespass* is pronounced normally with first syllable stress.

87. **access** here should be /ak SESS/.

108. **proselytes** /PRŎS ih līts/ converts.

153. ***paragon** US /PĂIR uh gŏn/ [-gun]; CN /-gŏn/; UK /-gun/ [-gn̩] most perfect example.

157. **Smalus** /SMAY lus/.

202. ***divers** various. Here should be stressed on the first syllable US, CN /DĪ vurss, -vurz/; UK /DĪ vurss/ [-vurz].

221. **advocate** /AD vuh kut/ someone who supports a person or cause.

Act 5 Scene 2

3, 116. **farthel** /FAR t̩hl̩/ bundle. Variant of **fardel** /FAR dl̩/.

21. **Rogero** /roh JĔR oh, ruh JĔR oh/. Some eds. prefer **Ruggiero** /rōoj YĔR oh/.

56. ***conduit** fountain or water channel. Here must be 2 syllables /CŎN dwit/; UK *also* [CUN dwit, CŎN dywit, CŎN dit, CUN dit].

64. **avouches** /uh VOWCH iz/ affirms.

87. **dolor** (UK **dolour**) /DOH lur/; UK *also* /DŎL ur/ pain. See App. D *-or*.

91. **swounded** archaic variant of **swooned**. In Shk's time the vowel could be either /ow/ or /ōo/.

97. **Julio** (**Giulio**) **Romano** /JOOL ee yoh roh MAHN oh/.

160. ***boors** US, CN /bōorz/, *sometimes* [borz]; UK /bōorz, borz/ peasants.

ă-bat, ăir-**marry**, air-**pair**, a̩r-**far**, ĕr-**merry**, ĝ- **get**, ī-**high**, ĭr-**mirror**, l̩-**little**, n̩-**listen**, ŏ-**hot**, oh-**go**, ōō-**wood**, ōo-**moon**, oor-**tour**, ōr- **or**, ow-**how**, t̩h-**that**, ~~th-thin~~, Ŭ-**but**, UR-**fur**, ur-**under**.   ( ) - suppress the syllable   see p. xiii for complete list.

Act 5 Scene 3

67. **fixure** /FIK shur/; UK *also* /-syoor/ fixedness. Some eds. prefer **fixture**. See App. D *-ure*.

77. **cordial** US /COR jł/; UK /COR dył/ cheering.

155. **dissever'd** /dih SEV urd/ severed.

The Poems

A Lover's Complaint

1. **concave** here should be /CŎN-, CŎNG kayv/.

5. **espied** /ess SPĪD/ saw.

8, 29. **platt(ed)** /PLAT id/ variant form of **plait(ed)** 'braided,' pronounced the same way, or US *also* /PLAY tid/.

15. **eyne** /īn/ dialect form of *eyes*.

19. **contents** here /cŏn TENTS/.

28. *****commix'd** mixed. US /cuh MIKST/ [coh-], *rarely* [cŏm-]; UK /coh-/ [cŏm-, cuh-]. Q **comixt** /coh-, cuh MIKST/.

33. **fillet** /FILL it/ ribbon.

36. **maund** /mawnd/ wicker basket.

39. **margent** /MAR junt/ archaic variant of **margin**.

40. **usury** /YŌŌ zhur ee/; UK *also* [-zhyoor ee, -zhoor ee] lending money for interest.

42. **excess** here should be /ek SESS/, the most common UK form.

46. **sepulchres** /SEP ł kurz/ tombs.

48. **sleided** /SLEED id/ untwisted.

49. *****Enswath'd** wrapped. US, CN /en SWŎTHD/ [-SWAYTHD]; UK /-SWAYTHD/.

56. **contents** here should be /cŏn TENTS/.

94. **unshorn** here should be /UN shorn/.

104. **authoriz'd** here should be /aw THOR īzd/.

ă-bat, ăir-m**arry**, air-**pair**, ạr-**far**, ĕr-**merry**, ĝ- get, ī-high, ĭr-m**irror**, ł-little, ṇ-listen, ŏ-hot, oh-go, ŏŏ-wood, ōō-moon, oor-**tour**, ōr- or, ow-how, ṭh-that, ŧħ-thin, ŭ-but, UR-**fur**, ur-under.   ( ) - suppress the syllable   see p. xiii for complete list.

110. **controversy** here should be /CŎN truh vur see/, the normal US pronunciation.

112. **manage**. Some eds. prefer **manège** which here has 1st syllable stress US /MAH nezh, -nayzh/; UK /MAN ayzh/ [-ezh]; Fr. /MAH nezh/. Both words mean 'horsemanship.'

152. ***bulwarks** structures for defense. US, CN /BŲLL wurks/ [BŬL wurks]; UK /BŲLL WURKS, -wurks/. The vowels /or/, /ahr/ not recommended in the final syllable, and are non-standard in the UK.

155. ***precedent** /PRESS ih dunt/ example.

156. **assay** /uh-, ass SAY/ attempt.

164. **forbod** /for BŎD/ archaic variant of *forbidden*. Some eds. prefer **forbade** /for BAD, -BAYD/. The latter is newer.

165. **behoof** /bih-, bee HOOF/ profit, advantage.

175. **adulterate** /uh DULL trayt, -trut/ adulterous. /-ut / is more usual for an adj.

185. **with acture** /AK chur/ by physical act. See App. D -*ure*.

211. **diamond** here should be /DĪ mund/, the most common US form.

217. **blazon'd** /BLAY zund, -zṇd/ described.

223. **oblations** /uh BLAY shunz/ [oh-, ŏb-] religious offerings.

231. **distract** separate. Here 1st syllable stress is indicated.

242. **gyves** /jīvz/ chains, fetters.

244. **scapeth** /SKAY pith/ escapeth.

251. **enur'd** hardened. /en YOORD/; US *also* [en OORD], US, CN *rarely* [en YURD]. Some eds. prefer **inur'd** /in-/, others **immured** /ih MYOORD/ 'imprisoned.'

265. **confine** /cŏn-, cun FĪN/ limit.

270. **filial fear** /FIL yɫ/ a child's fear.

273. **aloes** /AL ohz/ bitterness.

279. **credent** /CREED n̩t/ trusting.

284. **brinish** /BRĪ nish/ referring to salt water, i.e., tears.

297. **daff'd** /dăft/ archaic variant of **doffed** /dŏft/; US *also* /dawft/ took off, put aside.

302. **plenitude** abundance. US /PLEN ih to͞od/ [-tyo͞od]; UK /-tyo͞od/. /-cho͞od/ is considered non-standard in the UK.

303. **cautels** /KAWT ł z/ deceits.

305, 308. **sound(ing)** archaic variant of **swooning**. In Shk's time the vowel could be either /ow/ or /o͞o/.

319. *__cherubin__ angel. US, CN /CHĔR uh bin/ [-yuh-]; UK uses both equally. /KĔR-/ not recommended.

326. **spungy** archaic variant of **spongy**, both pronounced /SPUN jee/.

ă-bat, ăir-ma**rry**, air-**pair**, a̱r-**far**, ĕr-me**rry**, ĝ- **get**, ī-**high**, ĭr-**mirror**, ł-**little**, n̩-**listen**, ŏ-**hot**, oh-**go**, o͝o-**wood**, o͞o-**moon**, oor-**tour**, ōr- **or**, ow-**how**, t̠h-**that**, t̶h̶-**thin**, ŭ-**but**, UR-f**ur**, ur-und**er**.   ( ) - suppress the syllable   see p. xiii for complete list.

The Passionate Pilgrim

People in the Poem

*Adonis US, CN /uh DŎN iss/, *rarely* [-DOHN-]; UK /uh DOHN iss/, *rarely* [-DŎN-] Venus' lover.
   Adon US, CN /uh DŎN/, *rarely* [uh DOHN]; UK /uh DOHN/, *rarely* [uh DŎN].

3.11. **Exhal 'st** here stress could fall on the 1st or 2nd syllable, the former is the usual US form, the latter is normal in the UK.

4.1. **Cytherea** /si~~th~~ uh REE uh/ Venus.

4.9. **unripe** here should be /UN rīp/.

4.13. **toward** /TOH wurd, -urd/ willing.

4.14. **froward** /FROH wurd, FROH urd/ peevish.

5.4, 6.5 *osier(s) US /OH zhur(z)/ [OH zyur(z)]; UK /OH zyur(z)/ willow(s).

6.3. **Cytherea** /si~~th~~ uh REE uh/ Venus.

7.5. **damask** /DAM usk/ pink or light red.

8.5. **Dowland** /DOW lund/ John Dowland, composer.

8.10. **Phoebus'** /FEE bus/ god of the sun.

10.1., 13.2- 8. **vaded, -eth** /VAY did, -di~~th~~/ variant of **faded, -eth**.

12.2. **pleasance** (F1) /PLEZ unss/ pleasantness, delight. Q1 has **pleasure**.

13.3. **gins** /ĝinz/ begins.

13.10. **cement** here with 1st syllable stress /SEE ment, SEM ent/.

14.3 **daff'd** /dăft/ archaic variant of **doffed** /dŏft/; US *also* /dawft/ discarded.

14.4. **descant** here should be /DES kănt/ sing variations.

14.8. **conster** /CŎN stur/ understand.

14.17. **Philomela** /fill oh MEE luh, fill uh-/ the nightingale.

14.23. **solace** /SŎL us/ comfort.

14.28. **succor** (UK **succour**) /SUCK ur/ help. See App. D *-or*.

16.16. **Ethiope** /EE̶T̶H̶ yohp/ person from Ethiopia.

17.19. **curtal dog** /CURT ł/ dog with tail cut short.

17.35. **Corydon** a love-sick shepherd. US /COR ih dŏn, -dun/;
UK, E.COAST US /CŎR-/. /-ŏn/ is usual in the US and is increasingly common in
the UK. See App. D *-on*.

18.26, 29. **yer** /yair/, archaic variant of **ere**.

18.54. **bewray'd** /bih-, bee RAYD/ revealed.

19.11. **kirtle** /KURT ł/ long gown.

20.14. **Tereu** /tee-, tih RŌŌ/ song of the nightingale.

20.23. **Pandion** /pan DĪ un/ Philomel's father. Sometimes newer /-ŏn/ is used,
but is not recommended. See App. D *-on*.

20.44. **commandement, commandment** here an archaic form in 4 syllables is
indicated /-uh munt/.

ă-bat, ăir-**marry**, air-**pair**, ạr-**far**, ĕr-**merry**, ĝ- **get**, ī-**high**, ĭr-**mirror**, ł-**little**, ṇ-**listen**,
ŏ-**hot**, oh-**go**, ōō-**wood**, ōō-**moon**, oor-**tour**, ŏr- **or**, ow-**how**, t̪h-**that**, t̶h̶-**thin**, ŭ-**but**,
UR-**fur**, ur-**under**.   ( ) - suppress the syllable   see p. xiii for complete list.

The Phoenix and the Turtle

5. **harbinger** /HAR bin jur/ advance messenger.

6. **precurrer** /pree-, prih CUR ur/ precursor.

7. *__Augur__ /AWG yur/ [-ur]; UK *also* /-yoor/ augurer, prophet.

12. **obsequy** /ŎB suh kwee/ burial service.

13. **surplice** /SUR pliss/ white priest's garment.

16. *__requiem__ /REK w(ee) yum/ funeral music.

49. **threne** /threen/ threnody, a funeral song.

Heading after 52. **Threnos** Gk. form of *threne*. Angl. /THREE nus, -ŏss/. Normal development would favor /-us/. A newer form /THRAY nohss/ is also used.

The Rape of Lucrece

People in the Poem

Brutus see **Junius Brutus.**

Collatinus /cŏl uh TĪ nus/.
  Collatine /CŎL uh tīn/.

Junius Brutus /JOON ee us BROO tus/. *Junius* appears in the argument only.

Lucius Tarquinius /LOO shus tar KWIN ee us/, /LOO s(ee) yus/. The former is nearly universal in the US, the latter is the most common form in the UK. Normal development would favor /LOO shus/ (for /lyoo-/ see App. D *lu-*). In the argument only.

Lucrece Shk intended first syllable stress /LOO creess/ in all instances. In some cases, in the first foot, for example, the usual mod. pronunciation /loo CREESS/ may be used, producing a regular line instead of an inversion (for /lyoo-/ see App. D *lu-*).
  Lucretia /loo CREE shuh/ (for /lyoo-/ see App. D *lu-*).

Lucretius /loo CREE shus/ (for /lyoo-/ see App. D *lu-*).

Publius Valerius /PUB lee us vuh LEER ee us/. In the argument only.

Servius Tullius /SUR vee us TŬLL ee us/. In the argument only.

Sextus Tarquinius /SEKS tus tar KWIN ee us/. In the argument only.

Superbus (Lucius Tarquinius) /soo PUR bus/; UK, SOUTH. US *also* [syoo-]. In the argument only.

Tarquin (Sextus Tarquinius) /TAR kwin/.

---

1. **Ardea** /ĄRD yuh/.

4, 50. **Collatium** /cŏl AY shum/.

---

26. **expir'd** here should be /EK spīrd/.

ă-bat, ăir-**marry**, air-**pair**, ąr-**far**, ĕr-**merry**, ĝ- **get**, ī-**high**, ĭr-**mirror**, ł-**little**, n̦-**listen**, ŏ-**hot**, oh-**go**, oo-**wood**, oo-**moon**, oor-**tour**, ŏr- **or**, ow-**how**, țh-**that**, th-**thin**, ŭ-**but**, UR-**fur**, ur-**under**.   ( ) - suppress the syllable   see p. xiii for complete list.

30. ***orator** US, CN /OR uh tur/; UK, E.COAST US /ŎR-/. Sometimes /OR ayt ur/ is used, but it is not recommended.   See App. D *-or*.

57. **entituled** /en TIT yoo led/; US *also* /-TITCH ł ed] having a claim. Some eds. prefer ***intituled** /in-/.

79. **niggard** /NIG urd/ miserly.

87. **unstain'd** here should be /UN staynd/.

88. **lim'd** /līmd/ caught in a trap of lime paste.

102. **margents** /MAR junts/ archaic variant of **margins**.

103. **unknown** here should be /UN nohn/.

138. **excess** here should be /ek SESS/, the most common UK form.

140. ***bankrout** /BANK rowt/ [-rut] archaic variant of **bankrupt.**

148. **vent'ring** /VEN tring/ archaic variant of **venturing.**

151. **defect** here should be /dih-, dee FECT/.

164. **comfortable** here should be /CUM fur tuh bł/.

176. ***falchion** type of sword. /FĂL chun/ [-shun]; *older* [FAWL chun].

179. **lodestar** /LOHD star/ pole star, guiding star.

199. **impious** /IM pyus/ profane.

200. **martial** /MAR shł/ warlike.

217. **strooken** /STRo͞oK in/ or perhaps simply a variant spelling of **strucken.**

221. **engirt** /en GURT/ surrounded.

224. **ever-during** /-DYOOR-/; US *also* [-Do͞oR-, -DUR-] everlasting.

230. **extreme** here should be /EK streem/.

268. ***orators** US, CN /OR uh turz/; UK, E.COAST US /ŎR-/. Sometimes /OR ayt urz/ is used, but it is not recommended.   See App. D *-or*.

274. **avaunt** /uh VAWNT/ begone!

276. ***countermand** revoke a command. /COWNT ur mănd/;
E.NEW ENG., UK /-mahnd/. More rarely the stress falls on the last syllable.

285. **servitors** /SURV (ih) turz/ servants. See App. D *-or*.

295. ***servile** /SUR vīl/, *rarely* [SUR vł] slave-like.

296. ***jocund** /JŎCK und/; US, CN *rarely* [JOHK-] merry.

299. **slavish** /SLAY vish/ slave-like.

300. **reprobate** /REP ruh bayt, -but/ depraved. /-ut / is more usual for an adj.

321. **inur'd** /in YOORD/; US *also* [in OORD], US, CN *rarely* [in YURD]
accustomed.

324. **consters** /CŎN sturs/ construes.

333. **sneaped** /SNEEP id/ nipped with cold.

361. **espied** /ess SPĪD/ seen.

367. **close** /clohss/ secure.

419. ***azure** blue. US /AZH oor/ [AZ yoor, AZH ur]; UK /AZH oor, AZ yoor/
[AY zyoor, -zhyoor]. Normal development would favor /AZH ur, AY zhur/.
See App. D *-ure*.

419. **alablaster** a type of white rock. US /AL uh blăss tur/;
E. NEW ENG., UK /-blahss-/ [-blăss-]. Archaic variant of **alabaster**
/-băss-, -bahss-/.

425. **Slak'd** /slaykt/ diminished.

429. ***Obdurate** unmoveable. Elsewhere in Shk with 2nd syll. stress
/ŏb-, ub DYOOR it/; US *also* /-DYUR-/ [-DUR-], however here the foot may be
inverted to permit the usual mod. form /ŎB dyoor ut, -dyur-/ [-jur-];
US *sometimes* [-dur-].

429. **exploits** here should be /ek SPLOYTS/.

ă-bat, ăir-ma**rry**, air-**pair**, ạr-**far**, ĕr-**merry**, ĝ- **get**, ī-**high**, ĭr-**mirror**, ł-**little**, n̩-**listen**,
ŏ-**hot**, oh-**go**, o͞o-**wood**, o͞o-**moon**, oor-**tour**, ōr- **or**, ow-**how**, t̩h-**that**, t̶h̶-**thin**, ŭ-**but**,
UR-**fur**, ur-**under**.   ( ) - suppress the syllable   see p. xiii for complete list.

433. *alarum US, CN /uh LAHR um/ [-LĂIR-]; UK /uh LĂIR um, uh LAHR um/ a call to arms.

447. *tumult turmoil. US /TO͞OM ult/; SOUTH.US *also* /TYO͞OM-/; CN /TYO͞OM-/ [TO͞OM-]; UK /TYO͞OM-/. /CHO͞OM-/ considered non-standard in the UK. A newer pronunciation /TUM ult/ is not recommended.

471. *parley /PAR lee/ conference with an enemy. Newer [-lay] not recommended.

509. *falchion type of sword. /FĂL chun/ [-shun]; *older* [FAWL chun].

523. obloquy /ŎB luh kwee/ disgrace.

537. slavish wipe /SLAY vish/ slave's brand.

538. descried /dih SKRĪD/ seen.

540. *cockatrice' /CŎCK uh triss, -trīss/ a monster whose gaze kills.

543. hind /hīnd/ doe.

553. *Orpheus here should be 2 syllables /OR fyus/ [-fyo͞oss]. See App. D -*eus*.

568. *conjures entreats earnestly. Here should be the usual mod. pronunciation with first syllable stress. US, CN /CŎN jurz/, *rarely* [CUN-]; UK /CUN-/ [CŎN-]. However, the older pronunciation for this meaning is /cun JOORZ/, now rarely used.

605. outrage here with 2nd syllable stress /owt RAYJ/.

637. askaunce at a sideways angle. Archaic variant of askance US /uh SKĂNSS/; UK, E. NEW ENG. /uh SKAHNSS/ [uh SKĂNSS]. See App. D -*aun*-.

643. eyne /īn/ dialect form of *eyes*.

710. recreant /REK r(ee) yunt/ cowardly.

711. *bankrout /BANK rowt/ [-rut] archaic variant of bankrupt.

727. *prescience foreknowldge. US /PRESS yunss/ [PRESH unss]; CN, UK /PRESS yunss/, *rarely* [PRESH unss]. Here should be two syllables, but the 3 syllable form /PRESS ee unss/ is the most common in all countries.

743. **convertite** /CŎN vur tīt/ a penitent.

753, 763, 827. **unseen** here should be /UN seen/.

779. **exhal'd** here with 2nd syllable stress, /eks HAYLD/, the normal UK form.

780. **supreme** here should be US /SOO preem/; UK, SOUTH. US *also* [SYOO-].

805. **sepulcher'd** here should be /suh-, sep PŬL kurd/ entombed.

807. **character'd** written. Here with second syllable stress.

809. **impious** /IM pyus/ profane.

815. *****orator** US, CN /OR uh tur/; UK, E.COAST US /ŎR-/. Sometimes /OR ayt ur/ is used, but it is not recommended.   See App. D -*or*.

824. **alloted** /uh LŎT id/ dealt.

828. **unfelt** here should be /UN felt/.

830. **mot** /mŏt/ motto.

858. **Tantalus** /TAN tuh lus/ he was tormented with hunger and thirst in Hades.

897. **suppliant's** /SUP lyunts/ someone who asks humbly for something.

910. *****heinous** /HAYN us/ hateful.   /HEEN us/ is non-standard though common in the UK.

914. *****gratis** unrewarded.   US, UK /GRAHT iss/ [GRAT-], UK *rarely* [GRAYT-]; CN /GRAT-/ [GRAHT-].

922. **accessary** here should be US /AK sess ĕr ee/; UK /-uh ree/.

925. **copesmate** /COHPS mayt/ companion.

940. **unmask** here should be US, CN /UN mask/; UK /-mahsk/.

943. **wronger** US /RAWNG ur/; UK /RŎNG-/ someone who does wrong.

ă-bat, ăir-**marry**, air-**pair**, ạr-**far**, ĕr-**merry**, ĝ- **get**, ī-**high**, ĭr-**mirror**, ł-**little**, ṇ-**listen**, ŏ-**hot**, oh-**go**, ōō-**wood**, ōō-**moon**, oor-**tour**, ōr- **or**, ow-**how**, ṭh-**that**, t̶h̶-**thin**, ŭ-**but**, UR-**fur**, ur-**under**.   ( ) - suppress the syllable   see p. xiii for complete list.

948. **contents** here /cŏn TENTS/.

953. ***beldame, beldam** old woman. US /BEL dam, -dum/; UK /BEL dam/, *rarely* [-dum]. /-daym/ is also used, but normal development would probably favor /-dam, -dum/.

975. **bedred** archaic variant of **bedrid** 'bedridden.' Both pronounced /BED rid/.

976. ***mischances** here with 2nd syllable stress.

986. **alms** charity for the poor. /ahmz/ is older; /ahlmz, awlmz/ are newer. In the UK the latter are non-standard.

1025. **cavil** /KAV ł/; UK *also* /KAV il/ quibble.

1042. **Aetna** /ET nuh/ volcano in Sicily.

1046. ***falchion** type of sword. /FĂL chun/ [-shun]; *older* [FAWL chun].

1062. **graff** shoot grafted to another stem. US /grăf/; E.NEW ENG., UK /grahf/. Archaic variant of **graft**.

1078. **impure** here should be /IM pyoor/; US *also* /-pyur/.

1079, 1128. **Philomele** /FILL uh meel, -oh-/ the nightingale. Variant of **Philomel** /-mel/.

1093. **cavils** US /KAV łz/; UK *also* [KAV ilz] quibbles.

1116. ***salve** ointment. US /sav/ [salv]; NEW ENG. /sahv/; CN /sav, salv/ [sahlv]; UK /salv/. Normal development would favor the *l*-less form (cf. *halve, calve*).

1129. **dishevell'd** /dih SHEV łd/ hanging loosely and disorderly.

1132. ***diapason** US /dī uh PAY sun, -sn̩/ [-zun, -zn̩]; UK /-z-/ [-s-] harmonious bass sound.

1134. **Tereus** he raped Philomel. /TEER yus/ [-yōōss]. See App. D -*eus*.

1134. **descants** here /DES kănts/ sings a treble part. The correct form would be *descant'st*.

1173. **engirt** /en GURT/ enclosed, surrounded.

1213. **brinish** /BRĪ nish/ referring to salt water, i.e., tears.

1214. **untun'd** here with 1st syllable stress.

1218. **meads** /meedz/ meadows.

1229. **eyne** /īn/ dialect form of *eyes*.

1234. ***conduits** water pipes or channels. Here must be 2 syllables /CŎN dwits/; UK *also* [CUN dwits, CŎN dywits, CŎN dits, CUN dits].

1234. **cesterns** /SESS turnz/ archaic variant of **cisterns** /SISS turnz/.

1247. ***champaign** level. Here should have 1st syllable stress /SHAM payn/; US *sometimes* [CHAM payn]. The latter form is older.

1254. **inveigh** /in VAY/ protest.

1257. **hild** /hild/ archaic variant of **held**.

1261. **president** example. Archaic variant of ***precedent**, both /PRESS ih dunt/. It is not clear whether /PREZ-/ was used in Shk's time.

1310. **tenure** archaic variant of **tenor** 'summary statement,' both /TEN ur/.

1332. **Ardea** /ĄRD yuh/.

1345. **defect** here should be /dih-, dee FECT/.

In lines 1367-1564 the following names appear several times:

***Priam('s)** King of Troy. US, CN /PRĪ um/ [-am]; UK /-am/, *rarely* [-um].
Normal development would favor /-um/.

Hecuba /HEK yoo buh/ Queen of Troy.

Pyrrhus(') /PĬR us/ Achilles' son.

Sinon traitor who caused Troy's fall. /SĪ nun/, but /-nŏn/ is becoming more common. See App. D *-on*.

1370. ***Ilion** Troy. /ILL yun/; UK *sometimes newer* [Ī lyun].

ă-bat, ăir-ma**rr**y, air-**pair**, ąr-**far**, ĕr-me**rr**y, ĝ- **get**, ī-**high**, ĭr-mi**rr**or, ł-**little**, ṇ-**listen**,
ŏ-**hot**, oh-**go**, o͞o-**wood**, o͞o-**moon**, oor-**tour**, ōr- **or**, ow-**how**, ţh-**that**, ~~th~~-**thin**, ŭ-**but**,
UR-**fur**, ur-**under**.   ( ) - suppress the syllable   see p. xiii for complete list.

1373. ***lamentable** here should be /LAM un tuh bł/ the usual UK pronunciation.

1374. **liveless** /LĪV liss/ archaic variant of **lifeless.**

1380. **pioner** soldier who dug trenches and planted mines. Archaic variant of **pioneer** /pī uh NEER/. Here rhymes with *appear.*

1388. **triumphing** here /trī UM fing/.

1394,1399. **Ulysses** /yōō LISS eez/; US *also* /yōō-/. The less common UK pronunciation /YŌŌ lih seez/ will not fit the meter.

1395. **physiognomy** /fiz ee ŎG nuh mee/, *rarely older* [fiz ee ŎN uh mee] face.

1401, 1420. **Nestor('s)** /NEST ur(z)/ oldest of the Greeks at Troy. See App. D -*or.*

1407. **winding** /WĪN ding/ spiraling.

1417. **boll'n** /bohln/ swollen with anger.

1423. **compact** here /cum-, cŏm PACT/ solid.

1424. **Achilles'** /uh KILL eez/ Gk. hero.

1430, 1486. **Hector** /HEK tur/ Trojan hero. See App. D -*or.*

1436. **strond** /strŏnd/ shore. Archaic variant of **strand.**

1436. **Dardan** /DAR dun/ district in which Troy lay.

1437,1442. **Simois'** /SIM (oh) wiss/ river near Troy.

1446. **dolor** (UK **dolour**) /DOH lur/; UK *also* /DŎL ur/ pain. See App. D -*or.*

1458. ***beldame's, beldam's** old woman's. US /BEL damz, -dumz/; UK /BEL damz/, *rarely* [-dumz]. /-daymz/ is also used, but normal development would probably favor /-damz, -dumz/.

1486. **Troilus** /TROY lus/ prince of Troy.

1486. **sounds** archaic variant of **swoons.** In Shk's time the vowel could be either /ow/ or /ōō/.

1486-9. sounds : wounds: confounds. The rhymes here rested on /ow/ in Shk's time.

1502. Phrygian /FRIJ un, -yun/. Normal development would favor the former.

1515. ensconc'd /en SKŎNST/ hid, sheltered.

1524. *Ilion Troy. /ILL yun/; UK *sometimes newer* [Ī lyun],

1533. belied /bih-, bee LĪD/ misrepresented.

1543. *travail here should be /TRAV ayl/ difficult labor.

1558. contraries /CŎN truh reez/ opposites.

1582. dolor (UK **dolour**) /DOH lur/; UK *also* /DŎL ur/ pain. See App. D -*or*.

1598. uncouth here should be /UN cōōth/ strange.

1609. consorted /cun SORT id/ assembled.

1612. dirge /durj/ funeral song.

1625. midnight here with 2nd syllable stress.

1626. *falchion type of sword. /FĂL chun/ [-shun]; *older* [FAWL chun].

1643. record here should be /rek-, rik ORD/.

1645. Th' adulterate /ṭhʸuh DULL trayt, -trut/ defiled. /-ut / is more usual for an adj.

1648. forbod probably /for BŎD/ archaic variant of **forbade**. /for BAD/ is older, /-BAYD/ newer.

1658. accessary here should be US /AK sess ĕr ee/; UK /-uh ree/.

1698. bewray'd /bih-, bee RAYD/ revealed.

1700. *protestation US /proh tess-, prŏt ess TAY shun/; CN /prŏt ess-/ [proh tess-]; UK /prŏt ess-/.

ă-bat, ăir-**marry**, air-**pair**, ạr-**far**, ĕr-**merry**, ĝ- **get**, ī-**high**, ĭr-**mirror**, ł-**little**, ṇ-**listen**, ŏ-**hot**, oh-**go**, ōō-**wood**, ōō-**moon**, oor-**tour**, ōr- **or**, ow-**how**, ṭh-**that**, th-**thin**, ŭ-**but**, UR-**fur**, ur-**under**.　　( ) - suppress the syllable　　see p. xiii for complete list.

1720. **assays** /uh-, ass SAYZ/. Some eds. prefer **essays** /es SAYZ/. Both mean 'attempts.'

1727. **contrite** here should be /CŎN trīt/ remorseful.

1745. ***rigol** /RIG ohl/ [RĪ gł, RIG ł, RĪ gohl] circle. The ending /-ohl/ is a newer, spelling pronunciation. /RĪ gł/ is recommended to avoid confusion with *wriggle*.

1754. **unlived** deprived of life. /un LĪVD/, rhymes with *derived*.

1756. **progenitors** /proh-, pruh JEN ih turz/ ancestors. See App. D *-or*.

1766. **surcease** /sur SEESS/ cease.

1805. **dispers'd** here with 1st syllable stress.

1844. ***protestation** US /proh tess-, prŏt ess TAY shun/;
CN /prŏt ess-/ [proh tess-]; UK /prŏt ess-/.

1851. **thorough** archaic variant of *through*, used when the meter demands two syllables. It is often pronounced as *thorough* on stage, but using /-o͞o/ in the final syllable will bring it closer to mod. *through*.

The Sonnets

1.1. **increase** here should be /in CREESS/ offspring.

1.12. **chorl** /chorl/ archaic variant of **churl**.

1.12. **niggarding** /NIG urd ing/ hoarding.

3.5. **unear'd** here should be /UN eerd/ unplowed.

4.5. **niggard** /NIG urd/ miser.

4.6. **The bounteous *largess given thee to give** 'liberal gifts.' If *bounteous* is two syllables, then *largess* should be stressed on the 1st syllable as elsewhere in Shk: US /LAR jess/ [-zhess]; CN, UK /LAR zhess/ [-jess]. But if *bounteous* is three syllables, then *largess* is stressed on the second syllable, as is more usual today. *Given* then becomes one syllable. Some eds. prefer **largesse**, pronounced the same way. Forms with /j/ are older.

4.7. **usurer** /Y$\overline{OO}$ zhur ur/; UK *also* [-zhyoor ur, -zhoor ur] someone who lends money for interest.

4.12. **acceptable** here should be /AK sep tuh bł/.

4.13. **unus'd** here should be /UN y$\overline{oo}$zd/.

5.14. **Leese** /leez/ an archaic form, related to **lose**.

6.5. **usury** /Y$\overline{OO}$ zhur ee/; UK *also* [-zhyoor ee, -zhoor ee] lending money for interest.

7.3. ***homage** /HŎM ij/; US *also* /ŎM ij/ acknowledgement of allegience.

11.5. **increase** here should be /in CREESS/ offspring.

12.6. **erst** /urst/ formerly.

12.8. **bier** /beer/ coffin.

14.13. **prognosticate** foretell. US /prŏg NŎSS tih kayt/; UK /prug-/ [prŏg-].

17.12. ***antique** ancient. Here /AN teek/, *rarely older* [AN tik].

ă-bat, ăir-**marry**, air-**pair**, ạr-**far**, ĕr-**merry**, ĝ- get, ī-high, ĭr-mirror, ł-little, ṇ-listen, ŏ-hot, oh-go, $\overline{oo}$-wood, $\overline{oo}$-moon, oor-**tour**, ōr- or, ow-how, ţh-that, ŧħ-thin, ŭ-but, UR-**fur**, ur-under.　　　() - suppress the syllable　　　see p. xiii for complete list.

19.4. **long-liv'd** /-livd/; US *also older* [līvd].

19.8. ***heinous** /HAYN us/ hateful. /HEEN us/ is non-standard though common in the UK.

19.10. ***antique** ancient. Here /AN teek/, *rarely older* [AN tik].

21.8. **rondure** sphere. US, CN /RŎN jur, -dyoor, -dyur/; UK /-dyoor/ [-dyur, -jur]. See App. D *-ure.*

22.4. **expiate** /EK spee ayt/ put an end to.

22.11. **chary** /CHAIR ee/; E.COAST US *also* /CHĂIR ee/ carefully.

23.10. ***presagers** /pree-, prih SAY jurz/ indicators.

24.4. **perspective** here should be /PUR spek tiv/.

25.11. **rased** /RAY sid/ erased. Some eds. prefer a variant **razed** /RAY zid/ which could also mean 'erased.'

26.3. **ambassage** /AM buh sij/ ambassador's message. Variant of **embassage** /EM-/.

28.11. **swart-complexioned** /swŏrt/ dark complexioned.

28.12. **twire** /twīr/ peer, peep.

31.5. **obsequious** /ub-, ŏb SEE kw(ee) yus/ dutifully mourning.

32.3. **re-survey** here should be /REE sur VAY/.

32.9. **voutsafe** /vowt SAYF/ grant. Archaic variant of **vouchsafe** /vowch SAYF/.

32.12. **equipage** accoutrements, dress. Usually /EK wih pij/ today, but here rhymes with *age.*

33.4. **alcumy** archaic variant of **alchemy** the study of the transformation of base metals to gold. Both pronounced /AL kuh mee/.

33.7. **forlorn** here should be /FOR lorn/.

34.7. ***salve** ointment. US /sav/ [salv]; NEW ENG. /sahv/; CN /sav, salv/ [sahlv]; UK /salv/. Normal development would favor the *l*-less form (cf. *halve, calve*).

35.6. **Authorizing** here /aw ~~THOR~~ ī zing/.

35.7. *****salving** applying a healing oinment. US /SALV ing/ [SAV ing];
E. NEW ENG. [SAHV ing]; CN /SALV ing/ [SAHLV ing, SAV ing, SAHV ing];
UK /SALV ing/. Normal development would favor the *l*-less form (cf. *halve, calve*).

35.10. **advocate** someone who supports a person. Normally /AD vuh kut/ but here rhymes with *hate*.

35.13. **accessary** here should be US /AK sess ĕr ee/; UK /-uh ree/.

38.10. **invocate** /IN voh kayt/ call upon.

40.13. **Lascivious** /luh SIV yus/ lustful.

45.9. **recured** cured, recovered. /ree-, rih KYOORD/; US *also* [-KYURD].

46.12. **moiety, moi'ty** /MOY tee/ portion.

49.2. **defects** here should be /dih-, dee FECTS/.

49.9. **insconce** /in SKŎNSS/ take shelter. Most eds. prefer **ensconce** /en-/.

50.7. **instinct** here /in STINCT/.

52.8. **carcanet** /CAR kuh net/ necklace.

53.5. *****Adonis** Venus' lover. US, CN /uh DŎN iss/, *rarely* [-DOHN-];
UK /-DOHN-/, *rarely* [-DŎN-].

53.8. **tires** /tīrz/ clothing.

53.9. **foison** /FOY zun, -zṇ/ harvest.

55.3. **contents** here should be /cŏn TENTS/.

55.4. **unswept** here should be /UN swept/.

56.3. **allay'd** /uh LAYD/ diminished.

57.9. **jealious** /JEL yus/ archaic variant of **jealous**.

ă-bat, ăir-**marry**, air-**pair**, ạr-**far**, ĕr-**merry**, ĝ- get, ī-**high**, ĭr-**mirror**, ļ-**little**, ṇ-**listen**, ŏ-**hot**, oh-**go**, ōō-**wood**, ōō-**moon**, oor-**tour**, ŏr- **or**, ow-**how**, ṭh-**that**, ~~th~~-**thin**, ŭ-**but**, UR-**fur**, ur-**under**.   ( ) - suppress the syllable   see p. xiii for complete list.

59.5. **record** here should be /rek-, rik ORD/.

59.7. *****antique** ancient. Here /AN teek/, *rarely older* [AN tik].

60.4. **sequent toil** /SEE kwunt/ unbroken toil.

61.8. **tenure** archaic variant of **tenor**, both /TEN ur/.

61.13. **elsewhere** here with 2nd syllable stress, a form still used in the UK, but unknown in the US.

64.3. **rased**, **razed** here /RAY zid/ destroyed.

67.9. *****bankrout** /BANK rowt/ [-rut] archaic variant of **bankrupt.**

67.11. *****exchequer** /eks CHEK ur/ treasury.

68.6. **sepulchres** /SEP ł kurz/ tombs.

68.9. *****antique** ancient. Here /AN teek/, *rarely older* [AN tik].

70.1. **defect** here should be /dih-, dee FECT/.

72.8. **niggard** /NIG urd/ miser.

74.6. **consecrate** /CŎN suh crut, -crayt/ consecrated.

78.4. *****poesy** US /POH ih see/ [-zee]; UK, CN /POH ih zee/ [-see] poetry.

79.6. *****travail** here should be /TRAV ayl/ labor.

83.6. *****extant** in existence. Here stressed on the 1st syllable
US /EK stunt/ [-stănt]; UK /-stănt/, *rarely* [-stunt]; in CN both are used equally.
In the UK /ek STĂNT/ is usual.

84.3. **confine** /cŏn-, cun FĪN/ confines, limits of an area.

84.3. **immured** /ih MYOOR id/ imprisoned.

84.5. **penury** /PEN yur ee/; UK *also* /PEN yoor ee/ poverty.

85.12. **hindmost** /HĪND mohst/ furthest behind.

86.7. **compeers** /cŏm-, cum PEERZ/ close associates.

87.2. *estimate US /ES tih mut/ [-mayt]; UK /-mayt/ [-mut] reputation. Rhymes with *determinate,* which may have been either /-ut/ or /-ayt/. Today nouns of this sort usually are /-ut/.

87.4. **determinate** /dih-, dee TUR mih nut, -ayt/ expired.

87.8. **patent** US /PAT ņt/; UK /PAYT ņt/ [PAT-] privilege, title to something.

87.11. **misprision** /mis PRIZH un, -ņ/ mistake.

95.6. **lascivious** /luh SIV yus/ lustful.

96.8, 10. **translate(d)** here should be stressed on the 2nd syllable, the normal UK pronunciation. US /trănss LAYT, trănz-/; UK /trănss-/ [trănz-, trahnz-, trahnss-, trunss-, trunz-].

97.6. **increase** here should be /in CREESS/ crops.

98.2. **proud-pied** /-pīd/ two or more colors in splotches.

99.7. **marjerom** type of herb. Archaic variant of **marjoram**, both pronounced /MAR jur rum/.

99.13. **eat** /et/ dialect variant of **ate**, which is also commonly /et/ in the UK.

102.7. **Philomel** /FILL oh mel, -uh-/ the nightingale.

106.5. **blazon** /BLAY zun, -zņ/ showy praise.

106.7. *antique ancient. Here /AN teek/, *rarely older* [AN tik].

107.4. **confin'd** here with 1st syllable stress /CŎN fīnd/.

107.6. *augurs /AWG yurz/ [-urz]; UK *also* /-yoorz/ augurers, prophets.

107.6. *presage here should be /pree-, prih SAYJ/ prediction.

108.12. **aye** /ay/ ever. /ī/ is often used, but not recommended.

110. 2. **motley** /MŎT lee/ fool (*motley* was the costume of different colored cloth worn by fools).

ă-bat, ăir-marry, air-pair, ạr-far, ĕr-merry, ĝ- get, ī-high, ĭr-mirror, ł-little, ņ-listen, ŏ-hot, oh-go, ōō-wood, ōō-moon, oor-tour, ōr- or, ow-how, ṭh-that, ᵵh-thin, ŭ-but, UR-fur, ur-under.　　( ) - suppress the syllable　　see p. xiii for complete list.

110.6. **Askaunce** at a sideways angle. Archaic variant of **Askance**
US /uh SKĂNSS/; UK, E. NEW ENG. /-SKAHNSS/ [-SKĂNSS]. See
App. D -*aun*-.

110.8. **essays** here with 2nd syllable stress /ess AYZ/ attempts.

111.10. ***eisel** US, CN /EE zł/ [AY zł]; UK /AY zł, EE zł/ vinegar. /ĪZ ł/ not
recommended.

112.9. **abysm** /uh BIZM/ variant of **abyss** /uh BISS/.

114.3. **saith** says. Here should be one syllable US /sayth/, *rarely* [seth];
UK /seth/ [sayth]. The older form is /seth/.

114.4. **alcumy** archaic variant of **alchemy** the study of the transformation of
base metals to gold. Both pronounced /AL kuh mee/.

114.5. **indigest** /in dih JEST/; US *also* /-dī-/ formless.

114.6. ***cherubins** angels. US, CN /CHĔR uh binz/ [-yuh-]; UK uses both
equally. /KĔR-/ not recommended.

116.8. **highth** /hīth/ archaic variant of **height**. /hītth/ is still used today, though
non-standard.

117.5. **unknown** here should be /UN nohn/.

119.2. **limbecks** /LIM beks, -biks/ archaic variant of *alembics*, upper parts of a
distillery.

120.12. ***salve** ointment. US /sav/ [salv]; NEW ENG. /sahv/;
CN /sav, salv/ [sahlv]; UK /salv/. Normal development would favor the
l-less form (cf. *halve, calve*).

121.5. **adulterate** /uh DULL trayt, -trut/ defiled. /-ut / is more usual for an adj.

123.11. **records** here should be /rek-, rik ORDZ/.

124.9. **heretic** /HĔR ih tik/ dissenter.

124.11. **politic** /PŎL ih tik/ cunning.

125.2. **extern** /ek STURN/ exterior.

125.7. **savor** (UK **savour**) /SAY vur/ smell, taste.

125.8. **thrivers** /~~THR~~Ī vurz/ those who thrive.

125.9. **obsequious** /ub-, ŏb SEE kw(ee) yus/ dutiful.

125.10. **oblation** /uh BLAY shun/ [oh-, ŏb-] religious offering.

125.13. **suborn'd** /sub ORND/ bribed.

126.12. ***quietus** final payment on a debt. /kwī EE tus/ is older and in the UK less frequently used; /kwī AY tus, kwee AY tus/ are newer and in the US less frequently used; in CN all three are equally used.

128.5 **envy** here with 2nd syllable stress /en VEE/.

130.5. **damask'd** /DAM uskt/ colored light red or pink.

130.14. **belied** /bih-, bee LĪD/ misrepresented.

134.7. ***surety-like** guarantee. Here should be two syllables, though in mod. English, three syllables are more common, /SHUR (ih) tee, SHOOR-, SHOR-/ (see App. D).

134.10. **usurer** /YOO zhur ur/; UK *also* [-zhyoor ur, -zhoor ur] someone who lends money for interest.

139.5, 12. **elsewhere** here with 2nd syllable stress, a form still used in the UK, but unknown in the US.

140.13. **belied** /bih-, bee LĪD/ slandered.

142.8. **revenues** here should be /ruh VEN yooz/.

142.10. ***importune** /im POR chun/ ask insistently. See App. D.

143.1. ***huswife** /HUZ if/ is traditional, /HUSS wīf/ is a newer, spelling pronunciation. The former is the most common form in the UK, the latter in the US. In CN both are used equally. In North America /HUSS wif/ is also sometimes used. Some eds. prefer mod. **housewife**.

143.4. **pursuit** here should be US /PUR soot/; UK, SOUTH. US /-syoot/.

146.7. **excess** here should be /ek SESS/, the most common UK form.

ă-bat, ăir-**marry**, air-**pair**, ạr-**far**, ĕr-**merry**, ĝ- **get**, ī-**high**, ĭr-**mirror**, ł-**little**, ṇ-**listen**, ŏ-**hot**, oh-**go**, ōō-**wood**, ōō-**moon**, oor-**tour**, ōr- **or**, ow-**how**, ṭh-**that**, ~~th~~-**thin**, Ŭ-**but**, UR-**fur**, ur-**under**.　　( ) - suppress the syllable　　see p. xiii for complete list.

146.11. **dross** /drŏss/; US *also* /drawss/ impure matter, rubbish.

147.12. **randon** /RAN dun/ archaic form of **random**.

149.7. **thou low'r'st, lourest** thou frownest. /lowrst/ with the vowel of *how*.

149.11. **defect** here should be /dih-, dee FECT/.

150.7. **warrantise, -ize** guarantee. US /WŌR un tīz/;
UK, E.COAST US /WŎR un tīz/.

154.5. **votary** /VOHT uh ree/ someone devoted to something or someone.

Venus and Adonis

People in the Poem

*Adonis US, CN /uh DŎN iss/, *rarely* [-DOHN-]; UK /uh DOHN iss/,
rarely [-DŎN-] Venus' lover.
  Adon US, CN /uh DŎN/, *rarely* [uh DOHN]; UK /uh DOHN/, *rarely* [uh DŎN].

The following words occur several times in this poem:

saith says. Here should be one syllable US /sayth/, *rarely* [seth];
UK /seth/ [sayth]. The older form is /seth/. Today the most common US form is
/SAY ith/.

courser /COR sur/ warhorse.

5. **amain** /uh MAYN/ with full speed.

6, 46. **gins** /ĝinz/ begins.

15. **deign** /dayn/ accept.

19. **saciety** /suh SĪ uh tee/ fullness. Archaic variant of **satiety** /suh TĪ uh tee/.

26. **president** sign. Archaic variant of ***precedent**, both /PRESS ih dunt/. It is
not clear whether /PREZ-/ was used in Shk's time.

28. *salve ointment. US /sav/ [salv]; NEW ENG. /sahv/; CN /sav, salv/ [sahlv];
UK /salv/. Normal development would favor the *l*-less form (cf. *halve, calve*).

75. **low'rs, lours** frowns. /lowrz/ with the vowel of how.

84. **comptless** /COWNT liss/ archaic variant of **countless**. See App. D
accompt.

99. **sinowy** /SIN (oh) wee/ muscular. Archaic variant of **sinewy**
/SIN y(oo) wee/; US *also* [SIN (oo) wee].

107. *ensign flag. US, CN /EN sn̩/, US *rarely* [-sīn]; UK /-sn̩, -sīn/.

112. *servile /SUR vīl/, *rarely* [SUR vl̩] slave-like.

ă-bat, ăir-marry, air-pair, ạr-far, ĕr-merry, ĝ- get, ī-high, ĭr-mirror, l̩-little, n̩-listen,
ŏ-hot, oh-go, ōō-wood, ōō-moon, oor-tour, ōr- or, ow-how, th-that, th-thin, ŭ-but,
UR-fur, ur-under.   ( ) - suppress the syllable   see p. xiii for complete list.

135. **rheumatic** here must be /RŌŌM uh tik/ suffering from colds.

138. **defects** here should be /dih-, dee FECTS/.

147. **dishevelled** /dih SHEV łd/ hanging loosely and disorderly.

149. **compact** /cum-, cŏm PACT/ composed of.

169, 170. **increase** here should be /in CREESS/ offspring, harvest.

183. **low'ring, louring** frowning. /LOWR ing/, with the vowel of *how*.

199. *****obdurate** unmoveable. Here with 2nd syll. stress /ŏb-, ub DYOOR it/; US *also* /-DYUR-/ [-DUR-]. 1st syllable stress is more usual today.

211. **liveless** /LĪV liss/ archaic variant of **lifeless**.

213. **Statuë** elsewhere this indicates a 3 syllable pronunciation /STATCH oo wuh/, but here 2 syllables is required and the mod. form can be used. If the older form is used it must be /STATCH wuh/ here.

260. **jennet** /JEN it/ small Sp. horse.

261. **espy** /ess PĪ/ see.

265. **Imperiously** /im PEER yus lee/ imperially.

275. **glisters** /GLIS turz/ glistens.

279. **curvets** hops on hind legs. Here may be /CUR vets, -vits/ or the more usual /cur VETS/.

284. **Holla** here should be /HŎL uh/ whoa.

286. **caparisons** /kuh PĂIR ih sn̩z/ ornamental cloth coverings for a horse.

290. *****limning** /LIMM ing/, *sometimes newer* [LIM ning] drawing.

313. *****malcontent** /MAL cun tent/; CN, UK *rarely* [mal cun TENT] person who is displeased.

320. **unback'd** here /UN backt/ never having had a rider.

325. **chafing** /CHAY fing/ anger.

342. **askance** US /uh SKĂNSS/; UK, E. NEW ENG. /uh SKAHNSS/ [uh SKĂNSS] at a sideways angle.

363. **alablaster** a type of white rock. US /AL uh blăss tur/; E. NEW ENG., UK /-blahss-/ [-blăss-]. Archaic variant of **alabaster** /-băss-, -bahss-/.

364. **engirts** /en GURTS/ besieges, surrounds.

384, 385. **palfrey** /PAWL free/; UK *also* [PŎL-] saddle horse.

392. *__Servilely__ /SUR vīl ee /, *rarely* [SUR vł ee] in a slave-like manner.

443. **stillitory** here should be two syllables /STILL (ih) tree/ distillery.

457. *__presage__ here should be /pree-, prih SAYJ/ omen.

466. *__bankrout__ /BANK rowt/ [-rut] archaic variant of **bankrupt.**

477. **chafes** /chayfs/ rubs.

500. **shrowd** /shrohd/ harsh. Archaic variant of **shrewd.**

507. **verdour** archaic form of *__verdure__ 'freshness.'
US, CN /VUR jur, -dyoor, -dyur/; UK /-dyoor/ [-dyur, -jur]. See App. D *-ure.*

526. **ungrown** here should be /UN grohn/.

540. **Incorporate** /in CORP rut, -rayt/ made into one body. /-ut / is more usual for an adj.

544. **drouth** /drowth/ variant of **drought** /drowt/ still used in some US dialects.

551. **vultur** /VŬL tur/ archaic variant of **vulture.**

562. **froward** /FROH wurd, FROH urd/ difficult to deal with.

567. **vent'ring** /VEN tring/ archaic variant of **venturing.**

570. **froward** difficult to deal with. Today normally /FROH wurd, FROH urd/ but here shows an archaic variant that rhymes with *coward.*

ă-bat, ăir-**marry**, air-**pair**, ạr-**far**, ĕr-**merry**, ĝ- **get**, ī-**high**, ĭr-**mirror**, ł-**little**, ṇ-**listen**, ŏ-**hot**, oh-**go**, ōŏ-**wood**, ōō-**moon**, oor-**tour**, ōr- **or**, ow-**how**, ţh-**that**, ŧħ-**thin**, ŭ-**but**, UR-**fur**, ur-**under**.　　　( ) - suppress the syllable　　　see p. xiii for complete list.

599. **Tantalus'** /TAN tuh lus/ king tormented with hunger and thirst in Hades.

600. ***Elysium** the realm of the blessed in the after-life. US /ih LEEZH yum/ [-LIZ-, -LIZH-, -LEESS-, -LISS-]; UK /-LIZ-/; *also* /ee-/ in all countries. The oldest forms still in use are /-LIZ-/, /-LIZH-/. The historic form is /ih LIZH um/.

603. **mishaps** here should be /mis HAPS/.

608. **assay'd** /uh-, ass SAYD/ tried.

616. **javeling's** variant spelling of **javelin's**, both pronounced /JAV (uh) linz/.

617, 624. **tushes** /TŬSH iz/ archaic form of **tusks** still used in some southern US dialects.

622. **sepulchres** /SEP ł kurz/ tombs.

628. **venter** /VEN tur/ archaic variant of **venture**.

633. **eyne** /īn/ dialect form of *eyes*.

636. **mead** /meed/ meadow.

657. **dissentious** /dih SEN shus/ creating ill-will.

662. **chafing** /CHAY fing/ enraged.

671. **prophesy** /PRŎF uh sī/ predict the future.

674. **timorous** /TIM (uh) rus/ frightened.

679. **purblind** /PUR blīnd/ partly-blind.

683. **musits, musets** /MYŌŌ zits/ gaps in a hedge.

697. **Wat** /wŏt/ the hare.

698. **hinder-legs** /HĪN dur/ hind legs.

700. ***alarums** US, CN /uh LAHR umz/ [-LĂIR-]; UK /uh LĂIR umz, uh LAHR umz/ calls to arms.

738. ***mischances** in verse normally with 2nd syllable stress.

739. **agues** /AY gyōōz/ malarial fevers.

740. **wood** /wo͞od/ crazy, distraught. It was also /wo͞od, wohd/ in the dialects of North. Eng. Here rhymes with *blood*, which was either /blo͞od/ or /blŏod/.

743. *__impostumes, imposthumes__ /im PŎS tyo͞omz/ [-cho͞omz]; US *also* [-to͞omz] abcesses.

747. **savor** (UK **savour**) /SAY vur/ character, style.

766. **reaves** /reevz/ bereaves, robs.

774. *__treatise__ speech. US /TREET iss/, *rarely* [-iz]; CN /-iss/; UK both /s/ and /z/ forms used equally.

791. **increase** here should be /in CREESS/ offspring.

806. *__orator__ US, CN /OR uh tur/; UK, E.COAST US /ŎR-/. Sometimes /OR ayt ur/ is used, but it is not recommended. See App. D *-or*.

813. **laund** /lawnd/ glade.

825. **stonish'd** /STŎN isht/ astonished.

836. **extemporally** /ek STEM p(uh) ruh lee/ composed on the spur of the moment.

848. **parasits** /PĂIR uh sits/ archaic form of **parasites**.

869. **chaunt** archaic variant of **chant** US /chănt/; E. NEW ENG, UK /chahnt/. See App. D *-aun-*.

875. **milch** /milch/ milk.

881. **timorous** /TIM (uh) rus/ frightened.

914. **caitiff** /KAYT if/ wretch.

940. **randon** /RAN dun/ archaic form of **random**.

948. **ebon** /EB un/ black.

987. **weal** /weel/ welfare.

ă-bat, ăir-**marry**, air-**pair**, ạr-**far**, ĕr-**merry**, ĝ- g**e**t, ī-high, ĭr-**mirror**, ł-little, ṇ-listen, ŏ-hot, oh-go, o͝o-wood, o͞o-moon, oor-**tour**, ōr- **or**, ow-how, th̪-**that**, th̶-**thin**, ŭ-but, UR-**fur**, ur-und**er**.　　　( ) - suppress the syllable　　see p. xiii for complete list.

995. **clepes** /cleeps/ calls.

996. **Imperious** /im PEER yus/ imperial.

996. **supreme** ruler. Here should be US /S$\overline{OO}$ preem/;
UK, SOUTH. US *also* [SY$\overline{OO}$-].

1002. **decesse, decess** /dee-, dih SESS/ poetic variant of **decease** 'death.'

1004. **wreak'd** /reekt/ revenged.

1041. **consort** /cun SORT/ keep company.

1095. **recreate himself** /REK ree ayt/ amuse himself.

1115. **nousling** archaic variant of **nuzzling**, both pronounced /NUZ ling/.

1135. **prophesy** /PRŎF uh sī/ predict the future.

1161. ***servile** /SUR vīl/, *rarely* [SUR vł] slave-like.

1193. **Paphos** place on Cyprus sacred to Venus. US /PAY fus, -fŏs/;
UK /-fŏs/ [-fus]. Normal development would favor /-us/. A newer ending
/-ohss/ is also used, especially in the US. A more recent restored pronunciation
with /PAH-/ is also used.

1194. **immure** /ih MYOOR/ imprison.

Appendices

APPENDIX A: COMMON WORDS WITH MORE THAN ONE STANDARD PRONUNCIATION IN TODAY'S ENGLISH

Some common words have two or more pronunciations in Standard American or British English today, or the same word may vary between countries. Here is a list of some that occur in Shakespeare. All of the pronunciations given in the chart are acceptable as Standard English within the listed country, that is, large numbers of educated speakers pronounce the words in the given way, though some may be newer forms based on spelling.

It is important to remember that speakers from one part of the country often look with scorn on pronunciations they do not use. An example is *catch* which many Americans know only as /ketch/ while others say /katch/; there are many within each group who believe theirs is the only correct pronunciation.

There are also groups of words that vary between North America and the UK. The British and some New Englanders generally use /ah/ before /f, th, s/, and /n/ plus consonant in words like *laugh, bath, fast, can't* where most North Americans use /ă/. These words are not included in this list.

Evidence for the pronunciations listed here comes primarily from the surveys conducted for this study (indicated by an asterisk) supplemented by older dialect studies and the dictionaries.

	United States	UK (RP)
accomplish	/uh CŎMP lish/	/-CUMP-/ [-CŎMP-]
again(st)	/uh GEN(ST)/, rarely [uh GAYN(st)]	/uh GEN(ST)/ [uh GAYN(ST)]
***agile**	/AJ ł/ [-īl]	/AJ īl/
***balk**	/bawk, bawlk/	/bawk/ [bawlk]
battery	/BAT ur ee/	/BAT ree/
been	/bin, ben/, rarely [been]	/been/ [bin]
borrow	/BAHR oh/ [-uh, BŌR-]	/BŌR oh/
braggart	/BRAG urt/	/-ut/ [-aht]
***buoy**	/BOO ee/ [boy]	/boy/
calm	/kahm, kahlm, kawlm/	/kahm/ [kahlm]
catch	/katch, ketch/	/katch/
***celestial**	/suh LEST ee ł, -chł/	/suh LEST YŁ/
circumstance	/SUR cum stanss/	/SUR cum stᵘnss/ [-stahnss, -stanss]
clerk	/clurk/	/clahk/
***compost**	/CŎM pohst/ [-pŏst]	/CŎM pŏst/
counterfeit	/COWN tur fit/	/COWN tuh fit/ [-feet]
***deity**	/DEE ih tee/	/DAY ih tee/ [DEE-]
desolation, desolate	/DESS-/, rarely [DEZ-]	/DESS-/
***direct**	/dur-, dih REKT/ [dī-]	/dih REKT/ [dī-]

	United States	UK (RP)
*disdain	/dis DAYN/ [diz-]	/dis DAYN/ [diz-]
disguise	/dis SKĪZ/	/dis SKĪZ/ [diz ĜĪZ]
dog	/dawg, dŏg/	/dŏg/
either	/EE ᵗhur/ [Ī ᵗhur]	/Ī ᵗhuh/ [EE-]
*exile	/EK sīl, EGG zīl/	/EK sīl/ [EGG zīl/
experiment	/ek SPĔR ih ment, -SPĬR-/	/ek SPĔR ih ment/
*falcon	/FAL kun/ [FAWL-]	/FAL kun, FAWL-/
*fantasy	/FANT uh see/	/FANT uh see/ [-zee]
*fertile	/FURT ł/ [-īl]	/FUR tīl/
figure	/FIG yur/	/FIG uh/
*forehead	/FOR hed/ [FOR id] E. Coast [FAHR-]	/FŎR id/ [FOR hed]
*fragile	/FRAJ ł/ [-īl]	/FRAJ īl/
gone	/gawn, gŏn/	/gŏn/
herbs	/urbz/ [hurbz]	/HURBZ/
*homicide	/HŎM ih sīd/ rarely [HOHM-]	/HŎM ih sīd/
*hostile	/HŎST ł/ [-īl]	/HŎST īl/
*hover	/HUV ur/	/HŎV uh/ [HUV uh]
human,huge, etc.	/HYŌŌ-/, [YŌŌ-]	/HYŌŌ-/
*(after-) inquiry	/ING kwur ee/ [ing KWĪ ree]	/ing KWĪ ree/
*interest	/IN trist/ [IN tur ist]	/INT rist/ [IN tuh rist]
issue	/ISH ōō/	/ISH ōō/ [ISS yōō, ISH yōō]
*jury	/JUR ee, JŌŌR ee/	/JŌŌR ee/
*leisure	/LEE zhur/ [LEZH ur]	/LEZH uh/
*lever	/LEV ur/ [LEE vur]	/LEE vuh/
*luxury	/LUCK shur ee, LUG zhur ee/	/LUCK shuh ree/
madman	/MAD man/	/MAD mun/
medicine	/MED ih sin/	/MED sn/ [MED sin, MED ih sin]
melancholy	/MEL un cŏl ee/	/MEL un cuh lee/ [-cŏl-]
*minority	/mih NŎR it ee/ [mī-] E.COAST /-NAHR-/	/mī NŎR it ee/ [mih-]
*mongrel	/MŎNG grł/ [MAWNG-, MUNG-]	/MUNG grł/
*negotiate	/nuh GOH shee ayt/, rarely [-see ayt]	/nuh GOH shee ayt/ [-see ayt]
neither	/NEE ᵗhur/ [NĪ ᵗhur]	/NĪ ᵗhuh/ [NEE-]

	United States	UK (RP)
*oaths	/oht̪hs, oht̪hz/	/oht̪hs, oht̪hz/
often	/AWF ṇ, -tun/	/ŎF ṇ/ [-tun]
on	/ŏn, awn/	/ŏn/
orange	/OR inj, ornj/; E.COAST /AHR inj/	/ŎR inj/
*poor	/pŏŏr, por/	/pŏŏr, por/
*posterior	/pŏs STEER ee ur/ [pohst-]	/pŏs STEER ee uh/
princess	/PRIN sess/	/prin SESS/
privacy	/PRĪ vuh see/	/PRIV uh see/
*process	/PRŎS ess/ [PROH sess]	/PROH sess/ [PRŎS ess]
*progress	/PRŎG ress/ [PROH gress]	/PROH gress/ [PRŎG ress]
rather	/RĂT̪H ur/ [RUH t̪hur, RAH-]	/RAH t̪huh/
roof	/rŏŏf/ [rŏŏf, ruff]	/rŏŏf/ [rŏŏf]
room	/rŏŏm/ [rŏŏm, rum]	/rŏŏm/ [rŏŏm]
root	/rŏŏt/ [rŏŏt, rut]	/rŏŏt/ (/rŏŏt/ is non-standard)
*sliver	/SLĬV ur/	/SLĬV uh/ [SLĪ vuh]
sorrow	/SAHR oh/[-uh, SŌR-]	/SŎR oh/
sorry	/SAHR ee/ [SŌR ee]	/SŎR ee/
*sterile	/STĔR ł/ [-īl]	/STĔR īl/
suggest	/sug JEST/	/suh JEST/
syrup	/SĬR up, SUR-/	/SĬR up/
tomorrow	/tŏŏ MAHR oh, -uh/ [tuh-, -MŌR-]	/tŏŏ MŌR oh/, /tuh-/
*tournament	/TUR nuh munt/ [TOOR-, TOR-]	/TOOR nuh munt/ [TOR-, TUR-]
toward (prep.)	/twōrd, tord/ [tuh WÂRD]	/tuh WÂRD/ [tord]
*tresspass	/TRESS păss, -pus/	/TRESS pus/; /-păss, -pahss/ are non-standard
were	/WUR/	/WUR/ [wair]
with	/wit̪h/ [wit̪h]	/wit̪h/; /wit̪h/ non-standard
wrath	/răt̪h/, E.NEW ENG. /ah/	/rŏt̪h/ [rawt̪h]; /raht̪h, răt̪h/ are non-standard

ă-bat, ăir-marry, air-pair, ạr-far, ĕr-merry, ĝ- get, ī-high, ĭr-mirror, ł-little, ṇ-listen, ŏ-hot, oh-go, ŏŏ-wood, ōō-moon, oor-tour, ōr- or, ow-how, t̪h-that, t̪h-thin, ŭ-but, UR-fur, ur-under.   ( ) - suppress the syllable   see p. xiii for complete list.

APPENDIX B: COMMON ARCHAIC FORMS IN SHAKESPEARE

alevan /uh LEV un/	**eleven**
beshrow /bee-, bih SHROH/	**beshrew** 'to curse'
burthen /BURṬH in/	**burden**
fadom /FAD um/	**fathom**
fift /fift/	**fifth**
lanthorn /LAN turn/, or possibly /LAN ~~th~~orn, ~~th~~urn, LANT horn/. Although a popular misconception led to the spelling with *-horn,* it was probably still pronounced /LAN turn/ (compare the breed of chicken, *Leghorn,* still /LEG urn/ today).	**lantern**
moe /moh/	**more**
murther /MUR ṭhur/	**murder**
sate /sat/ or possibly /sayt/	**sat**
shrike /shrīk/	**shriek**
shrowd /shrohd/	**shrewd**
sixt /sikst/	**sixth**
sound /sownd, sōōnd/	**swoon**
strook, -en /strŏŏk, struck/	**struck, stricken**
vild /vīld/	**vile**
wrastle /RĂSS ł/	**wrestle**

APPENDIX C: THE VOWEL SYSTEMS OF NORTH AMERICAN AND BRITISH ENGLISH

Some minor confusion in interpreting the pronunciation symbols may arise in certain instances because not all types of English have the same system of vowel sounds. One of the major differences now found in North American English centers around the so-called *cot-caught* merger: the vowel found in the group of words *cot, father, drama, body, Tommy* and the vowel found in the group of words *caught, awe, talk, audience, bought, broad* were once pronounced differently everywhere in the English speaking world, but in the twentieth century, speakers in some areas have merged them to the same sound. *Caught* and *cot* are now homonyms in those areas. Speakers from Canada, eastern New England, western Pennsylvania, and parts of the West Coast have exhibited merger for decades, but the change is now spreading to all parts of the United States, particularly among younger speakers. The difference is maintained most strongly along the East Coast of the United States, up to the Connecticut-Rhode Island border, and in the Great Lakes Region.[*]

In regions where *cot* and *caught* are pronounced alike there is one less vowel in the speaker's repertory. So when the *Guide* lists two of the possible pronunciations of *wont* as /wawnt/ and /wŏnt/, speakers who have merged the two sounds will be puzzled because /aw/ and /ŏ/ sound the same for them. Yet it must be listed in this way to inform those speakers who still maintain a distinction that they have a choice between those two pronunciations.

A parallel example is found in the consonants in words that begin with *wh-*. *Where, white, whale* are pronounced with /hw-/ in Scotland and in some parts of the United States, but in England and most of the United States, they have lost the initial breath, leaving simple /w-/. *Where, white, whale* are homonymous with *wear, wight, wail* in these areas. Using the symbol /wh-/ keyed to *why* instructs each group of speakers to supply whichever sound it normally would use.

Vowel-system differences also account for the use of two different symbols to describe what to most Americans is the same vowel in the first syllable of *father* and in *fop*. However British speakers and some New Englanders use distinct vowels for these two words, /AH/ for *father* (the same sound as in Standard British *bath, farm*), and /ŏ/ for *fop*, which in British English is shorter, rounder, and pronounced more toward the back of the mouth than /ah/. If *wan*, for example, were symbolized as /wahn/, speakers from the UK would use the vowel of *father*, the incorrect sound for British English. The correct vowel is that found in *fop* /ŏ/. By using the symbols /ah/ and /ŏ/ in the appropriate words, each speaker can supply the sound typically used in his or her speech community and produce the desired sound.

---

[*] Dale Coye, "A Linguistic Survey of College Freshmen: Keeping up with Standard American English," *American Speech* 69 (Fall 1994): 267.

Other American mergers are found in vowels before /r/ plus another vowel. The vowels of *marry, merry, Mary* are pronounced alike by most Americans, but since East Coast speakers, as well as some non-Americans, pronounce them differently, different symbols are needed: *marry* /MĂIR ee/, *merry* /MĔR ee/, and *Mary* /MAIR ee/. For most Americans these symbols will refer to the same sound, but others will be directed to the correct vowel in their repertory. Similarly, *mirror* and *mere* contain the same vowel for most Americans, which could simply be symbolized as /eer/, but again some speakers from the East Coast and some non-Americans distinguish the two sounds, here given as /ir/ and /eer/.

A further point of confusion lies in the pronunciation of words like *sure, pure, cure*. In everyday speech many Americans pronounce these words to rhyme with *fur*, while others pronounce them to rhyme with *tour*. However in formal contexts many of the former group shift their pronunciation so they also rhyme them with *tour*. This category of words includes several that are common in elevated or literary styles: *assure, inure, endure, penurious*. In the *Guide* they will all be listed to rhyme with *tour*, though the Survey indicated some support for pronouncing them to rhyme with *fur*, even in formal contexts like the stage.[+]

Most dictionaries list the vowel of *tour* as /to͞or/, but as it is spoken in North America there are several variations. In some parts of the United States it is approximately the same as in *too* /o͞o/, in others it is more like the vowel in *took* /o͝o/, and in some areas (southern New Jersey, southeastern Pennsylvania) it has the vowel of *tore*. In Standard British it also has merged with the vowel in *tore* for many speakers (J.C. Wells 1982, 1: 236-7; 2: 287-8). In this volume it will be symbolized without a diacritic mark, /oor/, or in ambiguous cases /o͞or/ (e.g., in a word like *durance* where to symbolize the American pronunciation as /DOOR unss/ makes the first syllable look like *door*).

A few Americans speakers, particularly older ones, may maintain a distinction between the vowels in words like *horse* and those in *hoarse*, which affects a large number of words, but the merger of these two sounds is now virtually universal among middle-aged and younger Americans. Though some dictionaries indicate this distinction by using different symbols for these two types of vowels, the *Guide* symbolizes both as /or/.

[+] North American professors in the Survey were asked to advise a foreigner on the pronunciation of this class of words ending in *-ure*, with the results listed below. If the question had been put to a group lower on the education scale, for example, those who had only completed four years of college, the results would very likely have shown a greater preference for rhyming these words with *fur*, even at the formal level.

Words like *endure, assure* are pronounced to rhyme with . . .

	United States	Canada
tour always	80%	64%
tour formally, *fur* informally	11%	36%
fur always, even formally	9%	0

Another potential point of confusion arises from the American vs. British difference in the vowel of *fur*. For most Americans this vowel is the same as the weak vowel of *mother*, but in British English and some American dialects they are different sounds. The notation allows for this difference in its upper vs. lower case distinction /UR/ vs. /ur/. *Murmer* would be /MUR mur/, where the two vowels are the same for most Americans, but different for British speakers. However, in British English /UR/ sometimes occurs in unstressed positions, making it necessary at times to use small caps to indicate the correct vowel. In most varieties of American English *peradventure* could be symbolized with the same vowel in the first and last syllables, /pur ad VEN chur/, but because these are two different sounds in the UK system, and because the upper case letters must be reserved for the third syllable where the main stress usually falls, the first vowel is written with small caps, /UR/, and the last /ur/, /PUR ad VEN chur/.

A similar confusion may arise when British speakers confront the notation for the weak vowel in words like *very, enough, Julia*. In most types of North American English, this weak vowel has the same quality as the strong vowel of *bee*, that is, the two vowels of *weedy* are the same, and the symbols /EE/ and /ee/ are used for the stressed and weak vowels respectively. But in the UK this weak vowel was traditionally the same as the vowel of *bit* in RP. Today some RP speakers still use the vowel of *bit*, some the vowel of *bee*, and others use something in between. The symbol /ee/, keyed to *very*, is used to represent whichever of these sounds the speaker normally uses.* The same is true for the weak vowel of words like *stimulate* which may be the vowel of *moon, took*, or something in between (*LPD*, 476). In the *Guide* this range of sounds is symbolized by lower case /oo/.

---

* In the event that RP demands the vowel of *bee* in unstressed position, small caps are used: *Aeneus* US /ih NEE us/; UK *also* /EE NEE us/.

ă-bat, ăir-marry, air-pair, ạr-far, ĕr-merry, ĝ- get, ī-high, ĭr-mirror, ł-little, n̩-listen, ŏ-hot, oh-go, ŏŏ-wood, ōō-moon, oor-tour, ōr- or, ow-how, th-that, th-thin, ŭ-but, UR-fur, ur-under.   ( ) - suppress the syllable   see p. xiii for complete list.

APPENDIX D: SPECIAL NOTES ON SELECTED WORDS, WORD ENDINGS, AND PREFIXES

Accompt 'account.' This word was borrowed into Middle English from French as *acount* and was pronounced /uh COWNT/ throughout the Elizabethan era. However, scholars decided in the 16th century that the correct written form should be *accompt* from the Latin, and spelled it this way up to the end of the 17th century. In Shakespeare both spellings are used. Some educated Elizabethans may have switched to a spelling pronunciation /uh CŎMPT/, but how common it was is not clear, and the older pronunciation was certainly popular enough to eventually win the spelling contest. /uh CŎMPT/ is sometimes heard today because of the unfortunate decision of so many editors to retain the ending *-ompt* (cf. *comptroller*, traditionally /kun TROLL ur/).

An hundred, an heretic. In Elizabethan English *h* at the beginning of a word was pronounced by some speakers, but not by others and the usage of *a* vs. *an* was not yet established according to the rules we follow today. Consequently many words beginning with *h* were preceded by *an* instead of modern *a*. These could have been pronounced /an UN drid/, etc. but the reader may choose to modernize by substituting our usual *a* and pronouncing the /h/. A parallel can be found before the sound /yo͞o-/ in words that begin with *eu-, u-*: *an eunuch, an union, an urinal*. In Elizabethan English these did not begin with /y-/, but with a diphthong /ih-oo/ (*eunuch* was also pronounced /EV nook/ by some).

-ate endings. Words ending in unstressed *-ate* in Shakespeare deserve careful attention, especially in instances such as *all thy goods are confiscate*. The usual modern form would be *confiscated*, a past participle in *-ed*, and the first impulse might be to use the pronunciation /-ayt/. However, in general, English words ending in *-ate* have /ay/ when they are verbs, and /-uh/ if nouns or adjectives. Note the verbs *fabricate, indicate, vacate*; nouns *confederate, subordinate* and adjectives *delicate, intricate*. Note also that some of these words are spelled the same, whether verbs, nouns, or adjectives, but their pronunciations differ accordingly: *deliberate, separate, associate, graduate*. There are however exceptions: *reprobate, magistrate, ingrate* are all nouns that usually have /ay/ and the Survey showed the noun *estimate* 'reputation,' and adjectives *illustrate* 'illustrious,' *prostrate* and *situate* all were divided between /ay/ and /uh/ in the US, but overwhelmingly were /ay/ in the UK.

The recommendation in the *Guide* will be, if a word ends in *-ate* and is a noun it should be /-ut/ except for *reprobate, magistrate, runagate*, and *estimate* 'reputation,' which are usually /-ayt/. If the word is an adjective (*fatigate, exsufflicate*) it should follow the pattern of *delicate, intricate*, etc. and be pronounced /-ut/, the exceptions being *intestate, prostrate* and in the UK *situate, illustrate*, which the Survey and dictionaries showed to be /-ayt/. In cases where modern English would use a past participle after a form of *to be* (*being so* *frustrate, thy goods are confiscate*), either /ay/ or /uh/ may be used, but the former is preferred by the vast majority of those in the Survey.

The earliest pronunciation evidence we have dating from the 16th century shows that even then there was no agreement. Some experts recommended /ay/ and some /ă/ (which today has been reduced to /uh/ or /ih/) for verbs, nouns, and adjectives alike (Dobson 1968, 2: 838, 918).   Shakespeare's rhymes show several instances where modern /-ut/ was pronounced /-ayt/: *compassionate : gate, degenerate : hate, fortunate : mate* (Cercignani 1981, 301) which the reader may observe or ignore as he or she pleases.

-aun- vs. -an-. Words like *chant, chantry, askance* are given in *Riverside* with an older variant spelled *chaunt, chauntry, askaunce.* The *-au-* spelling reflects the Anglo-Norman development of Old French nasal *a,* and in Early Modern English was also found in words like *grant / graunt, dance / daunce, hant / haunt* which are now modernized in most editions. The *-an-* variant was pronounced /ăn/ and gives rise to the pronunciations still used in North America in *chant, grant, dance.* The *-aun-* variant was pronounced in Middle English with the vowel in modern *how,* but in some dialects became /ayn/ (whence the pronunciation of *ancient, strange, etc.*), or in others /awn/, which gives us the current pronunciation in *haunt, staunch.* After the Elizabethan period, this /awn/ became /ahn/ in some dialects, heard today in Eastern New England and Standard British in *branch, dance, grant, chant.* Today standard spellings have normalized the pronunciations in most instances, with the exception of *staunch / stanch,* which still may have either /aw/, /ă/, or /ah/, and *aunt* which is /ă/ in most of North America, but /ah/ in the United Kingdom, New England and for many African-American speakers in the United States. Also showing variation is the archaic word *vaward* 'vanguard' from *vaunt-* which the Survey showed may be /VAW urd, VAY wurd-, VOW urd/, the latter perhaps derived from /VĂ-/.

-eus endings.   Greek names ending in *-eus* with main stress on the antepenultimate syllable (*Perseus, Theseus, Proteus, Orpheus*) generally have the anglicized ending /-ee us/, which in verse may reduce to /PUR syus/, etc. However, a restored pronunciation is used by a small percentage of speakers (/PUR syōōss/, etc.) which in North American may exhibit the typical loss of glide after dental consonants (/t,d,n,s,z/ as in *sue* /sōō/, *tune* /tōōn/) to produce /PUR sōōss/, etc., but not after other consonants (e.g., /f/ in *Orpheus*). Names with main stress on the penultimate (*Machabeus, Egeus*) are not subject to this restoration. *Zeus,* on the other hand (which does not appear in Shakespeare), is only pronounced in the United States with restored /zōōss/, or in the South /zyōōss/. As always in the *Guide,* the restored pronunciations are not normally recommended for names, and will not fit the meter when three syllables are needed.

importune 'ask insistently, urge, beg.'   The best choice from a historical standpoint is /im POR chun/ (cf. *fortune*), but /-ch$\overline{oo}$n, -ty$\overline{oo}$n, -tyun/ and in the US, CN /-t$\overline{oo}$n/ are also used.   About half the respondents in each country of the Survey reported third syllable stress /im por TY$\overline{OO}$N/; US *also* /-T$\overline{OO}$N/; UK, CN *also* /-CH$\overline{OO}$N/, which is fairly recent, perhaps modeled after *opportune*. However this will not fit the meter in verse.

In the Survey professors were asked how they would recommend pronouncing *importune* in a prose passage, where meter was not a consideration:

	US	CN	UK
im por T$\overline{OO}$N	10	1	
im por TY$\overline{OO}$N	8	4	7
im por CH$\overline{OO}$N		1	3
im POR chun	3	1	1
im POR ch$\overline{oo}$n	4	1	4
im POR t$\overline{oo}$n	4	1	
im POR ty$\overline{oo}$n	3	1	5
im POR tyun	2	1	2
im POR chun, -tyun	1		
im POR ty$\overline{oo}$n, -tyun		1	
im POR ty$\overline{oo}$n, im por TY$\overline{OO}$N	1		
Not sure			1
percentage with 3rd syll. stress	50	50	44
percentage with 2nd syll. stress	47	50	52

lu-, lew-. Words beginning with this combination are nearly always /l$\overline{oo}$-/ in the US (*lunatic, lucid, lute, lewd*).   In the UK this class of words was formerly pronounced /ly$\overline{oo}$-/ in Standard British (cf. /dy$\overline{oo}$-/ in *duke*, /ny$\overline{oo}$/ in *new*, etc.), but many of them have now lost the glide and are pronounced as in North America.   Some UK speakers may still use /ly$\overline{oo}$-/ in certain *lu*- words, like *lubricate, lucid, lucrative, illuminate, lute*, and especially *lure, lurid* and *alluring* (*LPD, EPD* 14, s.vv.).

-on endings. Words ending in unstressed *-on* fall into several categories.   The general rule is that traditional English words with unstressed *-on* are pronounced /-un/: *canon, lion, person, prison, poison, Fenton, London*.   Biblical names like *Solomon, Simeon, Gideon, Aaron* are pronounced /-un/, but *Lebanon, Hebron* sometimes have a newer pronunciation with /-ŏn/.   Greek names with stress

---

ă-bat, ăir-**marry**, air-**pair**, ạr-**far**, ĕr-**merry**, ĝ- **get**, ī-**high**, ĭr-**mirror**, ł-**little**, ṇ-**listen**, ŏ-**hot**, oh-**go**, $\overline{oo}$-**wood**, $\overline{oo}$-**moon**, oor-**tour**, ōr- **or**, ow-**how**, ţh-**that**, ŧħ-**thin**, ŭ-**but**, UR-**fur**, ur-**under**.   ( ) - suppress the syllable   see p. xiii for complete list.

directly before *-on*, whether three or two syllables, were formerly always pronounced /-un/ in English: *Jason, Gorgon, Orion, Arion* /uh RĪ un/, and by rights *Typhon, Triton, Solon* should be also, but a pronunciation with /-ŏn/ has become quite common recently, especially in two-syllable words in which *-on* is immediately preceded by a stressed vowel (*Creon, Cleon, Dion, Leon*). Greek names in three syllables with first syllable stress are pronounced with /-ŏn/ in the US, with [-un] used to a lesser degree, mainly by older speakers: *Marathon, Xenophon, Myrmidon, Babylon, Amazon, Pantheon.* In the UK /-un/ prevails in these words, but the newer ending /-ŏn/ is increasingly heard, especially for younger speakers. However in three- and four-syllable words ending in *-ion* or *-eon* in which stress falls on the antepenultimate, /-un/ is still by far the most common everywhere: *Ilion, Pygmalion, Deucalion, Hyperion.*

Words of recent vintage are usually /-ŏn/: *electron, neutron, rayon, fouton, freon, crouton*, which adds to the interference with the older forms. *Paragon* is overwhelmingly /-ŏn/ in the US, CN, but /-un/ in the UK, and *capon*, like all older, native words, would ordinarily be /-un/, but because it has become less familiar, it is treated like a newer word with /-ŏn/ predominating everywhere and /-un/ preserved to a lesser degree. *Charon* is a special case. The oldest form is /CAIR un/ but /-ŏn/ is also used to a greater extent than in other Greek words of its type. Both forms are used equally in the US. In the first syllable the newer form /CĂIR-/ is also used on the East Coast and the restored form /CAR-/ with /-ŏn/ is increasing everywhere, probably partly driven by a desire to avoid the older pronunciation's resemblance to the girl's name *Karen*.

-or endings. Common words in English that end in *-or* are pronounced /-ur/: *doctor, actor, junior, professor.* If it were not for interference from spelling, the more unusual words (*proditor, succor, servitor*) would also be pronounced in this way, but because of their unfamiliarity or their perception as foreign words (*lictor, Nestor*), or in the case of *succor*, the fact that it is identical to the quasi-taboo word *sucker*, the tendency is to pronounce them /-or/. Actors and singers sometimes extend this practice to even the most common words in *-or* ("I am an /AK tor/!", "And I that lowly suitor"), but it is difficult to call it anything but an affectation. The recommendation is that this entire class of words be pronounced /-ur/.

Prefixes *re-, de-, be-, pre-* (*request, defeat, betide, predict*). Standard British English recommends /rih-, dih-, bih-/, though some speakers use the vowel of *bee*. *Pre-*, however, according to the dictionaries, sometimes has /ee/ in Standard British. In the United States and Canada both /ih/ and /ee/ are used interchangeably in all of these prefixes.

puissance 'power,' (often meaning 'army'); **puissant** 'powerful.' Today these words show a mixture of forms in all countries, often doubtlessly based on guesswork. Traditionally /PWISS ņss/ and /PYOO̅ (ih) sņss/ were used. Today in the UK and CN these forms are virtually non-existent, while in the US each of these two pronunciations was recommended by less than 10 percent of those surveyed. The most common first syllable in all countries is now /PWEE-/ based on modern French. The British sometimes use a French nasal vowel for the second syllable as well. In verse *puissant* always has two syllables while *puissance* may have two or three, but in all cases they are stressed on the first syllable.

In the Survey professors were asked how they would recommend pronouncing *puissance* in a prose passage, where meter was not a consideration:

	US	CN	UK
PWEE snss	17	2	4
PWEE sahnss	4	7	3
PWEE sah^nss			4
PWEE sŏnss			2
PWEE sănss	3		2
PWEE sahnss, -sah^nss			1
pwee SAHNSS	6		1
pwee SAH^NSS			4
PWISS nss	4		
PYOO sahnss	1		
PYOO snss	1		
PWEE ih snss		1	
PYOO ih sahnss	2		1
PYOO snss, pyoo IH snss	1		
PWEE snss, pwee SAHNSS	1		
PWEE snss, -sănss		1	
Not sure	2	2	

surety 'collateral.' In verse *surety* is always two syllables (unless in a triple ending), though in modern English a pronunciation with three syllables is more common in all countries.

ă-bat, ăir-ma**rry**, air-**pair**, ạr-**far**, ĕr-**merry**, ĝ- **get**, ī-**high**, ĭr-**mirror**, ł-**little**, ṇ-**listen**, ŏ-**hot**, oh-**go**, ōō-**wood**, ōō-**moon**, oor-**tour**, ōr- **or**, ow-**how**, ṭh-**that**, th-**thin**, ŭ-**but**, UR-**fur**, ur-**under**.   ( ) - suppress the syllable   see p. xiii for complete list.

In the Survey, professors were asked how they would recommend pronouncing *surety* in a prose passage, where meter was not a consideration:

	US	CN	UK
SHOOR tee	2		2
SHUR tee	1		1
SHOOR ih tee	8	1	3
SHUR ih tee	5	6	
3 syllables, and the vowel SHOOR=SHUR*	3		
SHOR ih tee	1		6
SHOR ih tee, SHOR tee			1

*Some North Americans pronounce the vowel of *tour* the same as the vowel of *fur*

-ure endings. When unstressed, this ending is normally /-ur/ in English, and the general recommendation is for most Shakespearean words to follow suit. For example the *-ture* ending is regularly /-chur/: *feature, stature, forfeiture, venture, adventure* and this should be the ending for *discomfiture, wafture, exposture* as well. However in the UK there are some who prefer /-tyoor/ in certain words: *pasture, posture* (*LPD*, s.vv.). This pronunciation is not used in the US, and would be considered somewhat affected by many in the UK, especially if extended to words like *venture* as is sometimes heard on recordings. Unstressed *-dure*, however, which might be expected to become regularly /-jur/ (cf. *soldier*), tends to resist this development, perhaps because the words in this class are not normally used in everyday speech. *Verdure* is almost evenly divided between /-jur, -dyoor, -dyur/ in North America, while /-dyoor/ is slightly favored in the UK.   *Ordure* is most commonly /-dyoor/ in the US, or less often /-jur, -joor, -dyur/, while CN reported /-dyoor, -dyur/, and the UK overwhelmingly preferred the ending /-dyoor/, or rarely [-jur]. *Fixure, flexure* are usually /-shur/, with some UK speakers also using /-syoor/. The *-sure* ending is /-zhur/ in *pleasure, measure*. *Erasure* (and by extention *embrasure*) is /-shur/ in North America, but in the UK is /-zhur/.   *Censure* is overwhelmingly /-shur/ in all countries of the Survey with /-syoor/ used to a much smaller degree. In the US and CN a small minority also use /-chur/.

APPENDIX E: PRONUNCIATION IN ELIZABETHAN ENGLAND

It is difficult to describe Shakespeare's speech in terms of modern pronunciation for several reasons. First, because of the dialect differences in today's English. A statement like "vowel x sounded much like the vowel in present day *awe*" is often misleading because *awe* is pronounced differently in London, New York, and Toronto. There were also many dialects of Elizabethan English, both regionally and socially. Finally, no one really knows exactly how English was spoken in Shakespeare's day. We can come close because there were several writers in the sixteenth and seventeenth centuries who wrote in some detail on how words were pronounced. At times, however, it is difficult to interpret their descriptions.

It is clear, however, that the consonants were much the same as they are today. Those Elizabethans interested in "proper" English still pronounced the *gh* inherited from Old English in *night, weigh, neighbor,* (pronounced as in German *ich,* that is, like an extended /h/ in *he*), and in *bough, daughter* (pronounced as in Scottish *loch*). Words with initial *kn-, gn-* like *knot* and *gnat* were pronounced with /k/ and /g/ before /n/ until sometime in the seventeenth century. Words spelled *wh-* were pronounced with a breath, /hw-/, which is still retained in some US dialects, particularly in the South, and in Scottish English, whereas in most American speech and in standard British it has become simple /w-/. Words spelled *th* that were borrowed from Latin or French were pronounced with /t/ (*author, orthography, Katherine*). *Sure* could be pronounced either /SIH-oor/ or /shoor/, and *sugar, suit, sue* varied in a similar way. Elizabethan English also had /r/ after most vowels in words like *bark, dear, her,* which today has been lost in Standard British and most dialects in England, as well as in some East Coast American dialects. What exactly Shakespeare's /r/ sounded like is difficult to say for certain, but it was probably much like that found in North America and SW England, though it may have been trilled as in Scottish at the beginnings of words.

The vowels were much the same too, with some notable exceptions. The diphthongs heard in words like *mouse* and *mice* were pronounced more like /UH-oo/, /UH-ee/, rather than modern /AH-oo/, /AH-ee/. The long *a* in words like *trail, day, mate* was pronounced like the vowel of modern *get, fed,* but held longer. Words with long *e* spelled *ea* (*meat, eat, speak*) were pronounced as they are today with /ee/ by some Elizabethans, but another, perhaps more formal pronunciation, equal to the vowel just described in *trail, day,* was also used by some segments of the population.* It is also possible that for some the vowel in

---

*In modern English the words *break, steak, great, yea* are still pronounced with long *a* today, as are all *ea* words of this sort in Irish English.

meat was a long /ĕ/, different from both the vowel in *meet* /ee/ and the vowel in *mate* (long /ă/) (Cercignani 1981, 154–161). Long *o* was slightly diphthongized as it is today in many northern US dialects or was a monophthong rather like standard British *awe* (or in North American English, the vowel before /r/ in *oar*), not as in Standard British *owe* where the diphthong has become /EH-oo/. Most of the words spelled *oi, oy* could be pronounced as in modern /oy/, or as Elizabethan long *i* /UH-ee/, so *point* and *pint* were homonyms. Modern short *u* in words spelled with *o* could be /ōo/ in Elizabethan English (*blood, done, dost, doth, love, come*), but could also be /uh/.

Words spelled *-ir-, -er-, -ur-* which today are all pronounced alike with the vowel of *her*, may have maintained their distinct Middle English vowel sounds into this era, so *fir* may have still been /fĭr/, *refer* /-fĕr/, and *fur* /fur/. Many words spelled *-er-* which are now pronounced /ur/ were then pronounced /ahr/: *heard, German, person, merchant* (and still are in UK *Derby, clerk*). *War, warm, reward* had the short *a* of *wax* or possibly the sound /ah/. Words which today have /ahr/ (*harm, arm, barn*) may also have had the short /ă/. The /ah/ used in Standard British in *staff, father, fast* was probably /ă/ as well, perhaps held longer.

In addition there were some differences in syllables that did not bear the main stress:

fortune, actual ⇒	/-tih-oon/, /-tih-ooł/ or /-tyoon/, /-tyool/
educate ⇒	/-dih-oo-/, /-dyoo-/
action, martial ⇒	/-sih-un/, /-sih-ŭl/, or /-syun/, /-sył/ or mod. /-shun/, /-shł/
occasion, measure ⇒	/-zih-un/, /-zih-oor/ or /-zyun/, /-zyur/ or mod. /-zhun/, /-zhur/
nature, venture, pasture ⇒	/-tur/ as in *enter* or /-tih-oor/
verdure, ordure ⇒	/-dur/ as in *order* or /-dih-oor/
temperate, fortunate ⇒	rhymed with *hate* or with *hat*
embassage, pilgrimage ⇒	rhymed with *age* or with *badge*
Titania, Bianca, Hermia ⇒	ended in /ă/ or the vowel of *say*, still heard in some US dialects in *Ioway* (*Iowa*)

There are also many examples of individual words that differed from modern English. *One* and *gone* rhymed with *moan*, *Rome* was /rōōm/, *whore* was /hōōr/ (still found in Canada), *schedule* was /SED yooł/. *Eunuch* had several pronunciations, one of the most common being /EV nook/. In stressed positions *should, would, could* were pronounced with /l/.

Some other differences like word stress are discussed in the introduction.

References

DICTIONARIES

The American Heritage Dictionary of the English Language, 3rd ed. 1992. Boston: Houghton Mifflin.

BBC English Dictionary. 1992. London: BBC English and HarperCollins.

Collins Cobuild English Language Dictionary. 1987. London: Collins.

English Pronouncing Dictionary, 14th ed. 1988. Eds. A. C. Gimson and Susan Ramsaran. Cambridge, UK: Cambridge University Press.

Everyman's English Pronouncing Dictionary, 12th ed. 1964. Ed. Daniel Jones. London: J. M. Dent.

Irvine, Theodora. 1945. *A Pronouncing Dictionary of Shakespearean Proper Names*. New York : Barnes and Noble.

Kökeritz, Helge. 1959. *Shakespeare's Names: A Pronouncing Dictionary*. New Haven, Conn.: Yale University Press.

Longman Pronunciation Dictionary. 1990. Ed. J. C. Wells. London: Longman.

Merriam-Webster's Collegiate Dictionary, 10th ed. 1993. Springfield, Mass.: Merriam-Webster.

Onions, C. T. *A Shakespeare Glossary*, revised by Robert D. Eagleson. 1986. Oxford: Clarendon.

The Oxford English Dictionary, 2nd ed. 1989. 20 vols. Oxford: Clarendon.

A Pronouncing Dictionary of American English. 1953. John Samuel Kenyon and Thomas Albert Knott, eds. Springfield, Mass.: Merriam.

A Pronouncing Dictionary of English Place-Names. 1981. Ed. Klaus Forster. London: Routledge and Kegan Paul.

Pronouncing Dictionary of Proper Names. 1993. Ed. John K. Bollard. Detroit: Omnigraphics.

The Random House Dictionary of the English Language, 2nd ed. 1987. New York: Random House.

Webster's New International Dictionary of the English Language. 1934. Springfield, Mass.: Merriam.

Webster's Third New International Dictionary of the English Language. 1961. Springfield, Mass.: Merriam.

A Universal Critical and Pronouncing Dictionary of the English Language. 1856. Ed. Joseph E. Worcester. London: Henry G. Bohn.

EDITIONS OF SHAKESPEARE'S WORKS

The basic text for the *Guide* is *The Riverside Shakespeare*. 1974. Ed. G. Blakemore Evans. Boston: Houghton Mifflin. *Edward III* was added from the second edition, 1997, eds. G. Blakemore Evans and J.J.M. Tobin.
Based on *Riverside* 1974 are:
A Complete and Systematic Concordance to the Works of Shakespeare. 1968–1980. Ed. Marvin Spevack. 9 vols. Hildesheim: Olms.
The Harvard Concordance to Shakespeare. 1973. Ed. Marvin Spevack. Cambridge, Mass.: Belknap Press of Harvard University Press.
Other editions that were used in the search for alternative readings, include:
The Arden Shakespeare. 1951–. General eds. Una Ellis-Fermor, Harold F. Brooks, Harold Jenkins, and Brian Morris. London: Methuen. Recent volumes published by Routledge.
The Complete Oxford Shakespeare 1987. 3 vols. General eds. Stanley Wells and Gary Taylor. Oxford: Clarendon.
The New Cambridge Shakespeare. 1984–. General eds. Philip Brockbank and Brian Gibbons. Cambridge: Cambridge University Press.
A New Variorum Edition of Shakespeare. 1871–. Ed. Horace Howard Furness. Philadelphia: Lippincott. A revised series is being published by the Modern Language Association of America.
The Oxford Shakespeare. 1982–. General ed. Stanley Wells. Oxford: Clarendon.
The Parallel King Lear 1608–1623. 1989. Prepared by Michael Warren. Berkeley: University of California.
Shakespeare's Edward III. 1996. Ed. Eric Sams. New Haven, Conn.: Yale University Press.
William Shakespeare: The Complete Works. 1986. General eds. Stanley Wells and Gary Taylor. Oxford: Clarendon.
William Shakespeare: A Textual Companion. 1987. Stanley Wells, et al. Oxford: Clarendon.
The Three-Text Hamlet. 1991. Eds. Paul Bertram and Bernice W. Kliman. New York.: AMS.

ON SHAKESPEARE'S TEXTS

Thompson, Ann, et al. 1992. *Which Shakespeare? A User's Guide to Editions*. Milton Keynes: Open University.
Wells, Stanley. 1979. *Modernizing Shakespeare's Spelling*. Oxford: Oxford University Press.
———. 1984. *Re-Editing Shakespeare for the Modern Reader*. Oxford: Clarendon.

ON LATIN AND GREEK PRONUNCIATION

Allen, W. Sidney. 1968. *Vox Graeca*. Cambridge, UK: Cambridge Univ. Press.
———. 1978. *Vox Latina*. Cambridge, UK: Cambridge Univ. Press.

Else, Gerald F. 1967. "The Pronunciation of Classical Names and Words in English." *Classical Journal* 62: 210–14.

Kelly, H. A. 1986. "Pronouncing Latin Words in English." *Classical World* 80: 33–37.

Moore-Smith, G. C. 1930. "The English Language and the 'Restored' Pronunciation of Latin" in *A Grammatical Miscellany offered to Otto Jespersen:* 167–78. Copenhagen: Levin and Munksgaard.

Sargeaunt, John. 1920. "The Pronunciation of English Words Dervied from the Latin." *Society for Pure English Tract No. IV.* Oxford: Clarendon Press.

Tucker, R. Whitney. 1973. "Why Don't Scholars Speak English?" *Classical Journal* 69: 145–48.

ON REGIONAL PRONUNCIATIONS

Bähr, Dieter. 1981. *Die englische Sprache in Kanada.* Tübingen: Gunter Narr.

Dictionary of American Regional English. 1985–. Chief ed. Frederick G. Cassidy. 3 vols. to date. Cambridge, Mass.: Belknap Press of Harvard University Press.

The English Dialect Dictionary. 1898–1904. Ed. Joseph Wright. 6 vols. London: Henry Frowde.

The Linguistic Atlas of New England. 1941–43. Ed. Hans Kurath, et al. 6 vols. Providence, RI: American Council of Learned Societies and Brown University.

Survey of English Dialects. 1962. 4 vols. Eds. Harold Orton, et al. Leeds: E. J. Arnold.

Wells, J. C. *Accents of English.* 1982. 3 vols. Cambridge, UK: Cambridge University Press.

ON ELIZABETHAN PRONUNCIATION

Cercignani, Fausto. 1981. *Shakespeare's Works and Elizabethan Pronunciation.* Oxford: Clarendon.

Dobson, E. J. 1968. *English Pronunciation, 1500–1700.* 2 volumes. Oxford: Clarendon.

Kökeritz, Helge. 1953. *Shakespeare's Pronunciation.* New Haven: Yale University Press.

Prins, A. A. 1974. *A History of English Phonemes.* Leiden: Leiden University Press.

Viëtor, Wilhelm. 1906. *Shakespeare's Pronunciation: A Shakespeare Phonology.* Marburg: N. G. Elwert.

ON READING SHAKESPEARE'S VERSE

Kökeritz, Helge. 1969. "Elizabethan Prosody and Historical Phonology" in *Approaches to English Historical Linguistics.* Ed. Roger Lass. New York: Holt, Rinehart, and Winston, 208–27.

Linklater, Kristin. 1992. *Freeing Shakespeare's Voice: The Actor's Guide to Talking the Text.* New York: Theatre Communications Group.

Sipe, Dorothy L. 1968. *Shakespeare's Metrics.* New Haven, Conn.: Yale University Press, Yale Studies in English, vol. 166.

Spain, Delbert. 1988. *Shakespeare Sounded Soundly.* Santa Barbara, Calif.: Capra.

Wright, George T. 1985. "Shakespeare's Poetic Techniques" in *William Shakespeare: His World, His Work, His Influence,* ed. John F. Andrews, vol. 2, 3 vols.   New York: Scribner, 363–87.

————. 1988.   *Shakespeare's Metrical Art.* Berkeley, Calif.: University of California Press.

Index of Words

annothanize, 341
anon, 33
an't, 160, 318, 354, 454
Antenor, 558
Anthony, 54, 212, 218, 280, 334, 364, 425, 477
Antiates, 97, 103, 107
Antigonus, 616
Antioch, 451
Antiochus, 450
Antipholus, 84
Antipodes, 267, 394, 419, 428, 470
antiquary, 567
antique, 75, 100, 135, 150, 163, 219, 310, 448, 497, 499, 584, 645, 646, 648, 649
Antium, 97, 101, 103, 104, 107
Antonio, 32, 47, 54, 293, 382, 425, 513, 514, 522, 578, 591
Antony, 54, 55, 212, 218, 257, 293, 364
antres, 438
Apemantus, 532
apoplex, 155
apoplexy, 105, 184, 194
aporn, 251
apostraphas, 345
apothecary, 255, 330, 457, 493, 506
appeach, 43, 474
appellant, 251, 464, 465, 472
apperil, 534
appertinent, 206, 337
apricock, 419, 471, 605
aqua-vitae, 89, 403, 502, 505, 585, 626
Aquitaine, 336, 337
Aragon, 382, 426, 430
arbiterment, arbitrament, arbitrement, 110, 177, 214, 332, 491, 587, 614
Archbishop, 168, 181, 274, 280
Archidamus, 616
Arcite, 601
Arden, 72, 680
ardor, ardure, 156, 529
argal, 160
argentine, 461
argo, 257, 383, 394
argosy, 271, 383, 385, 389, 394, 515
Argus, 340, 394, 561
Ariadne, 416, 574, 599
Ariel, 522, 529
Arion, 579, 674

arithmetician, 436
armada, armado, 89, 130, 309
Armado, 37, 334, 336, 339, 347, 348, 350, 354, 356
armipotent, 50, 356, 613
aroint, aroynt, 325, 360
a-row, 91
Arragon, 382, 426, 430
arrand, 183, 428
arrant, 67, 86, 106, 128, 146, 152, 170, 186, 195, 197, 212, 216, 217, 218, 322, 431, 433, 540, 575
arras, 148, 155, 156, 173, 176, 309, 405, 427, 515, 613
arrearages, 113
Artemidorus, 293
artere, 145
Artesius, 601
articulate, 179
artificer, 311
artire, 145
Artois, 123, 230
Arviragus, 108
as lief, 61, 73, 78, 80, 104, 152, 184, 191, 213, 295, 372, 404, 429, 473, 511, 586, 602
as lieve, 177, 500, 561
as live, 61, 104, 152, 184, 191, 213, 429
asinico, 565
askance, askaunce, 514, 560, 638, 650, 655, 672
askant, askaunt, 159
aslant, 159
asnego, 565
asnico, 565
aspect, 33, 310
aspic, 71, 445
aspray, 105
assay, 48, 74, 91, 133, 147, 151, 155, 159, 180, 203, 258, 267, 368, 372, 373, 376, 401, 438, 441, 443, 539, 630, 643, 656.
assubjugate, 567
Atalanta, 77, 78
Ate, 299, 305, 356, 428
Athenian, 326, 413, 532, 606
atomi, 496
atomy, 78, 79, 197, 496
Atropos, 188
attainder, 285

Subject Index